Lecture Notes in Computer Science 15942

The series Lecture Notes in Computer Science (LNCS), including its subseries Lecture Notes in Artificial Intelligence (LNAI) and Lecture Notes in Bioinformatics (LNBI), has established itself as a medium for the publication of new developments in computer science and information technology research, teaching, and education.

LNCS enjoys close cooperation with the computer science R & D community, the series counts many renowned academics among its volume editors and paper authors, and collaborates with prestigious societies. Its mission is to serve this international community by providing an invaluable service, mainly focused on the publication of conference and workshop proceedings and postproceedings. LNCS commenced publication in 1973.

Dexter Kozen · Ruy de Queiroz
Editors

Logic, Language, Information, and Computation

31st International Workshop, WoLLIC 2025
Porto, Portugal, July 14–17, 2025
Proceedings

Editors
Dexter Kozen
Cornell University
Ithaca, NY, USA

Ruy de Queiroz
Federal University of Pernambuco
Recife, Brazil

ISSN 0302-9743 ISSN 1611-3349 (electronic)
Lecture Notes in Computer Science
ISBN 978-3-031-99535-4 ISBN 978-3-031-99536-1 (eBook)
https://doi.org/10.1007/978-3-031-99536-1

This Springer imprint is published by the registered company Springer Nature Switzerland AG
The registered company address is: Gewerbestrasse 11, 6330 Cham, Switzerland

Preface

This volume contains the papers presented at the 31st Workshop on Logic, Language, Information and Computation (WoLLIC 2025), held on July 14–17, 2025 at the Department of Computer Science, Faculty of Sciences, University of Porto, Portugal. The WoLLIC series of workshops started in 1994 with the aim of fostering interdisciplinary research in pure and applied logic. The idea is to have a forum which is large enough in the number of possible interactions between logic and the sciences related to information and computation, and yet is small enough to allow for concrete and useful interaction among participants.

For WoLLIC 2025 there were 57 submissions. Each submission was reviewed by at least 2 program committee members. The committee decided to accept 21 papers. This volume includes all the accepted papers, together with the extended abstracts of the invited speakers at WoLLIC 2025:

- Tobias Kappé Leiden University
- Daniela Petrisan IRIF, Université Paris Cité

We would like to thank all the people who contributed to making WoLLIC 2025 a success. We thank the Program Committee and all additional reviewers for the work they put into reviewing the submissions. We thank the invited speakers and the tutorialists for their inspiring talks, the Steering Committee and the Advisory Committee for their advice, and the Local Organizing Committeeespecially Mário Florido and Sandra Alvesfor their great support. Finally, we thank all the authors for their excellent contributions.

The help provided by the EasyChair system created by Andrei Voronkov is gratefully acknowledged. We also would like to acknowledge the scientific sponsorship of the following organizations: Interest Group in Pure and Applied Logics (IGPL), Association for Logic, Language and Information (FoLLI), Association for Symbolic Logic (ASL), European Association for Theoretical Computer Science (EATCS), European Association for Computer Science Logic (EACSL), the Brazilian Logic Society (SBL), and Sociedade Portuguesa de Lógica (SPL).

July 2025

Dexter Kozen
Ruy de Queiroz

Organization

Program Committee Chair

Dexter Kozen	Cornell University, USA

General Chair

Ruy de Queiroz	Universidade Federal de Pernambuco, Brazil

Steering Committee

Samson Abramsky	University College London, UK
Agata Ciabattoni	Vienna University of Technology, Austria
Anuj Dawar	University of Cambridge, UK
Helle Hvid Hansen	University of Groningen, The Netherlands
Juliette Kennedy	University of Helsinki, Finland
Ulrich Kohlenbach	Technische Universität Darmstadt, Germany
Daniel Leivant	Indiana University Bloomington, USA
Leonid Libkin	University of Edinburgh, UK
Lawrence Moss	Indiana University Bloomington, USA
Luke Ong	Oxford University, UK
Valeria de Paiva	Topos Institute/PUC-Rio, USA/Brazil
Elaine Pimentel	University College London, UK
Ruy de Queiroz	Universidade Federal de Pernambuco, Brazil
Andre Scedrov	University of Pennsylvania, USA
Alexandra Silva	Cornell University, USA
Renata Wassermann	Universidade de São Paulo, Brazil

Advisory Committee

Johan van Benthem	University of Amsterdam, Netherlands and Stanford University, USA
Joe Halpern	Cornell University, USA
Wilfrid Hodges	Queen Mary University of London, UK
Angus Macintyre	University of Oxford, UK

Hiroakira Ono	Japan Advanced Institute of Science and Technology, Japan
Jouko Väänänen	University of Helsinki, Finland

Program Committee

Dexter Kozen (Chair)	Cornell University, USA
Juan Aguilera	TU Wien, Austria
Natasha Alechina	Utrecht University, The Netherlands
Maria Aloni	University of Amsterdam, The Netherlands
Steve Awodey	Carnegie Mellon University, USA
Dana Bartosova	University of Florida, USA
Marta Bilkova	Institute of Computer Science, Czech Academy of Sciences, Czech Republic
Katalin Bimbo	University of Alberta, Canada
Francesca Zaffora Blando	Carnegie Mellon University, USA
Mikolaj Bojanczyk	University of Warsaw, Poland
Hans van Ditmarsch	University of Toulouse, CNRS, IRIT, France
Amy Felty	University of Ottawa, Canada
Santiago Figueira	University of Buenos Aires, Argentina
Pietro Galliani	University of Insubria, Italy
Sam van Gool	IRIF, Université Paris Cité, France
Marie Kerjean	LIPN, Université Sorbonne Paris Nord, France
Dorel Lucanu	Alexandru Ioan Cuza University, Romania
Radu Mardare	Heriot-Watt University, UK
Wim Martens	University of Bayreuth, Germany
José Meseguer	University of Illinois Urbana-Champaign, USA
Anca Muscholl	LaBRI, Université Bordeaux, France
Alessandra Palmigiano	Vrije Universiteit Amsterdam, The Netherlands
R. Ramanujam	Institute of Mathematical Sciences, India
Peter Selinger	Dalhousie University, Canada
Michael Shulman	University of San Diego, USA
Sonja Smets	University of Amsterdam
Andres Villaveces	Universidad Nacional de Colombia

Additional Reviewers

Matteo Acclavio
Andrei Arusoaie
Philippe Balbiani
Alexi Block Gorman
Horatiu Cheval
Florence Clerc
Tiziano Dalmonte
Andrea De Domenico
Ronald de Haan Samuel Fish
Benjamin Lucien Kaminsk
Jędrzej Kołodziejski
Serafina Lapenta
Ioana Leustean
Dean McHugh
Luka Mikec
Chunyan Mu
Nina Pardal
Tin Perkov
Simone Picenni
Umberto Rivieccio
Alexis Saurin
Ezra Schoen
Andrei Sipos
Tachio Terauchi
Diana Trandabat
Apostolos Tzimoulis
Niels van der Weide
Ruoding Wang

Invited talks

- Tobias Kappé (Leiden University, The Netherlands): On propositional program equivalence
- Daniela Petrisan (IRIF, Université Paris Cité, France): Functorial Mealy machines

Contents

Invited paper

Contributed papers

Invited paper

On Propositional Program Equivalence (Extended Abstract)

Tobias Kappé(✉)

LIACS, Leiden University, Leiden, The Netherlands
t.w.j.kappe@liacs.leidenuniv.nl

Abstract. General program equivalence is undecidable. However, if we abstract away the semantics of statements, then this problem becomes not just decidable, but practically feasible. For instance, a program of the form `if` b `then` e `else` f should be equivalent to `if not` b `then` f `else` e—no matter what b, e and f are. This kind of equivalence is known as *propositional equivalence*. In this extended abstract, we discuss recent developments in propositional program equivalence from the perspective of (Guarded) Kleene Algebra with Tests, or (G)KAT.

1 Introduction

Modern programming languages offer a wealth of techniques to implement a desired computation. The resulting flexibility also means that some changes to a program do not (and should not) change its semantics. As such, there are circumstances where one would like to check whether a rearrangement of the source code is equivalent to the original. Because this problem is undecidable in general, there are two options: we can to focus on specific fragments of programming languages where equivalence is decidable, or we can adjust our notion of equivalence to make it decidable. This extended abstract is about the latter approach, using *(Guarded) Kleene Algebra with Tests* [29,35,49].

More specifically, the notion of equivalence under study is called *propositional equivalence*. In a nutshell, two programs are propositionally equivalent if their semantics coincide, independently of the interpretation of the primitive statements. As an example, consider a program in an imperative programming language with traditional branches and loops, such as `if` b `then {` e`; while` b `do` e `}`. It should be clear that this program has the same effect as `while` b `do` e, regardless of the actual test filled in for b, or the actual statement (or indeed, program) that appears at e.[1] Of course, equivalences like this one are relatively easy to grasp, and most programmers will have an intuitive understanding of them. On the other hand, equivalences between more involved programs are harder to justify by themselves; in such cases, it would be preferable if we could establish them as consequences of simpler rules, or check them mechanically.

[1] For the sake of simplicity, let's assume that e does not contain any context-dependent control flow, like `break`. This assumption can be relaxed [54].

D. Kozen and R. de Queiroz (Eds.): WoLLIC 2025, LNCS 15942, pp. 3–18, 2026.
https://doi.org/10.1007/978-3-031-99536-1_1

```
s := new stack();
node := root;
while node != nil do
  s.push(node);
  node := node.left;
end
while !s.empty do
  node = s.pop();
  visit(node);
  node = node.right;
  while node != nil do
    s.push(node);
    node := node.left;
  end
end
```

(a) Triple-loop version

```
s := new stack();
node := root;
while node != nil or !s.empty do
  if node != nil then
    s.push(node);
    node = node.left;
  else
    node = s.pop();
    visit(node);
    node = node.right;
  end
end
```

(b) Single-loop version

Fig. 1. Two algorithms for an in-order walk of a binary tree.

As an example of such a nontrivial equivalence, consider a program meant to visit the nodes of a binary tree in-order, i.e., by visiting each node after its left child, but before its right child. A plausible implementation appears in Fig. 1a.

While this implementation is not entirely straightforward, it implements a correct in-order traversal. Nevertheless, there is something to be desired: the first loop is the same as the third (inner) loop. We could abstract this code into a function, but a different approach is possible too, unifying the three loops into one. The underlying idea is that each "step" of the algorithm either visits the current node, or remembers a node to be visited later, with the latter action taking priority. This yields the implementation in Fig. 1b [26, §2.3.1].

If these implementations are equivalent, then the second program must also be correct—but how do we prove this? Perhaps surprisingly, propositional equivalence can help: regardless of what `s.push(node)` and other actions do, these programs achieve the same outcome. Put differently: e`;` `while` b `do` f`;` `while` c `do {` g`;` `while` b `do` f `}` is equivalent to e`;` `while` b `or` c `do { if` b `then` f `else` g `}`, for all programs e, f and g, and tests b and c. In fact, these programs perform the same actions (stack manipulations, node visits, variable assignments), in the same order, when given the same input. As hinted at, we would like to be able to prove this far-from-trivial equivalence using simpler laws. This is where *Guarded Kleene Algebra with Tests* [35,49], or *GKAT*, can help, as an algebraic system to prove equivalences such as this one.

The extended abstract will go over the syntax, semantics, and metatheory of GKAT. The objective is not to give a comprehensive, textbook-like treatment, but rather to serve as a starting point for further study to those interested in learning more, with plenty of references for further reading. We start in Sect. 2 with an overview of Kleene Algebra with Tests; next, we delve into the specifics of GKAT in Sect. 3. We discuss connections with process algebra in Sect. 4, and conclude in Sect. 5 with some suggestions for future work.

2 Kleene Algebra with Tests

To properly explain GKAT, we need to spend some time discussing, *Kleene Algebra with Tests* (*KAT*) [8,28,29,34]. As the name might suggest, KAT is an extension of Kleene Algebra [9,27,36,45]; it is a powerful algebraic system to reason about propositional equivalence between programs that include non-deterministic composition and loops. This non-determinism makes KAT extremely expressive. However, as we will see, it also comes at the cost of a high (theoretical) complexity when deciding equivalence [8] (although a practically feasible equivalence checking algorithm does exist[40]).

The syntax of KAT is defined in two stages. First, there are the *tests*, which represent a propositional abstraction of the conditions that might occur in branches (such as `node != nil` in our motivating example). These are generated by a set of *primitive tests* T, which we fix for the remainder, as follows:

$$\mathsf{BExp} \ni b, c ::= 0 \mid 1 \mid t \in T \mid b + c \mid b \cdot c \mid \overline{b}$$

Within these tests, $+$ is meant to model disjunction, $\cdot$ models conjunction, and $\overline{}$ is negation. Using tests as well as a similarly fixed set of *primitive programs* Σ, we can then build the set of KAT expressions Exp as follows:

$$\mathsf{Exp} \ni e, f ::= b \in \mathsf{BExp} \mid p \in \Sigma \mid e + f \mid e \cdot f \mid e^*$$

Here, tests represent assertions: when $b \in \mathsf{Exp}$, b as a program does nothing when b is true, and aborts otherwise. The operator $+$ represents non-deterministic composition: $e+f$ non-deterministically runs e or f; in the same vein, * represents non-deterministic loops: e^* runs e some non-deterministic (possibly zero) number of times. Finally, $\cdot$ is sequential composition, i.e., $e \cdot f$ first runs e, and then f.

This syntax is close to that of regular expressions, and of course this is no accident, as Kleene Algebra proper was developed to study their equational theory [9]. We will treat KAT expressions using the precedence rules of regular expressions: * binds more tightly than $\cdot$, which takes priority over $+$.

2.1 Encoding Programs

One way to think of KAT expressions is as regular expressions instrumented with assertions, describing the "language" of traces representing possible ways of executing a program—we will make this more precise momentarily. For now though, we should make clear that in spite of this non-determinism, traditional program compositions can still be modelled in KAT [28].

- Branches like `if` b `then` e `else` f can be modelled with the expression $b \cdot e + \overline{b} \cdot f$. Intuitively, this program non-deterministically chooses between asserting that b is true, and then executing e, or asserting that b is false, and then executing f. The branch that matches the truth value of b "survives".

- Loops like `while` b `do` e can be modelled with the expression $(b \cdot e)^* \cdot \overline{b}$. The intuition here is that $b \cdot e$ is executed some non-deterministic number of times, with each iteration asserting that the condition b is true before running e; finally, when the loop is done, the expression asserts that b is false.

With these encodings in mind, the program in Fig. 1a can be written as a KAT expression: $e \cdot (b \cdot f)^* \cdot \overline{b} \cdot (c \cdot g \cdot (b \cdot f)^* \cdot \overline{b})^* \cdot \overline{c}$. Here, e stands in for the two lines of code before the first loop, f is the body of the first (and third) loop, and g represents the first three lines of the second loop; b is the condition of the first and third loops, while c is the condition of the second loop. Similarly, the program in Fig. 1b can be encoded as $e \cdot ((b + c) \cdot (b \cdot f + \overline{b} \cdot g))^* \cdot \overline{b + c}$.

2.2 Semantics

To further clarify what we mean when we say that two programs are equivalent regardless of how primitive statements interpreted, we first define semantics that *does* involve the meaning of the statements; next we abstract from this interpretation. Because KAT programs model non-deterministic programs, it seems most reasonable to model their semantics in terms of relations, connecting initial states of the program to the states that can be reached by running it [34].

Given a set S of states, suppose we had an interpretation σ that assigns to each $p \in \Sigma$ a relation $\sigma(p)$ on S representing the action of p. Furthermore, suppose that we had for each $t \in T$ a predicate $\tau(t) \subseteq T$ describing the states where t is true. We can then derive a relation $[\![e]\!]_I$ to model the behavior of the program e, provided its primitives are interpreted according to $I = (\sigma, \tau)$: [34]

$$[\![0]\!]_I = \emptyset \qquad [\![1]\!]_I = \mathsf{id}_S \qquad [\![t]\!]_I = \{(s,s) \mid s \in \tau(t)\} \qquad [\![\overline{b}]\!]_I = \mathsf{id}_S \setminus [\![b]\!]_I$$

$$[\![p]\!]_I = \sigma(p) \qquad [\![e + f]\!]_I = [\![e]\!]_I \cup [\![f]\!]_I \qquad [\![e \cdot f]\!]_I = [\![e]\!]_I \circ [\![f]\!]_I \qquad [\![e^*]\!]_I = [\![e]\!]_I^*$$

Here, we write id_S for the identity relation on S, and R^* for the reflexive-transitive closure of a relation $R \subseteq S \times S$—overloading the Kleene star operator. The operator $+$ (resp. $\cdot$) is interpreted the same way, whether it is applied to programs or tests. It is not too hard to prove that $[\![b]\!]_I$ is always a subset of id_S, for any $b \in \mathsf{BExp}$, and in fact, for $b, c \in \mathsf{Exp}$ we have $[\![b \cdot c]\!]_I = [\![b]\!]_I \cap [\![c]\!]_I$. At this point, the reader may want to verify that our encoding of traditional flow control aligns with this semantics—for instance, that $[\![t \cdot p_1 + \overline{t} \cdot p_2]\!]_I$ is exactly

$$\{(s, s') \mid s \in \tau(t) \land (s, s') \in \sigma(p_1)\} \cup \{(s, s') \mid s \notin \tau(t) \land (s, s') \in \sigma(p_2)\}$$

With all of this in place, our claim from the introduction can finally be made formal: for all interpretations I, it holds that the two encodings (presented above) of the programs in Fig. 1 are mapped to the same relation by $[\![-]\!]_I$. More broadly, we are interested in all pairs of programs related similarly for all I—that is to say, in the *equational theory* induced by this semantics.

When further advancing our understanding, quantifying over all interpretations can become cumbersome. This is where the *language semantics* of KAT

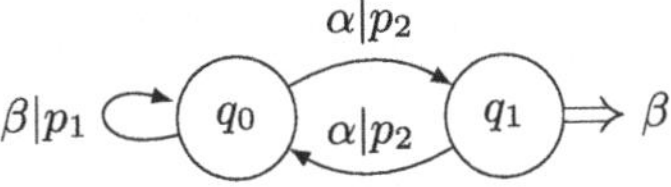

Fig. 2. An example automaton on guarded strings

comes in [34]. In a nutshell, the language semantics of a KAT expression gives an accounting of the possible ways the program *could* be executed, without making any assumptions about the interpretations of the primitive symbols. Among other things, this means that paths of execution that simply cannot happen—i.e., dead code—do not contribute to the language semantics.

Executions of a program are recorded in so-called *guarded strings* [34], which are plain words that alternate between actions and *atoms*. The latter record the truth value of each test at that point in the program. More formally, the set of atoms At is 2^T, and $\alpha \in \mathsf{At}$ is the atom signifying that all tests in α are true, whereas the primitive tests outside α are false. A guarded string is a word of the form $\alpha_0 p_0 \alpha_1 p_1 \cdots \alpha_n$, i.e., an element of the regular language $\mathsf{At} \cdot (\Sigma \cdot \mathsf{At})^*$. This guarded string records that the memory of the program was initially described by α_0, and after executing p_0 the description of the memory was reflected by α_1, and so on, until the program finally terminated with memory described by α_n.

A set of guarded strings is called a *guarded language*. To give a semantics of KAT in terms of such languages, we need some formal tools. Given two guarded languages L_1 and L_2, their *fusion product* $L_1 \diamond L_2$ is the guarded language $\{w\alpha x \mid w\alpha \in L_1 \wedge \alpha x \in L_2\}$. If we then write $L^{(0)}$ for At and $L^{(n+1)}$ for $L^{(n)} \diamond L$, with $L^{(*)} = L^{(0)} \cup L^{(1)} \cup \cdots$, then the guarded language semantics $[\![e]\!]$ of a KAT expression e can be defined inductively, as follows: [34]

$$[\![0]\!] = \emptyset \qquad [\![1]\!] = \mathsf{At} \qquad [\![t]\!] = \{\alpha \in \mathsf{At} \mid t \in \alpha\} \qquad [\![\bar{b}]\!] = \mathsf{At} \setminus [\![b]\!]$$

$$[\![p]\!] = \mathsf{At} \cdot \{p\} \cdot \mathsf{At} \qquad [\![e+f]\!] = [\![e]\!] \cup [\![f]\!] \qquad [\![e \cdot f]\!] = [\![e]\!] \diamond [\![f]\!] \qquad [\![e^*]\!] = [\![e]\!]^{(*)}$$

The guarded language semantics of KAT is connected to its relational semantics in the intended way: for all $e, f \in \mathsf{Exp}$, we have that $[\![e]\!] = [\![f]\!]$ if and only if for all interpretations I, we have $[\![e]\!]_I = [\![f]\!]_I$ [34]. Importantly, this means that to decide whether e and f coincide relationally for all interpretations I is equivalent to deciding whether their guarded language semantics is the same.

Because regular languages correspond precisely to automata, and language equivalence of automata is decidable, this suggests a strategy to decide equivalence in KAT: convert expressions to some kind of automata, and check equivalence there. The relevant kind of automata are called *automata on guarded strings*; these label transitions with an atom and an action [5,31] (see Fig. 2). Moreover, acceptance is indicated for each combination of state and atom; double arrows pointing to an atoms signify acceptance of that atom. The language of a state is then defined by the guarded strings that are read along transitions to some state, and terminated by an atom accepted at that state.

$$b + \bar{b} \equiv 1 \qquad b \cdot \bar{b} \equiv 0 \qquad b \cdot b \equiv b \qquad b \cdot c \equiv c \cdot b \qquad b + c \cdot d \equiv (b + c) \cdot (b + d)$$

$$e + 0 \equiv e \qquad e + e \equiv e \qquad e + f \equiv f + e \qquad e \cdot 1 \equiv e \equiv 1 \cdot e \qquad e \cdot 0 \equiv 0 \equiv 0 \cdot e$$

$$e + (f + g) \equiv (e + f) + g \qquad e \cdot (f \cdot g) \equiv (e \cdot f) \cdot g$$

$$e \cdot (f + g) \equiv e \cdot f + e \cdot g \qquad (e + f) \cdot g \equiv e \cdot g + f \cdot g$$

$$1 + e \cdot e^* \equiv e^* \equiv 1 + e^* \cdot e \qquad e + f \cdot g \leqq g \implies f^* \cdot e \leqq g \qquad e + f \cdot g \leqq f \implies e \cdot g^* \leqq f$$

Fig. 3. The axioms of KAT. Here, $\equiv$ is the smallest congruence on KAT that satisfies the laws above for all $e, f, g \in \mathsf{Exp}$ and $b, c, d \in \mathsf{BExp}$. We also write $e \leqq f$ as a shorthand for $e + f \equiv f$; this makes $\leqq$ a partial order (up to $\equiv$).

The conversion from KAT expressions to automata is beyond the scope of this work—suffice it to say that it is not too different from the well-known conversion of regular expressions to finite automata [53]; the procedure to decide language equivalence of (states in) automata on guarded strings is also similar. We only remark here that checking language equivalence in KAT is PSPACE-complete [8], although a practically efficient algorithm exists [40].

2.3 Axiomatization

Besides using the decision procedure sketched above to find out whether two KAT terms are equivalent, we can also reason about them equationally. The relevant axioms (in Fig. 3) combine Boolean Algebra [3] and Kleene Algebra [27].

It is not too difficult to prove soundness of these axioms: when $e \equiv f$, it also holds that $[\![e]\!] = [\![f]\!]$, by induction on $\equiv$. In contrast, *completeness*—i.e., when $[\![e]\!] = [\![f]\!]$, we have that $e \equiv f$—is far from trivial [34]. Known proofs all seem to hinge on a version of Kleene's theorem for KAT.[2] An example of such a proof follows. First, we cast automata as systems of equations in KAT, with a variable for each state. For example, the automaton in Fig. 2 corresponds to

$$\alpha \cdot p_2 \cdot x_1 + \beta \cdot p_1 \cdot x_0 \equiv x_0 \qquad \alpha \cdot p_2 \cdot x_0 + \beta \equiv x_1$$

where x_i is the variable for state q_i, and we used atoms γ to denote the test asserting that $t \in T$ is true if and only if $t \in \gamma$. Such a system of equations admits a *least* solution (w.r.t. $\leqq$) [9,27]; this can be seen as an algebraic take on the construction to convert an automaton to an expression [38]. Moreover, we have a *round trip theorem*: the least solution to the variable for the initial state in the system obtained from the automaton for e is always equivalent to e [27].

Now, given an expression e (resp. f), we can come up with an automaton on guarded strings for e (resp. f), whose language is $[\![e]\!]$ (resp. $[\![f]\!]$). Since $[\![e]\!] = [\![f]\!]$,

[2] More accurately, the usual proof of completeness for KAT [34] relies on a reduction to completeness of Kleene Algebra [27]. The latter typically follows a tactic very close to the one outlined here [21,27,30]. Importantly, the two-way correspondence between expressions and automata is crucial in alternative proofs, too [25].

the automata for e and f have the same language. With some effort, we can then prove that the systems of equations corresponding to equivalent automata must have equivalent least solutions [21,27]. This allows us to conclude that e and f are equivalent, because the least solutions to their automata are, too.

3 Determinism

With the theory discussed so far, it is possible to encode the two programs from Fig. 1, and then either mechanically check that they are equivalent, or prove that this is the case using the laws from Fig. 3. But why should we need to use non-determinism to encode control flow that is essentially deterministic? To explore this question further, we shift gears to talk about GKAT [35,49], the fragment of KAT that can be built using the embeddings of `if` b `then` e `else` f and `while` b `to` e. Formally, the syntax of GKAT is generated as follows:

$$\mathsf{GExp} \ni e, f ::= b \in \mathsf{BExp} \mid p \in \Sigma \mid e +_b f \mid e \cdot f \mid e^{(b)}$$

We use $e +_b f$ as a shorthand for `if` b `then` e `else` f, and $e^{(b)}$ to denote `while` b `do` e. Also, $^{(b)}$ takes precedence over $\cdot$, which has a higher priority than $+_b$.

The semantics of GKAT can be defined by embedding of GKAT into KAT, sending $e +_b f$ to $b \cdot e + \bar{b} \cdot f$, and $e^{(b)}$ to $(b \cdot e)^* \cdot \bar{b}$ [28]. Going forward, when e is a GKAT expression we will simply write $[\![e]\!]$ (resp. $[\![e]\!]_I$) for the guarded language obtained by viewing e as a KAT expression and taking its guarded language (resp. relational semantics w.r.t. I). Alternatively, we can interpret the primitive actions in Σ as functional relations (i.e., partial functions) [4]. If $I = (\sigma, \tau)$ with $\sigma(p)$ a functional relation for each $p \in \Sigma$, then $[\![e]\!]_I$ is also a partial function for each $e \in \mathsf{GExp}$.[3] The connection between the language semantics and relational semantics specializes to partial functions for GKAT: for all $e, f \in \mathsf{GExp}$, we have that $[\![e]\!] = [\![f]\!]$ if and only if $[\![e]\!]_I = [\![f]\!]_I$ for each functional interpretation I.

By treating these constructs as first-class citizens, the automata obtained satisfy a special property: they are *deterministic* [35,49], in the sense that for every atom there is exactly one possibility between accepting, not accepting, or transitioning to a state. Furthermore, when an atom causes a transition to another state, it does so with only one action, and to only one state. The automaton drawn in Fig. 2 is an example of a deterministic automaton. Note that an automaton on guarded strings can be classically deterministic (in that there is at most one transition exiting each state with a given atom and action), while being non-deterministic in our sense—for instance, by having a transition labeled $\alpha|p_1$ to one state, and one labeled $\alpha|p_2$ to another (or the same) state.

This property of automata obtained for GKAT expressions gives rise to a specialized conversion from expressions to automata, in the style of Thompson [51]. Unlike the general conversion from KAT expressions to automata on

[3] We can also directly define a partial function semantics of GKAT expressions, e.g., by sending $e \cdot f$ to $[\![f]\!]_I \circ [\![e]\!]_I$ [4]. The only slightly tricky (but still doable) part is the semantics of loops, which require directed-completeness of partial function inclusion.

$$e +_b e \equiv e \qquad e +_b f \equiv f +_{\overline{b}} e \qquad (e +_b f) +_c \equiv e +_{b \cdot c} (f +_c g) \qquad e +_b f \equiv b \cdot e +_b f$$

$$e \cdot g +_b f \cdot g \equiv (e +_b f) \cdot g \qquad (e \cdot f) \cdot g \equiv e \cdot (f \cdot g) \qquad 0 \cdot e \equiv 0 \equiv e \cdot 0$$

$$1 \cdot e \equiv e \equiv e \cdot 1 \qquad e^{(b)} \equiv e \cdot e^{(b)} +_b 1 \qquad (c \cdot e)^{(b)} \equiv (e +_c 1)^{(b)}$$

Fig. 4. Some axioms of GKAT [49]. Here, $\equiv$ is the smallest congruence on GExp generated by the laws above, for all $e, f, g \in \mathsf{GExp}$ and $b, c \in \mathsf{BExp}$.

guarded strings, this does *not* involve a determinization step, and hence avoids the exponential blowup that may occur. Indeed, the automata produced have a number of states that is *linear* in the size of the expression [49]. We can combine this with an efficient algorithm to check language equivalence of automata [20] to obtain a decision procedure whose complexity is *nearly linear* (thanks to the union-find data structure [50]) in the size of the expressions involved [49].

3.1 Axiomatization

Because GKAT specializes KAT, a natural question is whether the same type of results can be achieved. Previously, we already indicated that an efficient decision procedure exists. Moreover, we can also translate GKAT expressions to KAT expressions, and reason about them there—but can we prove these equivalences *within GKAT*? To this end, we need laws expressed in the language of GKAT itself; some candidates appear in Fig. 4 [49]. For instance, $e \cdot g +_b f \cdot g \equiv (e +_b f) \cdot g$ says that actions common to the end of a conditional can be factored out. Each of these laws can be shown to be sound w.r.t. the semantics [49].

One thing missing from these laws is a description of loops as a least fixed point, like how KAT describes $e^* \cdot f$ as the least fixed point (w.r.t. $\leqq$) of $x \mapsto e \cdot x + f$. The only problem is that, unlike KAT, GKAT does not have a native partial order—for the simple reason that it lacks the $+$ operator from KAT.

The first way to resolve this issue is to axiomatize loops as *unique* fixed points. To a first approximation, it may seem reasonable to stipulate that, if $g \equiv e \cdot g +_b f$, we should be able to conclude that $g \equiv e^{(b)} f$—after all, g seems to be a program that, when b is true, executes e and then restarts, and otherwise executes f. Unfortunately, this rule would be unsound; take for instance $e = f = g = b = 1$: in this case, the premise is true by the laws in Fig. 4, but the consequence $1 \equiv 1^{(1)} \cdot 1$ cannot be accepted. Intuitively, this is because 1 succeeds immediately, while $1^{(1)} \cdot 1$ describes a (non-productive) infinite loop; formally, the relational semantics maps the former to the identity function, and the latter to the empty partial function. More broadly, this issue occurs when the loop body e may be non-productive. To get around this problem, we can take inspiration from the approach championed by Salomaa [45], and define a side-condition to our rule to stipulate that the loop body must be productive. This can be done by defining a function $E : \mathsf{GExp} \to \mathsf{BExp}$ that sends each GKAT program e to a test $E(e)$, describing the circumstances under which e can be "skipped"—i.e.,

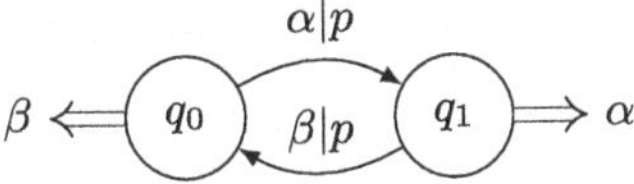

Fig. 5. A deterministic automaton on guarded strings without a solution [46].

executed without performing any action. Formally, E is defined as follows.

$$E(b) = b \qquad E(p) = 0 \qquad E(e +_b f) = b \cdot E(e) + \overline{b} \cdot E(f)$$

$$E(e \cdot f) = E(e) \cdot E(f) \qquad E(e^{(b)}) = \overline{b}$$

We can now state our *unique fixed point* rule as follows: if $g \equiv e \cdot g +_b f$ and $E(e) \equiv 0$, then $g \equiv e^{(b)} \cdot f$. This prevents the earlier pathological case [49].

An alternative approach to the lack of order is to not axiomatize equivalence, but rather inclusion of programs—given e and f, we could look at when $[\![e]\!] \subseteq [\![f]\!]$. To achieve this, we can simply think of the axioms in Fig. 4 as syntactic sugar for two inclusions of this form, i.e., $e +_b e \equiv e$ stands in for $e +_b e \leqq e$ *and* $e \leqq e +_b e$. With that in mind, we can define a least fixed point rule to state that, if $e \cdot g +_b f \leqq g$, then $e^{(b)} \cdot f \leqq g$; this rule is sound w.r.t. the semantics.

Although both approaches produce a sound reasoning system, it is an open problem whether they are *complete*, i.e., whether they can be used to prove any valid equivalence or containment. The root of the problem is that the systems of equations induced by deterministic automata do not always admit a GKAT expression as a solution [35] (we will explore this issue momentarily). As such, the strategies to prove completeness for KAT, which all hinge on being able to solve systems of equations, cannot be cleanly applied in the setting of GKAT.

One way to circumvent this issue and obtain a complete axiomatization is to strengthen the unique fixed point axiom. This axiom states that an equation with one unknown of the form $x \equiv e \cdot x +_b f$ has exactly one solution up to equivalence, namely $e^{(b)}$, provided that $E(e) \equiv 0$. While systems with more than one unknown may not admit any solution, it is sound to say that finite systems of equations with more than one variable (in a similar format), admit *at most* one solution, provided a similar side condition is satisfied [49]. This leads to an infinite number of rules, one for each number of variables; including this infinitary axiom scheme is sufficient to axiomatize equivalence of GKAT [49].

3.2 Expressivity

A moment ago, we noted that not all deterministic automata on guarded strings give rise to a system of equations solvable within GKAT [35,46]. An example of such an automaton is depicted in Fig. 5. Intuitively, the problem there is that there is no condition that terminates the loop: on the left, the atom α resumes the loop while β terminates execution, whereas on the right this is reversed [46].

One might wonder whether the behavior exemplified by this automaton is the *only* deterministic behavior not expressed by GKAT—in other words, can

$$\frac{\alpha \leqq E(e)}{e \Downarrow \alpha} \qquad \frac{}{p \xrightarrow{\alpha|p} 1} \qquad \frac{e \xrightarrow{\alpha|p} e' \quad \alpha \leqq b}{e +_b f \xrightarrow{\alpha|p} e'} \qquad \frac{f \xrightarrow{\alpha|p} f' \quad \alpha \leqq \bar{b}}{e +_b f \xrightarrow{\alpha|p} f'}$$

$$\frac{e \xrightarrow{\alpha|p} e'}{e \cdot f \xrightarrow{\alpha|p} e' \cdot f} \qquad \frac{e \Downarrow \alpha \quad f \xrightarrow{\alpha|p} f'}{e \cdot f \xrightarrow{\alpha|p} f'} \qquad \frac{e \xrightarrow{\alpha|p} e' \quad \alpha \leqq b}{e^{(b)} \xrightarrow{\alpha|p} e' \cdot e^{(b)}}$$

Fig. 6. Operational semantics of GKAT terms [46]. Here, $\alpha \in \mathsf{At}$, $e, f \in \mathsf{GExp}$, and $b \in \mathsf{BExp}$. We use $\leqq$ to denote containment (implication) in Boolean algebra.

we perhaps extend our language with an operation $\mathsf{twostate}(b, c, e)$ corresponding to this automaton? Unfortunately, extending our language like this gets us only so far: it can be shown that there is an infinite hierarchy of automata like this one, each with behavior inexpressible in terms of the ones that came before [4]. Thus, a finite extension of the language of GKAT will not allow us to express all deterministic behaviors. The best we can hope for is a characterization of the class of automata on guarded strings that can be solved within GKAT.

The strongest result that we have to relate GKAT expressions to deterministic automata on guarded strings goes as follows. First, given a deterministic automaton on guarded strings A that is *well-nested* (in a sense not elaborated upon here), we can find a solution e [49]. Conversely, for each GKAT expression e, we can derive a well-nested deterministic automaton on guarded strings A [35,49]. While this is a two-way correspondence between a fragment of deterministic automata on guarded strings, it is somewhat unsatisfactory because well-nestedness is only a sufficient condition for the existence of a solution—we know of automata that do admit a solution, but which are not well-nested [46].

A proper characterization of solvable automata would go a long way towards proving a completeness theorem for GKAT, simply because unique (or least) solutions to automata are such a powerful tool. At the time of writing, a characterization along these lines remains elusive, and so our labor continues.

The problem of characterizing solvable automata is also related to the age-old discussion of which programs can (not) be expressed without `goto` [12,13]. We could therefore think about extending GKAT with *non-local control flow*, i.e., primitives that affect control flow dependent on their context. The automaton in Fig. 5 could be captured by a program like `while` α `do { `p`; if `α` then break; `p` }`. In particular, if we include a `goto` statement in our syntax, then *all* deterministic GKAT automata can be converted to expressions. While such an extension maintains fairly favorable decidability properties [54], it is unclear how the context-dependent semantics of the added control flow statements can be incorporated in the axiomatization. More advanced reasoning techniques, beyond the traditional algebraic ones, may be necessary.

$$\frac{}{1\downarrow} \qquad \frac{e\downarrow}{e+f\downarrow} \qquad \frac{f\downarrow}{e+f\downarrow} \qquad \frac{e\downarrow \quad f\downarrow}{e\cdot f\downarrow} \qquad \frac{}{e^*\downarrow} \qquad \frac{p\in\Sigma}{p\xrightarrow{p}1} \qquad \frac{e\xrightarrow{p}e'}{e+f\xrightarrow{p}e'}$$

$$\frac{f\xrightarrow{p}f'}{e+f\xrightarrow{p}f'} \qquad \frac{e\xrightarrow{p}e'}{e\cdot f\xrightarrow{p}e'\cdot f} \qquad \frac{e\downarrow \quad f\xrightarrow{p}f'}{e\cdot f\xrightarrow{p}f'} \qquad \frac{e\xrightarrow{p}e'}{e^*\xrightarrow{p}e'\cdot e^*}$$

Fig. 7. Transition rules for regular expressions. All of these are quantified over regular expressions e and f, and letters $p \in \Sigma$.

3.3 Bisimilarity

One reasonable objection to the axioms and semantics of GKAT is that it equates programs that fail immediately (e.g., 0) to programs that inevitably fail later (e.g., $e \cdot 0$). This becomes particularly apparent when we realize that the axioms of GKAT allow us to prove that $e^{(b)} \equiv e^{(b)} \cdot \overline{b}$—after all, a loop condition should be false when the loop has ended—and thus $e^{(1)} \equiv e^{(1)} \cdot 0 \equiv 0$. In other words, infinite loops are equivalent to programs that fail immediately [46].

To address this problem, we can instead choose to study the equivalence on GKAT terms induced by *bisimilarity* in the transition system generated by the rules in Fig. 6. More precisely, e and f are bisimilar if there exists a bisimulation that relates them, i.e., a relation R on GExp such that if $e' \mathrel{R} f'$, then $e' \Downarrow \alpha$ implies $f' \Downarrow \alpha$, and if $e' \xrightarrow{\alpha|p} e''$, then $f' \xrightarrow{\alpha|p} f''$ with $e'' \mathrel{R} f''$.[4]

The results that we do have regarding axiomatization of GKAT—i.e., that a generalized unique fixed point rule suffices to obtain completeness—can be recovered for this setting. The only requirement is that we drop the right-annihilation axiom $e \cdot 0 \equiv 0$, because it is incompatible with bisimilarity ($p \cdot 0$ is not bisimilar to 0) [46]. Indeed, from this result we can even recover the original claim about the axiomatization of the language semantics [46]. This suggests that bisimilarity might be more interesting as a primary equivalence for GKAT, which can then be coarsened when language equivalence is more desirable.

4 Connections to Process Algebra

We finish with some exposition on a potential connection to process algebra, and how recent results there can be leveraged to partially answer our questions.

Language equivalence of regular expressions has a well-known axiomatization in the form of Kleene Algebra [27]. However, *bisimilarity* of regular expressions is a different beast altogether, and one that has eluded characterization for quite some time. This problem, first posed by Milner [39], revolves around the transition system on regular expressions induced by the rules in Fig. 7.

It is not too hard to see that, if e and f are bisimilar, then they represent the same regular language. Nevertheless, language equivalence does not imply

[4] Because of determinism, the converse requirement ("back condition") usually included for bisimilarity turns out not to be necessary [49].

bisimilarity—consider for instance the expressions $p_1 \cdot (p_2 + p_3)$ and $p_1 \cdot p_2 + p_1 \cdot p_3$. This example also tells us that the usual distributivity rule for regular expressions does not apply in this setting. Milner recognized this, and conjectured that dropping distributivity and the right annihilation rule $e \cdot 0 \equiv 0$ would give rise to a complete axiomatization of bisimilarity for regular expressions [39].

However, when adapting Salomaa's proof for completeness of regular expressions, an issue very similar to the one encountered above arises: there exist non-deterministic automata that are not bisimilar to any regular expression [39]. This lack of a proper back-and-forth correspondence between expressions and automata proved to be a roadblock towards proving completeness.

Relatively recent work by Grabmayer and Fokkink has made an important step in resolving Milner's conjecture: if we restrict ourselves to the 1-free fragment of regular expressions, i.e., where the constant 1 does not appear and the Kleene star is restricted to be a binary operator (written $e^* f$), then bisimilarity can be axiomatized [18]. Indeed, this result hinges on carving out a class of automata that corresponds to regular expressions up to bisimilarity, but that is also stable under bisimulation collapse [18] (and in fact, under homomorphic images [47]). This property is key to axiomatizing bisimilarity in this fragment.

The theme of characterizing a certain class of automata suggests that perhaps these results about 1-free regular expressions can be adapted to the setting of GKAT, and indeed: a suitably restricted fragment of GKAT, called *skip-free GKAT*, can be axiomatized using the same techniques [24]. Crucially, the result that the class of automata under study is closed under bisimulation collapse, which is extremely tricky to prove, can be reused as-is. Moreover, the techniques can be generalized using a coalgebraic approach to obtain an abstract completeness result that characterizes equivalence of 1-free regular expressions, skip-free GKAT, and even the skip-free fragment of GKAT's probabilistic extension [23].

Finally, a full proof of Milner's conjecture was announced by Grabmayer [17]. While the arguments in that work are highly intricate, and more work is necessary to clarify the details in the accompanying appendices, we remain hopeful that the mathematical essence of this work has the potential for abstraction along the same way as the preceding work on 1-free regular expressions.

5 New Horizons

Besides the two central questions on axiomatization and equivalence, several other worthwhile avenues of research exist. We highlight a few of these now.

First, we can flip the question about expressivity to ask whether we can restrict KAT to express *all* deterministic automata. As indicated before, this is not possible by just adding deterministic composition operators that occur within KAT itself [4]. Nevertheless, it may be possible to devise new deterministic composition operators that do not have an equivalent in KAT. One candidate is the *domain* operator, which turns a program e into a test $D(e)$ that describes the circumstances under which e may terminate successfully [11,48].

Intuitively, we can think of $D(e)$ as a program that calls a function whose body is e, and returns whether e was able to terminate successfully. The hope is that this operator could potentially be used to achieve the deterministic behavior that is normally modelled in KAT by non-deterministic compositions that turn out to behave deterministically, because at most one branch survives. In essence, D might help resolve non-determinism ahead of time, by peeking ahead.

Second, one could try and take another look at the behaviors expressible by GKAT terms from a coalgebraic point of view. Collectively, these behaviors induce a *covariety* of automata [46]. The automata in this covariety can be viewed as Eilenberg-Moore coalgebras for a comonad [15]. One may then ask: can we describe the *coequations* that characterize this comonad? While these notions have well-understood duals (varieties, monads, Eilenberg-Moore algebras), their mathematics leave something to be desired. In particular, there are different methods for "writing down" a coequation [10], and it is not clear which of these (if any) would be appropriate to characterize the automata of GKAT expressions.

Third, Kleene algebra can be extended with hypotheses [14,19,22,32,41,42]. In this setting, we have one or more hypotheses $H = \{e_1 \equiv f_1, \ldots, e_1 \equiv f_n\}$, and we ask whether H, in conjunction with the usual laws of Kleene algebra, is sufficient to prove some equivalence $e \equiv f$. In general, this problem is not decidable [1,28,37], but for special cases, such as when $f_i = 0$ for all i, it is [7]. Moreover, completeness results can also be obtained, usually via a series of reductions to the base completeness theorem for Kleene algebra [41]. We wonder whether similar results can be obtained for GKAT, by leveraging the existing completeness theorem that relies on the infinitary unique solutions axiom. Unfortunately, the answer is not obvious—whereas completeness results about KA with hypotheses typically rely on *saturating* an expression to include all of the behavior deemed equivalent by the hypotheses [14], such an approach is not immediately possible in GKAT, for lack of the $+$ operator.

Fourth, perhaps the most applied direction to take GKAT lies in analyzing (de)compilers. On the one hand, a compiler typically performs a great number of non-trivial program transformations; perhaps the theory of GKAT can aid in verifying some of these—as was done with KAT [33]. On the other hand, *decompilers* are tasked with analyzing binary code, with the aim of obtaining a more high-level representation of the intended behavior in a programming language [6]. Part of the challenge there lies in structuring control flow that is essentially represented in the form of an automaton. New developments in characterizations of solvable automata could help improve decompilers. Conversely, we believe there is much to be learned from modern decompilers, and that perhaps GKAT could one day serve as the theoretical backbone of a verified decompiler [54].

Finally, there are interesting developments further afield, such as probabilistic [44], relational [16] and weighted [52] extensions of GKAT, as well as connections to modal logic [2] and cyclic proof systems [43].

Acknowledgements. I am grateful to Balder ten Cate, Nate Foster, Justin Hsu, Dexter Kozen, David E. Narváez, Nico Naus, Wojciech Różowski, Todd Schmid, Alexandra Silva, Steffen Smolka, and Cheng Zhang for the wonderful collaborations on this topic, and Todd Schmid in particular for helpful commentary on a first draft of this manuscript. I would furthermore like to thank Jurriaan Rot and Jana Wagemaker for their thoughtful insights, and Hendrik Jan Hoogeboom for proposing the example of the two in-order tree traversal algorithms.

This work was supported by the Dutch Research Council (NWO) under grant no. VI.Veni.232.286 (ChEOpS).

References

1. Azevedo de Amorim, A., Zhang, C., Gaboardi, M.: Kleene algebra with commutativity conditions is undecidable. In: CSL, pp. 36:1–36:25 (2025). https://doi.org/10.4230/LIPICS.CSL.2025.36
2. Benevides, M., Gomes, L., Lopes, B.: Towards determinism in PDL: relations and proof theory. J. Logic Comput., exae022 (2024)
3. Birkhoff, G., Bartee, T.C.: Modern Applied Algebra. McGraw-Hill, Boston (1970)
4. ten Cate, B., Kappé, T.: Algebras for deterministic computation are inherently incomplete. In: POPL, pp. 25:1–25:27 (2025). https://doi.org/10.1145/3704861
5. Chen, H., Pucella, R.: A coalgebraic approach to Kleene algebra with tests. Theor. Comput. Sci. **327**(1–2), 23–44 (2004). https://doi.org/10.1016/j.tcs.2004.07.020
6. Cifuentes, C.: Reverse compilation techniques. Ph.D. thesis, Queensland University of Technology (1994)
7. Cohen, E.: Hypotheses in Kleene algebra. Technical report, Bellcore (1994)
8. Cohen, E., Kozen, D., Smith, F.: The complexity of Kleene algebra with tests. Technical Report. TR96-1598, Cornell University (1996)
9. Conway, J.H.: Regular Algebra and Finite Machines. Chapman and Hall Ltd., London (1971)
10. Dahlqvist, F., Schmid, T.: How to write a coequation ((co)algebraic pearls). In: CALCO, pp. 13:1–13:25 (2021). https://doi.org/10.4230/LIPICS.CALCO.2021.13
11. Desharnais, J., Möller, B., Struth, G.: Kleene algebra with domain. ACM Trans. Comput. Log. **7**(4), 798–833 (2006). https://doi.org/10.1145/1183278.1183285
12. Dijkstra, E.W.: Letters to the editor: go to statement considered harmful. Commun. ACM **11**(3), 147–148 (1968). https://doi.org/10.1145/362929.362947
13. Dijkstra, E.W.: On a somewhat disappointing correspondence (1987). http://www.cs.utexas.edu/users/EWD/ewd10xx/EWD1009.PDF
14. Doumane, A., Kuperberg, D., Pous, D., Pradic, P.: Kleene algebra with hypotheses. In: FoSSaCS, pp. 207–223 (2019). https://doi.org/10.1007/978-3-030-17127-8_12
15. Goldblatt, R.: A comonadic account of behavioural covarieties of coalgebras. Math. Struct. Comput. Sci. **15**(2), 243–269 (2005). https://doi.org/10.1017/S096012950400458X
16. Gomes, L., Baillot, P., Gaboardi, M.: BiGKAT: an algebraic framework for relational verification of probabilistic programs. In: FoSSaCS, pp. 243–264 (2025). https://doi.org/10.1007/978-3-031-90897-2_12
17. Grabmayer, C.: Milner's proof system for regular expressions modulo bisimilarity is complete. In: LICS, pp. 34:1–34:13. ACM (2022). https://doi.org/10.1145/3531130.3532430. https://arxiv.org/abs/2209.12188
18. Grabmayer, C., Fokkink, W.J.: A complete proof system for 1-free regular expressions modulo bisimilarity. In: LICS, pp. 465–478. ACM (2020). https://doi.org/10.1145/3373718.3394744
19. Hardin, C.: The Horn theory of relational Kleene algebra. Ph.D. thesis, Cornell University (2005)

20. Hopcroft, J.E., Karp, R.M.: A linear algorithm for testing equivalence of finite automata. Technical Report. TR71-114, Cornell University (1971)
21. Jacobs, B.: A bialgebraic review of deterministic automata, regular expressions and languages. In: Algebra, Meaning, and Computation, Essays Dedicated to Joseph A. Goguen on the Occasion of His 65th Birthday, pp. 375–404 (2006). https://doi.org/10.1007/11780274_20
22. Kappé, T., Brunet, P., Silva, A., Wagemaker, J., Zanasi, F.: Concurrent Kleene algebra with observations: from hypotheses to completeness. In: FoSSaCS, pp. 381–400 (2020). https://doi.org/10.1007/978-3-030-45231-5_20
23. Kappé, T., Schmid, T.: A general completeness theorem for skip-free star algebras. In: FoSSaCS, pp. 265–286 (2025). https://doi.org/10.1007/978-3-031-90897-2_13
24. Kappé, T., Schmid, T., Silva, A.: A complete inference system for skip-free guarded Kleene algebra with tests. In: ESOP, pp. 309–336 (2023). https://doi.org/10.1007/978-3-031-30044-8_12. https://arxiv.org/abs/2301.11301
25. Kappé, T.: An elementary proof of the FMP for Kleene algebra (2024). https://arxiv.org/abs/2212.10931
26. Knuth, D.E.: The Art of Computer Programming, Volume I: Fundamental Algorithms, 3rd edn. Addison-Wesley, Boston (1997)
27. Kozen, D.: A completeness theorem for Kleene algebras and the algebra of regular events. Inf. Comput. **110**(2), 366–390 (1994). https://doi.org/10.1006/inco.1994.1037
28. Kozen, D.: Kleene algebra with tests and commutativity conditions. In: TACAS, pp. 14–33 (1996). https://doi.org/10.1007/3-540-61042-1_35
29. Kozen, D.: Kleene algebra with tests. ACM Trans. Program. Lang. Syst. **19**(3), 427–443 (1997). https://doi.org/10.1145/256167.256195
30. Kozen, D.: Myhill-Nerode relations on automatic systems and the completeness of Kleene algebra. In: STACS, pp. 27–38 (2001). https://doi.org/10.1007/3-540-44693-1_3
31. Kozen, D.: Automata on guarded strings and applications. Matematica Contemporanea **24**, 117–139 (2003)
32. Kozen, D., Mamouras, K.: Kleene algebra with equations. In: ICALP, pp. 280–292 (2014). https://doi.org/10.1007/978-3-662-43951-7_24
33. Kozen, D., Patron, M.C.: Certification of compiler optimizations using Kleene algebra with tests. In: CL, pp. 568–582 (2000). https://doi.org/10.1007/3-540-44957-4_38
34. Kozen, D., Smith, F.: Kleene algebra with tests: completeness and decidability. In: CSL, pp. 244–259 (1996). https://doi.org/10.1007/3-540-63172-0_43
35. Kozen, D., Tseng, W.D.: The Böhm-Jacopini theorem is false, propositionally. In: MPC, pp. 177–192 (2008). https://doi.org/10.1007/978-3-540-70594-9_11
36. KROB, D.: A complete system of B-rational identities. In: Paterson, M.S. (ed.) ICALP 1990. LNCS, vol. 443, pp. 60–73. Springer, Heidelberg (1990). https://doi.org/10.1007/BFb0032022
37. Kuznetsov, S.L.: On the complexity of reasoning in Kleene algebra with commutativity conditions. In: ICTAC, pp. 83–99 (2023). https://doi.org/10.1007/978-3-031-47963-2_7
38. McNaughton, R., Yamada, H.: Regular expressions and state graphs for automata. IRE Trans. Electron. Comput. **9**(1), 39–47 (1960). https://doi.org/10.1109/TEC.1960.5221603
39. Milner, R.: A complete inference system for a class of regular behaviours. J. Comput. Syst. Sci. **28**(3), 439–466 (1984). https://doi.org/10.1016/0022-0000(84)90023-0

40. Pous, D.: Symbolic algorithms for language equivalence and Kleene algebra with tests. In: POPL, pp. 357–368 (2015). https://doi.org/10.1145/2676726.2677007
41. Pous, D., Rot, J., Wagemaker, J.: On tools for completeness of Kleene algebra with hypotheses. Log. Methods Comput. Sci. **20**(2) (2024). https://doi.org/10.46298/LMCS-20(2:8)2024
42. Pous, D., Wagemaker, J.: Completeness theorems for Kleene algebra with tests and top. Log. Methods Comput. Sci. **20**(3) (2024). https://doi.org/10.46298/LMCS-20(3:27)2024
43. Rooduijn, J., Kozen, D., Silva, A.: A cyclic proof system for guarded Kleene algebra with tests. In: IJCAR, pp. 257–275 (2024). https://doi.org/10.1007/978-3-031-63501-4_14
44. Różowski, W., Kappé, T., Kozen, D., Schmid, T., Silva, A.: Probabilistic guarded KAT modulo bisimilarity: completeness and complexity. In: ICALP (2023). https://doi.org/10.4230/LIPIcs.ICALP.2023.136
45. Salomaa, A.: Two complete axiom systems for the algebra of regular events. J. ACM **13**(1), 158–169 (1966). https://doi.org/10.1145/321312.321326
46. Schmid, T., Kappé, T., Kozen, D., Silva, A.: Guarded Kleene algebra with tests: coequations, coinduction, and completeness. In: ICALP, pp. 142:1–142:14 (2021). https://doi.org/10.4230/LIPICS.ICALP.2021.142
47. Schmid, T., Rot, J., Silva, A.: On star expressions and coalgebraic completeness theorems. In: MFPS, pp. 242–259 (2021). https://doi.org/10.4204/EPTCS.351.15
48. Sedlár, I.: Kleene algebra with dynamic tests: completeness and complexity (2023). https://arxiv.org/abs/2311.06937
49. Smolka, S., Foster, N., Hsu, J., Kappé, T., Kozen, D., Silva, A.: Guarded Kleene algebra with tests: verification of uninterpreted programs in nearly linear time. In: POPL, pp. 61:1–61:28 (2020). https://doi.org/10.1145/3371129
50. Tarjan, R.E.: Efficiency of a good but not linear set union algorithm. J. ACM **22**(2), 215–225 (1975). https://doi.org/10.1145/321879.321884
51. Thompson, K.: Regular expression search algorithm. Commun. ACM **11**(6), 419–422 (1968). https://doi.org/10.1145/363347.363387
52. Van Koevering, S., Rozowski, W., Silva, A.: Weighted GKAT: completeness and complexity (2025). https://arxiv.org/abs/2504.20385
53. Watson, B.W.: A taxonomy of finite automata construction algorithms. Technical report, Technische Universiteit Eindhoven (1993). https://research.tue.nl/files/2482472/9313452
54. Zhang, C., Kappé, T., Narváez, D.E., Naus, N.: CF-GKAT: efficient validation of control-flow transformations. In: POPL, pp. 21:1–21:27 (2025). https://doi.org/10.1145/3704857

Contributed papers

Deep Induction for Inductive Families

Patricia Johann(✉) and Edward Morehouse

Appalachian State University, Boone, NC 28608, USA
johannp@appstate.edu, edward.morehouse@gmail.com

Abstract. Deep induction provides induction rules for deep data types, i.e., data types that are defined over, or mutually recursively with, (other) such data types. Deep induction is currently defined only for type-indexed types, such as ADTs, nested types, and GADTs. In this paper we show how to extend deep induction from data types with only type indices to data types with term indices as well. Specifically, we extend to inductive families—as found in dependently typed systems such as Agda, Epigram, and Idris—the methodology for deriving sound deep induction rules that was originally developed for nested types and has recently been extended to GADTs.

Keywords: Deep induction · inductive families · proof assistants

1 Introduction

Indexed programming is the practice of programming with indexed types. Perhaps the most common form of indexing indexes types by (other) types. Type-indexed types are found in, e.g., the functional languages Haskell [17] and ML [15]. The essential idea is that a type like List can be indexed by another type that classifies the data it contains. For example, lists of integers, lists of booleans, and lists of lists of data of type t can be modeled by the type-indexed types $\mathsf{List\,Int}$, $\mathsf{List\,Bool}$, and $\mathsf{List\,(List\,t)}$, respectively. More modern programming languages allow types to be indexed not just by types, but also by terms. The essential idea is that a type like List can be indexed by a term that represents, e.g., the length of the list or a proof that it satisfies some property. For instance, lists of length 3 and lists that a proof term p proves are sorted can be modeled by term-indexed types such as $\mathsf{List\,3}$ and $\mathsf{List\,p}$, respectively. (Type- and) term-indexed types are supported as inductive families (IFs) [7] in dependently typed systems such as Agda [1,16], Epigram [13,14], and Idris [9].

Deep induction was introduced in [11] to give induction rules for type-indexed data types that are *deep*, i.e., defined over, or mutually recursively with, (other) such data types. Examples of such data types include, trivially, ordinary algebraic data types (ADTs) and nested types; data types, like that of forests from [11], whose recursive occurrences appear below other type constructors; so-called *truly* nested types, like that of bushes from [2], whose recursive occurrences can appear below their own type constructors; and generalized algebraic data types

D. Kozen and R. de Queiroz (Eds.): WoLLIC 2025, LNCS 15942, pp. 21–37, 2026.
https://doi.org/10.1007/978-3-031-99536-1_2

(GADTs) [3,22], as found in Haskell and Agda. Of course, term-indexed types such as IFs can also be deep, both in the type-indexed data types that underlie them—i.e., the data types obtained by erasing their term indices—and in the data types (which can also be IFs) that index those underlying data types.

In this paper we show how deep induction can be extended from data types that allow only type indexing to those that also allow term indexing. In fact, we extend to IFs the entire methodology for deriving sound deep induction rules that was developed for nested types in [11] and extended to GADTs in [10]. The structural induction rules currently generated by proof assistants for deep data types induct only over their top-level structures and leave any data internal to that top-level structure untouched; as a result, proof assistants currently provide insufficient support for inducting over deep data types. By contrast, deep induction inducts over *all* of the structured data present in a data type. This opens the way for incorporating automatic generation of truly useful induction rules for deep data types, including deep IFs, into state-of-the-art proof assistants.

The remainder of this paper is structured as follows. The rest of this section discusses deep induction for IFs in the context of related work. Section 2 reviews the current state-of-the-art of deep induction for GADTs. These are the most general data types having type indices only. Section 3 illustrates our methodology for extending deep induction from GADTs to *proper* IFs, i.e., IFs that involve term-indexing, and thus are not GADTs. In Sect. 4 we present our general methodology for deriving deep induction rules for IFs, show that both our methodology and the deep induction rules it delivers generalize those for GADTs, and observe that each concrete instance of a deep induction rule appearing in this paper has been derived by instantiating our methodology. Section 5 contains an application of deep induction for IFs. Our Agda implementation containing all of the deep induction rules appearing in this paper (and proof terms that witness their soundness) is available at https://cs.appstate.edu/johannp/.

Related Work. Deep induction was introduced for nested types in [11] and extended to GADTs in [10]. The methodology for deriving deep induction rules developed in this paper further extends that in [10] to IFs. The relationship between our results and those of [10,11] are discussed in detail throughout this paper.

To the best of our knowledge, other work on generating induction rules for IFs is either restricted to structural induction (see, e.g., [4–7]) or fails to adequately account for depth in term indices. For example, both [20] and [21] derive induction rules that are deep for nested types and some IF's whose underlying data types and indexing types are containers. But since they generate only trivial predicates for types such as the natural numbers, the derived induction rule for, e.g., vectors (length-indexed lists), is reduced to that for their underlying lists.

2 The State-of-the-Art in Deep Induction

To illustrate the difference between structural induction and deep induction, consider the following data type of lists:[1]

$$\begin{array}{l} \mathsf{data\,List\,(a : Set) : Set\,where} \\ \quad [\,] : \mathsf{List\,a} \\ \quad \_::\_ \;:\; \mathsf{a} \to \mathsf{List\,a} \to \mathsf{List\,a} \end{array}$$

Since it uses a predicate P on entire lists, the data inside an element of type List a are essentially ignored by the standard structural induction rule for lists:

$$\begin{array}{l} (\mathsf{P} : \mathsf{List\,a} \to \mathsf{Set}) \to \mathsf{P}\,[\,] \to \\ \quad ((\mathsf{x} : \mathsf{a}) \to (\mathsf{xs} : \mathsf{List\,a}) \to \mathsf{P\,xs} \to \mathsf{P}\,(\mathsf{x} :: \mathsf{xs})) \to \\ \quad (\mathsf{xs} : \mathsf{List\,a}) \to \mathsf{P\,xs} \end{array} \tag{1}$$

By contrast, the deep induction rule for lists traverses not just the outer list structure with P, but also each element of that list with a custom predicate Q:

$$\begin{array}{l} (\mathsf{P} : \mathsf{List\,a} \to \mathsf{Set}) \to (\mathsf{Q} : \mathsf{a} \to \mathsf{Set}) \to \\ \quad \mathsf{P}\,[\,] \to ((\mathsf{x} : \mathsf{a}) \to (\mathsf{xs} : \mathsf{List\,a}) \to \mathsf{Q\,x} \to \mathsf{P\,xs} \to \mathsf{P}\,(\mathsf{x} :: \mathsf{xs})) \to \\ \quad (\mathsf{xs} : \mathsf{List\,a}) \to \mathsf{List}^\wedge\,\mathsf{Q\,xs} \to \mathsf{P\,xs} \end{array} \tag{2}$$

Here, the lifting $\mathsf{List}^\wedge$ lifts its argument predicate Q on data of type a to a predicate on data of type List a by asserting that $\mathsf{List}^\wedge$ Q holds of xs : List a precisely when Q holds for every element of xs. It can be defined in Agda by:

$$\begin{array}{l} \mathsf{List}^\wedge : (\mathsf{a} \to \mathsf{Set}) \to \mathsf{List\,a} \to \mathsf{Set} \\ \mathsf{List}^\wedge\,\mathsf{Q}\,[\,] \;=\; \top \\ \mathsf{List}^\wedge\,\mathsf{Q}\,(\mathsf{x} :: \mathsf{xs}) \;=\; \mathsf{Q\,x} \times \mathsf{List}^\wedge\,\mathsf{Q\,xs} \end{array}$$

The structural induction rule for lists can be recovered by taking the custom predicate Q in their deep induction rule to be the constantly $\top$-valued predicate.

Just as structural induction can be extended to nested types, so can deep induction. Consider, for example, the following type of perfect trees from [2]:

$$\begin{array}{l} \mathsf{data\,PTree\,(a : Set) : Set\,where} \\ \quad \mathsf{pleaf} \;:\; \mathsf{a} \to \mathsf{PTree\,a} \\ \quad \mathsf{pnode} \;:\; \mathsf{PTree}\,(\mathsf{a} \times \mathsf{a}) \to \mathsf{PTree\,a} \end{array}$$

Since the constructor pnode uses data of type PTree (a × a) to construct data of type PTree a, the instances of PTree at various indices cannot be defined independently, and the entire inductive family of types must be defined at once. This

[1] We use Agda syntax for concreteness of exposition in this paper. Specifically, to avoid repetition our development uses Agda's facility for generalizing declared variables whose types are easily inferred. Thus, throughout the paper, implicitly bound occurrences of a, b, c, and d have type Set and implicitly bound occurrences of m and n have type Nat. We emphasize, however, that our results are not Agda-specific.

intertwinedness of the instances of nested types is reflected in their both their structural and their deep induction rules, which, as explained in [11], must necessarily involve polymorphic predicates rather than the monomorphic predicates that suffice for lists and other ADTs. The deep induction rule for perfect trees is thus:

$$\begin{array}{l}(\mathsf{P} : \{\mathsf{a} : \mathsf{Set}\} \to (\mathsf{a} \to \mathsf{Set}) \to \mathsf{PTree\,a} \to \mathsf{Set}) \to \\ \quad (\{\mathsf{a} : \mathsf{Set}\} \to (\mathsf{Q} : \mathsf{a} \to \mathsf{Set}) \to (\mathsf{x} : \mathsf{a}) \to \mathsf{Q\,x} \to \mathsf{P\,Q\,(pleaf\,x)}) \to \\ \quad (\{\mathsf{a} : \mathsf{Set}\} \to (\mathsf{Q} : \mathsf{a} \to \mathsf{Set}) \to (\mathsf{xs} : \mathsf{PTree\,(a \times a)}) \to \mathsf{P\,(\times^\wedge\,Q\,Q)\,xs} \to \mathsf{P\,Q\,(pnode\,xs)}) \to \\ \quad (\mathsf{Q} : \mathsf{a} \to \mathsf{Set}) \to (\mathsf{xs} : \mathsf{PTree\,a}) \to \mathsf{PTree^\wedge\,Q\,xs} \to \mathsf{P\,Q\,xs}\end{array} \tag{3}$$

where the lifting $\times^\wedge : (\mathsf{a} \to \mathsf{Set}) \to (\mathsf{b} \to \mathsf{Set}) \to \mathsf{a} \times \mathsf{b} \to \mathsf{Set}$ is given by $\times^\wedge\, \mathsf{Q_a}\, \mathsf{Q_b}\, (\mathsf{x}, \mathsf{y}) = \mathsf{Q_a}\, \mathsf{x} \times \mathsf{Q_b}\, \mathsf{y}$, and the lifting $\mathsf{PTree}^\wedge$ is given by:

$$\begin{array}{lcl}\mathsf{PTree}^\wedge : (\mathsf{a} \to \mathsf{Set}) \to \mathsf{PTree\,a} \to \mathsf{Set} \\ \mathsf{PTree}^\wedge\,\mathsf{Q}\,(\mathsf{pleaf\,x}) & = & \mathsf{Q\,x} \\ \mathsf{PTree}^\wedge\,\mathsf{Q}\,(\mathsf{pnode\,xs}) & = & \mathsf{PTree}^\wedge\,(\times^\wedge\,\mathsf{Q\,Q})\,\mathsf{xs}\end{array}$$

The structural induction rule for perfect trees is obtained by taking Q in (3) to be the constantly $\top$-valued predicate. Similar instantiation shows that the deep induction rule for *any* nested type (indeed, any IF considered in this paper) syntactically generalizes its structural induction rule. The two rules have exactly the same computational power, however.

On the other hand, deep induction actually *is* central to generating genuinely useful induction rules for deep data types. Among these are the truly nested type of bushes, and the data type of forests, which is deep but not truly nested:

```
data Bush (a : Set) : Set where
  bnil : Bush a
  bcons : a → Bush (Bush a) → Bush a

data Forest (a : Set) : Set where
  fempty : Forest a
  fnode  : a → List (Forest a) → Forest a
```

The structural induction rule generated by Coq for forests is

$$\begin{array}{l}(\mathsf{P} : \mathsf{Forest\,a} \to \mathsf{Set}) \to \mathsf{P\,fempty} \to \\ \quad ((\mathsf{x} : \mathsf{a}) \to (\mathsf{xss} : \mathsf{List\,(Forest\,a)}) \to \mathsf{P\,(fnode\,x\,xss)}) \to (\mathsf{xs} : \mathsf{Forest\,a}) \to \mathsf{P\,xs}.\end{array}$$

But this is neither the intuitively expected induction rule for them, nor is it expressive enough to prove even basic properties of forests that ought to be amenable to inductive proof. The deep induction rule for forests from [11] is:

$$\begin{array}{l}(\mathsf{P} : \mathsf{Forest\,a} \to \mathsf{Set}) \to (\mathsf{Q} : \mathsf{a} \to \mathsf{Set}) \to \mathsf{P\,fempty} \to \\ \quad ((\mathsf{x} : \mathsf{a}) \to (\mathsf{xss} : \mathsf{List\,(Forest\,a)}) \to \mathsf{Q\,x} \to \mathsf{List^\wedge\,P\,xss} \to \mathsf{P\,(fnode\,x\,xss)}) \to \\ \quad (\mathsf{xs} : \mathsf{Forest\,a}) \to \mathsf{Forest^\wedge\,Q\,xs} \to \mathsf{P\,xs}\end{array}$$

where

$$\begin{array}{lcl}\mathsf{Forest}^\wedge : (\mathsf{a} \to \mathsf{Set}) \to \mathsf{Forest\,a} \to \mathsf{Set} \\ \mathsf{Forest}^\wedge\,\mathsf{Q\,fempty} & = & \top \\ \mathsf{Forest}^\wedge\,\mathsf{Q}\,(\mathsf{fnode\,x\,xss}) & = & \mathsf{Q\,x} \times \mathsf{List}^\wedge\,(\mathsf{Forest}^\wedge\,\mathsf{Q})\,\mathsf{xss}\end{array}$$

This rule is of much more use. The special case when Q is the constantly $\top$-valued predicate is equivalent to the expected induction rule as classically stated in Coq.

In [11], deep induction was also shown to be the key to defining *structural* induction rules for truly nested types like Bush. The deep induction rule for any nested type must account for the potentially different instances at which it is instantiated in its definition; for a truly nested type some of these may be itself. As detailed in [11], taking Q to be the constantly $\top$-valued predicate in the following deep induction rule for Bush gives the structural induction rule for Bush:

$$
\begin{aligned}
&(\mathsf{P} : \{\mathsf{a} : \mathsf{Set}\} \to (\mathsf{a} \to \mathsf{Set}) \to \mathsf{Bush\,a} \to \mathsf{Set}) \to\\
&\quad(\{\mathsf{a} : \mathsf{Set}\} \to (\mathsf{Q} : \mathsf{a} \to \mathsf{Set}) \to \mathsf{P\,Q\,bnil}) \to\\
&\quad(\{\mathsf{a} : \mathsf{Set}\} \to (\mathsf{x} : \mathsf{a}) \to (\mathsf{xss} : \mathsf{Bush\,(Bush\,a)}) \to (\mathsf{Q} : \mathsf{a} \to \mathsf{Set}) \to\\
&\qquad\mathsf{Q\,x} \to \mathsf{P\,(P\,Q)\,xss} \to \mathsf{P\,Q\,(bcons\,x\,xss)}) \to\\
&\quad(\mathsf{Q} : \mathsf{a} \to \mathsf{Set}) \to (\mathsf{xs} : \mathsf{Bush\,a}) \to \mathsf{Bush}^\wedge\,\mathsf{Q\,xs} \to \mathsf{P\,Q\,xs}
\end{aligned}
$$

where

$$
\begin{aligned}
&\mathsf{Bush}^\wedge : (\mathsf{a} \to \mathsf{Set}) \to \mathsf{Bush\,a} \to \mathsf{Set}\\
&\mathsf{Bush}^\wedge\,\mathsf{Q\,bnil} \;=\; \top\\
&\mathsf{Bush}^\wedge\,\mathsf{Q\,(bcons\,x\,xss)} = \mathsf{Q\,x} \times \mathsf{Bush}^\wedge\,(\mathsf{Bush}^\wedge\,\mathsf{Q})\,\mathsf{xss}
\end{aligned}
$$

Deep induction has been recently extended to GADTs in [10]. A simple example of a GADT is the data type Seq of sequences:[2]

$$
\begin{aligned}
&\mathsf{data\,Seq} : \mathsf{Set} \to \mathsf{Set\,where}\\
&\quad\mathsf{inj} : \mathsf{a} \to \mathsf{Seq\,a}\\
&\quad\mathsf{pair} : \mathsf{Seq\,b} \to \mathsf{Seq\,c} \to \mathsf{Seq\,(b \times c)}
\end{aligned}
$$

Note that Seq's data constructor pair constructs only sequences of data whose types are pair-structured, rather than sequences of any type, as does its data constructor inj. It can be fruitful to capture this kind of non-uniformity in the return types of GADTs' data constructors via their so-called *Henry Ford encodings* [3,8,12,18,19]. These encodings use the following equality type from Agda's standard library to, in essence, turn GADTs into nested types:

$$\mathsf{data}\ \_\!\equiv\!\_\ (\mathsf{x} : \mathsf{a}) : \mathsf{a} \to \mathsf{Set\,where\,refl} : \mathsf{x} \equiv \mathsf{x}$$

The Henry Ford encoding for Seq, for example, replaces the requirement that the data constructor pair produce data at an instance of Seq that is a product type with the requirement that pair produce data at an instance of Seq that is *equal* to a product type. It is:

$$
\begin{aligned}
&\mathsf{data\,Seq\,(a : Set)} : \mathsf{Set\,where}\\
&\quad\mathsf{inj} : \mathsf{a} \to \mathsf{Seq\,a}\\
&\quad\mathsf{pair} : (\mathsf{b} \times \mathsf{c}) \equiv \mathsf{a} \to \mathsf{Seq\,b} \to \mathsf{Seq\,c} \to \mathsf{Seq\,a}
\end{aligned}
\tag{4}
$$

Henry Ford encodings for other GADTs are obtained similarly.

[2] The type of Seq is actually $\mathsf{Set} \to \mathsf{Set}_1$, but to aid readability we elide the explicit tracking of Agda universe levels in this paper.

Deep induction rules for GADTs can now be defined using the lifting

$$\begin{aligned}&\equiv^\wedge : (\mathsf{a} \to \mathsf{Set}) \to (\mathsf{b} \to \mathsf{Set}) \to \mathsf{a} \equiv \mathsf{b} \to \mathsf{Set}\\ &\equiv^\wedge \ \mathsf{Q}\,\mathsf{Q}'\,\mathsf{refl} \ = \ (\mathsf{x} : \mathsf{a}) \to \mathsf{Q}\,\mathsf{x} \equiv \mathsf{Q}'\,\mathsf{x}\end{aligned}$$

for equality types, together with existentially quantified predicates[3] and the original methodology for nested types, to define their predicate liftings via their Henry Ford encodings. This approach gives the following lifting $\mathsf{Seq}^\wedge$ for Seq:

$$\begin{aligned}&\mathsf{Seq}^\wedge : (\mathsf{a} \to \mathsf{Set}) \to \mathsf{Seq}\,\mathsf{a} \to \mathsf{Set}\\ &\mathsf{Seq}^\wedge\,\mathsf{Q_a}\,(\mathsf{inj}\,\mathsf{x}) = \mathsf{Q_a}\,\mathsf{x}\\ &\mathsf{Seq}^\wedge\,\mathsf{Q_a}\,(\mathsf{pair}\,\mathsf{p}\,\mathsf{s_b}\,\mathsf{s_c}) = \exists[\mathsf{Q_b}]\exists[\mathsf{Q_c}] \ \equiv^\wedge (\times^\wedge\,\mathsf{Q_b}\,\mathsf{Q_c})\,\mathsf{Q_a}\,\mathsf{p} \times \mathsf{Seq}^\wedge\,\mathsf{Q_b}\,\mathsf{s_b} \times \mathsf{Seq}^\wedge\,\mathsf{Q_c}\,\mathsf{s_c}\end{aligned} \tag{5}$$

The lifting for Seq introduces new predicates on the new types introduced by its Henry Ford encoding, and then enforces the necessary connections between them and the predicates on the types present in the original data type declaration. For pair, e.g., it introduces predicates $\mathsf{Q_b}$ and $\mathsf{Q_c}$ on the types b and c introduced by Seq's Henry Ford encoding, and then ensures that $\mathsf{Q_b} \times \mathsf{Q_c}$ and $\mathsf{Q_a}$ are equal. Otherwise it simply performs the usual two tasks of liftings, namely (i) ensuring that any new primitive data used to construct a data element satisfy their predicates, and (ii) ensuring that all of that data element's recursive subdata also satisfy appropriate liftings of those predicates. The deep induction rule for Seq is:

$$\begin{aligned}&(\mathsf{P} : \{\mathsf{a} : \mathsf{Set}\} \to (\mathsf{a} \to \mathsf{Set}) \to \mathsf{Seq}\,\mathsf{a} \to \mathsf{Set}) \to\\ &\quad (\{\mathsf{a} : \mathsf{Set}\} \to (\mathsf{x} : \mathsf{a}) \to (\mathsf{Q_a} : \mathsf{a} \to \mathsf{Set}) \to \mathsf{Q_a}\,\mathsf{x} \to \mathsf{P}\,\mathsf{Q_a}\,(\mathsf{inj}\,\mathsf{x})) \to\\ &\quad (\{\mathsf{a}\,\mathsf{b}\,\mathsf{c} : \mathsf{Set}\} \to (\mathsf{p} : (\mathsf{b} \times \mathsf{c}) \equiv \mathsf{a}) \to (\mathsf{s_b} : \mathsf{Seq}\,\mathsf{b}) \to (\mathsf{s_c} : \mathsf{Seq}\,\mathsf{c}) \to (\mathsf{Q_a} : \mathsf{a} \to \mathsf{Set}) \to\\ &\qquad (\mathsf{Q_b} : \mathsf{b} \to \mathsf{Set}) \to (\mathsf{Q_c} : \mathsf{c} \to \mathsf{Set}) \to \mathsf{P}\,\mathsf{Q_b}\,\mathsf{s_b} \to \mathsf{P}\,\mathsf{Q_c}\,\mathsf{s_c} \to \mathsf{P}\,\mathsf{Q_a}\,(\mathsf{pair}\,\mathsf{p}\,\mathsf{s_b}\,\mathsf{s_c})) \to\\ &\quad (\mathsf{Q_a} : \mathsf{a} \to \mathsf{Set}) \to (\mathsf{s} : \mathsf{Seq}\,\mathsf{a}) \to \mathsf{Seq}^\wedge\,\mathsf{Q_a}\,\mathsf{s} \to \mathsf{P}\,\mathsf{Q_a}\,\mathsf{s}\end{aligned} \tag{6}$$

This Paper

In this paper we extend deep induction from GADTs to IFs. Unlike GADTs, whose indices are always *types*, IFs also allow indices that are *terms*. The predicate in the deep induction rule for an IF must therefore take as input predicates not only on its type indices but on the types of its term indices as well. To obtain an IF's deep induction rule, all of these predicates must be appropriately propagated to all of the primitive data in the IF's data elements. Properly accounting for conditions under which term indices must satisfy their predicates is thus the central challenge in extending deep induction from GADTs to proper IFs.

We do exactly this in this paper. Moreover, we account for term indices in such a way that the deep induction rules for IFs we develop specialize to the

[3] The suggestive notation $\exists[\mathsf{x}]\,\mathsf{F}\,\mathsf{x}$ is syntactic sugar for the type of dependent pairs (x, b) with $\mathsf{x} : \mathsf{a}$, $\mathsf{b} : \mathsf{F}\,\mathsf{x}$, and $\mathsf{F} : \mathsf{a} \to \mathsf{Set}$.

rules of [10] for those IFs that can be seen as GADTs (and thus to the rules of [11] for those IFs that can be seen as nested types and ADTs). We consider such specialization to be a minimal success criterion for our deep induction rules since it ensures that our methodology for producing them is a conservative extension of all those that have come before. Other important success criteria are that our deep induction rules for IFs specialize to the structural induction rules of [7], and properly extend the deep induction rules for IFs in [21], which are deep only on their type indices, to be deep on their term indices as well. The former is seen, as usual, by taking the parameterizing predicates (on *both* the type and term indices) to be constantly $\top$-valued. This is a second success criterion because the structural induction rule for a given data type should always be a special case of its deep induction rule. The latter is seen by specializing the parameterizing predicates on IFs' *term* indices to constantly $\top$-valued predicates. This is a third success criterion because it guarantees that our deep induction rules for IFs are more general than those found in other conjectured approaches.

Overall, then, this paper gives the first-ever deep induction rules for proper IFs and demonstrates their soundness. But it actually delivers far more: it gives a *general methodology* for deriving sound deep induction rules for IFs that can be instantiated to particular IFs of interest. This methodology can serve as a basis for conservatively extending proof assistants' automatic generation of structural induction rules for IFs to automatic generation of deep induction rules for them.

3 Predicates for Term Indices: The Key Idea

The key to deriving deep induction rules for type-indexed-only data types is to define predicate liftings for them that perform the tasks (i) and (ii) identified just before (6) above. We now show how to generalize liftings for GADTs—i.e., type-indexing-only IFs—to predicate liftings suitable to IFs that also allow *term* indexing. To this end, consider the proper IF Vec defining the data type of vectors over a type a taken (essentially) from Agda's standard library:

```
data Vec (a : Set) : Nat → Set where          data Nat : Set where
  [] : Vec a zero                                zero : Nat              (7)
  _::_ : a → Vec a n → Vec a (suc n)             suc : Nat → Nat
```

The data type underlying Vec—i.e., the data type obtained from Vec by erasing its term indices—is the List ADT. Its term indices are of type Nat, and thus do not have interesting traversable structure. Although Vec is a particularly simple proper IF, it cleanly isolates the process of tracking term indices in deriving deep induction rules for IFs. The same principled, uniform methodology we illustrate here delivers deep induction rules for IFs with *both* more complex underlying data types, *and* more complex index types ranging all the way from built-in ones to IFs themselves. For example, the IF of Fin-indexed-sequences in Fig. 1, which has the GADT Seq as its underlying data type and the IF Fin of finite sets from Agda's standard library as its index type, has both a maximally general underlying data type and a maximally general index type. Our predicate lifting and deep induction rule for it are given in Fig. 1. They are derived using the methodology illustrated here using Vec and described more fully in the next section.

Since [ ] constructs vectors of length zero, any useful deep induction rule for vectors must ensure that zero satisfies the predicate on their natural number indices. Moreover, since a vector of length suc n is made from a vector of length n and a new data element of the vector's parameter type, such a rule must also ensure that suc n satisfies this predicate whenever n does. Similar implications must obtain between the term indices of other IFs, so we add to tasks (i) and (ii) identified above for predicate liftings that of also (iii) ensuring that the[4] term index of every data element constructed using a data constructor of an IF satisfies the predicate on the type of the IF's indices provided the term indices of the element's recursive subdata do. For Vec, this results in the following predicate lifting and deep induction rule:

$$
\begin{aligned}
&\mathsf{Vec}^\wedge : (\mathsf{a} \to \mathsf{Set}) \to (\mathsf{Nat} \to \mathsf{Set}) \to \mathsf{Vec\,a\,n} \to \mathsf{Set}\\
&\mathsf{Vec}^\wedge\,\{\mathsf{n} = \mathsf{zero}\}\,\mathsf{Q_a}\,\mathsf{Q_n}\,[\,] \;=\; \mathsf{Q_n}\,\mathsf{zero}\\
&\mathsf{Vec}^\wedge\,\{\mathsf{n} = \mathsf{suc\,m}\}\,\mathsf{Q_a}\,\mathsf{Q_n}\,(\mathsf{x} :: \mathsf{xs}) \;=\; \mathsf{Q_a}\,\mathsf{x} \times \mathsf{Vec}^\wedge\,\mathsf{Q_a}\,\mathsf{Q_n}\,\mathsf{xs} \times (\mathsf{Q_n m} \to \mathsf{Q_n}(\mathsf{suc\,m}))
\end{aligned}
$$

$$
\begin{aligned}
&(\mathsf{Q_a} : \mathsf{a} \to \mathsf{Set}) \to (\mathsf{Q_n} : \mathsf{Nat} \to \mathsf{Set}) \to (\mathsf{P} : \{\mathsf{n} : \mathsf{Nat}\} \to \mathsf{Vec\,a\,n} \to \mathsf{Set}) \to\\
&\quad (\mathsf{Q_n}\,\mathsf{zero} \to \mathsf{P}\,[\,]) \to\\
&\quad (\{\mathsf{n} : \mathsf{Nat}\} \to (\mathsf{x} : \mathsf{a}) \to (\mathsf{xs} : \mathsf{Vec\,a\,n}) \to \mathsf{Q_a}\,\mathsf{x} \to \mathsf{P\,xs} \to \mathsf{Q_n}\,(\mathsf{suc\,n}) \to \mathsf{P}\,(\mathsf{x} :: \mathsf{xs})) \to\\
&\quad (\mathsf{xs} : \mathsf{Vec\,a\,n}) \to \mathsf{Vec}^\wedge\,\mathsf{Q_a}\,\mathsf{Q_n}\,\mathsf{xs} \to \mathsf{P\,xs}
\end{aligned}
\tag{8}
$$

Of course, just as the data in an IF's underlying data type can be structured, so can the data in elements of its indexing data type be structured. Propagation of predicates on both the primitive data in an IF's underlying data type and on the primitive data in its indexing IF's elements are handled in the standard way. This is explicated in [10,11] and also recalled above. The presence or absence of structure in the IF's underlying data type or term indices in no way affects how satisfaction of the predicates on term indices must be preserved in the clauses of the IF's lifting for its data constructors. Indeed, propagation of predicates on primitive data through all of the structure in an IF's underlying data type and indices on the one hand, and presevation of predicate satisfaction for all of that IF's term indices (and, implicitly, preservation of well-formedness of its type indices) on the other, are orthogonal concerns when constructing its deep induction rule.

4 Deriving Liftings and Deep Induction Rules for IFs

That satisfaction of the predicates on a proper IF's term indices must be appropriately preserved to derive deep induction rules for these data types is the key observation of this paper. Detailing and justifying the uniform and principled

[4] For ease of exposition, we assume throughout that IFs have exactly one term index. The generalization to more than one term index is straightforward, if slightly tedious.

manner in which this is done is its main technical contribution. This results in a general methodology for defining liftings and deep induction rules for proper IFs that generalize those from [10,11] for IFs that are type-indexed only.

Since our methodology will handle an IF's type indices as they are handled in [10,11], the only new thing we need to account for is satisfaction of predicates on its term indices. In the most general situation we consider, an IF can have a GADT as its underlying indexed data type and, recursively, an IF as its indexing data type. In this paper we consider IFs whose underlying GADTs, and whose indexing IFs' underlying GADTs, are of the same form as those in [10], namely:

$$\mathsf{data}\ \mathsf{G} : \mathsf{Set}^{\alpha} \to \mathsf{Set}\ \mathsf{where}\ \mathsf{c}\ :\ \forall\{\overline{\mathsf{B} : \mathsf{Set}}\} \to \mathsf{F}\,\mathsf{G}\,\overline{\mathsf{B}} \to \mathsf{G}(\overline{\mathsf{K}\,\overline{\mathsf{B}}}) \tag{9}$$

For brevity and clarity we indicate only one data constructor c in (9), even though a GADT can have any finite number of them, each with a type of the same form as c's. In (9), F and each K in $\overline{\mathsf{K}}$ are type constructors with signatures $(\mathsf{Set}^{\alpha} \to \mathsf{Set}) \to \mathsf{Set}^{\beta} \to \mathsf{Set}$ and $\mathsf{Set}^{\beta} \to \mathsf{Set}$, respectively. If T is a type constructor with signature $\mathsf{Set}^{\gamma} \to \mathsf{Set}$ then the overline notation denotes a finite list whose length is exactly γ. The number of type constructors in $\overline{\mathsf{K}}$ (resp., $\overline{\mathsf{B}}$) is thus α (resp., β). In addition, the type constructor F must be constructed inductively according to the following grammar from [10]:

$$\mathsf{F}\,\mathsf{G}\,\overline{\mathsf{B}} := \mathsf{F}_1\,\mathsf{G}\,\overline{\mathsf{B}} \times \mathsf{F}_2\,\mathsf{G}\,\overline{\mathsf{B}} \,|\, \mathsf{F}_1\,\mathsf{G}\,\overline{\mathsf{B}} + \mathsf{F}_2\,\mathsf{G}\,\overline{\mathsf{B}} \,|\, \mathsf{F}_1\,\overline{\mathsf{B}} \to \mathsf{F}_2\,\mathsf{G}\,\overline{\mathsf{B}} \,|\, \mathsf{G}\,(\overline{\mathsf{F}_1\,\overline{\mathsf{B}}}) \,|\, \mathsf{H}\,\overline{\mathsf{B}} \,|\, \mathsf{H}\,(\overline{\mathsf{F}_1\,\mathsf{G}\,\overline{\mathsf{B}}})$$

As in [10], this grammar is subject to the following restrictions. In the third clause the type constructor F_1 does not use G, so G is omitted from the call to F_1. Similarly, in the fourth clause, none of the α-many type constructors in $\overline{\mathsf{F}_1}$ use G. This prevents nesting, which would make it impossible to give an induction rule for G; see Sect. 6 of [10] for details. In the fifth and sixth clauses, H is the syntactic reflection of some functor, and thus has an associated map function. Note that the fifth clause subsumes the cases in which $\mathsf{F}\,\mathsf{G}\,\overline{\mathsf{B}}$ is a closed type or one of the B_i, and that H can be the data type constructor for any (truly) nested type.

Focusing on the same class of GADTs as in [10] guarantees that the techniques of that paper apply to the type indices both of the GADT underlying an IF and of the GADT underlying the IF's indexing IF. We thus need only additionally ensure that each of an IF's data constructors appropriately preserves satisfaction of the predicate on the type of the IF's term indices in order to arrive at a conservative extension to proper IFs of the techniques in [10,11], and thus at a uniform methodology for deriving deep induction rules for such IFs.

Given an IF D, a predicate on the type of its term indices, and predicates on each of the primitive types appearing in D, the lifting $\mathsf{D}^{\wedge}$ for D includes one clause for each of its data constructors. The clause for the data constructor c is constructed via the steps described below. We illustrate each step using the fpair constructor for the IF FSeq from Fig. 1. As in the case of FSeq, the GADT underlying the IF of interest may first need to be converted into its Henry Ford encoding to accommodate its type indices; see [10] for details. The following steps can then be taken directly for that converted IF, exactly as illustrated below. The liftings from [10] can be newly understood as liftings that accomplish all three of the tasks below for GADTs (the last trivially), so our methodology for IFs subsumes that for GADTs in [10] (and, hence, that for nested types in [11]) when no term indices are present.

The clause of $\mathsf{D}^\wedge$ for a data constructor c of an IF D is constructed as follows:

1. Check that all non-recursive data used by c to construct elements of D satisfy the liftings for their types of the given predicates on D's type indices. (But in our examples we omit checks for term indices here when they already arise in checks in Steps 2 and 3.) In the definition of FSeq, e.g., the data constructor fpair requires a non-recursive non-term-index argument $\mathsf{p} : (\mathsf{b} \times \mathsf{c}) \equiv \mathsf{a}$, so the clause of $\mathsf{FSeq}^\wedge$ for fpair requires a corresponding term $\equiv^\wedge (\times^\wedge\, \mathsf{Q_b}\, \mathsf{Q_c})\, \mathsf{Q_a}\, \mathsf{p}$.
2. Check that all recursive subdata of the element of D that c constructs satisfy the lifting being defined of the predicates on D's type indices and the type of its term indices. In the definition of FSeq, e.g., fpair requires recursive arguments $\mathsf{sbi} : \mathsf{FSeq\, b\, i}$ and $\mathsf{scj} : \mathsf{FSeq\, c\, j}$, so the clause of $\mathsf{FSeq}^\wedge$ for fpair requires corresponding terms $\mathsf{FSeq}^\wedge\, \mathsf{Q_b}\, \mathsf{Q_f}\, \mathsf{sbi}$ and $\mathsf{FSeq}^\wedge\, \mathsf{Q_c}\, \mathsf{Q_f}\, \mathsf{scj}$.
3. Check that the term index of the element of D that c constructs satisfies the predicate on its type provided the term indices of the element's recursive subdata do. In the definition of FSeq, e.g., fpair constructs an element with term index $\mathsf{i} +_\mathsf{f} \mathsf{j}$ from recursive subdata with indices i and j, where $+_\mathsf{f}$ is the addition function for elements of Fin defined in Agda's standard library. The clause of $\mathsf{FSeq}^\wedge$ for fpair thus requires the corresponding satisfaction preservation condition $\mathsf{Q_f\, i} \to \mathsf{Q_f\, j} \to \mathsf{Q_f}\, (\mathsf{i} +_\mathsf{f} \mathsf{j})$.

Altogether this gives the clause of $\mathsf{D}^\wedge$ for c. The clause of $\mathsf{FSeq}^\wedge$ for fpair, e.g., is:

$$\begin{aligned}\mathsf{FSeq}^\wedge\, \mathsf{Q_a}\, \mathsf{Q_f}\, (\mathsf{fpair\, p}\, \{\mathsf{i}\}\, \{\mathsf{j}\}\, \mathsf{sbi\, scj}) \;=\; & \exists[\mathsf{Q_b}]\, \exists[\mathsf{Q_c}]\, \equiv^\wedge (\times^\wedge\, \mathsf{Q_b}\, \mathsf{Q_c})\, \mathsf{Q_a}\, \mathsf{p} \times & \text{(Step 1)}\\ & \mathsf{FSeq}^\wedge\, \mathsf{Q_b}\, \mathsf{Q_f}\, \mathsf{sbi} \times \mathsf{FSeq}^\wedge\, \mathsf{Q_c}\, \mathsf{Q_f}\, \mathsf{scj} \times & \text{(Step 2)}\\ & (\mathsf{Q_f\, i} \to \mathsf{Q_f\, j} \to \mathsf{Q_f}\, (\mathsf{i} +_\mathsf{f} \mathsf{j})) & \text{(Step 3)}\end{aligned}$$

Once we have its lifting, the deep induction rule for D is derived as follows:

1. The first input to D's deep induction rule is a predicate P to be shown to hold for all elements of D. It must be parameterized by predicates on D's type indices and a predicate on the type of D's term indices. For example, the first input to the deep induction rule for FSeq is a predicate

$$\begin{aligned}\mathsf{P} : \{\mathsf{a} : \mathsf{Set}\} \to \{\mathsf{n} : \mathsf{Nat}\} \to \{\mathsf{i} : \mathsf{Fin\, n}\} \to (\mathsf{Q_a} : \mathsf{a} \to \mathsf{Set}) \to\\ (\mathsf{Q_f} : \{\mathsf{n} : \mathsf{Nat}\} \to \mathsf{Fin\, n} \to \mathsf{Set}) \to \mathsf{FSeq\, a\, i} \to \mathsf{Set}\end{aligned}$$

   that is parameterized by a predicate $\mathsf{Q_a}$ on the primitive type a and a predicate $\mathsf{Q_f}$ on the type $\mathsf{Fin\, n}$ of term indices appearing in FSeq's definition. Similarly, the first input to the deep induction rule for Vec is a predicate P of type $\{\mathsf{a} : \mathsf{Set}\} \to \{\mathsf{n} : \mathsf{Nat}\} \to (\mathsf{Q_a} : \mathsf{a} \to \mathsf{Set}) \to (\mathsf{Q_n} : \mathsf{Nat} \to \mathsf{Set}) \to \mathsf{Vec\, a\, n} \to \mathsf{Set}$ that is parameterized by predicates $\mathsf{Q_a}$ on the primitive type a and $\mathsf{Q_n}$ on

```
data Fin : Nat → Set where
  fz : Fin (suc n)
  fs : Fin n → Fin (suc n)

data FSeq (a : Set) : Fin n → Set where
  finj : a → (i : Fin n) → FSeq a i
  fpair : (b × c) ≡ a → {i : Fin m} → {j : Fin n} → FSeq b i → FSeq c j → FSeq a (i +_f j)

FSeq^ : (a → Set) → ({n : Nat} → Fin n → Set) → {i : Fin n} → FSeq a i → Set
FSeq^ Q_a Q_f (finj x i) = Q_a x × Q_f i
FSeq^ Q_a Q_f (fpair p {i} {j} sbi scj) = ∃ [Q_b] ∃ [Q_c] ≡^ (×^ Q_b Q_c) Q_a p × FSeq^ Q_b Q_f sbi ×
                                           FSeq^ Q_c Q_f scj × (Q_f i → Q_f j → Q_f (i +_f j))

(P : {a : Set} → {n : Nat} → {i : Fin n} →
   (Q_a : a → Set) → (Q_f : {n : Nat} → Fin n → Set) → FSeq a i → Set) →        (Step 1)
  ({a : Set} → (x : a) → {n : Nat} → (i : Fin n) → (Q_a : a → Set) →
   (Q_f : {n : Nat} → Fin n → Set) → Q_a x → Q_f i → P Q_a Q_f (finj x i)) →     (Step 2)
  ({a b c : Set} → (p : (b × c) ≡ a) → {m n : Nat} → {i : Fin m} → {j : Fin n} →
   (sbi : FSeq b i) → (scj : FSeq c j) → (Q_a : a → Set) → (Q_b : b → Set) →
   (Q_c : c → Set) → (Q_f : {n : Nat} → Fin n → Set) →
   P Q_b Q_f sbi → P Q_c Q_f scj → Q_f (i +_f j) → P Q_a Q_f (fpair p sbi scj)) →  (Step 2)
  (Q_a : a → Set) → (Q_f : {n : Nat} → Fin n → Set) → {i : Fin n} → (s : FSeq a i) →
   FSeq^ Q_a Q_f s → P Q_a Q_f s                                                  (Step 3)
```

Fig. 1. Deep induction rule for Fin-indexed sequences.

the type Nat of term indices appearing in Vec's definition. However, in this case the predicate arguments Q_a and Q_n are the same at all call sites, so they can be factored out of P as in (8). This simplification can be applied to the deep induction rules for other IFs, such as FSeq in Fig. 1, as well.

2. Include one induction hypothesis in D's deep induction rule for each of its data constructors c. The induction hypothesis for c must:
   (a) take as its first arguments all of the ingredients needed to construct an element of D using c.
   (b) take as additional arguments predicates on the type indices and the type of the term index appearing in the clause of D^ for c.
   (c) take as further arguments terms checking that each argument of c introducing new data of primitive type satisfies the lifting for its type of P's parameterizing predicates (for those that exist), and that each recursive argument of c satisfies (an appropriate instance of) P.
   (d) take as its final arguments terms checking that the term index of the element constructed using c satisfies the predicate for its type parameterizing P.
   (e) have as its conclusion that the term constructed using c satisfies P.

The induction hypothesis for fpair in the deep induction rule for FSeq, e.g., is:

$$\{\mathsf{a\,b\,c} : \mathsf{Set}\} \to (\mathsf{p} : (\mathsf{b} \times \mathsf{c}) \equiv \mathsf{a}) \to \{\mathsf{m\,n} : \mathsf{Nat}\} \to \{\mathsf{i} : \mathsf{Fin\,m}\} \to \{\mathsf{j} : \mathsf{Fin\,n}\} \to \\ (\mathsf{sbi} : \mathsf{FSeq\,b\,i}) \to (\mathsf{scj} : \mathsf{FSeq\,c\,j}) \to (\mathsf{Q_a} : \mathsf{a} \to \mathsf{Set}) \to (\mathsf{Q_b} : \mathsf{b} \to \mathsf{Set}) \to \\ (\mathsf{Q_c} : \mathsf{c} \to \mathsf{Set}) \to (\mathsf{Q_f} : \{\mathsf{n} : \mathsf{Nat}\} \to \mathsf{Fin\,n} \to \mathsf{Set}) \to \\ \mathsf{P\,Q_b\,Q_f\,sbi} \to \mathsf{P\,Q_c\,Q_f\,scj} \to \mathsf{Q_f}\,(\mathsf{i} +_\mathsf{f} \mathsf{j}) \to \mathsf{P\,Q_a\,Q_f}\,(\mathsf{fpair\,p\,sbi\,scj})$$

3. Conclude that, given an arbitary element of D and the ingredients needed to construct it, if the element satisfies D's lifting of P's parameterizing predicates then it satisfies P. For example, the conclusion for FSeq is:

$$(\mathsf{Q_a} : \mathsf{a} \to \mathsf{Set}) \to (\mathsf{Q_f} : \{\mathsf{n} : \mathsf{Nat}\} \to \mathsf{Fin\,n} \to \mathsf{Set}) \to \\ \{\mathsf{i} : \mathsf{Fin\,n}\} \to (\mathsf{s} : \mathsf{FSeq\,a\,i}) \to \mathsf{FSeq}^\wedge\,\mathsf{Q_a\,Q_f\,s} \to \mathsf{P\,Q_a\,Q_f\,s}$$

Exactly this methodology has yielded all of the deep induction rules in this paper. The accompanying code file contains additional examples illustrating our methodology (but note that when the term index of an IF is given by a GADT, we can choose to obtain the predicate on it by lifting predicates on its type indices rather than giving it directly). The file contains deep induction rules for IFs with term indices given by primitive types (natural number indexed lists, i.e., vectors); ADTs (list-indexed sequences); nested types (perfect-tree-indexed sequences); GADTs (LType-indexed LTerms); and IFs (finite-set-indexed and vector-indexed sequences). Due to space limitations, only the first and final two of these examples appear in the text of this paper, in (8) and Figs. 1 and 2, respectively.

We call to attention some particular features of our methodology. Firstly, as in [10,11], there is no need to reflect predicates as data types. Secondly, a predicate on a type (either a type index or the type of a term index) appearing in an IF D need not hold for *all* elements of that type, but rather only for those elements that actually *can be* indices of elements of D. This observation was not highlighted in [10] but obtains (for type indices) there as well. Thirdly, the previous point is in stark contrast to the methods of [20,21], which use only trivial predicates for types of term indices. This has the effect of reducing the deep induction principle for an IF to that for its underlying GADT. For example, in [21] the deep induction rule for vectors is reduced to that for lists. Finally, the combining function that makes the term index of an element of D constructed using a data constructor c from the term indices of its recursive subdata determines the term-index predicate satisfaction preservation requirement in the clause of D^ for c. For example, the term-index predicate satisfaction preservation requirement in the clause of Vec^ for _::_ is $\mathsf{Q_n\,m} \to \mathsf{Q_n\,(suc\,m)}$ precisely because the type of _::_ is (up to variable renaming) $\mathsf{a} \to \mathsf{Vec\,a\,m} \to \mathsf{Vec\,a\,(suc\,m)}$.

5 Case Study

We now show how deep induction can be used to prove a non-trivial property of GADTs indexed by terms of an IF that is deep in its own type indices. Let _++_

be Agda's vector concatenation, and consider the type VSeq of vector-indexed sequences analogous to the type FSeq of finite-set-indexed sequences in Fig. 1:

```
data VSeq (a : Set) {d : Set} : Vec d n → Set where
  vinj : a → (xs : Vec d n) → VSeq a xs
  vpair : (b × c) ≡ a → {ys : Vec d m} → {zs : Vec d n} →
            VSeq b ys → VSeq c zs → VSeq a (ys ++ zs)
```

The lifting and deep induction rule for VSeq are shown in Fig. 2 in the appendix. We can use the latter to prove that, for every xs : Vec Nat n and every s : VSeq a xs for some a : Set, if every subterm of s constructed using vinj is indexed by a vector of even length all of whose elements are odd, then s itself is indexed by such a vector. To state this proposition, we use the predicate eloe : Vec Nat n → Set defined by eloe xs = even (length xs) × all odd xs, where even and odd are the standard predicates on Nat, length computes the length of its vector argument, and the predicate all on vectors with elements of type a checks that each of its elements satisfies a given predicate on a. The proposition prop to be proved can then be stated as:

```
{xs : Vec Nat n} → (s : VSeq a xs) → Tree^ (QvOnVec eloe) (leaves s) → eloe xs
```

Here, Tree is the type of binary trees with data only at the leaves, Tree^ checks that every datum of in a tree satisfies a given predicate on the type of its elements, leaves : {xs : Vec d n} → VSeq a xs → Tree (Σ Set id × Σ Nat (Vec d)) collects into a binary tree the data-index pairs in the vinj-constructed subterms of a vector-indexed sequence[5], and QvOnVec : ({n : Nat} → Vec d n → Set) → Σ Set id × Σ Nat (Vec d) → Set applies a given predicate on vectors to the vector inside such a pair. Now, in order to use the deep induction rule for VSeq to prove prop, we need to construct a term of type VSeq^ KT eloe s from prop's argument of type Tree^ (QvOnVec eloe) (leaves s). The function

```
mkVSeq^ : (Qv : {n : Nat} → Vec d n → Set) →
  ({m n : Nat} → (ys : Vec d m) → (zs : Vec d n) → Qv ys → Qv zs → Qv (ys ++ zs)) →
  {xs : Vec d n} → (s : VSeq a xs) → Tree^ (QvOnVec Qv) (leaves s) → VSeq^ KT Qv s
```

does exactly this.

Note that the even predicate does not hold for all indices of type Nat in indices of type Vec that index elements of VSeq. But it *does* hold for all indices of type Nat that can index indices of type Vec that index elements of VSeq provided it holds for all of their subterms constructed using vinj.

The code for the complete application appears in the appendix, and is also included in the code file accompanying this paper. How to use deep induction rules to prove properties of more general IFs should be apparent.

---

[5] We use the constantly ⊤-valued predicate KT as our predicate on a since using a non-trivial predicate on a here wouldn't introduce anything new over [10].

Appendix

```
– The IF VSeq
data VSeq (a : Set) {d : Set} : Vec d n → Set where
  vinj : a → (xs : Vec d n) → VSeq a xs
  vpair : (b × c) ≡ a → {ys : Vec d m} → {zs : Vec d n} → VSeq b ys → VSeq c zs → VSeq a (ys ++ zs)

– The lifting for VSeq
VSeq^ : (a → Set) → ({n : Nat} → Vec d n → Set) → {xs : Vec d n} → VSeq a xs → Set
VSeq^ Qa Qv (vinj x xs) = Qa x × Qv xs
VSeq^ Qa Qv (vpair p {ys} {zs} sbys sczs) = ∃[Qb] ∃[Qc] ≡^ (×^ Qb Qc) Qa p × VSeq^ Qb Qv sbys ×
                                            VSeq^ Qc Qv sczs × (Qv ys → Qv zs → Qv (ys ++ zs))

– The deep induction rule for VSeq
VSeqInd :
  (P : {a d : Set} → {n : Nat} → {xs : Vec d n} →
    (Qa : a → Set) → (Qv : {n : Nat} → Vec d n → Set) → VSeq a xs → Set) →
  ({a d : Set} → (x : a) → {n : Nat} → (xs : Vec d n) → (Qa : a → Set) →
    (Qv : {n : Nat} → Vec d n → Set) → Qa x → Qv xs → P Qa Qv (vinj x xs)) →
  ({a b c d : Set} → (p : (b × c) ≡ a) → {m n : Nat} → {ys : Vec d m} → {zs : Vec d n} →
    (sbys : VSeq b ys) → (sczs : VSeq c zs) →
    (Qa : a → Set) → (Qb : b → Set) → (Qc : c → Set) → (Qv : {n : Nat} → Vec d n → Set) →
    P Qb Qv sbys → P Qc Qv sczs → Qv (ys ++ zs) → P Qa Qv (vpair p sbys sczs)) →
  (Qa : a → Set) → (Qv : {n : Nat} → Vec d n → Set) → {xs : Vec d n} →
    (s : VSeq a xs) → VSeq^ Qa Qv s → P Qa Qv s
VSeqInd P hinj hpair Qa Qv (vinj x xs) (Qax, Qvxs) = hinj x xs Qa Qv Qax Qvxs
VSeqInd P hinj hpair Qa Qv seq@(vpair p sbys sczs) lft@(Qb, Qc, e, ^Qsbys, ^Qsczs, hQv) =
  hpair p sbys sczs Qa Qb Qc Qv
    (VSeqInd P hinj hpair Qb Qv sbys ^Qsbys)
    (VSeqInd P hinj hpair Qb Qv sczs ^Qsczs)
    (QvOnIndex Qa Qv seq lft)
  where
    QvOnIndex : {a d : Set} → {n : Nat} → {xs : Vec d n} →
      (Qa : a → Set) → (Qv : {n : Nat} → Vec d n → Set) →
      (s : VSeq a xs) → VSeq^ Qa Qv s → Qv xs
    QvOnIndex Qa Qv (vinj x xs) (Qax, Qvxs) = Qvxs
    QvOnIndex Qa Qv (vpair x sbys scjs) (Qb, Qc, e, ^Qsbys, ^Qsczs, hQv) =
      hQv (QvOnIndex Qb Qv sbys ^Qsbys) (QvOnIndex Qc Qv scjs ^Qsczs)
```

Fig. 2. Deep induction rule for VSeq.

(See Figs. 3 and 4)

```
– the evenness predicates on Nats:
data even : Nat → Set where
  zeven : even zero
  sseven : even n → even (suc (suc n))

– the sum of even Nats is even:
sumEvens : even m → even n → even (m + n)
sumEvens zeven neven = neven
sumEvens (sseven meven) neven = sseven (sumEvens meven neven)

– the oddness predicate on Nats:
odd : Nat → Set
odd n = ¬(even n)

– the trivial predicate on a type:
KT : a → Set
KT = const ⊤

– identifies the singleton types ⊤ × ⊤ and ⊤
postulate
  preunit : (⊤ × ⊤) ≡ ⊤

– the data type of leaf-labeled binary trees
data Tree (a : Set) : Set where
  leaf : a → Tree a
  node : Tree a → Tree a → Tree a

– predicate lifting for leaf-labeled binary trees:
Tree^ : (a → Set) → Tree a → Set
Tree^ Q (leaf x) = Q x
Tree^ Q (node xs ys) = Tree^ Q xs × Tree^ Q ys

– function that collects the label-index pairs from the vinj constuctors of a VSeq:
leaves : {xs : Vec d n} → VSeq a xs → Tree (Σ Set id × Σ Nat (Vec d))
leaves {n = n} {a = a} (vinj x xs) = leaf ((a, x), (n, xs))
leaves (vpair p sbys sczs) = node (leaves sbys) (leaves sczs)

– apply a Vec predicate to the Vec inside such a label-index pair:
QvOnVec : ({n : Nat} → Vec d n → Set) → Σ Set id × Σ Nat (Vec d) → Set
QvOnVec Qv (_, (_, xs)) = Qv xs

– construct a VSeq lifting from the hypotheses of our desired proposition,
– which is about a certain predicate holding for all vinj leaf constructors of a given VSeq term.
mkVSeq^ : (Qv : {n : Nat} → Vec d n → Set) →
  ({m n : Nat} → (ys : Vec d m) → (zs : Vec d n) → Qv ys → Qv zs → Qv (ys ++ zs)) →
  {xs : Vec d n} → (s : VSeq a xs) → Tree^ (QvOnVec Qv) (leaves s) → VSeq^ KT Qv s
mkVSeq^ Qv pres (vinj x xs) Qvxs = (tt, Qvxs)
mkVSeq^ Qv pres (vpair refl {ys} {zs} sbys sczs) (^Qsbys, ^Qsczs) =
(KT, KT, const preunit, mkVSeq^ Qv pres sbys ^Qsbys, mkVSeq^ Qv pres sczs ^Qsczs, pres ys zs)
```

Fig. 3. Code for Sect. 5.

```
– predicate transformer to extend an element predicate to all elements of a Vec:
all : (a → Set) → Vec a n → Set
all Q [] = ⊤
all Q (x :: xs) = Q x × all Q xs

– if all elements of two Vecs satisfy an element predicate
– then so do all elements of their concatenation:
allConcat : (Q : a → Set) → (xs : Vec a m) → (ys : Vec a n) → all Q xs → all Q ys → all Q (xs ++ ys)
allConcat Q [] ys hxs hys = hys
allConcat Q (x :: xs) ys (Qx, Qxs) Qys = (Qx, allConcat Q xs ys Qxs Qys)

– an example of a predicate on vectors of Nats:
– having even length and only odd entries.
eloe : Vec Nat n → Set
eloe xs = even (length xs) × all odd xs

– this predicate is preserved under vector concatenation:
eloePres : (ys : Vec Nat m) → (zs : Vec Nat n) → eloe ys → eloe zs → eloe (ys ++ zs)
eloePres ys zs (meven, ysodd) (neven, zsodd) = (sumEvens meven neven, allConcat odd ys zs ysodd zsodd)

– Finally, we can use deep induction to prove a propositition about VSeqs:
– If all of the vinj subterms of an VSeq have indices that are even-length Vecs with odd Nat entries
– then the whole VSeq term does as well.
prop : {xs : Vec Nat n} → (s : VSeq a xs) → Tree^ (QvOnVec eloe) (leaves s) → eloe xs
prop s hyp = VSeqInd P hinj hpair KT eloe s (mkVSeq^ eloe eloePres s hyp)
  where
  P : {xs : Vec d n} → (Qa : a → Set) → (Qv : {n : Nat} → Vec d n → Set) → VSeq a xs → Set
  P {xs = xs} Qa Qv s = Qv xs
  –
  hinj : (x : a) → {n : Nat} → (xs : Vec d n) → (Qa : a → Set) → (Qv : {n : Nat} → Vec d n → Set) →
    Qa x → Qv xs → P Qa Qv (vinj x xs)
  hinj x xs Qa Qv Qax Qvxs = Qvxs
  –
  hpair : (p : (b × c) ≡ a) → {m n : Nat} → {ys : Vec d m} → {zs : Vec d n} →
    (sbys : VSeq b ys) → (sczs : VSeq c zs) →
    (Qa : a → Set) → (Qb : b → Set) → (Qc : c → Set) → (Qv : {n : Nat} → Vec d n → Set) →
    P Qb Qv sbys → P Qc Qv sczs →
    Qv (ys ++ zs) → P Qa Qv (vpair p sbys sczs)
  hpair p sbys sczs Qa Qb Qc Qv Psbys Psczs Qvyszs = Qvyszs
```

Fig. 4. Code for Sect. 5 (continued).

References

1. The Agda Wiki. https://wiki.portal.chalmers.se/agda/pmwiki.php
2. Bird, R., Meertens, L.: Nested datatypes. In: Jeuring, J. (ed.) MPC 1998. LNCS, vol. 1422, pp. 52–67. Springer, Heidelberg (1998). https://doi.org/10.1007/BFb0054285
3. Cheney, J., Hinze, R.: First-class phantom types. Technical Report. CUCIS TR2003-1901, Cornell University (2003)
4. Christensen, D.: Practical Reflection and Metaprogramming for Dependent Types. Ph.D. thesis, IT University of Copenhagen (2015)
5. Coq Development Team: The Coq proof assistant, version 8.19.2 (2024)
6. Coquand, T., Paulin-Mohring, C.: Inductively defined types. In: COLOG-88, pp. 50–66 (1990). https://doi.org/10.1007/3-540-52335-9_47

7. Dybjer, P.: Inductive families. Formal Aspects Comput. **6**(4), 440–465 (1994). https://doi.org/10.1007/BF01211308
8. Hinze, R.: Fun with phantom types. In: The Fun of Programming, pp. 245–262. Palgrave Macmillan (2003)
9. Idris: A language for type-driven development. https://www.idris-lang.org/
10. Johann, P., Ghiorzi, E.: (Deep) induction rules for GADTs. In: Certified Programs and Proofs, pp. 324–337 (2022). https://doi.org/10.1145/3497775.3503680
11. Johann, P., Polonsky, A.: Deep induction: induction rules for (truly) nested types. In: Foundations of Software Science and Computation Structures, pp. 339–358 (2020). https://doi.org/10.1007/978-3-030-45231-5_18
12. McBride, C.: Dependently Typed Programs and their Proofs. Ph.D. thesis, University of Edinburgh (1999)
13. McBride, C.: Epigram: practical programming with dependent types. In: Advanced Functional Programming, pp. 130–170 (2005). https://doi.org/10.1007/11546382_3
14. McBride, C., McKinna, J.: The view from the left. J. Funct. Program. **14**(1), 69–111 (2004). https://doi.org/10.1017/S0956796803004829
15. Milner, R., Tofte, M., Harper, R., MacQueen, D.: The Definition of Standard ML, Revised edn. MIT Press, Cambridge (1997). https://doi.org/10.7551/mitpress/2319.001.0001
16. Norell, U.: Dependently typed programming in Agda. Lecture Notes, Advanced Functional Programming Summer School (2008)
17. Peyton Jones, S.L. (ed.): Haskell 98 Language and Libraries: The Revised Report. Cambridge University Press, Cambridge (2003)
18. Schrijvers, T., Peyton Jones, S.L., Sulzmann, M., Vytiniotis, D.: Complete and decidable type inference for GADTs. In: International Conference on Functional Programming, pp. 341–352 (2009). https://doi.org/10.1145/1596550.1596599
19. Sheard, T., Pasalic, E.: Meta-programming with built-in type equality. In: Proceedings of the Fourth International Workshop on Logical Frameworks and Meta-languages, pp. 49–65 (2008). https://doi.org/10.1016/j.entcs.2007.11.012
20. Tassi, E.: Deriving proved equality tests in Coq-elpi: stronger induction principles for containers in Coq. In: 10th International Conference on Interactive Theorem Proving, pp. 1–18 (2019). https://doi.org/10.4230/LIPIcs.ITP.2019.29
21. Ullrich, M.: Generating induction principles for nested induction types in MetaCoq. Bachelor thesis, Saarland University (2020)
22. Xi, H., Chen, C., Chen, G.: Guarded recursive datatype constructors. In: Principles of Programming Languages, pp. 224–235 (2003). https://doi.org/10.1145/604131.604150

Asymptotic Reasoning With Two Variables

J. Andres Montoya(✉)

Universidad Nacional de Colombia, Bogota, Colombia
jamontoyaa@unal.edu.co

Abstract. We study asymptotic probabilities of formal languages specified by logical formulas. We focus on first-order sentences. We prove several results related to the asymptotic tractability of the two-variable fragment. Those results amount to show that asymptotic reasoning with two variables is feasible. We study some applications that are related to temporal reasoning.

We study asymptotic probabilities of regular languages. We focus on the problem of computing those limit probabilities when the input languages are specified by logical formulas. The study of asymptotic densities of formal languages has a long history that can be traced back to Chomsky and Miller; see [3]. There are many potential applications of those asymptotic densities, including but not limited to: probabilistic reasoning, asymptotic and temporal reasoning, and approximation of nonregular languages. Let us introduce the main definitions.

Definition 1. *Let $L, T \subset \Sigma^*$ be two languages.*

1. *Set* $\Pr_n(L) = \frac{|\Sigma^n \cap L|}{|\Sigma|^n}$. *Suppose that* $\lim_{n\to\infty} \Pr_n(L)$ *exists. We use the symbol* $\Pr(L)$ *to denote this limit.* $\Pr(L)$ *is the asymptotic density of* L.
2. *Let* $\Pr_n(L \mid T)$ *be equal to* $\frac{|\Sigma^n \cap L \cap T|}{|\Sigma^n \cap T|}$. *Suppose that* $\lim_{n\to\infty} \Pr_n(L \mid T)$ *exists. We use the symbol* $\Pr(L \mid T)$ *to denote this limit. We say that* $\Pr(L \mid T)$ *is the conditional probability of* L *given* T *(also the relative density of* L *in* T*).*

Chomsky and Miller studied the analytical behavior of asymptotic densities. They proved that asymptotic densities of regular languages are computable. We study the complexity of computing those limit probabilities when the input languages are specified by logical formulas.

Organization of the Work and Contributions. This work is organized into six sections besides this introduction. In Sect. 1, we study the relative densities of regular languages. We prove that there exist aperiodic languages whose relative densities do not exist. Then, we begin the search for a robust class of regular languages for which relative densities always exist. We introduce the

D. Kozen and R. de Queiroz (Eds.): WoLLIC 2025, LNCS 15942, pp. 38–55, 2026.
https://doi.org/10.1007/978-3-031-99536-1_3

class of star-free unambiguous languages, and we provide a new characterization of this important variety of regular languages that we denote with the symbol **UL**. We prove that **UL** equals the class of languages accepted by partially ordered unambiguous automata, (poUFA's, for short). In Sect. 2, we introduce geodesic languages, and we show that many different classes of geodesic languages are contained in the variety **UL**. In Sect. 3, we prove that for all L and T in **UL**, the limit probability $\Pr(L \mid T)$ exists and can be computed in time $2^{O(|\alpha|+|\beta|)}$, when the languages are specified by sentences of the two-variable fragment $\mathrm{FO}^2[<]$. In Sect. 4, we study some potential applications related to the monitoring of agents that explore Cayley graphs, probabilistic model-checking of partially ordered automata, and temporal planning. In Sect. 5, we study the parameterized complexity of model-checking problems related to $\mathrm{FO}^2[<]$ and some higher levels of the Straubing-Therien hierarchy of star-free languages; see [15]. We finish in Sect. 6, with a few concluding remarks.

1 Regular, Aperiodic, and Star-Free Unambiguous Languages

Let L be equal to $(11)^*$. The sequence $\{\Pr_n(L)\}_{n\geq 1}$ oscillates between 0 and 1. We get that regular languages exist without asymptotic density. Let us then focus on the class of regular languages that can be defined by sentences of $\mathrm{FO}[<]$. This is the class of aperiodic, (also star-free), languages; see [13]. Lynch proved that for all aperiodic language L, the limit probability $\Pr(L)$ exists; see [12]. Let α be a sentence of $\mathrm{FO}[<]$, and let L_α be the aperiodic language defined by this sentence. We use the symbol $\Pr(\alpha)$ to denote the limit probability $\Pr(L_\alpha)$. We use the symbol $\Pr(\alpha \mid \beta)$ accordingly. Let us observe that there exist sentences of $\mathrm{FO}[<]$, say α and β, such that the limit probability $\Pr(\alpha \mid \beta)$ does not exist.

Example 1. Let $L = (ab)^*$ and let $T = (ab)^* \cup (ab)^* a$. Those two languages are aperiodic and the limit probability $\Pr(L \mid T)$ does not exist.

Moreover, we have:

Theorem 1. *Let α and β be sentences of $FO^3[<]$, the problem of deciding whether the limit probability $\Pr(\alpha \mid \beta)$ exists and is different from zero has nonelementary complexity.*

Proof. Let α be a sentence of $\mathrm{FO}^3[<]$ and suppose $L_\alpha \subset \Sigma^*$. Let c be a fresh character not in Σ. Let α_c be the three-variable sentence that defines the language $L_\alpha c(\Sigma \cup \{c\})^*$. We have that α has finite models if and only if the limit probability $\Pr(\alpha_c \mid \forall x (x = x))$ exists and is different from zero. We get that the finite satisfiability problem for $\mathrm{FO}^3[<]$ is ptime reducible to the problem of computing limit probabilities of three-variable sentences. The former problem has nonelementary complexity; see [17]. The theorem is proved.

Let us focus on detecting a fragment $\mathcal{L}$ of $\mathrm{FO}[<]$, such that for all sentences α and β in $\mathcal{L}$, the limit probability $\Pr(\alpha \mid \beta)$ exists and can be *efficiently* computed.

1.1 Star-Free Unambiguous Languages

Let r be a regular expression. We say that r is *a monomial* if and only if there exists $h \geq 1$, there exist sets $\Sigma_0, \Sigma_1, ..., \Sigma_h \subseteq \Sigma$, and there exist $a_1, ..., a_h \in \Sigma$ such that the equality

$$r = \Sigma_0^* a_1 \Sigma_1^* \cdots \Sigma_{h-1}^* a_h \Sigma_h^*$$

holds. We say that $\Sigma_0, ...\Sigma_h$ are the *factors* of r.

Definition 2. *Let r be a monomial, and let L_r be the language defined by r. We say that r is an unambiguous monomial if and only if for all $w \in L_r$ this string can be parsed in only one way as an element of L_r.*

Example 2. The monomial $\emptyset^* a_1 \emptyset^* \cdots \emptyset^* a_h \emptyset^*$ is an unambiguous monomial that defines the language $\{a_1 \cdots a_h\}$.

Definition 3. *Let $r_1, ..., r_N$ be unambiguous monomials. Suppose that the languages $L_{r_1}, ..., L_{r_N}$ are pairwise disjoint. Let $R = \bigcup_{i \leq N} r_i$, we say that the regular expression R is an unambiguous polynomial, and we say that L_R is a star-free unambiguous language, (also unambiguous in the sense of Schützenberger [14], or simply unambiguous). We use the symbol* **UL** *to denote the class (variety) of unambiguous languages.*

Example 3. Any finite language is star-free unambiguous. The language Σ^* is an example of a star-free unambiguous language that is infinite.

Definition 4. *Let $\mathcal{M}$ be a NFA. We say that $\mathcal{M}$ is unambiguous if and only if for all input string w the number of accepting accepting computations of $\mathcal{M}$, on w, is not greater than* 1.

Let $\mathcal{M}$ be a NFA, and let p and q be two states of $\mathcal{M}$. We write $p \cdot w = q$ to indicate that string w sends state p in state q. We use the symbol $p \preceq_{\mathcal{M}} q$ to denote that there exists w such that $p \cdot w = q$.

Definition 5. *Let $\mathcal{M}$ be a NFA. We say that $\mathcal{M}$ is a partially ordered NFA if and only if the set of states of $\mathcal{M}$ is partially ordered by the relation $p \preceq_{\mathcal{M}} q$. We use the symbol poNFO to denote the class of partially ordered NFA's; see [16]. We say that $\mathcal{M}$ is a partially ordered unambiguous automaton (poUFA, for short) if and only if $\mathcal{M}$ is a poNFA that is unambiguous.*

The class **UL** enjoys many different characterizations. We provide a new characterization of this important class of regular languages. We prove that **UL** equals the class of languages accepted by poUFA's. We have:

Theorem 2. *The following classes of languages are all equal.*

1. *The class* **UL***, which is the class of regular languages denoted by unambiguous polynomials.*

2. *The class of languages recognized by finite monoids in the variety* $\mathbf{DA}$.
3. *The class of languages defined by sentences of* $FO^2[<]$.
4. *The class of languages defined by formulas of the unary temporal logic* $LTL[F, P]$.
5. *The class of languages accepted by partially ordered deterministic two-way automata, (po2DFA's, for short; see [16]).*
6. *The class of languages accepted by poUFA's.*

Proof. The first five items are known; see the references [14], [15], [16] and [10]. We prove the sixth item. We prove that **UL** equals the class of languages accepted by poUFA's.

Let us first introduce a restricted class of poUFA's. We refer to the class of linearly ordered unambiguous automata, (loUFA's, for short). A loUFA is, naively, a poUFA that is linearly ordered by the relation $\preceq_{\mathcal{M}}$. We use a slightly more restricted notion. Let $\mathcal{M}$ be an unambiguous automaton. Let us suppose that the set of states of $\mathcal{M}$ is equal to $\{1, ..., m\}$. We say that $\mathcal{M}$ is a linearly ordered unambiguous one-way automaton (loUFA) if and only if the following conditions hold:

1. The initial state is equal to 1, and the set of accepting states is equal to $\{m-1\}$.
2. Let $\delta \subset Q \times \Sigma \times Q$ be the set of transitions of $\mathcal{M}$. Let $i \leq m-1$. There exist $\Sigma_{1,i}, \Sigma_{2,i} \subseteq \Sigma$ such that:
   (a) $(i, a, i) \in \delta$ if and only if $a \in \Sigma_{1,i}$.
   (b) $(i, a, i+1) \in \delta$ if and only if $a \in \Sigma_{2,i}$.
   (c) The set δ is equal to the union of two sets, namely: the set of transitions listed in the previous items and the set $\{(i, a, m) : i \leq m \text{ and } a \in \Sigma\}$.

Let L be a star-free unambiguous language. Let $R = \bigsqcup_{i \leq N} r_i$ be an unambiguous polynomial that defines the language L. This representation of L yields a disjoint union of loUFA's accepting this language. Note that any disjoint union of loUFA's gives place to a poUFA.

Let $\mathcal{M}$ be a partially ordered unambiguous automaton, and let L be the language accepted by $\mathcal{M}$. We prove that L is an unambiguous language. First, we prove that L is accepted by a disjoint union of loUFA's. Let 1 be the initial state of $\mathcal{M}$, and let $\preceq_{\mathcal{M}}$ be the partial order determined by this automaton. A *chain* in $\mathcal{M}$ is an ordered sequence of states, say $1 = q_1 \prec \cdots \prec q_n$, such that q_n is an accepting state. Let $\overrightarrow{q} = q_1 \prec \cdots \prec q_n$ be a chain, we define

$$L_{\overrightarrow{q}} = \left\{ \begin{array}{c} w \in L : \text{the ordered sequence of states visited during the accepting} \\ \text{computation of } \mathcal{M}, \text{ on input } w, \text{ is precisely the sequence } \overrightarrow{q} \end{array} \right\}$$

Recall that $\mathcal{M}$ is unambiguous. This ensures that L equals the disjoint union of the languages in the set $\{L_{\overrightarrow{q}} : \overrightarrow{q} \text{ is a chain for } \mathcal{M}\}$. It remains to prove that for all chain $\overrightarrow{q}$ the language $L_{\overrightarrow{q}}$ is unambiguous. Let us first observe that $L_{\overrightarrow{q}}$

is accepted by a linear ordered unambiguous automaton $\mathcal{M}_{\overrightarrow{q}}$. This automaton is built by taking the restriction of $\mathcal{M}$ to the set $\{q_1, ..., q_n\} \cup \{*\}$, where $*$ is a sink that represents all the states of $\mathcal{M}$ that are not included in $\{q_1, ..., q_n\}$. We obtain that L is accepted by a disjoint union of loUFA's.

Let $\mathcal{M}$ be a loUFA. We prove that $L_{\mathcal{M}}$ can be defined by a disjoint union of unambiguous monomials. Let us suppose that the set of states of $\mathcal{M}$ is equal to $\{1, ..., m\}$. Let

$$\Sigma_{1,1}, \Sigma_{2,1}, ..., \Sigma_{1,m-1}, \Sigma_{2,m-1} \subseteq \Sigma$$

be as above. Notice that $L(\mathcal{M})$ is equal to $L(r_{\mathcal{M}})$, where $r_{\mathcal{M}}$ is the regular expression

$$\Sigma_{1,1}^* \left(\bigsqcup_{a \in \Sigma_{2,1}} a \right) \Sigma_{1,2}^* \cdots \Sigma_{1,m-2}^* \left(\bigsqcup_{a \in \Sigma_{2,m-2}} a \right) \Sigma_{1,m-1}^*$$

Let us check that $r_{\mathcal{M}}$ is an unambiguous polynomial. A choice function for $r_{\mathcal{M}}$ is a function

$$f : \{1, \ldots, m-2\} \to \bigsqcup_{i \leq m-2} \Sigma_{2,i}$$

such that for all $i \leq m-2$ the condition $f(i) \in \Sigma_{2,i}$ holds. The equality

$$r_{\mathcal{M}} = \bigsqcup_{\substack{f \text{ is a choice} \\ \text{function}}} \Sigma_{1,1}^* f(1) \Sigma_{1,2}^* f(2) \cdots \Sigma_{1,m-2}^* f(m-2) \Sigma_{1,m-1}^*$$

holds. It follows from the unambiguity of $\mathcal{M}$ that this union is disjoint. It follows, for the same reason, that for all choice function f the monomial

$$r_f = \Sigma_{1,1}^* f(1) \Sigma_{1,2}^* \cdots \Sigma_{1,m-2}^* f(m-2) \Sigma_{1,m-1}^*$$

is unambiguous. The sixth item and the theorem are proved.

2 Autonomous Vehicles and Discrete Geometry

We are interested in the class of star-free unambiguous languages. Let us ask: where do unambiguous languages and poUFA's come from?

Remark 1. The notion of unambiguity might seem suspect. Let us observe that this restricted notion of nondeterminism has played a major role in theoretical computer science. Unambiguous finite state automata arise naturally from many different sources, let us just mention: sofic systems and codes [1], and finitely generated virtually Abelian groups, (see below).

Definition 6. *Let G be a finitely generated group. Let X be a spanning set for G, let $X^{-1} = \{g^{-1} : g \in X\}$, and let $R_X = X \cup X^{-1}$. The pair (G, R_X) determines a labeled graph that we call the Cayley graph of (G, X). We use the symbol $\mathcal{K}(G, R_X)$ to denote this graph. $\mathcal{K}(G, R_X)$ is defined as follows:*

- *The nodes of* $\mathcal{K}(G, R_X)$ *are the elements of* G.
- *Let* $g, h \in G$, *there exists an edge from* g *to* h, *with label* x, *if and only if the equality* $g \cdot x = h$ *holds in* G.

$\mathcal{K}(G, R_X)$ is endowed with a metric, the *graph metric*, that is defined as follows:

$$d_{R_X}(g, h) = \min\{|\gamma| : \text{where } \gamma \text{ is a path from } g \text{ to } h\}$$

This metric yields, in turn, a notion of shortest paths or *geodesics* .

Example 4. Let G be the group of symmetries of the Rubik cube. The elements of G are in bijective correspondence with the configurations of the cube. The configuration with all the six faces monochromatic corresponds to the identity e_G. Let X be the set of four canonical generators of G. Let $g \in G$, and let γ be a shortest path from e_G to g. Let w_γ be the string that labels this path, and let $w_\gamma^{-1} = w[|w_\gamma|]^{-1} \cdots w[1]^{-1}$. Notice that w_γ^{-1} corresponds to an optimal way of producing e_G from g. Let

$$\mathcal{L}(G, R_X) = \left\{ \begin{matrix} w_\gamma : \gamma \text{ is a shortest path from } e \\ \text{to some } g \in G \end{matrix} \right\}$$

We say that $\mathcal{L}(G, R_X)$ is the *geodesic language* of G. This language is finite and hence unambiguous. Let $\mathcal{L}(G, R_X)^R$ be the reversal of $\mathcal{L}(G, R_X)$, and let a be a Rubik cube gamer. Notice that a can be modeled as an agent that moves over $\mathcal{K}(G, R_X)$, trying to get back to e_G, and trying to stay as close as possible to the star-free unambiguous language $\mathcal{L}(G, R_X)^R$.

Let a be an autonomous vehicle that moves over $\mathcal{K}(G, R_X)$. Suppose a is asked to go from e_G to g. Suppose we can only see the labels of the edges that are being traversed by a. Can we determine whether a does not deviate from the set $\mathcal{G}_g(G, R_X)$? It depends on G and X. We have:

Theorem 3. *The following assertion hold:*

1. *Let* G *be a finitely generated Abelian group, for all spanning set* X , *the languages* $\mathcal{L}(G, R_X)$ *and* $\mathcal{L}(G, R_X)^R$ *are unambiguous.*
2. *Let* G *be a finitely generated Abelian group, and let* H *be a finite group. Let* Y *be the canonical basis of the module* G, *and let* Z *be a spanning set of* H. *The languages* $\mathcal{L}(G, R_{Y \times Z})$ *and* $\mathcal{L}(G, R_{Y \times Z})^R$ *are unambiguous.*
3. *Let* G *be a finitely generated group that is virtually Abelian. There exists* X *such that* $\mathcal{L}(G, R_X)$ *and* $\mathcal{L}(G, R_X)^R$ *are both unambiguous.*

Remark 2. Let G be a finitely generated hyperbolic group, and let X be a spanning set. Gromov showed that $\mathcal{K}(G, R_X)$ is a discrete model of hyperbolic Geometry; see [8]. The class of finitely generated hyperbolic groups is a large class of groups that includes the class of finite groups and the class of virtually Abelian groups. Cannon proved that for all finitely generated hyperbolic group G, and for all spanning set X, the language $\mathcal{L}(G, R_X)$ is regular; see [2].

Remark 3. Let us think for a while about the ordered sequences of traces we use in order to lead someone somewhere in the city. Those strings are unambiguous monomials.

3 $\mathrm{FO}^2[<]$ Is Strongly-Stationary

We use the symbol $\mathrm{FO}^2[<]$ to denote the two-variable fragment of FO[<]. We prove that for all α and β in $\mathrm{FO}^2[<]$ the limit probability $\Pr(\alpha \mid \beta)$ exists and can be computed in time $2^{poly(|\alpha|+|\beta|)}$. We say that $\mathrm{FO}^2[<]$ is strongly-stationary.

Definition 7. *Let $\mathcal{M}$ be a DFA with input alphabet Σ. Suppose $Q = \{1, ..., n\}$. The transition matrix of $\mathcal{M}$ is the $n \times n$ matrix that is defined as follows*

$$T_{\mathcal{M}}[i,j] = |\{a \in \Sigma : \delta(i,a) = j\}|$$

Theorem 4. *The following assertions hold*

1. *$\mathrm{FO}^2[<]$ is strongly-stationary.*
2. *Let α and β be sentences of $\mathrm{FO}^2[<]$. The limit probability $\Pr(\alpha \mid \beta)$ can be computed in time $2^{poly(|\alpha|+|\beta|)}$.*

Proof. Let us proceed:

1. Let α and β be sentences of $\mathrm{FO}^2[<]$. Let $L = L_{\alpha\wedge\beta}$ and let $T = L_\beta$. The condition $L \subseteq T$ holds. Let $c_L(n)$ and $c_T(n)$ be the census functions of L and T. Those functions are defined by the equations

$$c_L(n) = |L \cap \Sigma^n| \text{ and } c_T(n) = |T \cap \Sigma^n|$$

Let $\mathcal{M}$ and $\mathcal{N}$ be poUFA's accepting the unambiguous languages L and T. Let $T(\mathcal{M})$ and $T(\mathcal{N})$ be the transition matrices of those automata, and let $Spec(T(\mathcal{M}))$ and $Spec(T(\mathcal{N}))$ be the spectra of those two matrices. We can express $c_L(n)$ and $c_T(n)$ as

$$\sum_{\lambda\in\mathrm{Spec}(T(\mathcal{M}))} p_\lambda(n)\lambda^n \quad \text{and} \quad \sum_{\lambda\in\mathrm{Spec}(T(\mathcal{N}))} q_\lambda(n)\lambda^n$$

where the p's and the q's are polynomials with rational coefficients that can be easily computed from the Jordan canonical forms of $T(\mathcal{M})$ and $T(\mathcal{N})$; see [6]. There are two key observations to be made, namely:

(a) The entries of $T(\mathcal{M})$ and $T(\mathcal{N})$ are included in the set $\{0, ..., |\Sigma|\}$.
(b) $T(\mathcal{M})$ and $T(\mathcal{N})$ can be triangulated by permuting some rows.

We get that $Spec(T(\mathcal{M}))$ and $Spec(T(\mathcal{N}))$ are included in $\{0, ..., |\Sigma|\}$. Let $d_{\mathcal{M}} = \max\{\lambda : \lambda \in Spec(T(\mathcal{M}))\}$. We define $d_{\mathcal{N}}$ accordingly. The inequality $d_{\mathcal{M}} \leq d_{\mathcal{N}}$ holds. Then, we express $c_L(n)$ and $c_T(n)$ as

$$p(n)\, d_{\mathcal{N}}^n + \sum_{0 \leq s < d_{\mathcal{N}} - 1} p_s(n)\, s^n \text{ and}$$

$$q(n)\, d_{\mathcal{N}}^n + \sum_{0 \leq s < d_{\mathcal{N}} - 1} q_s(n)\, s^n$$

Let $p(n) = a_k n^k + \cdots + a_0$, and let $q(n) = b_k n^k + \cdots + b_0$. The condition $b_k \neq 0$ holds. We obtain the equalities

$$\Pr(L \mid T) = \lim_{n \to \infty} \frac{c_L(n)}{c_T(n)} = \lim_{n \to \infty} \frac{p(n)}{p(n)} = \frac{a_k}{b_k}$$

We get that $\Pr(\alpha \mid \beta)$ exists. Notice that $\frac{a_k}{b_k}$ is a rational number that can be computed exactly.

2. Let be a sentence of $FO^2[<]$. Weis proved that one can compute in time $2^{poly(|\alpha|)}$ a NFA $\mathcal{M}_\alpha$ that accepts L_α; see [18]. It can be checked that $\mathcal{M}_\alpha$ is poUFA. Thus, given α and β be sentences of $FO^2[<]$, we compute in time $2^{poly(|\alpha|+|\beta|)}$ two poUFA's $\mathcal{M}_{\alpha\wedge\beta}$ and $\mathcal{M}_\alpha$ that accept the languages $L_{\alpha\wedge\beta}$ and L_β. We can assume that the transition matrices of $\mathcal{M}_{\alpha\wedge\beta}$ and $\mathcal{M}_\beta$ are triangular matrices with entries in the set $\{0, ..., |\Sigma|\}$. Then, we compute in time $2^{poly(|\alpha|+|\beta|)}$ the Jordan canonical forms of those two matrices. We use those canonical forms to compute the limit probability $\Pr(\alpha \mid \beta)$. The theorem is proved.

4 Proposed Applications

Let us explore a few applications of the asymptotic tractability of $FO^2[<]$.

4.1 Regular Language Distance and Model Checking

Let G be a finitely generated group and let X be a spanning set for G. Suppose that $\mathcal{L}(G, R_X)$ is regular. Let a be an agent that moves over $\mathcal{K}(G, R_X)$. Can we measure the distance from a to the ideal itinerary represented by $\mathcal{L}(G, R_X)$? Let us assume we know a poUFA $\mathcal{G}$ that accepts the language $co\text{-}\mathcal{L}(G, R_X)$. This corresponds to knowing the set (a set) of nongeodesic executions. The conditional probability $\Pr(L_{\mathcal{N}} \mid L_\alpha)$ tells us how many executions of α are wrong. This limit probability can be computed in time $2^{poly(|\alpha|)}\,|\mathcal{N}|$.

Definition 8. *Let $\mathcal{L}$ be a set of sentences, and let $\mathcal{C}$ be a class of automata. We use the symbol $p\text{-}PMCA_1(\mathcal{L}, \mathcal{C})$ to denote the parameterized problem that is defined as follows:*

- *Input: $(\alpha, \mathcal{N})$, where $\alpha \in \mathcal{L}$ and $\mathcal{N} \in \mathcal{C}$.*

- *Parameter:* $|\alpha|$.
- *Problem: decide whether the conditional probability* $\Pr(L_{\mathcal{N}} \mid L_\alpha)$ *exists, and in that case compute this limit probability.*

Theorem 5. *The problem p-PMCA*$_1$ $(FO^2[<], poUFA)$ *can be solved in time* $2^{poly(|\alpha|)}|\mathcal{N}|$.

Let G be a finitely generated group whose word problem is undecidable. The geodesic languages of G are undecidable. On the other hand, there exist finitely generated groups whose word problems are decidable and whose geodesic languages are all nonregular. The best-studied examples correspond to groups whose geodesic languages are linear unambiguous context-free languages (LUCFL's, for short). It is an interesting fact that the relative densities of LUCFL's with respect to star-free unambiguous languages can be computed. We have:

Theorem 6. *Let L be a linear unambiguous context-free language and let T be a star-free unambiguous language. The limit probability* $\Pr(L \cap T \mid T)$ *can be effectively computed.*

4.2 Sampling From Word Structures and Abductive Diagnosis

Suppose we do not know the program of a. Suppose we can monitor the movement of a and see the labels of the edges traversed by this agent. Suppose that a moves fast and we can only see traces, (subsequences and short factors), of the words that label the paths of a. Can we measure the quality of a's performance?

Definition 9. *Let $L \subset \Sigma^*$ be a language. Let $s \in \Sigma^k$ and let $n \geq k$. We define* $\Pr_n^S(s \mid L)$ *as*

$$\Pr_{i_1 < \cdots < i_k \leq n}\left(w[i_1]\cdots w[i_k] = s \mid w \in L \cap \Sigma^n\right)$$

Then, we define $\Pr^S(s \mid L)$ *as* $\lim_{n\to\infty}\Pr_n^S(s \mid L)$. *We define* $\Pr_n^F(s \mid L)$ *as*

$$\Pr_{i \leq n-k}\left(w[i,...,i+k-1] = s \mid w \in L \cap \Sigma^n\right)$$

Finally, we define $\Pr^F(s \mid L)$ *as* $\lim_{n\to\infty}\Pr_n^F(s \mid L)$.

There exist aperiodic languages that do not behave well under the above notion of asymptotic sampling.

Example 5. Let $L \subset \Sigma^*$ and $T \subset \Gamma^*$ be two languages. We use the symbol $L \times T$ to denote the language

$$\left\{w \in (\Sigma \times \Gamma)^* : \pi_1(w) \in L \text{ and } \pi_2(w) \in T\right\}$$

Let

$$L = (ab)^* \times \{a\}^* \cup (ab)^* a \times \{b\}^*$$

Notice that the limit probabilities $\Pr^S((a,a) \mid L)$ and $\Pr^F((a,a) \mid L)$ do not exist.

Theorem 7. *Let α be a sentence of $FO^2[<]$. For all $k \geq 1$ and all $s \in \Sigma^k$ the limit probabilities $\Pr^S(s \mid L_\alpha)$ and $\Pr^F(s \mid L_\alpha)$ exist and can be computed in time $2^{kpoly(|\alpha|)}$.*

Definition 10. *Let α be a sentence of $FO^2[<]$. This sentence determines a probability distribution over the set Σ^k. We use the symbol $\mu_{\alpha,k}$ to denote this distribution which is defined by the equation $\mu_{\alpha,k}(s) = \Pr(s \mid L_\alpha)$.*

Remark 4. Let S be the multiset constituted by all the traces of a we got to observe. It is important to emphasize that S is a multiset (a list with repeated items): each string s can appear more than once in S, and the number of occurrences of s in S is related to the frequency of pattern s among the strings belonging to L_α.

Let S be the multiset of observed traces. Suppose the traces in S have length k. Multiset S determines an empirical distribution μ_S over the set Σ^k. Let α be the program of a, and let μ_α the distribution over the set Σ^k that is determined by this unambiguous program. Suppose S is large. The empirical distribution μ_S is expected to be close to μ_α. Suppose the norm $\|\mu_{L_\mathcal{M}} - \mu_S\|$ is large. Then, the norm $\|\mu_{L_\mathcal{M}} - \mu_\alpha\|$ should be large, and we can conclude with a high confidence level that α deviates drastically from the optimal itinerary represented by $L_\mathcal{M}$.

Definition 11. *Let $v \in \mathbb{Q}^{|\Sigma|^k}$, we use the symbol $\|v\|$ to denote the norm of v, we define this norm as follows*

$$\|v\| = \max\left\{|v[i]| : i \leq |\Sigma|^k\right\}$$

We define the bit-norm of v as

$$\|v\|_b = \max\left\{|v[i]|_b : i \leq |\Sigma|^k\right\},$$

where $|v[i]|_b$ denotes the size in bits of $v[i]$.

Theorem 8. *The following assertions hold:*

1. *Let α be a sentence of $FO^2[<]$. The probability distribution $\mu_{\alpha,k}$ can be computed in time $2^{kpoly(|\alpha|)}$.*
2. *Let μ_k be an empirical distribution over the set Σ^k , let α be a sentence of $FO^2[<]$, and let $\varepsilon > 0$. The inequality $\|\mu_{S_k} - \mu_\alpha\| < \varepsilon$ can be checked in time $2^{kpoly(|\alpha|)}\|\mu_{S_k}\|_b^2$.*

4.3 Temporal Planning

Suppose a has been walking the graph $\mathcal{K}(G, R_X)$ during t time units. Let γ be the traversed path, and let w_γ be the string that labels this path. Suppose we could observe the prefix $w[1, ..., t]$. Can we use this knowledge of the past, and the knowledge of $\mathcal{M}_{G,R_X}$, to predict the future of this walk?

We can represent some properties of the observed traces using FO[<]. We can also express hypotheses about the future of the walk using this logic. Let α be a sentence of FO[<] that represents our observations about the past. Let β be a sentence of FO[<] that expresses a hypothesis about the future. We would like to compute the conditional probability $\Pr(\beta \mid \alpha; \mathcal{M}_{G,R_X})$.

Definition 12. *Let α and β be sentences of FO[<], and let $\mathcal{M}$ be an automaton. We set*

$$\Pr(\beta \mid \alpha; \mathcal{M}) = \Pr(L_\beta \mid L_\alpha \cap L_{\mathcal{M}})$$

Theorem 9. *Let α and β be formulas of $FO^2[<]$, and let $\mathcal{M}$ be a poUFA. The limit probability $\Pr(\beta \mid \alpha; \mathcal{M})$ exists and can be computed in time $2^{poly(|\alpha|+|\beta|)}|\mathcal{M}|^4$.*

5 Parameterized Intractability Beyond $\mathbf{FO^2}[<]$

We studied, in the previous section, three potential applications of our research work. In all three cases, we found algorithms that run in time $2^{poly(|\alpha|)}poly(|\mathcal{O}|)$. This corresponds to a strong form of fixed parameter tractability. This strong form is called *bounded fixed parameter tractability*; see [19]. This seems to be the characteristic behavior of the fragment $\mathrm{FO}^2[<]$.

Definition 13. *Let $\mathcal{L}$ be a set of sentences of FO[<], and let $\mathcal{C}$ be a class of automata. We use the symbol p-PMCA$(\mathcal{L},\mathcal{C})$ to denote the parameterized problem:*

- *Input: $(\alpha,\beta,\mathcal{M},\mathcal{N})$, where $\alpha,\beta \in \mathcal{L}$ and $\mathcal{M},\mathcal{N} \in \mathcal{C}$.*
- *Parameter: $|\alpha| + |\beta|$.*
- *Problem: decide whether the limit probability $\Pr(L_\alpha \cap L_{\mathcal{M}} \mid L_\beta \cap L_{\mathcal{N}})$ exists, and in that case compute this probability.*

We will prove that *p-PMCA*$\left(\mathrm{FO}^2[<], \mathrm{poUFA}\right)$ is bounded fixed parameter tractable, (belongs to PPT; see [19]). On the other hand, we will prove that some small *perturbations* of this problem yield intractability.

Note 1. We use the symbol loDFA to denote the class of linearly ordered DFA's. We use the symbol $\top$ to denote the trivial fragment $\{\forall x\,(x = x), \forall x\,(x \neq x)\}$.

We prove that *p-PMCA*$(\Pi_3[<], \mathrm{loDFA})$ is hard for #PW[1]. We also prove that *p-PMCA*$(\top, \mathrm{poNFA})$ does not belong to XP. We say that $\mathrm{FO}^2[<]$, and the related class of partially ordered UFA's, lie *at the edge of intractability*. Let us introduce some definitions.

Definition 14. *Let L and T be two parameterized problems. We say that L is ppt-reducible to T if and only if there exists an algorithm $\mathcal{M}$ which, on input (x,k), works as follows:*

1. *Decides in time time* $2^{poly(k)} poly(|x|)$ *whether* (x, k) *belongs to* T.
2. *There exist* c *and* d *such that for all input* (x, k) *and all query* (y, r) *computed by* $\mathcal{M}$ *during the processing of* (x, k), *the condition* $r \in O\left(\log^c(|x|) + k^d\right)$ *holds.*

Definition 15. *Let* P *be a parameterized problem. We use the symbol* $\langle P \rangle^{ppt}$ *to denote the closure of* $\{P\}$ *under ppt reductions. We use the symbol* $PW[1]$ *to denote the parameterized class* $\left\langle WSAT\left(\Gamma^+_{1,2}\right)\right\rangle^{ppt}$*; see [19].*

We use the symbol #PW[1] to denote the counting version of PW [1], we are referring to the class $\left\langle \#WSAT\left(\Gamma^+_{1,2}\right)\right\rangle^{ppt}$. Let us recall that the symbol $\Gamma^+_{1,2}$ denotes the class of positive 2CNF's. A typical instance of $\#WSAT\left(\Gamma^+_{1,2}\right)$ is a pair

$$\left(\bigwedge_i (p_{i,1} \vee p_{i,2}), k\right).$$

The problem is to count the number of satisfying assignments of $\bigwedge_i (p_{i,1} \vee p_{i,2})$ of *weight* k. The weight of an assignment is the number of propositional letters that are sent to 1.

Definition 16. *Let* T *be a parameterized problem. We say that* T *belongs to XP if and only if for any value of the parameter, say* r_0, *the subproblem (fiber)*

$$\{x : \textit{the parameter } k(x) \textit{ equals } r_0\}$$

can be solved in polynomial time.

Remark 5. The classes EPT, PPT, PW[1], and #PW[1] are all included in XP.

Theorem 10. *The following assertions hold:*

1. *p-PMCA* $(\Pi_1[<], poUFA)$ *can be solved in time* $poly(|\alpha|, |\beta|, |\mathcal{M}|, |\mathcal{N}|)$.
2. *p-PMCA* $\left(FO^2[<], poUFA\right)$ *can be solved in time* $2^{poly(|\alpha|+|\beta|)} poly(|\mathcal{M}|, |\mathcal{N}|)$.
3. *p-PMCA* $(\Pi_3[<], loDFA)$ *is hard for* $\#PW[1]$.
4. *If P is different from NP, the problem p-PMCA* $(\top,$ *poNFA) does not belong to XP.*

Let us recall that $\mathrm{FO}^2[<]$ is expressively equivalent to $\Delta_2[<]$. The proof of the above fourth item shows that *p*-DC($\forall^*\exists^*\forall[<]$, loDFA) is hard for #PW[1]. This leaves one gap in our classification. We are referring to the fragment $\Pi_2[<]$.

Question 1. Is *p-PMCA* $(\Pi_2[<]$, poUFA) hard for *PW* [1]?

6 Concluding Remarks

We conjecture that $\Pi_2[<]$ and $\Sigma_2[<]$ are hard for #PW[1]. Let us suppose, for the sake of discussion, that the problem $p\text{-}PMCA(\Pi_2[<], \text{poUFA})$ belongs to PPT. This does not mean that the fragments $\text{FO}^2[<]$ and $\Pi_2[<]$ are equally tractable. Let us use the symbol $\text{SAT}(\text{FO}^2[<])$ to denote the satisfiability problem for $\text{FO}^2[<]$. This problem is NP-complete; see [5]. On the other hand, the problem SAT $(\Pi_2[<])$ is hard for PSPACE. We would like to point out the following two facts:

1. The satisfiability problem for $\text{FO}^2[<]$ is NP-complete, the same complexity of SAT.
2. The problems $\#\text{SAT}(\text{FO}^2[<])$ and $CCP(\text{FO}^2[<])$ are #P-complete, the same complexity of #SAT.

Acknowledgement. I would like to thank Centro de Investigaciones Antonio Sanchez de Cozar, Vereda los Egidos, San Gil Colombia. Most of this work was written while the author was visiting this charming research center.

Appendix

Proof. (Proof of Theorem 3)

Let G be a finitely generated Abelian group, and let X be a spanning set for G. The language $\mathcal{L}(G, R_X)$ is *piecewise testable*; see [9]. The class of piecewise testable languages is included in the class of unambiguous languages. This latter class is closed under reversals. We get that $\mathcal{L}(G, X)$ and $\mathcal{L}(G, X)^R$ are both unambiguous.

Let us prove the second item. We prove something stronger. Let G be equal to $H \times K$, where K admits an unambiguous geodesic language and H is a finitely generated Abelian group. We prove that there exists a spanning set for G such that the corresponding geodesic language is unambiguous. We can assume that There exists a k such that $H = \mathbb{Z}^k$. Let $X = \{e_1, \dots, e_k\}$ be the canonical basis of the finite-dimensional module $\mathbb{Z}^k$, and let Y be a spanning set of K such that $\mathcal{L}(G, R_Y)$ is unambiguous. Suppose that for all $i \leq N$, the monomial r_i is unambiguous. Let $r_i = \Sigma_0^* a_1 \Sigma_1^* \cdots \Sigma_{n-1}^* w[n] \Sigma_n^*$. Let $\varepsilon \in \{0,1\}^k$, and let Σ_ε be equal to $\left\{e_1^{\varepsilon(1)}, ..., e_k^{\varepsilon(k)}\right\}$, where

$$e_i^{\varepsilon(i)} = \begin{cases} e_i, \text{ if } \varepsilon(i) = 1 \\ -e_i, \text{ otherwise} \end{cases}$$

Let $r_{i,\varepsilon}$ be equal to the unambiguous monomial

$$(\Sigma_0 \cup \Sigma_\varepsilon)^* a_1 (\Sigma_1 \cup \Sigma_\varepsilon)^* \cdots (\Sigma_{n-1} \cup \Sigma_\varepsilon)^* a_n (\Sigma_n \cup \Sigma_\varepsilon)^*$$

The equality $\mathcal{L}(G \times K, R_{X \cup Y}) = \bigcup_{i,\varepsilon} r_{i,\varepsilon}$ holds. It is easy to check that this union is disjoint. This shows that $\mathcal{L}(G \times K, R_{X \cup Y})$ is unambiguous.

Let G be a finitely generated group that is virtually Abelian. There exists X such that $\mathcal{L}(G, X)$ is piecewise testable; see [9]. The theorem is proved.

Proof. (Proof of Theorem 6)

Let L be a linear unambiguous context-free language and let R be a regular language, (LUCFL, for short). The language $L \cap R$ is a LUCFL. Let $G = (V, T, S, \mathcal{R})$ be linear unambiguous context-free grammar for this latter language. Let us suppose $V = \{X_1, ...X_m\}$ and $S = X_1$. Let $i \leq m$, and let

$$X_i \to a_{i_1} X_{i_1} \mid \cdots \mid a_{i_p} X_{i_p} \mid X_{j_1} a_{j_1} \mid \cdots \mid X_{j_r} a_{j_r} \mid a_{k_1} \mid \cdots \mid a_{k_l}$$

be the set of production rules in $\mathcal{R}$ that have the nonterminal X_i as root. We use the symbol $\mathcal{R}_i$ to denote this finite set of production rules. We apply the Chomsky-Schützenberger method to compute, from $\mathcal{R}_i$, the functional equation:

$$X_i(x) = x\left(\sum_{s=1}^{p} X_{i_s}(x) + \sum_{s=1}^{r} X_{j_r}(x)\right) + lx + \varepsilon_i,$$

where $\varepsilon_i = 1$ if and only if $X_i \to \varepsilon$ is a production rule in $\mathcal{R}$. We do the same with all the nonterminal symbols in V. We obtain a system

$$\overrightarrow{X} = (I - xA)^{-1} (x\Delta + \overrightarrow{\varepsilon})$$

The solution for $X_1(x)$, (i.e. $\overrightarrow{X}[1]$), is a rational function that can be effectively computed. We use the symbol $m(x)$ to denote this rational function. Function $m(x)$ is the generating function of $L \cap R$. Let us point out a key fact: the set of poles of $m(x)$ equals the set of roots of its denominator.

We can also compute a generating function for the star-free unambiguous language R. We can compute this latter function using an easier method. Let us use the symbol $f_R(z)$ to denote the generating function of L_R. We compute a closed formula for $f_R(x)$ using the following substitutions:

1. Replace any constant symbol with x.
2. Replace union with sum.
3. Replace concatenation with multiplication.
4. Given β and given $f_\beta(x)$, compute $f_{\beta^*}(x)$ as $\frac{1}{1-f_\beta(x)}$.

Let $n(x)$ be the generating function of L_R. Let $d \leq |\Sigma|$ be the dominating eigenvalue of R. It is easy to check that the poles of $n(x)$ are included in the set $\left\{1, ..., \frac{1}{d}\right\}$. We get that $n(x)$ has a dominating root at $\frac{1}{d}$, (this means that the norm of any other pole is strictly larger than $\frac{1}{d}$; see [11]). We have three possibilities, namely:

1. Either $m(x)$ does not have poles of norm $\frac{1}{d}$. In this case, $\Pr(L \cap R \mid R)$ equals zero.
2. Or $m(x)$ has many poles of norm $\frac{1}{d}$. In this case, $\Pr(L \cap R \mid R)$ does not exist.

3. Or $m(x)$ has exactly one pole of norm $\frac{1}{d}$. In this case, $\Pr(L \cap R \mid R)$ equals $\lim_{x \to \frac{1}{d}} \frac{m(x)}{n(x)}$; see [11].

Let us observe that the above three cases can be easily checked from a rational representation of $m(x)$. We obtain that the limit probability $\Pr(L \cap R \mid R)$ can be effectively computed. The theorem is proved.

Proof. (Proof of Theorem 7)

We write down the proof for $\Pr^S(s \mid L_\alpha)$. The proof for $\Pr^F(s \mid L_\alpha)$ is analogous and we omit it.

Let $\mathcal{M}$ be a poUFA. Let $(Q, \preceq_{\mathcal{M}})$ be the ordered set of states of $\mathcal{M}$. The *depth* of $\mathcal{M}$ is the length of the longest chain occurring in this ordered set. Let α be a sentence of $\mathrm{FO}^2[<]$. We can compute in time $2^{poly(|\alpha|)}$ a poUFA $\mathcal{M}_\alpha$ of depth $poly(|\alpha|)$ that accepts L_α. Then, we can compute in time $2^{poly(|\alpha|)}$ a disjoint union of LOUFA's, say $\bigcup_{i \leq N} \mathcal{M}_i$, such that for all $i \leq N$ the size of $\mathcal{M}_i$ belongs to $poly(|\alpha|)$. Let $k \geq 1$, and let $s \in \Sigma^k$. The limit probability $\Pr^S(s \mid L_\alpha)$ equals

$$\sum_{i \leq N} \Pr(L_{\mathcal{M}_i} \mid L_\alpha) \Pr(s \mid L_{\mathcal{M}_i})$$

We know that for all $i \leq N$, the limit probability $\Pr\left(L_{L_{\mathcal{M}_i}} \mid L_\alpha\right)$ exists and can be computed in time $2^{O(poly(|\alpha|))}$. Recall that N belongs to $2^{poly(|\alpha|)}$. Then, it suffices if we prove that for all $i \leq N$ the limit probability $\Pr(s \mid L_{\mathcal{M}_i})$ can be computed in time $|\alpha|^{O(k)}$. Let us do this. Let $i \leq N$, we can represent $\mathcal{M}_i$ as a *generalized monomial*

$$r_i = \Sigma_0^* \Gamma_1 \Sigma_2^* \cdots \Sigma_{m-1}^* \Gamma_m \Sigma_m^*,$$

where $\Gamma_1, \ldots, \Gamma_m \subseteq \Sigma$. We assume the inequality $m \leq |\alpha|$. Let $\Sigma_{i_1}, \ldots, \Sigma_{i_r}$ be the factors of maximum size in r_i. The equality

$$\Pr(s \mid r_i) = \frac{1}{N_{k,r}} \Pr(s \mid f),$$

holds, where the sum ranges over the set

$$\left\{ \begin{array}{c} f : f \text{ is a non-decreasing function from} \\ \{1, \ldots, k\} \text{ in } \{1, \ldots, r\} \end{array} \right\},$$

and $\Pr(s \mid f)$ is defined by the equation

$$\Pr(s \mid f) = \begin{cases} \frac{1}{|\Sigma_{i_1}|^k}, \text{ if for all } j \leq k \text{ the condition } s[j] \in \Sigma_{i_{f(j)}} \text{ holds} \\ \qquad 0, \text{ otherwise} \end{cases}$$

Notice that $\Pr(s \mid r_i)$ can be computed in time $O\left(|\alpha|^k\right)$. The theorem is proved.

Proof. (Proof of Theorem 10)
Let us proceed:

1. Let α be a sentence of $\Pi_1[<]$. We can compute in polynomial time a poUFA $\mathcal{M}_\alpha$ that accepts L_α. Thus, if we are given $(\alpha, \beta, \mathcal{M}, \mathcal{M})$, an instance of p-DC$(\Sigma_1[<], \text{poUFA})$, we compute in polynomial time two product automata $\mathcal{M}_\alpha \times \mathcal{M}_\beta \times \mathcal{M} \times \mathcal{N}$ and $\mathcal{M}_\beta \times \mathcal{N}$ accepting the languages $L_\alpha \cap L_\beta \cap L_{\mathcal{M}} \cap L_{\mathcal{N}}$ and $L_\beta \cap L_{\mathcal{N}}$. These product automata are poUFA's, and we can use them to compute in polynomial time the limit probability $\Pr(L_\alpha \cap L_{\mathcal{M}} \mid L_\beta \cap L_{\mathcal{N}})$.
2. The proof of this item is analogous to the proof of the previous one.
3. Let (α, k) be an instance of p-$\#WSAT(\Gamma^+_{1,2})$. Let α be equal to

$$\bigwedge_{i \leq n} (p_{i,1} \vee p_{i,2}),$$

where for all $i \leq n$, the subformulas $p_{i,1}$ and $p_{i,2}$ are propositional letters. We use

$$\bigwedge_{i \leq n} (p_{i,1} \vee p_{i,2})$$

to compute a pair $(\phi_\alpha, \mathcal{M}_{\alpha,k})$. This pair is constituted by a $\Pi_3[<]$-sentence ϕ_α, and a loDFA. $\mathcal{M}_{\alpha,k}$. Automaton $\mathcal{M}_{\alpha,k}$ accepts a language L^α that encodes the structure of α. Let us define this language. We use the input alphabet $\Sigma = \{0, 1, V, \#, C, D\}$. Let $\{p_1, ..., p_m\}$ be the set of propositional letters in α. Let $i \leq m$, we use the symbol $\langle i \rangle$ to denote the binary code of i. Let $r = \lceil \log_2 m \rceil$. We assume that for all i the equality $|\langle i \rangle| = r$ holds. Let $w_\alpha \in \{C, D, 0, 1\}^*$ be the string

$$C \langle k_1 \rangle D \langle s_1 \rangle C \cdots C \langle k_n \rangle D \langle s_n \rangle C,$$

where for all $i \leq n$ the equalities $p_{i,1} = p_{k_1}$ and $p_{i,2} = p_{s_i}$ hold. We set

$$L = (V\{0,1\}^m)^k \#w_\alpha c (\Sigma \cup \{c\})^*$$

Notice that $\mathcal{M}_{\alpha,k}$ can be computed in time $2^{poly(k)}|\alpha|$. It remains to define the sentence ϕ_α. We set

$$\phi_\alpha = \psi \wedge \forall y_0 \forall y_1 \cdots \forall y_{2r+1} \forall y_{2r+2} \exists z_0 \cdots \exists z_r \forall u \Psi ,$$

where:
- ψ is a $\Pi_1[<]$ sentence asserting that given the prefix $Vu_1V \cdots Vu_k\#$, the factors $u_1, \ldots, u_k$ are pairwise different.

- Ψ is the quantifier-free formula:

$$\left(C(y_0) \wedge \left(\bigwedge_{0\leq i\leq 2r} y_i < y_{i+1}\right) \wedge \right.$$

$$\left.\left(\bigwedge_{0\leq i\leq 2r} (y_i < y_{2r+2} \leq y_{i+1} \Rightarrow y_{2r+2} = y_{i+1})\right)\right)$$

$$\Rightarrow$$

$$\left(V(z_0) \wedge \left(\bigwedge_{i<r} (z_i < z_{r+1} \leq z_{i+1} \Rightarrow z_{r+1} = y_{i+1})\right)\right.$$

$$\left.\wedge \left(\bigwedge_{i\leq r} ((0(y_i) \Leftrightarrow 0(z_i)) \wedge (1(y_i) \Leftrightarrow 1(z_i)))\right.\right.$$

- Let us prove the fourth item. Let $\mathcal{M}$ be a poNFA, and let n be a positive integer. Let $\mathcal{M}_n$ be a poNFA that accepts the language $\Sigma^n c (\Sigma \cup \{c\})^*$. Let $\mathcal{M}_c$ the poNFA that accepts the language $(L_{\mathcal{M}} \cap \Sigma^n)\, c\, (\Sigma \cup \{c\})^*$. The equality

$$c_{L_{\mathcal{M}}}(n+1) = \Pr(\mathcal{M}_n \mid \mathcal{M}_c)\,(|\Sigma|+1)^{n+1}$$

holds. The problem of computing the census functions of poNFA's is hard for #P. Thus, if we suppose P is different from NP, we get that the set

$$\{(\forall x\,(x=x), \forall x\,(x=x), \mathcal{M}, \mathcal{N}) : \mathcal{M} \text{ and } \mathcal{N} \text{ are poNFA's}\}$$

cannot be recognized in polynomial time. We conclude that *p*-DC($\top$, poNFA) does not belong to XP. The theorem is proved.

References

1. Béal, M.-P., Perrin, D.: Codes, unambiguous automata and sofic systems. Theor. Comput. Sci. **356**(1–2), 6–13 (2006)
2. Cannon, J.: The combinatorial structure of cocompact discrete hyperbolic groups. Geom. Dedicata **16**(2) (1984)
3. Chomsky, N., Miller, G.: Finite state languages. Inf. Control **1**(2), 91–112 (1958)
4. De Giacomo, G., Di Stasio, A., Fuggitti, F., Rubin, S.: Pure-past linear temporal and dynamic logic on finite traces. In: Proceedings of IJCAI 20 (2020)
5. Etessami, K., Vardi, M., Wilke, T.: First-order logic with two variables and unary temporal logic. Inf. Comput. **179**(2), 279–295 (2002)

6. Flajolet, P., Sedgewick, R.: Analytic Combinatorics. Princenton University Press, Boston (2009)
7. Göös, M., Kiefer, S., Yuan, W.: Lower bounds for unambiguous automata via communication complexity. ICALP **126**(1–126), 13 (2022)
8. Gromov, M.: Hyperbolic groups. In: Gersten, S.M. (ed.). Essays in Group Theory. Mathematical Sciences Research Institute Publications, vol. 8, pp. 75–263. Springer, New York (1987)
9. Hermiller, S., Holt, D., Rees, S.: Star-free geodesic languages for groups. Int. J. Algebra Comput. **17**(2), 329–345 (2007)
10. Kieronski, E., Kuusisto, A.: One-dimensional fragment over words and trees. J. Log. Comput. **32**(5), 902–941 (2022)
11. Kozik, J.: Conditional densities of regular languages. In: Proceedings of CLA 2004, pp. 67–79 (2004)
12. Lynch, J.: Convergence laws for random words. Aust. J. Comb. **7**, 145–156 (1993)
13. McNaughton, R., Papert, S.: Counter-Free Automata. M.I.T Press, Cambridge (1971)
14. Schützenberger, M.: Sur le produit de concatenation non ambigu. Semigroup Forum **13**, 47–75 (1976)
15. Therien, D., Wilke, Th.: Over words, two variables are as powerful as one quantifier alternation. In: Proceedings of STOC, pp. 234–240 (1998)
16. Schwentick, T., Thérien, D., Vollmer, H.: Partially-ordered two-way automata: a new characterization of DA. In: Proceedings of DLT 2001, pp. 239–250 (2001)
17. Stockmeyer, L.: The Complexity of Decision Problems in Automata Theory and Logic. Ph.D. dissertation, Massachusetts Institute of Technology (1974)
18. Weis, P.: Expressiveness and Succinctness of First-Order Logic on Finite Words. PhD thesis, University of Massachusetts (2011)
19. Weyer, M.: Bounded fixed-parameter tractability: the case 2poly(k). In: IWPEC 2004, pp. 49–60 (2004)

Logics of Import and Export for the Implicative Conditional

Eric Raidl(✉)

Cluster of Excellence 'Machine Learning for Science', Eberhard Karls Universität, Tübingen, Germany
eric.raidl@uni-tuebingen.de

Abstract. The implicative conditional $A \Rightarrow C := \Diamond A \wedge \Diamond \neg C \wedge \Box(A \supset C)$ strengthens the strict conditional and circumvents the paradoxes of the latter, all by remaining modally interpretable. This paper extends the analysis from Raidl and Gomes (2025) where Import (IM) and Export (EX) are analyzed for $\Rightarrow$, as well as possibilistic versions, where either the possibility of the antecedent of the consequent conditional (P1X) or the consequent of it (P2X) or both (PPX) are added as antecedent of the principle (X= IM or EX). In reflexive Kripke models, $\Rightarrow$ only validates PPIM. Thus no Gibbardian collapse arises, i.e. $\Rightarrow$ remains distinct from material implication, since the collapse theorem requires at least EX and Simplification (SI), which are both invalid for $\Rightarrow$.

Here I investigate the other principles and their modal counterparts. I show that, in reflexive Kripke models, P1IM corresponds to the modal axiom 4, and IM to 4 together with the provability axiom Grz. On the other hand, in Kripke models, P2EX (and hence PPEX) corresponds to the modal axiom 5 together with shift-discreteness $\Box(A \supset \Box A)$. It is then easily shown that all Exportations imply the collapse $\Diamond A \supset \Box A$. Hence, although there are non-trivial ways to validate Importation(s), without implying a collapse, there is no non-trivial way for $\Rightarrow$ to validate Exportation from a normal modal logic perspective.

Keywords: Implicative conditional · Import · Export · Gibbard's collapse · Simplification · Conjunction Elimination · Grz · S4

1 Introduction

The implicative conditional $A \Rightarrow C := \Diamond A \wedge \Diamond \neg C \wedge \Box(A \supset C)$ was proposed as a strengthening of the strict conditional.[1] It was shown to circumvent the paradoxes of the latter, all by remaining modally interpretable.[2] The implicative conditional logic IC, introduced and investigated by Raidl and Gomes (2024), was shown to be translationally equivalent to the modal logic KT, due to the fact that $\Box$ is definable by $\Rightarrow$ as $\Box A := A \wedge \neg(A \Rightarrow A)$ in reflexive Kripke

[1] Burks (1955); Gherardi and Orlandelli (2021); Gomes (2005, 2020); Priest (1999).
[2] Gomes, Pizzi, and Raidl (2025); Raidl and Gomes (2024).

D. Kozen and R. de Queiroz (Eds.): WoLLIC 2025, LNCS 15942, pp. 56–70, 2026.
https://doi.org/10.1007/978-3-031-99536-1_4

models. IC preserves many principles from strict conditional and variably strict conditionals, all by avoiding certain shortcomings of the latter. In particular, IC can be seen as obtained from David Lewis' (1973) logic VW from which we remove CN ($A > \top$), RW (Right-Weakening), ID ($A > A$), RM (Rational Monotonicity), but add AT (Aristotle Thesis), TR (Transitivity) and C (Contraposition), yet without adding M ([Antecedent] Monotonicity). Although not connexive (as it invalidates Strong Boethius thesis), it was shown to be a weakly connexive logic and even Boethian, as it validates both Aristotle's thesis, weak Boethius thesis and invalidates Symmetry (Gomes et al., 2025). Hence from a logical perspective, it is very interesting classical, but non-normal, conditional logic (in Chellas' (1980) sense).

The implicative conditional was also argued to be an adequate representation of natural language indicative conditionals.[3] As such, it potentially faces a forceful objection: natural language behavior of indicative conditionals is thought to license Import (IM) and Export (EX) (here written for $\Rightarrow$):

$$((A \wedge B) \Rightarrow C) \supset (A \Rightarrow (B \Rightarrow C)) \qquad \text{EX}$$
$$(A \Rightarrow (B \Rightarrow C)) \supset ((A \wedge B) \Rightarrow C) \qquad \text{IM}$$

However, any conditional which strengthens the material conditional ($\supset$)[4] and validates these principles collapses with the material conditional, under mild assumptions (henceforth 'Gibbardean collapse').[5] How does the implicative conditional behave with respect to these collapse theorems? The question was treated by Raidl and Gomes (2025). We showed that the implicative conditional validates neither EX nor IM, and also invalidates the major assumption of the collapse theorem – Simplification (SI). Hence the known proofs of the Gibbardean collapse are blocked. We also argued that while natural language examples support the failure of EX, similar examples speak in favor of IM. We accommodated this by showing that $\Rightarrow$ does in fact validate a possibilistic version of IM (PPIM), where two possibility assumptions are added to the antecedent of IM, namely $\Diamond(A \wedge B)$– the possibility of the antecedent of the consequent conditional – and $\Diamond \neg C$– the possibility of the consequent of the consequent conditional. Weaker versions of IM – P1IM where only $\Diamond(A \wedge B)$ is added and P2IM where only $\Diamond \neg C$ is added – remain invalid. Furthermore, all possibilistic versions of EX (PPEX, P1EX, P2EX constructed similarly) are invalid. Thus the implicative conditional behaves well with respect to the natural language data – validating a version of Importation all by invalidating Exportation –, without leading to collapse. However, for this we need to accept that the antecedent of Importation essentially presupposes two further possibilistic assumptions.

In this article, I ask whether these presuppositions can be turned into implicatures. On the one hand, I take the remark seriously that IM (but not EX) is a natural inference behavior of indicative conditionals. I thus ask, if we can strengthen the implicative conditional semantically, so that the original IM is

[3] Gherardi and Orlandelli (2021); Gomes (2005; 2020); Raidl and Gomes (2024).

[4] Or even some weaker 'logical conditional'.

[5] Egré, Rossi, and Sprenger (2023); Fitelson (2013); Gibbard (1981).

valid, not only the possibilistic version. On the other hand, I examine what happens when we add EX or any of the possibilistic versions to the logic of the implicative conditional, and show that, although the Gibbardean collapse fails, another collapse arises – one between necessity and possibility, and in fact between necessity and truth.

Section 2 rehearses the collapse theorems and Sect. 3 presents the possibilistic versions of IM and EX and recalls the results from Raidl and Gomes (2025). The remaining sections, develop the new material. Section 4 examines P1IM, and shows that it is equivalent to the modal axiom 4 in reflexive models. And in transitive reflexive models, P1IM is equivalent to PPIM, and P2IM to IM. Section 5 examines IM, and shows that it is equivalent to 4 together with the provability axiom Grz in reflexive models. I also show that IM remains valid in shift-reflexive, transitive, conversely well-founded models, showing that $\Rightarrow$ supports IM without implying the material conditional (and hence avoiding the minor part of the collapse). Section 6 examines P2EX and shows that it is equivalent to the modal axiom 5 together with the axiom $\Box(A \supset \Box A)$ which characterizes shift-discreteness (Appendix 7 contains the proofs).

From the results, we can also conclude that all Exportations imply the collapse $\Diamond A \supset \Box A$, and hence the collapse of modalities in serial models and the collapse of modalities with truth in reflexive models. Hence, while there are non-trivial ways to validate not only PPIM (Raidl & Gomes, 2025), but also P1IM and even IM, there is no non-trivial way to validate any Exportation in Kripke models. The questions left open by this article are: (i) are there non-normal models in which EX is non-trivially valid? (ii) does PPIM (and the other Importations) imply reflexivity or (iii) only the weaker shift reflexivity? My conjecture is 'yes' for (i) and (iii).

2 Collapse Theorems

Import and Export seem natural principles that dictate the interaction of conjunction and the conditional, and allow to handle nested conditionals. In particular, Import allows to reduce a nested conditional to an unnested one. However, Import-Export lead to triviality given some mild assumptions:[6]

$$(A \wedge B) > B \qquad \text{SI}$$
$$(A > B) \supset (A \supset B) \qquad \text{MI}$$
$$((A \wedge B) > C) \supset (A > (B > C)) \qquad \text{EX}$$
$$\vdash A \equiv B, \text{ then } \vdash (A > C) \supset (B > C) \qquad \text{LLE}$$

where SI is Simplification, MI is the law of Material Implication, EX is Export, LLE is Substitution of Left Logical Equivalents, and $\equiv$ stands for material bi-implication.

Theorem 1. SI, MI, EX, LLE $\vdash (A \supset B) \equiv (A > B)$.

[6] (Egré et al., 2023; Fitelson, 2013; Gibbard, 1981).

This was taken to mean that there can be no non-trivial indicative conditional strengthening the material implication which satisfies EX. The proof establishes $(A \supset B) \supset (A > B)$ based solely on SI, MI, EX, LLE and EX (hence 'Exportation-based collapse'). IM is not needed, and the reverse implication is one of the assumptions (MI).

The premisses can be weakened:

$\vdash A > B$ then $\vdash A \supset B$ MI*
$(A \wedge B) > C \vdash A > (B > C)$ EX*
$B \dashv\vdash A$, then $A > C \vdash B > C$ LLE*

These still lead to an Exportation-based collapse:

Theorem 2. SI, MI*, EX*, LLE* $\vdash (A \supset B) \supset (A > B)$.

An analogue result proves the converse (MI), using IM* instead of EX* (hence I call it 'Import-based collapse'):

Theorem 3. SI, MI*, IM*, LLE* $\vdash (A > B) \supset (A \supset B)$.

Together we obtain:

Corollary 4. SI, MI*, EX*, IM*, LLE* $\vdash (A > B) \equiv (A \supset B)$.

The results can be generalized replacing $\supset$ by a conditional $\to$ that is sufficiently strong to allow the derivation. For this, we need to have $A \wedge C \dashv\vdash (A \to C) \wedge A$ (see proof of Theorem 2) and Exportation for $\to$ (see proof of Theorem 3).[7] These are essentially the additional assumptions of Fitelson (2013) and Egré et al. (2023). As the assumptions on $\to$ can be argued to encode 'logicality' of $\to$, and those for $>$ are thought to hold for the indicative conditional, the result has been taken to support the view that there can be no non-trivial indicative conditional satisfying Export and Import while strengthening a logical conditional. In brief: the strengthening strategy combined with Export and Import collapses.

As the implicative conditional does not validate the central assumption SI, the proofs of these collapse theorems are blocked, even if we added EX or IM or variants of these to the logic of $\Rightarrow$. The implicative conditional is a strengthening of a logical conditional (material or strict conditional) and it is a promising representation of natural language implicative conditionals. Thus the strengthening strategy might work after all, and we may ask whether $\Rightarrow$ could support IM or EX while avoiding the collapse. On the one hand, I show that there is a version of the implicative conditional that validates IM without implying the IM-collapse MI. On the other hand, I show that the problem of adding EX persists in a different manner – this results in a collapse of modalities, and of necessity with truth.

[7] Another way to put it, is that $A, C \vdash A$, and $\to$ satisfies the deduction theorem, Modus Ponens and Exportation.

3 Possibilistic Importation and Exportation

In what follows 'models' refers to normal Kripke models (with an accessibility relation R to interpret $\Box$). Here I briefly recall the basis of my investigation (Raidl & Gomes, 2025), where Import and Export are analyzed for $\Rightarrow$ in reflexive models:

$$((A \wedge B) \Rightarrow C) \supset (A \Rightarrow (B \Rightarrow C)) \qquad \text{EX}$$
$$(A \Rightarrow (B \Rightarrow C)) \supset ((A \wedge B) \Rightarrow C) \qquad \text{IM}$$

Raidl and Gomes (2025, Thm. 1 & 2) proved that

Theorem 5. EX *is invalid for* $\Rightarrow$ *in reflexive models.*

Theorem 6. IM *is invalid for* $\Rightarrow$ *in reflexive models.*

Given this, there are principally two strategies for accommodating Importation or Exportation. The first consists in considering weaker versions of Importation and Exportation (Raidl & Gomes, 2025). The second strategy consists in strengthening the semantics. I combine both strategies.

Along the lines of the first strategy, Raidl and Gomes (2025) consider the following weaker possibilistic versions:

$$(((A \wedge B) \Rightarrow C) \wedge \Diamond A \wedge \Diamond \neg(B \Rightarrow C)) \supset (A \Rightarrow (B \Rightarrow C)) \qquad \text{PPEX}$$
$$(((A \wedge B) \Rightarrow C) \wedge \Diamond A) \supset (A \Rightarrow (B \Rightarrow C)) \qquad \text{P1EX}$$
$$(((A \wedge B) \Rightarrow C) \wedge \Diamond \neg(B \Rightarrow C)) \supset (A \Rightarrow (B \Rightarrow C)) \qquad \text{P2EX}$$
$$((A \Rightarrow (B \Rightarrow C)) \wedge \Diamond(A \wedge B) \wedge \Diamond \neg C) \supset ((A \wedge B) \Rightarrow C) \qquad \text{PPIM}$$
$$((A \Rightarrow (B \Rightarrow C)) \wedge \Diamond(A \wedge B)) \supset ((A \wedge B) \Rightarrow C) \qquad \text{P1IM}$$
$$((A \Rightarrow (B \Rightarrow C)) \wedge \Diamond \neg C) \supset ((A \wedge B) \Rightarrow C) \qquad \text{P2IM}$$

Generally, X implies P1X, P2X, and each of these imply PPX. The converse implications need not hold, but sometimes do, when one of the added possibilistic assumptions are redundant. Raidl and Gomes showed that P2EX is equivalent to PPEX, and P1EX equivalent to EX, and that while all Exportations are invalid for $\Rightarrow$ in reflexive models, PPIM *is* valid for $\Rightarrow$ in these models (Raidl & Gomes, 2025, Fact 1, Thm. 3 & 4). The stronger P1IM and P2IM remain invalid:

Theorem 7. P1IM *is invalid for* $\Rightarrow$ *in reflexive models.*

Theorem 8. P2IM *is invalid for* $\Rightarrow$ *in reflexive models.*

Thus, the first strategy yields a clear mismatch between Importation and Exportation. It is easier to validate Importation than Exportation. All possibilistic exportations are invalid, while (only) the weakest possibilistic Importation PPIM is valid.

However, from a natural language perspective, one might argue that Importation for sentences A, B, C, should not only hold under the auxiliary assumptions of PPIM that $A \wedge B$ is possible and $\neg C$ is possible, but also without these. The possibility of the antecedent and/or negated consequent of the consequent conditional should follow from the assumed antecedent conditional. In other words, possibilistic assumptions should not be presupposed but implicated by the antecedent conditional. Consider the example from Raidl and Gomes (2025):

(1) If you sell your car, then if you buy a bike, you'll have money for the trip.
(2) If you sell your car and buy a bike, you'll have money for the trip.

In reflexive Kripke models, the implication from (1) to (2) holds, provided it is assumed possible that you sell your car and buy a bike, and it's also possible that you will not have money for the trip (in some other imaginable situation). But these possibilities (at least the second) should be contained in (1) or implied by it, and not required to be explicitly assumed additionally or implicitly presupposed. To accommodate for these possibility-free inferences, we need to find a way for $\Rightarrow$ to validate P1IM or even IM. For this I deploy the second strategy, to ask in which kind of models, P1IM and IM are valid. Similarly for EX and P2EX. I also ask a converse question: what kind of modal conditions do the different Importations and Exportations impose? And what kind of implicative conditional or modal logics arise from these principles?

4 P1Imp and Transitivity

Until now I restricted attention to interpreting $\Rightarrow$ in reflexive models. Thereby the Truth axiom T, $\Box A \supset A$, is valid. But we could consider stronger models. A standard choice, with the corresponding characteristic axiom, is:

transitive $\Box A \supset \Box\Box A$ 4

R is *transitive* iff for all x, y, z, if $xRyRz$ then xRz. We can add 4 to the modal logic KT and obtain the well known system KT4, also known as C.I. Lewis' system S4, which is sound and complete for preorder (i.e., reflexive transitive) models.

The axiom 4 is particularly interesting, as addition to T, when $\Box$ is interpreted as knowledge. T says that knowledge implies truth – a minimal requirement which distinguishes knowledge from mere belief. 4 says that knowledge is positively introspective: if A is known, then it is known that A is known. The knowledge interpretation of $\Box$ is also available for $A \Rightarrow C$. Under that interpretation, $A \Rightarrow C$ means that the speaker knows $A \supset C$, and A as well as $\neg C$ are each compatible with what the speaker knows.

In transitive reflexive models, the previous four distinct Importation principles now also reduce to just two versions – IM and P1IM:

Fact 9. *In preorder models:*

1. P1IM *is equivalent to* PPIM,
2. P2IM *is equivalent to* IM.

As a consequence:

Theorem 10. P1IM *is valid in preorder models.*

One can show that the other Importations (IM, P2IM) remain invalid. From the previous result an interesting question arises: Is P1IM equivalent to imposing the modal axiom 4? In fact it is:

Theorem 11. P1IM $\vdash_{\mathsf{KT}}$ 4.

Corollary 12. $\vdash_{\mathsf{KT}}$ P1IM $\equiv$ 4.

In the following IC refers to any of the equivalent axiomatization of the logic of $\Rightarrow$ for reflexive models:[8]

Corollary 13. IC +P1IM *is translationally equivalent to* $\mathsf{S4}$.

Corollary 14. IC +P1IM *is sound and complete for* $\Rightarrow$ *w.r.t. preorder models.*

Thus, in the context of the logic of the implicative conditional, P1IM characterizes transitive models and is equivalent to positive modal introspection. The above also provides a translationally equivalent axiomatization of $\mathsf{S4}$, in the language of $\Rightarrow$.

5 Importation and the Provability Logic Grz

IM is invalid in transitive reflexive models. But maybe it is valid in stronger models. What kind of modal constraints does IM impose?

Consider the following axiom

$$\Box(\Box(A \supset \Box A) \supset A) \supset \Box A \qquad \text{Grz}$$

The label refers to Grzegorczyk (1967) who introduced it through a slightly different formula which however is equivalent to Grz in $\mathsf{S4}$. The scheme has been investigated in provability logic as an alternative to Löb's formula G $(\Box(\Box A \supset A) \supset \Box A)$, and the logic $\mathsf{Grz} = \mathsf{S4}$ +Grz has been studied as an alternative to the standard provability logic $\mathsf{G} = \mathsf{K4}$ +G. In preorder frames, Grz corresponds to converse well-foundedness ($R \setminus \mathrm{id}$ has no infinite ascending chains).[9] And $\mathsf{Grz} = \mathsf{S4}+$ Grz is known to be sound and complete for reflexive, transitive and conversely well-founded frames, or equivalently, for finite partial order models.[10] In Grz, $\Box$ is interpreted as 'provable and true'. The wit of Grz is that Grz proves A iff G proves A', where $(\Box A)' = A' \wedge \Box A'$ and other connectives are translated simplistically ($(\neg\varphi)' = \neg\varphi'$, etc.).

Consider the following law:

$$\Diamond A \supset (\Diamond \Box A \vee \Box \Diamond A) \qquad \text{w5}$$

This is a weak version of 5 where the premiss $\Box\Diamond\neg A$ is added: $(\Diamond A \wedge \Box\Diamond\neg A) \supset \Box\Diamond A$.

---

[8] See Gomes et al. (2025); Raidl andGomes (2024).

[9] The equivalence of well-foundedness and no infinite chains requires the axiom of dependent choice, which I shall assume in what follows. Hence the correspondence of Grz with no infinite ascending chains rests on that assumption, and does in fact depend on it Jěrábek(2003).

[10] See Boolos 1979); Avron (1984); Segerberg (1971).

Fact 15. Grz $\vdash_{\mathsf{K4}}$ w5.

Theorem 16. *In reflexive, transitive conversely well-founded models,* IM *is valid.*

What about the converse? We already know that IM implies 4 (corollary to Theorem 11). Furthermore we have:

Theorem 17. *In reflexive, transitive frames,* IM *implies converse well-foundedness.*

From the previous we can conclude:

Corollary 18. $\vdash_{\mathsf{KT}}$ IM $\equiv$ 4 + Grz.

Corollary 19. IC +IM *is translationally equivalent to* Grz.

Corollary 20. IC +IM *is sound and complete for finite partial order models.*

The consequence of these results may be of interest for the implicative conditional but also for provability logic, but the discussion of this exceeds the scope of this paper. To put it briefly: for modal logic, the result shows that Grz has an equivalent conditional axiomatization, which is well motivated and routed in the natural language analysis of conditionals, thus Grz is not only a provability logic, but (read in terms of $\Rightarrow$) also (equivalent to) a valuable conditional logic. From the perspective of the implicative conditional, the result shows that when we add IM to the logic of the implicative conditional, we force the models to be finite and partial orders. But both these assumptions are actually cognitively justifiable: after all when we evaluate conditionals in a modal way (as for $\Rightarrow$) we might consider only finite models, and that the necessity satisfies 4 simply reflects positive knowledge introspection. Furthermore, under the Grz-provability interpretation of $\Box$, an implicative conditional $A \Rightarrow C$ says that $A \supset C$ is true and provable, and both A and C are Gödel sentences, i.e. undecidable.

Here we conclude that PPIM is valid in reflexive models, P1IM is valid in transitive reflexive models and characterizes transitivity (given reflexivity), and IM (hence P2IM) is valid in well-founded (or finite) partial order models and characterizes these (given reflexivity). An open question is whether PPIM (and the other axioms) also characterize reflexivity. The conjecture is that they don't, but do characterize shift reflexivity ($\Box(\Box A \supset A)$, ST).

With respect to the collapse theorem we may note that

Theorem 21. IM *remains valid in shift-reflexive, transitive, conversely well-founded models.*

This exemplifies that there is a conditional ($\Rightarrow$) which (i) strengthens the material conditional, (ii) can be used as representing the natural language indicative conditional, and (iii) for which the IM-collapse (Theorem 3) does not hold. That is, IM is valid without $\Rightarrow$ implying $\supset$ (as $\Rightarrow$ invalidates that implication in shift reflexive models, even if these are transitive and conversely well-founded). An open question is whether adding IM to K characterizes the logic G + ST = K4 + G + ST. We conjecture that it does (by reconfiguring the above proofs).

6 Exportation and Collapses

We may ask a similar question for exportation(s): what kind of constraints do these principles impose, and are there models validating one or the other version?

Consider the following properties of the accessibility relation and their corresponding axioms

euclidean	$\Diamond A \supset \Box\Diamond A$	5
symmetric	$A \supset \Box\Diamond A$	B
shift-discrete	$\Box(A \supset \Box A)$	ST$^-$

R is *euclidean* iff for all x, y, z, if xRy and xRz then yRz. We can add 5 to the modal logic KT and obtain the well known system KT5, also known as C.I. Lewis' system S5, where 4 and B are derivable. In this logic, we do not only have positive introspection, but also negative introspection (due to 5): if B is not known ($\neg\Box B$, i.e. $\Diamond A$ for $A = \neg B$), then it is known that B is not known ($\Box\neg\Box B$, i.e., $\Box\Diamond A$ for $A = \neg B$.

R is *shift-discrete* iff $\forall x\forall y\forall z$ if $xRyRz$, then $y = z$. The term comes from the stronger *discrete* relation: $\forall x\forall y$, if xRy then $x = y$, with the characteristic axiom T$^-$: $A \supset \Box A$ (the converse of T). While discreteness says that the accessibility relation reduces to identity, shift-discreteness only requires that accessibility reduces to identity in accessible worlds. ST$^-$ is quite strong. For example, ST$^-$ implies 4.[11] Furthermore, ST$^-$ together with T implies discreteness T$^-$, and hence the collapse of truth and modalities $A \equiv \Box A \equiv \Diamond A$. We will shortly see that a similar collapse is unavoidable in the presence of Exportation(s), even without T.

Theorem 22. P2EX *(hence* PPEX*) is valid in shift-discrete, euclidean models.*

Theorem 23. P2EX *corresponds to euclidicity + shift-discreteness.*

As a consequence, it is equivalent to impose P2EX or 5 + ST$^-$. Thus P2EX (as well as EX) forces 5+ST$^-$. While this is an interesting fact from the perspective of modality (P2EX is a conditional interpretation of 5 + ST$^-$), we will shortly see that it is detrimental for the implicative conditional.

Consider the following property and corresponding axiom:
partial function $\Diamond A \supset \Box A$ D$^-$
R is a *partial function* iff $\forall x, y, z$ if xRy, xRz then $y = z$. And D$^-$ is the converse of the seriality axiom D.

Fact 24. ST$^- \vdash_{\mathsf{K}} 5 \equiv$ D$^-$.

By the above, 5 + ST$^-$ is equivalent to D$^-$ + ST$^-$. And one can further show that this is equivalent to D$^-$ + ST $\Box(\Box A \supset A)$ (where the latter is the characteristic axiom of shift-reflexivity). Thus

Corollary 25. $\vdash_{\mathsf{K}}$ P2Exp $\equiv 5 +$ ST$^- \equiv$ D$^-$ + ST$^- \equiv$ D$^-$ + ST

[11] $\Box(A \supset \Box A)$ by ST$^-$. Thus $\Box A \supset \Box\Box A$ by K,MP.

By this we see that P2EX trivializes the semantics. Indeed, partial, shift-reflexive models are such that for each world w, if w accesses v, it does not access any other world, and v itself only accesses v. Thus the only possibilities are wRw, $wRvRv$ or w accesses no other world and is accessed from no world.

By the above results, we further have:

Corollary 26. *All Exportations imply* D^-.

D^- is detrimental for the theory of implicative conditionals. Indeed, by D^- all implicative conditionals $A \Rightarrow C$ imply $\Box(A \supset C) \wedge \Box A \wedge \Box \neg C$ – a contradiction. Thus all implicative conditionals are false, since inconsistent (not only invalid as in reflexive models). Thereby, although shift-discreteness, together with euclidicity allows validity of P2EX, this validity is trivial, since the antecedent of P2EX (and all Exportations) is always false. Hence

Corollary 27. *There is no non-trivial way to validate Exportation(s) in Kripke models.*

In particular, in serial models, $\Diamond A \supset \Box A$ implies the collapse of modalities $\Diamond A \equiv \Box A$, and in reflexive models, it also implies the collapse with truth $A \equiv \Diamond A \equiv \Box A$. We may also conclude, that in reflexive models, all Exportations are equivalent to discreteness: $A \supset \Box A$. Hence

Corollary 28. IC+P2EX *(or* +EX*) is sound and complete for discrete reflexive models.*

But this is only interesting from a modal perspective (as it provides an alternative conditional characterization of the mentioned models), not from the perspective of the implicative conditional (as it trivializes the conditional).

With respect to the collapse theorem for EX (Theorem 2), the questions arises whether we can find a version of the implicative conditional which satisfies EX but without collapse with the material implication. Such a version will need to have a non-normal modal logic for the underlying necessity. It remains an open question, whether such a construction is possible.

7 Proofs

Proof of Theorem 1: $(A \wedge C) > C$ by SI. Hence $((A \supset C) \wedge A) > C$ by LLE. Therefore $(A \supset C) > (A > C)$ by EX. Thus $(A \supset C) \supset (A > C)$ by MI. Hence by MI again $(A \supset C) \equiv (A \Rightarrow C)$. □

Proof of Theorem 2: $\vdash (A \wedge C) > C$ by SI. But $A \wedge C \dashv\vdash (A \supset C) \wedge A$. Thus $\vdash ((A \supset C) \wedge A) > C$ by LLE*. Therefore $\vdash (A \supset C) > (A > C)$ by EX*. Thus $\vdash (A \supset C) \supset (A > C)$ by MI*. □

Proof of Theorem 3: $\vdash ((A > B) \wedge A) > (A > B)$ by SI. $\vdash (((A > B) \wedge A) \wedge A) > B$ by IM*. $\vdash ((A > B) \wedge A) > B$ by LLE*. $\vdash ((A > B) \wedge A) \supset B$ by MI*. $\vdash ((A > B) \supset (A \supset B)$ (by EX for $\supset$). □

Proof of Theorem 7: In the following reflexive model (where A, B, C are propositional variables and a propositional variable is true in a world x iff it is listed in its index)

$$\begin{array}{ccccc} w_{BC} & \longrightarrow & v_{ABC} & \longrightarrow & u \\ & \searrow & & & \\ & & x_{BC} & \longrightarrow & y_B \end{array} \tag{1}$$

at w:

1. $A \Rightarrow (B \Rightarrow C)$ ($\Diamond A$, $\Diamond \neg(B \Rightarrow C)$, $\Box(A \supset (B \Rightarrow C))$), and $\Diamond(A \wedge B)$ are true (the second since $B \wedge \neg C$ is true in y),
2. but $(A \wedge B) \Rightarrow C$ (i.e. one of $\Diamond(A \wedge B)$, $\Diamond \neg C$, $\Box((A \wedge B) \supset C)$), is false, namely $\Diamond \neg C$ (since C in w, v, x).

□

Proof of Theorem 8: The same model as Raidl and Gomes (2025) used in the proof of invalidity of IM (Theorem 6) can be used to prove invalidity of P2IM (no smaller model is possible). Consider the reflexive model

$$w_C \longrightarrow v_A \longrightarrow u_{BC} \tag{2}$$

at w:

1. $A \Rightarrow (B \Rightarrow C)$ (i.e. all of $\Diamond A$, $\Box(A \supset (B \Rightarrow C))$, $\Diamond \neg(B \Rightarrow C)$, namely $\Diamond \Box \neg B$) as well as $\Diamond \neg C$ are true
2. but $(A \wedge B) \Rightarrow C$ is false (namely $\Diamond(A \wedge B)$).

□

Proof of Fact 9: Consider the shared antecedent $A \Rightarrow (B \Rightarrow C)$ of all IM-Principles. Thus $\Box(A \supset (B \Rightarrow C))$. In particular $\Box(A \supset \Diamond \neg C)$. But since the antecedent also implies $\Diamond A$, we obtain $\Diamond(A \wedge \Diamond \neg C)$. Therefore $\Diamond \Diamond \neg C$. The contraposed of axiom 4 is $\Diamond \Diamond A \supset \Diamond A$. Hence $\Diamond \neg C$ by 4. Therefore this conjunct is redundant in PPIM as in P2IM. The two above claims follow. □

Proof of Theorem 10: PPIM is valid in reflexive models (Raidl & Gomes, 2025, see), hence valid in transitive ones. But in these P1IM is equivalent to PPIM (Fact 9). Hence P1IM is valid as well. □

Proof of Theorem 11: Assume P1IM. We show 4 in the form $\Diamond \Diamond A \supset \Diamond A$. Note that $\Diamond A = A \vee (A \Rightarrow A)$. Also note that $A \Rightarrow A$ is equivalent to $\neg A \Rightarrow \neg A$. 4 can then be rewritten as

$$(A \vee (A \Rightarrow A) \vee ((A \vee (A \Rightarrow A)) \Rightarrow (A \vee (A \Rightarrow A)))) \supset (A \vee (A \Rightarrow A))$$

It suffices to prove

$$(((A \vee (A \Rightarrow A)) \Rightarrow (A \vee (A \Rightarrow A))) \wedge \neg A) \supset (A \Rightarrow A)$$

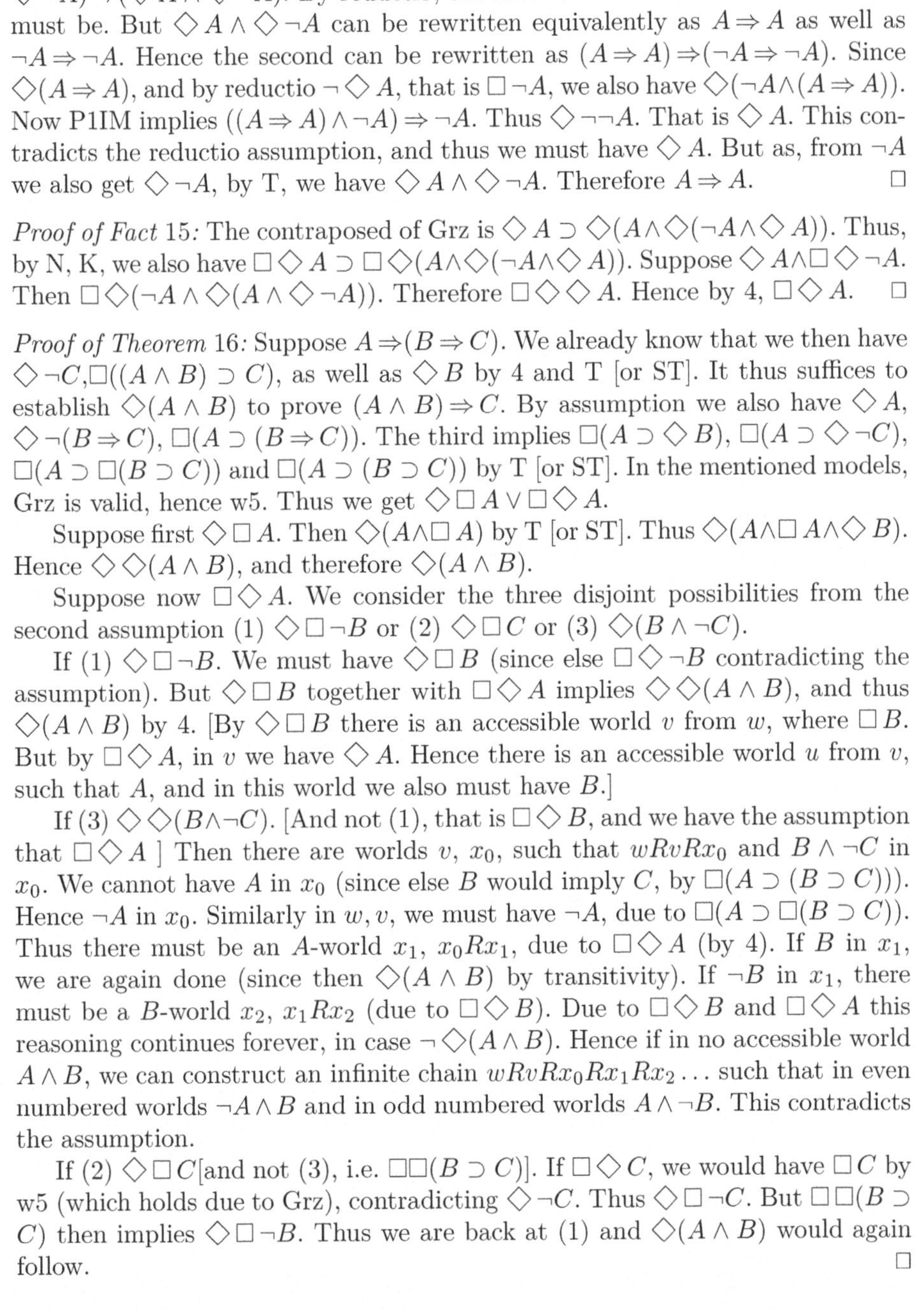

Assume $(A \vee (A \Rightarrow A)) \Rightarrow (A \vee (A \Rightarrow A))$ and $\neg A$. From the first we obtain $\Diamond(A \vee (A \Rightarrow A))$. Thus $\Diamond A \vee \Diamond(A \Rightarrow A)$. Suppose for reductio that $\neg \Diamond A$. Hence $\Diamond(A \Rightarrow A)$, that is $\Diamond(\Diamond A \wedge \Diamond \neg A)$. This is $\Diamond A \wedge \Diamond \neg A$ or $(\Diamond A \wedge \Diamond \neg A) \Rightarrow (\Diamond A \wedge \Diamond \neg A)$. By reductio, the first can't be true. Hence the second must be. But $\Diamond A \wedge \Diamond \neg A$ can be rewritten equivalently as $A \Rightarrow A$ as well as $\neg A \Rightarrow \neg A$. Hence the second can be rewritten as $(A \Rightarrow A) \Rightarrow (\neg A \Rightarrow \neg A)$. Since $\Diamond(A \Rightarrow A)$, and by reductio $\neg \Diamond A$, that is $\Box \neg A$, we also have $\Diamond(\neg A \wedge (A \Rightarrow A))$. Now P1IM implies $((A \Rightarrow A) \wedge \neg A) \Rightarrow \neg A$. Thus $\Diamond \neg\neg A$. That is $\Diamond A$. This contradicts the reductio assumption, and thus we must have $\Diamond A$. But as, from $\neg A$ we also get $\Diamond \neg A$, by T, we have $\Diamond A \wedge \Diamond \neg A$. Therefore $A \Rightarrow A$. □

Proof of Fact 15*:* The contraposed of Grz is $\Diamond A \supset \Diamond(A \wedge \Diamond(\neg A \wedge \Diamond A))$. Thus, by N, K, we also have $\Box \Diamond A \supset \Box \Diamond(A \wedge \Diamond(\neg A \wedge \Diamond A))$. Suppose $\Diamond A \wedge \Box \Diamond \neg A$. Then $\Box \Diamond(\neg A \wedge \Diamond(A \wedge \Diamond \neg A))$. Therefore $\Box \Diamond \Diamond A$. Hence by 4, $\Box \Diamond A$. □

Proof of Theorem 16*:* Suppose $A \Rightarrow (B \Rightarrow C)$. We already know that we then have $\Diamond \neg C, \Box((A \wedge B) \supset C)$, as well as $\Diamond B$ by 4 and T [or ST]. It thus suffices to establish $\Diamond(A \wedge B)$ to prove $(A \wedge B) \Rightarrow C$. By assumption we also have $\Diamond A$, $\Diamond \neg(B \Rightarrow C)$, $\Box(A \supset (B \Rightarrow C))$. The third implies $\Box(A \supset \Diamond B)$, $\Box(A \supset \Diamond \neg C)$, $\Box(A \supset \Box(B \supset C))$ and $\Box(A \supset (B \supset C))$ by T [or ST]. In the mentioned models, Grz is valid, hence w5. Thus we get $\Diamond \Box A \vee \Box \Diamond A$.

Suppose first $\Diamond \Box A$. Then $\Diamond(A \wedge \Box A)$ by T [or ST]. Thus $\Diamond(A \wedge \Box A \wedge \Diamond B)$. Hence $\Diamond \Diamond(A \wedge B)$, and therefore $\Diamond(A \wedge B)$.

Suppose now $\Box \Diamond A$. We consider the three disjoint possibilities from the second assumption (1) $\Diamond \Box \neg B$ or (2) $\Diamond \Box C$ or (3) $\Diamond(B \wedge \neg C)$.

If (1) $\Diamond \Box \neg B$. We must have $\Diamond \Box B$ (since else $\Box \Diamond \neg B$ contradicting the assumption). But $\Diamond \Box B$ together with $\Box \Diamond A$ implies $\Diamond \Diamond(A \wedge B)$, and thus $\Diamond(A \wedge B)$ by 4. [By $\Diamond \Box B$ there is an accessible world v from w, where $\Box B$. But by $\Box \Diamond A$, in v we have $\Diamond A$. Hence there is an accessible world u from v, such that A, and in this world we also must have B.]

If (3) $\Diamond \Diamond(B \wedge \neg C)$. [And not (1), that is $\Box \Diamond B$, and we have the assumption that $\Box \Diamond A$] Then there are worlds v, x_0, such that $wRvRx_0$ and $B \wedge \neg C$ in x_0. We cannot have A in x_0 (since else B would imply C, by $\Box(A \supset (B \supset C))$). Hence $\neg A$ in x_0. Similarly in w, v, we must have $\neg A$, due to $\Box(A \supset \Box(B \supset C))$. Thus there must be an A-world x_1, x_0Rx_1, due to $\Box \Diamond A$ (by 4). If B in x_1, we are again done (since then $\Diamond(A \wedge B)$ by transitivity). If $\neg B$ in x_1, there must be a B-world x_2, x_1Rx_2 (due to $\Box \Diamond B$). Due to $\Box \Diamond B$ and $\Box \Diamond A$ this reasoning continues forever, in case $\neg \Diamond(A \wedge B)$. Hence if in no accessible world $A \wedge B$, we can construct an infinite chain $wRvRx_0Rx_1Rx_2 \ldots$ such that in even numbered worlds $\neg A \wedge B$ and in odd numbered worlds $A \wedge \neg B$. This contradicts the assumption.

If (2) $\Diamond \Box C$[and not (3), i.e. $\Box\Box(B \supset C)$]. If $\Box \Diamond C$, we would have $\Box C$ by w5 (which holds due to Grz), contradicting $\Diamond \neg C$. Thus $\Diamond \Box \neg C$. But $\Box\Box(B \supset C)$ then implies $\Diamond \Box \neg B$. Thus we are back at (1) and $\Diamond(A \wedge B)$ would again follow. □

Proof of Theorem 17*:* We prove the contraposed (assuming the axiom of dependent choice). Consider a reflexive transitive frame where $R^- \setminus \mathrm{id}$ is not well-founded. Hence, by the axiom of dependent choice, there is an infinite ascending chain (reflexive connections excluded) $x_0 R x_1 R x_2 \ldots$.

Then we can construct a model on that frame, where IM is false in x_0: In x_0 only B is true. And for $n \geq 0$, we set: in x_{2n}, only B, C are true ($n \neq 0$), in x_{2n+1}, only A is true. Then in x_0 we have $A \Rightarrow (B \Rightarrow C)$. Indeed, $\Diamond A$ since A in x_1. $\Diamond \Diamond(B \wedge \neg C)$ since $B \wedge \neg C$ in x_0 and by reflexivity. Hence $\Diamond \neg(B \Rightarrow C)$. $\Box(A \supset \Diamond \neg C)$, since every A-world (odd world) is also a $\neg C$-world. $\Box(A \supset \Diamond B)$, since every A-world (odd worlds) has a succeeding B-world. $\Box(A \supset \Box(B \supset C))$, since in every A-world (odd world) all accessible B-worlds (even successors) are C-worlds.

However the consequent of IM, $(A \wedge B) \Rightarrow C$, is false, since in no world $A \wedge B$, hence $\neg \Diamond(A \wedge B)$ in x_0. □

Proof of Theorem 21*:* In the results on validity of IM, T and reflexivity can be replaced by ST and shift reflexivity. (This is marked in the proofs.) Here is the proof sketch of this replacement. Assume $A \Rightarrow (B \Rightarrow C)$. Thus $\Box(A \supset (B \Rightarrow C))$, $\Diamond A$ and $\Diamond \neg(B \Rightarrow C)$.

From the first we have $\Box(A \supset \Box(B \supset C))$. But this implies $\Box(A \supset (B \supset C))$ by ST and hence $\Box((A \wedge B) \supset C)$.

From the first, we also have $\Box(A \supset \Diamond \neg C)$. But $\Diamond A \wedge \Box(A \supset \Diamond \neg C)$ implies $\Diamond \neg C$ just by 4 (see Fact 9).

Finally, that we also obtain $\Diamond(A \wedge B)$ can be seen from the reasoning in Theorem 16, where whenever we use reflexivity (or T) we can use shift reflexivity (or ST). And the use of w5 does not require T (as w5 was shown from the axiom Grz without T in Fact 15). □

Proof of Theorem 22*:* Assume $(A \wedge B) \Rightarrow C$, and $\Diamond \neg(B \Rightarrow C)$. From the first, we obtain $\Diamond(A \wedge B)$, $\Diamond \neg C$ and $\Box((A \wedge B) \supset C)$. Thus $\Diamond A$, $\Diamond B$. By 5, we get $\Box \Diamond B$. Hence $\Box(A \supset \Diamond B)$. Similarly $\Box \Diamond \neg C$. Hence $\Box(A \supset \Diamond \neg C)$. Furthermore, from $\Box((A \wedge B) \supset C)$ we obtain $\Box(A \supset (B \supset C))$. But $\Box((B \supset C) \supset \Box(B \supset C))$ by ST$^-$. Thus $\Box(A \supset \Box(B \supset C))$. Thus we have $\Box(A \supset (B \Rightarrow C))$. Since additionally $\Diamond A$, and we have assumed $\Diamond \neg(B \Rightarrow C)$, we obtain $A \Rightarrow (B \Rightarrow C)$.

That PPEX is also valid, follows from the equivalence of P2EX and PPEX (Raidl & Gomes, 2025). □

Proof of Theorem 23*:* The previous Theorem showed that P2EX is valid in euclidean + shift-discrete frames. Thus it suffices to show the converse: if P2EX is valid in a class of frames, these are euclidean and shift-discrete. We show the contraposed. Let C be a class of frames and suppose it is either not euclidean or not shift-discrete. Then there is a frame F in that class that is not euclidean or that is not shift-discrete. We show that then P2EX is invalid in F.

Suppose F is not euclidean. Then there are worlds x, y, z in F such that xRy, xRz but not-yRz. We can then construct a model on that frame where P2EX is invalid. Let y be an A, B, C- world, and z a $\neg A, B, \neg C$ world, and x a

$\neg A, B, \neg C$-world. Then $(A \wedge B) \Rightarrow C$ is true in x. To also satisfy $\Diamond \neg(B \Rightarrow C)$, we need to differentiate three possibilities at z. Either z is a terminal world which accesses no other world. Then $\Box C$ is true at z and hence $\Diamond \neg(B \Rightarrow C)$ true at x. Or z is not a terminal world, and does access another world t. Either $t = y$ or $t = x$ or $t = z$, or $t \notin \{x, y, z\}$. If $t = x$, then $\Diamond(B \wedge \neg C)$ at y hence $\Diamond\Diamond(B \wedge \neg C)$ at x, so that $\Diamond \neg(B \Rightarrow C)$. Similarly if $t = z$. If $t \notin \{x, y, z\}$, we can alway put $\neg A, B, \neg C$ at t. If $t = y$, we need to distinguish two cases. Either z accesses another world $t' \neq y$ and then we proceed with t' as above with t. Or z only accesses y. In the last case, we have $\Box C$ at z and hence $\Diamond \Box C$ at x, thus $\Diamond \neg(B \Rightarrow C)$ at x. Thus overall, the antecedent of P2EX is true at x. However the consequent is false. Either y accesses no world, in which case $A \supset \Diamond \neg C$ is false at y, or y does access another world (but does not access z by assumption). In the latter case, either x is among the worlds or not. If not, we can put C at all the accessed worlds from y (including potentially y itself), and then $A \supset \Diamond \neg C$ is false at y, hence $\Box(A \supset \Diamond \neg C)$ false at x. If x is among the accessed worlds, then $A \supset \Box(B \supset C)$ is false at y, hence $\Box(A \supset \Box(B \supset C))$ false at x. Thus overall, $\Box(A \supset (B \Rightarrow C))$ is false at x, hence $A \Rightarrow (B \Rightarrow C)$ is false at x.

Now suppose that F is not shift-discrete, but euclidean. Then there are worlds x, y, z such that $xRyRz$ such that $y \neq z$. By euclidicity, yRy, zRz and zRy. x is irrelevant for the argument. Let ABC at y and $\neg A, B, \neg C$ at z. Then $A \wedge B \Rightarrow C$ is true at z. And $\Diamond \neg(B \Rightarrow C)$ is also true at z, since $B \wedge \neg C$ is true at z, hence $\Diamond\Diamond(B \wedge \neg C)$. Yet $\Box(A \supset \Box(B \supset C))$ is false at z, since $\Box(B \supset C)$ is false at y, due to $B \wedge \neg C$ being true at z. Hence overall $A \Rightarrow (B \Rightarrow C)$ is false at z. □

Proof of Fact 24*:* 5 corresponds to euclidicity and ST^- to shift-discreteness. But these two imply that R is a partial function. Indeed, if xRy, xRz then by euclidicity yRz. But by shift-discreteness $z = y$. Yet R being a partial function corresponds to the axiom $\Diamond A \supset \Box A$.

Conversely, a partial function is euclidean, hence D^- implies 5. □

Acknowledgement. Eric Raidl's work was funded by the Deutsche Forschungsgemeinschaft (EXC number 2064/1, project no. 390727645). I am grateful to 3 anonymous reviewers whose questions led me to further develop the relation of the investigation with the Gibbardian collapse, and to Gilberto Gomes for suggesting to investigate IM and EX for $\Rightarrow$.

Disclosure of Interests. The authors have no competing interests to declare that are relevant to the content of this article.

References

Avron, A.: On modal systems having arithmetical interpretations. J. Symb. Logic **49**(3), 935–942 (1984)

Boolos, G.: The Unprovability of Consistency. Cambridge University Press, Cambridge (1979)

Burks, A.W.: Dispositional statements. Philos. Sci. **22**(3), 175–193 (1955). https://doi.org/10.1086/287422

Chellas, B.F.: Modal Logic: An Introduction. Cambridge University Press (1980)

Egré, P., Rossi, L., Sprenger, J.: Gibbardian collapse and trivalent conditionals. In: Kaufmann, S., Over, D.E., Sharma, G. (eds.) Conditionals. Palgrave MacMillan (2023)

Fitelson, B.: Gibbard's collapse theorem for the indicative conditional: an axiomatic approach. In: Bonacina, M.P., Stickel, M.E. (eds.) Automated Reasoning and Mathematics. LNCS (LNAI), vol. 7788, pp. 181–188. Springer, Heidelberg (2013). https://doi.org/10.1007/978-3-642-36675-8_10

Gherardi, G., Orlandelli, E.: Super-strict implications. Bull. Sect. Logic **50**(1), 1–34 (2021). https://doi.org/10.18778/0138-0680.2021.02

Gibbard, A.: Two recent theories of conditionals. In: Harper, W.L., Stalnaker, R., Pearce, G. (eds.) Ifs: Conditionals, Belief, Decision, Chance and Time, pp. 211–247. Springer, Dordrecht (1981). https://doi.org/10.1007/978-94-009-9117-0_10

Gomes, G.: Ordinary language conditionals (2005). https://www.academia.edu/93865496/Ordinary_Language_Conditionals_2005 (Manuscript)

Gomes, G.: Concessive conditionals without 'even if' and nonconcessive conditionals with 'even if'. Acta Analytica **35**(1), 1–21 (2020). https://doi.org/10.1007/s12136-019-00396-y

Gomes, G., Pizzi, C., Raidl, E.: Consequential implication and the implicative conditional. Logic Logical Philos. (2025). https://doi.org/10.12775/LLP.2025.001

Grzegorczyk, A.: Some relational systems and the associated topological spaces. Fundam. Math. **60**(3), 223–231 (1967)

Jěrábek, E.: A note on Grzegorczyk's logic (2003)

Lewis, D.: Counterfactuals. Blackwell, Oxford (1973). https://doi.org/10.1007/978-94-009-9117-0_3

Priest, G.: Negation as cancellation, and connexive logic. Topoi **18**, 14–148 (1999). https://doi.org/10.1023/A:1006294205280

Raidl, E., Gomes, G.: The implicative conditional. J. Philos. Log. **53**, 1–47 (2024). https://doi.org/10.1007/s10992-023-09715-6

Raidl, E., Gomes, G.: Counterexamples to import-export in conditionals: a logical analysis (2025). (Manuscript)

Segerberg, K.: An essay in classical modal logic. Uppsala Universitet. (Ph.D. dissertation) (1971)

Paraconsistent Constructive Modal Logic

Han Gao(✉), Daniil Kozhemiachenko, and Nicola Olivetti

Aix-Marseille University, CNRS, LIS, Marseille, France
{gao.han,daniil.kozhemiachenko,nicola.olivetti}@lis-lab.fr

Abstract. We present a family of paraconsistent counterparts of the constructive modal logic CK. These logics aim to formalise reasoning about contradictory but non-trivial propositional attitudes like beliefs or obligations. We define their Kripke-style semantics based on intuitionistic frames with two valuations which provide independent support for truth and falsity; they are connected by strong negation as defined in Nelson's logic. A family of systems is obtained depending on whether both modal operators are defined using the same or by different accessibility relations for their positive and negative support. We propose Hilbert-style axiomatisations for all logics determined by this semantic framework. We also propose a family of modular cut-free sequent calculi that we use to establish decidability.

Keywords: constructive modal logic · paraconsistent logic · Nelson logic · sequent calculi · decidability

1 Introduction

The aim of developing an intuitionistic or constructive notion of modalities is old: it goes back to Fitch [8] and Prawitz [16]. Among the different proposals, the so-called Constructive modal logic based on the work by Wijesekera [20] and then De Paiva et al. [1,3] is motivated by applications to computer sciences, such as type-theoretic interpretation and Curry-Howard correspondence, but also by contextual reasoning [11,15], where $\Box\phi$ and $\Diamond\phi$ are interpreted as 'ϕ holds in all contexts' and 'ϕ holds in some contexts', respectively. The constructive view is also relevant for the epistemic [21], doxastic, and deontic [5] reading of modalities, for instance in the latter case it is customary to distinguish the 'strong' permission that ϕ, supported explicitly by some norm, from a 'weak' permission asserting only that $\neg\phi$ is not obligatory.

Constructive modal logics are characterised by their simple proof-theoretic presentation in terms of (cut-free) Gentzen sequent calculi (cf., e.g., [4,18,20]). Their semantics can be specified in terms of bi-relational Kripke models containing both a preorder, as in Kripke frames for propositional intuitionistic logic (Int), and an accessibility relation. The main difference with other proposals such as IK by Fisher-Servi [7] and Simpson [18] is that no properties are assumed to relate the preorder and the accessibility relation. Both Wijesekera's logic and constructive modal logic CK satisfy some of the conditions stated by Simpson [18]: they

D. Kozen and R. de Queiroz (Eds.): WoLLIC 2025, LNCS 15942, pp. 71–88, 2026.
https://doi.org/10.1007/978-3-031-99536-1_5

are conservative extensions of Int, they have the disjunction property, and the two modalities are independent. Notice that the hereditary condition, necessary to ensure the conservativity over Int is built in by the forcing conditions, without the need for specific frame conditions (as, e.g., is done in IK, recent **FIK** [2] and Došen's $\mathbf{HK}_\Box$ [6]).

In this work, we aim to define a paraconsistent counterpart of CK. The logic we are seeking must have the following features:

1. it has the property of constructive falsity: if $\neg(\phi \wedge \chi)$ is provable then either $\neg\phi$ or $\neg\chi$ is provable;
2. $\phi \wedge \neg\phi$ does not entail every proposition (paraconsistency);
3. contradictions are not equivalent: $p \wedge \neg p$ is not equivalent to $q \wedge \neg q$.

Intuitionistic logic with its standard negation $\neg$ satisfies none of the three conditions. Our starting point for the interpretation of propositional connectives is the well-known logic N4 by Nelson [12]. In this logic, intuitionistic negation and falsity are replaced by so-called strong negation $\sim$ that satisfies the properties above.

On the other hand, paraconsistent modal logics provide a more intuitive doxastic and deontic interpretations of modalities. Classically (and intuitionistically), to account for contradictory beliefs or obligations, one may consider a non-normal or non-regular logic. In the first case, $\Box(\phi \wedge \chi)$ is not equivalent to $\Box\phi \wedge \Box\chi$. In the second case, $\Box\phi \rightarrow \Box\chi$ does not follow from $\phi \rightarrow \chi$. Still, even in these cases, all contradictions are equivalent. Hence, if an agent believes in one contradiction, they believe in *all contradictions*. If an agent has one conflicting obligation, then all obligations are contradictory. In addition to that, even in the presence of contradictory beliefs and obligations, one might want to utilise characteristic features of normal and regular modalities. Both options are possible when using paraconsistent logics.

The aim of this paper is to define a family of paraconsistent constructive modal logics of increasing strength, all of which can be considered N4-like counterparts of CK in a loose sense. We get several systems from the weakest to strongest according to the relation between the two modal operators $\Box$, $\Diamond$ and their strong negations: $\sim\Box$, $\sim\Diamond$. In the weakest system, there is no relation among the four. In the strongest one, $\Box$ and $\Diamond$ are reducible to one another via strong negation.

The corresponding semantic picture is to consider N4-models having one or more accessibility relations for defining the modal operators. Namely, the models of the weakest system contain *four* independent accessibility relations (one for each modality and for their negations); the models of the strongest logic interpret all modalities using the same relation.

We provide strongly complete Hilbert axiomatisations for all logics and construct cut-free sequent calculi which we use to establish the decidability of our systems. Due to the limited space, some proofs are put in the appendix.

2 Nelson's Logic and Its Modal Expansions

We begin with the presentation of the propositional Nelson's logic (N4). Fix a countable set Prop of propositional variables and define its language $\mathcal{L}^{\sim}$:

$$\mathcal{L}^{\sim} \ni \phi := p \in \mathsf{Prop} \mid {\sim}\phi \mid (\phi \wedge \phi) \mid (\phi \vee \phi) \mid (\phi \to \phi)$$

The semantics of N4 is defined on intuitionistic frames *with two independent valuations* corresponding to the *support of truth* (positive support) and *support of falsity* (negative support) of formulas in states.

Definition 1 (Semantics of N4). *An* N4 model *is a tuple* $\mathfrak{M} = \langle W, \leq, v^+, v^- \rangle$ *with* $W \neq \varnothing$, $\leq$ *being a partial preorder on* W, *and* $v^+, v^- : \mathsf{Prop} \to 2^W$ *s.t.* $w \in v^+(p)$, $w \leq w'$ *imply* $w' \in v^+(p)$ *and* $w \in v^-(p)$, $w \leq w'$ *imply* $w' \in v^-(p)$. *The notions of* positive *and* negative support *of a formula in a state* ($\mathfrak{M}, w \Vdash^+ \phi$ *and* $\mathfrak{M}, w \Vdash^- \phi$, *respectively) are defined as follows.*

$$\mathfrak{M}, w \Vdash^+ p \textit{ iff } w \in v^+(p) \quad \mathfrak{M}, w \Vdash^- p \textit{ iff } w \in v^-(p)$$
$$\mathfrak{M}, w \Vdash^+ {\sim}\phi \textit{ iff } \mathfrak{M}, w \Vdash^- \phi \quad \mathfrak{M}, w \Vdash^- {\sim}\phi \textit{ iff } \mathfrak{M}, w \Vdash^+ \phi$$
$$\mathfrak{M}, w \Vdash^+ \phi \wedge \chi \textit{ iff } \mathfrak{M}, w \Vdash^+ \phi \textit{ and } \mathfrak{M}, w \Vdash^+ \chi$$
$$\mathfrak{M}, w \Vdash^- \phi \wedge \chi \textit{ iff } \mathfrak{M}, w \Vdash^- \phi \textit{ or } \mathfrak{M}, w \Vdash^- \chi$$
$$\mathfrak{M}, w \Vdash^+ \phi \vee \chi \textit{ iff } \mathfrak{M}, w \Vdash^+ \phi \textit{ or } \mathfrak{M}, w \Vdash^+ \chi$$
$$\mathfrak{M}, w \Vdash^- \phi \vee \chi \textit{ iff } \mathfrak{M}, w \Vdash^- \phi \textit{ and } \mathfrak{M}, w \Vdash^- \chi$$
$$\mathfrak{M}, w \Vdash^+ \phi \to \chi \textit{ iff } \forall w' \geq w : \mathfrak{M}, w' \Vdash^+ \phi \Rightarrow \mathfrak{M}, w' \Vdash^+ \chi$$
$$\mathfrak{M}, w \Vdash^- \phi \to \chi \textit{ iff } \mathfrak{M}, w \Vdash^+ \phi \textit{ and } \mathfrak{M}, w \Vdash^- \chi$$

We say that $\phi \in \mathcal{L}^{\sim}$ *is* N4-valid *if* $\mathfrak{M}, w \Vdash^+ \phi$ *in each* N4*-model* $\mathfrak{M}$ *and* $w \in \mathfrak{M}$.

As one can see, the positive support conditions coincide with the semantics of Intuitionistic logic. The negative support conditions are dual to them via the *classical* De Morgan laws. Thus, N4 is a conservative extension of the positive Intuitionistic logic. Thus, it possesses disjunctive property and its dual *constructive falsity property*: if ${\sim}(\phi \wedge \chi)$ is N4-valid, then ${\sim}\phi$ or ${\sim}\chi$ is N4-valid. Note, however, that there are other ways of treating the falsity condition of constructive implications [19]. Still, they either lead to a contradictory logic or define the negation of the implication via *co-implication*. We choose the Nelsonian negation of $\to$ because it does not result in the language expansion.

The Hilbert-style axiomatisation of N4 can be obtained as follows.

Definition 2 ($\mathcal{H}$N4—the Hilbert calculus for N4). $\mathcal{H}$N4 *contains the following axiom schemes and rules* ($\phi \leftrightarrow \chi$ *stands for* $(\phi \to \chi) \wedge (\chi \to \phi)$).

Int$^+$: *Instantiations of the axioms for the* positive *Intuitionistic logic in* $\mathcal{L}^{\sim}$.

$$\sim\sim := {\sim}{\sim}\phi \leftrightarrow \phi \qquad \mathbf{DeM}_{\wedge} := {\sim}(\phi \wedge \chi) \leftrightarrow ({\sim}\phi \vee {\sim}\chi)$$
$$\mathbf{DeM}_{\vee} := {\sim}(\phi \vee \chi) \leftrightarrow ({\sim}\phi \wedge {\sim}\chi) \qquad \mathbf{DeM}_{\to} := {\sim}(\phi \to \chi) \leftrightarrow (\phi \wedge {\sim}\chi)$$
$$\mathbf{mp} := \frac{\phi \quad \phi \to \chi}{\chi}$$

Let us now consider $\mathsf{CN4K}$—a modal expansion of $\mathsf{N4}$. As expected, the language $\mathcal{L}^{\sim}_{\Box,\Diamond}$ of $\mathsf{CN4K}$ expands $\mathcal{L}^{\sim}$ with two modalities: $\Box$ and $\Diamond$. Semantically, $\mathsf{CN4K}$ is defined on intuitionistic frames with additional relations used to compute the support of truth and falsity of modalities.

Definition 3 ($\mathsf{CN4K}$ **frames**). *A* $\mathsf{CN4K}$ frame *is a tuple of the following form:* $\mathfrak{F} = \langle W, \leq, R^+_\Box, R^-_\Box, R^+_\Diamond, R^-_\Diamond \rangle$ *with* $W \neq \varnothing$*,* $\leq$ *being a partial preorder on* W*, and* $R^\bullet_\heartsuit$ *binary relations on* W *with* $\bullet \in \{+, -\}$ *and* $\heartsuit \in \{\Box, \Diamond\}$*.*

A frame is called $\pm$-birelational *if* $R^+_\Box = R^+_\Diamond$ *and* $R^-_\Box = R^-_\Diamond$*,* $\curlyvee$-birelational *if* $R^+_\Box = R^-_\Box$ *and* $R^+_\Diamond = R^-_\Diamond$*,* $\bowtie$-birelational *if* $R^+_\Box = R^-_\Diamond$ *and* $R^+_\Diamond = R^-_\Box$*, and* monorelational *if all four relations coincide.*

For a relation R *on* W *and* $w \in W$*, we set* $R(w) = \{w' \mid wRw'\}$*.*

In the definition above, we have five different classes of frames. In the most general case, $\Box$ and $\Diamond$ are interpreted with two independent relations corresponding to the support of truth and the support of falsity. Birelational frames are obtained by identifying two pairs of accessibility relations. Finally, in monorelational frames, all accessibility relations coincide. Note that it makes sense to use different accessibility relations to treat positive and negative support of modalities. Indeed, if one assumes *proofs* (i.e., finding evidence *in favour of something*) to be independent of *refutations* (finding evidence *against something*), it is also reasonable to assume that the states used to *prove* a modal statement are different from the states used to *refute* it.

Definition 4 ($\mathsf{CN4K}$ **models**). *A* $\mathsf{CN4K}$ model *is a tuple* $\mathfrak{M} = \langle \mathfrak{F}, v^+, v^- \rangle$ *with* $\mathfrak{F}$ *being a* $\mathsf{CN4K}$ *frame and* $v^+, v^- : \mathsf{Prop} \to 2^W$ *being such that*

$$w \in v^+(p) \text{ and } w \leq w' \Rightarrow w' \in v^+(p) \quad w \in v^-(p) \text{ and } w \leq w' \Rightarrow w' \in v^-(p)$$

The notions of positive *and* negative support *for propositional connectives are the same as in Definition 1. The semantics of modalities is as follows.*

$$\mathfrak{M}, w \Vdash^+ \Box\phi \text{ iff } \forall w' \geq w\ \forall w'' \in R^+_\Box(w') : \mathfrak{M}, w'' \Vdash^+ \phi$$
$$\mathfrak{M}, w \Vdash^- \Box\phi \text{ iff } \forall w' \geq w\ \exists w'' \in R^-_\Box(w') : \mathfrak{M}, w'' \Vdash^- \phi$$
$$\mathfrak{M}, w \Vdash^+ \Diamond\phi \text{ iff } \forall w' \geq w\ \exists w'' \in R^+_\Diamond(w') : \mathfrak{M}, w'' \Vdash^+ \phi$$
$$\mathfrak{M}, w \Vdash^- \Diamond\phi \text{ iff } \forall w' \geq w\ \forall w'' \in R^-_\Diamond(w') : \mathfrak{M}, w'' \Vdash^- \phi$$

Definition 5. *We say that* $\Gamma \subseteq \mathcal{L}^{\sim}_{\Box,\Diamond}$ entails χ *(*$\Gamma \models_{\mathsf{CN4K}} \chi$*) if: for every* $\mathfrak{M} = \langle \mathfrak{F}, v^+, v^- \rangle$ *and* $w \in \mathfrak{M}$ *s.t.* $\mathfrak{M}, w \Vdash^+ \phi$ *for all* $\phi \in \Gamma$*, then* $\mathfrak{M}, w \Vdash^+ \chi$*. If* $\Gamma = \varnothing$*, we write* $\mathsf{CN4K} \models \chi$ *and say that* χ *is* valid*.*

We note briefly that $\Box$ and $\Diamond$ are dual to one another via $\sim$. Namely, $\sim\Box\sim$ behaves like $\Diamond$ w.r.t. $R^-_\Box$ and $\sim\Diamond\sim$ like $\Box$ w.r.t. $R^-_\Diamond$.

In what follows, we use the following notation: $\mathsf{CN4K}$ stands for the logic of all $\mathsf{CN4K}$ frames, $\mathsf{CN4K}^*$ for the logic of all $*$-birelational frames with $* \in \{\pm, \curlyvee, \bowtie\}$, and $\mathsf{CN4K}^1$ for the logic of all monorelational frames. The notions of validity and entailment in these logics are obtained in the same way as in Definition 5.

It is important to note that apart from the number of relations in the frame, there are no other conditions on the accessibility relations themselves. This differentiates our logics from those studied in [13,14] and [17] as in both these cases, the accessibility relations defining modalities and the ordering of the states in the frame were connected via the confluence condition. This means that our logics are weaker than those of Odintsov, Wansing, and Sherkhonov. In particular, $\mathsf{DK}^{dd\sim}$ from [17] extends $\mathsf{CN4K}^{\pm}$ and $\mathcal{CALC}^{\mathsf{C}}$ from [14] extends $\mathsf{CN4K}^{1}$. Still, as expected, all CN4K logics have persistence.

Proposition 1. *Let $\mathfrak{M}$ be a* CN4K *model $w \leq w'$, and $\phi, \chi \in \mathcal{L}^{\sim}_{\Box,\Diamond}$. Then:*

$$\text{if } \mathfrak{M}, w \Vdash^{+} \phi, \text{ then } \mathfrak{M}, w' \Vdash^{+} \phi \qquad \text{if } \mathfrak{M}, w \Vdash^{-} \chi, \text{ then } \mathfrak{M}, w' \Vdash^{-} \chi$$

We finish the section by observing that every $\mathcal{L}^{\sim}_{\Box,\Diamond}$ theory is satisfiable. Consider a model with one state w, all relations being equal to $\{\langle w, w\rangle\}$, and all variables both true and false at w. It is easy to check by the induction on formulas that every $\phi \in \mathcal{L}$ is true (and false) at w.

Proposition 2. *There is a monorelational* CN4K *model $\mathfrak{M}$ and s.t. $\mathfrak{M}, w \Vdash^{+} \phi$ for every $\phi \in \mathcal{L}^{\sim}_{\Box,\Diamond}$ and $w \in \mathfrak{M}$.*

3 Hilbert Calculi for CN4K and Its Extensions

Let us now axiomatise Nelson's modal logics over the different classes of frames we introduced in Definition 3. To facilitate the presentation, we first introduce the following technical notion.

Definition 6. *Let $\mathcal{C}$ be a calculus and* **R** *a set of rules and axioms. We use $\mathcal{C} \oplus \mathbf{R}$ to denote the calculus obtained by adding the rules and axioms in* **R** *to $\mathcal{C}$.*

Definition 7 (Hilbert calculi for CN4K and its extensions). *Consider the following axiom schemes and rules.*

$$\top_{\Box} :- \Box(\phi \to \phi) \qquad \top_{\Diamond} :- {\sim}\Diamond{\sim}(\phi \to \phi)$$

$$\wedge_{\Box} :- (\Box\phi \wedge \Box\chi) \to \Box(\phi \wedge \chi) \qquad \wedge_{\Diamond} :- ({\sim}\Diamond\phi \wedge {\sim}\Diamond\chi) \to {\sim}\Diamond(\phi \vee \chi)$$

$$\pm_{\Box} :- \Box(\phi \to \chi) \to (\Diamond\phi \to \Diamond\chi) \qquad \pm_{\Diamond} :- {\sim}\Diamond{\sim}({\sim}\phi \to {\sim}\chi) \to ({\sim}\Box\phi \to {\sim}\Box\chi)$$

$$\curlyvee_{\Box} :- \Box(\phi \to \chi) \to ({\sim}\Box{\sim}\phi \to {\sim}\Box{\sim}\chi) \qquad \curlyvee_{\Diamond} :- {\sim}\Diamond{\sim}(\phi \to \chi) \to (\Diamond\phi \to \Diamond\chi)$$

$$\bowtie_{\Box} :- \Box\phi \leftrightarrow {\sim}\Diamond{\sim}\phi \qquad \bowtie_{\Diamond} :- \Diamond\phi \leftrightarrow {\sim}\Box{\sim}\phi$$

$$\mathbf{r}_{\Box} :- \frac{\vdash \phi \to \chi}{\vdash \Box\phi \to \Box\chi} \quad \mathbf{r}_{\Diamond} :- \frac{\vdash \phi \to \chi}{\vdash \Diamond\phi \to \Diamond\chi} \qquad \mathbf{r}^{\sim}_{\Box} :- \frac{\vdash {\sim}\phi \to {\sim}\chi}{\vdash {\sim}\Box\phi \to {\sim}\Box\chi} \quad \mathbf{r}^{\sim}_{\Diamond} :- \frac{\vdash {\sim}\phi \to {\sim}\chi}{\vdash {\sim}\Diamond\phi \to {\sim}\Diamond\chi}$$

The calculi are as follows:

$$\mathcal{H}\mathsf{CN4K} = \mathcal{H}\mathsf{N4} \oplus \{\top_{\Box}, \wedge_{\Box}, \mathbf{r}_{\Box}, \mathbf{r}^{\sim}_{\Box}, \top_{\Diamond}, \wedge_{\Diamond}, \mathbf{r}_{\Diamond}, \mathbf{r}^{\sim}_{\Diamond}\}$$

$$\mathcal{H}\mathsf{CN4K}^{\pm} = \mathcal{H}\mathsf{CN4K} \oplus \{\pm_{\Box}, \pm_{\Diamond}\} \qquad \mathcal{H}\mathsf{CN4K}^{\curlyvee} = \mathcal{H}\mathsf{CN4K} \oplus \{\curlyvee_{\Box}, \curlyvee_{\Diamond}\}$$

$$\mathcal{H}\mathsf{CN4K}^{\bowtie} = \mathcal{H}\mathsf{CN4K} \oplus \{\bowtie_{\Box}, \bowtie_{\Diamond}\} \qquad \mathcal{H}\mathsf{CN4K}^{1} = \mathcal{H}\mathsf{CN4K}^{\pm} \oplus \mathcal{H}\mathsf{CN4K}^{\curlyvee} \oplus \mathcal{H}\mathsf{CN4K}^{\bowtie}$$

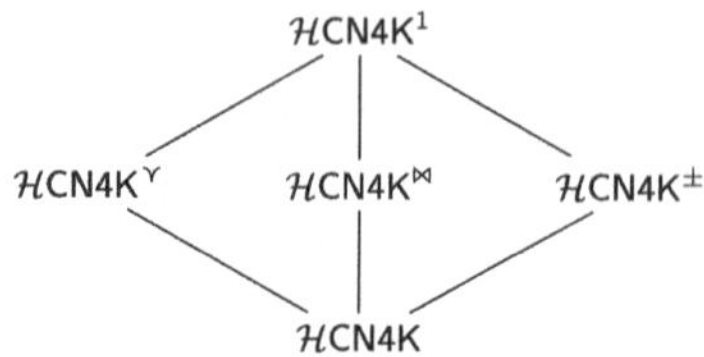

Fig. 1. Hilbert calculi for CN4K and its extensions.

An $\mathcal{H}$L-derivation of ϕ from Γ *($\Gamma \vdash_{\mathcal{H}\mathsf{L}} \phi$) is a finite sequence of formulas ϕ_1, ..., $\phi_n = \phi$ s.t. every ϕ_i is an instance of an axiom scheme, belongs to Γ, or obtained from previous formulas by an application of a rule (with modal rules being applied to theorems only). If ϕ is derivable from $\Gamma = \varnothing$, we write $\mathcal{H}\mathsf{L} \vdash \phi$ and say that ϕ is* $\mathcal{H}$L-provable.

In the text below, we let $\mathsf{L} \in \{\mathsf{N4}, \mathsf{CN4K}, \mathsf{CN4K}^{\curlyvee}, \mathsf{CN4K}^{\pm}, \mathsf{CN4K}^{\bowtie}, \mathsf{CN4K}^{1}\}$ *and use* $\mathcal{H}\mathsf{L}$ *to denote its Hilbert calculus (Fig. 1).*

Observe that $\top_\heartsuit$, $\wedge_\heartsuit$, and $\mathbf{r}_\heartsuit$ ($\heartsuit \in \{\Box, \Diamond\}$) can be replaced with the following axioms and rules.

$$\mathbf{K}_\Box :- \Box(\phi \to \chi) \to (\Box\phi \to \Box\chi) \qquad \mathbf{K}_\Diamond :- {\sim}\Diamond{\sim}(\phi \to \chi) \to ({\sim}\Diamond{\sim}\phi \to {\sim}\Diamond{\sim}\chi)$$

$$\mathbf{nec}_\Box :- \frac{\vdash \phi}{\vdash \Box\phi} \qquad \mathbf{nec}_\Diamond :- \frac{\vdash \phi}{\vdash {\sim}\Diamond{\sim}\phi}$$

Furthermore, as one can see from Definition 4 [3], and [4], the positive support conditions of all connectives except $\sim$ coincide with the semantics of CK. Thus, *positive (i.e., $\sim$-free) mono-modal fragments* of CN4K coincide with the positive ($\perp$-free) mono-modal fragments of CK. Moreover, the positive fragments of CN4K$^\pm$ and CN4K^1 coincide with the positive fragment of CK.

The soundness can be obtained by checking the validity of axioms and that the rules preserve truth.

Theorem 1 (Soundness). *Let $\Gamma \vdash_{\mathcal{H}\mathsf{L}} \phi$. Then $\Gamma \models_{\mathsf{L}} \phi$.*

For the completeness, we follow the method of [20]. We begin with an observation and some technical notions.

Lemma 1. $\mathcal{H}\mathsf{CN4K} \vdash \bigwedge_{i=1}^{n}\Box\phi_i \leftrightarrow \Box\bigwedge_{i=1}^{n}\phi_i$ *and* $\mathcal{H}\mathsf{CN4K} \vdash \bigwedge_{i=1}^{n}{\sim}\Diamond\phi_i \leftrightarrow {\sim}\Diamond\bigvee_{i=1}^{n}\phi_i$.

Definition 8. *We call $\Xi \subseteq \mathcal{L}$* saturated *if it is* deductively closed *(i.e., $\xi \in \Xi$ for $\Xi \vdash_{\mathcal{H}\mathsf{CN4K}} \xi$) and* prime *(i.e., $\xi \vee \xi' \in \Xi$ entails that $\xi \in \Xi$ or $\xi' \in \Xi$).*

The next statement is proved by a standard argument for the Lindenbaum lemma. Note that we do not need the usual requirement of *consistency* since every $\Xi \subseteq \mathcal{L}$ has a model (recall Proposition 2).

Proposition 3. *If $\Gamma \nvdash_{\mathcal{H}\mathsf{CN4K}} \phi$, there is a saturated set $\Gamma' \supseteq \Gamma$ s.t. $\Gamma' \nvdash_{\mathcal{H}\mathsf{CN4K}} \phi$.*

Definition 9. *A* segment *is a tuple* $\mathfrak{s} = \langle \Xi, \Phi^+_\Box, \Phi^-_\Box, \Phi^+_\Diamond, \Phi^-_\Diamond \rangle$ *s.t.* Ξ *is a saturated set that we call* head *of* $\mathfrak{s}$ *(*$\mathbf{h}(\mathfrak{s})$*) and* $\Phi^\bullet_\heartsuit$*'s are families of saturated sets s.t. the following holds:*

- *if* $\Box\phi \in \Xi$*, then* $\phi \in \Delta$ *for every* $\Delta \in \Phi^+_\Box$*;*
- *if* $\sim\Box\phi \in \Xi$*, then* $\sim\phi \in \Delta$ *for some* $\Delta \in \Phi^-_\Box$*;*
- *if* $\Diamond\phi \in \Xi$*, then* $\phi \in \Delta$ *for some* $\Delta \in \Phi^+_\Diamond$*;*
- *if* $\sim\Diamond\phi \in \Xi$*, then* $\sim\phi \in \Delta$ *for every* $\Delta \in \Phi^-_\Diamond$*.*

Definition 10. *A* canonical CN4K-model *is the following tuple:* $\mathfrak{M}^\mathsf{C} = \langle W^\mathsf{C}, \leq^\mathsf{C}, R^{+\mathsf{C}}_\Box, R^{-\mathsf{C}}_\Box, R^{+\mathsf{C}}_\Diamond, R^{-\mathsf{C}}_\Diamond, v^{+\mathsf{C}}, v^{-\mathsf{C}} \rangle$ *s.t.* W^C *is the set of all segments and for any segments* $\mathfrak{s} = \langle \Xi, \Phi^+_\Box, \Phi^-_\Box, \Phi^+_\Diamond, \Phi^-_\Diamond \rangle$ *and* $\mathfrak{s}' = \langle \Xi', \Phi^{+\prime}_\Box, \Phi^{-\prime}_\Box, \Phi^{+\prime}_\Diamond, \Phi^{-\prime}_\Diamond \rangle$*, we have:*

$$\mathfrak{s} \leq^\mathsf{C} \mathfrak{s}' \text{ iff } \mathbf{h}(\mathfrak{s}) \subseteq \mathbf{h}(\mathfrak{s}') \qquad \mathfrak{s} R^{\bullet\mathsf{C}}_\heartsuit \mathfrak{s}' \text{ iff } \mathbf{h}(\mathfrak{s}') \in \Phi^\bullet_\heartsuit$$

$$\mathfrak{M}^\mathsf{C}, \mathfrak{s} \Vdash^+ p \text{ iff } p \in \mathbf{h}(\mathfrak{s}) \qquad \mathfrak{M}^\mathsf{C}, \mathfrak{s} \Vdash^- p \text{ iff } \sim p \in \mathbf{h}(\mathfrak{s})$$

Lemma 2 (Truth lemma for $\mathcal{H}$CN4K). *For every* $\phi \in \mathcal{L}^\sim_{\Box,\Diamond}$ *and* $\mathfrak{s} \in \mathfrak{M}^\mathsf{C}$*, it holds that (1)* $\mathfrak{M}^\mathsf{C}, \mathfrak{s} \Vdash^+ \phi$ *iff* $\phi \in \mathbf{h}(\mathfrak{s})$*; (2)* $\mathfrak{M}^\mathsf{C}, \mathfrak{s} \Vdash^- \phi$ *iff* $\sim\phi \in \mathbf{h}(\mathfrak{s})$*.*

Proof. We proceed by induction on $\phi \in \mathcal{L}^\sim_{\Box,\Diamond}$. If $\phi = p$, then the statement holds by the construction of $\mathfrak{M}^\mathsf{C}$. For the induction steps, we only consider the case $\phi = \sim\Diamond\chi$. We assume that $\mathfrak{s} = \langle \Xi, \Phi^+_\Box, \Phi^-_\Box, \Phi^+_\Diamond, \Phi^-_\Diamond \rangle$.

Let $\phi = \sim\Diamond\chi$ and assume for contradiction that $\mathfrak{M}^\mathsf{C}, \mathfrak{s} \Vdash^- \Diamond\chi$ but $\sim\Diamond\chi \notin \mathbf{h}(\mathfrak{s})$. Consider $\Xi^{\sim!} = \{\sim\tau \mid \sim\Diamond\tau \in \mathbf{h}(\mathfrak{s})\}$. Let us show that $\Xi^{\sim!} \nvdash_{\mathcal{H}\mathsf{CN4K}} \sim\chi$. Suppose for contradiction that there is some finite $\Xi' \subseteq \Xi^{\sim!}$ s.t. $\Xi' \vdash_{\mathcal{H}\mathsf{CN4K}} \sim\chi$. Then applying the deduction theorem, De Morgan laws for $\wedge$ and $\vee$, and $\mathbf{r}^\sim_\Diamond$, we have $\mathcal{H}\mathsf{CN4K} \vdash \sim\Diamond \bigvee\limits_{\sim\tau' \in \Xi'} \tau' \rightarrow \sim\Diamond\chi$. Now, we use Lemma 1 which gives us $\mathcal{H}\mathsf{CN4K} \vdash \bigwedge\limits_{\sim\tau' \in \Xi'} \sim\Diamond\tau' \rightarrow \sim\Diamond\chi$. But as $\sim\Diamond\tau$'s belong to $\mathbf{h}(\mathfrak{s})$ which is deductively closed, this means that $\sim\Diamond\chi \in \mathbf{h}(\mathfrak{s})$ as well which contradicts our assumption. Thus, we can extend $\Xi^{\sim!}$ to a saturated $\Xi^{\sim\sharp}$ s.t. $\Xi^{\sim\sharp} \nvdash_{\mathcal{H}\mathsf{CN4K}} \sim\chi$ and consider $\mathfrak{s}' = \langle \Xi, \Phi^+_\Box, \Phi^-_\Box, \Phi^+_\Diamond, \{\Xi^{\sim\sharp}\} \rangle$. Now let $\mathfrak{s}''$ be a segment with $\mathbf{h}(\mathfrak{s}'') = \Xi^{\sim\sharp}$. It is easy to see that $\mathfrak{s}' R^{-\mathsf{C}}_\Diamond \mathfrak{s}''$ and that $\mathfrak{M}^\mathsf{C}, \mathfrak{s}'' \nVdash^- \chi$ by the induction hypothesis. Hence, using that $\mathfrak{s} \leq^\mathsf{C} \mathfrak{s}'$, we obtain $\mathfrak{M}^\mathsf{C}, \mathfrak{s} \nVdash^- \Diamond\chi$, contrary to the assumption.

Conversely, let $\sim\Diamond\chi \in \mathbf{h}(\mathfrak{s})$. We have that $\sim\Diamond\chi \in \mathbf{h}(\mathfrak{s}')$ for every $\mathfrak{s}' \geq^\mathsf{C} \mathfrak{s}$. Hence, $\sim\chi \in \mathbf{h}(\mathfrak{s}'')$ for every $\mathfrak{s}'' \in R^{-\mathsf{C}}_\Diamond(\mathfrak{s}')$. Applying the induction hypothesis, we have $\mathfrak{M}^\mathsf{C}, \mathfrak{s}'' \Vdash^- \chi$ for every such $\mathfrak{s}''$ as required. □

We can now adapt the proof of Lemma 2 to obtain the completeness of extensions of $\mathcal{H}$CN4K. To do that, we introduce additional types of segments.

Definition 11. *We say that* $\mathfrak{s}$ *is a* $\pm$-segment *if* $\Phi^+_\Box = \Phi^+_\Diamond$ *and* $\Phi^-_\Box = \Phi^-_\Diamond$*;* $\curlyvee$-segment *if* $\Phi^+_\Box = \Phi^-_\Box$ *and* $\Phi^+_\Diamond = \Phi^-_\Diamond$*;* $\bowtie$-segment *if* $\Phi^+_\Box = \Phi^-_\Diamond$ *and* $\Phi^+_\Diamond = \Phi^-_\Box$*;* 1-segment *if* $\Phi^+_\Box = \Phi^-_\Diamond = \Phi^+_\Diamond = \Phi^-_\Box$.

We let $* \in \{\pm, \curlyvee, \bowtie, 1\}$*. The canonical models* $\mathfrak{M}^\mathsf{C}_*$ *of* CN4K**'s can be defined as before (cf. Definition 10) but over the corresponding set of* $*$*-segments.*

Lemma 3. *It holds that (1)* $\mathfrak{M}^{\mathsf{C}}_{*}, \mathfrak{s} \Vdash^{+} \phi$ *iff* $\phi \in \mathbf{h}(\mathfrak{s})$*, and (2)* $\mathfrak{M}^{\mathsf{C}}_{*}, \mathfrak{s} \Vdash^{-} \phi$ *iff* ${\sim}\phi \in \mathbf{h}(\mathfrak{s})$*, for every* $\phi \in \mathcal{L}^{\sim}_{\Box,\Diamond}$ *and* $\mathfrak{s} \in \mathfrak{M}^{\mathsf{C}}_{*}$.

The following statement now follows from Theorem 1 and Lemmas 2, and 3.

Theorem 2. $\Gamma \models_{\mathsf{L}} \phi$ *iff* $\Gamma \vdash_{\mathcal{H}\mathsf{L}} \phi$.

We finish the section by noting an important asymmetry between the pairs of axioms extending $\mathcal{H}\mathsf{CN4K}$. While one could expect that adding any two pairs of axioms $\pm$, $\curlyvee$, and $\bowtie$ proves the remaining pair, this is not always the case.

Theorem 3.

1. $\mathcal{H}\mathsf{CN4K}^{\pm} \oplus \{\bowtie_{\Box}, \bowtie_{\Diamond}\} \vdash \curlyvee_{\Box} \wedge \curlyvee_{\Diamond}$ *and* $\mathcal{H}\mathsf{CN4K}^{\curlyvee} \oplus \{\bowtie_{\Box}, \bowtie_{\Diamond}\} \vdash \pm_{\Box} \wedge \pm_{\Diamond}$.
2. $\mathcal{H}\mathsf{CN4K}^{\pm} \oplus \{\curlyvee_{\Box}, \curlyvee_{\Diamond}\} \nvdash \bowtie_{\Box}$ *and* $\mathcal{H}\mathsf{CN4K}^{\pm} \oplus \{\curlyvee_{\Box}, \curlyvee_{\Diamond}\} \nvdash \bowtie_{\Diamond}$.

Proof. Item 1 is straightforward since $\bowtie$-axioms establish the interdefinability of $\Box$ and $\Diamond$. We tackle Item 2. Consider the following two frames over $W = \{w_0, w_1\}$ s.t. $w_0 \leq w_1$:

$$\mathfrak{F}_1 = \langle W, \leq, R^{+}_{\Box}, R^{-}_{\Box}, R^{+}_{\Diamond}, R^{-}_{\Diamond} \rangle : R^{+}_{\Diamond} = R^{-}_{\Box} = \varnothing, R^{+}_{\Box} = \{(w_0, w_0)\}, R^{-}_{\Diamond} = \{(w_0, w_1)\}$$
$$\mathfrak{F}_2 = \langle W, \leq, S^{+}_{\Box}, S^{-}_{\Box}, S^{+}_{\Diamond}, S^{-}_{\Diamond} \rangle : S^{+}_{\Box} = S^{-}_{\Box} = S^{-}_{\Diamond} = \{(w_0, w_1), (w_1, w_1)\}, S^{+}_{\Diamond} = \varnothing$$

We show that $\mathfrak{F}_1 \models_{\mathsf{CN4K}} \mathcal{H}\mathsf{CN4K}^{\pm} \oplus \mathcal{H}\mathsf{CN4K}^{\curlyvee}$. Indeed, since both $R^{+}_{\Diamond}$ and $R^{-}_{\Box}$ are empty, $\pm$'s and $\curlyvee$'s axioms are vacuously valid (and other axioms and rules are valid on every frame). Now let $\mathfrak{M}_1$ be a model on $\mathfrak{F}_1$ s.t. $\mathfrak{M}_1, w_0 \Vdash^{+} p$ and $\mathfrak{M}_1, w_1 \nVdash^{+} p$. Clearly, $\mathfrak{M}_1, w_0 \Vdash^{+} \Box p$. On the other hand, $\mathfrak{M}_1, w_0 \nVdash^{-} \Diamond{\sim}p$ (whence, $\mathfrak{M}_1, w_0 \nVdash^{+} {\sim}\Diamond{\sim}p$). Thus, $\mathfrak{F}_1 \not\models_{\mathsf{CN4K}} \Box p \leftrightarrow {\sim}\Diamond{\sim}p$.

Similarly, $\mathfrak{F}_2 \models_{\mathsf{CN4K}} \curlyvee_{\Diamond}$ because $S^{+}_{\Diamond} = \varnothing$. The validity of other axioms is also straightforward to establish. Now, assume $\mathfrak{M}_2$ to be a model on $\mathfrak{F}_2$ s.t. $\mathfrak{M}_2, w_1 \Vdash^{+} p$. It is clear that $\mathfrak{M}_2, w_1 \Vdash^{-} \Box{\sim}p$ (i.e., $\mathfrak{M}_2, w_1 \Vdash^{+} {\sim}\Box{\sim}p$) but $\mathfrak{M}_2, w_1 \nVdash^{+} \Diamond p$ (as $S^{+}_{\Diamond} = \varnothing$). Thus, $\mathfrak{F}_2 \not\models_{\mathsf{CN4K}} \Diamond p \leftrightarrow {\sim}\Box{\sim}p$. □

4 Sequent Calculi

In this section, we present sequent calculi for all logics under consideration. Below $\mathcal{G}\mathsf{L}$ denotes the sequent calculus of L.

Definition 12. *A sequent is an expression* $\Gamma \Rightarrow \phi$*, where* Γ *is a finite multi-set of formulas and* ϕ *is a formula. The* formula interpretation *of* $\Gamma \Rightarrow \phi$ *is the formula* $\bigwedge_{\psi \in \Gamma} \psi \to \phi$*. A sequent is* L-valid *if so is its formula interpretation.*

Given a multiset of formulas Γ*, we let* $\Gamma^{\Box} = \{\phi \mid \Box\phi \in \Gamma\}$ *and* $\Gamma^{\Diamond}_{\sim} = \{{\sim}\phi \mid {\sim}\Diamond\phi \in \Gamma\}$*. We define the following calculi:*

$$\mathcal{G}\mathsf{CN4K} = \mathcal{G}\mathsf{N4} \oplus \{\Box, \Diamond, \Box_{\sim}, \Diamond_{\sim}\} \quad \mathcal{G}\mathsf{CN4K}^{\curlyvee} = \mathcal{G}\mathsf{N4} \oplus \{\Box, \Diamond^{\curlyvee}, \Box^{\curlyvee}_{\sim}, \Diamond_{\sim}\}$$
$$\mathcal{G}\mathsf{CN4K}^{\pm} = \mathcal{G}\mathsf{N4} \oplus \{\Box, \Diamond^{\pm}, \Box^{\pm}_{\sim}, \Diamond_{\sim}\} \quad \mathcal{G}\mathsf{CN4K}^{\bowtie} = \mathcal{G}\mathsf{N4} \oplus \{\Box^{\bowtie}, \Diamond, \Diamond^{\bowtie}, \Box_{\sim}, \Box^{\bowtie}_{\sim}, \Diamond^{\bowtie}_{\sim}\}$$
$$\mathcal{G}\mathsf{CN4K}^{1} = \mathcal{G}\mathsf{N4} \oplus \{\Box^{\bowtie}, \Diamond^{1}, \Diamond^{1,\bowtie}, \Box^{1}_{\sim}, \Box^{1,\bowtie}_{\sim}, \Diamond^{\bowtie}_{\sim}\}$$

Propositional rules which constitute $\mathcal{G}\mathsf{N4}$ *are found in Fig. 2 and modal rules are found in Fig. 3.*

$$
\mathrm{Ax}\,\frac{}{p,\Gamma\Rightarrow p}\quad
\mathrm{Ax}_{\sim}\,\frac{}{\sim p,\Gamma\Rightarrow\sim p}\quad
{\sim\sim_l}\,\frac{\phi,\Gamma\Rightarrow\psi}{\sim\sim\phi,\Gamma\Rightarrow\psi}\quad
{\sim\sim_r}\,\frac{\Gamma\Rightarrow\phi}{\Gamma\Rightarrow\sim\sim\phi}
$$

$$
\wedge_l\,\frac{\phi,\chi,\Gamma\Rightarrow\psi}{\phi\wedge\chi,\Gamma\Rightarrow\psi}\quad
\wedge_r\,\frac{\Gamma\Rightarrow\phi\quad\Gamma\Rightarrow\chi}{\Gamma\Rightarrow\phi\wedge\chi}\quad
\vee_l\,\frac{\phi,\Gamma\Rightarrow\psi\quad\chi,\Gamma\Rightarrow\psi}{\phi\vee\chi,\Gamma\Rightarrow\psi}\quad
\vee_{r1}\,\frac{\Gamma\Rightarrow\phi}{\Gamma\Rightarrow\phi\vee\chi}
$$

$$
\vee_{r2}\,\frac{\Gamma\Rightarrow\chi}{\Gamma\Rightarrow\phi\vee\chi}\quad
{\sim\vee_l}\,\frac{\sim\phi,\sim\chi,\Gamma\Rightarrow\psi}{\sim(\phi\vee\chi),\Gamma\Rightarrow\psi}\quad
{\sim\vee_r}\,\frac{\Gamma\Rightarrow\sim\phi\quad\Gamma\Rightarrow\sim\chi}{\Gamma\Rightarrow\sim(\phi\vee\chi)}\quad
{\sim\wedge_{r1}}\,\frac{\Gamma\Rightarrow\sim\phi}{\Gamma\Rightarrow\sim(\phi\wedge\chi)}
$$

$$
{\sim\wedge_{r2}}\,\frac{\Gamma\Rightarrow\sim\chi}{\Gamma\Rightarrow\sim(\phi\wedge\chi)}\quad
{\sim\vee_l}\,\frac{\sim\phi,\Gamma\Rightarrow\psi\quad\sim\chi,\Gamma\Rightarrow\psi}{\sim(\phi\wedge\chi),\Gamma\Rightarrow\psi}\quad
\to_l\,\frac{\phi\to\chi,\Gamma\Rightarrow\phi\quad\chi,\Gamma\Rightarrow\psi}{\phi\to\chi,\Gamma\Rightarrow\psi}
$$

$$
\to_r\,\frac{\Gamma,\phi\Rightarrow\chi}{\Gamma\Rightarrow\phi\to\chi}\quad
{\sim\to_l}\,\frac{\phi,\sim\chi,\Gamma\Rightarrow\psi}{\sim(\phi\to\chi),\Gamma\Rightarrow\psi}\quad
{\sim\to_r}\,\frac{\Gamma\Rightarrow\phi\quad\Gamma\Rightarrow\sim\chi}{\Gamma\Rightarrow\sim(\phi\to\chi)}
$$

Fig. 2. Rules of $\mathcal{G}$N4

$$
\Box\,\frac{\Gamma^{\Box}\Rightarrow\chi}{\Gamma\Rightarrow\Box\chi}\quad
\Diamond\,\frac{\phi\Rightarrow\chi}{\Gamma,\Diamond\phi\Rightarrow\Diamond\chi}\quad
\Box_{\sim}\,\frac{\sim\phi\Rightarrow\sim\chi}{\Gamma,\sim\Box\phi\Rightarrow\sim\Box\chi}\quad
\Diamond_{\sim}\,\frac{\Gamma^{\Diamond}_{\sim}\Rightarrow\sim\chi}{\Gamma\Rightarrow\sim\Diamond\chi}
$$

$$
\Diamond^{\pm}\,\frac{\Gamma^{\Box},\phi\Rightarrow\chi}{\Gamma,\Diamond\phi\Rightarrow\Diamond\chi}\quad
\Box^{\pm}_{\sim}\,\frac{\Gamma^{\Diamond}_{\sim},\sim\phi\Rightarrow\sim\chi}{\Gamma,\sim\Box\phi\Rightarrow\sim\Box\chi}\quad
\Diamond^{\curlyvee}\,\frac{\Gamma^{\Diamond}_{\sim},\phi\Rightarrow\chi}{\Gamma,\Diamond\phi\Rightarrow\Diamond\chi}\quad
\Box^{\curlyvee}_{\sim}\,\frac{\Gamma^{\Box},\sim\phi\Rightarrow\sim\chi}{\Gamma,\sim\Box\phi\Rightarrow\sim\Box\chi}
$$

$$
\Box^{\bowtie}\,\frac{\Gamma^{\Box},\Gamma^{\Diamond}_{\sim}\Rightarrow\chi}{\Gamma\Rightarrow\Box\chi}\quad
\Diamond^{\bowtie}\,\frac{\sim\phi\Rightarrow\chi}{\Gamma,\sim\Box\phi\Rightarrow\Diamond\chi}\quad
\Box^{\bowtie}_{\sim}\,\frac{\phi\Rightarrow\sim\chi}{\Gamma,\Diamond\phi\Rightarrow\sim\Box\chi}\quad
\Diamond^{\bowtie}_{\sim}\,\frac{\Gamma^{\Box},\Gamma^{\Diamond}_{\sim}\Rightarrow\sim\chi}{\Gamma\Rightarrow\sim\Diamond\chi}
$$

$$
\Diamond^{1}\,\frac{\Gamma^{\Box},\Gamma^{\Diamond}_{\sim},\phi\Rightarrow\chi}{\Gamma,\Diamond\phi\Rightarrow\Diamond\chi}\quad
\Box^{1}_{\sim}\,\frac{\Gamma^{\Box},\Gamma^{\Diamond}_{\sim},\sim\phi\Rightarrow\sim\chi}{\Gamma,\sim\Box\phi\Rightarrow\sim\Box\chi}\quad
\Diamond^{1,\bowtie}\,\frac{\Gamma^{\Box},\Gamma^{\Diamond}_{\sim},\sim\phi\Rightarrow\chi}{\Gamma,\sim\Box\phi\Rightarrow\Diamond\chi}
$$

$$
\Box^{1,\bowtie}_{\sim}\,\frac{\Gamma^{\Box},\Gamma^{\Diamond}_{\sim},\phi\Rightarrow\sim\chi}{\Gamma,\Diamond\phi\Rightarrow\sim\Box\chi}
$$

Fig. 3. Modal rules for CN4K-style logics

As usual, we define a $\mathcal{G}$L-*derivation* as an upwards-branching tree of sequents s.t. each node is obtained from its parents via an application of a rule from $\mathcal{G}$L. A *proof* is a finite derivation whose leaves are axioms. The *height* of a sequent in a finite derivation is the height of the corresponding node in the derivation (that is the height of the subtree rooted in that node).

Definition 13. *A rule is* height-preserving (hp) invertible *if, in case the conclusion has a proof of height at most n, so do all its premises. A rule is* height-preserving (hp) admissible *if, in case the premises have a proof of height at most n, so does the conclusion.*

We can show by induction on the complexity of a formula that

Proposition 4. *For any ϕ and Γ, $\Gamma,\phi\Rightarrow\phi$ is provable in $\mathcal{G}$L.*

Note that the context changes from the conclusion of a modal rule to its premise depending on which accessibility relations coincide. E.g., as in CN4K all four relations are distinct, the $\Box$ rule only proceeds from Γ to $\Gamma^{\Box}$. On the other hand, as $R^{+}_{\Box}=R^{-}_{\Diamond}$ in $\bowtie$-birelational frames, $\Box^{\bowtie}$ proceeds from Γ to $\Gamma^{\Box}\cup\Gamma^{\Diamond}_{\sim}$.

We show that axioms $\bowtie_{\Box}$ and $\curlyvee_{\Diamond}$ are provable in $\mathcal{G}$CN4K$^{\bowtie}$ and $\mathcal{G}$CN4K$^{\curlyvee}$,

$$\wedge_r \dfrac{\to_r \dfrac{\Diamond^{\bowtie}_{\sim} \dfrac{{\sim}{\sim}_r \dfrac{\text{Prop 4} \dfrac{}{\phi \Rightarrow \phi}}{\phi \Rightarrow {\sim}{\sim}\phi}}{\Box\phi \Rightarrow {\sim}\Diamond{\sim}\phi}}{\Rightarrow \Box\phi \to {\sim}\Diamond{\sim}\phi} \qquad \to_r \dfrac{\Box^{\bowtie} \dfrac{{\sim}{\sim}_l \dfrac{\text{Prop 4} \dfrac{}{\phi \Rightarrow \phi}}{{\sim}{\sim}\phi \Rightarrow \phi}}{{\sim}\Diamond{\sim}\phi \Rightarrow \Box\phi}}{\Rightarrow {\sim}\Diamond{\sim}\phi \to \Box\phi}}{\Rightarrow (\Box\phi \to {\sim}\Diamond{\sim}\phi) \wedge ({\sim}\Diamond{\sim}\phi \to \Box\phi)}
\qquad
\to_r \times 2 \dfrac{\Diamond^{\curlyvee} \dfrac{{\sim}{\sim}_l \dfrac{\to_l \dfrac{\text{Prop 4} \dfrac{}{\phi \to \chi, \phi \Rightarrow \phi} \qquad \text{Prop 4} \dfrac{}{\phi, \chi \Rightarrow \chi}}{\phi \to \chi, \phi \Rightarrow \chi}}{{\sim}{\sim}(\phi \to \chi), \phi \Rightarrow \chi}}{{\sim}\Diamond{\sim}(\phi \to \chi), \Diamond\phi \Rightarrow \Diamond\chi}}{\Rightarrow {\sim}\Diamond{\sim}(\phi \to \chi) \to (\Diamond\phi \to \Diamond\chi)}$$

The soundness of calculi can be shown by checking that the validity of sequents is preserved from the premises to the conclusion of every rule.

Theorem 4. *For any* L, *it holds that* $\mathcal{G}\mathsf{L} \vdash \Gamma \Rightarrow \phi$ *implies* $\mathsf{L} \models \bigwedge_{\psi \in \Gamma} \psi \to \phi$.

We prove the completeness of $\mathcal{G}\mathsf{L}$ calculi in the following section as a consequence of the admissibility of the cut rule.

$$\mathsf{cut} \dfrac{\Gamma \Rightarrow \phi \qquad \phi, \Delta \Rightarrow \chi}{\Gamma, \Delta \Rightarrow \chi}$$

5 Cut-Admissibility

In order to prove the admissibility of cut for all systems, we first observe that the calculus $\mathcal{G}\mathsf{N4}$ in Fig. 2 is a variant of the one for logic $\mathsf{N4}$ provided in [9,10]. For convenience, we refer to the latter as $\mathcal{C}\mathsf{N4}$. To compare the two calculi, in $\mathcal{C}\mathsf{N4}$, structural rules like weakening and contraction are primitive rules, initial sequents (or 'axioms') are simply $p \Rightarrow p$ and ${\sim}p \Rightarrow {\sim}p$ and $\to_l$ is of the following form where the implication formula is no longer kept in the left premise and the two premises have independent contexts Γ and Δ:

$$\to_l \dfrac{\Gamma \Rightarrow \phi \qquad \chi, \Delta \Rightarrow \psi}{\phi \to \chi, \Gamma, \Delta \Rightarrow \psi}$$

As a result, $\mathcal{C}\mathsf{N4}$ is shown to admit cut-elimination but is neither weakening-free nor contraction-free. However, with the modification on $\to_l$, we can show that both rules are *hp admissible* in $\mathcal{G}\mathsf{N4}$. This relies on the fact that the modified $\to_l$ is height-preserving invertible on the right premise and all the other left rules in $\mathcal{G}\mathsf{N4}$ are hp invertible. Besides, all the right rules except $\vee_{r_i}$ and ${\sim}\wedge_{r_i}$ are also hp invertible. We will use this property to prove cut-admissibility and obtain decidability for the logics we consider. The proof for the basic $\mathcal{G}\mathsf{N4}$ relies on cut-elimination of $\mathcal{C}\mathsf{N4}$ (see the appendix).

Proposition 5. *The following rules are height-preserving admissible in* $\mathcal{G}\mathsf{L}$*:*

$$\textit{weakening} \dfrac{\Gamma \Rightarrow \chi}{\phi, \Gamma \Rightarrow \chi} \qquad\qquad \textit{contraction} \dfrac{\phi, \phi, \Gamma \Rightarrow \chi}{\phi, \Gamma \Rightarrow \chi}$$

Let us compare rules in Fig. 3. We say that $\mathcal{R}$ is *weaker* than $\mathcal{R}'$ ($\mathcal{R} \lessdot \mathcal{R}'$) if $\mathcal{R}$ and $\mathcal{R}'$ have the same conclusion while the premise of $\mathcal{R}$ is a subset (in the sense of multiset) of that of $\mathcal{R}'$. We have the following relations:

$$\Box \lessdot \Box^{\bowtie} \qquad \Box_{\sim}^{\bowtie} \lessdot \Box_{\sim}^{1,\bowtie} \qquad \Diamond \lessdot \Diamond^{\curlyvee} \lessdot \Diamond^{1} \qquad \Box_{\sim} \lessdot \Box_{\sim}^{\pm} \lessdot \Box_{\sim}^{1}$$

$$\Diamond_{\sim} \lessdot \Diamond_{\sim}^{\bowtie} \qquad \Diamond^{\bowtie} \lessdot \Diamond^{1,\bowtie} \qquad \Diamond \lessdot \Diamond^{\pm} \lessdot \Diamond^{1} \qquad \Box_{\sim} \lessdot \Box_{\sim}^{\curlyvee} \lessdot \Box_{\sim}^{1}$$

The 'weaker' rules are derivable in calculi containing the 'stronger' rules by applying weakening to the premises.

Definition 14. *In a $\mathcal{G}\mathsf{L}$-derivation, we say an occurrence of a formula in the conclusion of an application of $\mathcal{R}$ is* side *if it is irrelevant to the rule application and also kept in one of the premises;* weak *if it is irrelevant to the rule application and does not occur in any of the premises;* principal, *otherwise.*

For example, in $\wedge_r$, formulas in Γ occur as side formulas while $\phi \wedge \chi$ is principal; in $\rightarrow_l$, formulas in Γ and formula ψ occur as side formulas while $\phi \rightarrow \chi$ is principal. In modal rules like $\Diamond^{1,\bowtie}$, formula $\Diamond\chi, {\sim}\Box\phi$ and all the $\Box$ or ${\sim}\Diamond$-prefixed formulas in Γ are principal while other formulas in Γ are weak. No side formulas occurs in any application of modal rules.

Theorem 5 (Cut-admissibility). *The* cut *rule is admissible in* $\mathcal{G}\mathsf{L}$.

Proof. We provide the proof for $\mathcal{G}\mathsf{CN4K}^1$. For other systems, a proof can be obtained by taking a subset of cases presented in this proof, as all the other rules from Fig. 3 are derivable in $\mathcal{G}\mathsf{CN4K}^1$ with applications of weakening.

For each application of cut, we associate a pair (h, d) as its *rank*, where h denotes the sum of the heights of the two premise of cut in the derivation and d denotes complexity of the cut formula. We proceed by double induction on the rank of cut. Consider a derivation $\mathcal{D}$ in $\mathcal{G}\mathsf{CN4K}^1$ that has the form

$$\dfrac{\begin{array}{c}\mathcal{D}_1\\ \Gamma \Rightarrow \phi\end{array} \qquad \begin{array}{c}\mathcal{D}_2\\ \phi, \Delta \Rightarrow \chi\end{array}}{\Gamma, \Delta \Rightarrow \chi}\ \mathsf{cut}$$

We denote the last rule application in $\mathcal{D}_1$ and $\mathcal{D}_2$ as $\mathcal{R}_1$ and $\mathcal{R}_2$ respectively and discuss possible different roles of the cut formula ϕ in $\mathcal{R}_1$ and $\mathcal{R}_2$. We omit details in the cases when both $\mathcal{R}_1$ and $\mathcal{R}_2$ are $\mathsf{N4}$ rules as they are covered by the cut-admissibility of $\mathcal{G}\mathsf{N4}$, for which the proof can be found in the appendix.

Given a cut formula ϕ, we have four cases. (1) one of the premises is an axiom; (2) ϕ is principal in *both* premises; (3) ϕ is principal in the left premise *only*; (4) ϕ is *not principal* in the left premise. We only consider the second case here while other cases are shown in the appendix.

If ϕ is a propositional formula, all cases are part of the cut-elimination of $\mathcal{G}\mathsf{N4}$. If $\phi = \Box\psi$, we have $\mathcal{R}_1 = \Box^{\bowtie}$ and $\mathcal{R}_2$ is any modal rule. All cases can be done by applying cut first and then a suitable modal rule. We only provide one example with $\mathcal{R}_1 = \Box^{\bowtie}$ and $\mathcal{R}_2 = \Box_{\sim}^{1}$ as other cases are similar. In this case, χ is some ${\sim}\Box\theta$ and $\Delta = \Sigma, {\sim}\Box\mu$. We unfold $\mathcal{D}$ and transform it as follows.

$$\dfrac{\dfrac{\dfrac{\mathcal{D}'_1}{\Gamma^{\Box}, \Gamma^{\Diamond}_{\sim} \Rightarrow \psi}}{\Gamma \Rightarrow \Box\psi}\,\Box^{\bowtie} \quad \dfrac{\dfrac{\mathcal{D}'_2}{\psi, \Sigma^{\Box}, \Sigma^{\Diamond}_{\sim}, {\sim}\mu \Rightarrow {\sim}\theta}}{\Box\psi, \Sigma, {\sim}\Box\mu \Rightarrow {\sim}\Box\theta}\,\Box^{1}_{\sim}}{\Gamma, \Sigma, {\sim}\Box\mu \Rightarrow {\sim}\Box\theta}\,\mathsf{cut} \dashrightarrow \dfrac{\dfrac{\dfrac{\mathcal{D}'_1}{\Gamma^{\Box}, \Gamma^{\Diamond}_{\sim} \Rightarrow \psi} \quad \dfrac{\mathcal{D}'_2}{\psi, \Sigma^{\Box}, \Sigma^{\Diamond}_{\sim}, {\sim}\mu \Rightarrow {\sim}\theta}}{\Gamma^{\Box}, \Gamma^{\Diamond}_{\sim}, \Sigma^{\Box}, \Sigma^{\Diamond}_{\sim}, {\sim}\mu \Rightarrow {\sim}\theta}\,\mathsf{cut}}{\Gamma, \Sigma, {\sim}\Box\mu \Rightarrow {\sim}\Box\theta}\,\Box^{1}_{\sim}$$

If $\phi = \Diamond\psi$, then $\mathcal{R}_1 \in \{\Diamond^1, \Diamond^{1,\bowtie}\}$ and $\mathcal{R}_2 \in \{\Diamond^1, \Box^{1,\bowtie}\}$. The proof for all four combinations proceeds as in the case of $\phi = \Box\psi$. The cases when $\phi = {\sim}\Box\psi$ and $\phi = {\sim}\Diamond\psi$ are dual to the cases of $\Diamond\psi$ and $\Box\psi$, respectively. $\Box$

Completeness of sequent calculi, decidability of CN4K and its extensions, and disjunctive and constructive falsity properties now follow by standard arguments from Theorem 5.

Theorem 6. $\mathsf{L} \models \bigwedge_{\psi \in \Gamma} \psi \to \phi$ *implies* $\mathcal{G}\mathsf{L} \vdash \Gamma \Rightarrow \phi$.

Theorem 7. *Validity in* CN4K *and its extensions is decidable.*

Proof. Since contraction is admissible in all calculi we can consider their set-based formulation where in a sequent $\Gamma \Rightarrow \phi$, Γ is a set rather than a multiset. All rules are 'weakly' analytical in the sense that for every rule $\mathcal{R}$ with conclusion $\Gamma \Rightarrow \phi$, all formulas occurring in the premises of $\mathcal{R}$ are either subformulas of formulas in $\Gamma \cup \{\phi\}$ or obtained by prefixing a negation-free subformula in this set with at most two $\sim$. Therefore if we consider any derivation $\mathcal{D}$ with a root sequent $\Gamma \Rightarrow \chi$, there are only finitely many distinct sequents that can occur in $\mathcal{D}$ (as they can contain only a subset of subformulas of $\Gamma \cup \{\chi\}$ and their negations $\sim$). We can w.l.o.g. restrict the proof search to derivations (let us call them 'regular') such that no branch contains the same sequent twice. As a consequence, given a sequent $\Gamma \Rightarrow \chi$, there are only finitely many regular derivations with root $\Gamma \Rightarrow \chi$. Thus the (obvious) decision procedure for $\Gamma \Rightarrow \chi$ generates subsequently each regular derivation $\mathcal{D}$ testing whether it is a proof or not and reporting Success as soon as it finds a proof or Failure after having exhausted all derivations without finding a proof. $\Box$

Theorem 8. *Let* $\mathsf{L} \in \{\mathsf{CN4K}, \mathsf{CN4K}^{\curlyvee}, \mathsf{CN4K}^{\pm}, \mathsf{CN4K}^{\bowtie}, \mathsf{CN4K}^{1}\}$. *Then:*

$$\mathsf{L} \models \phi \vee \chi \textit{ iff } \mathsf{L} \models \phi \textit{ or } \mathsf{L} \models \chi \qquad \mathsf{L} \models {\sim}(\phi \wedge \chi) \textit{ iff } \mathsf{L} \models {\sim}\phi \textit{ or } \mathsf{L} \models {\sim}\chi$$

6 Conclusion and Perspectives

There are several axes of further research. First, even though we established the decidability of CN4K logics, their exact complexity remains open. We conjecture that all our logics are PSpace-complete. It would be also instructive to construct analytic calculi that produce *counter-models* witnessing non-validity.

From a semantical perspective, a natural development would be the study of other Nelson-like paraconsistent modal logics such as those presented in [17] and [13,14]. In particular, we are interested in establishing a hierarchy of paraconsistent constructive logics corresponding to the frame conditions connecting accessibility relations and preordering of the states.

Another extension would be to consider the usual properties of the accessibility relations that characterise the epistemic, doxastic, or deontic interpretation of the modalities. In all cases, the study of semantic and axiomatic extensions should be accompanied by the development of analytic proof systems which can provide a decision procedure for the respective logics.

Appendix

Proposition 2. *There is a monorelational* CN4K *model* $\mathfrak{M}$ *and s.t.* $\mathfrak{M}, w \Vdash^+ \phi$ *for every* $\phi \in \mathcal{L}^{\sim}_{\Box,\Diamond}$ *and* $w \in \mathfrak{M}$.

Lemma 2 (Truth lemma for $\mathcal{H}$CN4K). *For every* $\phi \in \mathcal{L}^{\sim}_{\Box,\Diamond}$ *and* $\mathfrak{s} \in \mathfrak{M}^{\mathsf{C}}$, *it holds that (1)* $\mathfrak{M}^{\mathsf{C}}, \mathfrak{s} \Vdash^+ \phi$ *iff* $\phi \in \mathbf{h}(\mathfrak{s})$; *(2)* $\mathfrak{M}^{\mathsf{C}}, \mathfrak{s} \Vdash^- \phi$ *iff* $\sim\phi \in \mathbf{h}(\mathfrak{s})$.

Proof. We consider the remaining cases of modal formulas: $\phi = \Box\chi$, $\phi = \sim\Box\chi$, and $\phi = \Diamond\chi$. First, let $\phi = \Box\chi$. Again, we assume for contradiction that $\mathfrak{M}^{\mathsf{C}}, \mathfrak{s} \Vdash^+ \Box\chi$ but $\Box\chi \notin \mathbf{h}(\mathfrak{s})$. Consider $\Xi^! = \{\tau \mid \Box\tau \in \mathbf{h}(\mathfrak{s})\}$. It is clear that $\Xi^! \nvdash_{\mathcal{H}\mathsf{CN4K}} \chi$ because otherwise we would have $\mathcal{H}\mathsf{CN4K} \vdash \bigwedge \Xi' \rightarrow \chi$ for some finite subset of $\Xi^!$, whence, $\mathcal{H}\mathsf{CN4K} \vdash \Box \bigwedge\limits_{\tau' \in \Xi'} \tau' \rightarrow \Box\chi$ by $\mathbf{r}_\Box$ and $\mathcal{H}\mathsf{CN4K} \vdash \bigwedge\limits_{\tau' \in \Xi'} \Box\tau' \rightarrow \Box\chi$ using Lemma 1. But then, we would have that $\{\Box\tau' \mid \tau' \in \Xi'\} \vdash_{\mathcal{H}\mathsf{CN4K}} \Box\chi$ which contradicts the assumption that $\Box\chi \notin \mathbf{h}(\mathfrak{s})$. Thus, again, using Proposition 3, we extend $\Xi^!$ to a saturated set $\Xi^\sharp$ s.t. $\Xi^\sharp \nvdash_{\mathcal{H}\mathsf{CN4K}} \chi$ and let $\mathfrak{s}' = \langle \Xi, \{\Xi^\sharp\}, \Phi^-_\Box, \Phi^+_\Diamond, \Phi^-_\Diamond \rangle$. Now let $\mathfrak{s}''$ be a segment s.t. $\mathbf{h}(\mathfrak{s}'') = \Xi^\sharp$. Clearly, $\mathfrak{s}' R^{+\mathsf{C}}_\Box \mathfrak{s}''$ and by the induction hypothesis, $\mathfrak{M}^{\mathsf{C}}, \mathfrak{s}'' \nVdash^+ \chi$. But as $\mathfrak{s} \leq^{\mathsf{C}} \mathfrak{s}'$, we have that $\mathfrak{M}^{\mathsf{C}}, \mathfrak{s} \nVdash^+ \Box\chi$, contrary to the assumption.

Conversely, let $\Box\chi \in \mathbf{h}(\mathfrak{s})$. It follows that $\Box\chi \in \mathbf{h}(\mathfrak{s}')$ for every $\mathfrak{s}' \geq^{\mathsf{C}} \mathfrak{s}$. But then $\chi \in \mathbf{h}(\mathfrak{s}'')$ for every $\mathfrak{s}'' \in R^{+\mathsf{C}}_\Box(\mathfrak{s}')$. Hence, by the induction hypothesis, we have that $\mathfrak{M}^{\mathsf{C}}, \mathfrak{s}'' \Vdash^+ \chi$ for every such $\mathfrak{s}''$, as required.

Let $\phi = \sim\Box\chi$. We show that $\sim\Box\chi \in \mathbf{h}(\mathfrak{s})$ iff $\mathfrak{M}^{\mathsf{C}}, \mathfrak{s} \Vdash^- \Box\chi$. Assume for contradiction that $\mathfrak{M}^{\mathsf{C}}, \mathfrak{s} \Vdash^- \Box\chi$ but $\sim\Box\chi \notin \mathbf{h}(\mathfrak{s})$. Similarly to the case of $\Diamond$, we can see that $\sim\varrho \nvdash_{\mathcal{H}\mathsf{CN4K}} \sim\chi$ for every $\sim\Box\varrho \notin \mathbf{h}(\mathfrak{s})$. Indeed, otherwise, we would infer $\sim\Box\varrho \vdash_{\mathcal{H}\mathsf{CN4K}} \sim\Box\chi$ (whence, $\mathbf{h}(\mathfrak{s}) \vdash_{\mathcal{H}\mathsf{CN4K}} \sim\Box\chi$, contrary to the assumption) using $\mathbf{r}^{\sim}_\Box$ and the deduction theorem. Now, we can extend $\{\sim\varrho\}$ to a saturated set $\Xi_{\sim\varrho}$ s.t. $\Xi_{\sim\varrho} \nvdash_{\mathcal{H}\mathsf{CN4K}} \sim\chi$ and see that $\mathfrak{s}' = \left\langle \Xi, \Phi^+_\Box, \{\Xi_{\sim\varrho} \mid \sim\Box\varrho \in \Xi\}, \Phi^+_\Diamond, \Phi^-_\Diamond \right\rangle$ is a segment s.t. $\mathfrak{s}' \geq^{\mathsf{C}} \mathfrak{s}$. Moreover, $\mathfrak{s}' R^{-\mathsf{C}}_\Box \mathfrak{s}''$ implies that $\mathbf{h}(\mathfrak{s}'') = \Xi_{\sim\varrho}$ for some $\sim\varrho$. As $\sim\chi \notin \Xi_{\sim\varrho}$ for every $\Xi_{\sim\varrho}$, we have that $\mathfrak{M}^{\mathsf{C}}, \mathfrak{s}'' \nVdash^+ \sim\chi$ (whence, $\mathfrak{M}^{\mathsf{C}}, \mathfrak{s}'' \nVdash^- \chi$) for every $\mathfrak{s}'' \in R^{-\mathsf{C}}_\Box(\mathfrak{s}')$. This, however, contradicts the assumption that $\mathfrak{M}^{\mathsf{C}}, \mathfrak{s} \Vdash^- \Box\chi$.

Conversely, let $\sim\Box\chi \in \mathbf{h}(\mathfrak{s})$. Thus, for every $\mathfrak{s}' \geq^{\mathsf{C}} \mathfrak{s}$, we have $\sim\Box\chi \in \mathbf{h}(\mathfrak{s}')$, whence, $\sim\chi \in \Phi^{-\prime}_\Box$. This means that there is some $\mathfrak{s}''$ s.t. $\mathbf{h}(\mathfrak{s}'') = \Phi^{-\prime}_\Box$

(i.e., $\mathfrak{s}' R_{\Box}^{-\mathsf{C}} \mathfrak{s}''$) and $\sim\chi \in \mathbf{h}(\mathfrak{s}'')$. By the induction hypothesis, we obtain that $\mathfrak{M}^{\mathsf{C}}, \mathfrak{s}'' \Vdash^{+} \sim\chi$ and hence, $\mathfrak{M}^{\mathsf{C}}, \mathfrak{s}'' \Vdash^{-} \chi$, as required.

Let $\phi = \Diamond\chi$. Assume for contradiction that $\mathfrak{M}^{\mathsf{C}}, \mathfrak{s} \Vdash^{+} \Diamond\chi$ but $\Diamond\chi \notin \mathbf{h}(\mathfrak{s})$. Now, for $\Diamond\varrho \in \Xi$, one can see that $\varrho \nvdash_{\mathcal{H}\mathsf{CN4K}} \chi$, for otherwise we would infer $\Diamond\varrho \vdash_{\mathcal{H}\mathsf{CN4K}} \Diamond\chi$ by $\mathbf{r}_{\Diamond}$ and the deduction theorem, whence, $\Xi \vdash_{\mathcal{H}\mathsf{CN4K}} \Diamond\chi$, contrary to the assumption. Hence, using Proposition 3 we can extend $\{\varrho\}$ to a saturated set Ξ_{ϱ} s.t. $\Xi_{\varrho} \nvdash_{\mathcal{H}\mathsf{CN4K}} \chi$. Clearly, $\mathfrak{s}' = \langle \Xi, \Phi_{\Box}^{+}, \Phi_{\Box}^{-}, \{\Xi_{\varrho} \mid \Diamond\varrho \in \Xi\}, \Phi_{\Diamond}^{-} \rangle$ is a segment and $\mathfrak{s} \leq^{\mathsf{C}} \mathfrak{s}'$. Moreover, $\mathfrak{s}' R_{\Diamond}^{+\mathsf{C}} \mathfrak{s}''$ implies that $\mathbf{h}(\mathfrak{s}'') = \Xi_{\varrho}$ for some ϱ. As $\chi \notin \Xi_{\varrho}$ (for every Ξ_{ϱ}), we have by the application of the induction hypothesis, that $\mathfrak{M}^{\mathsf{C}}, \mathfrak{s}'' \nVdash^{+} \chi$ for every $\mathfrak{s}'' \in R_{\Diamond}^{+\mathsf{C}}(\mathfrak{s}')$. But this contradicts the assumption that $\mathfrak{M}^{\mathsf{C}}, \mathfrak{s} \Vdash^{+} \Diamond\chi$ as now $\mathfrak{s}'$ is the required $\leq^{\mathsf{C}}$-successor of $\mathfrak{s}$ s.t. χ is *not true* in any of its $R_{\Diamond}^{+\mathsf{C}}$-successors.

Conversely, let $\Diamond\chi \in \mathbf{h}(\mathfrak{s})$. Then for every $\mathfrak{s}' \geq^{\mathsf{C}} \mathfrak{s}$, we have that $\Diamond\chi \in \mathbf{h}(\mathfrak{s}')$, whence $\chi \in \Phi_{\Diamond}^{+\prime}$, and thus, there is some $\mathfrak{s}''$ s.t. $\mathbf{h}(\mathfrak{s}'') = \Phi_{\Diamond}^{+\prime}$ (hence, $\mathfrak{s}' R_{\Diamond}^{+\mathsf{C}} \mathfrak{s}''$) and $\chi \in \mathbf{h}(\mathfrak{s}'')$. By the induction hypothesis, we get $\mathfrak{M}^{\mathsf{C}}, \mathfrak{s}'' \Vdash^{+} \chi$, as required.□

Lemma 3. *It holds that (1)* $\mathfrak{M}^{\mathsf{C}}_{*}, \mathfrak{s} \Vdash^{+} \phi$ *iff* $\phi \in \mathbf{h}(\mathfrak{s})$, *and (2)* $\mathfrak{M}^{\mathsf{C}}_{*}, \mathfrak{s} \Vdash^{-} \phi$ *iff* $\sim\phi \in \mathbf{h}(\mathfrak{s})$, *for every* $\phi \in \mathcal{L}^{\sim}_{\Box,\Diamond}$ *and* $\mathfrak{s} \in \mathfrak{M}^{\mathsf{C}}_{*}$.

Proof. The only detail in the proof of Lemma 2 that we need to change is the treatment of modalities. For $\mathcal{H}\mathsf{CN4K}^{\bowtie}$, the difference is in the treatment of the $\Box\chi$ and $\sim\Diamond\chi$ cases. Namely, we set $\Xi^{!} = \{\tau \mid \Box\tau \in \Xi\} \cup \{\sim\sigma \mid \sim\Diamond\sigma \in \Xi\}$. Again, it is clear that $\Xi \nvdash_{\mathcal{H}\mathsf{CN4K}^{\bowtie}} \chi$. Otherwise, we would have $\Xi' \vdash_{\mathcal{H}\mathsf{CN4K}^{\bowtie}} \chi$ for some finite $\Xi' \subseteq \Xi^{!}$. But then $\mathcal{H}\mathsf{CN4K}^{\bowtie} \vdash \left(\bigwedge\limits_{\tau' \in \Xi'} \Box\tau' \wedge \bigwedge\limits_{\sim\sigma' \in \Xi'} \Box{\sim}\sigma'\right) \to \Box\chi$ using $\mathbf{r}_{\Box}$ and Lemma 1, whence, applying $\bowtie_{\Box}$ and $\mathbf{r}^{\sim}_{\Diamond}$ which give us $\Box{\sim}\sigma' \leftrightarrow \sim\Diamond{\sim}{\sim}\sigma'$ and $\sim\Diamond{\sim}{\sim}\sigma' \leftrightarrow \sim\Diamond\sigma'$, we would get $\mathcal{H}\mathsf{CN4K}^{\bowtie} \vdash \left(\bigwedge\limits_{\tau' \in \Xi'} \Box\tau' \wedge \bigwedge\limits_{\sim\sigma' \in \Xi'} \sim\Diamond\sigma'\right) \to \Box\chi$ contrary to the assumption. Note, alternatively, that due to the deductive closure of Ξ, the two halves of $\Xi^{!}$ coincide. This can be seen by showing that $\mathcal{H}\mathsf{CN4K}^{\bowtie} \vdash \sim\Diamond\psi \leftrightarrow \Box{\sim}\psi$ using $\mathbf{r}^{\sim}$ and $\bowtie_{\Box}$. Thus, if $\Xi^{\sharp}$ is a saturation of $\Xi^{!}$ s.t. $\Xi^{\sharp} \nvdash_{\mathcal{H}\mathsf{CN4K}^{\bowtie}} \chi$, $\mathfrak{s}' = \langle \Xi, \Xi^{\sharp}, \Phi_{\Box}^{-}, \Phi_{\Diamond}^{+}, \Xi^{\sharp} \rangle$ and $\mathbf{h}(\mathfrak{s}'') = \Xi^{\sharp}$, it follows that $\mathfrak{s}' R_{\Box}^{+\mathsf{C}} \mathfrak{s}''$ and $\mathfrak{s}' R_{\Diamond}^{-\mathsf{C}} \mathfrak{s}''$. Whence, $\mathfrak{M}^{\mathsf{C}}, \mathfrak{s} \nVdash^{+} \Box\chi$, as required.

The proof of the $\sim\Diamond\chi$ case is similar. The rest of the proof is the same as for $\mathcal{H}\mathsf{CN4K}$. Note also that it is possible to treat $\Diamond$ as a shorthand for $\sim\Box\sim$ and provide a mono-modal axiomatisation of $\mathsf{CN4K}^{1}$.

Let us now consider the case of $\mathcal{H}\mathsf{CN4K}^{\pm}$. Assume that $\mathfrak{s}$ is a $\pm$-segment. We show that $\Diamond\chi \in \mathbf{h}(\mathfrak{s})$ iff $\mathfrak{M}^{\mathsf{C}}, \mathfrak{s} \Vdash^{+} \Diamond\chi$. Suppose for contradiction that $\mathfrak{M}^{\mathsf{C}}, \mathfrak{s} \Vdash^{+} \Diamond\chi$ but $\Diamond\chi \notin \mathbf{h}(\mathfrak{s})$. For $\Diamond\varrho \in \Xi$, consider $\Xi^{\pm}_{\varrho} = \{\varrho\} \cup \{\tau \mid \Box\tau \in \Xi\}$ and observe that $\Xi^{\pm}_{\varrho} \nvdash_{\mathcal{H}\mathsf{CN4K}^{\pm}} \chi$ (the reasoning is the same as in Lemma 2). Thus, we extend $\Xi^{\pm}_{\varrho}$ to a saturated Ξ'_{ϱ} s.t. $\Xi'_{\varrho} \nvdash_{\mathcal{H}\mathsf{CN4K}^{\pm}} \chi$ and consider $\mathfrak{s}' = \langle \Xi, \{\Xi'_{\varrho} \mid \Diamond\varrho \in \Xi\}, \Phi_{\Box}^{-}, \{\Xi'_{\varrho} \mid \Diamond\varrho \in \Xi\}, \Phi_{\Diamond}^{-} \rangle$. It is easy to see that $\mathfrak{s}'$ is a segment s.t. $\mathfrak{s}' \geq^{\mathsf{C}} \mathfrak{s}$. The proof of the rest of the case is the same as for $\mathcal{H}\mathsf{CN4K}$. The case of $\sim\Box\chi$ is dual: we consider the saturation of $\Xi^{\pm}_{\sim\varrho} = \{\sim\varrho\} \cup \{\sim\tau \mid \sim\Diamond\tau \in \Xi\}$.

The main difference in the case of $\mathcal{H}\mathsf{CN4K}^{\curlyvee}$ is the treatment of $\Diamond$ and $\sim\Box$. For every $\Diamond\varrho \in \Xi$, we consider the saturation of $\Xi^{\curlyvee}_{\varrho} = \{\varrho\} \cup \{\sim\tau \mid \sim\Diamond\tau \in \Xi\}$. Dually, for every $\sim\Box\varrho \in \Xi$, we consider the saturation of $\Xi^{\curlyvee}_{\sim\varrho} = \{\sim\varrho\} \cup \{\tau \mid \Box\tau \in \Xi\}$. The rest of the proof is the same as for $\mathcal{H}\mathsf{CN4K}$. □

Theorem 5 (Cut-admissibility). *The* cut *rule is admissible in* $\mathcal{G}\mathsf{L}$.

Proof. We first show the cut-admissibility for $\mathcal{G}\mathsf{N4}$. We establish the proof by transforming an arbitrary derivation in $\mathcal{G}\mathsf{N4}+\mathsf{cut}$ into another one in $\mathcal{G}\mathsf{N4}$ without applications of cut. The transformation is further divided into the following steps: (1) from $\mathcal{G}\mathsf{N4}+\mathsf{cut}$ to $\mathcal{C}\mathsf{N4}+\mathsf{cut}$; (2) from $\mathcal{C}\mathsf{N4}+\mathsf{cut}$ to $\mathcal{C}\mathsf{N4}$; (3) from $\mathcal{C}\mathsf{N4}$ to $\mathcal{G}\mathsf{N4}$. (2) is due to the fact that $\mathcal{C}\mathsf{N4}$ has cut-admissibility [9], thus it suffices to show (1) and (3). For (1), to transform a derivation $\mathcal{D}$ in $\mathcal{G}\mathsf{N4}+\mathsf{cut}$, we keep all the other rule applications and only need to modify axioms and $\rightarrow_l$. Recall weakening and contraction are primitive rules in $\mathcal{C}\mathsf{N4}$, thus we have

$$(\sim)p, \Gamma \Rightarrow (\sim)p \quad \dashrightarrow \quad w\,\frac{(\sim)p \Rightarrow (\sim)p}{(\sim)p, \Gamma \Rightarrow (\sim)p}$$

$$\rightarrow_l \frac{\phi \rightarrow \chi, \Gamma \Rightarrow \phi \qquad \chi, \Gamma \Rightarrow \psi}{\phi \rightarrow \chi, \Gamma \Rightarrow \psi} \quad \dashrightarrow \quad c\,\frac{\rightarrow_l \dfrac{\phi \rightarrow \chi, \Gamma \Rightarrow \phi \qquad \chi, \Gamma \Rightarrow \psi}{\phi \rightarrow \chi, \phi \rightarrow \chi, \Gamma \Rightarrow \psi}}{\phi \rightarrow \chi, \Gamma \Rightarrow \psi}$$

For (3), note that initial sequents in $\mathcal{C}\mathsf{N4}$ are also initial in $\mathcal{G}\mathsf{N4}$, and for an application of $\rightarrow_l$, we have

$$\rightarrow_l \frac{\Gamma \Rightarrow \phi \qquad \chi, \Delta \Rightarrow \psi}{\phi \rightarrow \chi, \Gamma, \Delta \Rightarrow \psi} \quad \dashrightarrow \quad \rightarrow_l \frac{w\,\dfrac{\Gamma \Rightarrow \phi}{\phi \rightarrow \chi, \Gamma, \Delta \Rightarrow \phi} \qquad w\,\dfrac{\chi, \Delta \Rightarrow \psi}{\chi, \Gamma, \Delta \Rightarrow \psi}}{\phi \rightarrow \chi, \Gamma, \Delta \Rightarrow \psi}$$

In this way, we obtain a derivation in $\mathcal{G}\mathsf{N4}$ with (possibly) applications of weakening and contraction. According to Proposition 5, weakening and contraction are admissible in $\mathcal{G}\mathsf{N4}$, thus we can further eliminate these applications and in the end, obtain one derivation in $\mathcal{G}\mathsf{N4}$.

Next, we finish the proof of cut-admissibility of $\mathcal{G}\mathsf{CN4K}^{1}$. It remains to consider the first, third, and fourth cases.

If $\phi \in \{p, \sim p\}$ for some $p \in \mathsf{Prop}$ and $\phi \in \Gamma$, we obtain the conclusion $\Gamma, \Delta \Rightarrow \chi$ from the right premise $\phi, \Delta \Rightarrow \chi$ by weakening. If $\phi \in \{p, \sim p\}$ for some $p \in \mathsf{Prop}$ and $\phi = \chi$, we obtain the conclusion $\Gamma, \Delta \Rightarrow \chi$ from the left premise $\Gamma \Rightarrow \phi$ by weakening. Otherwise, $\Delta \Rightarrow \chi$ is an axiom, we apply weakening to it and obtain the conclusion as required.

In the **third case**, ϕ is principal in the left premise *only*. If ϕ is *weak* in the right premise, which means $\mathcal{R}_2$ is one of the modal rules and is neither $\Box$-prefixed nor $\sim\Diamond$-prefixed. We obtain the conclusion of cut from the right premise directly. For example, if $\mathcal{R}_2 = \Box^{\bowtie}$ and $\chi = \Box\theta$, we transform the derivation as follows:

$$\dfrac{\begin{array}{c}\mathcal{D}_1\\ \Gamma \Rightarrow \phi\end{array} \qquad \Box^{\bowtie}\dfrac{\begin{array}{c}\mathcal{D}'_2\\ \Delta^{\Box}, \Delta^{\Diamond}_{\sim} \Rightarrow \theta\end{array}}{\phi, \Delta \Rightarrow \Box\theta}}{\Gamma, \Delta \Rightarrow \Box\theta}\,\mathsf{cut} \quad \dashrightarrow \quad w\dfrac{\Box^{\bowtie}\dfrac{\begin{array}{c}\mathcal{D}'_2\\ \Delta^{\Box}, \Delta^{\Diamond}_{\sim} \Rightarrow \theta\end{array}}{\Delta \Rightarrow \Box\theta}}{\Gamma, \Delta \Rightarrow \Box\theta}$$

If ϕ is *side* in the right premise, note that there are no side formulas in a modal rule, so $\mathcal{R}_2$ is a rule in $\mathcal{G}\mathsf{N4}$. By the invertibility of $\mathcal{G}\mathsf{N4}$ rules, we unfold $\mathcal{D}$ and transform it as follows:

$$\dfrac{\begin{array}{c}\mathcal{D}_1\\ \Gamma \Rightarrow \phi\end{array} \qquad \mathcal{R}_2\dfrac{\begin{array}{c}\mathcal{D}'_2\\ \phi, \Delta' \Rightarrow \chi'\end{array}}{\phi, \Delta \Rightarrow \chi}}{\Gamma, \Delta \Rightarrow \chi}\,\mathsf{cut} \quad \dashrightarrow \quad \mathcal{R}_2\dfrac{\dfrac{\begin{array}{c}\mathcal{D}_1\\ \Gamma \Rightarrow \phi\end{array} \qquad \begin{array}{c}\mathcal{D}'_2\\ \phi, \Delta' \Rightarrow \chi'\end{array}}{\Gamma, \Delta' \Rightarrow \chi'}\,\mathsf{cut}}{\Gamma, \Delta \Rightarrow \chi}$$

Finally, in the **fourth case**, ϕ is *not principal* in the left premise. Since sequents have only one formula on the right, ϕ can only occur as *side* formula in the application of $\mathcal{R}_1$, which implies $\mathcal{R}_1$ must be a left rule in the basic calculus $\mathcal{G}\mathsf{N4}$ (for $\rightarrow_l$ only occur as side formula in the right branch). We have the following general form of $\mathcal{D}$ that we transform as shown below (weakening is omitted):

$$\dfrac{\mathcal{R}_1\dfrac{\begin{array}{c}\mathcal{D}'_1\\ \Gamma' \Rightarrow \phi\end{array}}{\Gamma \Rightarrow \phi} \qquad \begin{array}{c}\mathcal{D}_2\\ \phi, \Delta \Rightarrow \chi\end{array}}{\Gamma, \Delta \Rightarrow \chi}\,\mathsf{cut} \quad \dashrightarrow \quad \mathcal{R}_1\dfrac{\dfrac{\begin{array}{c}\mathcal{D}'_1\\ \Gamma' \Rightarrow \phi\end{array} \qquad \begin{array}{c}\mathcal{D}_2\\ \phi, \Delta \Rightarrow \chi\end{array}}{\Gamma', \Delta \Rightarrow \chi}\,\mathsf{cut}}{\Gamma, \Delta \Rightarrow \chi}$$

This completes the proof. □

Theorem 6. *$\mathsf{L} \models \bigwedge_{\psi \in \Gamma} \psi \rightarrow \phi$ implies $\mathcal{G}\mathsf{L} \vdash \Gamma \Rightarrow \phi$.*

Proof. The completeness is obtained as follows. $\mathcal{H}\mathsf{L}$-axioms can be proved in the corresponding $\mathcal{G}\mathsf{L}$ (cf. Sect. 4 for examples). The modal rules can be derived by corresponding rules in $\mathcal{G}\mathsf{L}$ with the invertibility of $\rightarrow_r$. Finally, **mp** can be simulated via the cut rule which is admissible by Theorem 5. □

References

1. Alechina, N., Mendler, M., de Paiva, V., Ritter, E.: Categorical and Kripke semantics for constructive S4 modal logic. In: Fribourg, L. (ed.) CSL 2001. LNCS, vol. 2142, pp. 292–307. Springer, Heidelberg (2001). https://doi.org/10.1007/3-540-44802-0_21
2. Balbiani, P., Gao, H., Gencer, Ç., Olivetti, N.: A natural intuitionistic modal logic: axiomatization and bi-nested calculus. In: 32nd EACSL Annual Conference on Computer Science Logic (CSL 2024). Leibniz International Proceedings in Informatics (LIPIcs), vol. 288, pp. 13:1–13:21. Schloss Dagstuhl — Leibniz-Zentrum für Informatik (2024)
3. Bellin, G., Paiva, V.D., Ritter, E.: Extended Curry-Howard correspondence for a basic constructive modal logic. In: Proceedings of Methods for Modalities, vol. 2 (2001)
4. Dalmonte, T., Grellois, C., Olivetti, N.: Terminating calculi and countermodels for constructive modal logics. In: Das, A., Negri, S. (eds.) TABLEAUX 2021. LNCS (LNAI), vol. 12842, pp. 391–408. Springer, Cham (2021). https://doi.org/10.1007/978-3-030-86059-2_23
5. Dalmonte, T., Grellois, C., Olivetti, N.: Towards an intuitionistic deontic logic tolerating conflicting obligations. In: Ciabattoni, A., Pimentel, E., Queiroz, R.D. (eds.) Logic, Language, Information, and Computation — 28th International Workshop, WoLLIC 2022, pp. 280–294. Springer (2022)
6. Došen, K.: Models for stronger normal intuitionistic modal logics. Stud. Logica **44**(1), 39–70 (1985)
7. Fisher Servi, G.: Semantics for a class of intuitionistic modal calculi. In: Dalla Chiara, M. (ed.) Italian Studies in the Philosophy of Science, pp. 59–72. Springer, Netherlands (1980)
8. Fitch, F.: Intuitionistic modal logic with quantifiers. J. Symb. Logic **14**(4) (1950)
9. Kamide, N., Wansing, H.: Proof theory of Nelson's paraconsistent logic: a uniform perspective. Theoret. Comput. Sci. **415**, 1–38 (2012)
10. López-Escobar, E.: Refutability and elementary number theory. Indagationes Mathematicae (Proceedings) **75**(4), 362–374 (1972)
11. Mendler, M., Paiva, V.D.: Constructive CK for contexts. In: Context Representation and Reasoning (CRR-2005), vol. 13. Citeseer (2005)
12. Nelson, D.: Constructible falsity. J. Symb. Logic **14**(1), 16–26 (1949)
13. Odintsov, S., Wansing, H.: Inconsistency-tolerant description logic: motivation and basic systems. Stud. Logica. **31**, 301–335 (2003)
14. Odintsov, S., Wansing, H.: Inconsistency-tolerant description logic. Part II: a tableau algorithm for $\mathcal{CALCC}^{\mathsf{C}}$. J. Appl. Logic **6**(3), 343–360 (2008)
15. Paiva, V.: Natural deduction and context as (constructive) modality. In: Blackburn, P., Ghidini, C., Turner, R.M., Giunchiglia, F. (eds.) CONTEXT 2003. LNCS (LNAI), vol. 2680, pp. 116–129. Springer, Heidelberg (2003). https://doi.org/10.1007/3-540-44958-2_10
16. Prawitz, D.: An interpretation of intuitionistic predicate logic in modal logic. In: Contributions to Mathematical Logic, Proceedings of the Logic Colloquium (1966)
17. Sherkhonov, E.: Modal operators over constructive logic. J. Log. Comput. **18**(6), 815–829 (2008)
18. Simpson, A.: The proof theory and semantics of intuitionistic modal logic. Ph.D. thesis, University of Edinburgh. College of Science and Engineering. School of Informatics (1994)

19. Wansing, H.: Constructive negation, implication, and co-implication. J. Appl. Non-Classical Logics **18**(2–3), 341–364 (2008). https://doi.org/10.3166/jancl.18.341-364
20. Wijesekera, D.: Constructive modal logics I. Ann. Pure Appl. Logic **50**(3), 271–301 (1990)
21. Williamson, T.: On intuitionistic modal epistemic logic. J. Philos. Log. **21**(1), 63–89 (1992)

Denotation of Sentential Complements

R. Zuber(✉)

CNRS, Paris, France
Richard.Zuber@linguist.univ-paris-diderot.fr

Abstract. It is proposed that sentential complements such as *that S* or *whether S* denote sentential quantifiers where a sentential quantifier is a set of sentential predicates (like *is a rumour, is strongly believed*) and a sentential predicate is a set of (declarative) sentences. Some properties of sentential predicates are studied and an analogy with nominal quantifiers is pointed out. An application to the analysis of questions (interrogative sentences) is made. Questions are rogative sentential predicates (which are semantically defined). No reference to possible worlds is made in the proposed analysis.

1 Introduction

The ontological richness of natural languages in conjunction with methodological principles of simplicity and adequacy makes it that the question concerning basic logical types and the type forming mechanisms is still open (cf. Sutton 2024). For instance, to take a very simple example, the fact that in natural languages some expressions can apply (as syntactic functional expressions) to various expressions each of which is of different category is well-known. A good example of such "categorially ambiguous" expressions are the negative particle *not* and the conjunction *and*: they can apply to verbs, noun phrases, determiners, adjectives, adverbs, etc. In order to account for such facts, classical categorial grammar has been extended by rules and principles allowing for the semantic flexibility of grammatical categories. According to these principles a grammatical category can be interpreted not only by its basic type but also additionally, in some contexts, by various types obtained by specific derivational rules usually logically or empirically justified (see van Benthem 1986 for some discussion).

A well-known rule allowing for such a multiple type assignment is the lifting rule proposed by Montague (1974) and indicated in (1):

(1) If an expression is interpreted in a type a then it may also be interpreted in any type of the form $\langle\langle a, b\rangle, b\rangle\rangle$, for any type b.

When a in (1) corresponds to e - the type in which denote proper names and b corresponds to t - the type of sentences, then rule (1) lifts proper names (in the subject position) from type e to type $\langle\langle e, t\rangle, t\rangle\rangle$. Consequently proper names can be said to denote also sets of sets of entities that is type $\langle 1\rangle$ quantifiers in the same way as quantified noun phrases. This fact has been explicitly used

D. Kozen and R. de Queiroz (Eds.): WoLLIC 2025, LNCS 15942, pp. 89–100, 2026.
https://doi.org/10.1007/978-3-031-99536-1_6

by Partee (1987) to account for the fact that NPs (in English) can have three different interpretations: they can be used as referring expressions, in (2a), as predicates, in (2b), and as quantified NPs, in (2c):

(2) a. The logician smiled
   b. Dan is a logician
   c. Most logicians are funny

Montague lift of proper names is sometimes said to be based on the Leibnitz's principle which identifies an entity with the set of properties it has. Its mathematical justification is obviously the fact that an element belongs to a set if and only if this set belongs to the ultra-filter generated by this element.

Observe that the type shifting rule (1) can be iterated, that is it can apply to already shifted types. In particular rule (1) says that any expression of type $\langle\langle e,t\rangle,t\rangle\rangle$ can also have the type $\langle\langle\langle e,t\rangle,t\rangle\rangle,t\rangle\rangle t\rangle\rangle$. This means that we can lift not only noun phrases (in the subject position) but also verb phrases VPs (or predicates). In this case a verb phrase which denotes before the lift in the type $\langle e,t\rangle$ will denote after the lift, in the type $\langle\langle e,t\rangle,t\rangle\rangle,t\rangle\rangle$. Thus a verb phrase can also denote a set of type $\langle 1\rangle$ quantifiers. In this case a sentence of the form $NP + VP$ is true iff the quantifier denoted by the NP belongs to the set of quantifiers denoted by the (lifted) VP.

Interestingly some complex verb phrases also seem to necessitate their lift. It has been shown in Zuber (2017) that verb phrases formed with "higher order noun phrases" in the object position such as *the same CN*, where *CN* is a common noun, need to be lifted in order to account for some of their logical properties. Similarly with complex verb phrases formed with the reciprocal pronoun *each other* used in the subject position (see Zuber 2016, Chow 2023).

In this article I make a proposal in which the lift will be used to analyse semantically a complex syntactic category similar in many respects to (nominal) NPs. The category that will be studied is the category of sentential complement corresponding in (3) to the *that*-complement *that life is sad*:

(3) That life is sad is true

Sentential complements occur in particular with verbs of propositional attitudes and their analysis is related to various traditional problems in the formal semantics and the philosophy of language. I present an analysis without making use of possible worlds and using a version of rule (1) applied to the category S of sentences.

2 Sentential Categories

We are interested in the possibility of lifting sentences and such lift can occur in sentential categories. Sentential complements also occur with sentential categories. Informally, sentential categories are grammatical categories which explicitly contain (declarative) sentences as their part and, also, grammatical categories whose syntax and semantics depend on such categories. Declarative sentences occurring as parts of mother sentences can have a "degenerated" form We distinguish sentential noun phrases, SNPs for short, on the one hand, from sentential predicates, SPRs for short, on the other hand. The fact that the grammatical subject of a sentence can be occupied by expressions which are not typical NPs, that is (complex) expressions which do not denote type ⟨1⟩ quantifiers, is well-known. Such non-standard noun phrase-like expressions are precisely SNPs, and typical SNPs that we will first consider are constituted by sentences headed by complementizers *that* and the complementizer *whether*. In order to form a sentence, SNPs have to go with specific SPRs. When SPRs are unary, SNPs play the role of sentential subjects. SPRs can also be binary and in this case SNPs can additionally occur in the (direct) object position of the sentence.

Let us see some examples. In (4) we have a sentence with the SNP *that life is sad* in the subject position and with SPRs such as *is a rumour/is true/a serious hypothesis*, and in (5) we have a sentence with the SNP *whether life is sad* in the subject position and a sentential predicate *is not known/is being investigated*. SNPs occurring on the direct object position will be called sentential complements; when they are of the form *whether S*, they will be called (polar) *interrogative complements*:

(4) That life is sad is a rumour/true/a serious hypothesis/a myth.

(5) Whether life is sad is not known/is being investigated.

In (6) and (7) we have binary sentential predicates:

(6) That life is sad is more probable than that life is not sad.

(7) Whether life is sad depends on whether logic is funny.

The above examples are clear from purely syntactic point of view since SNP contains a standard form of declarative sentences. We want to consider also indirect non-declaratives as being susceptible to "sentential syntactic analysis". and such complex sentences may contain "degenerated" embedded sentences as their part. For instance sentences corresponding to embedded imperatives and embedded exclamatives are usually given in a "degenerated" form. Since we are not interested in the internal structure of simple sentences we will accept that embedded sentences can have such a "degenerated" form.

As in the case of ordinary predicates one can distinguish nominal predicates formed from sentential common noun phrases or adjectives preceded by a copula such as *is a truth, is a fake truth, is a rumour, is a an interesting result, is a bad prediction, is interesting*, etc. from "purely verbal" sentential predicates which contain in particular an "ordinary" noun phrase in the subject position. I will consider in particular that verbs of propositional attitude with their (grammatical) subject taking a sentential complement form also SPRs. This is the case in (8), (9) and (10):

(8) Dan believes/suspects that life is sad.

(9) Dan wonders/forgot whether life is said.

(10) That life is sad is suspected/believed by Dan.

In (8) the SPR is *Dan believes*, in (9) - *Dan wonders/forgot* and in (10) - *is suspected by Dan/is believed by Dan.*

In addition to sentential complements of the form *that S* or *whether S* there are also SNPs with overt quantifiers occurring in them such as *everything Dan wrote, whatever Bo believes, much more than Ed conjectured* or even *nothing that Bo said/believes except that life is sad* as it occurs in (11).

(11) Dan believes nothing that Bo said/believes except that life is sad.

It seems quite natural to suppose that such SNPs should be assigned to the same category as SNPs with the complementizers *that* and *whether.* Though such complex SNPs will not be analysed here I mention their existence in order to indicate the analogy with many aspects of the generalised quantifier theory.

In order to form a (complex) sentence (containing sentential categories), SNPs have to go with sentential predicates. There are many syntactic ways of forming SPRs, not all of them being equally productive. I mention only two types of SPRs: those formed from sentential common nouns (SCNs) and those formed from verbs taking sentential complements. SCN are expressions like *truth, fact, strange assumption, possibility, necessity, usual rumour and frequent belief, something obvious*, etc. When preceded by a copula (possibly with an indefinite article) SCNs form SPRs. An SNP following an SPR it will be called a *sentential complement* or SC.

To be able to discuss some semantic aspects of complex sentences we need to present the syntactic relations that exist between various sentential categories. For simplicity we distinguish the category of simple sentences S from the category of complex sentences CSS: simple sentences do not contains sentential categories. The general syntactic form of complex sentences is indicated by the rule in (12) and the rule in (13) indicates the syntactic structure of one type of SNP (where + is the concatenation sign)

(12) $CSS = SNP + SPR.$

(13) $SNP = COMP + S.$

The category $COMP$ corresponds in English to items like *that* or *whether.* which are called *complementizers.* In the domain of declarative sentences complementizers allow us to make a difference between whole sentential complements and the sentences occurring in such complements. In classical logical theories of attitude reports, which usually involve sentential predicates, initiated by Hintikka (1969), no semantic difference between whole sentential complements and the sentences they contain has been made and thus no meaning has been assigned to the complementizer *that* (cf. Thomason 1980). More linguistically oriented work shows that there is not only a syntactic difference between SNPs and sentences related to them, that is between for instance *that (S)* and *S*. Consider the following examples (Zuber, forthcoming):

(14) a. Dan believes that (either) life is sad or the earth is flat.

b. Dan believes that life is sad or that the earth is flat.

(15) Dan believes that life is sad or Dan believes that the earth is flat.

There is a clear semantic difference between (14a) and (14b): (14a) says that Dan believes that a certain disjunction holds; (he may have no opinion of which disjunct is in true and (14b) indicates that Dan believes one of the disjuncts. For this reason (15) is a paraphrase of (14b) and not of (14a). The following examples illustrate this difference in the context of the verb *to know*:

(16) a. Dan knows that life is sad or life is not sad.
b. Dan knows that life is sad or that life is not sad

Only (16a) indicates that Dan knows a logical truth

Thus complementizers will play an essential role in our analysis of sentential predicates characterising different types of non-declaratives. As we will see they will allow us to make the semantic difference between non-declarative sentences and sentences on which these non-declaratives are based.

Among sentential predicates we will essentially analyse SPRs formed from verbs, in particular verbs expressing propositional attitudes. Such SPRs will be treated as syntactically (and, to some extent, semantically) in-decomposable wholes even if all of them will contain a subject NP given in the form of a proper name. Among SPRs formed from SCN we will consider *is a truth/is true* which will be denoted by T. We will also use predicates K and K_a with their traditional meaning *It is known* and *a knows*.

The fact that we will consider only sentential predicates with proper nouns in the subject position should not be considered as an important restriction because the denotation of any NP is a Boolean combination of denotations of some proper nouns. In other words any type $\langle 1 \rangle$ quantifier is a Boolean combination of some individuals (cf. Keenan and Faltz 1985).

In the next section we define denotational algebras for different sentential categories and distinguish semantically various sub-classes of SPRs.

3 Denotations of Sentential Categories

Following Zuber (2023), the universe from which we construct the denotations of sentential predicates (and, indirectly, of SNPs) is formed from (declarative) sentences of a given, fixed, natural language. Strictly speaking, not all sentences will belong to the universe of our model. We will exclude sentences with free variables, with indexicals and sentences with externally bound pronouns. In addition many sentences should be "identified". For instance we identify sentences with an even number of negations with corresponding sentences without negation (in the same clause) or sentences with conjunctions (but without anaphors) which differ just by the order of conjuncts. This means that the universe of our model will contain non-negated sentences, say, S and negated sentences with only one main negation sign, noted nS.

Let Σ be such a simplified set of sentences. Denotations of SPRs and of SNPs will be constructed from elements of the power set algebra of Σ and $\wp(\Sigma)$ can be considered as a Boolean algebra whose elements are sets of sentences and Boolean operations correspond to operations on sets. The unit of this algebra is the set Σ itself and the zero element is the empty set. Entailment corresponds to set inclusion between sets of sentences.

Sentential predicates will be interpreted as sets of sentences, sub-sets of the universe Σ given by the "simplified" set of sentences. Thus any set of sentences is (the denotation of) a sentential predicate. For instance the sentential predicate *is true* denotes a set of true sentences and the predicate *Dan believes* corresponds to the set of sentences that Dan believes to be true. This approach avoids in particular the problem of intensionality of SPRs formed from verbs of propositional attitude (cf. Zuber 2023).

Since SPRs are sets of Boolean objects they have two negations, the Boolean complement and the post-complement which corresponds to the set of their negated elements. More precisely:

Definition 1. *Let P be a sentential predicate. Then $\neg P$, the Boolean complement of P is defined as $\neg P = \{S : S \notin P\}$. The post-complement of P, noted $P\neg$, is defined as $P\neg = \{nS : S \in P\} \cup \{S : nS \in P\}$.*

The notion of post-complement corresponds to the negation of the sentential argument of a sentence forming operator. It will be used to determine various properties of sentential predicates. For instance the relationship between the predicates K_a and KW_a can be expressed, as we will see, with the help of the post-complement as $KW_a = K_a \cup K_a\neg$ (where $S \in KW$ corresponds to *a knows whether* S).

A natural class of SPRs corresponds to consistent predicates:

Definition 2. *A sentential predicate P is consistent, $P \in CNST$, iff for no sentence S it is the case that $S \in P$ and $nS \in P$.*

SPRs formed from verbs of propositional attitude are in general consistent, This is not the case with some predicates formed from SCNs, For instance (17a) and (17b) are not contradictory:

(17) a. That life is sad is a plausible hypothesis
 b. That life is not sad is a plausible hypothesis

Post-negation of a SPR can be used to define a class of sentential predicates called *midpoint* predicates (Zuber 2023):

Definition 3. *A sentential predicate P is a midpoint predicate, $P \in MPP$, iff $P = P\neg$.*

It follows from the definition of the post-complement that MPP predicates can be defined as in Fact 1:

Fact 1. $P \in MPP$ *iff* $\forall_S (S \in P) \equiv (nS \in P)$.

Observe first that, given the properties of the post-complement and definition D2, the set of MPP operators is closed under Boolean operations and the post-complement. Consequently, given that the unit element Σ and the zero element 0_Σ are MPPs it the set of MPP predicates forms an atomic Boolean algebra, a sub-algebra of $\wp(\Sigma)$. Atoms of this algebra are sets $\{S, nS\}$, for any $S \in \Sigma$. We will use this fact in the next section when discussing the denotation of SNPs headed by the complementizer *whether*.

Facts 1 allows us to show that MPPs are specific unions and intersections of sets of sentences as indicated in Fact 2 (Zuber 2023):

Fact 2. *A sentential predicate* P_1 *is an* MPP *predicate iff there exists a sentential predicate* P_2 *such that* $P_1 = P_2 \cup P_2\neg$ *(or* $P_1 = P_2 \cap P_2\neg$*).*

Clearly non-empty MPPs are not consistent. They are, however, "strongly" inconsistent in the sense that for every sentence S that they contain they contain also its negation nS. We will consider that all sentential predicates in which an implicit reference to a human is made are either consistent or midpoint. If an agent has a contradictory thought or belief this does not mean that she/he thinks or believes that some sentence and its negation are true.

Among sentential predicates we distinguish the class of *intensional* predicates. They are defined as follows:

Definition 4. P *is intensional,* $P \in INT$*, iff* $P \neq \emptyset$ *and* $\forall S \in P \exists S_0 (v(S) = v(S_0)) \wedge S_0 \notin P$*, where* $v(S)$ *is the truth-value of* S*.*

Definition 4 says that a sentential predicate is intensional if and only if it is not empty and for any of its members (which is a sentence) there exists a logically equivalent sentence which does not belong to the predicate. For instance predicates Σ, T and $\emptyset$ are not intensional.

We divide intensional predicates into mixed and non-mixed predicates:

Definition 5. *An intensional predicate* P *is mixed,* $P \in MIX$*, iff* $P \cap T \neq \emptyset$ *and* $P \cap \neg T \neq \emptyset$

Veridical SPR, that is predicates P such that $P \subseteq T$, are not mixed.

For intensional predicates we define their *intensional negation* $\sim$:

Definition 6. *Let* $P \in INT$*. Then* $\sim P$*, the intensional negation of* P *is defined as follows:* $\sim P = \neg P \cap U$ *if* $P \in MIX$*,* $\sim P = \neg P \cap U \cap T$ *if* $P \subseteq T$ *and* $\sim P = \neg P \cap U \cap \neg T$ *if* $P \subseteq \neg T$*.*

An important subset of INT is the set $FACT$ of factive predicates:

Definition 7. $P \in FACT$ *iff* $P \subseteq T$ *and* $\sim P \subseteq T$*.*

For veridical intensional predicates we have (Zuber, forthcoming):

Fact 3. *If* $P \in INT$ *and* P *is veridical (that is* $P \subseteq T$*) then* P *is factive.*

What is the denotation of the sentential noun phrase *that* S? The basic idea uses the observation that the property expressed by the predicate *to be true (sentence)* can be equivalently expressed as *be a member of the set of true sentences.* This is in agreement with the fact that in an (extended) categorial grammar the syntactic counterpart of the operation of lifting permits to replace the rule of syntactic composition (i) in (18) by the rule (ii) in (18):

(18) (i) $S/S + S$; (ii) $(S/S) + S/(S/S)$

This category change is done for syntactic and semantic reasons. Syntactically, we want to interpret complex sentences (indirect non-declaratives) as sequences of SNP and SPR (or of SPR and SNPs). Semantically, sentential predicates will be interpreted as sets of sentences and sentential noun phrases will be interpreted as sets of sentential predicates. Sets of sentential predicates, that is denotations of SNPs (which are, thus, sets of sets of sentences) will be called sentential quantifiers. Consequently the (complex) sentence given in (19a) will be true iff the condition given in (19b) is satisfied:

(19) a. $SNP + SPR$.
  b. The set of sentences denoted by SPR is a member of the quantifier denoted by SNP.

The denotation of sentential complements is determined by their category: since they are of category S/SPR they denote a set of sentential predicates. The denotation of the sentential complement headed by the complementizet *that* is defined as follows:

Definition 8. *The SNP* that S, *where* S *is a sentence, denotes the sentential quantifier* $THAT(S)$ *defined as follows:* $THAT(S) = \{P : P \in SPR \wedge S \in P\}$.

Thus *that* S denotes a set of sentential predicates each of which contains S.

Observe that there is an interesting analogy between "ordinary" predicates and "ordinary" NPs on the one hand, and SPRs and sentential complements on the other hand. Indeed, in the generalised quantifier theory, enriched by Montague's insight concerning the interpretation of proper names, subject NPs are interpreted as sets of "ordinary" predicates or as type $\langle 1 \rangle$ quantifiers. Thus, by analogy, SNPs will denote sets of sentential predicates, that is sets of sets of sentences. It follows from this that the denotational algebra of sentential predicates is the Boolean algebra $\wp(\Sigma)$. Similarly, the SNPs denote *sentential quantifiers*, which are elements of the algebra $\wp(\wp(\Sigma))$.

Technically this means that the SNP *that S* denotes the ultra-filter, generated by $\{S\}$, in the algebra of sentential predicates. In other words, *that* S is like a Montagovian individual: it is a function from the algebra of SPRs to the algebra $\{0, 1\}$. This function is a homomorphism. Consequently the following facts hold:

Fact 4. *(i)* $P \notin THAT(S)$ *iff* $\neg P \in THAT(S)$, *(ii)* $P_1 \cap P_2 \in THAT(S)$ *iff* $P_1 \in THAT(S) \wedge P_2 \in THAT(S)$, *(iii)* $P_1 \cup P_2 \in THAT(S)$ *iff* $P_1 \in THAT(S) \vee P_2 \in THAT(S)$.

The fact that *that*-complements may denote a kind of individual has been often advocated for by philosophers, though usually in metaphorical terms.

The second consequence of D8 is indicated in:

Fact 5. *The sentence* That S is true *is true iff S is true.*

There is thus a one-to-one correspondence between the sentence S and the sentential individual denoted by *that S*, We will use this observation to explain the fact that declarative sentences can be conjoined with interrogative sentences and that the conjunction thus obtained entails each of its conjuncts, even if these conjuncts are of different "sentential" category.

4 An Application: Interrogatives with Declaratives

I will apply now the notion of sentential quantifier to the analysis of interrogatives (questions) and to the analysis of complex expressions in which interrogative and declarative sentences co-occur as Boolean compounds. It will also be shown that some intuitively natural logical relations between two interrogative sentences can be easily described with the help of the notion of sentential quantifier since sentential individuals and denotations of interrogatives are sentential quantifiers.

One of the thing we will try to explain is the fact that a conjunction of a declarative sentence with an interrogative one is possible and consequently we want such a conjunction entails every of its conjuncts: (20) entails, in the sense to be specified below, (21) (i) and (21) ii):

(20) Life is sad but is Dan sad?

(21) (i) Life is sad, (ii) Is Dan sad?

As we have seen the sentential quantifier $THAT(S)$ is characterised by the set of sentential predicates and, informally, in linguistic terminology, these predicates form "indirect declarative sentences" in which sentential complements headed by sentential quantifiers are embedded. For instance if (8) is true then one of the SPR which characterises the sentential predicate *that life is sad* is the predicate *Dan believes.*

Since questions (interrogatives) can also be embedded we can similarly consider that predicates forming indirect questions characterise questions which are embedded in them: if (9) is true then the SPR *Dan wonders* is one of the predicates which characterise the embedded interrogative *whether life is sad.*

The general form of the function denoting an SNPs headed by the complementizer *whether* is given in Definition 9 (cf. Zuber, forthcoming):

Definition 9. *The SNP* whether S *denotes the sentential quantifier* $WH(S)$ *defined as follows:* $WH(S) = \{P : P \in CNST \wedge (S \in P \vee nS \in P)\} \cup \{P \in MPP \wedge (S \in P \wedge nS \in P)\}$

The following fact is an obvious consequence of Definition 9 (Zuber, forthcoming):

Fact 6. $WH(S) = WH(nS)$.

According to definition D9 the set of predicates denoted by the *whether* complement can be divided into two (disjoint) sub-sets: a set of consistent and a set of inconsistent predicates. Every predicate in the sub-set of consistent predicates contains the sentence S or the sentence nS and every predicate in the sub-set of inconsistent predicates contains S and nS. This sub-division is related to the distinction between indirect interrogatives which, intuitively, express a question or are compatible with a question and indirect interrogatives which, intuitively, do not express a question or are not compatible with a question. Consider the following examples:

(22) Dan knows whether life is sad (or not).

(23) Dan does not know whether life is sad (or not)

Informally, we can say that only (23) is compatible with the question based on the embedded sentence; when sentence (22) is true the corresponding question in some sense does not arise.

Recall that from the syntactic point of view one can distinguish two types of predicates taking *whether*-complements: responsive predicates (*know, forget*) and rogative predicates (*inquire, ask*).. Responsive predicates can in addition take *that*-complements. We will consider that responsive predicates, whose properties are indicated in the first part of definition D9, cannot characterise interrogatives since they cannot be inconsistent. The second part of D9 describes rogative predicates that is those which properly characterise sentences expressing questions. Semantically, these predicates are strongly inconsistent and correspond to midpoint predicates such as *investigate (whether), find out (whether)*, etc. They are semantically characterised in Definition 10 and the interrogative complement to which they give rise is made precise in Definition 11:

Definition 10. *A sentential predicate P is rogative, $P \in ROG$, iff $P \in MPP \wedge P \subseteq \neg K \cap \neg K \neg$.*

This is a semantic definition of rogative predicates. According to it the set of rogative predicates is not closed with respect to the Boolean complement. For instance $\neg(K_a \wedge K_a \neg)$ is a rogative predicate and $K_a \vee K_a \neg$ is not a rogative predicate,

Definition 11. $QWH(S) = \{P : P \in ROG \wedge \{S, nS\} \subseteq P\}$.

Thus an interrogative based on the sentence S denotes the set of rogative predicates defined in Definition 11. Since Definition 10 of rogative predicates explicitly uses the negation of knowledge our idea of the meaning of a question explicitly introduces the "ignorance ingredient" to the semantics of questions.

An important consequence of Definition 11 is that interrogative sentences and lifted declarative sentences denote in the same denotational algebra since both denote sets of sentential predicates. Consequently we can Booleanly combine them and naturally express semantic relations between them as relations between elements of the corresponding denotational algebras. Thus (20) denotes the intersection of the set of SPRs (the sentential individual) with the set of SPRs denoted by the second conjunct (which is an interrogative). This move gives the desired result.

In the similar way we can explain various entailments between interrogative sentences which are not Boolean complexes. This is in particular the case of entailment between the constituent questions (or *wh*-questions) and *yes-no*-questions. It is usually assumed (cf. Groenendijk and Stokhof 1989) that (24) entails, in some generalised sense, (25):

(24) Who solved the problem?

(25) Did Dan solve the problem?

Observe now that constituent questions like (24) can also be characterised by the set of rogative predicates, because, roughly, they can be embedded in them. Furthermore, any predicate characterising (24) also characterises (25); for instance inquiring who solved the problem entails inquiring whether Dan solved the problem. Hence the set of SPRs (the sentential quantifier) denoted by the interrogative complement (24) is included in the set of SPRs (the sentential quantifier) denoted by the interrogative complement (25) and consequently (24) entails (25).

5 Conclusive Remarks

Lifting rules admitted in formal semantics generally concern sub-sentential syntactic units. In order to obtain the semantics of sentential complements I propose to apply specific lifts to sentences. As a result we obtain a kind of generalisation of the notion of the sentence. Usually sentences are considered as basic and "ultimate" syntactic units which have the property of being true or false. Lifted sentences denote sets of sentential predicates where a sentential predicate is a set of "classical" sentences. Thus generalised sentences correspond to sets of sentential predicates In particular the sentential individual, that is the ultra-filter generated by some sentence, corresponds to a declarative sentence. By varying the properties of sentential predicates grouped together we obtain other types of sentences. For instance if all sentential predicates of a given set are rogative then this set of predicates corresponds to a question. This move allows us to analyse semantically in an uniform way mixed constructions in which classical declarative and interrogative sentences occur and to describe entailments between different interrogative sentences and between conjunctions of interrogative and declarative sentences.

References

van Benthem, J.: Essays in Logical Semantics. D. Reidel Publishing Company (1986)
Chow, K.: Internal reading and reciprocity. In: Bekki, D., et al. (eds.) Logic and Engineering of Natural Language Semantics. LENLS 20 Conference, pp. 155–174. Springer (2023)
Hintikka, J.: Semantics for propositional attitudes. In: Models for Modalities, Synthese Library, pp. 87–111. Springer (1969)
Groenendijk, J., Stokhof, M.: Type-shifting rulers and the semantics of interrogatives. In: Chierchia, G., et al. (eds.) Properties, Types and Meaning II, pp. 21–68. Kluwer Academic Publishers (1989)
Keenan, E.L., Faltz, L.M.: Boolean Semantics for Natural Language. D. Reidel Publishing Company, Dordrecht (1985)
Montague, R.: Formal philosophy, (R. Thomason, ed.). Yale University Press (1974)
Partee, B.: Noun phrase interpretation and type-shifting principles. In: Groenendijk, J., et al. (eds.) Studies in Discourse Representation Theory-and the Theory of Generalized Quantifiers, GRASS 8, pp. 115–143. Foris, Dordrecht (1987)
Sutton, R.P.: Types and type theories in natural language analysis. Ann. Rev. Linguist. **10**, 107–126 (2024)
Thomason, R.H.: A model theory for propositional attitudes. Linguist. Philos. **4–1**, 47–70 (1980)
Zuber, R.: Anaphors and quantifiers. In: Väänänen, J., Hirvonen, Å., de Queiroz, R. (eds.) WoLLIC 2016. LNCS, vol. 9803, pp. 432–445. Springer, Heidelberg (2016). https://doi.org/10.1007/978-3-662-52921-8_26
Zuber, R.: Set partitions and the meaning of the same. J. Logic Lang. Inform. **26**, 1–20 (2017)
Zuber, R.: Properties of propositional attitude operators. Linguist. Philos. **46–2**, 237–257 (2023)
Zuber, R.: More on semantic restrictions on certain complementizers. J. Semantics (2025, forthcoming)

Convergence Laws for Expansions of Linear Preorders

Vera Koponen(✉) and Edward Karlsson

Uppsala University, Uppsala, Sweden
vera.koponen@math.uu.se, edward.karlsson.7342@student.uu.se

Abstract. We consider a sequence $\mathcal{L}_n$, $n = 1, 2, 3, \ldots$, of linear *pre*orders, a finite relational signature σ including the signature $\{\preceq\}$ of the linear preorders $\mathcal{L}_n$, and the set $\mathbf{W}_n$ of all expansions of $\mathcal{L}_n$ to σ. A probability distribution $\mathbb{P}_n$ is defined on each $\mathbf{W}_n$ (it can be e.g. the uniform distribution, but many other distributions are possible). We prove that if all equivalence classes of the preorder $\mathcal{L}_n$ grow (as $n \to \infty$) faster than every logarithm but slower than some polynomial, then every first-order formula is almost surely equivalent to a (in general) simpler formula that only expresses distances between variables and which atomic formulas they satisfy. As a corollary we get a convergence law for formulas, and zero-one law for sentences, of first-order logic. If we also assume that for some positive $\lambda \in \mathbb{N}$ the number of equivalence classes of every $\mathcal{L}_n$ is exactly λ and that all equivalence classes have roughly the same size, then we can also almost surely eliminate "proportion quantifiers" that express, for some $0 < r < 1$, that the proportion of elements satisfying a formula is larger than r; and we get a convergence law for first-order logic extended by such quantifiers.

Keywords: finite model theory · convergence law · almost sure elimination of quantifiers · linear preorder

1 Introduction

Most logical convergence laws have considered some context in which all relations under consideration are uncertain, or random, in some sense which is specified by a probability distribution on finite structures with a common domain (see e.g. [6,11–13,16,23,25] to mention only very few of them). However, in contexts related to "real world" situations one may know some things with certainty while having uncertain information about other things. This perspective is relevant from the point of view of data mining, machine learning and artificial intelligence. We can represent such a situation model theoretically by considering a specific "base structure" $\mathcal{B}$ which contains the certain information. For some signature σ which contains the signature of $\mathcal{B}$ we can let $\mathbf{W}$ be the set of all expansions of $\mathcal{B}$ to σ and consider some probability distribution $\mathbb{P}$ on $\mathbf{W}$. The relations of σ that are not part of the signature of $\mathcal{B}$, and properties that are defined

D. Kozen and R. de Queiroz (Eds.): WoLLIC 2025, LNCS 15942, pp. 101–118, 2026.
https://doi.org/10.1007/978-3-031-99536-1_7

by using these relations, are now described in a probabilistic way and we can formulate properties that depend on both the certain and the uncertain relations by using some formal logic, for example first-order logic.

We are interested in understanding the asymptotic behaviour of a query defined by a formula of some logic as the domain size tends to infinity. So instead of one base structure we consider a sequence $(\mathcal{B}_n : n \in \mathbb{N}^+)$ (where $\mathbb{N}^+ = \{1, 2, 3, \dots\}$) of base structures, with signature τ say, where the domain size of $\mathcal{B}_n$ tends to infinity, and for each n, $\mathbf{W}_n$ is the set of all σ-structures ($\tau \subset \sigma$) that expand $\mathcal{B}_n$, and $\mathbb{P}_n$ is a probability distribution on $\mathbf{W}_n$. If for a sentence φ of some formal logic the probability that it is true in a random $\mathcal{A} \in \mathbf{W}_n$ converges as $n \to \infty$, then we typically get a (possibly probabilistic) algorithm for estimating that probability for all large enough n. It also means that knowledge about that (approximate) probability on one large domain can be transferred to another large domain, which is relevant in the context of machine learning and artificial intelligence. So what kind of sequences of base structures would be interesting to study?

Various kinds of orders are common in theory and in the physical and virtual worlds. Let $\tau = \{\preceq\}$ where $\preceq$ is a binary relation symbol. Already in 1987 Compton, Henson and Shelah [8] proved that if, for all $n \in \mathbb{N}^+$, $\mathcal{B}_n = (\{1, \dots, n\}, \preceq)$ is a linear order, $\sigma = \{\preceq, R\}$ where R is a binary relation symbol, and $\mathbb{P}_n$ is the uniform probability distribution on $\mathbf{W}_n$, then there is a first-order sentence φ such that $\mathbb{P}_n(\varphi) := \mathbb{P}_n\big(\{\mathcal{A} \in \mathbf{W}_n : \mathcal{A} \models \varphi\}\big)$ does *not* converge as $n \to \infty$. Their result was later strengthened by Niemistö [24] who proved that a logic capable of defining a linear order on almost all graphs cannot have a convergence law with the uniform distribution. But what about other kinds of orders? Here we consider the case when the τ-structure $\mathcal{B}_n$ is a linear *pre*order, meaning that $\preceq$ is interpreted as a reflexive and transitive relation such that every pair of elements is comparable with respect to $\preceq$. In this context the formula $x \preceq y \wedge y \preceq x$ defines an equivalence relation on the domain of $\mathcal{B}_n$. So one can view a linear preorder as a linear order of (equivalence) classes of objects. Linear preorders arise naturally. For example, if all people are ordered according to the year of birth and persons who where born in the same year are considered "equivalent" then we get a linear preorder. As another example, suppose that a group of test persons have their blood pressure measured and, for some partition of the set of positive reals into intervals, two persons belong to the same equivalence class if their blood pressures are in the same interval. If the equivalence classes are linearly ordered then we get a linear preorder on the test persons.

In general we do not have a first-order convergence result in the context of $\mathcal{B}_n$ being a linear preorder, because it may be a linear order. But we will prove results about convergence and "almost sure equivalence" in the following context, informally described. Suppose that $\sigma \supset \tau$, for every n, $\mathcal{B}_n$ is a finite τ-structure in which $\preceq$ is interpreted as a linear preorder such that, as $n \to \infty$, all equivalence classes of $\mathcal{B}_n$ grow faster than $\log(n)$ for every choice of base, but slower than $P(n)$ for some polynomial P. Then, we consider a sequence $\mathbb{P}_n$ of distributions (on $\mathbf{W}_n$) where, for $R \in \sigma \setminus \tau$, say of arity ν_R, and $a_1, \dots, a_{\nu_R}$

from the domain of some $\mathcal{B}_n$, the probability that $R(a_1, \dots, a_{\nu_R})$ holds may (but need not) depend on the order of $a_1, \dots, a_{\nu_R}$ and the distances between the different a_i and a_j (elements in the same equivalence class have distance 0 from each other). Let $FO(\tau)$ and $FO(\sigma)$ denote the sets of first-order sentences that can be formed with τ and with σ, respectively.

The first main result, Theorem 1, is that for every $\varphi(\bar{x}) \in FO(\sigma)$ ($\bar{x} = (x_1, \dots, x_k)$ a sequence of variables) there is a (typically simpler) $\psi(\bar{x}) \in FO(\sigma)$ which is almost surely equivalent to $\varphi(\bar{x})$ and, for some $k \in \mathbb{N}$, the quantifiers that occur in $\psi(\bar{x})$ (if any) are only used to express distances up to k between variables in $\bar{x}$ and to the endpoints of the linear preorder. For any choice of parameters $\bar{a} = (a_1, \dots, a_k)$ from the domain of $\mathcal{B}_n$, for any n, the probability that $\psi(\bar{a})$ holds in a random $\mathcal{A} \in \mathbf{W}_n$ can be computed by only using $\psi(\bar{x})$, the distances, up to k, between elements in $\bar{a}$ and from them to the endpoints, and the fixed information that defines $\mathbb{P}_n$ for all n; hence there is no dependence on n. Moreover, the proof shows how to transform the original $\varphi(\bar{x})$, step by step, until one gets $\psi(\bar{x})$ with the described properties, and the transformation does not depend on n. Using Theorem 1 we can derive the following convergence law, Corollary 1: For every $\varphi(\bar{x}) \in FO(\sigma)$ there is $k \in \mathbb{N}$ such that if $\theta(\bar{x})$ is a formula which only expresses distances, up to k, between variables in $\bar{x}$ and to the endpoints, then there is β (depending on φ and θ) such that for every $\varepsilon > 0$, if n is large enough and $\mathcal{B}_n \models \theta(\bar{a})$, then the probability that $\varphi(\bar{a})$ holds is within distance ε from β. Moreover, β can be computed from φ, θ and the fixed information that defines $\mathbb{P}_n$ for all n. Thus, for every error marginal $\varepsilon > 0$, and all sufficiently large n, we can estimate the probability that $\varphi(\bar{a})$ holds in a random $\mathcal{A} \in \mathbf{W}_n$ with an error at most ε and the computation is independent of n. If φ is a sentence then β is 0 or 1. In general we cannot remove the condition that β depends also on $\theta(\bar{x})$ as above. This is because if, for example, R is a binary relation symbol, then the probability that $R(a_1, a_2)$ holds may depend on the distance between a_1 and a_2 (as well as on the distance from a_i to the endpoints, and on whether $a_i \preceq a_j$, for $i, j = 1, 2$).

Our second main result, Theorem 2, extends the above results to the case when first-order logic is extended by proportion quantifiers of the form $\exists^{>r} x \varphi$, interpreted as "the proportion of x such that φ holds is larger than r". For this we need stronger assumptions, namely we assume (in addition to previous assumptions) that, for some $\lambda \in \mathbb{N}^+$, every linear preorder $\mathcal{B}_n$ has exactly λ equivalence classes and all equivalence classes of $\mathcal{B}_n$ have roughly the same size.

Related Work. Already in 1980 Lynch [22] identified a condition (k-extendibility) that makes sense for base structures $\mathcal{B}_n$ in general and which guarantees that a convergence law holds for first-order logic and the uniform probability distribution. In particular he [22, Corollary 2.16] and later Abu Zaid, Dawar, Grädel and Pakusa [1] and Dawar, Grädel and Hoelzel [9] considered the context where $\mathcal{B}_n$ is a product of finite cyclic groups and the probability distribution considered is the uniform one. Baldwin [4] and Shelah [26] considered a base sequence where each $\mathcal{B}_n$ is a directed path of length n. In both cases $\mathbf{W}_n$ consists of all expansions of $\mathcal{B}_n$ to a new binary relation symbol R interpreted as an irreflexive and symmetric relation. In [4] the probability distribution on $\mathbf{W}_n$ is defined by letting an $R(x, y)$ be true with probability $n^{-\alpha}$ for some irrational $\alpha \in (0, 1)$, independently of whether it is true for other pairs. In [26] the probability of $R(x, y)$ is $d^{-\alpha}$ where d is the distance in $\mathcal{B}_n$ between x and y and $\alpha \in (0, 1)$ is irrational. Ahlman and Koponen [2] considered base structures $\mathcal{B}_n$ with a (nicely behaved) pregeometry. Koponen [19] studied base structures with bounded degree. Koponen and Tousinejad [20] considered base structures that were trees with bounded height. In both [19] and [20] the probability distributions $\mathbb{P}_n$ where determined by a so-called probabilistic graphical model [15], [5,17]. Convergence laws for the extension of first-order logic with "proportion quantifiers", but without underlying base structures, have been proved by Keisler and Lotfallah [14] and later Koponen [18] for a wider range of distributions.

2 Preliminaries

We refer to [10] for basics about first-order logic and finite model theory. Structures in the sense of first-order logic are denoted by calligraphic letters $\mathcal{A}, \mathcal{B}, \mathcal{C}, \ldots$ and their domains (universes) by the corresponding noncalligraphic letter $A, B, C, \ldots$. Finite sequences (tuples) of objects are denoted by $\bar{a}, \bar{b}, \ldots, \bar{x}, \bar{y}, \ldots$. We usually denote logical variables by x, y, z. When $\bar{x}$ is a sequence of variables we assume that $\bar{x}$ does not repeat a variable. But if $\bar{a}$ denotes a sequence of elements from the domain of a structure then repetitions may occur. We let $\mathbb{N}$ and $\mathbb{N}^+$ denote the set of nonnegative integers and the set of positive integers, respectively. For a set S, $|S|$ denotes its cardinality. For a finite sequence $\bar{s}$, $|\bar{s}|$ denotes its length and $\text{rng}(\bar{s})$ denotes the set of elements in $\bar{s}$. Let σ be a *signature*, that is, a set of relation symbols, and let $\mathcal{A}$ be a σ-structure. If $\tau \subseteq \sigma$ then $\mathcal{A}{\upharpoonright}\tau$ denotes the *reduct* of $\mathcal{A}$ to τ. If $R \in \sigma$ is a relation symbol then $R^{\mathcal{A}}$ denotes the interpretation of R in $\mathcal{A}$. For a signature σ, $FO(\sigma)$ denotes the set of all first-order formulas that can be formed with σ.

Definition 1. For any finite relational signature σ let $FOP(\sigma)$ (for "first-order logic with proportion quantifiers") be the extension of $FO(\sigma)$ where we add the following way of constructing new formulas:

If $\varphi(\bar{x}, y) \in FOP(\sigma)$ and $r \in (0, 1)$ then $\exists^{>r} y \varphi(\bar{x}, y)$ is a formula of $FOP(\sigma)$.

The semantics of this construction is that if $\mathcal{A}$ is a finite σ-structure and $\bar{a} \in A^{|\bar{x}|}$, then $\mathcal{A} \models \exists^{>r} y \varphi(\bar{x}, y)$ if and only if the number of $b \in A$ such that $\mathcal{A} \models \varphi(\bar{a}, b)$ divided by $|A|$ is larger than r.

If a formula of $FO(\sigma)$, or $FOP(\sigma)$, is denoted by $\varphi(\bar{x})$ then it is assumed that all free variables of $\varphi(\bar{x})$ are listed in $\bar{x}$ but we do not require that every variable of $\bar{x}$ occurs in $\varphi(\bar{x})$. If $\varphi(\bar{x}, y) \in FO(\sigma)$ (or $FOP(\sigma)$), $\mathcal{A}$ is a finite σ-structure, and $\bar{a} \in A^{|\bar{x}|}$, then $\varphi(\bar{a}, \mathcal{A}) = \{b \in A : \mathcal{A} \models \varphi(\bar{a}, b)\}$. For $\varphi(\bar{x}), \psi(\bar{x}) \in FOP(\sigma)$, '$\varphi(\bar{x}) \models \psi(\bar{x})$' means that $\forall \bar{x}(\varphi(\bar{x}) \rightarrow \psi(\bar{x}))$ is true in all finite σ-structures.

We will use the following which is a direct consequence of [3, Corollary A.1.14], which in turn follows from the Chernoff bound [7]:

Lemma 1. *Let Z be the sum of n independent 0/1-valued random variables, each one with probability p of having the value 1, where $p > 0$. For every $\varepsilon > 0$ there is $c_\varepsilon > 0$, depending only on ε, such that the probability that $|Z - pn| > \varepsilon pn$ is less than $2e^{-c_\varepsilon pn}$. (If $p = 0$ then the same statement holds if '$2e^{-c_\varepsilon pn}$' is replaced by (for example) 'e^{-n}'.)*

3 Linear Preorders and the Main Results

For the rest of this article we let $\tau = \{\preceq\}$ where $\preceq$ is a binary relation symbol. Moreover, σ will always denote a finite signature with only relation symbols such that $\tau \subset \sigma$, and for every $R \in \sigma \setminus \tau$, ν_R denotes its arity. We write $x \preceq y$ and $x \npreceq y$ instead of $\preceq(x, y)$ and $\neg\preceq(x, y)$, respectively, and we let $x \prec y$ be an abbreviation of '$x \preceq y \ \wedge \ y \npreceq x$'.

Definition 2. By a *linear preorder* we mean a *finite* τ-structure $\mathcal{L}$ such that

1. $\mathcal{L} \models \forall x(x \preceq x)$,
2. $\mathcal{L} \models \forall x, y\big((x \preceq y \wedge y \preceq z) \rightarrow x \preceq z\big)$, and
3. $\mathcal{L} \models \forall x, y\big(x \preceq y \vee y \preceq x\big)$.

Note that the formula $x \preceq y \wedge y \preceq$ defines an equivalence relation on the domain of every linear preorder $\mathcal{L}$, and we call the equivalence classes of this equivalence relation *the classes of* $\mathcal{L}$. Also observe that, by our definition, all linear preorders are finite so we do not need to repeat the finiteness condition.

Definition 3. Let $\mathcal{L}$ be a linear preorder.

(i) An element $a \in L$ is called *smallest* (respectively *largest*) if for all $b \in L$, $\mathcal{L} \models a \preceq b$ (respectively $\mathcal{L} \models b \preceq a$).
(ii) For $a, b \in L$ the *distance* from a to b (in $\mathcal{L}$) is 0 if $\mathcal{L} \models a \preceq b \wedge b \preceq a$, and otherwise the *distance* from a to b is the maximal natural number m such that either

1. there are $c_0, \ldots, c_m \in L$ such that $a = c_0 \prec \ldots \prec c_m = b$, or
2. there are $c_0, \ldots, c_m \in L$ such that $b = c_0 \prec \ldots \prec c_m = a$.

It is straightforward to see that for every $m \in \mathbb{N}$ there is a formula in $FO(\tau)$, which we denote by $\text{dist}_m(x, y)$ such that for every linear preorder $\mathcal{L}$ and all $a, b \in L$, $\mathcal{L}_n \models \text{dist}_m(a, b)$ if and only if the distance from a to b is m. For each m we let $\text{dist}_{>m}(x, y)$ be the formula $\bigwedge_{i=0}^{m} \neg\text{dist}_i(x, y)$ which expresses that the distance from x to y is larger than m.

For each $m \in \mathbb{N}$ there is also a formula $\text{dist}_m^{\text{sm}}(x) \in FO(\tau)$ such that for every linear preorder $\mathcal{L}$ and $a \in L$, $\mathcal{L}_n \models \text{dist}_m^{\text{sm}}(a)$ if and only if the distance from a to a smallest element is m. Similarly, there is a formula $\text{dist}_m^{\text{la}}(x) \in FO(\tau)$ which expresses that the distance from x to a largest element is m. We let $\text{dist}_{>m}^{\text{sm}}(x)$ and $\text{dist}_{>m}^{\text{la}}(x)$ denote the formulas $\bigwedge_{i=0}^{m} \neg\text{dist}_i^{\text{sm}}(x)$ and $\bigwedge_{i=0}^{m} \neg\text{dist}_i^{\text{la}}(x)$, respectively.

Finally, for each $m \in \mathbb{N}$, there is a sentence $\text{length}_m \in FO(\tau)$ which is true in a linear preorder $\mathcal{L}$ if and only the distance from a smallest element in $\mathcal{L}$ to a largest element in $\mathcal{L}$ is m. We also let $\text{length}_{>m}$ be the sentence $\bigwedge_{i=0}^{m} \neg\text{length}_m$. The notation just introduced for formulas that express distances will be used in the rest of the paper.

Now we are ready to specify the properties of the base sequences of linear preorders (from now on denoted $\mathcal{L}_n$) to which the results presented here apply.

Definition 4. We fix functions $g_1, g_2, g_3 : \mathbb{N} \to \mathbb{R}$ such that

- g_1 and g_3 are polynomials,
- $g_2(n) < g_1(n)$ for all $n \in \mathbb{N}^+$, and
- for every $\alpha \in \mathbb{R}$, $\lim_{n\to\infty}(g_2(n) - \alpha \ln(n)) = \infty$.

For each $n \in \mathbb{N}^+$ we let $\mathcal{L}_n$ be a linear preorder such that

1. the domain L_n of $\mathcal{L}_n$ is nonempty and $\mathcal{L}_n$ has at most $g_3(n)$ classes, and
2. for each class $C \subseteq L_n$ of $\mathcal{L}_n$, $g_2(n) \leq |C| \leq g_1(n)$.

Observe that for all n, $|L_n| \leq g_3(n)\cdot g_1(n)$ where $g_3(n)\cdot g_1(x)$ is a polynomial.

Definition 5. For every $n \in \mathbb{N}^+$, $\mathbf{W}_n$ denotes the set of all σ-structures that expand $\mathcal{L}_n$, or equivalently, $\mathbf{W}_n = \{\mathcal{A} : \mathcal{A} \text{ is a } \sigma\text{-structure and } \mathcal{A}{\restriction}\tau = \mathcal{L}_n\}$.

For $k \in \mathbb{N}$, the intuitive meaning of a "(τ, k)-type" is a formula $p(x_1, \ldots, x_k)$ which expresses distances, up to k, between variables in $x_1, \ldots, x_k$, between $x_1, \ldots, x_k$ and the largest/smallest elements, and the length of the linear preorder. A (σ, k)-type extends a (τ, k)-type by also saying that certain relations from $R \in \sigma \setminus \tau$ hold, or does not hold.

Definition 6. Let $\tau \subseteq \sigma' \subseteq \sigma$ and $k \in \mathbb{N}$. A formula $p(x_1, \ldots, x_s) \in FO(\sigma')$ is called a *(σ', k)-type* if the following hold:

1. There are $n \in \mathbb{N}^+$, $a_1, \ldots, a_s \in L_n$, and $\mathcal{A} \in \mathbf{W}_n$ such that $\mathcal{A} \models p(a_1, \ldots, a_s)$.
2. $p(x_1, \ldots, x_s)$ is a conjunction of σ'-literals and formulas of the following forms where $m \leq k$ and $i, j \in \{1, \ldots, s\}$: $\text{dist}_m(x_i, x_j)$, $\neg\text{dist}_m(x_i, x_j)$, $\text{dist}_m^{\text{sm}}(x_i)$, $\neg\text{dist}_m^{\text{sm}}(x_i)$, $\text{dist}_m^{\text{la}}(x_i)$, $\neg\text{dist}_m^{\text{la}}(x_i)$, length_m, and $\neg\text{length}_m$.
3. For all $i, j \in \{1, \ldots, s\}$ and $m \leq k$,
   (a) either $x_i = x_j$ or $x_i \neq x_j$ is a conjunct of p,
   (b) either $x_i \preceq x_j$ or $x_i \not\preceq x_j$ is a conjunct of p,
   (c) either $\text{dist}_m(x_i, x_j)$ or $\neg\text{dist}_m(x_i, x_j)$ is a conjunct of p,
   (d) either $\text{dist}_m^{\text{sm}}(x_i)$ or $\neg\text{dist}_m^{\text{sm}}(x_i)$ is a conjunct of p,
   (e) either $\text{dist}_m^{\text{la}}(x_i)$ or $\neg\text{dist}_m^{\text{la}}(x_i)$ is a conjunct of p, and
   (f) either length_m or $\neg\text{length}_m$ is a conjunct of p.

If, in addition, for every $R \in \sigma' \setminus \tau$ and all $i_1, \ldots, i_{\nu_R} \in \{1, \ldots, s\}$, either $R(x_{i_1}, \ldots, x_{i_\nu})$ or $\neg R(x_{i_1}, \ldots, x_{i_\nu})$ is a conjunct of p, then we call $p(x_1, \ldots, x_s)$ a *complete (σ', k)-type*. (Vacuously, every (τ, k)-type is a complete (τ, k)-type.)

Note that in Definition 6 we allow the special case when p is a sentence and in this case p is a conjunction of formulas of the form length_m or $\neg\text{length}$ for $0 \leq m \leq k$.

Definition 7. For all $k, m \in \mathbb{N}$ let $S_{k,m}$ be a finite set of pairwise nonequivalent (τ, k)-types with free variables $x_1, \ldots, x_m$ such that every (τ, k)-type with free variables $x_1, \ldots, x_m$ is equivalent to a (τ, k)-type in $S_{k,m}$.

We now define the probability distribution $\mathbb{P}_n$ in such a way that, for some $\kappa \in \mathbb{N}$, for every $R \in \sigma \setminus \tau$, every n, and all $a_1, \ldots, a_{\nu_R} \in L_n$, the probability that $R(a_1, \ldots, a_{\nu_R})$ holds is determined (only) by the (unique) (τ, κ)-type that $(a_1, \ldots, a_{\nu_R})$ satisfies.

Definition 8. (The probability distribution on $\mathbf{W}_n$) Fix some $\kappa \in \mathbb{N}$.

(i) To each $R \in \sigma \setminus \tau$ and every $q(x_1, \ldots, x_{\nu_R}) \in S_{\kappa,\nu_R}$ we associate a real number $\alpha_{R,q} \in [0, 1]$.
(ii) For each $n \in \mathbb{N}^+$ and $\mathcal{A} \in \mathbf{W}_n$ we define

$$\mathbb{P}_n(\mathcal{A}) = \prod_{R \in \sigma \setminus \tau} \prod_{q \in S_{\kappa,\nu_R}} \Big(\prod_{\bar{a} \in q(\mathcal{A}) \cap R^{\mathcal{A}}} \alpha_{R,q} \Big) \Big(\prod_{\bar{a} \in q(\mathcal{A}) \setminus R^{\mathcal{A}}} (1 - \alpha_{R,q}) \Big).$$

(iii) For every $n \in \mathbf{W}_n$ and $\mathbf{X} \subseteq \mathbf{W}_n$ let $\mathbb{P}_n(\mathbf{X}) = \sum_{\mathcal{A} \in \mathbf{X}} \mathbb{P}_n(\mathcal{A})$.

Example 1. Suppose that $R \in \sigma \setminus \tau$ has arity 2, so $\nu_R = 2$. We can define the parameters $\alpha_{R,q}$ in part (i) of Definition 8 in such a way that the probability that $R(a, b)$ holds depends on whether $a \preceq b$, or $b \preceq a$, and on the whether the distance between a and b is 0, 1, 2, or more. Let $\beta_{i,j} \in [0, 1]$ for $i = 0, 1, 2, 3$ and $j = 0, 1$, and suppose that $\beta_{0,0} = \beta_{0,1}$ as $\beta_{0,0}$ and $\beta_{0,1}$ will correspond to the same case below. Let $\kappa = 2$ (as we want to express distances up to 2) and let $q(x_1, x_2) \in S_{\kappa,\nu_R}$. Now define $\alpha_{R,q}$ as follows:

- If $q(x_1, x_2) \models x_1 \preceq x_2 \wedge \text{dist}_i(x_1, x_2)$ where $i \in \{0, 1, 2\}$ then let $\alpha_{R,q} := \beta_{i,0}$.
- If $q(x_1, x_2) \models x_1 \preceq x_2 \wedge \text{dist}_{>2}(x_1, x_2)$ then let $\alpha_{R,q} := \beta_{3,0}$.
- If $q(x_1, x_2) \models x_2 \preceq x_1 \wedge \text{dist}_i(x_1, x_2)$ where $i \in \{0, 1, 2\}$ then let $\alpha_{R,q} := \beta_{i,1}$.
- If $q(x_1, x_2) \models x_2 \preceq x_1 \wedge \text{dist}_{>2}(x_1, x_2)$ then let $\alpha_{R,q} := \beta_{3,1}$.

Intuitively speaking, this means, for example, that if $a \preceq b$ and the distance between a and b is 2, then the probability that $R(a, b)$ holds is $\beta_{2,0}$, independently of whether $R(a', b')$ holds if (a', b') is a different ordered pair than (a, b) (and independently of whether $Q(b_1, \ldots, b_{\nu_Q})$ holds if $Q \in \sigma \setminus \tau$ is different from R and $b_1, \ldots, b_{\nu_Q}$ are any elements from the domain). It is possible to also let the probability of $R(a, b)$ to depend on the distance (up to 2, as we set $\kappa = 2$) of a, respectively b, to the maximal and/or minimal elements, and/or on the length (up to 2) of the linear preorder.

Definition 9. (i) A formula $\varphi(\bar{x}) \in FOP(\sigma)$ is called *cofinally satisfiable* if there are arbitrarily large n such that, for some $\mathcal{A} \in \mathbf{W}_n$, $\mathcal{A} \models \exists \bar{x} \varphi(\bar{x})$.
(ii) For a sentence $\varphi \in FOP(\sigma)$ define $\mathbb{P}_n(\varphi) = \mathbb{P}(\{\mathcal{A} \in \mathbf{W}_n : \mathcal{A} \models \varphi\})$.

(iii) For a sentence $\varphi \in FOP(\sigma)$, we say that φ is almost surely true, respectively false, if $\lim_{n\to\infty} \mathbb{P}_n(\varphi) = 1$, respectively $\lim_{n\to\infty} \mathbb{P}_n(\varphi) = 0$.

(iv) Two formulas $\varphi(\bar{x}), \psi(\bar{x}) \in FOP(\sigma)$ are *almost surely equivalent* if $\forall \bar{x}(\varphi(\bar{x}) \leftrightarrow \psi(\bar{x}))$ is almost surely true.

Note that since $FO(\sigma) \subset FOP(\sigma)$ the above definition makes sense for $FO(\sigma)$ too. The assumptions on the sequence $(\mathcal{L}_n : n \in \mathbb{N}^+)$ do not guarantee that every formula in $FO(\sigma)$ is almost surely equivalent to a formula without quantifiers (as in e.g. [12,14] or [18] where all relations are random). For example, if $\mathcal{L}_n$ has at least 2 classes for all n, then the formula $\text{dist}_1^{\text{sm}}(x)$ expressing that "the distance from x to a smallest element is 1" cannot be equivalent to formula without quantifiers, because if $\psi(x) \in FO(\sigma)$ is quantifier-free and satisfiable in some $\mathcal{A} \in \bigcup_{n\in\mathbb{N}^+} \mathbf{W}_n$, then it only expresses (besides $x = x$ and/or $x \preceq x$) that $R(x, \ldots, x)$ or $\neg R(x, \ldots, x)$ for some $R \in \sigma \setminus \tau$, and if all $\alpha_{R,q}$ in Definition 8 are positive and less than 1 (or if they are all 0) then $\psi(x)$ cannot be almost surely equivalent to $\text{dist}_1^{\text{sm}}(x)$.

Neither do the assumptions guarantee that $\lim_{n\to\infty} \mathbb{P}_n(\varphi)$ exists for every sentence $\varphi \in FO(\sigma)$. Because if $\mathcal{L}_n$ has only one class for all odd n and $\mathcal{L}_n$ has at least two classes for all even $n > 1$, then the sentence length_0 (expressing that the length of the linear preorder is 0, that is, it has only one class) is true in $\mathcal{L}_n$ (hence true in all $\mathcal{A} \in \mathbf{W}_n$) for odd n and false in $\mathcal{L}_n$ for even n. It is possible to avoid this problem by imposing further conditions on the sequence $(\mathcal{L}_n : n \in \mathbb{N}^+)$ which rule out such examples. But we prefer to formulate the convergence result, Corollary 1, for a formula $\varphi(\bar{x})$ by "conditioning" on the truth of formulas that express distances between between elements (and to the endpoints of the linear preorder) up to some k (that depends ony on φ and κ from Definition 8).

Recall that the main results below depend on the assumptions made in Definitions 4 and 8.

Theorem 1. *Let $\varphi(\bar{x}) \in FO(\sigma)$ be cofinally satisfiable. Then there is $k \geq \kappa$ and a disjunction $\bigvee_{i=1}^{s} p_i(\bar{x})$ such that each $p_i(\bar{x})$ is a (σ, k)-type and $\varphi(\bar{x})$ is almost surely equivalent to $\bigvee_{i=1}^{s} p_i(\bar{x})$. In particular, every cofinally satisfiable sentence $\varphi \in FO(\sigma)$ is almost surely equivalent to a sentence of the form $\bigvee_{i=1}^{s} p_i$ where each p_i has the form* length_m *for some $m \leq k$ or the form* $\text{length}_{>k}$.

We cannot remove the assumption in Theorem 1 that $\varphi(\bar{x})$ is cofinally satisfiable (unless we change some other assumption). To see this, consider the case when $\bar{x}$ is empty, so that φ is a sentence, and note that it is possible to choose the sequence $(\mathcal{L}_n : n \in \mathbb{N}^+)$ so that, for every $k \in \mathbb{N}$, every (σ, k)-type p (without free variables) is cofinally satisfiable. In this case, if φ is an inconsistent formula then it can not be almost surely equivalent to a disjunction of (σ, k)-types.

Corollary 1. *Let $\varphi(\bar{x}) \in FO(\sigma)$ be cofinally satisfiable. Then there is $k \geq \kappa$ such that for every (τ, k)-type $p(\bar{x})$ there is $\beta \in [0, 1]$ such that for all $\varepsilon > 0$, if $n \in \mathbb{N}^+$ is large enough, $\bar{a} \in (L_n)^{|\bar{x}|}$ and $\mathcal{L}_n \models p(\bar{a})$, then*

$$\left| \mathbb{P}_n(\{\mathcal{A} \in \mathbf{W}_n : \mathcal{A} \models \varphi(\bar{a})\}) \; - \; \beta \right| \; \leq \; \varepsilon.$$

If φ is a sentence (i.e. if $\bar{x}$ is empty) then β can always be taken to be 0 or 1.

Property 1. In addition to the assumptions in Definition 4 suppose that there is $\lambda \in \mathbb{N}^+$ such that $g_3(n) = \lambda$ for all n, meaning that $\mathcal{L}_n$ has exactly λ classes for all n. Also suppose that there is $h : \mathbb{N}^+ \to \mathbb{R}$ such that $g_2(n) \leq h(n) \leq g_1(n)$ for all n and, for all reals $\delta > 0$, if $n \in \mathbb{N}^+$ is sufficiently large then every class of $\mathcal{L}_n$ has at least $(1 - \delta)h(n)$ elements and at most $(1 + \delta)h(n)$ elements.

Theorem 2. *Suppose that the sequence of $\mathcal{L}_n$, $n \in \mathbb{N}^+$, also satisfies Property 1. Let $\varphi(\bar{x}) \in FOP(\sigma)$ be cofinally satisfiable and suppose that if $\exists^{>r} y\psi(\bar{z}, y)$ is a subformula of φ then $r \neq \frac{\alpha}{\lambda}$ whenever α is a sum of numbers $\alpha_{R,q}$ as in Definition 8.*

If $k = \lambda$ where λ is as in Property 1 then either $\exists\bar{x}\varphi(\bar{x})$ is almost surely false, or there are complete (σ, k)-types $p_1(\bar{x}), \dots, p_m(\bar{x})$ such that $\varphi(\bar{x})$ is almost surely equivalent to $\bigvee_{i=1}^m p_i(\bar{x})$. Under the same assumptions, for every (τ, k)-type $p(\bar{x})$ there is $\beta \in [0, 1]$ such that the conclusion of Corollary 1 holds (now for $\varphi(\bar{x}) \in FOP(\sigma)$).

Property 1 is a necessary assumption in Theorem 2. For if the number of classes (of $\preceq$) is allowed to fluctuate, or if the sizes of the classes are allowed to fluctuate too much, then, as $n \to \infty$, the size of the sets of the form $\psi(\bar{a}, \mathcal{A})$ divided by the domain size need not "almost surely" converge, even if $\psi(\bar{x}, y)$ is quantifier-free, and then proportion quantifiers cannot almost surely be eliminated. We may also note that if $\lambda = 1$ (where λ is as in Property 1), then Theorem 2 implies the classical zero-one law for first-order logic [11,12].

4 Proofs

In the process of proving the main results we will prove some intermediate results. We begin with a small technical lemma which uses the assumption that g_2 does not grow too slowly, and it will be used to "preserve" exponential decay of certain probabilities. A proof of it is found in [20, Lemma 6.5] (which uses Assumption 6.3 of [20].

Lemma 2. *Let $k \in \mathbb{N}^+$. For every $\alpha > 0$, if n is sufficiently large then $\frac{n^k}{e^{\alpha g_2(n)}} \leq e^{-\frac{1}{2}\alpha g_2(n)}$.*

Definition 10. (i) Let $p(\bar{x})$ be a (σ, k)-type. The *restriction of $p(\bar{x})$ to τ*, denoted $p{\restriction}\tau$, is an (τ, k)-type $p'(\bar{x})$ such that $p(\bar{x}) \models p'(\bar{x})$, and for every (τ, k)-type $p^*(\bar{x})$, if $p(\bar{x}) \models p^*(\bar{x})$ then $p'(\bar{x}) \models p^*(\bar{x})$. (The restriction is not syntactically unique, but unique up to logical equivalence.)
(ii) Let $p(\bar{x})$ be a (σ, k)-type ((τ, k)-type) and let $\bar{y}$ be a subsequence of $\bar{x}$. The *restriction of $p(\bar{x})$ to $\bar{y}$*, denoted $p{\restriction}\bar{y}$, is a (σ, k)-type ((τ, k)-type) $p'(\bar{y})$ such that $p(\bar{x}) \models p'(\bar{y})$, and for every (σ, k)-type ((τ, k)-type) $p^*(\bar{y})$, if $p(\bar{x}) \models p^*(\bar{y})$ then $p'(\bar{y}) \models p^*(\bar{y})$.

Definition 11. Suppose that $\varphi(\bar{x}) \in FOP(\sigma)$ and $\bar{a} \in (L_n)^{|\bar{x}|}$ (for some n). Then

$$\mathbf{E}_n^{\varphi(\bar{a})} = \{\mathcal{A} \in \mathbf{W}_n : \mathcal{A} \models \varphi(\bar{a}))\}.$$

Lemma 3. *Let $k \geq \kappa$, let $p(\bar{x})$ be a (σ, k)-type and let $p'(\bar{x}) = p \restriction \tau$. Then there is $\beta \in [0, 1]$ such that if $n \in \mathbb{N}^+$, $\bar{a} \in (L_n)^{|\bar{x}|}$ and $\mathcal{L}_n \models p'(\bar{a})$, then $\mathbb{P}_n(\mathbf{E}_n^{p(\bar{a})}) = \beta$.*

Proof. Let $\bar{x} = (x_1, \dots, x_m)$. For each $k \geq \kappa$, each $R \in \sigma \setminus \tau$ and every $\bar{i} = (i_1, \dots, i_{\nu_R}) \in \{1, \dots, m\}^{\nu_R}$ there is a unique (τ, κ)-type $q_{\bar{i}}^R(x_1, \dots, x_{\nu_R}) \in S_{\kappa,\nu_R}$ such that $p(\bar{x}) \models q_{\bar{i}}^R(x_{i_1}, \dots, x_{i_{\nu_R}})$. Hence the probability that $R(a_{i_1}, \dots, x_{i_{\nu_R}})$ holds is $\alpha_{R,q_{\bar{i}}^R}$. Let $\alpha_{R,\bar{i}} = \alpha_{R,q_{\bar{i}}^R}$ if $p(\bar{x}) \models R(x_{i_1}, \dots, x_{i_{\nu_R}})$, let $\alpha_{R,\bar{i}} = 1 - \alpha_{R,q_{\bar{i}}^R}$ if $p(\bar{x}) \models \neg R(x_{i_1}, \dots, x_{i_{\nu_R}})$, and let $\alpha_{R,\bar{i}} = 1$ if none of the previous cases hold. Now we can let

$$\beta = \prod_{R \in \sigma \setminus \tau} \prod_{\bar{i} \in [m]^{\nu_R}} \alpha_{R,\bar{i}}.$$

□

Remark 1. Suppose that $\bar{x}$ in Lemma 3 is empty. Then it follows from Definition 6 of (σ, k)-types, respectively (τ, k)-types, that p (as in Lemma 3) is equivalent to $p \restriction \tau$. It follows that if $\bar{x}$ is empty in Lemma 3, then the lemma holds with $\beta = 1$.

The next concept to be defined is borrowed from [19] (and implicitly from [21]).

Definition 12. Let $\varphi(\bar{x}, y), \psi(\bar{x}, y), \chi(\bar{x}) \in FO(\sigma)$.

(i) Let $\alpha \in [0, 1]$, $\varepsilon > 0$ and let $\mathcal{A}$ be a finite σ-structure. The triple (φ, ψ, χ) is called (α, ε)-*balanced in* $\mathcal{A}$ if whenever $\bar{a} \in A^{|\bar{x}|}$ and $\mathcal{A} \models \chi(\bar{a})$, then

$$(\alpha - \varepsilon)|\psi(\bar{a}, \mathcal{A})| \leq |\varphi(\bar{a}, \mathcal{A}) \cap \psi(\bar{a}, \mathcal{A})| \leq (\alpha + \varepsilon)|\psi(\bar{a}, \mathcal{A})|.$$

(ii) Let $\alpha \in [0, 1]$. The triple (φ, ψ, χ) is α-*balanced* if for all $\varepsilon > 0$, if

$$\mathbf{X}_n^\varepsilon = \{\mathcal{A} \in \mathbf{W}_n : (\varphi, \psi, \chi) \text{ is } (\alpha, \varepsilon)\text{-balanced in } \mathcal{A}\}$$

then $\lim_{n \to \infty} \mathbb{P}_n(\mathbf{X}_n^\varepsilon) = 1$. The triple (φ, ψ, χ) is *balanced* if, for some $\alpha \in [0, 1]$, it is α-balanced. If, in addition, $\alpha > 0$ then we call (φ, ψ, χ) *positively balanced.*

Remark 2. Let $\varphi(\bar{x}, y), \psi(\bar{x}, y), \chi(\bar{x}) \in FO(\sigma)$. Suppose that $\varphi \wedge \psi \wedge \chi$ is not cofinally satisfiable. We claim that (φ, ψ, χ) is 0-balanced. It suffices to show that, for all sufficiently large n, if $\mathcal{A} \in \mathbf{W}_n$, $\mathcal{A} \models q(\bar{a})$, and $\mathcal{A} \models \psi(\bar{a}, b)$, then $\mathcal{A} \not\models \varphi(\bar{a}, b)$. But this is immediate from the assumption that $\varphi \wedge \psi \wedge \chi$ is not cofinally satisfiable.

In the proofs that follow it will be convenient to use the notation defined below:

Definition 13. For each n, the classes of $\mathcal{L}_n$ are denoted by $C_{n,1}, \dots, C_{n,g_4(n)}$ where $g_4(n) \leq g_3(n)$ for the polynomial g_3 in Definition 4, and where, for all $1 \leq i < j \leq g_4(n)$, all $a \in C_{n,i}$, and all $b \in C_{n,j}$, we have $\mathcal{L}_n \models a \prec b$.

Note that by Definition 4 we have $g_2(n) \leq |C_{n,i}| \leq g_1(n)$ for all n and all $1 \leq i \leq g_4(n)$, where g_1 and g_2 are specified in Definition 4. The next lemma is our main tool in the proofs of the main results when we want to eliminate quantifiers (except those appearing in (σ, k)-types) "almost surely".

Lemma 4. *Let $k \in \mathbb{N}$, let $p'(\bar{x}, y)$ be a (τ, k)-type, let $p(\bar{x}, y)$ be a (σ, k)-type, and let $q(\bar{x})$ be a $(\sigma, 2k+1)$-type. Then (p, p', q) is balanced. If $p(\bar{x}, y) \wedge p'(\bar{x}, y) \wedge q(\bar{x})$ is cofinally satisfiable then (p, p', q) is positively balanced.*

Proof. Let p', p and q be as assumed and suppose that $\bar{x} = (x_1, \dots, x_s)$. We will argue as if $\bar{x}$ is a nonempty sequence. The case when $\bar{x}$ is empty is simpler and uses the same kind of reasoning. By Remark 2 we may assume that $p \wedge p' \wedge q$ is cofinally satisfiable. If $p' \models \bigvee_{i=1}^{s} y = x_i$ then, as $p'(\bar{x}, y) \wedge p(\bar{x}, y) \wedge q(\bar{x})$ is cofinally satisfiable, we must have $q(\bar{x}) \wedge p'(\bar{x}, y) \models p(\bar{x}, y)$ and therefore (p, p', q) is 1-balanced. So from now on suppose that $p' \models \bigwedge_{i=1}^{s} y \neq x_i$.

Let $\hat{p}(\bar{x}, y)$ be the conjunction of every $(\sigma \setminus \tau)$-literal that

(a) contains y, and
(b) is implied by $p(\bar{x}, y)$ (or equivalently, is a conjunct of $p(\bar{x}, y)$).

Then $p(\bar{x}, y)$ is equivalent to $q(\bar{x}) \wedge p'(\bar{x}, y) \wedge \hat{p}(\bar{x}, y)$ and let

$$\tilde{p}(\bar{x}, y) := p'(\bar{x}, y) \wedge \hat{p}(\bar{x}, y) \text{ so } \tilde{p} \text{ is a } (\sigma, k)\text{-type.}$$

By Lemma 3, there is $\alpha \in [0, 1]$ such that for all n, if $\bar{a} \in (L_n)^s$, $b \in L_n$ and $\mathcal{L}_n \models p'(\bar{a}, b)$ then $\mathbb{P}_n\big(\mathbf{E}_n^{\tilde{p}(\bar{a}, b)}\big) = \alpha$. The assumption that $p \wedge p' \wedge q$ is cofinally satisfiable implies (by Lemma 3) that $\alpha > 0$.

Let $q'(\bar{x}) = q \restriction \tau$. By reordering $\bar{x}$ if necessary we may, without loss of generality, assume that for some $0 \leq t \leq s$ we have:

- $p' \models x_i \preceq x_{i+1}$ for all $i = 1, \dots, s-1$, and
- $p' \models x_t \preceq y \preceq x_{t+1}$, where '$x_t \preceq y$' is omitted if $t = 0$, and '$y \preceq x_{t+1}$' is omitted if $t = s$.

Now one of the following four cases must hold, where formulas containing x_t are removed if $t = 0$, and formulas containing x_{t+1} are removed if $t = s$:

1. For some $l, m \leq k$, $p' \models \mathrm{dist}_l(x_t, y) \wedge \mathrm{dist}_m(y, x_{t+1})$.
2. For some $l \leq k$, $p' \models \mathrm{dist}_l(x_t, y) \wedge \mathrm{dist}_{>k}(y, x_{t+1})$.
3. For some $m \leq k$, $p' \models \mathrm{dist}_{>k}(x_t, y) \wedge \mathrm{dist}_m(y, x_{t+1})$.
4. $p' \models \mathrm{dist}_{>k}(x_t, y) \wedge \mathrm{dist}_{>k}(y, x_{t+1})$.

First suppose that 1 holds and $1 \leq t < s$. Then $p' \models \mathrm{dist}_{l+m}(x_t, x_{t+1})$ where $l + m \leq 2k + 1$. As $q'(\bar{x})$ is a $(\tau, 2k+1)$-type and $p' \wedge q'$ is cofinally satisfiable it follows that $q' \models \mathrm{dist}_{l+m}(x_t, x_{t+1})$. For arbitrary n let $\bar{a} = (a_1, \dots, a_s) \in L_n^s$

and suppose that $\mathcal{L}_n \models q'(\bar{a})$, so $\mathcal{L}_n \models \text{dist}_{l+m}(a_t, a_{t+1})$ meaning that the distance from a_t to a_{t+1} is $l+m$. Let $C_{n,i}$ be the class to which a_t belongs. Then $\text{dist}_l(a_t, \mathcal{L}_n) = C_{n,i+l}$ and $\text{dist}_m(\mathcal{L}_n, a_{t+1}) = C_{n,i+1}$. Hence $p'(\bar{a}, \mathcal{L}_n) = C_{n,i+l} \setminus \text{rng}(\bar{a})$. It follows from Definition 4 that $|p'(\bar{a}, \mathcal{L}_n)| \geq g_2(n) - s$. From Definition 8 of $\mathbb{P}_n$ and the definition of $\tilde{p}$ it follows that for every $b \in p'(\bar{a}, \mathcal{L}_n)$ the event $\mathbf{E}_n^{\tilde{p}(\bar{a},b)}$ is independent from all events $\mathbf{E}_n^{\tilde{p}(\bar{a},b')}$ where $b' \in p'(\bar{a}, \mathcal{L}_n)$ is different from b.

As mentioned above, for all $b \in p'(\bar{a}, \mathcal{L}_n)$, $\mathbb{P}_n\big(\mathbf{E}_n^{\tilde{p}(\bar{a},b)}\big) = \alpha$. Let $\varepsilon > 0$. Lemma 1 implies that there is $c > 0$, depending only on ε and α such that the probability that the following does *not* hold is less than $e^{-cg_2(n)}$.

$$(\alpha - \varepsilon)|p'(\bar{a}, \mathcal{A})| \leq |\tilde{p}(\bar{a}, \mathcal{A})| \leq (\alpha + \varepsilon)|p'(\bar{a}, \mathcal{A})|. \tag{1}$$

As we observed after Definition 4, $|L_n| \leq f(n)$ for a polynomial $f(x)$. So we can choose $\bar{a} \in L_n^s$ in at most $f(x)^s$ ways where $f(x)^s$ is a polynomial. Therefore the probability that there is $\bar{a} \in L_n^s$ such that $\mathcal{L}_n \models q'(\bar{a})$ and (1) does *not* hold is at most $f(x)^s e^{-cg_2(n)}$. By Lemma 2, $f(x)^s e^{-cg_2(n)} \leq e^{-\frac{1}{2}cg_2(n)}$ if n is large enough. Hence the probability that (1) holds for all $\bar{a} \in L_n^s$ such that $\mathcal{L}_n \models q'(\bar{a})$ is at least $1 - e^{-\frac{1}{2}cg_2(n)}$ for large enough n where $1 - e^{-\frac{1}{2}cg_2(n)} \to 1$ as $n \to \infty$. Since $q(\bar{x}) \models q'(\bar{x})$ and $p(\bar{x}, y)$ is equivalent to $q(\bar{x}) \wedge \tilde{p}(\bar{x}, y)$ if follows that

$$\lim_{n\to\infty} \mathbb{P}_n\big(\{\mathcal{A} \in \mathbf{W}_n : (p, p', q) \text{ is } (\alpha, \varepsilon)\text{-balanced in } \mathcal{A}\}\big) = 1.$$

As the argument works for any $\varepsilon > 0$ it follows that (p, p', q) is α-balanced.

Still let us assume that 1 holds but now suppose that $t = s$, so $p' \models x_s \leq y \wedge \text{dist}_l(x_s, y)$. As $p'(\bar{x}, y)$ is a (τ, k)-type we either have $p' \models \text{dist}_m^{\text{la}}(y)$ for some $m \leq k$, or $p' \models \text{dist}_{>k}^{\text{la}}(y)$. First suppose that $p' \models \text{dist}_m^{\text{la}}(y)$ where $m \leq k$. Then $\mathcal{L}_n \models \forall\bar{x}(p'(\bar{x}, y) \to \text{dist}_{l+m}^{\text{la}}(x_s))$ for every n. Since $q'(\bar{x})$ is a $(\tau, 2k+1)$-type such that $p' \wedge q'$ is satisfiable in some $\mathcal{L}_n$ (in fact in infinitely many $\mathcal{L}_n$) it follows that $\mathcal{L}_n \models \forall\bar{x}(q'(\bar{x}) \to \text{dist}_{l+m}^{\text{la}}(x_s))$ for all n. So if $\bar{a} = (a_1, \dots, a_s) \in L_n^s$ and $\mathcal{L}_n \models q'(\bar{a})$ then $\mathcal{L}_n \models \text{dist}_{l+m}^{\text{la}}(a_s)$ so the distance from a_s to any element in the class $C_{n,g_4(n)}$ of largest elements is $l+m$. Then $p'(\bar{a}, \mathcal{L}_n) = C_{n,g_4(n)-m} \setminus \text{rng}(\bar{a})$ so (by Definition 4) $|p'(\bar{a}, \mathcal{L}_n)| \geq g_2(n) - s$. Now we can argue just as in the previous case (when we assumed that $1 \leq t < s$).

Now suppose $p' \models \text{dist}_{>k}^{\text{la}}(y)$ (and still 1 holds and $t = s$). Then $\mathcal{L}_n \models \forall\bar{x}(p'(\bar{x}, y) \to \text{dist}_{>l+k}^{\text{la}}(x_s))$ for every n. Since $q'(\bar{x})$ is a $(\tau, 2k+1)$-type such that $p' \wedge q'$ is satisfiable in some $\mathcal{L}_n$ it follows that $\mathcal{L}_n \models \forall\bar{x}(q'(\bar{x}) \to \text{dist}_{>l+k}^{\text{la}}(x_s))$ for all n. It follows that if $\bar{a} = (a_1, \dots, a_s) \in L_n^s$ and $\mathcal{L}_n \models q'(\bar{a})$ then $\mathcal{L}_n \models \text{dist}_{>l+k}^{\text{la}}(a_s)$ so the distance from a_s to any element in the class $C_{n,g_4(n)}$ of largest elements is greater than $l+k$. Let $C_{n,i}$ be the class to which a_s belongs. Then $p'(\bar{a}, \mathcal{L}_n) = C_{n,i+l} \setminus \text{rng}(\bar{a})$ so $|p'(\bar{a}, \mathcal{L}_n)| \geq g_2(n) - s$ and we can continue to argue as before.

If $t = 0$ then $p' \models y \leq x_1 \wedge \text{dist}_m(y, x_1)$, meaning (together with previous assumptions that are still in action) that "y is smaller than all x_i and the distance from y to x_1 is m". In this case we have two subcases: either $p' \models \text{dist}_l^{\text{sm}}(y)$ for some $l \leq k$, or $p' \models \text{dist}_{>k}^{\text{sm}}(y)$. These cases are treated similarly as we treated the corresponding subcases above (that is, the case $p' \models \text{dist}^{\text{la}}_m(y)$ for some $m \leq k$, and the case $p' \models \text{dist}^{\text{la}}_{>k}(y)$).

Now suppose that 2 holds, so for some $l \leq k$, $p' \models \text{dist}_l(x_t, y) \wedge \text{dist}_{>k}(y, x_{t+1})$. Suppose also that $1 \leq t < s$. Then $p'(\bar{x}, y) \models \text{dist}_{>l+k}(x_t, x_{t+1})$. As $q'(\bar{x})$ is a $(\tau, 2k+1)$-type such that $p' \wedge q'$ is satisfiable in some $\mathcal{L}_n$ it follows $q'(\bar{x}) \models \text{dist}_{>l+k}(x_t, x_{t+1})$. For arbitrary n let $\bar{a} = (a_1, \ldots, a_s) \in L_n^s$ and suppose that $\mathcal{L}_n \models q'(\bar{a})$. Let $C_{n,i}$ be the class containing a_t. From $\mathcal{L}_n \models q'(\bar{a})$ we get $\mathcal{L}_n \models \text{dist}_{>l+k}(a_t, a_{t+1})$ so the distance from any element in $C_{n,i+l}$ to a_{t+1} is greater than k. Hence $C_{n,i+l} \setminus \text{rng}(\bar{a}) \subseteq p'(\bar{a}, \mathcal{L}_n)$. By Definition 4 we get $|p'(\bar{a}, \mathcal{L}_n)| \geq g_2(n) - s$ and can continue to argue as in the first case. The other subcases of case 2, namely when $t = 0$ and when $t = s$, are treated similarly as the corresponding subcases of case 1.

The proofs in cases 3 and 4 are just minor variations of the arguments that we have seen and are thus left to the reader. □

Our last technical lemma before proving the main results is the following:

Lemma 5. *Let $p(\bar{x}, y)$ be a (τ, k)-type and let $q(\bar{x})$ be a $(\tau, 2k+1)$-type. Then either*

(a) for all n, $\mathcal{L}_n \models \forall \bar{x}\big(q(\bar{x}) \rightarrow \exists y p(\bar{x}, y)\big)$, or
(b) for all n, $\mathcal{L}_n \models \forall \bar{x}\big(q(\bar{x}) \rightarrow \neg \exists y p(\bar{x}, y)\big)$.

Proof. Let $p(\bar{x}, y)$ and $q(\bar{x})$ be as assumed and let $\bar{x} = (x_1, \ldots, x_s)$. We will reason similarly as in part of the proof of Lemma 4. Without loss of generality we may assume that

- $p \models x_i \preceq x_{i+1}$ for all $i = 1, \ldots, s-1$, and
- $p \models x_t \preceq y \preceq x_{t+1}$, where '$x_t \preceq y$' is omitted if $t = 0$, and '$y \preceq x_{t+1}$' is omitted if $t = s$.

If $q \models x_i \npreceq x_{i+1}$ for some i then we are in case (b), so suppose that $q \models x_i \preceq x_{i+1}$ for all $i = 1, \ldots, s-1$. One of the following four cases must hold, where formulas containing x_t are removed if $t = 0$, and formulas containing x_{t+1} are removed if $t = s$:

1. For some $l, m \leq k$, $p \models \text{dist}_l(x_t, y) \wedge \text{dist}_m(y, x_{t+1})$.
2. For some $l \leq k$, $p \models \text{dist}_l(x_t, y) \wedge \text{dist}_{>k}(y, x_{t+1})$.
3. For some $m \leq k$, $p \models \text{dist}_{>k}(x_t, y) \wedge \text{dist}_m(y, x_{t+1})$.
4. $p \models \text{dist}_{>k}(x_t, y) \wedge \text{dist}_{>k}(y, x_{t+1})$.

Suppose that case 1 holds and $1 \leq t < s$. Then $p \models \text{dist}_{l+m}(x_t, x_{t+1})$. Since q is a $(\tau, 2k+1)$-type and $l + m \leq 2k+1$ it follows that either $q \models \text{dist}_{l+m}(x_t, x_{t+1})$ or $q \models \neg\text{dist}_{l+m}(x_t, x_{t+1})$. In the first case we are in case (a), in the second case we are in case (b). The subcases when $t = 0$ and when $t = s$, as well as the cases 2–4 are treated in a similar way and follow the pattern of the corresponding cases in the proof of Lemma 4 so we leave the details to the reader. □

4.1 Proof of Theorem 1 and Corollary 1

Let $\varphi(\bar{x}) \in FO(\sigma)$ be cofinally satisfiable. We will show that there is $k \geq \kappa$ and a disjunction $\bigvee_{i=1}^{s} p_i(\bar{x})$ such that each $p_i(\bar{x})$ is a (σ, k)-type and $\varphi(\bar{x})$ is almost surely equivalent to $\bigvee_{i=1}^{s} p_i(\bar{x})$. We use induction on the complexity of formulas. First suppose that $\varphi(\bar{x})$ is quantifier-free. Then, for every complete (σ, κ)-type $p(\bar{x})$, either $p(\bar{x}) \models \varphi(\bar{x})$ or $p(\bar{x}) \models \neg\varphi(\bar{x})$. Let $p_1(\bar{x}), \ldots, p_s(\bar{x})$ be an enumeration of all, up to equivalence, complete (σ, κ)-types $p(\bar{x})$ in the variables $\bar{x}$ such that $p(\bar{x}) \models \varphi(\bar{x})$. The assumption that $\varphi(\bar{x})$ is cofinally satisfiable implies that the enumeration is not empty. Then $\varphi(\bar{x})$ is equivalent to $\bigvee_{i=1}^{s} p_i(\bar{x})$ in every $\mathcal{A} \in \bigcup_{n \in \mathbb{N}^+} \mathbf{W}_n$.

Suppose that $\varphi(\bar{x})$ has the form $\neg\psi(\bar{x})$ and $\psi(\bar{x})$ is almost surely equivalent to $\bigvee_{i=1}^{m} p_i(\bar{x})$ where, for some $k \geq \kappa$, each $p_i(\bar{x})$ is a complete (σ, k)-type. Then $\varphi(\bar{x})$ is almost surely equivalent to $\neg \bigvee_{i=1}^{m} p_i(\bar{x})$ and the later formula is equivalent (in all $\mathcal{A} \in \bigcup_{n \in \mathbb{N}^+} \mathbf{W}_n$) to $\bigvee_{i=1}^{m'} q_i(\bar{x})$ where $q_1(\bar{x}), \ldots, q_{m'}(\bar{x})$ is an enumeration of all, up to equivalence, complete (σ, k)-types in the variables $\bar{x}$ that are not equivalent to any of $p_1(\bar{x}), \ldots, p_m(\bar{x})$, which is equivalent to being inconsistent with each of them. Hence $\varphi(\bar{x})$ is almost surely equivalent to $\bigvee_{i=1}^{m'} q_i(\bar{x})$.

Suppose that $\varphi(\bar{x})$ has the form $\psi(\bar{x}) \wedge \theta(\bar{x})$ where, for some $k, k' \geq \kappa$, $\psi(\bar{x})$ and $\theta(\bar{x})$ are almost surely equivalent to $\bigvee_{i=1}^{m} p_i(\bar{x})$ and $\bigvee_{i=1}^{m'} p'_i(\bar{x})$, respectively, where each p_i is a complete (σ, k)-type and each p'_i is a complete (σ, k')-type. Without loss of generality suppose that $k \geq k'$. By considering "extensions" of the p'_i to complete (σ, k)-types we can assume that all p'_i are complete (σ, k)-types (i.e. that $k = k'$). Let $p_{j_1}, \ldots, p_{j_s}$ enumerate all p_i such that p_i is equivalent to some p'_l. As $\varphi(\bar{x})$ is cofinally satisfiable it follows that the enumeration is not empty, and it also follows that $\varphi(\bar{x})$ is almost surely equivalent to $\bigvee_{l=1}^{s} p_{j_l}(\bar{x})$.

Finally we consider the case when $\varphi(\bar{x})$ has the form $\exists y \psi(\bar{x}, y)$. Suppose, by the induction hypothesis, that $\psi(\bar{x}, y)$ is almost surely equivalent to $\bigvee_{i=1}^{s} p_i(\bar{x}, y)$ where, for some $k \geq \kappa$, each $p_i(\bar{x}, y)$ is a complete (σ, k)-type. It follows that $\varphi(\bar{x})$ is almost surely equivalent to $\exists y \bigvee_{i=1}^{s} p_i(\bar{x}, y)$. Since the later formula is logically equivalent to $\bigvee_{i=1}^{s} \exists y p_i(\bar{x}, y)$ is suffices to prove that for every $k \geq \kappa$ and every cofinally satisfiable complete (σ, k)-type $p(\bar{x}, y)$ there are complete $(\sigma, 2k+1)$-types $q_1(\bar{x}), \ldots, q_t(\bar{x})$ such that $\exists y p(\bar{x}, y)$ is almost surely equivalent to $\bigvee_{i=1}^{t} q_i(\bar{x})$.

So let $p(\bar{x}, y)$ be a cofinally satisfiable complete (σ, k)-type where $k \geq \kappa$. Let $p'(\bar{x}, y) = p{\restriction}\tau$, so $p \wedge p'$ is certainly cofinally satisfiable. We know from Lemma 4 that if $q(\bar{x})$ is a complete $(\sigma, 2k+1)$-type then (p, p', q) is balanced, and if $p \wedge p' \wedge q$ is cofinally satisfiable, then (p, p', q) is positively balanced. Let $q_1(\bar{x}), \ldots, q_t(\bar{x})$ enumerate all, up to equivalence, complete $(\sigma, 2k+1)$-types $q(\bar{x})$ such that $p \wedge p' \wedge q$ is cofinally satisfiable, and hence (p, p', q) is positively balanced. So suppose that (p, p', q_i) is α_i-balanced for some $\alpha_i > 0$. Let $q'_i(\bar{x}) = q_i{\restriction}\tau$ for $i = 1, \ldots, t$. Since $p' \wedge q$ is cofinally satisfiable it follows from Lemma 5 that, for all n and $i = 1, \ldots, t$, if $\bar{a} \in (L_n)^{|\bar{x}|}$ and $\mathcal{L}_n \models q'_i(\bar{a})$ for some i, then $\mathcal{L}_n \models \exists y p'(\bar{a}, y)$.

Let $\varepsilon > 0$ be smaller than all $\alpha_1, \ldots, \alpha_t$. Let

$$\mathbf{X}_n^{\varepsilon} = \big\{\mathcal{A} \in \mathbf{W}_n : \text{ for all } i = 1, \ldots, t, (p, p', q_i) \text{ is } (\alpha_i, \varepsilon)\text{-balanced in } \mathcal{A}\big\}.$$

Then $\lim_{n\to\infty}\mathbb{P}_n(\mathbf{X}_n^\varepsilon) = 1$ (because (p, p', q_i) is α_i-balanced for all i) and for all $\mathcal{A} \in \mathbf{X}_n^\varepsilon$, if $\mathcal{A} \models q_i(\bar{a})$ then $|p'(\bar{a}, \mathcal{L}_n)| \geq 1$ and $|p(\bar{a}, \mathcal{A})|/|p'(\bar{a}, \mathcal{A})| > \alpha_i - \varepsilon > 0$, so $p(\bar{a}, \mathcal{A}) \neq \emptyset$ and hence $\mathcal{A} \models \exists y p(\bar{a}, y)$. It follows that, for every n and $\mathcal{A} \in \mathbf{X}_n^\varepsilon$, $\mathcal{A} \models \bigvee_{i=1}^t q_i(\bar{x}) \to \exists y p(\bar{x}, y)$. Since $q_1, \ldots, q_t$ enumerate all, up to equivalence, complete $(\sigma, 2k+1)$-types such that $p \wedge p' \wedge q_i$ is cofinally satisfiable for all i it follows that, for all sufficiently large n and all $\mathcal{A} \in \mathbf{W}_n$, $\mathcal{A} \models \exists y p(\bar{x}, y) \to \bigvee_{i=1}^t q_i(\bar{x})$. Hence $p(\bar{x}, y)$ is almost surely equivalent to $\bigvee_{i=1}^t q_i(\bar{x})$. Thus Theorem 1 is proved.

Now we continue with the proof of Corollary 1. Let $\varphi(\bar{x}) \in FO(\sigma)$ be cofinally satisfiable. By Theorem 1, there is $k \geq \kappa$ and a disjunction $\bigvee_{i=1}^s p_i(\bar{x})$ such that each $p_i(\bar{x})$ is a complete (σ, k)-type and $\varphi(\bar{x})$ is almost surely equivalent to $\bigvee_{i=1}^s p_i(\bar{x})$. This means that if

$$\mathbf{X}_n = \big\{\mathcal{A} \in \mathbf{W}_n : \mathcal{A} \models \forall \bar{x}(\varphi(\bar{x}) \leftrightarrow \bigvee_{i=1}^s p_i(\bar{x}))\big\},$$

then $\lim_{n\to\infty}\mathbb{P}_n(\mathbf{X}_n) = 1$. We may assume that if $i \neq j$ then p_i is not equivalent to p_j, and hence $p_i \wedge p_j$ is inconsistent.

Let $p(\bar{x})$ be a (τ, k)-type. Suppose that $p \wedge p_i{\restriction}\tau$ is cofinally satisfiable for some i, and hence p is equivalent to $p_i{\restriction}\tau$. (If $\bar{x}$ is empty then p_i is equivalent to $p_i{\restriction}\tau$ so there is at most one such i.) Let $p_{j_1}, \ldots, p_{j_t}$ be an enumeration of all p_i such that $p \wedge p_i{\restriction}\tau$ is cofinally satisfiable, so p and $p_{j_l}{\restriction}\tau$ are equivalent for all $l = 1, \ldots, t$. By Lemma 3, for each $l = 1, \ldots, t$, there is $\beta_l \in [0, 1]$ such that if $n \in \mathbb{N}^+$, $\bar{a} \in (L_n)^{|\bar{x}|}$, and $\mathcal{L}_n \models p(\bar{a})$, then

$$\mathbb{P}_n\big(\{\mathcal{A} \in \mathbf{W}_n : \mathcal{A} \models p_{j_l}(\bar{a})\}\big) = \beta_l.$$

Consequently,

$$\mathbb{P}_n\big(\{\mathcal{A} \in \mathbf{W}_n : \mathcal{A} \models \bigvee_{l=1}^t p_{j_l}(\bar{a})\}\big) = \sum_{l=1}^t \beta_l.$$

Let $\beta = \sum_{l=1}^t \beta_l$. (If $\bar{x}$ is empty then $t = 1$, so $\beta = \beta_1$ and, by Remark 1, $\beta_1 = 1$). Let $\varepsilon > 0$. As $\lim_{n\to\infty}\mathbb{P}_n(\mathbf{X}_n) = 1$ it follows that if n is large enough then

$$\Big|\mathbb{P}_n\big(\{\mathcal{A} \in \mathbf{W}_n : \mathcal{A} \models \varphi(\bar{a})\}\big) \; - \; \beta\Big| \;\leq\; \varepsilon. \tag{2}$$

If, for all $i = 1, \ldots, s$, $p \wedge p_i{\restriction}\tau$ is not cofinally satisfiable, then for all sufficiently large n and $\bar{a} \in (L_n)^{|\bar{x}|}$, if $\mathcal{L}_n \models p(\bar{a})$, then,

$$\mathbb{P}_n\big(\{\mathcal{A} \in \mathbf{W}_n : \mathcal{A} \models \bigvee_{i=1}^s p_i(\bar{a})\}\big) = 0,$$

and, using that $\lim_{n\to\infty}\mathbb{P}_n(\mathbf{X}_n) = 1$, it follows that if we let $\beta = 0$ then (2) holds if n is large enough. □

4.2 Proof of Theorem 2

Suppose that the sequence of $\mathcal{L}_n$, $n \in \mathbb{N}^+$, also satisfies Property 1. Then each $\mathcal{L}_n$ has exactly λ classes, so $g_4(n) = \lambda$ for all n. Moreover, for each $\delta > 0$, all sufficiently large n, and all $i = 1, \dots, \lambda$, we have $(1-\delta)h(n) \leq |C_{n,i}| \leq (1+\delta)h(n)$, where $g_2(n) \leq h(n) \leq g_1(n)$ for all n.

Let $k = \lambda$ where λ is as in Property 1. Then every (τ, k)-type $p(x_1, \dots, x_l)$ (for arbitrary l) which is satisfiable in some $\mathcal{L}_n$ will, for all $1 \leq i, j \leq l$, express that the distance from x_i to x_j is exactly d for some $d \leq k$, and that the distance from x_i to any smallest element (largest element) is exactly e for some $e \leq k$. It will also express that the length of the linear preorder is k $(= \lambda)$.

Let $\varphi(\bar{x}) \in FOP(\sigma)$ be cofinally satisfiable and suppose that if $\exists^{>r} y \psi(\bar{z}, y)$ is a subformula of φ then $r \neq \frac{\alpha}{\lambda}$ whenever α is a sum of numbers $\alpha_{R,q}$ as in Definition 8. We use induction on the complexity of $\varphi(\bar{x})$. The cases when $\varphi(\bar{x})$ is quantifier-free or has one of the forms $\neg\psi(\bar{x})$, $\psi(\bar{x}) \wedge \theta(\bar{x})$, or $\exists y \psi(\bar{x}, y)$ were treated in the proof of Theorem 1, although here we can simplify the arguments by letting $k = \lambda$ all the time.

So now suppose that $\varphi(\bar{x})$ has the form $\exists^{>r} y \psi(\bar{x}, y)$ where (by the induction hypothesis) $\psi(\bar{x}, y)$ is almost surely equivalent to a formula $\bigvee_{i=1}^{s} p_i(\bar{x}, y)$ where each $p_i(\bar{x}, y)$ is a complete (σ, k)-type. By reordering and renaming the p_i if necessary we may assume that $\psi(\bar{x}, y)$ is almost surely equivalent to a formula $\bigvee_{i=1}^{s} \bigvee_{j=1}^{t_i} p_{i,j}(\bar{x}, y)$ where, for all $i = 1, \dots, s$, and all $j, j' = 1, \dots, t_i$, $p_{i,j} \restriction \bar{x}$ is equivalent to $p_{i,j'} \restriction \bar{x}$. For $i = 1, \dots, s$, let $q_i(\bar{x}) = p_{i,1} \restriction \bar{x}$, so $q_i(\bar{x})$ is equivalent to $p_{i,j} \restriction \bar{x}$ for all $j = 1, \dots, t_i$. Without loss of generality we assume that $q_i \wedge q_j$ is unsatisfiable if $i \neq j$ and that $p_{l,i} \wedge p_{l,j}$ is unsatisfiable if $i \neq j$.

If $p_{i,j}(\bar{x}, y)$ expresses that y equals some of the variables in $\bar{x}$, then $\mathcal{A} \models q_i(\bar{a})$ implies that $|p_{i,j}(\bar{a}, \mathcal{A})| = 1$ so the contribution of $p_{i,j}(\bar{a}, \mathcal{A})$ to $\bigcup_{i=1}^{s} \bigcup_{j=1}^{t_i} p_{i,j}(\bar{a}, \mathcal{A})$ is negligible for all sufficiently large n. If $p_{i,j}(\bar{x}, y)$ is not cofinally satisfiable then $p(\bar{a}, \mathcal{A}) = \emptyset$ for all sufficiently large n so again its contribution is negligible. Therefore we will now assume that for all i and j, $p_{i,j}(\bar{x}, y)$ is cofinally satisfiable and expresses that y is different from all variables in $\bar{x}$.

Let $p'_{i,j}(\bar{x}, y) = p_{i,j} \restriction \tau$. Then $p_{i,j} \wedge p'_{i,j} \wedge q_i$ is cofinally satisfiable for all i and j. By the assumption that there are always exactly k classes (with respect to $\preceq$) it follows that, for each $i = 1, \dots, s$, there is (up to equivalence) a unique complete $(\sigma, 2k+1)$-type $q_i^*(\bar{x})$ such that $q_i^* \wedge q_i$ is satisfiable in some $\mathcal{A} \in \bigcup_{n \in \mathbb{N}^+} \mathbf{W}_n$; in fact, it follows that q_i^* and q_i are equivalent in all such $\mathcal{A}$. Therefore Lemma 4 tells that, for all i and j, $(p_{i,j}, p'_{i,j}, q_i)$ is $\alpha_{i,j}$-balanced for some $\alpha_{i,j} > 0$. For every $\varepsilon > 0$ and n let

$$\mathbf{X}_n^{\varepsilon} = \{\mathcal{A} \in \mathbf{W}_n : \text{ for all } i \text{ and } j, (p_{i,j}, p'_{i,j}, q_i) \text{ is } (\alpha_{i,j}, \varepsilon)\text{-balanced in } \mathcal{A}\}.$$

Then $\lim_{n \to \infty} \mathbb{P}_n(\mathbf{X}_n^{\varepsilon}) = 1$ for all $\varepsilon > 0$. Fix any i and j. Then, for some $0 \leq l \leq k-1 (= \lambda - 1)$, $p'_{i,j}(\bar{x}, y) \models \text{dist}_l^{\text{sm}}(y)$, that is, $p'_{i,j}$ expresses that the distance to y from any one of the smallest elements is l. Since $p'_{i,j}(\bar{x}, y)$ cannot say anything more about y (except that it is different from all variables in $\bar{x}$) it follows that if $\mathcal{A} \in \mathbf{W}_n$ and $\mathcal{A} \models q_i(\bar{a})$ then $p'_{i,j}(\bar{a}, \mathcal{A}) = C_{n,l+1} \setminus \text{rng}(\bar{a})$.

As $(p_{i,j}, p'_{i,j}, q_i)$ is $\alpha_{i,j}$-balanced it follows that, for every $0 < \varepsilon < 1$, if n is sufficiently large, $\mathcal{A} \in \mathbf{X}_n^\varepsilon$, and $\mathcal{A} \models q_i(\bar{a}))$ then

$$\begin{aligned}|p_{i,j}(\bar{a}, \mathcal{A})| &\leq (\alpha_{i,j} + \varepsilon)|p'_{i,j}(\bar{a}, \mathcal{A})| \\ &\leq (\alpha_{i,j} + \varepsilon)(1+\varepsilon)h(n) \leq (\alpha_{i,j} + 3\varepsilon)h(n). \qquad \text{(by Property 1)}\end{aligned}$$

It follows that

$$\frac{\left|\bigcup_{j=1}^{t_i} p_{i,j}(\bar{a}, \mathcal{A})\right|}{|L_n|} \leq \frac{h(n)\sum_{j=1}^{t_i}(\alpha_{i,j} + 3\varepsilon)}{k(1-\varepsilon)h(n)} = \frac{\sum_{j=1}^{t_i}(\alpha_{i,j} + 3\varepsilon)}{k(1-\varepsilon)}.$$

In a similar way we get (for large enough n)

$$\frac{\left|\bigcup_{j=1}^{t_i} p_{i,j}(\bar{a}, \mathcal{A})\right|}{|L_n|} \geq \frac{\sum_{j=1}^{t_i}(\alpha_{i,j} - 3\varepsilon)}{k(1+\varepsilon)}.$$

Let $\alpha_i = \frac{1}{k}\sum_{j=1}^{t_i} \alpha_{i,j}$. It follows that, for every $\varepsilon > 0$, if n is large enough, $\mathcal{A} \in \mathbf{X}_n^\varepsilon$ and $\mathcal{A} \models q_i(\bar{a})$, then

$$\alpha_i - \varepsilon \leq \frac{\left|\bigcup_{j=1}^{t_i} p_{i,j}(\bar{a}, \mathcal{A})\right|}{|L_n|} \leq \alpha_i + \varepsilon.$$

So if $\varepsilon > 0$ is small enough, $\mathcal{A} \in \mathbf{X}_n^\varepsilon$ and $\bar{a} \in (L_n)^{|\bar{x}|}$, then $\mathcal{A} \models \exists^{>r} y \bigvee_{i=1}^{s} \bigvee_{j=1}^{t_i} p_{i,j}(\bar{a}, y)$ if and only if there is i such that $\mathcal{A} \models q_i(\bar{a})$ and $\alpha_i > r$. If there is no i such that $\alpha_i > r$ then $\exists^{>r} y \bigvee_{i=1}^{s} \bigvee_{j=1}^{t_i} p_{i,j}(\bar{x}, y)$ is false in every $\mathcal{A} \in \mathbf{X}_n^\varepsilon$ if $\varepsilon > 0$ is small enough and n large enough, and it follows that $\exists \bar{x} \varphi(\bar{x})$ is almost surely false. If there is some i such that $\alpha_i > r$ then we let $i_1, \ldots, i_\rho$ enumerate all such i. Then $\exists^{>r} y \bigvee_{i=1}^{s} \bigvee_{j=1}^{t_i} p_{i,j}(\bar{x}, y)$ is equivalent to $\bigvee_{j=1}^{\rho} q_{i_j}(\bar{x})$ in every $\mathcal{A} \in \mathbf{X}_n^\varepsilon$ if $\varepsilon > 0$ is small enough and n large enough, and it follows that $\varphi(\bar{x})$ is almost surely equivalent to $\bigvee_{j=1}^{\rho} q_{i_j}(\bar{x})$. □

Acknowledgement. Vera Koponen was partially supported by the Swedish Research Council, grant 2023-05238_VR.

Disclosure of Interests. The authors have no competing interests to declare that are relevant to the content of this article.

References

1. Abu Zaid, F., Dawar, A., Grädel, E., Pakusa, W.: Definability of summation problems for Abelian groups and semigroups. In: Proceedings of 32th Annual ACM/IEEE Symposium on Logic in Computer Science (LICS) (2017)
2. Ahlman, O., Koponen, V.: Random l-colourable structures with a pregeometry. Math. Log. Q. **63**, 32–58 (2017)
3. Alon, N., Spencer, J.H.: The Probabilistic Method, 2nd edn. Wiley (2000)
4. Baldwin, J.T.: Expansions of geometries. J. Symb. Log. **68**, 803–827 (2003)

5. Van den Broeck, G., Kersting, K., Natarajan, S., Poole, D. (eds.): An Introduction to Lifted Probabilistic Inference. The MIT Press (2021)
6. Burris, S.: Number Theoretic Density and Logical Limit Laws. Mathematical Surveys and Monographs Series. American Mathematical Society (2001)
7. Chernoff, H.: A measure of the asymptotic efficiency for tests of a hypothesis based on the sum of observations. Ann. Math. Stat. **23**, 493–509 (1952)
8. Compton, K.J., Henson, C.W., Shelah, S.: Nonconvergence, undecidability, and intractability in asymptotic problems. Ann. Pure Appl. Log. **36**, 207–224 (1987)
9. Dawar, A., Grädel, E., Hoelzel, M.: Convergence and nonconvergence laws for random expansions of product structures. In: Blass, A., et al. (eds.) Gurevich Festschrift. Lecture Notes in Computer Science, vol. 12180, pp. 118–132. Springer (2020)
10. Ebbinghaus, H.-D., Flum, J.: Finite Model Theory, 2nd edn. Springer (1999)
11. Fagin, R.: Probabilities on finite models. J. Symb. Log. **41**, 50–58 (1976)
12. Glebskii, Y., Kogan, D., Liogon'kii, M., Talanov, V.: Range and degree of realizability of formulas in the restricted predicate calculus. Cybernetics **5**, 142–154 (1969)
13. Haber, S., Krivelevich, M.: The logic of random regular graphs. J. Combin. **1**, 389–440 (2010)
14. Keisler, J.H., Lotfallah, W.B.: Almost everywhere elimination of probability quantifiers. J. Symb. Log. **74**, 1121–1142 (2009)
15. Kimmig, A., Mihalkova, L., Getoor, L.: Lifted graphical models: a survey. Mach. Learn. **99**, 1–45 (2015)
16. Kolaitis, P.G., Prömel, H.J., Rothschild, B.L.: K_{l+1}-free graphs: asymptotic structure and a $0 - 1$ law. Trans. Am. Math. Soc. **303**, 637–671 (1987)
17. Koller, D., Friedman, N.: Probabilistic Graphical Models: Principles and Techniques. MIT Press (2009)
18. Koponen, V.: Conditional probability logic, lifted Bayesian networks, and almost sure quantifier elimination. Theoret. Comput. Sci. **848**, 1–27 (2020)
19. Koponen, V.: Random expansions of finite structures with bounded degree (submitted). https://arxiv.org/abs/2401.04802
20. Koponen, V., Tousinejad, Y.: Random expansions of trees with bounded height. Theor. Comput. Sci. **1040**, 115201 (2025). https://doi.org/10.1016/j.tcs.2025.115201
21. Koponen, V., Weitkämper, F.: A general approach to asymptotic elimination of aggregation functions and generalized quantifiers (submitted). https://arxiv.org/abs/2304.07865
22. Lynch, J.F.: Almost sure theories. Ann. Math. Log. **18**, 91–135 (1980)
23. Gregory, L.: McColm, MSO zero-one laws on random labelled acyclic graphs. Discret. Math. **254**, 331–347 (2002)
24. Niemistö, H.: Zero-one law and definability of linear order. J. Symb. Log. **74**, 105–123 (2009)
25. Shelah, S., Spencer, J.: Zero-one laws for sparse random graphs. J. Am. Math. Soc. **1**, 97–115 (1988)
26. Shelah, S.: Zero-one laws for graphs with edge probabilities decaying with distance. Part I. Fundam. Math. **175**, 195–239 (2002)

Indicative Conditionals: Some Algebraic Considerations

Umberto Rivieccio(✉) and Miguel Muñoz Pérez(✉)

Departamento de Lógica, Historia y Filosofía de la Ciencia, UNED, Madrid, Spain
umberto@fsof.uned.es, mupemiguel99@gmail.com

Abstract. We consider a family of non-classical three-valued logics that have been proposed to model *indicative conditionals* – sentences of the *if-then* type that occur in natural language, and concern what could be true (as opposed to counterfactuals, which concern eventualities that are no longer possible). Among these, we study the systems introduced by B. De Finetti, W.S. Cooper, J. Cantwell and R.J. Farrell, as well as some variants that have not appeared in the literature but seem nevertheless to be natural objects of interest from a formal point of view. We determine which of these logics are *algebraizable* (in the sense of Blok and Pigozzi), providing for the corresponding algebraic counterparts equational presentations from which finite Hilbert-style calculi can be readily obtained. Even in the non-algebraizable cases we indicate how algebraic techniques may be employed to obtain further semantical insight into the logics and axiomatizations. In the concluding section we point to possible extensions of the present work, such as further analysis of the relevant classes of algebras via *twist-structure* representations.

Keywords: Indicative conditionals · Algebraizability · Axiomatization · Algebraic semantics · Connexive logics · Twist-structures

1 Introduction

Indicative conditionals are the simplest sentences of the *if-then* type that occur in natural language, concerning what could be true – in opposition to counterfactuals, which concern eventualities that are no longer possible. In Boolean propositional logic, an indicative conditional "if φ then ψ" is traditionally formalized as the material implication $\varphi \to \psi$, or equivalently the disjunction $\neg \varphi \vee \psi$. This approach has several limitations that have been remarked early on in the history of modern logic: in particular, a number of authors argued that conditionals having a false antecedent – which are true in Boolean logic, independently of the consequent – should instead be regarded as lacking a (classical) truth value. Such a proposal can be traced back at least to Reichenbach (1935), De Finetti (1936), and Quine (1950). "Uttering a conditional amounts to making a *conditional assertion*: the speaker is committed to the truth of the consequent when

D. Kozen and R. de Queiroz (Eds.): WoLLIC 2025, LNCS 15942, pp. 119–140, 2026.
https://doi.org/10.1007/978-3-031-99536-1_8

the antecedent is true, but committed to neither truth nor falsity of the consequent when the antecedent is false" [10, p. 188]; see also [12] and the references cited therein.

$\wedge_{\mathsf{OL}}$	**0**	**1/2**	**1**
0	**0**	**0**	**0**
1/2	**0**	**1/2**	**1**
1	**0**	**1**	**1**

$\vee_{\mathsf{OL}}$	**0**	**1/2**	**1**
0	**0**	**0**	**1**
1/2	**0**	**1/2**	**1**
1	**1**	**1**	**1**

	$\neg$
0	**1**
1/2	**1/2**
1	**0**

$\wedge_{\mathsf{K}}$	**0**	**1/2**	**1**
0	**0**	**0**	**0**
1/2	**0**	**1/2**	**1/2**
1	**0**	**1/2**	**1**

$\vee_{\mathsf{K}}$	**0**	**1/2**	**1**
0	**0**	**1/2**	**1**
1/2	**1/2**	**1/2**	**1**
1	**1**	**1**	**1**

$\to_{\mathsf{OL}}$	**0**	**1/2**	**1**
0	**1/2**	**1/2**	**1/2**
1/2	**0**	**1/2**	**1**
1	**0**	**1/2**	**1**

$\to_{\mathsf{DF}}$	**0**	**1/2**	**1**
0	**1/2**	**1/2**	**1/2**
1/2	**1/2**	**1/2**	**1/2**
1	**0**	**1/2**	**1**

$\to_{\mathsf{F}}$	**0**	**1/2**	**1**
0	**1/2**	**1/2**	**1/2**
1/2	**0**	**1/2**	**1/2**
1	**0**	**1/2**	**1**

Fig. 1. Tables of the three-valued connectives.

Among the possible ways of formalizing the above intuition, a very simple one consists in expanding the classical truth values $(\mathbf{0}, \mathbf{1})$ with a third "gap" value (here denoted by $\mathbf{1/2}$) to be assigned to conditional sentences with a false antecedent; extending then the truth tables of the propositional connectives in accordance with the above interpretation. In particular, with regard to the implication, one would certainly require $\mathbf{0} \to x = \mathbf{1/2}$, whereas in other cases (e.g. $\mathbf{1/2} \to x$) intuitions may differ (cf. Fig. 1). As for the designated elements to be preserved in derivations, it is natural to include (besides $\mathbf{1}$) also $\mathbf{1/2}$, at least if one wants to retain basic classical tautologies such as the law of identity $(\varphi \to \varphi)$[1].

The above constraints determine a range of three-valued propositional *logics of indicative conditionals* which turn out to be, in general, incomparable with classical two-valued logic rather than subclassical (i.e. weaker than classical logic). In particular, they may be *connexive* in that they validate the (classically contingent) formulas known as *Aristotle's* and *Boethius'* theses[2].

Logics of indicative conditionals are discussed at length in the papers [10–12], which constitute the main bibliographical source and the starting point for the

[1] A peculiar consequence of this setup is that there will be valid formulas whose negation is also valid: for instance the formula $\neg\varphi \to (\varphi \to \varphi)$, which turns out to be equivalent (within the systems considered here) to $\mathbf{1/2}$, viewed as a propositional constant. This makes the logics under consideration not only paraconsistent but actually *contradictory* in the sense of Wansing [30].

[2] Respectively: (i) $\neg(\varphi \to \neg\varphi)$ and (ii) $(\varphi \to \psi) \to \neg(\varphi \to \neg\psi)$; $(\varphi \to \neg\psi) \to \neg(\varphi \to \psi)$. One easily checks on Fig. 1 that (i) and (ii) are valid in all the systems under consideration. We note that Farrell's logic (alone) does not validate the converse of Boethius, $\neg(\varphi \to \neg\psi) \to (\varphi \to \psi)$, for one has $\mathbf{1/2} \to_{\mathsf{F}} \mathbf{0} = \mathbf{0}$ but $\neg(\mathbf{1/2} \to_{\mathsf{F}} \neg\mathbf{0}) = \mathbf{1/2}$.

present research, and to which we refer for further background and motivation. Here we shall look at these propositional systems from the formal standpoint of algebraic logic: in particular, we will determine which among them are algebraizable in the sense of Blok and Pigozzi [3], and look at the corresponding classes of algebra-based semantics. Besides the ones discussed in [10,12], we will also consider a few systems obtained by varying the basic parameters (in particular, the designated elements) that do not appear to have been considered in the existing literature. Our interest in the latter logics is also mainly formal, but we believe future research may prove them to be also relevant to the philosophical issues mentioned above.

As is well known, a standard way of introducing a propositional logic is to fix an algebra $\mathbf{A}$ – i.e. a set A endowed with a finite number of finitary operations (conveniently given by truth tables, when A is itself finite) – together with a subset $F \subseteq A$ of *designated elements* to be preserved in derivations. Such a pair $\langle \mathbf{A}, F \rangle$ is known as a *(logical) matrix* and (following e.g. [2]) we may unambiguously denote by $\mathrm{Log}\langle \mathbf{A}, F \rangle$ the propositional consequence relation determined by the matrix $\langle \mathbf{A}, F \rangle$. For the logics of interest here, the universe of the algebra is always going to be the three-element set $A_3 = \{\mathbf{0}, \mathbf{1/2}, \mathbf{1}\}$, with variations only in the algebraic operations considered, and possibly the set of designated values. The basic systems are the following (in all cases, $F = \{\mathbf{1/2}, \mathbf{1}\}$):

1. $\mathrm{Log}\langle \mathbf{DF_3}, F \rangle$, where $\mathbf{DF_3} = \langle A_3; \wedge_{\mathsf{K}}, \vee_{\mathsf{K}}, \to_{\mathsf{DF}}, \neg \rangle$, which is the logic proposed by De Finetti [16]. As we shall see, up to definitional equivalence, this system coincides with Priest's *logic of paradox* LP [26] expanded with the single propositional constant $\mathbf{1/2}$.
2. $\mathrm{Log}\langle \mathbf{OL_3}, F \rangle$, where $\mathbf{OL_3} = \langle A_3; \wedge_{\mathsf{OL}}, \vee_{\mathsf{OL}}, \to_{\mathsf{OL}}, \neg \rangle$. This is Cooper's *logic of ordinary discourse* [9], or, to be more precise, its structural version (denoted sOL), studied in the recent papers [20,28].
3. $\mathrm{Log}\langle \mathbf{CN_3}, F \rangle$, where $\mathbf{CN_3} = \langle A_3; \wedge_{\mathsf{K}}, \vee_{\mathsf{K}}, \to_{\mathsf{OL}}, \neg \rangle$. This is a variant of Cooper's system introduced by Cantwell [6] as the *logic of conditional negation* (CN), and independently considered by a number of other authors[3]. We shall prove that CN may be viewed as a term-definable subsystem of sOL.
4. $\mathrm{Log}\langle \mathbf{F_3}, F \rangle$, where $\mathbf{F_3} = \langle A_3; \wedge_{\mathsf{K}}, \vee_{\mathsf{K}}, \to_{\mathsf{F}}, \neg \rangle$, a logic introduced by Farrell [13]. We will see that this system is definitionally equivalent to CN, and may therefore also be viewed as a definable subsystem of sOL.
   Besides the above systems, we shall consider a few related ones that, as far as we are aware, have not yet appeared in the literature. These are obtained by:
5. Varying the set F of designated elements on A_3. For instance, logics that result from taking $F = \{\mathbf{1/2}\}$, which appears to be a natural choice – at least from a formal standpoint.
6. Considering a family of matrices based on the same algebra. As is well known, to any class of matrices one can associate the logic given by the intersection of

[3] This logic – or equivalent systems, with slight variations in the choice of primitive connectives – seems to have been introduced, independently, in a number of papers from the 1980s to the 2000s (see, e.g., [23,24]).

the consequence relations defined (as indicated above) by each matrix in the class. The particular case we will consider results from keeping the algebra fixed while letting the designated elements vary (e.g.) over all upsets of a given partial order. In this way one obtains *degree-preserving (semilattice-based) logics* associated to the above-mentioned algebras (see e.g. [21]).

Our main results may be summarized as follows. In each case we determine whether the given system is algebraizable or not, thereby settling some issues on the algebraization of logics of indicative conditionals that were raised but left unsolved in [12]. Algebraizable logics are well-behaved in many ways, in particular one may easily obtain a presentation of the algebraic semantics from an axiomatization of the logic, and vice-versa. These are built thanks to two mutually inverse maps (known as *transformers*, and usually denoted by τ and ρ) between formulas and equations[4]. While verifying that a given pair of transformers witnesses algebraizability is straightforward, coming up with suitable definitions for the two maps may require ingenuity and insight into the algebraic counterpart of the logic: this is our first main contribution. A second endeavor that may be not entirely straightforward is that of designing, with the help of the transformers, suitable Hilbert-style calculi for the logics under consideration: this is current work in progress, and will have to be left out from the present contribution due to space limitations.

On the other hand, proving that a given logic is not algebraizable is an even more tricky, *ad hoc* business. Fortunately, in the cases considered here, algebraizability fails for the banal reason that the given logic lacks valid formulas (see Footnote 5). In such cases, axiomatizing the logic and determining the class of algebras canonically associated with it may also turn out to be nontrivial tasks that need to be addressed in an *ad hoc* fashion: settling these issues is going to be the last main contribution to be included in the present paper.

Aside from the fact that the present space constraints do not allow for an extensive treatment of all the above-mentioned topics, it goes without saying that this contribution must be considered a preliminary report on a research project that we intend to explore fully in forthcoming publications. The concluding section contains some indications on which directions such future research may take.

Preliminaries and Notation. Let us briefly recall the logic and algebraic definitions we will need; for further background and all unexplained terminology, see [2,18,19]. Given a Tarskian[5] logic L, we denote by Mod(L) the class of all

[4] Standard examples of transformers (classical, intuitionistic and most fuzzy logics) are $\tau\colon x \mapsto x \approx \mathbf{1}$ and $\rho\colon \varphi \approx \psi \mapsto \{\varphi \leftrightarrow \psi\}$, but we shall here encounter more exotic ones, such as $\tau\colon x \mapsto x \vee \neg x = \mathbf{1}$ and $\rho\colon \varphi \approx \psi \mapsto \{\varphi \to \psi, \psi \to \varphi, \neg\varphi \to \neg\psi, \neg\psi \to \neg\varphi\}$.

[5] By this, we mean a logic satisfying the well-known Tarski postulates [19, Sect. 1.2], including *structurality*, i.e. invariance under uniform substitutions. As we will see, Cooper's logic OL violates this requirement, but all the other logics considered here are structural.

logical matrices $\langle \mathbf{A}, F\rangle$ that are *models* of L, i.e. such that $\mathbf{A}$ is an L-algebra and F is an L-*deductive filter*. A matrix $\langle \mathbf{A}, F\rangle$ whose *Leibniz congruence* is the identity relation on A is called *Leibniz-reduced*. Similarly, $\langle \mathbf{A}, F\rangle$ is *Suszko-reduced* if its *Suszko congruence* is the identity relation. The classes of Leibniz and Suszko-reduced models of L are denoted by $\mathrm{Mod}^*(\mathrm{L})$ and $\mathrm{Mod}^{\equiv}(\mathrm{L})$, respectively; these are key ingredients in the algebraic understanding of a Tarskian logic L, for every logic is complete with respect to both $\mathrm{Mod}^{\equiv}(\mathrm{L})$ and $\mathrm{Mod}^*(\mathrm{L})$. The corresponding classes of algebras, denoted $\mathrm{Alg}(\mathrm{L})$ (resp., $\mathrm{Alg}^*(\mathrm{L})$), are formed by all algebras $\mathbf{A}$ such that $\langle \mathbf{A}, F\rangle \in \mathrm{Mod}^{\equiv}(\mathrm{L})$ (resp., $\langle \mathbf{A}, F\rangle \in \mathrm{Mod}^*(\mathrm{L})$). These are the two classes of algebras canonically associated with a logic within the general theory of algebraization [18]. For a large family of logics, both are guaranteed to coincide (i.e. $\mathrm{Alg}(\mathrm{L}) = \mathrm{Alg}^*(\mathrm{L})$): these are the *protoalgebraic* systems, which may be said to be the largest class of logics that are relatively well-behaved from an algebraic point of view [18, Prop. 3.2][6]. Conversely, there is no general method for determining when $\mathrm{Alg}(\mathrm{L}) \neq \mathrm{Alg}^*(\mathrm{L})$: this may be a nontrivial issue, that in our context we shall be able to settle in some specific cases.

Of course, as mentioned earlier, the truly well-behaved logics are the *algebraizable* ones, which form a proper subclass of the protoalgebraic. Formally, L is algebraizable when there are a set of equations $\tau(x)$, a set of formulas $\rho(x, y)$ and a quasivariety $\mathbb{K}$ verifying: (i) $\Gamma \vdash_{\mathrm{L}} \varphi$ if and only if $\tau(\Gamma) \vDash_{\mathbb{K}} \tau(\varphi)$ and (ii) the equation $x \approx y$ is $\vDash_{\mathbb{K}}$-inter-derivable with $\tau(\rho(x, y))$. Algebraizability implies that the designated elements on each matrix $\langle \mathbf{A}, F\rangle \in \mathrm{Mod}^*(\mathrm{L})$ are definable by τ: logics satisfying only this weaker property have been dubbed *truth-equational*. An important fact – that we shall often use without further notice – is that the above-mentioned properties are preserved by strengthenings: thus, negatively, it suffices to show that a logic L is not algebraizable (protoalgebraic, truth-equational) to conclude that all weaker logics must also lack that property.

The notion of *selfextensionality* is orthogonal to the previous ones: L is *selfextensional* when its inter-derivability relation is a congruence on the formula algebra: for arbitrary formulas φ, ψ, χ, if $\varphi \dashv\vdash_{\mathrm{L}} \psi$, then $\chi(x/\varphi) \dashv\vdash_{\mathrm{L}} \chi(x/\psi)$. An important family of selfextensional logics, which will feature prominently in the present paper, is formed by those systems that preserve *degrees* of truth rather than "absolute truth": these have been the object of intense research in recent years within non-classical and especially fuzzy logics (see e.g. [2,4,19,21,22]). The formal definition is as follows: L is *semilattice-based* relative to a binary term & and a variety of algebras $\mathbb{K}$ (carrying a semilattice order $\leq$) when, for every finite set of formulas $\varphi_1, \ldots, \varphi_n, \varphi$, it holds that $\varphi_1, \ldots, \varphi_n \vdash_{\mathrm{L}} \varphi$ if and only if $v(\varphi_1) \& \ldots \& v(\varphi_n) \leq v(\varphi)$, for every $\mathbf{A} \in \mathbb{K}$ and every $\mathbf{A}$-valuation v. It is known [2, Thm. 2.13] that a logic L is semilattice-based (relative to some

[6] Formally, a logic L is *protoalgebraic* if it has a set $\rho(x, y)$ of formulas such that (i) $\varnothing \vdash_{\mathrm{L}} \rho(x, x)$ and (ii) $x, \rho(x, y) \vdash_{\mathrm{L}} y$. Intuitively, $\rho(x, y)$ may be thought of as a generalized biconditional connective that needs to satisfy the identity law (i) and a generalized version of the *modus ponens* rule (ii). Thus every protoalgebraic logics must have *theorems* – formulas derivable from the empty set of premisses (more on this below).

variety) if and only if L is selfextensional and has a *conjunction*, i.e. a term & for which the rules $x, y \vdash_{\mathrm{L}} x\&y$, $x\&y \vdash_{\mathrm{L}} x$ and $x\&y \vdash_{\mathrm{L}} y$ hold. In such a case, $\mathbb{K}$ is generated, as a variety, by $\mathsf{Alg}^*(\mathrm{L})$ [18, Prop. 1.23].

Semilattice-based logics are often contrasted (and come in a pair) with *assertional* logics. Given a class of algebras $\mathbb{K}$ and a transformer τ, the *τ-assertional logic* of $\mathbb{K}$ is defined as follows: $\Gamma \vdash \varphi$ holds if and only if $\tau(\Gamma) \vDash_{\mathbb{K}} \tau(\varphi)$ for every $\mathbf{A} \in \mathbb{K}$ (see, e.g., [1] for more details.). In case $\tau(x)$ is a single equation of the form $x \approx 1$, for a constant symbol 1, we refer to the τ-assertional logic as 1-assertional[7].

2 De Finettian Logics

In keeping with the interpretation of conditional sentences introduced in the preceding section, De Finetti views the formula $\varphi \to \psi$ as a kind of conditional bet on ψ given φ. The bet is lost when φ is realized while ψ is not, it is won when both φ and ψ are realized, but it is simply called off when φ is not realized (see [16] for De Finetti's original proposal, and [10,11] for a recent assessment of his logic).

Formally, De Finetti's logic DF is defined as $\mathrm{Log}\langle \mathbf{DF_3}, F\rangle$, where $F = \{\mathbf{1/2}, \mathbf{1}\}$ and $\mathbf{DF_3} = \langle A_3; \wedge_{\mathsf{K}}, \vee_{\mathsf{K}}, \to_{\mathsf{DF}}, \neg\rangle$. Alternatively, one may view $\mathbf{DF_3}$ as an algebra in the language $\{\wedge_{\mathsf{K}}, \vee_{\mathsf{K}}, \neg, \mathbf{1/2}\}$, replacing the implication by the constant $\mathbf{1/2}$. Both presentations are equivalent, for one can define (cf. [10, p. 231]):

$$x \to_{\mathsf{DF}} y = (\mathbf{1/2} \wedge_{\mathsf{K}} \neg x) \vee_{\mathsf{K}} (x \wedge_{\mathsf{K}} y), \qquad \mathbf{1/2} := \neg x \to_{\mathsf{DF}} (x \to_{\mathsf{DF}} x).$$

The implication-free presentation is more convenient for our purposes, for it allows us to view De Finetti's system as a conservative expansion of Priest's *Logic of Paradox* [26] obtained by just adding the propositional constant $\mathbf{1/2}$ to its language[8]. This, in turn, suggests the possibility of importing key results that are known to hold for Priest's logic (see especially [2]). Likewise, on an algebraic level, we will view the algebraic models of DF as a class of Kleene lattices enriched with an extra constant $\mathbf{1/2}$ (known as the *center*) required to satisfy $\neg\,\mathbf{1/2} = \mathbf{1/2}$: these algebras are known in the literature under the name of *centered Kleene lattices* [7].

Definition 1. *A* Kleene lattice *is an algebra* $\mathbf{A} = \langle A; \wedge, \vee, \neg\rangle$ *of type* $\langle 2, 2, 1\rangle$ *such that* $\langle A; \wedge, \vee\rangle$ *is a distributive lattice (with order* $\leq$*) and the following identities are satisfied:*

[7] Some familiar examples: classical propositional logic is both the 1-assertional and the semilattice-based logic of the variety of Boolean algebras (so both logics coincide); the same holds for intuitionistic logic/Heyting algebras. In contrast, in the case of modal (Boolean) algebras, the 1-assertional logic corresponds to the global consequence relation, and the semilattice-based to the local consequence.

[8] Note, however, that Priest's goal is to formalize reasoning with "true contradictions" rather than indicative conditionals; accordingly, the intended reading of $\mathbf{1/2}$ is *contradictory* (i.e. both true and false).

(K1) $\neg(x \vee y) \approx \neg x \wedge \neg y$,
(K2) $\neg(x \wedge y) \approx \neg x \vee \neg y$,
(K3) $\neg\neg x \approx x$,
(K4) $x \wedge \neg x \leq y \vee \neg y$.

A centered Kleene lattice *is an algebra* $\mathbf{A} = \langle A; \wedge, \vee, \neg, \mathbf{1/2} \rangle$ *of type* $\langle 2, 2, 1, 0 \rangle$ *such that* $\langle A; \wedge, \vee, \neg \rangle$ *is a Kleene lattice and* $\mathbf{1/2}$ *is a constant satisfying* $\neg\, \mathbf{1/2} \approx \mathbf{1/2}$. $\mathbb{CK}$ *will denote the class of centered Kleene lattices.*

The Logic of Paradox is known to be truth-equational and non-protoalgebraic [2, Thm. 5.1] – hence non-algebraizable. These properties are not altered by the introduction of the constant $\mathbf{1/2}$, as the following proposition shows.

Proposition 1. DF *is truth-equational (with* $\tau(x)$ *being* $x \approx x \rightarrow_{\mathsf{DF}} x$*, or* $\mathbf{1/2} \leq x$*, or also* $\neg x \leq x$*) and non-protoalgebraic.* A fortiori, DF *is not algebraizable.*

The proof of Proposition 1 suggests that adding the constants $\mathbf{0}, \mathbf{1}$ to DF does not change the picture: the resulting logic is still non-protoalgebraic. Later on we shall see examples where, in contrast, the addition of a single constant will turn a non-protoalgebraic logic into an algebraizable one.

Selfextensionality is useful in the algebraization process of a logic, for one may hope to prove algebraic completeness by factoring the formula algebra by the inter-derivability relation. This strategy, however, cannot be applied to DF.

Proposition 2. DF *is not selfextensional.*

It follows from [27, Lemma 3.1] that it suffices to add the extra condition of inter-derivability of negated formulas to obtain a congruence: indeed, the relation $\theta := \{\langle \varphi, \psi \rangle : \varphi \dashv\vdash \psi,\ \neg \varphi \dashv\vdash \neg \psi\}$ is a congruence on the formula algebra of DF (this fact is used in [27] to gain some algebraic insight on Priest's logic).

Proposition 2 entails that [12, Lemma 4.6] – in particular, the first item – cannot be correct (this first item is the one that makes the lemma fail). As Lemma 4.6 is used later in [12, Prop. 4.11] to provide an algebra-based semantics for De Finetti's logic, subsequent results might also be flawed. This, in turn, suggests that a new investigation of the algebraic models of DF may be in order. We will follow an approach alternative to that of [12], and more standard from an algebraic logic point of view.

Let $\vdash_{\mathrm{DF}}$ denote the logic determined by the Hilbert-style calculus extending any complete calculus for Priest's LP (see e.g. the one given in [2]) with the addition of the two rules $\vdash \mathbf{1/2}$ and $\vdash \neg\, \mathbf{1/2}$.

Theorem 1 (Completeness). $\vdash_{\mathrm{DF}}$ *axiomatizes* DF.

As a last observation on DF, we note that it is one case where we can disprove the equality $\mathsf{Alg}^*(\mathrm{DF}) = \mathsf{Alg}(\mathrm{DF})$ (see Corollary 1 below).

2.1 Variations on De Finettian Logics

Let us now briefly look at two alternative De Finettian logics that do not appear to have been considered in the literature: the semilattice-based logic $\mathrm{DF}^{\wedge_\mathsf{K}}$ and the **1**-assertional logic $\mathrm{DF}^{\mathbf{1}}$. The latter corresponds to the 'strict-strict' consequence relation of [10], also known in the context of super-Belnap logics as the 'exactly true logic' [25]. Both appear natural options to consider, at least from a formal point of view; we defer a discussion of their potential applications and motivations to a further stage of our research.

Let $\mathrm{DF}^{\wedge_\mathsf{K}} := \mathrm{Log}\{\langle \mathbf{DF_3}, \{\mathbf{1}\}\rangle, \langle \mathbf{DF_3}, \{\mathbf{1/2}, \mathbf{1}\}\rangle\}$. It is easy to verify that $\mathrm{DF}^{\wedge_\mathsf{K}}$ is the semilattice-based logic of the variety $\mathbb{CK}$, having $\wedge_\mathsf{K}$ as a conjunction. The semilattice-based logic of non-necessarily centered Kleene lattices (i.e. disregarding the constant $\mathbf{1/2}$) is the well-known *Kleene logic of order*, which is axiomatized by the Hilbert-style calculus introduced in [2, Thm. 3.4]. Denote by $\vdash_{\mathrm{DF}^{\wedge_\mathsf{K}}}$ the extension of this calculus by the following rules:

$$\mathbf{1/2} \vee_\mathsf{K} p \vdash \neg\, \mathbf{1/2} \vee_\mathsf{K} p \qquad\qquad \neg\, \mathbf{1/2} \vee_\mathsf{K} p \vdash \mathbf{1/2} \vee_\mathsf{K} p.$$

Theorem 2 (Completeness). $\vdash_{\mathrm{DF}^{\wedge_\mathsf{K}}}$ *axiomatizes* $\mathrm{DF}^{\wedge_\mathsf{K}}$.

It is easy to see that $\mathrm{DF}^{\mathbf{1}} := \mathrm{Log}\langle \mathbf{DF_3}, \{\mathbf{1}\}\rangle$ is the **1**-assertional logic associated to the variety $\mathbb{CK}$, which is, by its very definition, a strengthening of $\mathrm{DF}^{\wedge_\mathsf{K}}$. This logic may axiomatized by adding to $\vdash_{\mathrm{DF}^{\wedge_\mathsf{K}}}$ the single *disjunctive syllogism* rule: $p \wedge (\neg p \vee q) \vdash q$. Denoting by $\vdash_{\mathrm{DF}^{\mathbf{1}}}$ the resulting calculus, we have:

Theorem 3 (Completeness). $\vdash_{\mathrm{DF}^{\mathbf{1}}}$ *axiomatizes* $\mathrm{DF}^{\mathbf{1}}$.

Corollary 1. $\mathsf{Alg}^*(\mathrm{L}) \subsetneq \mathsf{Alg}(\mathrm{L}) = \mathbb{CK}$ *for every logic* $\mathrm{L} \in \{\mathrm{DF}, \mathrm{DF}^{\wedge_\mathsf{K}}, \mathrm{DF}^{\mathbf{1}}\}$.

3 Logics of Ordinary Discourse

The *Logic of Ordinary Discourse* (OL) introduced by Cooper [9] represents a more radical departure from classical reasoning than any of the systems mentioned in the Introduction. To begin with, OL is not Tarskian due to its non-structural character: valuations are forbidden to assign the middle value $\mathbf{1/2}$ to propositional letters. Furthermore, OL has not only a connexive implication ($\to_{\mathsf{OL}}$), but also a highly non-classical conjunction ($\wedge_{\mathsf{OL}}$) and disjunction ($\vee_{\mathsf{OL}}$). For instance, they fail to satisfy the distributive law (i.e. $(\varphi \wedge_{\mathsf{OL}} \psi) \vee_{\mathsf{OL}} (\varphi \wedge_{\mathsf{OL}} \chi) \nvdash \varphi \wedge_{\mathsf{OL}} (\psi \vee_{\mathsf{OL}} \chi)$) and the rule of disjunction introduction (i.e. $\varphi \nvdash \varphi \vee_{\mathsf{OL}} \psi$). For further examples, see Cooper's original paper, where these features are discussed at length, and proposed as better alternatives for modeling ordinary reasoning. For our purposes, let us just add the observation that $\wedge_{\mathsf{OL}}$ and $\vee_{\mathsf{OL}}$ are both semilattice operations (say, a meet and a join) on $\mathbf{O}_3$, but they are not lattice-theoretic duals of one another. We will presently return on this.

The recent papers [20,28] contain an algebraic study of OL, with a particular focus on its structural version (denoted by sOL), which is obtained in the standard way as $\mathrm{Log}\langle \mathbf{O}_3, \{\mathbf{1/2}, \mathbf{1}\}\rangle$. Let us briefly recall the main results on

OL/sOL before looking at some alternative logics that may also be defined from the three-element algebra $\mathbf{O}_3$.

As shown in [28, Thm. 3.1], sOL is algebraizable with transformers: $\tau\colon x \mapsto x \approx x \to_{\mathsf{OL}} x$ and $\rho\colon \varphi \approx \psi \mapsto \{\varphi \to_{\mathsf{OL}} \psi, \psi \to_{\mathsf{OL}} \varphi, \neg\varphi \to_{\mathsf{OL}} \neg\psi, \neg\psi \to_{\mathsf{OL}} \neg\varphi\}$. The equivalent algebraic semantics of sOL is a variety dubbed *OL-algebras* in [28], which we denote here by $\mathbb{OL}$. Every OL-algebra may be conveniently represented through a *twist* construction similar to the one introduced in [15] for C-algebras (see Sect. 4); this insight inspires several of our observations on the relations among the different algebras of indicative conditionals (see [28] for the details of the twist construction). Finite Hilbert-style axiomatizations for sOL have been introduced in [20,28], from which a calculus for OL can be obtained by adding the single *explosion* rule ($p \wedge_{\mathsf{OL}} \neg p \vdash q$) restricted to propositional variables.

The primitive language of OL/sOL (consisting of $\wedge_{\mathsf{OL}}, \vee_{\mathsf{OL}}, \to_{\mathsf{OL}}$ and $\neg$) allows us to recover as terms a number of well-known three-valued connectives, notably Kleene's ($\wedge_{\mathsf{K}}$ and $\vee_{\mathsf{K}}$) and those of Nelson logic[9]. The Kleene connectives may be defined as follows:

$$x \wedge_{\mathsf{K}} y := (x \to_{\mathsf{OL}} x) \vee_{\mathsf{OL}} ((x \to_{\mathsf{OL}} y) \to_{\mathsf{OL}} y)$$
$$x \vee_{\mathsf{K}} y := \neg(\neg x \wedge_{\mathsf{K}} \neg y).$$

In particular, the semilattice operations $\wedge_{\mathsf{K}}$, $\wedge_{\mathsf{OL}}$ and $\vee_{\mathsf{OL}}$ give rise to *three* independent orderings on $\mathbf{O}_3$ and three corresponding semilattice-based logics. In addition to the Kleene order ($\mathbf{0} < {}^1\!/_2 < \mathbf{1}$), we have an order having $\wedge_{\mathsf{OL}}$ as conjunction ($\mathbf{0} < \mathbf{1} < {}^1\!/_2$) and one determined by $\vee_{\mathsf{OL}}$ as a join-semilattice operation (${}^1\!/_2 < \mathbf{0} < \mathbf{1}$). Accordingly, we may consider three semilattice-based logics and the two corresponding assertional logics (namely, $\mathrm{Log}\langle \mathbf{O}_3, \{{}^1\!/_2\}\rangle$ and $\mathrm{Log}\langle \mathbf{O}_3, \{\mathbf{1}\}\rangle$). In the remaining part of this section, we take a look at these systems from an algebraic logic standpoint.

3.1 Variations on sOL

Denoting $A_3 := \{\mathbf{0}, {}^1\!/_2, \mathbf{1}\}$, we have that $\langle A_3; \wedge_{\mathsf{OL}}\rangle$ is a meet-semilattice with order $\mathbf{0} < \mathbf{1} < {}^1\!/_2$ and that $\langle A_3; \vee_{\mathsf{OL}}\rangle$ is a join-semilattice with order ${}^1\!/_2 < \mathbf{0} < \mathbf{1}$. In addition, we have the Kleene semilattice $\langle A_3; \wedge_{\mathsf{K}}\rangle$. These orderings induce the semilattice-based logics that are readily seen to be definable as follows:

(i) $\mathrm{OL}_{\wedge_{\mathsf{OL}}} := \mathrm{Log}\{\langle \mathbf{O}_3, \{{}^1\!/_2, \mathbf{1}\}\rangle, \langle \mathbf{O}_3, \{{}^1\!/_2\}\rangle\}$.
(ii) $\mathrm{OL}_{\wedge_{\mathsf{K}}} := \mathrm{Log}\{\langle \mathbf{O}_3, \{\mathbf{1}\}\rangle, \langle \mathbf{O}_3, \{{}^1\!/_2, \mathbf{1}\}\rangle$.
(iii) $\mathrm{OL}_{\vee_{\mathsf{OL}}} := \mathrm{Log}\{\langle \mathbf{O}_3, \{\mathbf{1}\}\rangle, \langle \mathbf{O}_3, \{\mathbf{0}, \mathbf{1}\}\rangle$.

These definitions suggest, for example, that the $\mathbf{1}$-assertional logic associated to the variety $\mathbb{OL}$ is $\mathrm{Log}\langle \mathbf{O}_3, \{\mathbf{1}\}\rangle$, which is by definition a strengthening common to

9 As pointed out in [20,28], other connectives (e.g. the Łukasiewicz, or the Heyting-Gödel implication) only become definable if we further expand $\mathbf{O}_3$ with the constant $\mathbf{1}$ (or, equivalently, $\mathbf{0}$), thereby achieving functional completeness.

$\mathrm{OL}_{\wedge_{\mathsf{K}}}$ and $\mathrm{OL}_{\vee_{\mathsf{OL}}}$. We shall consider this logic presently; in the meantime, let us note that the meet operation dual to $\vee_{\mathsf{OL}}$ (let us denote it by $\vee^{\delta}_{\mathsf{OL}}$) is definable in $\{\vee_{\mathsf{OL}}, \to_{\mathsf{OL}}, \neg\}$ as follows (recall that $\wedge_{\mathsf{K}}$ is itself term-definable):

$$x \vee^{\delta}_{\mathsf{OL}} y := ((x \vee_{\mathsf{K}} y) \to_{\mathsf{OL}} (x \vee_{\mathsf{OL}} y)) \to_{\mathsf{OL}} (x \wedge_{\mathsf{K}} y).$$

Similarly (keeping in mind that $x \wedge_{\mathsf{OL}} y = \neg(\neg x \vee_{\mathsf{OL}} \neg y)$), we have that the join operation dual to $\wedge_{\mathsf{OL}}$ (denote it by $\wedge^{\delta}_{\mathsf{OL}}$) is definable in $\{\vee_{\mathsf{OL}}, \to_{\mathsf{OL}}, \neg\}$ as follows:

$$x \wedge^{\delta}_{\mathsf{OL}} y := (\neg(x \wedge_{\mathsf{K}} y) \to_{\mathsf{OL}} \neg(x \wedge_{\mathsf{OL}} y)) \to_{\mathsf{OL}} (x \vee_{\mathsf{K}} y).$$

We thus have two lattices, $\langle A_3; \vee^{\delta}_{\mathsf{OL}}, \vee_{\mathsf{OL}} \rangle$ and $\langle A_3; \wedge_{\mathsf{OL}}, \wedge^{\delta}_{\mathsf{OL}} \rangle$, besides the Kleene lattice $\langle A_3; \wedge_{\mathsf{K}}, \vee_{\mathsf{K}} \rangle$, and all three semilattice-based logics have both a conjunction and a disjunction.

Theorem 4. *For each semilattice-based logic* L *among (i)–(iii), we have* $\mathsf{Alg}(\mathrm{L}) = \mathbb{OL}$. *In consequence, we also have* $\mathsf{Alg}(\mathrm{L}) = \mathbb{OL}$ *for*

$$\mathrm{L} \in \{\mathrm{Log}\langle \mathbf{O}_3, \{\mathbf{1/2}\} \rangle, \mathrm{Log}\langle \mathbf{O}_3, \{\mathbf{1}\} \rangle, \mathrm{Log}\langle \mathbf{O}_3, \{\mathbf{0}, \mathbf{1}\} \rangle\}.$$

Remark 1. The following logics are non-protoalgebraic, hence also non-algebraizable (due to the lack of valid formulas):

(i) $\mathrm{Log}\langle \mathbf{O}_3, \{\mathbf{1}\} \rangle$.
(ii) $\mathrm{Log}\langle \mathbf{O}_3, \{\mathbf{0}, \mathbf{1}\} \rangle$.
(iii) *A fortiori*, $\mathrm{OL}_{\wedge_{\mathsf{K}}}$ and $\mathrm{OL}_{\vee_{\mathsf{OL}}}$.

As mentioned earlier, the equality $\mathsf{Alg}^*(\mathrm{L}) = \mathsf{Alg}(\mathrm{L})$ is guaranteed in the protoalgebraic setting but need not hold more generally [18, §5.1]. Thus, Remark 1 suggests the question whether $\mathsf{Alg}^*(\mathrm{L}) = \mathsf{Alg}(\mathrm{L})$ for each of these logics. Theorem 5 below contains some answers in this direction, but does not settle the issue for $\mathrm{Log}\langle \mathbf{O}_3, \{\mathbf{0}, \mathbf{1}\} \rangle$ and $\mathrm{OL}_{\vee_{\mathsf{OL}}}$.

Theorem 5.

(i) $\mathsf{Alg}^*(\mathrm{L}) = \mathsf{Alg}(\mathrm{L}) = \mathbb{OL}$ *for* $\mathrm{L} \in \{\mathrm{OL}_{\wedge_{\mathsf{OL}}}, \mathrm{OL}_{\wedge_{\mathsf{K}}}, \mathrm{Log}\langle \mathbf{O}_3, \{\mathbf{1/2}\} \rangle\}$.
(ii) $\mathsf{Alg}^*(\mathrm{L}) \neq \mathsf{Alg}(\mathrm{L}) = \mathbb{OL}$ *for* $\mathrm{L} = \mathrm{Log}\langle \mathbf{O}_3, \{\mathbf{1}\} \rangle$.

For the subsequent results, it is useful to recall some abbreviations introduced in [28]:

$$\Diamond x := \neg x \to_{\mathsf{OL}} x, \qquad x \Rightarrow y := \neg(x \wedge_{\mathsf{OL}} \neg y), \qquad \uparrow x := \Diamond x \to (\neg x \wedge_{\mathsf{OL}} \mathbf{1}).$$

The following result shows that all the assertional logics based on $\mathbf{O}_3$ under consideration are algebraizable – provided we are willing to expand the language with the constants.

Theorem 6.

(i) $\mathrm{Log}\langle \mathbf{O}_3, \{\mathbf{1}\}\rangle$ *is not algebraizable (Remark 1) but, adding the constant* $\mathbf{1}$ *to the language, we achieve algebraizability through the following transformers:* $\tau\colon x \mapsto x \approx \mathbf{1}$ *and*

$$\rho\colon \varphi \approx \psi \quad \mapsto \quad \{(\varphi \rightarrow_{\mathsf{OL}} \psi) \wedge_{\mathsf{OL}} \mathbf{1}, (\psi \rightarrow_{\mathsf{OL}} \varphi) \wedge_{\mathsf{OL}} \mathbf{1}, (\neg\varphi \rightarrow_{\mathsf{OL}} \neg\psi) \wedge_{\mathsf{OL}} \mathbf{1}, (\neg\psi \rightarrow_{\mathsf{OL}} \neg\varphi) \wedge_{\mathsf{OL}} \mathbf{1}\}$$

or, alternatively, $\rho\colon \varphi \approx \psi \quad \mapsto \quad \{(\varphi \Rightarrow \psi) \wedge_{\mathsf{OL}} \mathbf{1}, (\psi \Rightarrow \varphi) \wedge_{\mathsf{OL}} \mathbf{1}\}$.

(ii) As above, $\mathrm{Log}\langle \mathbf{O}_3, \{\mathbf{1}, \mathbf{0}\}\rangle$ *is not algebraizable but, adding* $\mathbf{1}$ *to the language, we achieve algebraizability through the following transformers:* $\tau\colon x \mapsto x \vee_{\mathsf{OL}} \neg x \approx \mathbf{1}$ *and* $\rho\colon \varphi \approx \psi \quad \mapsto \quad \{\uparrow(\varphi \Rightarrow \psi), \uparrow(\psi \Rightarrow \varphi)\}$.

(iii) $\mathrm{Log}\langle \mathbf{O}_3, \{\mathbf{1/2}\}\rangle$ *is algebraizable with* $\tau\colon x \mapsto x \approx \mathbf{1/2}$ *(recall that the term* $\neg x \rightarrow (x \rightarrow x)$ *defines the algebraic constant* $\mathbf{1/2}$*) or* $\tau\colon x \mapsto x \approx \neg x$ *and*

$$\rho\colon \varphi \approx \psi \quad \mapsto \quad \{\diamond(\varphi \rightarrow_{\mathsf{OL}} \psi), \diamond(\psi \rightarrow_{\mathsf{OL}} \varphi), \diamond(\neg\varphi \rightarrow_{\mathsf{OL}} \neg\psi), \diamond(\neg\psi \rightarrow_{\mathsf{OL}} \neg\varphi)\}$$

or, alternatively, $\rho\colon \varphi \approx \psi \quad \mapsto \quad \{\diamond(\varphi \Rightarrow \psi), \diamond(\psi \Rightarrow \varphi)\}$.

It is an instance of a general phenomenon that, when the assertional logic associated to a class of algebras $\mathbb{K}$ is algebraizable, it is not selfextensional; whereas the semilattice-based logic of $\mathbb{K}$ is (obviously) self-extensional but non-algebraizable, for otherwise both logics would coincide. This applies to all such pairs of logics considered here (as well as to the algebraizable logics considered in Theorem 7 below).

In what follows, we abbreviate:

(i) $\mathrm{OL}^{\mathbf{1}} := \mathrm{Log}\langle \mathbf{O}_3^{\mathbf{1}}, \{\mathbf{1}\}\rangle$, where $\mathbf{O}_3^{\mathbf{1}}$ denotes $\mathbf{O}_3$ expanded with the $\mathbf{1}$ constant.
(ii) $\mathrm{OL}^{\mathbf{01}} := \mathrm{Log}\langle \mathbf{O}_3^{\mathbf{1}}, \{\mathbf{0}, \mathbf{1}\}\rangle$.
(iii) $\mathrm{OL}^{\mathbf{1/2}} := \mathrm{Log}\langle \mathbf{O}_3, \{\mathbf{1/2}\}\rangle$.

Remark 2. The matrix definitions of the different logics based on $\mathbf{O}_3$ determine interesting translations among the different systems whose meaning may be worthwhile investigating in future research. For the time being, let us just state these formal relationships (recall that Thm(L) denotes the set of valid formulas of a logic L):

(i) $\mathrm{Thm}(\mathrm{sOL}) = \mathrm{Thm}(\mathrm{OL}^{\mathbf{1}}) \cup \mathrm{Thm}(\mathrm{OL}^{\mathbf{1/2}})$ and, in fact, for any formula φ, we have $\vdash_{\mathrm{sOL}} \varphi$ if and only if $\vdash_{\mathrm{OL}^{\mathbf{1}}} \varphi \wedge_{\mathsf{OL}} \mathbf{1}$.
(ii) $\mathrm{Thm}(\mathrm{OL}^{\mathbf{1}}) = \mathrm{Thm}(\mathrm{sOL}) \cap \mathrm{Thm}(\mathrm{OL}^{\mathbf{01}})$. For any pair of formulas φ, ψ, we have $\varphi \vdash_{\mathrm{OL}^{\mathbf{01}}} \psi$ if and only if $\psi \vdash_{\mathrm{OL}^{\mathbf{1/2}}} \varphi$. In particular, $\mathrm{OL}^{\mathbf{01}}$ and $\mathrm{OL}^{\mathbf{1/2}}$ agree on inter-derivable formulas.
(iii) For any formula φ, we have $\vdash_{\mathrm{OL}^{\mathbf{1/2}}} \varphi$ if and only if both $\vdash_{\mathrm{sOL}} \varphi$ and $\vdash_{\mathrm{sOL}} \neg\varphi$.

The algebraic counterpart of every algebraizable logic L based on $\mathbf{O}_3$ – recall that in this case $\mathsf{Alg}(\mathrm{L}) = \mathsf{Alg}^*(\mathrm{L})$ – is the variety of OL-algebras or (if the constant $\mathbf{1}$ is included in the language) the variety of bounded OL-algebras. A finite Hilbert-style calculus for L can then be straightforwardly obtained by translating the algebraic presentation of (bounded) OL-algebras via the transformers τ, ρ that witness algebraizability of L. However, in some cases the calculi thus obtained are somewhat involved and not quite transparent. We get a fairly standard axiomatization for $\mathrm{OL}^{\mathbf{1}}$, whereas for $\mathrm{OL}^{\mathbf{01}}$ and $\mathrm{OL}^{\mathbf{1/2}}$ one seems to need (besides *modus pones*) a number of less standard inference rules; we do not currently know, but intend to further investigate in future research, wether these rules are eliminable. Alternative and potentially more transparent axiomatizations may be obtained via a detour through multiple-conclusion calculi, as we shall mention in the concluding section.

4 Conditional Negation and Farrell's Logic

The logic here called Conditional Negation CN (or slight variations thereof) seems to have been (re-)introduced independently by a number of authors at different times. CN may be defined as $\mathrm{Log}\langle \mathbf{CN_3}, \{\mathbf{1/2}, \mathbf{1}\}\rangle$, where $\mathbf{CN_3}$ is the three-element algebra in the language $\{\wedge_{\mathsf{K}}, \vee_{\mathsf{K}}, \rightarrow_{\mathsf{OL}}, \neg\}$.

CN's motivation and approach (as discussed, e.g., in [6]) are essentially the same as Cooper's – providing an adequate formal treatment of indicative conditionals, in particular those having a false antecedent, to be considered as lacking a truth value. In comparison to sOL, CN represents a less radical departure from classical logic, for while the implication is $\rightarrow_{\mathsf{OL}}$, the conjunction and disjunction are the more standard (and subclassical) Kleene connectives $\wedge_{\mathsf{K}}$ and $\vee_{\mathsf{K}}$. Hence, CN is by definition a conservative expansion of both Priest's logic and De Finetti's DF considered in Sect. 2. As an expansion of the $\{\rightarrow_{\mathsf{OL}}, \neg\}$-fragment of OL, it is clear that CN is also a connexive logic.

Another important observation is that CN may be viewed as an axiomatic strengthening of Wansing's connexive logic C [29, Sect. 4.5.1]. The recent paper [15] shows that C is algebraizable and admits a simple twist-algebra semantics akin to that of Nelson logics. It follows that CN is also algebraizable with the same transformers as C, and that its algebraic models may be represented as twist-algebras [15, Sec. 5.3]. For our purposes – e.g. comparing CN with the systems mentioned earlier – it may be interesting to give a presentation of the algebraic counterpart of CN that expands that of centered Kleene lattices[10].

Definition 2. *A* CN-algebra *is an algebra* $\mathbf{A} = \langle A; \wedge, \rightarrow, \neg, \mathbf{1/2}\rangle$ *of type* $\langle 2, 2, 1, 0\rangle$ *such that* $\langle A; \wedge, \neg, \mathbf{1/2}\rangle$ *is a centered Kleene lattice (with* $\vee$ *defined, as usual, through De Morgan's law) and the following equations hold (abbreviating* $\Diamond x := x \wedge \mathbf{1/2}$*):*

[10] Verifying that our presentation is equivalent to that of [15] would take too much space, but can be done easily once we have at out disposal twist representations for both classes of algebras (see [15, Defs. 6, 7] and [15, Thm. 50] for further details).

(CN1) $(x \wedge y) \to z = x \to (y \to z)$,
(CN2) $\mathbf{1/2} \leq x \to (y \to y)$,
(CN3) $\mathbf{1/2} \leq ((x \to y) \to x) \to x$,
(CN4) $\Diamond(x \to y) = \Diamond x \to \Diamond y$,
(CN5) $\neg(x \to y) = x \to \neg y$.

It follows from [15, Thm. 50] that CN is algebraizable with respect to the class of CN-algebras defined as above. As in the previous cases, one may consider variations of CN defined from the same underlying three-element algebra. Let us look at two assertional logics – those induced by the matrices $\langle \mathbf{CN}_3, \{\mathbf{1/2}\}\rangle$ and $\langle \mathbf{CN}_3, \{\mathbf{1}\}\rangle$; the study of associated semilattice-based systems is currently the object of ongoing research. We omit the proof of the following theorem, which is entirely analogous to the algebraizability results for Cooper's logic.

Theorem 7.

(i) Log$\langle \mathbf{CN}_3, \{\mathbf{1/2}\}\rangle$ *is algebraizable, as witnessed by* $\tau\colon x \mapsto x \approx \mathbf{1/2}$ *and (recall that* $\Diamond x := \neg x \to_{\mathsf{OL}} x$*):*

$$\rho\colon \varphi \approx \psi \quad \mapsto \quad \{\Diamond(\varphi \to_{\mathsf{OL}} \psi), \Diamond(\psi \to_{\mathsf{OL}} \varphi), \Diamond(\neg\varphi \to_{\mathsf{OL}} \neg\psi), \Diamond(\neg\psi \to_{\mathsf{OL}} \neg\varphi)\}.$$

(ii) Log$\langle \mathbf{CN}_3, \{\mathbf{1}\}\rangle$ *is not algebraizable (due to lack of valid formulas*[11]*). Adding the constant* $\mathbf{1}$ *in the language, algebraizability can is achieved by the translations* $\tau : x \mapsto x \approx \mathbf{1}$ *and*

$$\rho : \varphi \approx \psi \quad \mapsto \quad \{(\varphi \to_{\mathsf{OL}} \psi) \to_{\mathsf{OL}} \mathbf{1}, (\psi \to_{\mathsf{OL}} \varphi) \to_{\mathsf{OL}} \mathbf{1}, (\neg\varphi \to_{\mathsf{OL}} \neg\psi) \to_{\mathsf{OL}} \mathbf{1}, (\neg\psi \to_{\mathsf{OL}} \neg\varphi) \to_{\mathsf{OL}} \mathbf{1}\}.$$

Observe that, since the Kleene operations are definable in $\mathbf{O}_3$, every OL-algebra has a term-definable CN-algebra structure. Conversely, it is not hard to verify that the OL-algebra operations (e.g. $\wedge_{\mathsf{OL}}$) are not definable on CN-algebras. Having at one's disposal twist representation of CN-algebras [15], one can further show that OL-algebras may be defined as CN-algebras endowed with an extra operation $\wedge_{\mathsf{OL}}$ satisfying the following requirements:

(i) $\Diamond(x \wedge_{\mathsf{OL}} y) = \Diamond(x \wedge y)$.
(ii) $\Diamond\neg(x \wedge_{\mathsf{OL}} y) = (x \to \Diamond\neg y) \wedge (y \to \Diamond\neg x)$.

We conclude the section with a note on a logic introduced by R.J. Farrell [13] (see also [14]). The motivation and discussion in these papers are broader than in Cooper's and Cantwell's, for Farrell construes the middle value $\mathbf{1/2}$ as *inappropriate* (or, "to be ignored"), and considers inappropriate not only (composite) conditionals with a false antecedent (as in Cooper and Cantwell), but also

[11] The same argument as Remark 1 works, since $\mathbf{1/2}$ would have to be a designated element.

(atomic) propositions that are ambiguous or expressed in a language unfamiliar (to a given audient or reader).

Formally, Farrell's logic is identical with CN save for the table of the implication, which differs precisely in one output ($\mathbf{1/2} \to \mathbf{1}$ returns $\mathbf{1/2}$ instead of $\mathbf{1}$). However, both logics are definitionally equivalent, for one can construct $\to_{\mathsf{OL}}$ as a term in Farrell's system and, vice-versa, $\to_{\mathsf{F}}$ as a term in CN. Before demonstrating these terms, let us note that Farrell's logic may be algebraized without any detour through the language of CN (we omit the proof of this result, which is similar to that of Theorem 7).

Theorem 8. *Farrell's logic, i.e.* $\mathrm{Log}\langle \mathbf{F_3}, \{\mathbf{1/2}, \mathbf{1}\}\rangle$, *is algebraizable with the following transformers:* $\tau \colon x \mapsto x \approx x \to_{\mathsf{F}} x$ *and*

$$\rho \colon \varphi \approx \psi \quad \mapsto \quad \{\varphi \to_{\mathsf{F}} \psi, \psi \to_{\mathsf{F}} \varphi, \neg\varphi \to_{\mathsf{F}} \neg\psi, \neg\psi \to_{\mathsf{F}} \neg\varphi\}.$$

The following result is readily verified by direct inspection of the three-valued truth tables (Fig. 1).

Theorem 9. *Within Farrell's logic we can define:*

$$x \to_{\mathsf{OL}} y \;:=\; \neg((y \to_{\mathsf{F}} x) \to_{\mathsf{F}} \neg y) \to_{\mathsf{F}} ((x \vee_{\mathsf{K}} y) \to_{\mathsf{F}} y).$$

Conversely, in CN *we can define:*

$$x \to_{\mathsf{F}} y \;:=\; x \to_{\mathsf{OL}} (x \wedge_{\mathsf{K}} y).$$

In consequence, Farrell's logic and CN *are definitionally equivalent.*

5 Future Work

It is clear that the results contained in the preceding sections barely lay the foundations of a research project that we wish to further explore in the future. We mention below a few lines of investigation that seem to be especially promising.

1. *Axiomatizations.* It would be desirable to find simpler, more transparent axiomatizations for the algebraizable variants of sOL introduced in Sect. 3. This problem may also be tackled with a Set-Set approach (see Item 4 below).
2. *Axiomatizing the semilattice-based logics.* The logics mentioned in the previous item are the algebraizable ones. In the case of semilattice-based, we may hope to provide axiomatizations relative to their algebraizable (assertional) companion following the general method developed in [4]. However, to achieve this, some nontrivial adaptations may be in order, because the techniques of [4] are only guaranteed to work in the setting of logics defined from varieties of *integral residuated lattices.* Thus, one will need to show: (i) that the algebraic counterparts of our logic of interest may indeed be viewed as residuated structures of some kind (in the case of OL-algebras, this has been pointed out already in [28]), and (ii) that the integrality requirement, which certainly does not hold in our setting (see [4] for these technical definitions), can be dispensed with.

3. *Twist-algebra semantics.* The algebraic analysis of OL presented in [28] relies strongly on the possibility to represent OL-algebras as twist-algebras over generalized Boolean factors. Similar results may be extended to the classes of algebras considered in the present paper (cf. Definitions 1 and 2). Some cases (e.g. centered Kleene algebras) may be obtained as straightforward specializations of other well-known twist representations; in other cases, extra care and some ingenuity may be required in order to represent the new operations (e.g. Farrell's implication $\to_{\mathsf{F}}$). In turn, twist representations are insightful in that they may indicate where to find and how to establish term equivalences among the different classes of algebras/logics, and also, conversely, the cases where one should not expect any equivalence to exist.
4. *Set-Set consequence relations.* The paper [20] has shown that a deeper insight into sOL/OL can be obtained from the perspective of Set-Set (or: multiple-conclusion) consequence relations, where the conclusions of rules and derivations are finite sets rather than single formulas. This approach has several advantages: in particular – for finite matrices meeting certain requirements – it allows one to algorithmically construct (Set-Set) Hilbert-style axiomatizations that are modular and analytic (for a generalized notion of analyticity) both for the corresponding logic and for all its fragments that are sufficiently expressive (see e.g. [5] for details). Under further assumptions, the Set-Set calculi thus obtained may also be algorithmically converted into standard (i.e. Set-Formula) Hilbert calculi. This line of investigation appears to be particularly suited and insightful for the logics treated in the present paper, which are easily seen to meet all the above-mentioned requirements.

Acknowledgments. Umberto Rivieccio acknowledges support from the I+D+i research project PID2022-142378NB-I00 "PHIDELO", funded by the Ministry of Science and Innovation of Spain.

Appendix: Proofs

Proposition 1. DF is truth-equational (with $\tau(x)$ being $x \approx x \to_{\mathsf{DF}} x$, or $\mathbf{1/2} \leq x$, or also $\neg x \leq x$) and non-protoalgebraic. *A fortiori*, DF is not algebraizable.

Proof. It is enough to find a model of DF that falsifies the monotonicity condition of the Leibniz operator. For this, consider the five-element Kleene lattice chain $\mathbf{K_5}$ with $\mathbf{1/2}$ being the center, that is, $K_5 = \{\mathbf{0}, a, \mathbf{1/2}, \neg a, \mathbf{1}\}$ where $\mathbf{0} < a < \mathbf{1/2} < \neg a < \mathbf{1}$. This algebra has two homomorphisms into $f, g \colon K_5 \to A_3$ onto $\mathbf{DF_3}$ given as follows:

$$f : a, \mathbf{1/2}, \neg a \mapsto \mathbf{1/2}; \mathbf{1} \mapsto \mathbf{1}; \mathbf{0} \mapsto \mathbf{0},$$

$$g : \mathbf{1/2} \mapsto \mathbf{1/2}; \neg a, \mathbf{1} \mapsto \mathbf{1}; \mathbf{0}, a \mapsto \mathbf{0}.$$

Let $F := f^{-1}[\{\mathbf{1/2}, \mathbf{1}\}] = \{a, \mathbf{1/2}, \neg a, \mathbf{1}\}$ and $G := g^{-1}[(\{\mathbf{1/2}, \mathbf{1}\})] = \{\mathbf{1/2}, \neg a, \mathbf{1}\}$, so $G \subsetneq F$. Observe that $(K_5, F), (K_5, G)$ are models of DF, for they are (strict) homomorphic pre-images of the matrix $(\mathbf{DF_3}, \{\mathbf{1/2}, \mathbf{1}\})$. The Leibniz congruences associated to F and G are $\Omega^{K_5}F = [\mathbf{0}][\mathbf{1}][a, \mathbf{1/2}, \neg a]$ and $\Omega^{K_5}G = [\mathbf{0}, a][\mathbf{1}, \neg a][\mathbf{1/2}]$. Note that $\Omega^{K_5}G \nsubseteq \Omega^{K_5}F$, contradicting the monotonicity condition. For instance, $(a, \mathbf{0}) \notin \Omega^{K_5}F$ (for $a \in F$ and $\mathbf{0} \notin F$) but $(a, \mathbf{0}) \in \Omega^{K_5}G$. ∎

Lemma 1. $\mathbb{CK} = Q(\mathbf{DF_3}) = V(\mathbf{DF_3})$.

Proof. It is well known that there are only two subdirectly irreducible Kleene lattices, namely the two- and the three-element one. If $\mathbf{A} \in \mathbb{CK}$ is s.i., then its $\mathbf{1/2}$-free reduct must be either the two- or the three-element Kleene lattice. It is easy to see that there is no two-element centered Kleene lattice. Hence the only s.i. member of $\mathbb{CK}$ is $\mathbf{DF_3}$ itself, that is, $\mathbb{CK} = V(\mathbf{DF_3})$.

A sufficient condition for the equality $Q(\mathbf{DF_3}) = V(\mathbf{DF_3})$ is that all the s.i. algebras in $V(\mathbf{DF_3})$ be subalgebras of $\mathbf{DF_3}$ (see e.g. [8, Thm. 3.6.ii]), which is indeed the case. ∎

Proposition 2. DF is not selfextensional.

Proof. Recall that DF is a (conservative) expansion of LP, which is well known to be non selfextensional. For instance, in LP (and hence in DF) we have $p \vee_{\mathsf{K}} \neg p \dashv\vdash q \vee_{\mathsf{K}} \neg q$ (as both formulas are valid), but negating both sides we obtain $\neg(p \vee_{\mathsf{K}} \neg p) \dashv\vdash \neg(q \vee_{\mathsf{K}} \neg q)$ which does *not* hold (consider e.g. a valuation sending p to $\mathbf{1}$ and q to $\mathbf{1/2}$). ∎

Lemma 2. *For every reduced model* $\langle \mathbf{A}, F \rangle$ *of* $\vdash_{\mathrm{DF}}$*, we have that* $\mathbf{A}$ *is a centered Kleene lattice and* $F = \{a \in A : \neg a \leq a\}$.

Proof. Let $\langle \mathbf{A}, F \rangle$ be a reduced model of $\vdash_{\mathrm{DF}}$. Then $\mathbf{A}$ is a centered Kleene lattice, by Corollary 1. Denote by $\mathbf{A}_-$ the $\mathbf{1/2}$-free reduct of $\mathbf{A}$, which is obviously a Kleene lattice. Since $\mathrm{Con}(\mathbf{A}) = \mathrm{Con}(\mathbf{A}_-)$, the matrix $\langle \mathbf{A}_-, F \rangle$ is also reduced and it is (by the definition of $\vdash_{\mathrm{DF}}$) a model of LP. Then, by [2, Thm. 3.7], we have $F = \{a \in A : \neg a \leq a\}$. ∎

Theorem 1. $\vdash_{\mathrm{DF}}$ axiomatizes DF.

Proof. Soundness of $\vdash_{\mathrm{DF}}$ w.r.t. the matrix $\langle \mathbf{DF_3}, \{\mathbf{1/2}, \mathbf{1}\} \rangle$ is easily verified. For completeness, assume $\Gamma \nvdash_{\mathrm{DF}} \psi$. Note that it suffices to consider a finite Γ (for $\vdash_{\mathrm{DF}}$ is finitary, by definition), and by the rules of $\vdash_{\mathrm{DF}}$ we have $\Gamma \vdash_{\mathrm{DF}} \psi$ iff $\varphi \vdash_{\mathrm{DF}} \psi$, where $\varphi := \bigwedge \Gamma$. That is, it suffices to look at single-premise derivations. Now, by the assumption and Lemma 2, we have that there is a (reduced) matrix $\langle \mathbf{A}, F \rangle$, with $\mathbf{A}$ a centered Kleene lattice $\mathbf{A}$ and $F = \{a \in A : \neg a \leq a\}$, witnessing $\varphi \nvdash_{\mathrm{DF}} \psi$. This means that the quasi-equation $\neg \varphi \leq \varphi \rightsquigarrow \neg \psi \leq \psi$ fails in $\mathbf{A}$. But then this quasi-equation also fails in $\mathbf{DF_3}$, which generates centered Kleene lattices as a quasi-variety (Lemma 1). Hence, the matrix $\langle \mathbf{DF_3}, \{\mathbf{1/2}, \mathbf{1}\} \rangle$ also witnesses $\varphi \nvDash \psi$, as required. ∎

Lemma 3. *For every reduced model* $\langle \mathbf{A}, F\rangle$ *of* $\vdash_{\mathrm{DF}^{\wedge_\mathsf{K}}}$, *the algebra* $\mathbf{A}$ *is a centered Kleene lattice and* F *is a lattice filter of* $\mathbf{A}$.

Proof. Let $\langle \mathbf{A}, F\rangle$ be a reduced model of $\vdash_{\mathrm{DF}^{\wedge_\mathsf{K}}}$ and denote by $\mathbf{A}_{-}$ the $\mathbf{1/2}$-free reduct of $\mathbf{A}$. Since $\mathrm{Con}(\mathbf{A}) = \mathrm{Con}(\mathbf{A}_{-})$, the matrix $\langle \mathbf{A}_{-}, F\rangle$ is also reduced, and (by the definition of $\vdash_{\mathrm{DF}^{\wedge_\mathsf{K}}}$) it is a model of Kleene's degree-preserving logic $K^{\leq}$. Then, by [2, Thm. 3.7], $\mathbf{A}_{-}$ is a Kleene lattice[12] and F a lattice filter [2, Thm. 3.3]. Suppose $\mathbf{1/2} \neq \neg\,\mathbf{1/2}$. Then, by Font's characterization of reduced models (again [2, Thm. 3.3]), there is $a \in A$ such that $\mathbf{1/2} \vee a \notin F$ and $\neg\,\mathbf{1/2} \vee a \in F$ (or the other way round). But this is impossible if F must closed by the rule $\neg\,\mathbf{1/2} \vee p \vdash \mathbf{1/2} \vee p$. We conclude that $\mathbf{1/2} = \neg\,\mathbf{1/2}$ is the center of $\mathbf{A}$, as required. ■

Theorem 2. $\vdash_{\mathrm{DF}^{\wedge_\mathsf{K}}}$ axiomatizes $\mathrm{DF}^{\wedge_\mathsf{K}}$.

Proof. Soundness of $\vdash_{\mathrm{DF}^{\wedge_\mathsf{K}}}$ w.r.t. the matrices $\{\langle \mathbf{DF_3}, \{\mathbf{1}\}\rangle, \langle \mathbf{DF_3}, \{\mathbf{1/2}, \mathbf{1}\}\rangle\}$ is easily verified. For completeness, assume $\Gamma \nvdash_{\mathrm{DF}^{\wedge_\mathsf{K}}} \psi$. Note that it suffices to consider a finite Γ (for $\vdash_{\mathrm{DF}}$ is finitary, by definition), and by the rules of $\vdash_{\mathrm{DF}^{\wedge_\mathsf{K}}}$ we have $\Gamma \vdash_{\mathrm{DF}^{\wedge_\mathsf{K}}} \psi$ iff $\varphi \vdash_{\mathrm{DF}^{\wedge_\mathsf{K}}} \psi$, where $\varphi := \bigwedge \Gamma$. That is, it suffices to look at single-premise derivations. Now, by the assumption and Lemma 3, we have that there is a (reduced) matrix $\langle \mathbf{A}, F\rangle$, with $\mathbf{A}$ a centered Kleene lattice $\mathbf{A}$ and F a lattice filter, witnessing $\varphi \nvdash_{\mathrm{DF}^{\wedge_\mathsf{K}}} \psi$. This means that the equation $\varphi \approx \varphi \wedge_\mathsf{K} \psi$ fails in $\mathbf{A}$. But then this equation also fails in $\mathbf{DF_3}$, which generates centered Kleene lattices as a (quasi-)variety (Lemma 1). This means that there is a $\wedge_\mathsf{K}$-semilattice filter G on $\mathbf{DF_3}$ and a valuation $v\colon \mathbf{Fm} \to \mathbf{DF_3}$ such that $v(\varphi) \in G$ but $v(\psi) \notin G$. Since either $G = \{\mathbf{1/2}, \mathbf{1}\}$ or $G = \{\mathbf{1}\}$, we conclude that either $\langle \mathbf{DF_3}, \{\mathbf{1}\}\rangle$ or $\langle \mathbf{DF_3}, \{\mathbf{1/2}, \mathbf{1}\}\rangle$ witnesses $\varphi \nvdash \psi$, as required. ■

Lemma 4. *For every reduced model* $\langle \mathbf{A}, F\rangle$ *of* $\vdash_{\mathrm{DF}^{\mathbf{1}}}$, *the algebra* $\mathbf{A}$ *is a bounded centered Kleene lattice and* $F = \{\mathbf{1}\}$.

Proof. Let $\langle \mathbf{A}, F\rangle$ be a reduced model of $\vdash_{\mathrm{DF}^{\mathbf{1}}}$. Then $\mathbf{A} \in \mathbb{CK}$, by Corollary 1. Denote by $\mathbf{A}_{-}$ the $\mathbf{1/2}$-free reduct of $\mathbf{A}$. Since $\mathrm{Con}(\mathbf{A}) = \mathrm{Con}(\mathbf{A}_{-})$, the matrix $\langle \mathbf{A}_{-}, F\rangle$ is also reduced, and (by the definition of $\vdash_{\mathrm{DF}^{\mathbf{1}}}$) it is a model of strong Kleene's ($\mathbf{1}$-preserving) logic K. Then by [2, Thm. 3.7] we have $F = \{\mathbf{1}\}$. ■

Theorem 3. $\vdash_{\mathrm{DF}^{\mathbf{1}}}$ axiomatizes $\mathrm{DF}^{\mathbf{1}}$.

Proof. Soundness of $\vdash_{\mathrm{DF}^{\mathbf{1}}}$ with respect to the matrix $\langle \mathbf{DF_3}, \{\mathbf{1}\}\rangle$ is easily verified. For completeness, assume that $\Gamma \nvdash_{\mathrm{DF}^{\mathbf{1}}} \psi$. Note that it suffices to consider a finite Γ (for $\vdash_{\mathrm{DF}}$ is finitary, by definition) and, by the rules of $\vdash_{\mathrm{DF}^{\mathbf{1}}}$, we have that $\Gamma \vdash_{\mathrm{DF}^{\mathbf{1}}} \psi$ iff $\varphi \vdash_{\mathrm{DF}^{\mathbf{1}}} \psi$, where $\varphi := \bigwedge \Gamma$. That is, it suffices to look at single-premise derivations. Now, by the assumption and Lemma 4, we have that

[12] To be completely precise, [2, Thm. 3.7] gives us that $\mathbf{A}$ is a Kleene *algebra*, or bounded Kleene lattice, for in [2] all logics are considered in the language that includes the truth constants $\mathbf{0}, \mathbf{1}$. However, it is easy that all the results we need from [2] hold for the constant-free language as well.

there is a (reduced) matrix $\langle \mathbf{A}, \{\mathbf{1}\}\rangle$, where $\mathbf{A}$ a centered Kleene lattice, witnessing that $\varphi \nvdash_{\mathrm{DF}^{\mathbf{1}}} \psi$. Note that $\mathbf{A}$ is bounded, so we can view it as an algebra that includes the constant $\mathbf{1}$. That is, we can expand the language with the constant symbol $\mathbf{1}$ and consider the algebra $\mathbf{A}^{+}$. The assumptions then mean that the quasi-equation $\varphi \approx \mathbf{1} \rightsquigarrow \psi \approx \mathbf{1}$ fails in $\mathbf{A}^{+}$. But then this quasi-equation also fails in $\mathbf{DF_3}^{+}$, which also generates bounded centered Kleene lattices as a quasi-variety (i.e. the same proof as Lemma 1 works for $\mathbf{DF}_3^{+}$). Hence, the matrix $\langle \mathbf{DF_3}, \{\mathbf{1}\}\rangle$ also witnesses $\varphi \nvdash \psi$, as required. ■

Corollary 1. For every logic L in $\{\mathrm{DF}, \mathrm{DF}^{\wedge_{\mathsf{K}}}, \mathrm{DF}^{\mathbf{1}}\}$, we have $\mathsf{Alg}^*(\mathrm{L}) \subsetneq \mathsf{Alg}(\mathrm{L}) = \mathbb{CK}$.

Proof. Let us first consider $\mathrm{L} = \mathrm{DF}^{\wedge_{\mathsf{K}}}$. Since $\mathrm{DF}^{\wedge_{\mathsf{K}}}$ is semilattice-based, the equality $\mathsf{Alg}(\mathrm{DF}^{\wedge_{\mathsf{K}}}) = \mathbb{CK}$ is a particular instance of [2, Thm. 2.13].

In view of a contradiction, suppose $\mathsf{Alg}^*(\mathrm{DF}^{\wedge_{\mathsf{K}}}) = \mathsf{Alg}(\mathrm{DF}^{\wedge_{\mathsf{K}}}) = \mathbb{CK}$. Let $\mathbf{K_5} \in \mathbb{CK}$ be the 5-element linearly ordered centered Kleene lattice considered in the proof of Proposition 1. Reasoning as in Lemma 3, $\mathbf{K_5} \in \mathsf{Alg}^*(\mathrm{DF}^{\wedge_{\mathsf{K}}})$ would give us $\mathbf{A}_{-} \in \mathsf{Alg}^*(\mathrm{K}^{\leq})$, where $\mathrm{K}^{\leq}$ is Kleene's degree-preserving logic. But this is impossible, for we know (see e.g. [17, p. 427]) that the only chains in $\mathsf{Alg}^*(\mathrm{K}_{\leq})$ are the two- and the three-element one. Following the same reasoning as in [17, p. 427] we can also observe that $\mathsf{Alg}^*(\mathrm{DF}^{\wedge_{\mathsf{K}}})$ is not a quasi-variety.

Now, let $\mathrm{L} \in \{\mathrm{DF}, \mathrm{DF}^{\mathbf{1}}\}$. Since $\mathrm{DF}^{\wedge_{\mathsf{K}}} \leq \mathrm{L}$, we have $\mathsf{Alg}^*(\mathrm{L}) \subseteq \mathsf{Alg}^*(\mathrm{DF}^{\wedge_{\mathsf{K}}}) \subsetneq \mathbb{CK}$ and $\mathsf{Alg}(\mathrm{L}) \subseteq \mathsf{Alg}(\mathrm{DF}^{\wedge_{\mathsf{K}}}) = \mathbb{CK}$. To prove $\mathbb{CK} \subseteq \mathsf{Alg}(\mathrm{L})$, recall that $\mathsf{Alg}(\mathrm{L}) = P_S(\mathsf{Alg}^*(\mathrm{L}))$ for any logic L, where P_S is the operator that forms subdirect products [18, Thm. 2.23]. Since $\mathbf{DF_3} \in \mathsf{Alg}^*(\mathrm{L})$, we have $\mathbb{CK} = P_S(\mathbf{DF_3}) \subseteq P_S(\mathsf{Alg}^*(\mathrm{L})) = \mathsf{Alg}(\mathrm{L})$. Hence, $\mathbb{CK} = \mathsf{Alg}(\mathrm{L})$. ■

Theorem 4. For each semilattice-based logic L based on $\mathbf{O}_3$ among the above-mentioned ones (i.e. the ones induced, respectively, by $\wedge_{\mathsf{K}}, \wedge_{\mathsf{OL}}$ and $\vee_{\mathsf{OL}}$) we have $\mathsf{Alg}(\mathrm{L}) = \mathbb{OL}$. In consequence, for

$$\mathrm{L} \in \{\mathrm{Log}\langle \mathbf{O}_3, \{\mathbf{1/2}\}\rangle, \mathrm{Log}\langle \mathbf{O}_3, \{\mathbf{1}\}\rangle, \mathrm{Log}\langle \mathbf{O}_3, \{\mathbf{0}, \mathbf{1}\}\rangle\},$$

we also have $\mathsf{Alg}(\mathrm{L}) = \mathbb{OL}$.

Proof. Recall that every semilattice-based logic L among the ones we consider is (obviously) selfextensional, and has a conjunction in the sense of [18, Def. 2.45]. Then, by [18, Prop. 2.26, Thm. 4.27] we have that $V(\mathsf{Alg}(\mathrm{L})) = \mathsf{Alg}(\mathrm{L})$. It is known that $V(\mathsf{Alg}(\mathrm{L}))$ is generated by the class of algebraic reducts of any class of reduced matrices complete with respect to L [18, p. 30]. In our case, we can take this class to be the single algebra $\mathbf{O}_3$, so we have $\mathsf{Alg}(\mathrm{L}) = V(\mathsf{Alg}(\mathrm{L})) = V(\mathbf{O}_3) = \mathbb{OL}$.

Now let $\mathrm{L} \in \{\mathrm{Log}\langle \mathbf{O}_3, \{\mathbf{1/2}\}\rangle, \mathrm{Log}\langle \mathbf{O}_3, \{\mathbf{1}\}\rangle, \mathrm{Log}\langle \mathbf{O}_3, \{\mathbf{0}, \mathbf{1}\}\rangle\}$. By its matrix definition, any such L is stronger than some semilattice-based logic considered above, say, L′. So, $\mathsf{Alg}(\mathrm{L}) \subseteq \mathsf{Alg}(\mathrm{L}') = \mathbb{OL}$. For the converse inclusion, note that $\mathbf{O}_3 \in \mathsf{Alg}^*(\mathrm{L}) \subseteq \mathsf{Alg}(\mathrm{L})$. Then, recalling [18, Thm. 2.23], we have $\mathbb{OL} = P_S(\mathbf{O}_3) \subseteq P_S(\mathsf{Alg}(\mathrm{L})) = \mathsf{Alg}(\mathrm{L})$, where P_S is the operator forming subdirect products. Hence the claimed equality follows. ■

Lemma 5 (cf. [22], Prop. 1.24). *Suppose that* $\mathrm{L} := \mathrm{Log}\langle M\rangle$, *where* M *is a class of matrices such that, for each* $\langle \mathbf{A}, F\rangle \in M$, *it holds that* $|F| \leqslant 1$. *Then, for every* $\langle \mathbf{A}, F\rangle \in \mathrm{Mod}^*(\mathrm{L})$, *it holds that* $|F| \leqslant 1$.

Proof. Consider an arbitrary unary polynomial formula, i.e. of the form $p(x) := \varphi(x, \overline{z})$. Let $\langle \mathbf{A}, F\rangle \in M$ and f be an $\mathbf{A}$-valuation both verifying that $f(x), f(y), f(p(x)) \in F$. In particular, $F \neq \varnothing$, so $|F| = 1$ and hence $f(x) = f(y)$. As a consequence,

$$f(\varphi(y, \overline{z})) = \varphi^{\mathbf{A}}(f(y), f(\overline{z})) = \varphi^{\mathbf{A}}(f(x), f(\overline{z})) = f(\varphi(x, \overline{z})) \in F.$$

Therefore, we have seen that, for an arbitrary unary polynomial formula $p(x)$, it holds that

$$x, y, p(x) \vdash_{\mathrm{L}} p(y).$$

Now we can prove our claim. Take an arbitrary matrix $\langle \mathbf{A}, F\rangle \in \mathrm{Mod}^*(\mathrm{L})$ and $a, b \in F$. By our previous observation, for every unary polynomial function $p(x)$ it holds that $p(a) \in F$ if and only if $p(b) \in F$. Hence, $(a, b) \in \Omega^{\mathbf{A}} F = id_A$, so $a = b$, as desired. ■

Corollary 2 (cf. [22], Cor. 1.25). *If* L *is an assertional logic then, for every* $\langle \mathbf{A}, F\rangle \in \mathrm{Mod}^*(\mathrm{L})$ *it holds that* $|F| = 1$.

Proof. Since L is an assertional logic (of some class $\mathbb{K}$ of algebras), we already know that $\mathrm{L} = \mathrm{Log}\langle M\rangle$, where $M := \{\langle \mathbf{A}, \{1\}\rangle \mid \mathbf{A} \in \mathbb{K}\}$. By the preceding Lemma, $|F| \leqslant 1$ for every $\langle \mathbf{A}, F\rangle \in \mathrm{Mod}^*(\mathrm{L})$. On the other hand, that L is assertional logic implies, in general, that 1 is a theorem of the logic so that it appears in every deductive filter, that is, $|F| \geqslant 1$ for every $\langle \mathbf{A}, F\rangle \in \mathrm{Mod}^*(\mathrm{L})$. ■

Theorem 5. Given a logic L based on $\mathbf{O}_3$, we have:

(i) $\mathsf{Alg}^*(\mathrm{L}) = \mathsf{Alg}(\mathrm{L}) = \mathbb{OL}$ for $\mathrm{L} \in \{\mathrm{OL}_{\wedge_{\mathrm{OL}}}, \mathrm{OL}_{\wedge_{\mathrm{K}}}, \mathrm{Log}\langle \mathbf{O}_3, \{\mathbf{1/2}\}\rangle\}$.
(ii) $\mathsf{Alg}^*(\mathrm{L}) \neq \mathsf{Alg}(\mathrm{L}) = \mathbb{OL}$ for $\mathrm{L} = \mathrm{Log}\langle \mathbf{O}_3, \{\mathbf{1}\}\rangle$.

Proof. Recall that the equality $\mathsf{Alg}(\mathrm{L}) = \mathbb{OL}$ has been established for each of the above logics in Theorem 5. The equality $\mathsf{Alg}^*(\mathrm{Log}\langle \mathbf{O}_3, \{\mathbf{1/2}\}\rangle) = \mathsf{Alg}(\mathrm{Log}\langle \mathbf{O}_3, \{\mathbf{1/2}\}\rangle)$ is a consequence of algebraizability (see below).

Now consider the case where either $\mathrm{L} = \mathrm{Log}\{\langle \mathbf{O}_3, \{\mathbf{1/2}, \mathbf{1}\}\rangle, \langle \mathbf{O}_3, \{\mathbf{1/2}\}\rangle\}$ or $\mathrm{L} = \mathrm{Log}\{\langle \mathbf{O}_3, \{\mathbf{1}\}\rangle, \langle \mathbf{O}_3, \{\mathbf{1/2}, \mathbf{1}\}\rangle\}$. Notice that in both cases $\mathrm{L} \leq \mathrm{sOL}$, by definition. But then $\mathbb{OL} = \mathsf{Alg}^*(\mathrm{sOL}) \subseteq \mathsf{Alg}^*(\mathrm{L}) \subseteq \mathsf{Alg}(\mathrm{L}) = \mathbb{OL}$, so again we have an equality.

Now let $\mathrm{L} = \mathrm{Log}\langle \mathbf{O}_3, \{\mathbf{1}\}\rangle$. Since the designated set is a singleton, we know that every reduced model of $\mathrm{Log}\langle \mathbf{O}_3, \{\mathbf{1}\}\rangle$ is of the form $\langle \mathbf{A}, F\rangle$ with F also a singleton by Corollary 2. Then, since the rule $p \vdash p \vee_{\mathsf{K}} q$ is sound in $\mathrm{Log}\langle \mathbf{O}_3, \{\mathbf{1}\}\rangle$, it is easy to see that the unique element of F must be the top element of the $\vee_{\mathsf{K}}$-semilattice order, that is, $F = \{\mathbf{1}\}$. However, we know that there are unbounded algebras in $\mathbb{OL}$ (namely, any twist-algebra over a bottom-less generalized Boolean algebra). Hence, $\mathsf{Alg}^*(\mathrm{L}) \neq \mathbb{OL} = \mathsf{Alg}(\mathrm{L})$. ■

Theorem 6. The following holds:

1. $\text{Log}\langle \mathbf{O}_3, \{\mathbf{1}\}\rangle$ is not algebraizable (Remark 1). Adding the constant $\mathbf{1}$ to the language, we achieve algebraizability through the following translations: $\tau\colon x \mapsto x = \mathbf{1}$ and

$$\rho\colon \varphi \approx \psi \mapsto \{(\varphi \rightarrow_{\mathsf{OL}} \psi) \wedge_{\mathsf{OL}} \mathbf{1}, (\psi \rightarrow_{\mathsf{OL}} \varphi) \wedge_{\mathsf{OL}} \mathbf{1}, (\neg\varphi \rightarrow_{\mathsf{OL}} \neg\psi) \wedge_{\mathsf{OL}} \mathbf{1}, (\neg\psi \rightarrow_{\mathsf{OL}} \neg\varphi) \wedge_{\mathsf{OL}} \mathbf{1}\}$$

or, alternatively, $\rho\colon \varphi \approx \psi \mapsto \{(\varphi \Rightarrow \psi) \wedge_{\mathsf{OL}} \mathbf{1}, (\psi \Rightarrow \varphi) \wedge_{\mathsf{OL}} \mathbf{1}\}$.
2. As above, $\text{Log}\langle \mathbf{O}_3, \{\mathbf{1}, \mathbf{0}\}\rangle$ is not algebraizable. Adding $\mathbf{1}$ to the language, we achieve algebraizability through the following translations: $\tau\colon x \mapsto x \vee_{\mathsf{OL}} \neg x = \mathbf{1}$ and $\rho\colon \varphi \approx \psi \mapsto \{\uparrow(\varphi \Rightarrow \psi), \uparrow(\psi \Rightarrow \varphi)\}$.
3. $\text{Log}\langle \mathbf{O}_3, \{\mathbf{1/2}\}\rangle$ is algebraizable with $\tau\colon x \mapsto x \approx \mathbf{1/2}$ (recall that the term $\neg x \rightarrow (x \rightarrow x)$ defines the algebraic constant $\mathbf{1/2}$) or $\tau\colon x \mapsto x \approx \neg x$ and

$$\rho\colon \varphi \approx \psi \mapsto \{\Diamond(\varphi \rightarrow_{\mathsf{OL}} \psi), \Diamond(\psi \rightarrow_{\mathsf{OL}} \varphi), \Diamond(\neg\varphi \rightarrow_{\mathsf{OL}} \neg\psi), \Diamond(\neg\psi \rightarrow_{\mathsf{OL}} \neg\varphi)\}$$

or, alternatively, $\rho\colon \varphi \approx \psi \mapsto \{\Diamond(\varphi \Rightarrow \psi), \Diamond(\psi \Rightarrow \varphi)\}$.

Proof. The following argument establishes many cases for items (1) and (2). Recall that all protoalgebraic logics must have theorems (except for the quasi-inconsistent logic: see [19]). Since $\{\mathbf{1/2}\}$ forms a one-element subalgebra of all the algebras considered here, any valuation assigning $\mathbf{1/2}$ to all propositional variables will also assign $\mathbf{1/2}$ to all formulas. Hence, $\mathbf{1/2}$ must be designated for the logic to have theorems.

The strategy is similar for (3). Obviously, a valuation v over the matrix $\langle \mathbf{O}_3, \{\mathbf{1/2}\}\rangle$ satisfies an equation $\varphi \approx \mathbf{1/2}$ iff $v(\varphi) \in \{\mathbf{1/2}\}$. Thus, for all formulas Γ, φ, we have $\Gamma \vdash \varphi$ (where $\vdash$ is a Set-Formula calculus complete with respect to $\langle \mathbf{O}_3, \{\mathbf{1/2}\}\rangle$) iff $\tau(\Gamma) \vDash_{\langle \mathbf{O}_3, \{\mathbf{1/2}\}\rangle} \tau(\varphi)$. This is condition (ALG1) of algebraizability [19, Def. 3.11]. To establish algebraizability, it remains to prove (ALG4), i.e., that every equation $\varphi \approx \psi$ is inter-derivable in $\vDash_{\langle \mathbf{O}_3, \{\mathbf{1/2}\}\rangle}$ with $\tau(\rho(\varphi \approx \psi))$, which is the set $\{\Diamond(\varphi \Rightarrow \psi) \approx \mathbf{1/2}, \Diamond(\psi \Rightarrow \varphi) \approx \mathbf{1/2}\}$. This is easily verified in $\mathbf{O}_3$: indeed, if we assume that $v(\Diamond(\varphi \Rightarrow \psi)) = \mathbf{1/2}$ and $v(\Diamond(\psi \Rightarrow \varphi)) = \mathbf{1/2}$ hold for an arbitrary valuation v, it is not difficult to check (by direct inspection on the tables) that the only possible common cases for both equalities satisfy that $v(\varphi) = v(\psi)$, as desired. ∎

References

1. Albuquerque, H., Font, J.M., Jansana, R.: The strong version of a sentential logic. Stud. Log. **105**(4), 703–760 (2017). https://doi.org/10.1007/s11225-017-9709-0
2. Albuquerque, H., Přenosil, A., Rivieccio, U.: An algebraic view of super-belnap logics. Stud. Log. **105**(6), 1051–1086 (2017). https://doi.org/10.1007/s11225-017-9739-7

3. Blok, W., Pigozzi, D.: Algebraizable Logics. Memoirs of the AMS Series. American Mathematical Society (1989)
4. Bou, F., et al.: Logics preserving degrees of truth from varieties of residuated lattices. J. Log. and Comput. **19**(6), 1031–1069 (2009). https://doi.org/10.1093/logcom/exp030
5. Caleiro, C., Marcelino, S.: Analytic calculi for monadic PNmatrices. In: Iemhoff, R., Moortgat, M., de Queiroz, R. (eds.) WoLLIC 2019. LNCS, vol. 11541, pp. 84–98. Springer, Heidelberg (2019). https://doi.org/10.1007/978-3-662-59533-6_6
6. Cantwell, J.: The logic of conditional negation. Notre Dame J. Formal Log. **49**(3), 245–260 (2008). https://doi.org/10.1215/00294527-2008-010
7. Cignoli, R.: The class of Kleene algebras satisfying an interpolation property and nelson algebras. Algebra Univ. **23**, 262–292 (1986). https://doi.org/10.1007/BF01230621
8. Clark, D.M., Davey, B.A.: Natural Dualities for the Working Algebraist. Cambridge Studies in Advanced Mathematics, vol. 57. Cambridge University Press, Cambridge (1998)
9. Cooper, W.S.: The Propositional Logic of Ordinary Discourse. Inq. Interdiscip. J. Philos. **11**(1–4), 295–320 (1968). https://doi.org/10.1080/00201746808601531
10. Égré, P., Rossi, L., Sprenger, J.: De Finettian logics of indicative conditionals part I: trivalent semantics and validity. J. Philos. Log. **50**(2), 187–213 (2020). https://doi.org/10.1007/s10992-020-09549-6
11. Egré, P., Rossi, L., Spengler, J.: Certain and uncertain inference with indicative conditionals. Preprint available at the arXiv (2023)
12. Égré, P., Rossi, L., Sprenger, J.: De Finettian logics of indicative conditionals part II: proof theory and algebraic semantics. J. Philos. Log. **50**(2), 215–247 (2021). https://doi.org/10.1007/s10992-020-09572-7
13. Farrell, R.J.: Implication and presupposition. Notre Dame J. Formal Log. **27**(1) (1986)
14. Farrell, R.J.: Material implication, confirmation, and counterfactuals. Notre Dame J. Formal Log. **20**(2), 383–394 (1979)
15. Fazio, D., Odintsov, S.P.: An algebraic investigation of the connexive logic C. Stud. Logica. (2023). https://doi.org/10.1007/s11225-023-10057-2
16. de Finetti, B.: La logique de la probabilité. Actes du Congrés International de Philosophie Scientifique (1936)
17. Font, J.M.: Belnap's four-valued logic and de Morgan lattices. Log. J. IGPL **5**(3), 1–29 (1997). https://doi.org/10.1093/jigpal/5.3.1-e
18. Font, J.M., Jansana, R.: A General Algebraic Semantics for Sentential Logics. Springer (2009)
19. Font, J.M.: Abstract Algebraic Logic: An introductory textbook. College Publications (2016)
20. Greati, V., Marcelino, S., Rivieccio, U.: Axiomatizing the logic of ordinary discourse. Proceeding of IPMU24 (to appear) (2024)
21. Jansana, R.: Self-extensional logics with a conjunction. Stud. Log. **2006**(84), 63–104 (2006). https://doi.org/10.1007/s11225-006-9003-z
22. Moraschini, T.: Abstract algebraic logic. Teaching notes for the Master in Pure and Applied Logic at the University of Barcelona
23. Mortensen, C.: Aristotle's thesis in consistent and inconsistent logics. Stud. Log. **43**, 107–116 (1984)
24. Olkhovikov, G.K.: On a new three-valued paraconsistent logic. IfCoLog J. Log. Appl. **3**, 317–334 (2016)

25. Pietz, A., Rivieccio, U.: Nothing but the truth. J. Philos. Log. **42**(1), 125–135 (2013). https://doi.org/10.1007/s10992-011-9215-1
26. Priest, G.: The logic of paradox. J. Philos. Log. **8**(1), 219–241 (1979)
27. Pynko, A.P.: On priest's logic of paradox. J. Appl. Non-Classical Log. **5**(2), 219–225 (1995). https://doi.org/10.1080/11663081.1995.10510856
28. Rivieccio, U.: The algebra of ordinary discourse. On the semantics of Cooper's logic. Arch. Math. Log. (2025). https://doi.org/10.1007/s00153-024-00961-2
29. Wansing, H.: Connexive modal logic. In: Kracht, M., de Rijke, M., Wansing, H., Zakharyaschev, M. (eds.) Advances in Modal Logic, pp. 367–383. CSLI Publications (2005)
30. Wansing, H.: Constructive logic is connexive and contradictory. Log. Log. Philos. 1–27 (forthcoming). https://doi.org/10.12775/llp.2024.001

Abstracting Conceptual Models as a Weakening Process

Elena Romanenko[1(✉)], Oliver Kutz[1], Diego Calvanese[1], and Giancarlo Guizzardi[2]

[1] Free University of Bozen-Bolzano, 39100 Bolzano, Italy
{elena.romanenko,oliver.kutz,diego.calvanese}@unibz.it
[2] University of Twente, 7500 Enschede, The Netherlands
g.guizzardi@utwente.nl

Abstract. Utilizing abstractions of large conceptual models may enhance their clarity and comprehensibility. This work assesses an existing algorithm for generating abstractions of ontology-driven conceptual models. Although the algorithm has been empirically evaluated using the FAIR catalog of such models, it still lacks formal semantics. This paper addresses this gap by formalizing the basic transformations underlying the abstraction process in $\mathcal{SROIQ}$—the expressive and decidable description logic that underpins the Web Ontology Language (OWL 2). Specifically, it demonstrates that, under certain natural assumptions, these transformations are obtained by a formal procedure known as axiom weakening.

Keywords: Semantics for Abstraction · Ontology-Driven Conceptual Models · Axiom Weakening · $\mathcal{SROIQ}$

1 Introduction

Conceptual modeling is typically applied during the early stages of system development. The primary outcome of this process—a *conceptual model*, CM—not only accompanies the system throughout its subsequent development stages but also serves as a formal conceptual foundation for applications.

If we consider Chen's paper on the Entity-Relationship information model [13] as the starting point of conceptual modeling as a research discipline, then, as Akoka et al. [1] point out, this field has existed for nearly five decades by now. The authors also note that a distinct stage in the evolution of CMs was marked about 20 years ago by the emergence of *ontology-driven conceptual models*, ODCMs—those models that use ontological constructs to ground modeling elements. In principle, an ODCM can leverage semantics of any foundational ontology, but the focus of this paper is on models based on *Unified Foundational Ontology*, UFO [26].

D. Kozen and R. de Queiroz (Eds.): WoLLIC 2025, LNCS 15942, pp. 141–157, 2026.
https://doi.org/10.1007/978-3-031-99536-1_9

Both traditional and ontology-driven CMs aim to provide better communication between stakeholders with diverse backgrounds and knowledge, by offering a shared vocabulary and visual representation of a system's conceptual elements [10]. However, the complexity of the described domain reveals itself in the complexity of the corresponding (OD)CM, leading to models with hundreds of modeling elements. Examples of such large models[1], can be found in the FAIR catalog of ODCMs [42].

The problem of making (OD)CMs more comprehensible has been addressed in the literature for quite some time, and various complexity management approaches have been introduced, including modularization or clustering, ranking, summarization, and abstraction techniques [45]. In this paper, we analyze one of the abstraction methods for ODCMs, which aims to produce a reduced version of the original model while retaining its core content.

A first abstraction algorithm leveraging foundational ontological semantics for UFO-based models was introduced by Guizzardi et al. [27], followed by an enhanced one [38]. Although the generated abstractions were empirically evaluated for syntactical, semantic, and pragmatic quality aspects [39], the algorithm was not formally assessed. The main goal of this paper is to contribute to this line of research by answering the following research question:

How can we formally and semantically characterize the relation between the original model and its abstraction?

Both versions of the abstraction algorithm were introduced for models specified in OntoUML, a language that allows for conceptual modeling in compliance with the UFO semantics. OntoUML defines a set of constructs and semantically-motivated syntactical constraints tailored for ODCMs [12]. However, its constructs are limited to the elements of the underlying language, specifically to the components of UML class diagrams. Thus, within this paper, we consider the abstraction process in the context of UML class diagrams and use for formalization purposes the Web Ontology Language, OWL 2 [5], standardized by the W3C. The semantics that arise from the use of OntoUML requires a deep familiarity with the original algorithm and is beyond the scope of this paper.

Hence, to answer the stated question, we first analyze the latest version of the algorithm and formulate the basic graph transformations that are used to reach the desired abstraction. Then, we formalize these transformations in $\mathcal{SROIQ}$, the expressive and decidable description logic underlying OWL 2 [29]. We assume that *model abstraction is the process of reaching the desired granularity of the domain by means of axiom weakening*.

This work is not the first attempt to provide a formalization for models expressed in OntoUML. Braga et al. [11] validated conceptual models by means of Alloy, a "structural modelling language based on first-order logic for expressing complex structural constraints and behavior" [30]. Later, OntoUML pat-

[1] E.g., 'kritz2020ontobg' on https://github.com/OntoUML/ontouml-models/tree/master/models/kritz2020ontobg, and 'xhani2023xmlpo' on https://github.com/OntoUML/ontouml-models/tree/master/models/xhani2023xmlpo.

terns have been formally defined using a graph transformation approach [46], and implemented by means of the general-purpose graph transformation tool GROOVE[2] [18].

Still, our goal here is to *clarify formal relationships between models*, the original one and its abstraction. The remainder of the paper is organized as follows: Sect. 2 briefly describes the basic principles of the algorithm, presents our baseline in formalization approaches, and shows why $\mathcal{SROIQ}$ is enough for reaching our goal; Sect. 3 aims at formulating basic transformations that the algorithm applies to ODCMs; Sect. 4 analyzes under what conditions the process of abstraction can be considered as a weakening procedure; and Sect. 5 gives final considerations and discusses future work.

2 Background

2.1 UFO-Based Models and Their Abstractions

Unified Foundational Ontology [26] is an axiomatic domain-independent formal theory that builds on contributions from analytic metaphysics, cognitive sciences, linguistics, and philosophical logic. It leverages integration and revisitation of other foundational approaches and ontologies, specifically, OntoClean [22], DOLCE [8], and GFO [33]. UFO addresses fundamental ontological notions through a set of micro-theories representing types and taxonomic structures, part-whole relations, relations, and events, among others. It has been successfully used to model a wide range of domains, including legal relations, trust and risk, petroleum and gas, and genomics. Introduction of UFO concepts is beyond the scope of this paper, but interested readers can refer to the article by Guizzardi et al. [26], which serves as the most up-to-date specification of the ontology.

One of the reasons why the abstraction algorithm was developed for UFO-based models is the existence of OntoUML, a language designed to enrich the Unified Modeling Language, UML [36], with the concepts of UFO. In other words, it shifts the inherent complexity of reality towards the language's definition, so that *every syntactically valid OntoUML model should represent a sound ontology in terms of UFO* [17]. In fact, OntoUML serves as a metamodeling language, where every concept must instantiate exactly one leaf concept of the UFO taxonomy.

The latest version of the algorithm for abstracting UFO-based models leveraging the semantics of the foundational ontology defines 11 model-rewriting rules [38], which were grouped into three categories, namely, rules for abstracting *(1)* parthood relations (compositions and aggregations), *(2)* generalization relations, and *(3)* existentially dependent entities, namely, *Relators*, *Qualities*, and *Modes* in terms of UFO.

The rules can be applied together or separately, and modifications in an ODCM caused by each rule lead to the creation of a new abstracted version of

[2] https://groove.ewi.utwente.nl.

the original model (see [40] for details). These model-rewriting rules are, indeed, *patterns* for models expressed in OntoUML. Thus, to apply them, one needs to substitute the matching model with its replacement, where the placeholder concepts of the rule are changed to the concrete classes and relations of the model.

2.2 Formalizing UML Models in $\mathcal{SROIQ}$

Description Logics (DLs) were specifically designed as formalisms for representing knowledge, focusing on the conceptual representation of domains in terms of classes and their relationships, which admit decidable reasoning services [3].

As previously mentioned, OntoUML is an extension of UML that employs a stereotype mechanism to ensure model compliance with UFO. Botti Benevides et al. [9] formalized part of UFO in the DL $\mathcal{SROIQ}$, which is the formal underpinning of OWL 2. Formalizations of UML class diagrams in terms of first-order logic and various DLs also exist, e.g., [6]. However, these formalizations do not consider the use of a meta-level ontology, and therefore cannot be directly reused for OntoUML.

Still, since any UFO-based conceptual model has three levels—the foundational ontology level, the level of types, and the level of instances—and abstraction techniques are applied only at the level of types (see [40] for details), we do not consider metamodeling approaches to which $\mathcal{SROIQ}$ can be extended[3]. Instead, we focus solely on the level of types, representing it as a plain UML model (see later an example in Fig. 1), which—as shown further—can be formalized in $\mathcal{SROIQ}$. Furthermore, in the following discussion, we limit our scope to binary associations, even though UML also allows for n-ary associations.

Here we give a brief description of $\mathcal{SROIQ}$, which is suitable for our needs, for full details see [4,29]. The syntax of $\mathcal{SROIQ}$ is based on a vocabulary of two disjoint sets, N_C of concept names and N_R of role names. The sets of $\mathcal{SROIQ}$ roles and concepts are generated respectively by the following grammar:

$$R ::= U \mid r \mid r^-$$
$$C ::= \bot \mid \top \mid A \mid \neg C \mid C \sqcap D \mid C \sqcup D \mid \forall R.C \mid \exists R.C \mid \exists R.\mathit{Self} \mid \geqslant n\, R.C \mid \leqslant n\, R.C,$$

where $U \in N_R$ is the universal role, which always relates all pairs of individuals, $A \in N_C$ is a concept name, $r \in N_R$ is a role name, and $n \in \mathbb{N}_0$ is a non-negative integer. A *TBox* $\mathcal{T}$ is a finite set of concept inclusions of the form $C \sqsubseteq D$ where C and D are concepts. The TBox is used to store terminological knowledge concerning the relationship between concepts. An *RBox* $\mathcal{R}$ is a finite set of role inclusion axioms of the form $S \sqsubseteq R$, $R \circ S \sqsubseteq R$, where S and R are roles. The RBox represents knowledge about the relationships between roles. Note, that $\mathcal{SROIQ}$ requires regularity of role inclusion axioms, i.e., it prevents a role hierarchy from containing certain forms of cyclic dependencies. As we will see later, the same is required in UML models for composite aggregations.

[3] E.g., by Motik [34], De Giacomo et al. [15], Kubincová et al. [31] and others.

As usual in DLs, the semantics of $\mathcal{SROIQ}$ is specified through the notion of interpretation. An *interpretation* $\mathcal{I} = (\Delta^{\mathcal{I}}, \cdot^{\mathcal{I}})$ consists of an *interpretation domain* $\Delta^{\mathcal{I}}$ and an *interpretation function* $\cdot^{\mathcal{I}}$ that assigns to each concept C a subset $C^{\mathcal{I}} \subseteq \Delta^{\mathcal{I}}$ and to each role R a binary relation $R^{\mathcal{I}} \subseteq \Delta^{\mathcal{I}} \times \Delta^{\mathcal{I}}$ on the domain (see Table 1, where $\sharp P$ denotes the number of distinct elements in P).

In $\mathcal{SROIQ}$, a UML class C is represented by an atomic concept C.

Table 1. Expressions in $\mathcal{SROIQ}$.

Syntax	Semantics in $\mathcal{SROIQ}$	Syntax	Semantics in $\mathcal{SROIQ}$
$\neg C$	$\Delta^{\mathcal{I}} \setminus C^{\mathcal{I}}$	R^{-}	$\{\langle y, x\rangle \mid \langle x, y\rangle \in R^{\mathcal{I}}\}$
$C \sqcap D$	$C^{\mathcal{I}} \cap D^{\mathcal{I}}$	$R \circ S$	$\{\langle x, z\rangle \mid \exists y.\, \langle x, y\rangle \in R^{\mathcal{I}} \wedge \langle y, z\rangle \in S^{\mathcal{I}}\}$
$\exists R.C$	$\{x \mid \exists y.\langle x, y\rangle \in R^{\mathcal{I}} \wedge y \in C^{\mathcal{I}}\}$	$\geqslant n\, R.C$	$\{x \mid \sharp\{y \mid \langle x, y\rangle \in R^{\mathcal{I}} \wedge y \in C^{\mathcal{I}}\} \geq n\}$
$C \sqsubseteq D$	$C^{\mathcal{I}} \subseteq D^{\mathcal{I}}$	$S \sqsubseteq R$	$S^{\mathcal{I}} \subseteq R^{\mathcal{I}}$

UML defines a relationship as "an abstract concept that specifies some kind of relationship between elements" [36, p.54], and (if we leave out some details) distinguishes between *(1)* generalizations as direct relationships for organizing hierarchies, and *(2)* associations. OntoUML uses generalizations as specified in UML. Although UML allows for generalizations between both classes and relations, since the rules of the abstraction algorithm we consider do not cover generalizations between relations [38], we consider generalizations as *taxonomic relationships between classes*. In both languages, generalizations can be organized in sets with *covering* and *disjointness* properties. The covering property specifies whether the specific classes of the generalizations in a set are complete, in the sense that every instance of the general class is an instance of (at least) one of the specific classes. The disjoint property specifies whether the specific classes of the generalizations in a set may overlap.

In $\mathcal{SROIQ}$, a set of generalizations between a class C and its child classes $C_1, \ldots, C_n$ can be represented using the concept inclusion assertions $C_i \sqsubseteq C$, with $1 \leqslant i \leqslant n$. If the generalization is disjoint, it can be modeled by adding the assertions $C_i \sqsubseteq \sqcap_{j=i+1}^{n} \neg C_j$, with $1 \leqslant i \leqslant n-1$, and if it is covering, by adding the assertion $C \sqsubseteq \sqcup_{i=1}^{n} C_i$.

OntoUML distinguishes three sorts of *associations*: *(1)* an association without additional properties, *(2)* an association with derivation (see 'enrolled at' in Fig. 1), and *(3)* different *part-of* associations.

Table 2 shows how a standard association r (which has class C as domain and class D as range) can be formalized in $\mathcal{SROIQ}$. Of course, r is not necessarily the only relation of the model. If other relations exist for C or D, the corresponding assertions will change accordingly (as shown in Table 3).

According to the UML specification, an association with an association class not only connects objects but also defines a set of 'features' that belong to the association itself, rather than to any of the associated classes. OntoUML reuses

Table 2. Formalization of UML relation (adapted from [6]) and its trivialization (discussed in detail in Sect. 4).

UML	Formalization	Trivialization
C $a_1..a_n$ —— r▸ —— $b_1..b_n$ D	$\top \sqsubseteq \forall r.D \sqcap \forall r^{-}.C$	$\top \sqsubseteq \top$
	$C \sqsubseteq (\geqslant b_1\, r) \sqcap (\leqslant b_n\, r)$	$\bot \sqsubseteq \top$
	$D \sqsubseteq (\geqslant a_1\, r^{-}) \sqcap (\leqslant a_n\, r^{-})$	$\bot \sqsubseteq \top$

this notation for associations with derivation but *with different semantics*. Thus, to escape ambiguities, we formalize these associations as associations without additional properties, while the derived class is formalized as usual.

In UML each association end may receive an aggregation property, which could be shared or composite. *Composite aggregation* is a strong form of aggregation that requires a part object to be included in at most one composite object at a time, while "precise semantics of *shared aggregation* varies by application area and modeler" [36, p.112]. OntoUML, on its own, distinguishes different types of *part-of* relationships, which are also characterized by their transitivity (see discussion in [23–25]).

In $\mathcal{SROIQ}$ the *part-of* relation is formalized as a relation without additional properties, although it is assumed that the semantics is reified appropriately, e.g., for the transitive relations we may assume:

$$R \circ partOf \sqsubseteq R$$

Thus, if we consider the level of types of an OntoUML model as a standard UML class diagram, we can still use $\mathcal{SROIQ}$ for formalization purposes.

2.3 On Abstraction and Weakening

As mentioned before, the main goal of this paper is to conduct a formal evaluation of the existing algorithm used for generating ODCM abstractions. According to [41, p. 49], most existing theories identify abstraction with *a mapping from a ground* (original) *to an abstracted* (intended) *space*, but differ in the nature of spaces and the corresponding types of mappings.

Changes between the original and abstracted spaces may be introduced at different levels—syntax, semantics, axiomatic, and even at the level of the sustaining ontology (see [41] for details). Some of the foundational contributions to the field of semantics of abstraction were made by Plaisted [37], Hobbs [28], Tenenberg [43], Giunchiglia and Walsh [21], Nayak and Levy [35], Ghidini and Giunchiglia [19].

The notion of *granularity* in the context of abstraction was introduced by Hobbs [28]. According to him, two elements are indistinguishable if no relevant predicate differentiates them. For example, in the domain of legal relationships between parents and children, if our granularity is broad enough that predicate *Gender* is not considered relevant, predicates *Mother* and *Father* can fall into the same equivalence class, so the abstraction should only use predicate *Parent*.

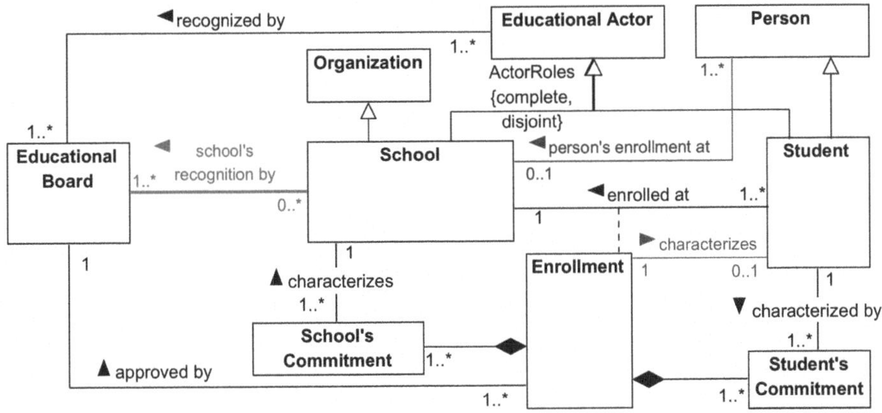

Fig. 1. Example of OntoUML types represented as UML model.

Tenenberg [43] defined abstracting at a syntactic level as a *restricted mapping between predicates, which preserved logical consistency.* Thus, all axioms from the original theory that serve to distinguish concepts and relations that are conflated at the abstract level should be removed.

Although simple deletion of axioms for a granularity increase leads to consistent theories, there is a need to receive useful and meaningful abstractions. It was noticed, that a similar problem arises during the debugging of inconsistent ontologies. In that case, removing axioms also makes the ontology consistent, but perhaps not very valuable [44].

Axiom weakening was thus developed as a technique that allows for a more fine-grained repair of inconsistent ontologies [7,44]. One of the advantages is that this approach repairs ontologies *by making axioms less restrictive* by employing refinement operators, rather than by deleting them. However, the problem with this approach is that there is initially no global guidance on *which* axioms should be weakened and *how* to do so. In theory, this can lead to endless chains of ever weaker axioms. However, this issue can be avoided in practice [14]. In the case of ODCMs, we aim to reuse their built-in semantics in order to guide this weakening process in a meaningful way.

The starting point of the axiom weakening approach is to stipulate that an axiom ϕ' is *weaker than* an axiom ϕ relative to a theory $\mathfrak{T}$: if $\mathfrak{T}, \phi \models \phi'$. Thus, we have an entailment guaranteeing that ϕ' conveys some of the meaning of ϕ, relative to $\mathfrak{T}$. In the case of terminological axioms in description logics of the form $C \sqsubseteq_{\mathcal{O}} D$ (where $\mathcal{O}$ is a fixed consistent background ontology), a weakening is any subsumption $C' \sqsubseteq_{\mathcal{O}} D'$ where C' is *specialization* of C and D' a *generalization* of D. The fine control over such a weakening procedure can then be given by specifying concrete rules to syntactically manipulate the space of specializations and generalizations. In particular, to control the granularity of such refinements, sets of most general specializations (downcover) and most specific generalizations (upcover) are syntactically generated, from which C' resp. D' are taken.

3 Model Transformations in the Abstraction Process

The next question that arises is what *basic transformations* are performed on a CM to reach the desired model when using the abstraction rules. To explore this, we again consider only the level of types and omit certain details introduced at the level of instances. For example, we leave aside enumerations [40]. Also, some rules that differ in OntoUML become indistinguishable in UML models.

An example of a model is given in Fig. 1. First, we can eliminate some elements of the model: a concept (e.g., 'Organization'), a relation, or a generalization set (e.g., 'ActorRoles')[4].

Second, we may *reduce the level of granularity*—that is, apply a kind of zoom-out approach—by revealing relationships at a higher level of the hierarchy, or at the level of a general concept rather than a more specific one. In the example, instead of modeling both 'Person' and its specialization 'Student', we might include only the more general 'Person' concept. This would not only eliminate 'Student' from the model but also require a reconstruction of the associated relationships. In particular, a relation derived from 'enrolled at' would need to be reconsidered at the higher level. One possible option—'person's enrollment at'—is shown in blue[5].

The same can be done with 'Student's Commitment'[6], which can be considered as part of 'Enrollment' serving as a characteristic of our 'Student'. In the example, the new 'characterizes' relation is shown in green.

Alternatively, we may decide to stay *more focused* on some precise concepts (e.g., 'School' and 'Student') and try to reveal those relationships in which these concepts participate implicitly. For instance, we may elaborate that our 'School' as an 'Educational Actor' is also recognized by the 'Educational Board' (the corresponding relation 'school's recognition by' is shown in red) to abstract from the more general concept, namely, 'Educational Actor'[7].

Finally, in some cases[8] we also need to establish a new relation between concepts that were not *explicitly* connected before. In the example, concepts 'Enrollment' and 'Educational Actor' may have an implicit connection, e.g., actors need to participate in the enrollment process, which is later approved by the 'Educational Board'. However, the semantics in cases where the relationship is non-trivial and must be explicitly defined can be verified only in OntoUML models. At the UML level, such cases cannot be distinguished.

Formalization of these basic model transformations (excluding elimination, which is discussed in the next section) can be found in Table 3, where the left part specifies the original model and its replacement is given on the right.

---

[4] For the readers familiar with the original algorithm, this is done in rules H.3 and H.5, A.1 and A.2. Here and further, the numbering of rules is kept as in [39].

[5] See rules H.2–H.5.

[6] Rule P.1 for the case of transitive part-of relations.

[7] Rule H.1.

[8] Rules A.1 and A.2, P.2–P.4 for the non-transitive version of part-of.

4 Abstracting as a Weakening Process

In some sense, the process of applying abstraction rules to CMs is similar to the *granularity adjustment*. Thus, we may expect this process to be an *iterative process*, where modifications in a model caused by each transformation lead to the development of new models, which all together form a hierarchy.

The idea that the original and abstracted models should be connected by some formal relationship is very intuitive. According to Tenenberg [43], there should be a logical consistency between models. Alternatively, we may expect a kind of compatibility relation as suggested by Ghidini and Giunchiglia [20]. Still, we assume that the process of applying those basic transformations with some additional assumptions can be considered as a *weakening process*.

First, imagine we would like to eliminate a concept C with all the relations it has. In ontology engineering, this operation is also known as *forgetting* [47]. Despite its apparent simplicity, the notion of forgetting allows many interpretations, starting from the original one suggested by Lin and Reiter [32]—which is currently known as *strong forgetting* in first-order logic—to many other forms, including concept-forgetting, TBox-forgetting, ontology-forgetting, etc. (see [16,47]). Regardless of the variant, forgetting intuitively should result in a theory that is weaker than the original one [16]. Let the concept C be related to another concept D via a relation r. Then, as shown in the right part of Table 2, we can always weaken the formulas in such a way, that they become trivial and can be omitted.

The first row of Table 3 shows a zoom-in operation in the case where a concept D has a generalization relation to the concept B. If we syntactically substitute B with the top concept in the right part of the formulas and with D in the left part, then we obtain the following:

$$
\begin{gathered}
D \sqsubseteq \top \\
\top \sqsubseteq \forall r.\top \sqcap \forall r^{-}.C \\
C \sqsubseteq (\geqslant a_1\, r) \sqcap (\leqslant a_n\, r) \\
D \sqsubseteq (\geqslant b_1\, r^{-}) \sqcap (\leqslant b_n\, r^{-})
\end{gathered}
$$

Here, the first formula is weaker than the original one $D \sqsubseteq B$, and simply states that D exists, therefore, it is trivial and can be omitted. The third and fourth formulas are part of a correct formalization of the relation's multiplicity constraints, and the latter is weaker than in the original set. Since we are not sure that the original relation implied a mandatory connection to a descendant of B, we have to relax the minimum multiplicity constraint from a_1 to 0, and this makes also the third formula weaker. A problem arises in the second formula, which is *not* a correct specification of the domain and range of the relation. It should be:

$$\top \sqsubseteq \forall r.\boldsymbol{D} \sqcap \forall r^{-}.C$$

In order to solve this issue, let us come back to the example in Fig. 1. One can expect that 'School' as an 'Educational Actor' has different functionality compared to another actor, i.e., 'Student'. Thus, we claim that the reconstructed relation has different semantics. Hence, there should be a relation $r_D \sqsubseteq r$ which is

Table 3. Formalization of model transformations.

Original model		Resulting model
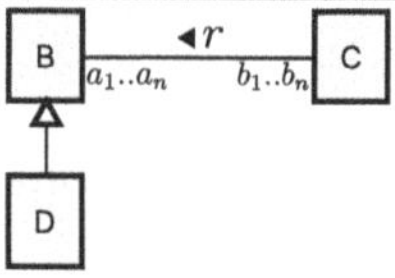	$r_D \sqsubseteq r$ ⇢	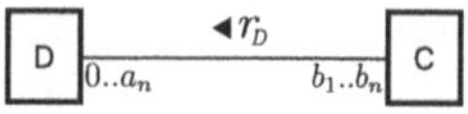
$D \sqsubseteq B$ $\top \sqsubseteq \forall r.B \sqcap \forall r^-.C$ $C \sqsubseteq (\geqslant a_1\, r) \sqcap (\leqslant a_n\, r)$ $B \sqsubseteq (\geqslant b_1\, r^-) \sqcap (\leqslant b_n\, r^-)$		$\top \sqsubseteq \forall r_D.D \sqcap \forall r_D^-.C$ $C \sqsubseteq (\leqslant a_n\, r_D)$ $D \sqsubseteq (\geqslant b_1\, r_D^-) \sqcap (\leqslant b_n\, r_D^-)$
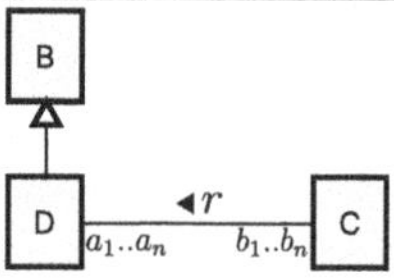	$r \sqsubseteq r_B$ ⇢	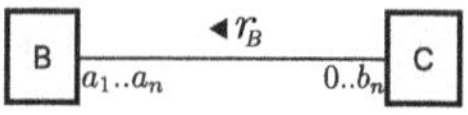
$D \sqsubseteq B$ $\top \sqsubseteq \forall r.D \sqcap \forall r^-.C$ $C \sqsubseteq (\geqslant a_1\, r) \sqcap (\leqslant a_n\, r)$ $D \sqsubseteq (\geqslant b_1\, r^-) \sqcap (\leqslant b_n\, r^-)$		$\top \sqsubseteq \forall r_B.B \sqcap \forall r_B^-.C$ $C \sqsubseteq (\geqslant a_1\, r_B) \sqcap (\leqslant a_n\, r_B)$ $B \sqsubseteq (\leqslant b_n\, r_B^-)$
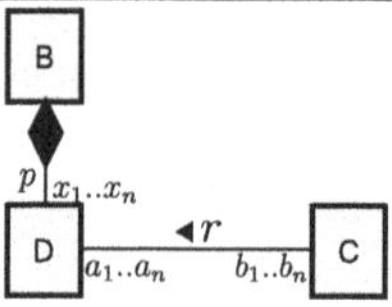	$r \circ p \sqsubseteq r_B$ ⇢	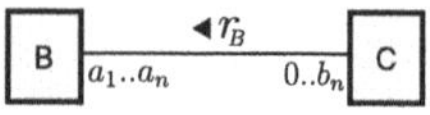
$\top \sqsubseteq \forall p.B \sqcap \forall p^-.D$ $\top \sqsubseteq \forall r.D \sqcap \forall r^-.C$ $B \sqsubseteq (\geqslant x_1\, p^-) \sqcap (\leqslant x_n\, p^-)$ $C \sqsubseteq (\geqslant a_1\, r) \sqcap (\leqslant a_n\, r)$ $D \sqsubseteq (\geqslant b_1\, r^-) \sqcap (\leqslant b_n\, r^-) \sqcap (= 1 p)$		$\top \sqsubseteq \forall r_B.B \sqcap \forall r_B^-.C$ $C \sqsubseteq (\geqslant a_1\, r_B) \sqcap (\leqslant a_n\, r_B)$ $B \sqsubseteq (\leqslant b_n\, r_B^-)$
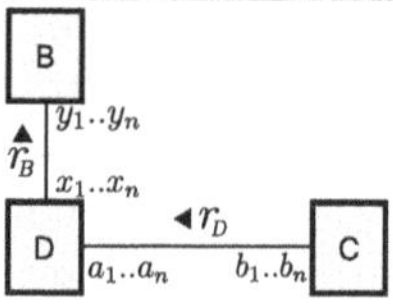	$r_D \circ r_B \sqsubseteq r$ ⇢	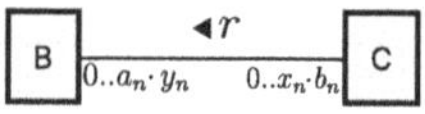
$\top \sqsubseteq \forall r_D.D \sqcap \forall r_D^-.C$ $\top \sqsubseteq \forall r_B.B \sqcap \forall r_B^-.D$ $C \sqsubseteq (\geqslant a_1\, r_D) \sqcap (\leqslant a_n\, r_D)$ $B \sqsubseteq (\geqslant x_1\, r_B^-) \sqcap (\leqslant x_n\, r_B^-)$ $D \sqsubseteq (\geqslant b_1\, r_D^-) \sqcap (\leqslant b_n\, r_D^-) \sqcap (\geqslant y_1\, r_B) \sqcap (\leqslant y_n\, r_B)$		$\top \sqsubseteq \forall r.B \sqcap \forall r^-.C$ $C \sqsubseteq (\leqslant a_n \cdot y_n\, r)$ $B \sqsubseteq (\leqslant x_n \cdot b_n\, r^-)$

valid for D. In the example, it could be *school's recognition by* $\sqsubseteq$ *recognized by*. Although this relation is not initially present in the model, it can be defined by modifying the domain of the original one. Then, the complete formalization of the original model is shown in Table 4, where the resulting model on the right is obviously weaker than the original one on the left. Note that, to obtain the final formalization of the abstracted model, we have left out the trivial formulas.

Table 4. Complete formalization of the zoom-in transformation.

$D \sqsubseteq B$	$D \sqsubseteq \top$
$\top \sqsubseteq \forall r.B \sqcap \forall r^{-}.C$	
$C \sqsubseteq (\geqslant a_1\, r) \sqcap (\leqslant a_n\, r)$	
$B \sqsubseteq (\geqslant b_1\, r^{-}) \sqcap (\leqslant b_n\, r^{-})$	
$r_D \sqsubseteq r$	$r_D \sqsubseteq U$
$\top \sqsubseteq \forall r_D.D \sqcap \forall r_D^{-}.C$	$\top \sqsubseteq \forall r_D.D \sqcap \forall r_D^{-}.C$
$C \sqsubseteq (\geqslant a_1\, r_D) \sqcap (\leqslant a_n\, r_D)$	$C \sqsubseteq (\leqslant a_n\, r_D)$
$D \sqsubseteq (\geqslant b_1\, r_D^{-}) \sqcap (\leqslant b_n\, r_D^{-})$	$D \sqsubseteq (\geqslant b_1\, r_D^{-}) \sqcap (\leqslant b_n\, r_D^{-})$

Let us denote the original model, defined on the vocabulary $\{B, C, D, r\}$ as theory $\mathfrak{T}_1$. Then, the abstracted model denoted as $\mathfrak{T}_2(D, C, r_D)$, cannot be directly entailed by $\mathfrak{T}_1$, because the relation r_D was not defined in the original model. However, if we assume the existence of an abstraction theory $\mathfrak{T}_A$:

$$\mathfrak{T}_A = \{r_D \sqsubseteq r,\ \top \sqsubseteq \forall r_D.D,\ \exists r_D.\top \sqsubseteq C\},$$

then $\mathfrak{T}_1 \oplus \mathfrak{T}_A \models \mathfrak{T}_2$. Moreover, as shown, $\mathfrak{T}_2$ is weaker than the original $\mathfrak{T}_1$.

Since the number of different situations that might occur is limited, we can examine each one individually to determine its prerequisites. Some details are provided in the Appendix.

For the second row in Table 3, in order to make an abstraction, we need to define a new relation r_B with $r \sqsubseteq r_B$, which relates C to B. We can always define this relation if we assume that participation in it for C is not mandatory. This will relax the minimum multiplicity constraint to 0. Then, by weakening the original relation r we obtain the correct formalization of the abstracted model.

The last two rows of the same table consider the situations when the new relation is defined based on the composition of two existing roles. For the third row we assumed the transitivity of the part-of relation p (see Sect. 3), but the resulting model can be entailed only if we define a new relation r_B so that $r \circ p \sqsubseteq r_B$.

Taking into account that a formalization of part-of relations in $\mathcal{SROIQ}$ is different from the formalization of ordinary relations only with respect to multiplicity/cardinality constraints, the last case is similar to the previous one. As mentioned before, at the level of UML we cannot guarantee participation to the new role r. The multiplicity constraints allow both concepts B and C *not* to participate in this new relation. Still, this relation can be defined, and the resulting model is weaker than the original one.

5 Conclusions

Ontology-driven conceptual models reflect the complexity of the domain in which they were created. Thus, understanding and comprehending such models can become challenging without the proper tools. Abstraction—the process of providing a summary of a given CM whilst preserving the gist of the conceptualization—is one of the key approaches to addressing this problem. According to Archer et al. [2], it is "probably the most powerful tool available for managing complexity".

Previously, abstractions of ODCMs were defined through model-rewriting rules [27,38]. The approach we have analyzed in this paper is operational, where the abstraction process is considered as a mapping from the original conceptual schema to a modified, more abstract, version. Abstraction formulated in this way can be seen as a meta-theoretical relationship between conceptual schemas, and, thus, endowed with corresponding formal semantics. We have formulated abstraction rules in $\mathcal{SROIQ}$, and we have shown that with some assumptions, an abstraction can be considered as a weakening of the original model.

Within this paper, we have considered models without individuals, i.e., without ABox assertions. Horrocks et al. [29] have shown that in $\mathcal{SROIQ}$, concept satisfiability with respect to ABoxes, RBoxes, and TBoxes is polynomially reducible to $\mathcal{SROIQ}$ concept satisfiability with respect to RBoxes and TBoxes only. Hence, this should not be considered as a constraint.

However, specifying OntoUML models using the same syntax results in inconsistent systems, since UFO classes are indeed meta-classes for OntoUML models. Metamodeling allows for referring to model concepts and roles as if they were individuals, e.g., allowing concepts to be instances of other concepts. Kubincová et al. [31] claimed that reaching an agreement on the structure of a DL suitable for metamodeling is challenging.

Still, we assume, that in the future to enrich domain models with meta-level notions of UFO, we can reuse an approach suggested by Kubincová et al. [31]. There, a higher-order variant of $\mathcal{SROIQ}$, called $\mathcal{HI}(\mathcal{SROIQ})$, allowing for individuals and concepts to be classified, has been proposed. This approach supports a basic level of separation between concepts and roles (concepts have only concept extensions and roles have only role extensions) and gains an advantage by using an 'instanceOf' role [31]. This approach would allow us to analyse the original algorithm without the simplification of the rules.

Acknowledgments. The authors thank the reviewers for their valuable comments, which helped to improve the clarity and quality of the paper.

This research is partially supported by the Autonomous Province of Bolzano through the 'Abstractron' project funded by the Research Südtirol/Alto Adige 2022 Call and the DFG through the project D2G2 (DFG grant n. 500249124), by the Autonomous Province of Bolzano and FWF through the project OnTeGra (FWF grant n. 10.55776/PIN8884924), by the HEU project CyclOps (under GA n. 101135513), by PNRR MUR project PE0000013-FAIR, by project EFRE-FESR 1047 AI-Lab, by project EFRE-FESR 1078 CRIMA, and by the Wallenberg AI, Autonomous Systems and Software Program (WASP), funded by the Knut and Alice Wallenberg Foundation.

Appendix: Complete Formalization of Transformations

Table 5 presents the complete formalization of the original models from Table 3 (including the underlying assumptions highlighted with a light gray background) and their abstracted counterparts. For clarity, trivialized formulas are omitted from the right-hand side of the table.

Table 5. Complete formalization of model transformations.

Original model with assumptions (in gray)	Resulting model
$D \sqsubseteq B$	
$\top \sqsubseteq \forall r.B \sqcap \forall r^-.C$	
$\top \sqsubseteq \forall r_D.D \sqcap \forall r_D^-.C$	$\top \sqsubseteq \forall r_D.D \sqcap \forall r_D^-.C$
$r_D \sqsubseteq r$	
$B \sqsubseteq (\geqslant b_1\, r^-) \sqcap (\leqslant b_n\, r^-)$	
$C \sqsubseteq (\geqslant a_1\, r) \sqcap (\leqslant a_n\, r)\ \sqcap (\geqslant a_1\, r_D) \sqcap (\leqslant a_n\, r_D)$	$C \sqsubseteq (\leqslant a_n\, r_D)$
$D \sqsubseteq (\geqslant b_1\, r_D^-) \sqcap (\leqslant b_n\, r_D^-)$	$D \sqsubseteq (\geqslant b_1\, r_D^-) \sqcap (\leqslant b_n\, r_D^-)$
$D \sqsubseteq B$	
$\top \sqsubseteq \forall r.D \sqcap \forall r^-.C$	
$\top \sqsubseteq \forall r_B.B \sqcap \forall r_B^-.C$	$\top \sqsubseteq \forall r_B.B \sqcap \forall r_B^-.C$
$r \sqsubseteq r_B$	
$D \sqsubseteq (\geqslant b_1\, r^-) \sqcap (\leqslant b_n\, r^-)$	
$C \sqsubseteq (\geqslant a_1\, r) \sqcap (\leqslant a_n\, r)\ \sqcap (\geqslant a_1\, r_B) \sqcap (\leqslant a_n\, r_B)$	$C \sqsubseteq (\geqslant a_1\, r_B) \sqcap (\leqslant a_n\, r_B)$
$B \sqsubseteq (\leqslant b_n\, r_B^-)$	$B \sqsubseteq (\leqslant b_n\, r_B^-)$
$\top \sqsubseteq \forall p.B \sqcap \forall p^-.D$	
$\top \sqsubseteq \forall r.D \sqcap \forall r^-.C$	
$r \circ p \sqsubseteq r_B$	
$\top \sqsubseteq \forall r_B.B \sqcap \forall r_B^-.C$	$\top \sqsubseteq \forall r_B.B \sqcap \forall r_B^-.C$
$D \sqsubseteq (\geqslant b_1\, r^-) \sqcap (\leqslant b_n\, r^-) \sqcap (= 1p)$	
$C \sqsubseteq (\geqslant a_1\, r) \sqcap (\leqslant a_n\, r)\ \sqcap (\geqslant a_1\, r_B) \sqcap (\leqslant a_n\, r_B)$	$C \sqsubseteq (\geqslant a_1\, r_B) \sqcap (\leqslant a_n\, r_B)$
$B \sqsubseteq (\geqslant x_1\, p^-) \sqcap (\leqslant x_n\, p^-)\ \sqcap (\leqslant b_n\, r_B^-)$	$B \sqsubseteq (\leqslant b_n\, r_B^-)$
$\top \sqsubseteq \forall r_D.D \sqcap \forall r_D^-.C$	
$\top \sqsubseteq \forall r_B.B \sqcap \forall r_B^-.D$	
$r_D \circ r_B \sqsubseteq r$	
$\top \sqsubseteq \forall r.B \sqcap \forall r^-.C$	$\top \sqsubseteq \forall r.B \sqcap \forall r^-.C$
$D \sqsubseteq (\geqslant b_1\, r_D^-) \sqcap (\leqslant b_n\, r_D^-) \sqcap (\geqslant y_1\, r_B) \sqcap (\leqslant y_n\, r_B)$	
$C \sqsubseteq (\geqslant a_1\, r_D) \sqcap (\leqslant a_n\, r_D)\ \sqcap (\leqslant a_n \cdot y_n\, r)$	$C \sqsubseteq (\leqslant a_n \cdot y_n\, r)$
$B \sqsubseteq (\geqslant x_1\, r_B^-) \sqcap (\leqslant x_n\, r_B^-)\ \sqcap (\leqslant x_n \cdot b_n\, r^-)$	$B \sqsubseteq (\leqslant x_n \cdot b_n\, r^-)$

References

1. Akoka, J., Comyn-Wattiau, I., Prat, N., Storey, V.C.: Unraveling the foundations and the evolution of conceptual modeling–intellectual structure, current themes, and trajectories. Data Knowl. Eng. **154**, 102351 (2024). https://doi.org/10.1016/j.datak.2024.102351
2. Archer, N., Head, M., Yuan, Y.: Patterns in information search for decision making: the effects of information abstraction. Int. J. Hum Comput Stud. **45**(5), 599–616 (1996). https://doi.org/10.1006/ijhc.1996.0069
3. Baader, F., Calvanese, D., McGuinness, D., Nardi, D., Patel-Schneider, P.F. (eds.): The Description Logic Handbook: Theory, Implementation and Applications, 2nd edn. Cambridge University Press (2007)
4. Baader, F., Horrocks, I., Lutz, C., Sattler, U.: Ontology languages and applications, pp. 205–227 (2017). https://doi.org/10.1017/9781139025355.008
5. Bao, J., et al.: OWL 2 Web Ontology Language Document Overview, 2nd edn. W3C Recommendation, W3C (2012). http://www.w3.org/TR/owl2-overview/
6. Berardi, D., Calvanese, D., De Giacomo, G.: Reasoning on UML class diagrams. Artif. Intell. **168**(1–2), 70–118 (2005). https://doi.org/10.1016/j.artint.2005.05.003
7. Bernard, R., Kutz, O., Troquard, N.: Making axiom weakening work in SROIQ. In: Proceedings of the 36th International Workshop on Description Logics(DL 2023) co-located with the 20th Int. Conference on Principles of Knowledge Representation and Reasoning and the 21st International Workshop on Non-Monotonic Reasoning (KR 2023 and NMR 2023), Rhodes, Greece, 2–4 September 2023, CEUR Workshop Proceedings, vol. 3515 (2023). https://ceur-ws.org/Vol-3515/paper-5.pdf
8. Borgo, S., et al.: DOLCE: a descriptive ontology for linguistic and cognitive engineering. Appl. Ontol. **17**(1), 45–69 (2022). https://doi.org/10.3233/ao-210259
9. Botti Benevides, A., Bourguet, J.R., Guizzardi, G., Peñaloza, R., Almeida, J.A.P.A.: Representing a reference foundational ontology of events in SROIQ. Appl. Ontol. **14**(3), 293–334 (2019). https://doi.org/10.3233/AO-190214
10. Braga, B., Almeida, J.: Modeling stories for conceptual model assessment. In: Jeusfeld, M.A., Karlapalem, K. (eds.) ER 2015. LNCS, vol. 9382, pp. 293–303. Springer, Cham (2015). https://doi.org/10.1007/978-3-319-25747-1_29
11. Braga, B., Almeida, J., Guizzardi, G., Benevides, A.B.: Transforming OntoUML into Alloy: towards conceptual model validation using a lightweight formal method. Innov. Syst. Softw. Eng. **6**(1), 55–63 (2010). https://doi.org/10.1007/s11334-009-0120-5
12. Carvalho, V.A., Almeida, J., Fonseca, C.M., Guizzardi, G.: Multi-level ontology-based conceptual modeling. Data Knowl. Eng. **109**, 3–24 (2017). https://doi.org/10.1016/j.datak.2017.03.002
13. Chen, P.: The entity-relationship model–toward a unified view of data. ACM Trans. Database Syst. **1**(1), 9–36 (1976). https://doi.org/10.1145/320434.320440
14. Confalonieri, R., Galliani, P., Kutz, O., Porello, D., Righetti, G., Troquard, N.: Almost certain termination for $\mathcal{ALC}$ weakening. In: EPIA 2022. LNCS, vol. 13566, pp. 663–675. Springer, Cham (2022). https://doi.org/10.1007/978-3-031-16474-3_54

15. De Giacomo, G., Lenzerini, M., Rosati, R.: Higher-order description logics for domain metamodeling. In: Proceedings of the Twenty-Fifth AAAI Conference on Artificial Intelligence, AAAI 2011, San Francisco, California, USA, 7–11 August 2011, pp. 183–188 (2011). https://doi.org/10.1609/AAAI.V25I1.7857
16. Fang, L., Liu, Y., van Ditmarsch, H.: Forgetting in multi-agent modal logics. Artif. Intell. **266**, 51–80 (2019). https://doi.org/10.1016/J.ARTINT.2018.08.003
17. Fonseca, C., Prince Sales, T., Viola, V., Fonseca, L., Guizzardi, G., Almeida, J.: Ontology-driven conceptual modeling as a service. In: Proceedings of the Joint Ontology Workshops 2021 Episode VII: The Bolzano Summer of Knowledge, CEUR Workshop Proceedings, vol. 2969 (2021). https://ceur-ws.org/Vol-2969/paper29-FOMI.pdf
18. Ghamarian, A.H., de Mol, M., Rensink, A., Zambon, E., Zimakova, M.: Modelling and analysis using GROOVE. Int. J. Softw. Tools Technol. Transf. **14**(1), 15–40 (2012). https://doi.org/10.1007/s10009-011-0186-x
19. Ghidini, C., Giunchiglia, F.: A semantics for abstraction. Technical report DIT-03-082, University of Trento (2003)
20. Ghidini, C., Giunchiglia, F.: What is local models semantics? In: Perspectives on contexts, pp. 19–42 (2008). https://web.stanford.edu/group/cslipublications/cslipublications/site/9781575865379.shtml
21. Giunchiglia, F., Walsh, T.: A theory of abstraction. Artif. Intell. **57**(2), 323–389 (1992)
22. Guarino, N., Welty, C.A.: An overview of OntoClean. In: Handbook on Ontologies, pp. 151–171 (2004). https://doi.org/10.1007/978-3-540-24750-0_8
23. Guizzardi, G.: The problem of transitivity of part-whole relations in conceptual modeling revisited. In: van Eck, P., Gordijn, J., Wieringa, R. (eds.) CAiSE 2009. LNCS, vol. 5565, pp. 94–109. Springer, Heidelberg (2009). https://doi.org/10.1007/978-3-642-02144-2_12
24. Guizzardi, G.: On the representation of quantities and their parts in conceptual modeling. In: Formal Ontology in Information Systems, Proceedings of the Sixth International Conference, FOIS 2010, Toronto, Canada, 11–14 May 2010, vol. 209, pp. 103–116 (2010). https://doi.org/10.3233/978-1-60750-535-8-103
25. Guizzardi, G.: Ontological foundations for conceptual part-whole relations: the case of collectives and their parts. In: Mouratidis, H., Rolland, C. (eds.) CAiSE 2011. LNCS, vol. 6741, pp. 138–153. Springer, Heidelberg (2011). https://doi.org/10.1007/978-3-642-21640-4_12
26. Guizzardi, G., Botti Benevides, A., Fonseca, C.M., Porello, D., Almeida, J.P.A., Prince Sales, T.: UFO: unified foundational ontology. Appl. Ontol. **17**(1), 167–210 (2022). https://doi.org/10.3233/AO-210256
27. Guizzardi, G., Figueiredo, G., Hedblom, M.M., Poels, G.: Ontology-based model abstraction. In: Proceedings of the 13th International Conference on Research Challenges in Information Science (RCIS), pp. 1–13 (2019). https://doi.org/10.1109/RCIS.2019.8876971
28. Hobbs, J.R.: Granularity. In: Proceedings of the 9th International Joint Conference on Artificial Intelligence (IJCAI), vol. 1, pp. 432–435 (1985)
29. Horrocks, I., Kutz, O., Sattler, U.: The even more irresistible SROIQ. In: Proceedings of the 10th International Conference on Principles of Knowledge Representation and Reasoning, Lake District of the United Kingdom, 2–5 June 2006, pp. 57–67 (2006). http://www.aaai.org/Library/KR/2006/kr06-009.php

30. Jackson, D.: Software Abstractions: Logic, Language, and Analysis. MIT Press (2006)
31. Kubincová, P., Kluka, J., Homola, M.: Towards expressive metamodelling with instantiation. In: Proceedings of the 28th International Workshop on Description Logics, Athens, Greece, 7–10 June 2015. CEUR Workshop Proceedings, vol. 1350 (2015). https://ceur-ws.org/Vol-1350/paper-32.pdf
32. Lin, F., Reiter, R.: Forget it! In: Proceedings of AAAI Fall Symposium on Relevance, pp. 154–159 (1994). https://www.cs.toronto.edu/kr/publications/forgetting.pdf
33. Loebe, F., Burek, P., Herre, H.: GFO: the general formal ontology. Appl. Ontol. **17**(1), 71–106 (2022). https://doi.org/10.3233/ao-220264
34. Motik, B.: On the properties of metamodeling in OWL. J. Log. Comput. **17**(4), 617–637 (2007). https://doi.org/10.1093/LOGCOM/EXM027
35. Nayak, P.P., Levy, A.Y.: A semantic theory of abstractions. In: Proceedings of the 14th International Joint Conference on Artificial Intelligence (IJCAI), vol. 1, pp. 196–202 (1995)
36. Object Management Group Standards Development Organization: OMG Unified Modeling Language (OMG UML) version 2.5.1. Standard (2017). https://www.omg.org/spec/UML/2.5.1/PDF
37. Plaisted, D.A.: Theorem proving with abstraction. Artif. Intell. **16**(1), 47–108 (1981). https://doi.org/10.1016/0004-3702(81)90015-1
38. Romanenko, E., Calvanese, D., Guizzardi, G.: Abstracting ontology-driven conceptual models: objects, aspects, events, and their parts. In: Guizzardi, R., Ralyté, J., Franch, X. (eds.) RCIS 2022. LNBIP, vol. 446, pp. 372–388. Springer, Cham (2022). https://doi.org/10.1007/978-3-031-05760-1_22
39. Romanenko, E., Calvanese, D., Guizzardi, G.: Evaluating quality of ontology-driven conceptual models abstractions. Data Knowl. Eng. **153**, 102342 (2024). https://doi.org/10.1016/J.DATAK.2024.102342
40. Romanenko, E., Kutz, O., Calvanese, D., Guizzardi, G.: Towards semantics for abstractions in ontology-driven conceptual modeling. In: Sales, T.P., Araújo, J., Borbinha, J., Guizzardi, G. (eds) ER 2023. LNCS, vol. 14319, pp. 199–209 (2023). https://doi.org/10.1007/978-3-031-47112-4_19
41. Saitta, L., Zucker, J.D.: Abstraction in Artificial Intelligence and Complex Systems. Springer, Cham (2013). https://doi.org/10.1007/978-1-4614-7052-6
42. Sales, T.P., et al.: A FAIR catalog of ontology-driven conceptual models. Data Knowl. Eng. **147**, 102210 (2023). https://doi.org/10.1016/j.datak.2023.102210
43. Tenenberg, J.D.: Preserving consistency across abstraction mappings. In: Proceedings of the 10th International Joint Conference on Artificial Intelligence (IJCAI), pp. 1011–1014 (1987). http://ijcai.org/Proceedings/87-2/Papers/090.pdf
44. Troquard, N., Confalonieri, R., Galliani, P., Peñaloza, R., Porello, D., Kutz, O.: Repairing ontologies via axiom weakening. In: Proceedings of the Thirty-Second AAAI Conference on Artificial Intelligence,(AAAI-18), the 30th Innovative Applications of Artificial Intelligence (IAAI-18), and the 8th AAAI Symposium on Educational Advances in Artificial Intelligence (EAAI-18), New Orleans, Louisiana, USA, 2–7 February 2018, pp. 1981–1988 (2018). https://doi.org/10.1609/AAAI.V32I1.11567
45. Villegas Niño, A.: A filtering engine for large conceptual schemas. Ph.D. thesis, Universitat Politècnica de Catalunya (2013)

46. Zambon, E., Guizzardi, G.: Formal definition of a general ontology pattern language using a graph grammar. In: Proceedings of the 2017 Federated Conference on Computer Science and Information Systems, FedCSIS 2017, Prague, Czech Republic, 3–6 September 2017, vol. 11, pp. 1–10 (2017). https://annals-csis.org/Volume_11/drp/pdf/001.pdf
47. Zhao, Y., Schmidt, R.A., Wang, Y., Zhang, X., Feng, H.: A practical approach to forgetting in description logics with nominals. In: The Thirty-Fourth AAAI Conference on Artificial Intelligence, AAAI 2020, The Thirty-Second Innovative Applications of Artificial Intelligence Conference, IAAI 2020, The Tenth AAAI Symposium on Educational Advances in Artificial Intelligence, EAAI 2020, New York, NY, USA, 7–12 February 2020, pp. 3073–3079 (2020). https://doi.org/10.1609/AAAI.V34I03.5702

Axiomatization and Decidability of Tense Information Logic

Timo Niek Franssen[(✉)] and Søren Brinck Knudstorp

ILLC, University of Amsterdam, Science Park 107, 1098 XG Amsterdam, The Netherlands
{t.n.franssen,s.b.knudstorp}@uva.nl

Abstract. Knudstorp [3] axiomatizes modal information logic (MIL) with a supremum operator on posets. Since infima naturally complement suprema, this raises the question: Can this result be extended to a modal logic that includes both operators and, if so, what axioms would govern the interaction between the two modalities? In this paper, we prove soundness and completeness of tense information logic (TIL)—a modal logic with two binary modalities, $\langle sup \rangle$ and $\langle inf \rangle$, interpreted as supremum and infimum operators over posets. Our axiomatization, which links $\langle sup \rangle$ and $\langle inf \rangle$ only through the standard tense-logic axioms, thereby resolves a question posed by van Benthem [6].

Completeness is proven using the step-by-step method [2] and as a corollary, we obtain completeness of TIL on preorders. Furthermore, we prove the finite model property (FMP) of TIL with respect to a generalized class of structures, which in turn establishes decidability of the logic.

By introducing both fusion ($\langle sup \rangle$) and refinement ($\langle inf \rangle$) within one logical framework, TIL provides an expressive paradigm for information dynamics.

Keywords: Tense information logic · Step-by-step · Completeness · Modal logic · Axiomatization · Polyadic modal logic · Decidability · Finite model property

1 Introduction

Modal information logic (MIL), introduced by van Benthem [5], models information flow using possible worlds semantics of modal logic by introducing additional modalities. Recently, Knudstorp [3] axiomatized MIL with a supremum modality on poset frames, enabling the modeling of fusion between two information states. In the context of posets, infima are equally natural to consider. This raises the following question: Can the axiomatization of MIL be extended to a version that includes both modalities—supremum and infimum—which we call tense information logic (TIL)? With TIL, we will be able to model refinement of information by identifying the shared content between information states with a second modality, the infimum operator, whose semantics is given by:

D. Kozen and R. de Queiroz (Eds.): WoLLIC 2025, LNCS 15942, pp. 158–174, 2026.
https://doi.org/10.1007/978-3-031-99536-1_10

$$\mathfrak{M}, x \Vdash \langle inf \rangle \varphi\psi \quad \textbf{iff} \quad \exists y, z : \mathfrak{M}, y \Vdash \varphi, \mathfrak{M}, z \Vdash \psi \text{ and } x = \inf\{y, z\}$$

This operator complements the $\langle sup \rangle$ operator, which has the semantics:

$$\mathfrak{M}, x \Vdash \langle sup \rangle \varphi\psi \quad \textbf{iff} \quad \exists y, z : \mathfrak{M}, y \Vdash \varphi, \mathfrak{M}, z \Vdash \psi \text{ and } x = \sup\{y, z\}$$

By axiomatizing this extended logic, we answer a natural second question: What axioms govern the relation between $\langle sup \rangle$ and $\langle inf \rangle$? This question was already posed by van Benthem in [6]. The main focus of this paper is to find a complete axiomatization of modal information logic with both modalities over poset frames, thereby addressing both questions simultaneously.

To arrive at a complete axiomatization of TIL, we first define its semantics over poset frames. We then apply the step-by-step method introduced by Burgess [2], which systematically repairs so-called "defects" of the canonical frame. This approach, also followed by [3], allows us to prove completeness by constructing, for a given consistent set of formulae, a poset model that witnesses its satisfiability. We then show that this result can easily be extended to TIL on the class of preorder frames.

Finally, we prove that TIL is decidable, thereby resolving an open problem raised in [7]. Since TIL lacks the finite model property with respect to posets, we instead consider a generalized class of structures. Since the axiomatization is also complete w.r.t. this class, we prove that TIL has the FMP by showing that every countermodel in this class can be transformed into a finite countermodel. This proof follows the approach outlined in Theorem 3.9 of [3], adapting it to the new setting.

Wang & Wang [9,10] prove completeness over lattices for a hybrid language with supremum and infimum operators as well as nominals. The completeness proof for TIL presented in this paper does not include nominals, and is over posets instead of lattices.

This paper is structured as follows. In Sect. 2, we provide the preliminaries and define the semantics. We give the axiomatization of TIL in Sect. 3. In Sect. 4, we show how the canonical model is constructed, setting the stage for the completeness proof, which is given in Sect. 5. The last section demonstrates that TIL has the FMP and is decidable.

2 Preliminaries

In this section, we introduce the formal setting of TIL and define the language. We then present the semantics.

2.1 The Language

Definition 1. *Given a countable set of propositional letters* $\mathbf{P}$*, we define the language* $\mathcal{L}_T$ *of tense information logic using two binary modalities* $\langle sup \rangle$ *and* $\langle inf \rangle$ *by the following BNF grammar:*

$$\varphi ::= p \mid \bot \mid \neg\varphi \mid \varphi \wedge \psi \mid \langle sup \rangle \varphi\psi \mid \langle inf \rangle \varphi\psi$$

2.2 The Semantics

Definition 2. *A (Kripke) poset model for $\mathcal{L}_T$ is a triple $\mathfrak{M} = (W, \leq, V)$, where W is a set, $\leq$ is a partial order and V is a valuation $V : \mathbf{P} \to \mathcal{P}(W)$.*

Given a poset frame ($\mathfrak{F} = (W, \leq)$), we say that x is the supremum of $\{y, z\}$ if x is an upper bound of y and z and the least such. We say that x is the infimum of $\{y, z\}$ if x is a lower bound of y and z and the greatest such.

The interpretation of a formula φ at a state $x \in W$ is then defined recursively as follows:

$$\begin{aligned}
\mathfrak{M}, x &\nVdash \bot \\
\mathfrak{M}, x \Vdash p &\text{ iff } x \in V(p) \\
\mathfrak{M}, x \Vdash \neg\varphi &\text{ iff } \mathfrak{M}, x \nVdash \varphi \\
\mathfrak{M}, x \Vdash \varphi \wedge \psi &\text{ iff } \mathfrak{M}, x \Vdash \varphi \text{ and } \mathfrak{M}, x \Vdash \psi \\
\mathfrak{M}, x \Vdash \langle sup \rangle \varphi\psi &\text{ iff there exist } y, z \in W \text{ such that } \mathfrak{M}, y \Vdash \varphi,\ \mathfrak{M}, z \Vdash \psi \\
&\qquad \text{and } x = \sup\{y, z\} \\
\mathfrak{M}, x \Vdash \langle inf \rangle \varphi\psi &\text{ iff there exist } y, z \in W \text{ such that } \mathfrak{M}, y \Vdash \varphi,\ \mathfrak{M}, z \Vdash \psi \\
&\qquad \text{and } x = \inf\{y, z\}
\end{aligned}$$

Definition 3. *With these semantics at hand we are able to define the standard past/future looking diamond/box of temporal logic [1] in the following way:*

$$\begin{aligned}
P\varphi &:= \langle sup \rangle \varphi \top && \textit{past looking diamond} \\
F\varphi &:= \langle inf \rangle \varphi \top && \textit{future looking diamond} \\
H\varphi &:= \neg \langle sup \rangle \neg\varphi \top && \textit{past looking box} \\
G\varphi &:= \neg \langle inf \rangle \neg\varphi \top && \textit{future looking box}
\end{aligned}$$

Based on these semantics, we define the following logic:

Definition 4. *Let TIL be the frame-based logic of all $\mathcal{L}_T$ validities on poset frames, i.e.*

$$TIL = \{\varphi \in \mathcal{L}_T : \textit{ for every poset model } \mathfrak{M} = (W, \leq, V) \textit{ and every } x \in W : \mathfrak{M}, x \Vdash \varphi\}$$

3 Axiomatisation and Soundness

To study modal information logics on posets in a symmetric way, we extended the language by including the infimum operator. However, it is not immediately clear how the interaction between these modalities should be reflected in the axiom system (see [6]). Surprisingly, it turns out that the relation between $\langle sup \rangle$ and $\langle inf \rangle$ can be fully captured by standard temporal axioms. To show this, we present the following logic:

Definition 5. *Let **TIL** be the least normal modal logic in the language $\mathcal{L}_T$ containing the following axioms:*

$$\begin{array}{rl} (Re.) & (p \wedge q \to \langle sup \rangle pq) \wedge (p \wedge q \to \langle inf \rangle pq) \\ (4) & (PPp \to Pp) \wedge (FFp \to Fp) \\ (Co.) & ((\langle sup \rangle pq \to \langle sup \rangle qp) \wedge ((\langle inf \rangle pq \to \langle inf \rangle qp) \\ (Dk1) & (p \wedge \langle sup \rangle qr) \to \langle sup \rangle pq \\ (Dk2) & (p \wedge \langle inf \rangle qr) \to \langle inf \rangle pq \\ (Sy.) & (p \to GPp) \wedge (p \to HFp) \end{array}$$

For each axiom in the axiomatization of MIL in [3] (namely (Re.), (4), (Co.) and (Dk)), we added the same axiom for the new $\langle inf \rangle$ operator. The only truly new axiom is the standard temporal axiom (Sy.) [8]. That this axiom is to be included is expected, since the temporal operators P, F, G and H are definable. We will proceed to show that this axiom system is complete for *TIL* and thus that the single axiom (Sy.) already suffices to capture the interaction between $\langle sup \rangle$ and $\langle inf \rangle$.

First off, the axiomatization is readily seen sound by checking that *TIL* is a normal modal logic validating all the axioms of **TIL**:

Theorem 1 (Soundness). ***TIL*** $\subseteq$ *TIL*

4 Canonical Model and Auxiliary Lemmas

To prove completeness, we will use a similar approach to the one presented in [3] (see Sect. 2). To avoid redundancy, and due to space constraints, we omit proofs that are identical (or nearly so) and instead focus on the aspects that provide insight into the relation between $\langle sup \rangle$ and $\langle inf \rangle$ in our extended system.

We begin by constructing the canonical model. However, this canonical model lacks the properties required to establish the necessary truth lemma for the completeness proof; in particular, the underlying frame is not a poset frame where the modalities refer to the induced supremum- and infimum-relations. We therefore make use of the step-by-step method (see [1]).

Definition 6. *Let $W_{\boldsymbol{TIL}}$ be the set that contains all maximally consistent **TIL**-sets. And let C_{sup} and C_{inf} be the two induced ternary relations of the canonical **TIL**-frame:*

$$C_{sup}\Gamma\Delta\Theta \iff \forall\delta \in \Delta, \theta \in \Theta(\langle sup \rangle \delta\theta \in \Gamma)$$

$$C_{inf}\Gamma\Delta\Theta \iff \forall\delta \in \Delta, \theta \in \Theta(\langle inf \rangle \delta\theta \in \Gamma)$$

We define the following binary relation on the canonical frame:

$$\leq_{pre} := \{(\Delta, \Gamma) \in W_{\boldsymbol{TIL}} \times W_{\boldsymbol{TIL}} \mid C_{sup}\Gamma\Gamma\Delta\}$$

It may appear bizarre that our definition of $\leq_{pre}$ only depends on C_{sup}, and indeed, we will need that it admits an equivalent characterization in terms of C_{inf}:

$$\leq_{pre} = \{(\Delta, \Gamma) \in W_{\mathbf{TIL}} \times W_{\mathbf{TIL}} \mid C_{inf}\Delta\Delta\Gamma\}. \quad (1)$$

To show this, we rely on two auxiliary lemmas (Lemma 1(1) and (2)). The equivalence itself is given by Lemma 1(3), while Lemma 1(4) and (5) are needed for later proofs.

Lemma 1. *1.* $p \to Pp$ *and* $p \to Fp$ *are derivable in* ***TIL***
2. $\forall \Gamma, \Delta, \Theta \in W_{\boldsymbol{TIL}} : C_{sup}\Gamma\Delta\Theta$ *iff* $C_{sup}\Gamma\Theta\Delta$ *and* $C_{inf}\Gamma\Delta\Theta$ *iff* $C_{inf}\Gamma\Theta\Delta$
3. $\forall \Gamma, \Delta \in W_{\boldsymbol{TIL}} : C_{sup}\Gamma\Gamma\Delta$ *iff* $C_{inf}\Delta\Delta\Gamma$
4. $\forall \Gamma, \Delta \in W_{\boldsymbol{TIL}} : \Delta \leq_{pre} \Gamma$ *iff* $(\forall \delta \in \Delta : P\delta \in \Gamma$ *and* $\forall \gamma \in \Gamma : F\gamma \in \Delta)$
5. $\leq_{pre}$ *is a preorder*
6. $\forall \Gamma, \Delta, \Theta \in W_{\boldsymbol{TIL}} : (C_{sup}\Gamma\Delta\Theta$ *only if* $\Delta \leq_{pre} \Gamma, \Theta \leq_{pre} \Gamma)$ *and* $(C_{inf}\Gamma\Delta\Theta$ *only if* $\Gamma \leq_{pre} \Delta, \Gamma \leq_{pre} \Theta)$

We explicitly present the proof of Lemma 1(3) in the appendix (see Sect. A.1), as the proofs of the other statements are analogous to the proofs of Observation 2.5 and Lemma 2.6 in [3]. In each case, the version involving the $\langle inf \rangle$ operator is proven in the same way as the version involving $\langle sup \rangle$.

In case C_{sup} and C_{inf} would correspond to the infimum and supremum relation w.r.t. $\leq_{pre}$, we would have completeness in our pocket. The following example shows that this is not the case.

Example 1. Suppose we have MCSs Γ and Δ for which it holds that $C_{inf}\Gamma\Delta\Delta$. If the canonical model was a poset, or preorder, model, we would then expect Γ to be the infimum of Δ under $\leq_{pre}$, so $\Gamma \leq_{pre} \Delta$ and $\Delta \leq_{pre} \Gamma$. We show that $C_{inf}\Gamma\Delta\Delta$ can hold without $\Delta \leq_{pre} \Gamma$ being true.

Consider the following model:

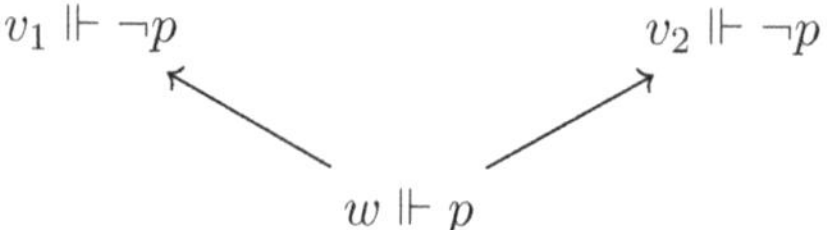

And let p be the only propositional variable that the states satisfy/dissatisfy. We define the following MCSs:

$$\Gamma := \{\varphi \in \mathcal{L}_T : \mathfrak{M}, w \Vdash \varphi\}$$

$$\Delta := \{\varphi \in \mathcal{L}_T : \mathfrak{M}, v_1 \Vdash \varphi\} = \{\varphi \in \mathcal{L}_T : \mathfrak{M}, v_2 \Vdash \varphi\}$$

We see that $p \in \Gamma$, but $Fp \notin \Delta$, so by Lemma 1(4) we get that $\Delta \nleq_{pre} \Gamma$. On the other hand, since $w = \inf\{v_1, v_2\}$ we see that $C_{inf}\Gamma\Delta\Delta$ holds.

5 Completeness Proof

To prove that syntactic consistency implies satisfiability (and hence completeness), we employ the step-by-step defect–repair construction to build a model $\mathfrak{M}$ whose worlds are labeled by a function l, assigning each world an MCS. The objective is then to ensure that the Truth Lemma

$$\mathfrak{M}, x \Vdash \varphi \Leftrightarrow \varphi \in l(x)$$

holds.

Concretely, we start with a single world labeled by our initial MCS Γ, so that if the truth lemma holds, then we have our satisfying model. For the truth lemma to hold, a world's label $l(x)$ can dictate that it should satisfy some formula involving $\langle sup \rangle$ or $\langle inf \rangle$; for example, if $\langle sup \rangle \varphi\psi \in l(x)$, then x should satisfy $\langle sup \rangle \varphi\psi$. If the model under construction does not yet provide points witnessing this (so $x \not\Vdash \langle sup \rangle \varphi\psi$), we call this shortfall a *defect*. These defects (Definitions 8 and 9) are *repaired* in stages. In case of the defect we just described, it is resolved by adjoining two fresh worlds y and z, s.t. $x = \sup\{y, z\}$, $\varphi \in l(y)$ and $\psi \in l(z)$. That the procedures we describe actually resolve the defects is proven in their respective repair lemmas (see Lemma 2 for example). Iterating this process until no defects remain yields our full model.

We will mostly use the outline as presented in Sect. 4.6 of [1] and Sect. 2.2 of [3]. We now turn to the formal definition of the partially labeled frames $(l, \leq)$ on which this construction is based:

Definition 7. *Let W be a countable set, and $\mathbb{P}$ the set of all tuples $(l, \leq)$ such that*

1. *l is a partial function from W to the set of all MCSs, $W_{\mathbf{TIL}}$.*
2. *$\mathrm{dom}(l)$ is finite.*
3. *$\leq$ is a partial order on $\mathrm{dom}(l)$, and the identity relation on $W \setminus \mathrm{dom}(l)$.*
4. *If $y \leq x$ then $l(y) \leq_{pre} l(x)$ (whenever $x, y \in \mathrm{dom}(l)$).*

There are four different types of defects that can occur. In addition to the two defects described in Definitions 2.8 and 2.9 of [3], there are now two additional defects involving the new $\langle inf \rangle$ operator. Since the $\langle inf \rangle$ and $\langle sup \rangle$ defects are mirror images of each other, we choose to define two representative cases.

Definition 8 ($\langle sup \rangle$-defect). *Let $(l, \leq) \in \mathbb{P}$. Then a pair $(\langle sup \rangle \chi\chi', x)$ is a $\langle sup \rangle$-defect (of $(l, \leq)$) iff*

(i) $x \in \mathrm{dom}(l)$
(ii) $\langle sup \rangle \chi\chi' \in l(x)$, *and*
(iii) *there are no* $y, z \in \mathrm{dom}(l)$ *s.t.:*

$$\begin{array}{lll} \chi \in l(y), & C_{sup}\, l(x)l(y)l(z), & \uparrow y = \uparrow x \cup \{y\} \cup (\uparrow y \cap \{w \mid \uparrow w \cap \uparrow x = \varnothing\}), \\ \chi' \in l(z), & x = \sup\{y, z\}, & \uparrow z = \uparrow x \cup \{z\} \cup (\uparrow z \cap \{w \mid \uparrow w \cap \uparrow x = \varnothing\}), \end{array}$$

where $\uparrow w = \{v | w \leq v\}$.

Definition 9 ($\neg$ inf-defect). *Let $(l, \leq) \in \mathbb{P}$. Then a quadruple $(\langle inf \rangle \psi\psi', x, y, z)$ is a $\neg\langle inf \rangle$-defect (of $(l, \leq)$) iff:*

$$\begin{array}{l} x \in \mathrm{dom}(l),\ x = \inf\{y, z\},\ \neg\langle inf \rangle \psi\psi' \in l(x), \\ \psi \in l(y), \quad \psi' \in l(z). \end{array}$$

[3] faces the same defects, but constrained to $(\neg)\langle sup\rangle$-defects. The question is whether a similar approach to resolving the defects in this setting would also work. It is not difficult to see that in the case of the $\langle sup\rangle$- and $\langle inf\rangle$-defects, the same solution as presented in Lemma 2.11 of [3] can be applied.

To repair $\neg\langle sup\rangle$-defect, Lemma 2.12 of [3] introduces dummy states that are not labeled. This does not work in this setting, since the $\langle sup\rangle$ and $\langle inf\rangle$ modality together can 'access' any point in the model by looking 'up' and 'down' with the $\langle inf\rangle$ and $\langle sup\rangle$ operator respectively. It thus matters with which MCS the new points get labeled. To resolve this, we duplicate the label of the point that constitutes the defect we are trying to resolve.

In this paper we only work out the $\neg\langle inf\rangle$-repair lemma. The $\neg\langle sup\rangle$-repair lemma is in fact a mirrored version of this one and for the proof of the $\langle sup\rangle$-repair lemma we refer to Lemma 2.11 of [3].

5.1 $\neg\langle inf\rangle$ Repair Lemma

Lemma 2 ($\neg\langle inf\rangle$ repair lemma). *Let $(\neg\langle inf\rangle\varphi\psi, x, y, z)$ be a $\neg\langle inf\rangle$-defect of $(l, \leq) \in \mathbb{P}$. Then we can resolve this defect by extending $(l, \leq)$ to $(l', \leq') \in \mathbb{P}$ in the following way:*
Take $d \in W \setminus dom(l)$ and let:

$$l' = l \cup \{(d, l(x))\} \quad \leq' = \leq \cup \{(d, u), (d, v) | y \leq u, z \leq v\}$$

So we get $x \neq \inf\{y, z\}$.

A diagram to get an intuition of this transition is included in the appendix, see Sect. A.2.

Proof. Take a fresh $d \in W$ and map it to $l(x)$. We must show that $(l', \leq') \in \mathbb{P}$ and that the defect is resolved.

- It is not difficult to show that $(l', \leq') \in \mathbb{P}$, the only step we highlight is showing that $y \leq' x$ implies $l(y) \leq_{pre} l(x)$ since this is where we see that the new way of labeling (different from what is done in [3]) plays a role. We go through all the cases:
  - $(d \leq' d)$: Then $l(d) \leq_{pre} l(d)$ follows from reflexivity of $\leq_{pre}$.
  - $(d \leq' y)$: Since $d \leq' y$, we should show that $l(d) = l(x) \leq_{pre} l(y)$. We know that $(l, \leq) \in \mathbb{P}$. So since we assumed $x = \inf_{\leq}\{y, z\}$, we have $x \leq y$, so $l(d) = l(x) \leq_{pre} l(y)$. We can replace y by z and repeat the same reasoning.
  - $(d \leq' u)$: If $y < u$ or $z < u$ we get $l(d) \leq_{pre} l(u)$ by transitivity of $\leq_{pre}$.
- We show that the $\neg\langle inf\rangle$ defect is resolved by showing that $d \not\leq' x$ (while d is a lower bound of $\{y, z\}$), which contradicts that $x = \inf_{\leq'}\{y, z\}$.
  Assume $d \leq' x$, then by definition of $\leq'$ this could only be the case if $x = y$ or $x = z$. Assume without loss of generality that $x = y$. Then since $x \leq z$, we get $l(x) \leq_{pre} l(z)$. So (1) $C_{sup}l(z)l(z)l(x)$ and (2) $C_{inf}l(x)l(x)l(z)$. By (2) we get $C_{inf}l(x)l(y)l(z)$ since $l(y) = l(x)$, but then we cannot have had a $\neg\langle inf\rangle$ defect, so we derived a contradiction.

5.2 Completeness Proof

Theorem 2 (Completeness). ***TIL*** *is strongly complete w.r.t TIL.*

We want to show that if Γ^* is a **TIL**-consistent set, then we can find a model defined on a poset-frame s.t. there is $x \in M$ for which $M, x \Vdash \gamma$ for all $\gamma \in \Gamma^*$. The structures $(l, \leq)$ will approximate such a model better at each step. We now explain how this approximation works.

First note that we can extend Γ^* to a **TIL**-MCS Γ. Let W be an arbitrary countable set and let $x \in W$ be arbitrary. Define $l_0 := \{(x, \Gamma)\}$ and let $\leq_0$ be the identity relation on W. Then $(l_0, \leq_0)$ satisfies all the conditions of Definition 7.

It is possible to enumerate all the potential $\langle sup \rangle$-, $\langle inf \rangle$-, $\neg\langle sup \rangle$- and $\neg\langle inf \rangle$-defects since the defects are defined as finite tuples, $\mathcal{L}_T$ is a countable language and W is countable. We construct a sequence

$$(l_0, \leq_0), ..., (l_n, \leq_n), ...$$

with $l_n \subseteq l_{n+1}$ and $\leq_n \subseteq \leq_{n+1}$, by constructing from $(l_n, \leq_n)$ the next element in the sequence $(l_{n+1}, \leq_{n+1})$ by taking the least tuple in our enumeration constituting a defect for $(l_n, \leq_n)$, and applying the corresponding repair-lemma to it.

Let

$$(l_\omega, \leq_\omega) := (\cup_{n \in \mathbb{N}} l_n, \cup_{n \in \mathbb{N}} \leq_n),$$

and define $V(p) = \{x \in dom(l_\omega) : p \in l_\omega(x)\}$. To prove completeness we want to prove the following:

Lemma 3 (Truth Lemma for labeled points)

$$\forall x \in dom(l_\omega) \ , \ \forall \varphi \in \mathcal{L}_T : \quad (W, \leq_\omega, V), x \Vdash \varphi \Leftrightarrow \varphi \in l_\omega(x)$$

Proof. We prove the lemma by induction on the complexity of φ. The base case and induction steps for $\neg$, $\wedge$ are routine arguments. We therefore focus on the case of $\langle sup \rangle$:

Left-to-Right: Assume $(W, \leq_\omega, V), x \Vdash \langle sup \rangle \varphi\psi$. By definition, there exist $y, z \in W$ s.t. $(W, \leq_\omega, V), y \Vdash \varphi$, $(W, \leq_\omega, V), z \Vdash \psi$ and $x = \sup_\omega\{y, z\}$. We know that $y, z \in dom(l_\omega)$, since if not, then as $\leq_\omega$ is the identity relation on $W \setminus dom(l_\omega)$, either $x = y$ and/or $x = z$ – contradicting $x \in dom(l_\omega)$. By the induction hypothesis, it follows that $\varphi \in l_\omega(y)$ and $\psi \in l_\omega(z)$. To conclude that $\langle sup \rangle \varphi\psi \in l_\omega(x)$, it would suffice that $(l_\omega, \leq_\omega)$ does not contain any $\neg\langle sup \rangle$-defects, which we will address later.

Right-to-Left: Assume now that $\langle sup \rangle \varphi\psi \in l_\omega(x)$. Then, again provided that $(l_\omega, \leq_\omega)$ does not contain any $\langle sup \rangle$-defects, there exist $y, z \in dom(l_\omega)$ s.t. $x = \sup_\omega\{y, z\}$ and $\varphi \in l_\omega(y)$ and $\psi \in l_\omega(z)$. By the induction hypothesis this implies that $(W, \leq_\omega, V), y \Vdash \varphi$ and $(W, \leq_\omega, V), z \Vdash \psi$, so by definition $(W, \leq_\omega, V), x \Vdash \langle sup \rangle \varphi\psi$.

The case of $\langle inf \rangle$ is proven similarly.

As pointed out in the proof, once we show that $(l_\omega, \leq_\omega)$ does not contain any defects, the truth lemma holds and completeness follows. The argument to show this closely follows the proof of Theorem 2.13 from [3], where necessary adjustments have to be made to handle the $\langle inf \rangle$-operator. In practice this comes down to adding repeating proofs in a mirrored way. Since this is not considered very informative and due to space constraints, we refer to [3] for these proofs.

Having established completeness of TIL on poset frames, a direct corollary is completeness w.r.t. another class of frames, namely preorders. $\mathfrak{M} = (W, \leq, V)$ is a preorder model if $\leq$ is a preorder on W. In this case, suprema and infima need not be unique, but can come in clusters. To account for this, we denote that x is a supremum or infimum of $\{y, z\}$ by writing $x \in \sup\{y, z\}$ or $x \in \inf\{y, z\}$, respectively. The semantics of the modal operators are then given by:

$$\mathfrak{M}, x \Vdash \langle inf \rangle \varphi\psi \quad \textbf{iff} \quad \exists y, z : \mathfrak{M}, y \Vdash \varphi, \mathfrak{M}, z \Vdash \psi \text{ and } x \in \inf\{y, z\}$$
$$\mathfrak{M}, x \Vdash \langle sup \rangle \varphi\psi \quad \textbf{iff} \quad \exists y, z : \mathfrak{M}, y \Vdash \varphi, \mathfrak{M}, z \Vdash \psi \text{ and } x \in \sup\{y, z\}$$

We define:

Definition 10

$$TIL_{pre} = \{\varphi \in \mathcal{L}_T : \textit{ for every preorder model } \mathfrak{M} = (W, \leq, V) \textit{ and every } x \in W : \mathfrak{M}, x \Vdash \varphi\}$$

Corollary 1

$$TIL_{pre} = TIL = \boldsymbol{TIL}$$

Proof. $TIL_{pre} \subseteq TIL$ follows from the fact that every poset frame is also a preorder frame. Since the soundness proof of **TIL** on poset frames carries over to preorders without significant changes, we also derive that $\mathbf{TIL} \subseteq TIL_{pre}$, which concludes the proof.

This result provides yet another example of how modal information logics cannot differentiate preorders from posets (see also [4]).

6 Finite Model Property and Decidability

Following the outline of [3, Section 3], we prove decidability of *TIL*. Since the logic does not have the finite model property (FMP) w.r.t. preorders, nor posets (see [3, Proposition 1.7]), we show that it does have the FMP w.r.t. a generalized class of frames. Again, we highlight the adjustments that have to be made to the proofs in [3], to make them work in the new setting with two modal operators: $\langle inf \rangle$ and $\langle sup \rangle$.

As we have already mentioned before, the ternary relations C_{sup} and C_{inf} induced by the canonical model need not coincide with the frame's supremum and infimum. We investigate whether there is a reinterpretation of $\langle sup \rangle$ and $\langle inf \rangle$ through frame correspondence of **TIL** on the class of all tuples

(W, C_{sup}, C_{inf}), where W is a set and C_{sup} and C_{inf} are arbitrary ternary relations on W. We call these structures $\tilde{\mathcal{C}}$-frames and denote with $\tilde{\mathcal{C}}$ the class of these frames.

Since the axioms of **TIL** are Sahlqvist, each has a first-order equivalent on $\tilde{\mathcal{C}}$-frames. Concretely, for every axiom Ax in our axiomatization of **TIL**, we denote by FOAx its first-order correspondent, i.e., a first-order sentence in the signature $\{C_{sup}, C_{inf}\}$ s.t.

$$(W, C_{sup}, C_{inf}) \Vdash \text{Ax} \Leftrightarrow (W, C_{sup}, C_{inf}) \vDash {}^{1}\text{FOAx}$$

Building on the suprema-only correspondences of Lemma 3.1 of [3], we add matching infimum clauses and introduce a new one for the (Sy.)-axiom.

$$(FORe) := \quad \forall x \left(C_{sup}\, x\, x\, x \wedge C_{inf}\, x\, x\, x\right)$$

$$(FO4') := \quad \forall x, y, z, u, v \Big(\big[C_{sup}\, x\, y\, z \wedge C_{sup}\, y\, u\, v \to \exists w\, C_{sup}\, x\, u\, w\big] \wedge \big[C_{inf}\, x\, y\, z \wedge C_{inf}\, y\, u\, v \to \exists z C_{inf}\, x\, u\, w)\big]\Big)$$

$$(FOCo) := \quad \forall x, y, z \Big(\big[C_{sup}\, x\, y\, z \to C_{sup}\, x\, z\, y\big] \wedge \big[C_{inf}\, x\, y\, z \to C_{inf}\, x\, z\, y\big]\Big)$$

$$(FODk1) := \forall x, y, z \left(C_{sup}\, x\, y\, z \to C_{sup}\, x\, x\, y\right)$$

$$(FODk2) := \forall x, y, z \left(C_{inf}\, x\, y\, z \to C_{inf}\, x\, x\, y\right)$$

$$(FOSy') := \quad \forall x, y \Big(\big[\exists z\, C_{sup}\, x\, y\, z \to \exists u\, C_{inf}\, y\, x\, u\big] \wedge \big[\exists z\, C_{inf}\, x\, y\, z \to \exists u\, C_{sup}\, y\, x\, u\big]\Big)$$

In addition to $(FO4')$ and $(FOSy')$, we introduce FO-sentences $(FO4)$ and $(FOSy)$ that, while equivalent only modulo the other axioms, have a simpler form and are easier to apply in arguments.

$$\text{(FO4)} \quad \forall w, v, u \Big([C_{sup}\, w\, w\, v \ \wedge\ C_{sup}\, v\, v\, u \ \to\ C_{sup}\, w\, w\, u] \wedge [C_{inf}\, w\, w\, v \ \wedge\ C_{inf}\, v\, v\, u \ \to\ C_{inf}\, w\, w\, u]\Big)$$

$$\text{(FOSy)}\ \forall w, v \Big([C_{sup}\, w\, w\, v \ \to\ C_{inf}\, v\, v\, w] \ \wedge\ [C_{inf}\, w\, w\, v \ \to\ C_{sup}\, v\, v\, w]\Big)$$

Using standard frame correspondence proofs, we can show the following:

$$(W, C_{sup}, C_{inf}) \Vdash \mathbf{TIL} \iff (W, C_{sup}, C_{inf}) \vDash (FORe) \wedge (FO4) \wedge (FOCo) \wedge (FODk1) \wedge (FODk2) \wedge (FOSy). \quad (2)$$

We want to show that if $\varphi \notin \mathbf{TIL}$, then it is falsified on a finite model. To do so we need the following definitions:

[1] In what follows, '$\vDash$' is used for frame validity for FO-sentences.

Definition 11

$$\tilde{\mathcal{C}} := \{(W, C_{sup}, C_{inf}) \vDash (FORe) \wedge (FO4) \wedge (FOCo) \wedge (FODk1) \\ \wedge (FODk2) \wedge (FOSy)\}$$

$$\tilde{\mathcal{C}}_F := \{(W, C_{sup}, C_{inf}) \in \tilde{\mathcal{C}} : W \text{ is finite}\}$$

$$Log(\tilde{\mathcal{C}}) := \{\varphi \in \mathcal{L}_T : (W, C_{sup}, C_{inf}) \Vdash \varphi, \forall (W, C_{sup}, C_{inf}) \in \tilde{\mathcal{C}}\}$$

$$Log(\mathcal{C}_{\mathcal{F}}) := \{\varphi \in \mathcal{L}_T : (W, C_{sup}, C_{inf}) \Vdash \varphi, \forall (W, C_{sup}, C_{inf}) \in \tilde{\mathcal{C}}_F\}$$

From the fact that poset frames are special cases of $\tilde{\mathcal{C}}$-frames together with (2), we can derive soundness and strong completeness of **TIL** w.r.t. the class $\tilde{\mathcal{C}}$. We see in particular that **TIL** $= Log(\tilde{\mathcal{C}})$.

Theorem 3. ***TIL*** *has the finite model property, i.e.* ***TIL*** $= Log(\mathcal{C}_{\mathcal{F}})$.

Proof. We show $Log(\tilde{\mathcal{C}}_F) \subseteq Log(\tilde{\mathcal{C}})$ by contraposition. Assume $\chi \notin Log(\tilde{\mathcal{C}})$, then we know that there is a $\tilde{\mathcal{C}}$-model based on a $\tilde{\mathcal{C}}$-frame (W, C_{sup}, C_{inf}, V) s.t. $(W, C_{sup}, C_{inf}, V) \nVdash \varphi$. We turn (W, C_{sup}, C_{inf}, V) into a finite model that refutes χ by a filtration argument.

The first step is to further extend the notion of a set of formulas being subformula closed, as already introduced in Definition 3.7 of [3].

Definition 12. *A set of $\mathcal{L}_T$ formulas Σ is $\tilde{\mathcal{C}}$-closed if:*

- *It is subformula closed (Sub)*
- *If $\langle sup\rangle\varphi\psi \in \Sigma$ then $\langle sup\rangle\psi\varphi \in \Sigma$ and if $\langle inf\rangle\varphi\psi \in \Sigma$ then $\langle inf\rangle\psi\varphi \in \Sigma$ (Com)*
- *If $\langle sup\rangle\varphi\psi \in \Sigma$ then $P\varphi \in \Sigma$ (S-P)*
- *If $\langle inf\rangle\varphi\psi \in \Sigma$ then $F\varphi \in \Sigma$ (S-F)*
- *If $\langle sup\rangle\varphi\psi \in \Sigma$ then $\langle inf\rangle\varphi\psi \in \Sigma$ and if $\langle inf\rangle\varphi\psi \in \Sigma$ then $\langle sup\rangle\varphi\psi \in \Sigma$ (Symm)*

Take $\Sigma' = \{\chi\}$ and let Σ be the least extension of Σ' s.t. it is $\tilde{\mathcal{C}}$-closed. We claim without proving that Σ is finite.

We now construct a finite model out of (W, C_{sup}, C_{inf}, V) that also falsifies χ: Define an equivalence relation $\sim_\Sigma$ on W as:

$$w \sim_\Sigma v \text{ iff } \forall \varphi \in \Sigma : (W, C_{inf}, C_{sup}, V), w \Vdash \varphi \Leftrightarrow \\ (W, C_{inf}, C_{sup}, V), v \Vdash \varphi.$$

Let $W_\Sigma = \{|w|_\Sigma : w \in W\}$ be the set of states.
Define

$$C^{\Sigma}_{sup}|w||v||u| \Leftrightarrow \quad \forall \langle sup\rangle\varphi\psi \in \Sigma :$$

(a) $(v \Vdash \varphi,\ u \Vdash \psi) \Rightarrow w \Vdash \langle sup\rangle\varphi\psi$ (b) $(v \Vdash P\varphi,\ u \Vdash P\psi) \Rightarrow w \Vdash P\varphi \wedge P\psi$

(c) $(w \Vdash \varphi,\ v \Vdash \psi) \Rightarrow v \Vdash \langle inf\rangle\varphi\psi$ (d) $(w \Vdash \varphi,\ u \Vdash \psi) \Rightarrow u \Vdash \langle inf\rangle\varphi\psi$

(e)$w \Vdash F\varphi \Rightarrow (v \Vdash F\varphi$ and $u \Vdash F\varphi)$

$$C^{\Sigma}_{inf}|x||y||z| \Leftrightarrow \quad \forall \langle inf\rangle\varphi\psi \in \Sigma:$$
$$\text{(a)} \quad (v \Vdash \varphi,\ u \Vdash \psi) \Rightarrow w \Vdash \langle inf\rangle\varphi\psi \qquad \text{(b)} \quad (v \Vdash F\varphi,\ u \Vdash F\psi) \Rightarrow w \Vdash F\varphi \wedge F\psi$$
$$\text{(c)} \quad (w \Vdash \varphi,\ v \Vdash \psi) \Rightarrow v \Vdash \langle sup\rangle\varphi\psi \qquad \text{(d)} \quad (w \Vdash \varphi,\ u \Vdash \psi) \Rightarrow u \Vdash \langle sup\rangle\varphi\psi$$
$$\text{(e)} \quad w \Vdash P\varphi \Rightarrow (v \Vdash P\varphi \text{ and } u \Vdash P\varphi)$$

and $V_\Sigma(p) := \{|x| \in W_\Sigma : x \in V(p)\}$.

If we show that $(W_\Sigma, C^{\Sigma}_{sup}, C^{\Sigma}_{inf}) \in \tilde{\mathcal{C}}_F$ and that $(W_\Sigma, C^{\Sigma}_{sup}, C^{\Sigma}_{inf}, V_\Sigma)$ is a filtration of (W, C_{sup}, C_{inf}, V) through Σ, so that for all $\varphi \in \Sigma$, $x \in W$:

$$(W_\Sigma, C^{\Sigma}_{sup}, C^{\Sigma}_{inf}, V_\Sigma), |x| \Vdash \varphi \Leftrightarrow (W, C_{sup}, C_{inf}, V), x \Vdash \varphi,$$

we have completed the proof.

Proposition 1. $(W_\Sigma, C^{\Sigma}_{sup}, C^{\Sigma}_{inf}) \in \tilde{\mathcal{C}}_F$

The proof of this proposition is given in the appendix, Sect. A.3.

Proposition 2. *$(W_\Sigma, C^{\Sigma}_{sup}, C^{\Sigma}_{inf}, V_\Sigma)$ is a filtration of (W, C_{sup}, C_{inf}, V) through Σ*

Proof. There are four things we need to show:

1. $C^{\Sigma}_{sup}|w||v||u|$ implies that for all $\langle sup\rangle\varphi\psi \in \Sigma$ we have that $v \Vdash \varphi$ and $u \Vdash \psi$ imply $w \Vdash \langle sup\rangle\varphi\psi$.
2. $C^{\Sigma}_{inf}|w||v||u|$ implies that for all $\langle inf\rangle\varphi\psi \in \Sigma$ we have that $v \Vdash \varphi$ and $u \Vdash \psi$ imply $z \Vdash \langle inf\rangle\varphi\psi$.
3. $C_{sup}wvu$ implies $C^{\Sigma}_{sup}|w||v||u|$.
4. $C_{inf}wvu$ implies $C^{\Sigma}_{inf}|w||v||u|$.

1. and 2. follow by definition of C^{Σ}_{sup} and C^{Σ}_{inf}. The proof of 3. and 4. is a technical proof that is included in the appendix, Sect. A.4.

This finishes the proof, showing that **TIL** $= Log(\tilde{\mathcal{C}}_F)$.

We conclude that

$$TIL = \mathbf{TIL} = Log(\tilde{\mathcal{C}}_F).$$

Since **TIL** is a finitely axiomatisable normal modal logic that has the FMP, we conclude that *TIL* is decidable. Note that from $TIL = TIL_{pre}$, we immediately get the same result for TIL_{pre}.

7 Conclusion

In this paper we considered tense information logic, an extension of modal information logic with a second modality: the infimum operator.

Following the outline and proofs of [3], we first gave an axiomatization of TIL on posets, showing that the only axioms linking $\langle sup\rangle$ and $\langle inf\rangle$ are the standard axioms of tense logic. We extended [3]'s completeness proof for MIL using the step-by-step method and showed that this result extends to TIL on preorder frames as well. Finally, we proved that TIL enjoys the FMP w.r.t. a generalized class of frames, thereby establishing decidability of the logic.

Acknowledgments. This work forms part of the first author's master's thesis, currently in progress, under the supervision of the second author and Nick Bezhanishvili. We thank Nick Bezhanishvili and the anonymous referees for helpful comments that significantly improved the presentation.

A Appendix

A.1 Proof of Lemma 1(3)

Proof. Throughout we use the standard properties of **TIL**–maximally consistent sets (MCSs), which hold because **TIL** is a normal modal logic.

Assume $C_{sup}\Gamma\Gamma\Theta$. To show that $C_{inf}\Delta\Delta\Gamma$, let $\delta \in \Delta$ and $\gamma \in \Gamma$ be arbitrary. By (Symm) and uniform substitution we get $\gamma \to \neg\langle sup\rangle(\neg\langle inf\rangle\gamma\top)\top \in \Gamma$. Since $\gamma \in \Gamma$, modus ponens yields $\neg\langle sup\rangle(\neg\langle inf\rangle\gamma\top)\top \in \Gamma$. Consistency then forces $\langle sup\rangle(\neg\langle inf\rangle\gamma\top)\top \notin \Gamma$. By Lemma 1(2), $C_{sup}\Gamma\Gamma\Delta$ implies $C_{sup}\Gamma\Delta\Gamma$, so it follows from $\langle sup\rangle(\neg\langle inf\rangle\gamma\top)\top \notin \Gamma$ that $\neg\langle inf\rangle\gamma\top \notin \Delta$ or $\top \notin \Gamma$. But $\top \in \Gamma$, so $\neg\langle inf\rangle\gamma\top \notin \Delta$, whence $\langle inf\rangle\gamma\top \in \Delta$.

Since $\delta \in \Delta$, an application of US and (Dk2) yields $\langle inf\rangle\delta\gamma \in \Delta$. Hence $C_{inf}\Delta\Delta\Gamma$.

The other direction is proven similarly.

A.2 Diagrams of Repair Lemmas

We give illustrations for the four repair lemmas that are used in the step-by-step method to give an intuition for how they help us to construct a satisfying model. In these diagrams, l denotes the labeling function, as described in Definition 7.
$\langle sup\rangle$-repair lemma

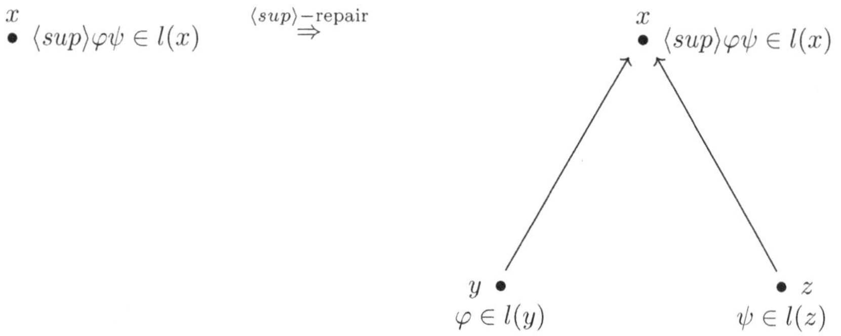

x • $\langle sup\rangle\varphi\psi \in l(x)$ $\overset{\langle sup\rangle-\text{repair}}{\Rightarrow}$ x • $\langle sup\rangle\varphi\psi \in l(x)$

y • $\varphi \in l(y)$ • z $\psi \in l(z)$

$\langle inf \rangle$-repair lemma

x
$\bullet\ \langle inf \rangle \varphi\psi \in l(x)$ $\overset{\langle inf \rangle-\text{repair}}{\Rightarrow}$

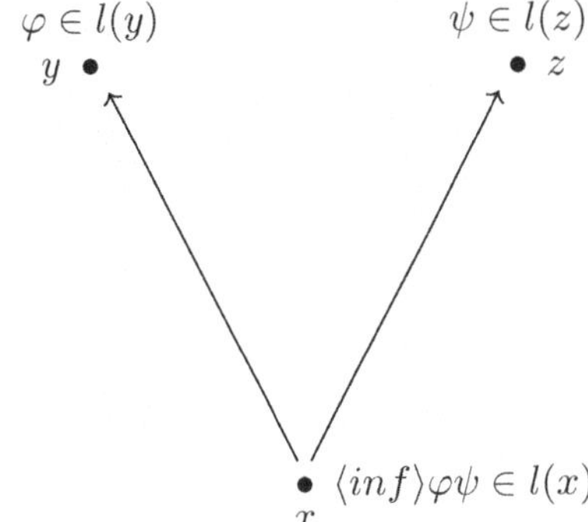

$\neg\langle sup \rangle$-repair lemma

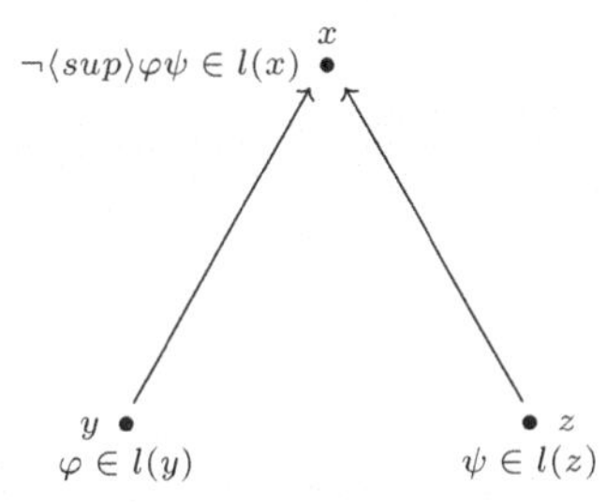

$\overset{\neg\langle sup \rangle-\text{repair}}{\Rightarrow}$

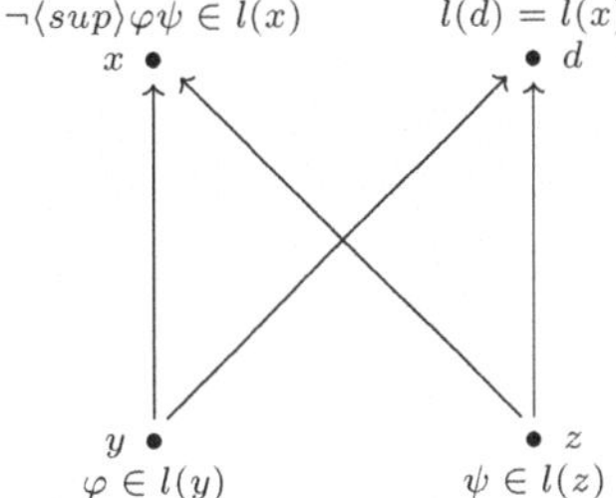

$\neg\langle inf \rangle$-repair lemma

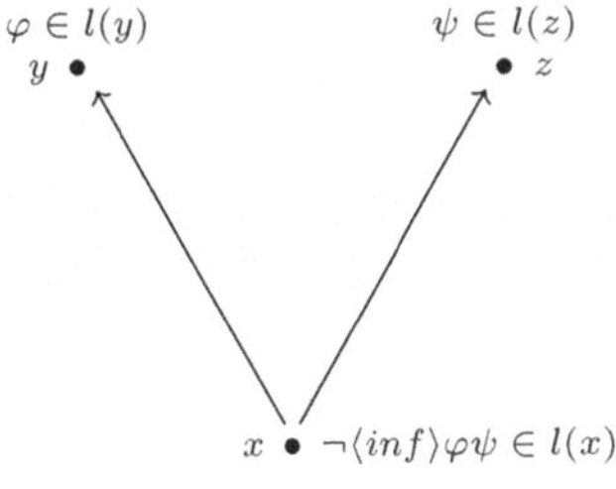

$\overset{\neg\langle inf \rangle-\text{repair}}{\Rightarrow}$

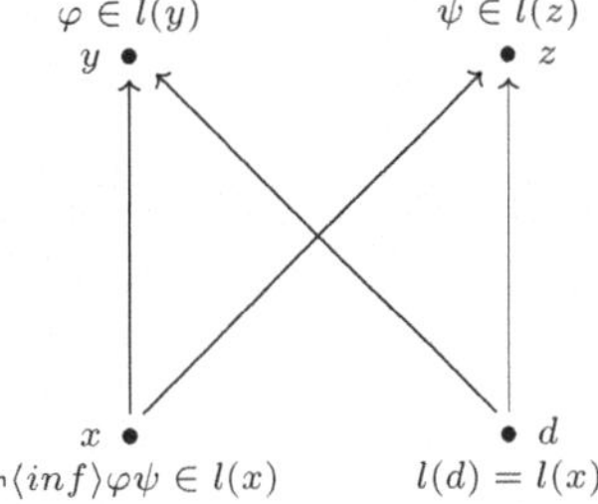

A.3 Proof of Proposition 1

To prove Proposition 1, we need to show that $(W_\Sigma, C^\Sigma_{sup}, C^\Sigma_{inf})$ satisfies all the frame correspondences:

- $(W_\Sigma, C^\Sigma_{sup}, C^\Sigma_{inf}) \models (FORe)$ follows from $(W_\Sigma, C^\Sigma_{sup}, C^\Sigma_{inf}) \Vdash (Re)$
- $(W_\Sigma, C^\Sigma_{sup}, C^\Sigma_{inf}) \models (FOCo)$ follows from (Com)-closure of Σ and $(W_\Sigma, C^\Sigma_{sup}, C^\Sigma_{inf}) \Vdash (Co.)$.

- For $(W_\Sigma, C^\Sigma_{sup}, C^\Sigma_{inf}) \vDash (FODk1)$, assume $C_{sup}|w||v||u|$ and let $\langle sup\rangle\varphi\psi \in \Sigma$ be arbitrary. We show that all clauses hold:
  (a) To show: $w \Vdash \varphi$, $v \Vdash \psi$ imply $w \Vdash \langle sup\rangle\varphi\psi$.
  By (Com)- and (S-P)-closure of Σ we get $\langle sup\rangle\psi\top = P\psi \in \Sigma$. Since $(W_\Sigma, C^\Sigma_{sup}, C^\Sigma_{inf}) \Vdash (Re)$ we get that $u \Vdash \langle sup\rangle\top\top = P\top$ and $v \Vdash \langle sup\rangle\psi\top = P\psi$. Then from $C_{sup}|w||v||u|$(b) we get $w \Vdash P\psi \wedge P\top$. So $w \Vdash P\psi = \langle sup\rangle\psi\top$. Then from $(W_\Sigma, C^\Sigma_{sup}, C^\Sigma_{inf}) \Vdash (Dk1)$ and $w \Vdash \varphi$ it follows that $w \Vdash \langle sup\rangle\varphi\psi$.
  (b) To show: $w \Vdash P\varphi$, $v \Vdash P\psi$ imply $w \Vdash P\varphi \wedge P\psi$.
  Again, since $u \Vdash P\top$, it follows from $v \Vdash P\psi$, (Com)- and (S-P)-closure of Σ (which implies $P\psi \in \Sigma$) and from $C_{sup}|w||v||u|$(b) that $w \Vdash P\psi \wedge P\top$. Thus $w \Vdash P\psi$ and we get that $w \Vdash P\varphi \wedge P\psi$.
  (c) To show: $w \Vdash \varphi$, $w \Vdash \psi$ imply $w \Vdash \langle inf\rangle\varphi\psi$.
  This follows from $(W_\Sigma, C^\Sigma_{sup}, C^\Sigma_{inf}) \Vdash (Re)$.
  (d) To show: $w \Vdash \varphi$, $v \Vdash \psi$ imply $v \Vdash \langle inf\rangle\varphi\psi$.
  From $C_{sup}|w||v||u|$(c) it follows that $v \Vdash \langle inf\rangle\varphi\psi$.
  (e) To show: $w \Vdash F\varphi$ implies $w \Vdash F\varphi$, $v \Vdash F\varphi$.
  Follows from $C_{sup}|w||v||u|$(e).
- $(W_\Sigma, C^\Sigma_{sup}, C^\Sigma_{inf}) \vDash (FODk2)$ is shown in the same way as $(W_\Sigma, C^\Sigma_{sup}, C^\Sigma_{inf}) \vDash (FODk1)$.
- For $(W_\Sigma, C^\Sigma_{sup}, C^\Sigma_{inf}) \vDash (FO4)$, assume $C_{sup}|w||w||v|$ and $C_{sup}|v||v||u|$ and let $\langle sup\rangle\varphi\psi \in \Sigma$ be arbitrary. We show that all clauses hold:
  (a) To show: $w \Vdash \varphi$, $u \Vdash \psi$ imply $w \Vdash \langle sup\rangle\varphi\psi$.
  By (Com)- and (S-P)-closure of Σ we get $\langle sup\rangle\psi\top = P\psi \in \Sigma$. From $C_{sup}|v||v||u|$(b), $u \Vdash P\psi$ and $v \Vdash P\top$ it follows that $v \Vdash P\psi$. Then from $C_{sup}|w||w||v|$, $w \Vdash P\top$, $v \Vdash P\psi$ it follows that $w \Vdash P\psi$. Since $(W_\Sigma, C^\Sigma_{sup}, C^\Sigma_{inf}) \Vdash (Dk1)$, it follows from $w \Vdash \langle sup\rangle\psi\top$ and $w \Vdash \varphi$ that $w \Vdash \langle sup\rangle\varphi\psi$.
  (b) To show: $w \Vdash P\varphi$, $u \Vdash P\psi$ imply $w \Vdash P\varphi \wedge P\psi$.
  Again, (Com)- and (S-P)-closure of Σ implies $P\psi \in \Sigma$. So again from (Com)-closure we get $\langle sup\rangle\top\psi \in \Sigma$. Since $v \Vdash \langle sup\rangle\top\top$, $u \Vdash \langle sup\rangle\psi\top$, it follows from $C_{sup}|v||v||u|$(b) that $v \Vdash P\psi$.
  By applying the exact same reasoning again but with $C_{sup}|w||w||v|$, we get that $w \Vdash P\psi$ since $v \Vdash P\psi$. Since we already assumed $w \Vdash P\varphi$, we derive that $w \Vdash P\varphi \wedge P\psi$.
  (c) To show: $w \Vdash \varphi$, $w \Vdash \psi$ imply $w \Vdash \langle inf\rangle\varphi\psi$.
  This follows from $(W_\Sigma, C^\Sigma_{sup}, C^\Sigma_{inf}) \Vdash (Re)$.
  (d) To show: $w \Vdash \varphi$, $u \Vdash \psi$ imply $u \Vdash \langle inf\rangle\varphi\psi$.
  From (Symm) and (S-F)-closure we get $F\varphi \in \Sigma$. From $C_{sup}|w||w||v|$(e) and $w \Vdash F\top$ (which we know since $(W_\Sigma, C^\Sigma_{sup}, C^\Sigma_{inf}) \Vdash (Re)$), it follows that $v \Vdash F\varphi$. We then apply the same reasoning using $v \Vdash F\varphi$ and $C_{sup}|v||v||u|$(e) to get $u \Vdash F\varphi$. Then from $u \Vdash \psi$ and $(W_\Sigma, C^\Sigma_{sup}, C^\Sigma_{inf}) \Vdash (Dk2)$ we get that $u \Vdash \langle inf\rangle\psi\varphi$. Since $(W_\Sigma, C^\Sigma_{sup}, C^\Sigma_{inf}) \Vdash (Co)$ we get $u \Vdash \langle inf\rangle\varphi\psi$
  (e) To show: $w \Vdash F\varphi$ implies $w \Vdash F\varphi$, $u \Vdash F\varphi$.
  We already got this result in (d).

- For $(W_\Sigma, C^\Sigma_{sup}, C^\Sigma_{inf}) \models (FOSy)$, assume $C_{sup}|w||w||v|$ and let $\langle inf\rangle\varphi\psi \in \Sigma$ be arbitrary. Then by (Symm)-closure of Σ we have that $\langle sup\rangle\varphi\psi \in \Sigma$. We show that all clauses hold:
  (a) To show: $v \Vdash \varphi$, $w \Vdash \psi$ imply $v \Vdash \langle inf\rangle\varphi\psi$.
  By (Com)-closure of Σ we get $\langle sup\rangle\psi\varphi \in \Sigma$. From $C_{sup}|w||w||v|$(d) and $(W_\Sigma, C^\Sigma_{sup}, C^\Sigma_{inf}) \Vdash (Co)$, we get $v \Vdash \langle inf\rangle\varphi\psi$
  (b) To show: $v \Vdash F\varphi$, $w \Vdash F\psi$ imply $v \Vdash F\varphi \wedge F\psi$.
  (Com)- and (S-F)-closure of Σ imply $F\psi \in \Sigma$. So from $C_{sup}|w||w||v|$(e) and $w \Vdash F\psi$ we get $v \Vdash F\psi$. Thus $v \Vdash F\varphi \wedge F\psi$.
  (c) To show: $v \Vdash \varphi$, $v \Vdash \psi$ imply $v \Vdash \langle sup\rangle\varphi\psi$.
  This follows from $(W_\Sigma, C^\Sigma_{sup}, C^\Sigma_{inf}) \Vdash (Re)$.
  (d) To show: $v \Vdash \varphi$, $w \Vdash \psi$ imply $w \Vdash \langle sup\rangle\varphi\psi$.
  From (S-F)-closure we get $F\varphi \in \Sigma$. Then from $C_{sup}|w||w||v|$(a), $w \Vdash \top$ and $v \Vdash \varphi$, it follows that $w \Vdash \langle sup\rangle\top\varphi$. Thus from $(W_\Sigma, C^\Sigma_{sup}, C^\Sigma_{inf}) \Vdash (Co.)$ we get that $w \Vdash \varphi\top$. Then $(W_\Sigma, C^\Sigma_{sup}, C^\Sigma_{inf}) \Vdash (Dk1)$, $(W_\Sigma, C^\Sigma_{sup}, C^\Sigma_{inf}) \Vdash (Co.)$ and $w \Vdash \psi$ imply $w \Vdash \langle sup\rangle\varphi\psi$.
  (e) To show: $v \Vdash P\varphi$ implies $v \Vdash P\varphi$, $w \Vdash P\varphi$. (S-P)- and (Com)-closure we get $\langle sup\rangle\top\varphi \in \Sigma$. Since $w \Vdash \langle sup\rangle\top\top$ and $v \Vdash \langle sup\rangle\varphi\top$ it follows from $C_{sup}|w||w||v|$(b) that $w \Vdash P\varphi$.

A.4 Proof of Proposition 2

To prove 3., we first make the following observations:

$$(W, C_{sup}, C_{inf}), w \Vdash P\varphi \quad \Leftrightarrow \quad \exists v \in W : C_{sup}wwv \text{ and } v \Vdash \varphi$$
$$(W, C_{sup}, C_{inf}), w \Vdash F\varphi \quad \Leftrightarrow \quad \exists v \in W : C_{inf}wwv \text{ and } v \Vdash \varphi$$

Now assume $C_{sup}wvu$ and let $\langle sup\rangle\varphi\psi \in \Sigma$ be arbitrary. We show that all clauses of $C^\Sigma_{sup}|w||v||u|$ hold:

(a) This clause follows by definition.
(b) Assume $v \Vdash P\varphi$ and $u \Vdash P\psi$. From $(W, C_{sup}, C_{inf}) \models (FODk1) \wedge (FOCo)$ we get $C_{sup}wwv$ and $C_{sup}wwu$. Thus by our previous observation, and by our assumptions, we get $w \Vdash PP\varphi \wedge PP\psi$. Then since $(W, C_{sup}, C_{inf}) \Vdash (4)$, it follows that $w \Vdash P\varphi \wedge P\psi$.
(c) Assume $w \Vdash \varphi$ and $v \Vdash \psi$. From $(W, C_{sup}, C_{inf}) \models (FODk1) \wedge (FOSy)$ we get that $C_{inf}vvw$, which implies $v \Vdash \langle inf\rangle\psi\varphi$. Since $(W, C_{sup}, C_{inf}) \Vdash (Co)$ we get $v \Vdash \langle inf\rangle\varphi\psi$.
(d) This clause is proven in a similar fashion as (c), but additionally relying on $(W, C_{sup}, C_{inf}) \models (FOCo)$
(e) Assume $w \Vdash F\varphi$. From $(W, C_{sup}, C_{inf}) \models$ FODk1 $\wedge$ FOSy, it follows that $C_{inf}vvw$. By our observation, we have $v \Vdash FF\varphi$. Since $(W, C_{sup}, C_{inf}) \Vdash (4)$, it follows that $v \Vdash F\varphi$. The result for u is obtained similarly, with an additional application of $(W, C_{sup}, C_{inf}) \models$ FOCo.

This finalizes the proof of 3.; 4. is proven similarly.

References

1. Blackburn, P., de Rijke, M., Venema, Y.: Modal Logic. Cambridge University Press, Cambridge (2001)
2. Burgess, J.P.: Basic tense logic. In: Gabbay, D., Guenthner, F. (eds.) Handbook of Philosophical Logic: Volume II: Extensions of Classical Logic, pp. 89–133. Springer, Dordrecht (1984). https://doi.org/10.1007/978-94-009-6259-0_2
3. Knudstorp, S.: Modal information logics: axiomatizations and decidability. J. Philos. Log. **52**(6), 1723–1766 (2023). https://doi.org/10.1007/s10992-023-09724-5
4. Knudstorp, S.: The modal logic of minimal upper bounds. Language, logic, and computation. In: 14th International Tbilisi Symposium, TbiLLC 2023, Telavi, Georgia, forthcoming
5. van Benthem, J.: Modal logic as a theory of information. In: Copeland J. (ed.) Logic and Reality. Essays on the Legacy of Arthur Prior, pp. 135–168. Oxford University Press, Oxford (1997). https://doi.org/10.1093/oso/9780198240600.003.0008
6. van Benthem, J.: Truth Maker Semantics and Modal Information Logic. Draft manuscript (2017). https://eprints.illc.uva.nl/id/eprint/1590/
7. van Benthem, J.: Constructive agents. Indag. Math. **29**(1), 23–35 (2018). https://doi.org/10.1016/j.indag.2017.10.004
8. Rescher, N., Urquhart, A.: Temporal Logic. Springer, Vienna (1971)
9. Wang, X., Wang, Y.: Modal Logics over Lattices. In: Annals of Pure and Applied Logic, vol. 176, no. 4. Elsevier BV (2025). https://doi.org/10.1016/j.apal.2025.103553
10. Wang, X., Wang, Y.: Tense logics over lattices. In: Logic, Language, Information, and Computation, pp 70–87. Springer, Cham (2022). https://doi.org/10.1007/978-3-031-15298-6_5

Infinitary Refinement Types for Temporal Properties in Scott Domains

Colin Riba(✉) and Alexandre Kejikian

ENS de Lyon, CNRS, Université Claude Bernard Lyon 1, LIP, UMR 5668, 69342 Lyon Cedex 07, France
colin.riba@ens-lyon.fr

Abstract. We discuss an infinitary refinement type system for input-output temporal specifications of functions that handle infinite objects like streams or infinite trees. Our system is based on a reformulation of Bonsangue and Kok's infinitary extension of Abramsky's Domain Theory in Logical Form to saturated properties. We show that in an interesting range of cases, our system is complete without the need of an infinitary rule introduced by Bonsangue and Kok to reflect the well-filteredness of Scott domains.

Keywords: Refinement Types · Scott Domains · Temporal Logic

1 Introduction

We are interested in input-output specifications of higher-order programs that handle infinite data, such as streams or non-wellfounded trees. Consider e.g.

$$\mathsf{filter} \ : \ (A \to \mathsf{Bool}) \ \longrightarrow \ \mathsf{Str}A \ \longrightarrow \ \mathsf{Str}A$$
$$\mathsf{filter}\ p\ (a :: x) = \mathsf{if}\ (p\ a)\ \mathsf{then}\ a :: (\mathsf{filter}\ p\ x)\ \mathsf{else}\ (\mathsf{filter}\ p\ x)$$

where $\mathsf{Str}A$ stands for the type of streams on A. Assume $p : A \to \mathsf{Bool}$ is a function that tests for a property ψ. If x is a stream on A, then $(\mathsf{filter}\ p\ x)$ retains those elements of x which satisfy ψ. The stream produced by $(\mathsf{filter}\ p\ x)$ is thus only partially defined if x has only finitely many elements satisfying ψ.

Logics like LTL (Linear Temporal Logic), CTL (Computation Tree Logic) or the modal μ-calculus are widely used to formulate, on infinite objects, safety and liveness properties (see e.g. [7,14]). Safety properties state that some "bad" event will not occur, while liveness properties specify that "something good" will happen (see e.g. [4]). One typically uses temporal modalities like $\Box$ (*always*) or $\Diamond$ (*eventually*) on streams in specifications of programs.

A possible specification for filter asserts that $(\mathsf{filter}\ p\ x)$ is a totally defined stream whenever x is a totally defined stream with infinitely many elements satisfying ψ. We express this as follows. Let A be finite and assume given, for each a of type A, a formula $[a]$ which holds on $b : A$ exactly when b is a. Then

D. Kozen and R. de Queiroz (Eds.): WoLLIC 2025, LNCS 15942, pp. 175–193, 2026.
https://doi.org/10.1007/978-3-031-99536-1_11

$\Box \bigvee_a [a]$ selects those streams on A which are totally defined. The formula $[\mathsf{hd}]\psi$ holds on a stream $(a :: x)$ when ψ holds on a. Hence $\Box\Diamond[\mathsf{hd}]\psi$ expresses that a stream has infinitely many elements satisfying ψ. We can thus state that

$$x \text{ satisfies } \Box \bigvee_a [a] \text{ and } \Box\Diamond[\mathsf{hd}]\psi \quad \Longrightarrow \quad (\mathsf{filter}\ p\ x) \text{ satisfies } \Box \bigvee_a [a] \tag{1}$$

It is undecidable whether a given higher-order program satisfies such an input-output temporal property written with formulae of the modal μ-calculus [20]. A previous work [18] provided a refinement type system for proving such properties. This type system handles the (negation-free) alternation-free modal μ-calculus on infinite types such as streams or trees. But it is based on guarded recursion and does not allow for non-productive functions such as filter.

In this paper, we consider a fragment of FPC equipped with general recursion (FPC extends PCF [27] with recursive types, see e.g. [26]). We are interested in specifications as in (1), but interpreted at the level of denotational semantics: In our view, since a stream (as opposed to e.g. an integer) is an inherently infinite object, the above specification for filter should hold for any stream whatsoever, and not only for those definable in a given programming language.

This leads us to consider temporal properties on infinite datatypes in Scott domains. We noted in [29] that the usual rule of Scott induction (see e.g. [3, §6.2]) does not prove liveness properties like (1) above. We instead resort to Abramsky's paradigm of "Domain Theory in Logical Form" (DTLF) [1]. We build on [6], in which Bonsangue and Kok extend DTLF to an infinitary type system which is sound and complete for a large family of infinitary properties, known as the *saturated* ones.[1] This includes the *negation-free* formulae of (suitable adaptations of) the modal μ-calculus [29], and thus the specification in (1).

We present an infinitary refinement type system for saturated properties. Our system is a reformulation of DTLF which, in contrast with [1,6] (see also [3, §10.5]), has no specific syntactic entity for compact open sets. We do isolate a finitary logical fragment, but it only consists of finite conjunctions and falsity, without non-empty disjunctions. As consequence, our version of Abramsky's *coprimeness predicate* is a *consistency* predicate, which selects those finite formulae with a non-empty interpretation. Besides, our consistency predicate has a *positive* (inductive) definition (cf. [3,6]).

Also, similarly as in [6], the completeness of our system relies on a topological property of Scott domains known as *well-filteredness*, and reflected in an infinitary rule ((WF) in Sect. 4). We show that this rule is actually not needed for an interesting range of specifications, including (1) for filter, as well as various specifications for functions on streams and trees (see Example 9 and Theorem 3).

Having some control on the rule (WF) is relevant in the context of this work. We ultimately target a finitary system in which, similarly as in [18], infinitary behaviours of fixpoint formulae are simulated by explicit quantifications over the number of unfoldings of these fixpoints. To this end, it is important to know that the rule (WF) can be avoided in many interesting cases.

---

[1] A subset of a domain is *saturated* when it is upward-closed.

$$\frac{\mathcal{E}, x : \tau \vdash M : \tau}{\mathcal{E} \vdash \mathsf{fix}\, x.M : \tau} \qquad \frac{\mathcal{E} \vdash M : \tau[\mathsf{rec}\,\alpha.\tau/\alpha]}{\mathcal{E} \vdash \mathsf{fold}(M) : \mathsf{rec}\,\alpha.\tau} \qquad \frac{\mathcal{E} \vdash M : \mathsf{rec}\,\alpha.\tau}{\mathcal{E} \vdash \mathsf{unfold}(M) : \tau[\mathsf{rec}\,\alpha.\tau/\alpha]}$$

$$\frac{}{\mathcal{E} \vdash a : A}\ (A \in \mathcal{B} \text{ and } a \in A) \qquad \frac{\mathcal{E} \vdash M : A \qquad \text{for each } a \in A,\quad \mathcal{E} \vdash N_a : \tau}{\mathcal{E} \vdash \mathsf{case}\ M\ [a \mapsto N_a \mid a \in A] : \tau}$$

Fig. 1. Typing rules of the pure calculus (excerpt).

Organization of the paper. We devise our refinement type system in Sect. 2. Its (Scott) semantics is presented in Sect. 3, and completeness is handled in Sect. 4. Finally, Sect. 5 discusses our results in the perspective of further works.

Appendix A contains additional technical material. Proofs are available in the Appendices of the full version [28].

2 A Refinement Type System

We assume given a collection of sets $\mathcal{B}$, which will play the role of *base types.*

2.1 The Pure System

The *pure types* (notation $\tau, \sigma, \ldots$) are the closed types over the grammar

$$\tau \ ::= \ A \mid \tau \times \tau \mid \tau \to \tau \mid \alpha \mid \mathsf{rec}\alpha.\tau$$

where $A \in \mathcal{B}$, where α ranges over an infinite supply of *type variables*, and where $\mathsf{rec}\alpha.\tau$ binds α in τ. We consider terms from the grammar

$$\begin{aligned} M, N \ ::= \ & x \mid \lambda x.M \mid MN \mid \mathsf{fix}x.M \mid \mathsf{fold}(M) \mid \mathsf{unfold}(M) \\ & \mid \langle M, N\rangle \mid \pi_1(M) \mid \pi_2(M) \mid a \mid \mathsf{case}\ M\ [a \mapsto N_a \mid a \in A] \end{aligned}$$

where $A \in \mathcal{B}$ and $a \in A$. The term formers $\mathsf{fold}, \mathsf{unfold}, \pi_1, \pi_2$ are often written in curried form: e.g. $(\mathsf{fold}M)$ stands for $\mathsf{fold}(M)$. Write $M \circ N$ for $\lambda x.M(N\,x)$.

Terms are typed as usual, with judgments of the form $\mathcal{E} \vdash M : \tau$, where $\mathcal{E}$ is a list $x_1 : \sigma_1, \ldots, x_n : \sigma_n$ with $x_i \neq x_j$ if $i \neq j$. Some typing rules are presented in Fig. 1.[2] Of course, each type τ is inhabited by the term $\Omega_\tau := \mathsf{fix}x.x : \tau$.

Example 1. The type of *streams over* σ is $\mathsf{Str}\sigma := \mathsf{rec}\alpha.\,\sigma \times \alpha$. It is equipped with the constructor $\mathsf{Cons} := \lambda h.\lambda t.\mathsf{fold}\langle h, t\rangle : \sigma \to \mathsf{Str}\sigma \to \mathsf{Str}\sigma$. We use the infix notation $(M :: N)$ for $(\mathsf{Cons}M\,N)$. The usual *head* and *tail* functions are $\mathsf{hd} := \lambda s.\,\pi_1(\mathsf{unfold}s) : \mathsf{Str}\sigma \to \sigma$ and $\mathsf{tl} := \lambda s.\,\pi_2(\mathsf{unfold}s) : \mathsf{Str}\sigma \to \mathsf{Str}\sigma$.

The type of *binary trees over* σ is $\mathsf{Tree}\sigma := \mathsf{rec}\alpha.\,\sigma \times (\alpha \times \alpha)$. The constructor $\mathsf{Node} : \sigma \to \mathsf{Tree}\sigma \to \mathsf{Tree}\sigma \to \mathsf{Tree}\sigma$ and the destructors $\mathsf{label} : \mathsf{Tree}\sigma \to \sigma$ and $\mathsf{left}, \mathsf{right} : \mathsf{Tree}\sigma \to \mathsf{Tree}\sigma$ are defined similarly as resp. $\mathsf{Cons}, \mathsf{hd}, \mathsf{tl}$ on streams.

[2] The set of all typing rules of the pure system is in Fig. 6, Sect. A.

Table 1. Functions on Streams and Trees.

$$\mathsf{map} := \lambda f.\mathsf{fix}g.\lambda x.\ (f\ (\mathsf{hd}x)) :: (g\ (\mathsf{tl}x))\ :\ (\tau \to \sigma) \longrightarrow \mathsf{Str}\tau \longrightarrow \mathsf{Str}\sigma$$

$$\begin{aligned}\mathsf{filter}\ &:\ (\sigma \to \mathsf{Bool}) \longrightarrow \mathsf{Str}\sigma \longrightarrow \mathsf{Str}\sigma \\ &:= \lambda p.\mathsf{fix}g.\lambda x.\ \mathsf{if}\ (p\ (\mathsf{hd}x))\ \mathsf{then}\ (\mathsf{hd}x) :: (g\ (\mathsf{tl}x))\ \mathsf{else}\ (g\ (\mathsf{tl}x))\end{aligned}$$

$$\mathsf{diag} := \mathsf{diagaux}(\lambda x.x)\ :\ \mathsf{Str}(\mathsf{Str}\sigma) \longrightarrow \mathsf{Str}\sigma$$

$$\begin{aligned}\mathsf{diagaux}\ &:\ (\mathsf{Str}\sigma \to \mathsf{Str}\sigma) \longrightarrow \mathsf{Str}(\mathsf{Str}\sigma) \longrightarrow \mathsf{Str}\sigma \\ &:= \mathsf{fix}g.\lambda k.\lambda x.\ \big((\mathsf{hd} \circ k)(\mathsf{hd}x)\big) :: \big(g\ (k \circ \mathsf{tl})\ (\mathsf{tl}x)\big)\end{aligned}$$

$$\begin{aligned}\mathsf{extract}\ &:\ \mathsf{Rou}\sigma \longrightarrow \sigma \qquad & \mathsf{Over}\ &:\ \mathsf{Rou}\sigma \\ &:= \mathsf{fix}e.\lambda c.\mathsf{unfold}\ c\ e & &:= \mathsf{fix}c.\mathsf{fold}(\lambda k.k\ c)\end{aligned}$$

$$\mathsf{bft} := \lambda t.\ \mathsf{extract}(\mathsf{bftaux}\ t\ \mathsf{Over})\ :\ \mathsf{Tree}\sigma \longrightarrow \mathsf{Str}\sigma$$

$$\begin{aligned}\mathsf{bftaux}\ &:\ \mathsf{Tree}\sigma \longrightarrow \mathsf{Rou}(\mathsf{Str}\sigma) \longrightarrow \mathsf{Rou}(\mathsf{Str}\sigma) \\ &:= \mathsf{fix}g.\lambda t.\lambda c.\mathsf{fold}\ \Big(\lambda k.\ (\mathsf{label}t) :: \Big(\mathsf{unfold}\ c\ \big(k \circ (g(\mathsf{left}t)) \circ (g(\mathsf{right}t))\big)\Big)\Big)\end{aligned}$$

$$\frac{\varphi \in \mathcal{L}(\tau_1)}{[\pi_1]\varphi \in \mathcal{L}(\tau_1 \times \tau_2)} \qquad \frac{\varphi \in \mathcal{L}(\tau_2)}{[\pi_2]\varphi \in \mathcal{L}(\tau_1 \times \tau_2)} \qquad \frac{\psi \in \mathcal{L}(\sigma) \quad \varphi \in \mathcal{L}(\tau)}{\psi \Vdash\!\!\!\to \varphi \in \mathcal{L}(\sigma \to \tau)}$$

$$\frac{\varphi \in \mathcal{L}(\tau[\mathsf{rec}\,\alpha.\tau/\alpha])}{[\mathsf{fold}]\varphi \in \mathcal{L}(\mathsf{rec}\,\alpha.\tau)} \qquad \frac{A \in \mathcal{B} \text{ and } a \in A}{[a] \in \mathcal{L}(A)}$$

Fig. 2. Modalities.

Example 2. Table 1 defines functions on streams and trees for which we will be able to derive specifications which improve on [18] (see Examples 9 and 13).

On streams, besides the usual map function, we consider the filter function from Sect. 1. This assumes that $\mathcal{B}$ contains a set Bool $= \{\mathsf{tt}, \mathsf{ff}\}$ of *Booleans*. The notation if M then N_{tt} else N_{ff} stands for the term case $M\ [a \mapsto N_a \mid a \in \mathsf{Bool}]$. Finally, the function diag computes the diagonal of a stream of streams. We refer to [18, Example 8.3] for explanations.

On trees, the function bft implements Martin Hofmann's breadth-first traversal (see e.g. [5,18]). It uses the recursive type $\mathsf{Rou}\sigma := \mathsf{rec}\alpha.\,(\alpha \to \sigma) \to \sigma$.

2.2 Negation-Free Infinitary Modal Logics

We consider negation-free infinitary formulae with modalities as in [1,6,18].

Definition 1 (Formulae). *Let τ be a pure type.*

The formulae $\varphi \in \mathcal{L}(\tau)$ are formed using the modalities in Fig. 2 together with arbitrary set-indexed conjunctions $\bigwedge_{i\in I} \varphi_i$ and disjunctions $\bigvee_{i\in I} \varphi_i$. We write True *(resp.* False*) for the empty conjunction (resp. disjunction).*

We let $\mathcal{L}_\wedge(\tau)$ consist of those $\varphi \in \mathcal{L}(\tau)$ in which all conjunctions are finite and all disjunctions are empty (False is the only disjunction allowed in $\mathcal{L}_\wedge(\tau)$).

The formulae $\varphi \in \mathcal{L}_\bigcirc(\tau)$ are formed from formulae in $\mathcal{L}_\wedge(\tau)$ using arbitrary disjunctions and finite conjunctions.

The normal forms *$\varphi \in \mathcal{N}(\tau)$ are the $\varphi = \bigwedge_{i \in I} \bigvee_{j \in J_i} \psi_{i,j}$ with $\psi_{i,j} \in \mathcal{L}_\wedge(\tau)$ and where I and the J_i's are arbitrary sets.*

The semantics of formulae is defined in Sect. 3. Their intended meaning is as follows. The formula $\psi \Vdash\!\!\rightarrow \varphi \in \mathcal{L}(\sigma \to \tau)$ is intended to select those $M : \sigma \to \tau$ such that φ holds on $MN : \tau$ whenever ψ holds on $N : \sigma$. Similarly, $[\mathsf{fold}]\varphi$ holds on M whenever φ holds on $\mathsf{unfold}M$. For $i = 1, 2$, the formula $[\pi_i]\varphi$ selects those $M : \tau_1 \times \tau_2$ such that φ holds on $\pi_i M$. With $\langle \varphi_1, \varphi_2 \rangle := [\pi_1]\varphi_1 \wedge [\pi_2]\varphi_2$, we have a formula which holds on those M such that φ_i holds on $\pi_i M$ for $i = 1, 2$.

Example 3. Given $A \in \mathcal{B}$ and $a \in A$, the formula $[a]$ is intended to hold on a but not on the $b \in A \setminus \{a\}$. For instance, given $S \subseteq A$, the formula $\bigwedge_{a \in S}([a] \Vdash\!\!\rightarrow [\mathsf{tt}])$ is intended to select the $p : A \to \mathsf{Bool}$ such that $(p\,a)$ is tt for all $a \in S$.

Example 4. On streams $\mathsf{Str}\sigma$, the composite modalities $[\mathsf{hd}]$ and $[\mathsf{tl}]$ are defined as $[\mathsf{hd}]\psi := [\mathsf{fold}][\pi_1]\psi$ and $[\mathsf{tl}]\varphi := [\mathsf{fold}][\pi_2]\varphi$. Given $\psi \in \mathcal{L}(\sigma)$ and $\varphi \in \mathcal{L}(\mathsf{Str}\sigma)$, the formulae $[\mathsf{hd}]\psi \in \mathcal{L}(\mathsf{Str}\sigma)$ and $[\mathsf{tl}]\varphi \in \mathcal{L}(\mathsf{Str}\sigma)$ select those streams M such that ψ holds on $(\mathsf{hd}M)$ and such that φ holds on $(\mathsf{tl}M)$, respectively. In the following, we write $\bigcirc\varphi$ for $[\mathsf{tl}]\varphi$.

Using $\mathbb{N}$-indexed connectives, we can define the usual LTL modalities $\Box$ and $\Diamond$ as $\Box\varphi := \bigwedge_{n \in \mathbb{N}} \bigcirc^n \varphi$ and $\Diamond\varphi := \bigvee_{n \in \mathbb{N}} \bigcirc^n \varphi$. Hence, $\Box\varphi$ (resp. $\Diamond\varphi$) is intended to hold on those $M : \mathsf{Str}\sigma$ such that φ holds on $\mathsf{tl}^n M$ for all $n \in \mathbb{N}$ (resp. for some $n \in \mathbb{N}$). In particular, $\Box\Diamond[\mathsf{hd}]\psi$ (resp. $\Diamond\Box[\mathsf{hd}]\psi$) selects those streams with infinitely many (resp. ultimately all) elements satisfying ψ.

Example 5. Similarly, on trees $\mathsf{Tree}\sigma$ one can define $[\mathsf{label}]$, $[\mathsf{left}]$ and $[\mathsf{right}]$ such that $[\mathsf{label}]\psi, [\mathsf{left}]\varphi, [\mathsf{right}]\varphi \in \mathcal{L}(\mathsf{Tree}\sigma)$ whenever $\psi \in \mathcal{L}(\sigma)$ and $\varphi \in \mathcal{L}(\mathsf{Tree}\sigma)$.

Moreover, the LTL stream modalities $\Box, \Diamond$ have their usual CTL counterparts $\forall\Box$, $\exists\Box$, $\forall\Diamond$ and $\exists\Diamond$. Namely, given $\varphi \in \mathcal{L}(\mathsf{Tree}\sigma)$,

$$\forall\Box\varphi := \bigwedge_{n \in \mathbb{N}}(\varphi \wedge \textcircled{\scriptsize$\wedge$}(-))^n(\mathsf{True}) \qquad \forall\Diamond\varphi := \bigvee_{n \in \mathbb{N}}(\varphi \vee \textcircled{\scriptsize$\wedge$}(-))^n(\mathsf{False})$$
$$\exists\Box\varphi := \bigwedge_{n \in \mathbb{N}}(\varphi \wedge \textcircled{\scriptsize$\vee$}(-))^n(\mathsf{True}) \qquad \exists\Diamond\varphi := \bigvee_{n \in \mathbb{N}}(\varphi \vee \textcircled{\scriptsize$\vee$}(-))^n(\mathsf{False})$$

with $\textcircled{\scriptsize$\wedge$}\theta := [\mathsf{left}]\theta \wedge [\mathsf{right}]\theta$ and $\textcircled{\scriptsize$\vee$}\theta := [\mathsf{left}]\theta \vee [\mathsf{right}]\theta$, and where $(\varphi \wedge \textcircled{\scriptsize$\vee$}(-))^0(\mathsf{True})$ is True and $(\varphi \wedge \textcircled{\scriptsize$\vee$}(-))^{n+1}(\mathsf{True})$ is the formula $\varphi \wedge \textcircled{\scriptsize$\vee$}((\varphi \wedge \textcircled{\scriptsize$\vee$}(-))^n(\mathsf{True}))$.

The intended meaning of $\forall\Box[\mathsf{label}]\psi$ is to select those trees whose node labels all satisfy ψ, while $\exists\Box[\mathsf{label}]\psi$ asks ψ to hold on all labels in some infinite path. The formula $\exists\Diamond[\mathsf{label}]\psi$ holds if there is a node whose label satisfies ψ, and $\forall\Diamond[\mathsf{label}]\psi$ requires that every infinite path has a node label on which ψ holds.

Examples 4 and 5 are generalized in Example 12 (Sect. 3) to (negation-free) least and greatest fixpoints in the style of the modal μ-calculus (see e.g. [7,8]).

$$\frac{\psi \vdash \theta \quad \theta \vdash \varphi}{\psi \vdash \varphi} \qquad \frac{a \neq b}{[a] \wedge [b] \vdash_A \mathsf{False}} \qquad (\mathsf{D})\frac{}{\bigwedge_{i\in I}\bigvee_{j\in J_i}\varphi_{i,j} \vdash \bigvee_{f\in\prod_{i\in I}J_i}\bigwedge_{i\in I}\varphi_{i,f(i)}}$$

$$\frac{}{\varphi \vdash \varphi} \qquad \frac{\text{for each } i \in I,\ \psi \vdash \varphi_i}{\psi \vdash \bigwedge_{i\in I}\varphi_i} \qquad \frac{\psi_i \vdash \varphi}{\bigwedge_{i\in I}\psi_i \vdash \varphi}\ (i \in I) \qquad \frac{}{\bigwedge_{i\in I}[\triangle]\varphi_i \vdash [\triangle]\bigwedge_{i\in I}\varphi_i}$$

$$\frac{\psi \vdash \varphi_i}{\psi \vdash \bigvee_{i\in I}\varphi_i}\ (i \in I) \qquad \frac{\text{for each } i \in I,\ \psi_i \vdash \varphi}{\bigvee_{i\in I}\psi_i \vdash \varphi} \qquad \frac{}{[\triangle]\bigvee_{i\in I}\varphi_i \vdash \bigvee_{i\in I}[\triangle]\varphi_i}$$

$$(\mathsf{F})\frac{\psi \in \mathcal{L}_\wedge(\sigma) \quad \varphi_i \in \mathcal{L}(\tau) \quad I \neq \emptyset}{\psi \mathrel{\|\!\!\to} (\bigvee_{i\in I}\varphi_i) \vdash \bigvee_{i\in I}(\psi \mathrel{\|\!\!\to} \varphi_i)} \qquad \frac{\psi' \vdash_\sigma \psi \quad \varphi \vdash_\tau \varphi'}{\psi \mathrel{\|\!\!\to} \varphi \vdash_{\sigma\to\tau} \psi' \mathrel{\|\!\!\to} \varphi'} \qquad \frac{\psi \vdash \varphi}{[\triangle]\psi \vdash [\triangle]\varphi}$$

$$\frac{}{\bigwedge_{i\in I}(\psi \mathrel{\|\!\!\to} \varphi_i) \vdash \psi \mathrel{\|\!\!\to} (\bigwedge_{i\in I}\varphi_i)} \qquad \frac{}{\bigwedge_{i\in I}(\psi_i \mathrel{\|\!\!\to} \varphi) \vdash (\bigvee_{i\in I}\psi_i) \mathrel{\|\!\!\to} \varphi}$$

Fig. 3. Basic deduction rules, where $\triangle$ is either π_1, π_2 or fold.

Table 2. Some judgments with refinement types (functions defined in Table 1).

Map on streams (with $\triangle$ either $\Box$, $\Diamond$, $\Diamond\Box$ or $\Box\Diamond$) $\mathsf{map} : \{\tau \to \sigma \mid \psi \mathrel{\|\!\!\to} \varphi\} \longrightarrow \{\mathsf{Str}\tau \mid \triangle[\mathsf{hd}]\psi\} \longrightarrow \{\mathsf{Str}\sigma \mid \triangle[\mathsf{hd}]\varphi\}$
Filter on streams (with $\triangle$ either $\Box$ or $\Box\Diamond$) $\mathsf{filter} : \{A \to \mathsf{Bool} \mid \bigwedge_{a\in S}([a] \mathrel{\|\!\!\to} [\mathsf{tt}])\} \longrightarrow \{\mathsf{Str}\sigma \mid \triangle[\mathsf{hd}]\bigvee_{a\in S}[a]\} \longrightarrow \{\mathsf{Str}\sigma \mid \Box[\mathsf{hd}]\bigvee_{a\in S}[a]\}$
Diagonal of streams of streams (with $\triangle$ either $\Box$ or $\Diamond\Box$) $\mathsf{diag} : \{\mathsf{Str}(\mathsf{Str}\sigma) \mid \triangle[\mathsf{hd}]\Box[\mathsf{hd}]\varphi\} \longrightarrow \{\mathsf{Str}\sigma \mid \triangle[\mathsf{hd}]\varphi\}$
Breadth-first tree traversal (see Example 9 for $\triangle$ and $\overline{\triangle}$) $\mathsf{bft} : \{\mathsf{Tree}\sigma \mid \triangle[\mathsf{label}]\varphi\} \longrightarrow \{\mathsf{Str}\sigma \mid \overline{\triangle}[\mathsf{hd}]\varphi\}$

Definition 2 (Deduction). *A* sequent *has the form* $\psi \vdash_\tau \varphi$ *where* $\varphi, \psi \in \mathcal{L}(\tau)$. *We often write* $\psi \vdash \varphi$ *for* $\psi \vdash_\tau \varphi$. Basic deduction *is defined by the rules in Fig. 3.*
We write $\psi \dashv\vdash \varphi$ *when the sequents* $\psi \vdash \varphi$ *and* $\varphi \vdash \psi$ *are both derivable.*

Note that $\varphi \vdash \mathsf{True}$ and $\mathsf{False} \vdash \varphi$ by definition of True and False. One can derive that $\vdash$ preserves conjunctions and disjunctions: if $\psi_i \vdash \varphi_i$ for all $i \in I$, then $\bigwedge_{i\in I}\psi_i \vdash \bigwedge_{i\in I}\varphi_i$ and $\bigvee_{i\in I}\psi_i \vdash \bigvee_{i\in I}\varphi_i$.

Example 6. Let $\triangle$ be either π_1, π_2 or fold. The modality $[\triangle]$ commutes over conjunctions and disjunctions ($\bigwedge_i[\triangle]\varphi_i \dashv\vdash [\triangle]\bigwedge_i\varphi_i$, and similarly for $\bigvee$). In particular, for each normal form φ there is a normal form ψ such that $[\triangle]\varphi \dashv\vdash \psi$.

Example 7. As usual, the converse of (D) is derivable, and so is the dual law $\bigwedge_{f\in\prod_{i\in I}J_i}\bigvee_{i\in I}\varphi_{i,f(i)} \dashv\vdash \bigvee_{i\in I}\bigwedge_{j\in J_i}\varphi_{i,j}$ (see e.g. [19, Lemma VII.1.10]).

Remark 1. Taking $I = \emptyset$ in the last two rules of Fig. 3 yields $\mathsf{True} \vdash (\psi \mathrel{\|\!\!\to} \mathsf{True})$ and $\mathsf{True} \vdash (\mathsf{False} \mathrel{\|\!\!\to} \varphi)$. The rule (F) would thus be unsound with $I = \emptyset$ and $\psi = \mathsf{False}$. Rule (F) differs from usual systems for DTLF (cf. [1, §4.2] [6, Figure 5] and [3, Figure 10.3]). The case of $I = \emptyset$ will be handled by rule (C) in (2), Sect. 4.

2.3 Refinement Types

Refinement types (or *types*), notation $T, U, \ldots$, are given by the grammar

$$T ::= \tau \mid \{\tau \mid \varphi\} \mid T \times T \mid T \to T$$

where τ is a pure type and $\varphi \in \mathcal{L}(\tau)$. We shall consider typing judgments of the form $\mathcal{E} \vdash M : T$, where $\mathcal{E}$ is allowed to mention refinement types. A judgment $M : \{\tau \mid \varphi\}$ is intended to mean that M is of pure type τ and satisfies φ.

Example 8. Given a base type $A \in \mathcal{B}$ and $S \subseteq A$, a judgment of the form $p : \{A \to \mathsf{Bool} \mid \bigwedge_{a \in S} ([a] \Vdash\!\!\to [\mathsf{tt}])\}$ expresses that $(p\,a)$ yields tt for all $a \in S$.

Example 9. Table 2 presents some specifications, expressed as refinement types, for functions defined in Table 1 (see Example 2).

For the map function, assuming $f : \{\sigma \to \tau \mid \psi \Vdash\!\!\to \varphi\}$, if $\triangle$ is $\Box$ (resp. $\Diamond, \Box\Diamond, \Diamond\Box$), then the judgment expresses that $(\mathsf{map} f)$ takes a stream with all (resp. some, infinitely many, ultimately all) elements satisfying ψ to a stream with all (resp. some, infinitely many, ultimately all) elements satisfying φ.

The specifications for filter are the expected ones. Let $p : A \to \mathsf{Bool}$ such that $(p\,a)$ yields tt for all $a \in S$. If $\triangle$ is $\Box$ (resp. $\Box\Diamond$) then the judgment means that $(\mathsf{filter} p)$ takes a stream with all (resp. infinitely many) elements in S to a stream with all elements in S. Recalling that the stream formula $\Box[\mathsf{hd}][a]$ amounts to $\bigwedge_{n \in \mathbb{N}} \bigcirc^n [\mathsf{hd}][a]$, note that none of the formulae $\bigcirc^n[\mathsf{hd}][a]$ hold on $\Omega_{\mathsf{Str}A} : \mathsf{Str}A$.

Concerning the diagonal, if $\triangle$ is $\Box$ (resp. $\Diamond\Box$), then the judgment expresses that diag takes a stream whose component streams all (resp. ultimately all) satisfy $\Box[\mathsf{hd}]\varphi$ to a stream whose elements all (resp. ultimately all) satisfy φ.

For the tree traversal bft we can allow for any sound combination of $\triangle$ and $\overline{\triangle}$. This includes all pairs $(\triangle, \overline{\triangle})$ among $(\forall\Box, \Box)$, $(\exists\Box, \Box\Diamond)$, $(\exists\Diamond, \Diamond)$, $(\forall\Diamond, \Diamond)$ and $(\forall\Box\exists\Diamond, \Box\Diamond)$. For instance, if $\triangle$ is $\forall\Box$ (resp. $\exists\Diamond, \forall\Box\exists\Diamond$), then the judgment says that bft takes a tree with all (resp. some, infinitely many) node labels satisfying φ to a stream with all (resp. some, infinitely may) elements satisfying φ.

Each refinement type T has an *underlying pure type* $|T|$ defined by induction from $|\tau| := \tau$ and $|\{\tau \mid \varphi\}| := \tau$. We write $|\mathcal{E}|$ for the extension of $|{-}|$ to $\mathcal{E}$.

We derive typing judgments $\mathcal{E} \vdash M : T$ using the rules in Fig. 5 augmented with all the typing rules of the pure system (Sect. 2.1). Deduction on formulae (Sect. 2.2) enters the type system via a subtyping relation $U \preceq T$. Subtyping rules are presented in Fig. 4, where $U \simeq T$ stands for the conjunction of $U \preceq T$ and $T \preceq U$. Note that for each τ we have $\tau \simeq \{\tau \mid \mathsf{True}\}$. Subtyping is extended to typing contexts: given $\mathcal{E} = x_1 : U_1, \ldots, x_n : U_n$ and $\mathcal{E}' = x_1 : U'_1, \ldots, x_n : U'_n$, we let $\mathcal{E} \preceq \mathcal{E}'$ when $U_i \preceq U'_i$ for all $i = 1, \ldots, n$. Note that if $\mathcal{E} \vdash M : T$ is derivable then so is $|\mathcal{E}| \vdash M : |T|$.

$$\frac{}{T \preceq |T|} \qquad \frac{}{\tau \preceq \{\tau \mid \mathsf{True}\}} \qquad \frac{\psi \vdash_\tau \varphi}{\{\tau \mid \psi\} \preceq \{\tau \mid \varphi\}} \qquad \frac{T \preceq U \qquad U \preceq V}{T \preceq V}$$

$$\frac{T \preceq T' \qquad U \preceq U'}{T \times U \preceq T' \times U'} \qquad \frac{}{\{\tau \mid \varphi\} \times \{\sigma \mid \psi\} \simeq \{\tau \times \sigma \mid \langle \varphi, \psi \rangle\}} \qquad \frac{}{T \preceq T}$$

$$\frac{U' \preceq U \qquad T \preceq T'}{U \to T \preceq U' \to T'} \qquad \frac{}{\{\sigma \mid \psi\} \to \{\tau \mid \varphi\} \simeq \{\sigma \to \tau \mid \psi \Vdash\!\!\to \varphi\}}$$

Fig. 4. Subtyping.

$$\frac{(x : T) \in \mathcal{E}}{\mathcal{E} \vdash x : T} \qquad \frac{\mathcal{E}, x : U \vdash M : T}{\mathcal{E} \vdash \lambda x.M : U \to T} \qquad \frac{\mathcal{E} \vdash M : U \to T \qquad \mathcal{E} \vdash N : U}{\mathcal{E} \vdash MN : T}$$

$$\frac{\mathcal{E} \vdash M : T \qquad \mathcal{E} \vdash N : U}{\mathcal{E} \vdash \langle M, N \rangle : T \times U} \qquad \frac{\mathcal{E} \vdash M : T \times U}{\mathcal{E} \vdash \pi_1(M) : T} \qquad \frac{\mathcal{E} \vdash M : T \times U}{\mathcal{E} \vdash \pi_2(M) : U}$$

$$\frac{\begin{array}{l}|\mathcal{E}| \vdash M : \tau \\ \text{for each } i \in I, \quad \mathcal{E} \vdash M : \{\tau \mid \varphi_i\}\end{array}}{\mathcal{E} \vdash M : \{\tau \mid \bigwedge_{i \in I} \varphi_i\}} \qquad \frac{\begin{array}{l}|\mathcal{E}|, x : \sigma, |\mathcal{E}'| \vdash M : |T| \\ \text{for each } i \in I, \quad \mathcal{E}, x : \{\sigma \mid \psi_i\}, \mathcal{E}' \vdash M : T\end{array}}{\mathcal{E}, x : \{\sigma \mid \bigvee_{i \in I} \psi_i\}, \mathcal{E}' \vdash M : T}$$

$$\frac{\mathcal{E}' \preceq \mathcal{E} \quad T \preceq T' \quad \mathcal{E} \vdash M : T}{\mathcal{E}' \vdash M : T'} \qquad \frac{\mathcal{E} \vdash \mathsf{fix}\, x.M : \{\tau \mid \psi\} \quad \mathcal{E}, x : \{\tau \mid \psi\} \vdash M : \{\tau \mid \varphi\}}{\mathcal{E} \vdash \mathsf{fix}\, x.M : \{\tau \mid \varphi\}} \ (\varphi, \psi \in \mathcal{L}_\wedge)$$

$$\frac{\mathcal{E} \vdash M : \{\tau_1 \times \tau_2 \mid [\pi_i]\varphi\}}{\mathcal{E} \vdash \pi_i(M) : \{\tau_i \mid \varphi\}} \ (i = 1, 2) \qquad \frac{\mathcal{E} \vdash M_i : \{\tau_i \mid \varphi\} \qquad \mathcal{E} \vdash M_{3-i} : \tau_{3-i}}{\mathcal{E} \vdash \langle M_1, M_2 \rangle : \{\tau_1 \times \tau_2 \mid [\pi_i]\varphi\}} \ (i = 1, 2)$$

$$\frac{}{\mathcal{E} \vdash a : \{A \mid [a]\}} \qquad \frac{\mathcal{E} \vdash M : \{A \mid [b]\} \qquad \mathcal{E} \vdash N_b : T \qquad \text{for each } a \in A, \quad |\mathcal{E}| \vdash N_a : |T|}{\mathcal{E} \vdash \mathsf{case}\ M\ [a \mapsto N_a \mid a \in A] : T}$$

$$\frac{\mathcal{E} \vdash M : \{\tau[\mathsf{rec}\,\alpha.\tau/\alpha] \mid \varphi\}}{\mathcal{E} \vdash \mathsf{fold}(M) : \{\mathsf{rec}\,\alpha.\tau \mid [\mathsf{fold}]\varphi\}} \qquad \frac{\mathcal{E} \vdash M : \{\mathsf{rec}\,\alpha.\tau \mid [\mathsf{fold}]\varphi\}}{\mathcal{E} \vdash \mathsf{unfold}(M) : \{\tau[\mathsf{rec}\,\alpha.\tau/\alpha] \mid \varphi\}}$$

Fig. 5. Typing with refinement types.

The rules in Figs. 5 and 4 are direct adaptations of those in [1,6,18]. In particular, the rule for fix (in which $\varphi, \psi \in \mathcal{L}_\wedge(\tau)$) comes from [1].

Example 10. The following rules are derived using the last rule in Fig. 4.

$$\frac{\mathcal{E}, x : \{\sigma \mid \psi\} \vdash M : \{\tau \mid \varphi\}}{\mathcal{E} \vdash \lambda x.M : \{\sigma \to \tau \mid \psi \Vdash\!\!\to \varphi\}} \qquad \frac{\mathcal{E} \vdash M : \{\sigma \to \tau \mid \psi \Vdash\!\!\to \varphi\} \quad \mathcal{E} \vdash N : \{\sigma \mid \psi\}}{\mathcal{E} \vdash MN : \{\tau \mid \varphi\}}$$

Lemma 1. *For each type T, there is a $\varphi \in \mathcal{L}(|T|)$ such that $T \simeq \{|T| \mid \varphi\}$.*

Our goal is to devise extensions of this type system which are sound and complete w.r.t. the usual Scott semantics, the sense that given $\vdash M : \tau$,

$$\vdash M : \{\tau \mid \varphi\} \quad \text{if, and only if,} \quad \varphi \text{ holds on } [\![M]\!] \text{ in the Scott semantics.}$$

The Scott semantics is recalled in Sect. 3, while Sect. 4 discusses completeness. In particular, all typing judgments in Table 2 (Example 9) will be derivable. Those for filter and bft improve on [18] (see Example 13).

3 Semantics

Scott Domains. We shall interpret pure types as Scott domains and terms as Scott-continuous functions. We mostly use the terminology of [3, §1]. A *dcpo* is a poset with all directed suprema. A *cpo* is dcpo with a least element (often denoted $\bot$). A function between dcpos is *Scott-continuous* if it preserves the order (i.e. is monotone) as well as directed suprema. A Scott-continuous function is *strict* if it preserves least elements.

Definition 3 (Scott Domain). *A* Scott domain *is a bounded-complete algebraic cpo.* **Scott** *is the category of Scott domains and Scott-continuous functions.*

Recall that a cpo X is bounded-complete if any two $x, y \in X$ have a sup (or *least* upper bound) $x \vee y \in X$ whenever they have an upper bound in X.

An element x of a dcpo X is *finite* if for all directed $D \subseteq X$ such that $x \leq \bigvee D$, we have $d \in \downarrow D$ (i.e. $x \leq d$ for some $d \in D$).[3] Note that $\bot$ is always finite, and that if $d, d' \in X$ are finite, then $d \vee d'$ is finite whenever it exists. A dcpo X is *algebraic* if for each $x \in X$, the set $\{d \in X \mid d \text{ finite and } \leq x\}$ is directed and has sup x.

The category **Scott** is Cartesian-closed (see e.g. [2, Corollary 4.1.6]).

Semantics of the Pure System. Typed terms $\mathcal{E} \vdash M : \tau$ of the pure system (Sect. 2.1) are interpreted as morphisms $[\![M]\!] \colon [\![\mathcal{E}]\!] \to [\![\tau]\!]$ in **Scott**, where $[\![\mathcal{E}]\!] = \prod_{i=1}^{n} [\![\sigma_i]\!]$ when $\mathcal{E} = x_1 : \sigma_1, \ldots, x_n : \sigma_n$. This is well-known.

Base types $A \in \mathcal{B}$ are interpreted as *flat domains* $[\![A]\!] := A_\bot$, where $A_\bot$ is $A + \{\bot\}$ with A discrete. For each $a \in A$, we let $[\![a]\!] \colon \mathbf{1} \to [\![A]\!]$ be the constant map of value a. The term $\mathsf{case}\ M\ [a \mapsto N_a \mid a \in A]$ is interpreted using the strict Scott-continuous function which takes $b \in A$ and $(y_a)_a \in X^A$ to y_b.

We refer to [2,3,33] for the interpretation of recursive types $\mathsf{rec}\alpha.\tau$.[4]

Term-level fixpoints $\mathsf{fix}x.M$ are interpreted using the usual fixpoint combinators $\mathsf{Y} \colon (X \to X) \to X$ taking $f \colon X \to X$ to $\mathsf{Y}(f) := \bigvee_{n \in \mathbb{N}} f^n(\bot)$.

Example 11. The domain $[\![\mathsf{Str}\sigma]\!]$ of streams (resp. $[\![\mathsf{Tree}\sigma]\!]$ of trees) is $[\![\sigma]\!]^K$ equipped with the pointwise order, where $K = \mathbb{N}$ (resp. $K = \mathbf{2}^*$). The finite elements are those $z \in [\![\sigma]\!]^K$ such that $z(p)$ is finite in $[\![\sigma]\!]$ for all $p \in K$, and $z(p) \neq \bot$ for at most finitely many $p \in K$.

Given $x \in [\![\mathsf{Str}\sigma]\!]$, we have $[\![\mathsf{hd}]\!](x) = x(0)$ while $[\![\mathsf{tl}]\!](x)$ is the stream taking $n \in \mathbb{N}$ to $x(n+1) \in [\![\sigma]\!]$. Moreover, $x = [\![\mathsf{Cons}]\!]([\![\mathsf{hd}]\!](x), [\![\mathsf{tl}]\!](x))$.[5]

Similarly, if $y \in [\![\mathsf{Tree}\sigma]\!]$ then $[\![\mathsf{label}]\!](y) = y(\varepsilon)$ is the root label of y, while $[\![\mathsf{left}]\!](y)$ and $[\![\mathsf{right}]\!](y)$ are the left- and right-subtrees of y, respectively.

---

[3] Finite elements are called *compact* in [3].

[4] See also [28] for details.

[5] Note that $[\![\mathsf{Str}A]\!]$ differs from the usual *Kahn domain* $A^* \cup A^\omega$ (see e.g. [35, Definition 3.7.5 and Example 5.4.4] or [10, §7.4], see also [36]).

Scott Topology. The semantics of refinement types involves some topology. We refer to e.g. [3, §1.2], [2, §2.3] or [11, §7.1]. See also [29].

Let $(X, \leq)$ be a dcpo. A set $S \subseteq X$ is *Scott-open* if S is upward-closed (if $x \in S$ and $x \leq y$ in X, then $y \in S$), and if moreover S is inaccessible by directed sups, in the sense that if $\bigvee D \in S$ with $D \subseteq X$ directed, then $D \cap S \neq \emptyset$. This equips X with a topology, called the *Scott topology*.[6] A function between dcpos is Scott-continuous precisely when it is continuous for the Scott topology.

If X is algebraic, then the Scott-opens are exactly the unions of sets of the form $\uparrow d = \{x \in X \mid d \leq x\}$, with d finite in X. Note that $\uparrow d$ is a compact subset of X when d is finite in X. If X is a Scott domain, then $\uparrow d \cap \uparrow d'$ is compact for all finite $d, d' \in X$ (by bounded-completeness, if $\uparrow d \cap \uparrow d'$ is non-empty, then $d \vee d'$ is defined, finite and such that $\uparrow(d \vee d') = \uparrow d \cap \uparrow d'$).[7]

A set $S \subseteq X$ is *saturated* if S is upward-closed, or equivalently if S is an intersection of Scott-open sets (see e.g. [12, Proposition 4.2.9]).

Semantics of Formulae. For each $\varphi \in \mathcal{L}(\tau)$ we define a set $[\![\varphi]\!] \subseteq [\![\tau]\!]$ using the following *semantic modalities*: $[\![[a]]\!] := \{a\} \subseteq [\![A]\!]$ for $A \in \mathcal{B}$ and $a \in A$, and

$$\begin{array}{rcl} S \in \mathcal{P}([\![\tau_i]\!]) & \longmapsto & [\![[\pi_i]]\!](S) \;:= \{x \in [\![\tau_1 \times \tau_2]\!] \mid \pi_i(x) \in S\} \\ S \in \mathcal{P}([\![\tau[\mathsf{rec}\alpha.\tau/\alpha]]\!]) & \longmapsto & [\![[\mathsf{fold}]]\!](S) := \{x \in [\![\mathsf{rec}\alpha.\tau]\!] \mid [\![\mathsf{unfold}]\!](x) \in S\} \\ S \in \mathcal{P}([\![\sigma]\!]),\, T \in \mathcal{P}([\![\tau]\!]) & \longmapsto & (S \Vdash\!\!\to T) \;:= \{f \in [\![\sigma \to \tau]\!] \mid \forall x \in S,\; f(x) \in T\} \end{array}$$

We let $[\![[\pi_i]\varphi]\!] := [\![[\pi_i]]\!]([\![\varphi]\!])$, $[\![[\mathsf{fold}]\varphi]\!] := [\![[\mathsf{fold}]]\!]([\![\varphi]\!])$, and $[\![\psi \Vdash\!\!\to \varphi]\!] := [\![\psi]\!] \Vdash\!\!\to [\![\varphi]\!]$. Conjunctions and disjunctions are interpreted as intersections and unions.

Example 12. Assume given *propositional variables* $p^\tau, \ldots$ for each pure type τ. If a formula $\varphi(p^\tau)$ of type τ is positive in p^τ, then it induces a monotone function on $(\mathcal{P}([\![\tau]\!]), \subseteq)$ with least and greatest fixpoints $[\![\mu p.\varphi]\!] = [\![\bigvee_{\alpha \leq |\mathcal{P}([\![\tau]\!])|} \varphi^\alpha(\mathsf{False})]\!]$ and $[\![\nu p.\varphi]\!] = [\![\bigwedge_{\alpha \leq |\mathcal{P}([\![\tau]\!])|} \varphi^\alpha(\mathsf{True})]\!]$ [13, §20]. This generalizes Examples 4, 5.

Lemmas 2, 3 below are semantic characterizations of the classes of formulae in Definition 1 (Sect. 2.2). This yields the soundness of the rule (F) in Fig. 3 (Sect. 2.2).

Lemma 2. *Given $\varphi \in \mathcal{L}_\wedge(\tau)$, if $[\![\varphi]\!] \neq \emptyset$ then $[\![\varphi]\!] = \uparrow d$ for some finite $d \in [\![\tau]\!]$. Conversely, if $d \in [\![\tau]\!]$ is finite, then $\uparrow d = [\![\varphi]\!]$ for some $\varphi \in \mathcal{L}_\wedge(\tau)$.*

Lemma 3. *A set $S \subseteq [\![\tau]\!]$ is saturated (resp. Scott-open) if, and only if, there is a formula $\varphi \in \mathcal{L}(\tau)$ (resp. $\varphi \in \mathcal{L}_{\mathcal{O}}(\tau)$) such that $S = [\![\varphi]\!]$.*

In particular, for each $\varphi \in \mathcal{L}(\tau)$ we have $[\![\varphi]\!] = [\![\psi]\!]$ for some $\psi \in \mathcal{N}(\tau)$.

Proposition 1 (Soundness of Deduction). *If $\psi \vdash \varphi$ is derivable in the basic deduction system in Fig. 3 (Sect. 2.2), then $[\![\psi]\!] \subseteq [\![\varphi]\!]$.*

---

6 Moreover, we have $x \leq y$ if, and only if, $x \in S$ implies $y \in S$ for every Scott-open S.

7 It is well-known that Scott domains are *coherent* topological spaces (see [2, Proposition 4.2.17, §4.2.3], and also [12, Definition 5.2.21] and [11, §2.3]).

Proof. We only detail the case of (F). If $[\![\psi]\!] = \emptyset$, then for all $S \subseteq [\![\tau]\!]$ we have $[\![\psi]\!] \Vdash\!\!\to S = [\![\sigma \to \tau]\!]$, and we are done since I is assumed to be non-empty.

Otherwise, we have $[\![\psi]\!] = \uparrow d$ by Lemma 2. Let $f \in [\![\sigma \to \tau]\!]$. If $\uparrow d$ is included in $f^{-1}([\![\bigvee_i \varphi_i]\!]) = \bigcup_i f^{-1}([\![\varphi_i]\!])$, then $d \in f^{-1}([\![\varphi_i]\!])$ for some i. Hence $\uparrow d \subseteq f^{-1}([\![\varphi_i]\!])$ as $f^{-1}([\![\varphi_i]\!])$ is saturated ($f^{-1}([\![\varphi_i]\!])$ is saturated since f is monotone and since $[\![\varphi_i]\!]$ is saturated by Lemma 3). □

Semantics of Refinement Types. The interpretation $[\![T]\!] \subseteq [\![|T|]\!]$ of a type T is defined as $[\![\{\tau \mid \varphi\}]\!] := [\![\varphi]\!]$, $[\![T \times U]\!] := [\![T]\!] \times [\![U]\!]$ and $[\![U \to T]\!] := [\![U]\!] \Vdash\!\!\to [\![T]\!]$.

Definition 4 (Sound Typing Judgement). *A judgment $\mathcal{E} \vdash M : T$ with $\mathcal{E} = x_1 : U_1, \dots, x_n : U_n$ is* sound *if $|\mathcal{E}| \vdash M : |T|$ is derivable and if moreover $[\![M]\!](u_1, \dots, u_n) \in [\![T]\!]$ whenever $u_i \in [\![U_i]\!]$ for all $i = 1, \dots, n$.*

The judgments in Table 2 (Example 9) are sound. Also, derivable judgments are sound.

Theorem 1 (Soundness of Typing). *If $\mathcal{E} \vdash M : T$ is derivable in the system of Sect. 2.3, then $\mathcal{E} \vdash M : T$ is sound.*

4 Completeness

The Finite Case. Since the rule (F) assumes $I \neq \emptyset$, it does not allow us to derive $(\psi \Vdash\!\!\to \mathsf{False}) \vdash \mathsf{False}$. This sequent is sound only when $[\![\psi]\!] \neq \emptyset$. In [1], Abramsky introduced *coprimeness predicates* which select those finite φ with $[\![\varphi]\!] \neq \emptyset$. We extend our basic deduction system (Fig. 3 in Sect. 2.2) with the predicate $\mathcal{C}$ and the rules in Eq. (2) below. Recall that $\langle \varphi, \psi \rangle = [\pi_1]\varphi \wedge [\pi_2]\psi$.

$$\frac{}{\mathcal{C}(\mathsf{True})} \qquad \frac{A \in \mathcal{B} \text{ and } a \in A}{\mathcal{C}([a])} \qquad \frac{\mathcal{C}(\varphi)}{\mathcal{C}([\mathsf{fold}]\varphi)} \qquad \frac{\mathcal{C}(\varphi) \quad \mathcal{C}(\psi)}{\mathcal{C}(\langle \varphi, \psi \rangle)} \qquad \frac{\mathcal{C}(\psi) \quad \psi \vdash \varphi \quad \varphi \in \mathcal{L}_\wedge}{\mathcal{C}(\varphi)}$$

$$(\mathsf{C})\frac{\mathcal{C}(\psi)}{(\psi \Vdash\!\!\to \mathsf{False}) \vdash \mathsf{False}} \qquad \frac{\begin{array}{c} I \text{ finite and } \forall i \in I,\ \mathcal{C}(\psi_i) \text{ and } \mathcal{C}(\varphi_i); \\ \forall J \subseteq I,\ \bigwedge_{j \in J} \psi_j \vdash \mathsf{False} \ \text{ or } \ \mathcal{C}\left(\bigwedge_{j \in J} \varphi_j\right) \end{array}}{\mathcal{C}\left(\bigwedge_{i \in I} (\psi_i \Vdash\!\!\to \varphi_i)\right)} \tag{2}$$

In contrast with [1,3,6], our $\mathcal{C}$ is a consistency predicate rather than a coprimeness predicate. Note that the clauses defining $\mathcal{C}$ are positive.[8]

Proposition 2. *In the extension of Fig. 3 (Sect. 2.2) with Eq. (2):*

(1) for all $\varphi, \psi \in \mathcal{L}_\wedge(\tau)$, we have $\psi \vdash_\tau \varphi$ if, and only if, $[\![\psi]\!] \subseteq [\![\varphi]\!]$;
(2) for all $\varphi \in \mathcal{L}_\wedge$, we have $\mathcal{C}(\varphi)$ if, and only if, $[\![\varphi]\!] \neq \emptyset$.

In particular, for each $\varphi \in \mathcal{L}_\wedge$, either $\mathcal{C}(\varphi)$ or $\varphi \vdash \mathsf{False}$ is derivable.

A type is *finite* if it only contains formulae $\varphi \in \mathcal{L}_\wedge$. A typing context $x_1 : U_1, \dots, x_n : U_n$ is finite if so are all U_i's. Completeness for finite types can be obtained from minor adaptations to [1].

[8] Compare with [6, Figure 3] and [3, Figure 10.3].

Theorem 2 (Abramsky [1]). *Assume $\mathcal{E}$ and T are finite. If $\mathcal{E} \vdash M : T$ is sound, then $\mathcal{E} \vdash M : T$ is derivable in the system of Sect. 2.3 extended with Eq.* (2).

Well-Filteredness. Following [6], completeness for types with infinitary formulae relies on the fact that Scott domains are *well-filtered* spaces. The latter is stated in [2, Corollary 7.1.11] and [12, Proposition 8.3.5] as a consequence of the Hofmann-Mislove (or Scott-open filter) Theorem. It can also be obtained from [11, Theorem 7.38]. A subset F of a poset P is *filtering* if F is directed in P^{op}.

Proposition 3 (Well-Filteredness). *Let X be an algebraic dcpo,*[9] *and let $\mathcal{F}$ be a set of compact saturated subsets of X. If $\mathcal{F}$ is filtering in $\mathcal{P}(X)$ and $\bigcap \mathcal{F} \subseteq S$ for some Scott-open S, then $Q \subseteq S$ for some $Q \in \mathcal{F}$.*

Proposition 3 yields the soundness of the following deduction rule.

$$(\mathsf{WF})\ \frac{\text{for all } i \in I,\ \psi_i \in \mathcal{L}_\wedge(\sigma) \qquad \varphi \in \mathcal{L}_{\mathcal{O}}(\tau)}{\left(\bigwedge_{i \in I} \psi_i\right) \Vdash\!\!\!\rightarrow \varphi \vdash \bigvee_{J \subseteq I,\ J \text{ finite}} \left(\left(\bigwedge_{j \in J} \psi_j\right) \Vdash\!\!\!\rightarrow \varphi\right)}$$

Lemma 4. *The rule* (WF) *is sound.*

Main Results. Theorem 3 below gives sufficient conditions for the completeness of the system in Sect. 2.3 extended with Eq. (2). This relies on Well-Filteredness (Proposition 3), but does not use the rule (WF). In Sect. 5, we discuss why it might be useful for future work to avoid that rule. Proofs of Lemma 5 and Theorem 3 are given in Appendix A.2.

Lemma 5. *Given $\varphi, \psi \in \mathcal{N}(\tau)$, if $[\![\psi]\!] \subseteq [\![\varphi]\!]$, then $\psi \vdash_\tau \varphi$ is derivable in the extension of Fig. 3 (Sect. 2.2) with Eq.* (2).

Definition 5. *A type is* normal *if it is pure or $\{\tau \mid \varphi\}$ with $\varphi \in \mathcal{N}(\tau)$. A typing context $x_1 : U_1, \ldots, x_n : U_n$ is* normal *if so are all U_i's.*

The first-order over normal forms *(*fonf*) types are generated by the grammar*

$$T \ ::= \ U \ \mid \ T \times T \ \mid \ U \to T$$

with U normal. A judgment $\mathcal{E} \vdash M : T$ is normal *if $\mathcal{E}$ is normal and T is fonf.*

We shall see that if $\mathcal{E} \vdash M : T$ is sound and normal, then it is derivable. The idea is to reduce to the finite case (Theorem 2) by using Proposition 3, but without using the rule (WF). We first show that T can be assumed to be normal.

[9] More generally, this result holds for any sober space X (with S open in X).

To each normal judgment $\mathcal{E} \vdash M : T$ we associate a set of normal judgments $\eta(\mathcal{E} \vdash M : T)$. We let $\eta(\mathcal{E} \vdash M : T) := \{\mathcal{E} \vdash M : T\}$ if T is normal, and

$$\begin{array}{rcl} \eta(\mathcal{E} \vdash M : T_1 \times T_2) & := & \eta(\mathcal{E} \vdash \pi_1 M : T_1) \cup \eta(\mathcal{E} \vdash \pi_2 M : T_2) \\ \eta(\mathcal{E} \vdash M : U \to T) & := & \eta(\mathcal{E}, x : U \vdash Mx : T) \end{array}$$

Note that for each $(\mathcal{E}' \vdash M' : T') \in \eta(\mathcal{E} \vdash M : T)$, the type T' is normal.

Proposition 4. *A normal judgment $\mathcal{E} \vdash M : T$ is sound (resp. derivable) if, and only if, so are all $(\mathcal{E}' \vdash M' : T') \in \eta(\mathcal{E} \vdash M : T)$.*

Theorem 3 (Main Result). *If $\mathcal{E} \vdash M : T$ is sound and normal then $\mathcal{E} \vdash M : T$ is derivable in the system of Sect. 2.3 extended with Eq.* (2).

Example 13. Using Examples 6 and 7, the judgments for filter, diag and bft in Table 2 (Example 9) can be assumed to be normal whenever so is φ. Hence our Main Theorem 3 applies and these judgments are derivable in the system of Sect. 2.3 extended with Eq. (2), but without the rule (WF). This improves on [18], which does not handle filter, and which handles bft only when $\triangle$ is $\forall\Box$.

As for map, one has to assume that $\psi \in \mathcal{L}_\wedge$ (in addition to $\varphi \in \mathcal{N}$).

The General Case. Using (WF) and Example 6, any formula is *provably* equivalent to a $\psi \in \mathcal{N}$. This yields the completeness result of Bonsangue & Kok [6].

Lemma 6. *For each $\varphi \in \mathcal{L}(\tau)$, there is a $\psi \in \mathcal{N}(\tau)$ such that $\varphi \dashv\vdash \psi$ in the extension of Fig. 3 (Sect. 2.2) with Eq.* (2) *and* (WF).

Corollary 1 (Bonsangue & Kok [6]). *If $\mathcal{E} \vdash M : T$ is sound then $\mathcal{E} \vdash M : T$ is derivable in the system of Sect. 2.3 extended with Eq.* (2) *and* (WF).

5 Future Work

We think of the present infinitary system as an intermediary between denotational semantics and finitary type systems in the style of [18]. In the latter, the logic uses fixpoints in the spirit of the modal μ-calculus (cf. Example 12). When fixpoints are *alternation-free*[10] (which includes LTL on Str$A$ and CTL on Tree$A$), their semantics can computed by iteration up to ω. In order to reason syntactically over (finite) unfoldings of alternation-free fixpoints, the system of [18] uses a term language over natural numbers (with quantifications over these).

We target a similar finitarization of our system, in which alternation-free fixpoints $\mu p.\varphi(p)$ and $\nu p.\varphi(p)$ would be seen as $(\exists k)\varphi^k(\mathsf{False})$ and $(\forall k)\varphi^k(\mathsf{True})$. Rules (WF) and (D) may turn out to be problematic. Our Main Theorem 3 shows that (WF) is not needed in an interesting range of cases. On the other hand,

[10] This corresponds to "alternation depth 1" in [8, §2.2 & §4.1]. See also [7, §7] and [30].

in view of Example 7 we think rule (D) could be handled (under appropriate assumptions) using enough fresh Skolem symbols, as in

$$\frac{(\forall k)\psi(k, f(k)) \ \vdash \ \varphi}{(\forall k)(\exists \ell)\psi(k, \ell) \ \vdash \ \varphi} \qquad \frac{\psi \ \vdash \ (\exists k)\varphi(k, f(k))}{\psi \ \vdash \ (\exists k)(\forall \ell)\varphi(k, \ell)} \qquad (f \text{ fresh function symbol})$$

Further, we expect to handle alternation-free modal μ-properties on (finitary) polynomial types, thus targeting a system which as a whole would be based on FPC. But polynomial types involve sums, and sums are not universal in **Scott**.[11] We think of working with Call-By-Push-Value (CBPV) [22,23] for the usual adjunction between dcpos and cpos with strict functions. In the long run, it would be nice if this basis could extend to enriched models of CBPV, so as to handle further computational effects. Print and global store are particularly relevant, as an important trend in proving temporal properties considers programs generating streams of events. Major works in this line include [15,16,21,24,31,32,34]. In contrast with ours, these approaches are based on trace semantics of syntactic expressions rather than denotational domains.[12]

In a different direction, we think the approach of this paper could extend to linear types [17,25,37], possibly relying on the categorical study of [9].

Acknowledgments. We thank the anonymous referees for constructive comments which have hopefully helped to improve the presentation of the paper. Research supported by the ANR project QuaReMe (ANR-20-CE48-0005).

A Additional Material

Figure 6 gathers all rules of the pure calculus.

$$\frac{(x : \tau) \in \mathcal{E}}{\mathcal{E} \vdash x : \tau} \qquad \frac{\mathcal{E}, x : \sigma \vdash M : \tau}{\mathcal{E} \vdash \lambda x.M : \sigma \to \tau} \qquad \frac{\mathcal{E} \vdash M : \sigma \to \tau \qquad \mathcal{E} \vdash N : \sigma}{\mathcal{E} \vdash MN : \tau}$$

$$\frac{\mathcal{E} \vdash M : \tau \qquad \mathcal{E} \vdash N : \sigma}{\mathcal{E} \vdash \langle M, N \rangle : \tau \times \sigma} \qquad \frac{\mathcal{E} \vdash M : \tau \times \sigma}{\mathcal{E} \vdash \pi_1(M) : \tau} \qquad \frac{\mathcal{E} \vdash M : \tau \times \sigma}{\mathcal{E} \vdash \pi_2(M) : \sigma}$$

$$\frac{\mathcal{E}, x : \tau \vdash M : \tau}{\mathcal{E} \vdash \mathsf{fix}\, x.M : \tau} \qquad \frac{\mathcal{E} \vdash M : \tau[\mathsf{rec}\, \alpha.\tau/\alpha]}{\mathcal{E} \vdash \mathsf{fold}(M) : \mathsf{rec}\, \alpha.\tau} \qquad \frac{\mathcal{E} \vdash M : \mathsf{rec}\, \alpha.\tau}{\mathcal{E} \vdash \mathsf{unfold}(M) : \tau[\mathsf{rec}\, \alpha.\tau/\alpha]}$$

$$\frac{}{\mathcal{E} \vdash a : A}\ (A \in \mathcal{B} \text{ and } a \in A) \qquad \frac{\mathcal{E} \vdash M : A \qquad \text{for each } a \in A,\ \ \mathcal{E} \vdash N_a : \tau}{\mathcal{E} \vdash \mathsf{case}\ M\ [a \mapsto N_a \mid a \in A] : \tau}$$

Fig. 6. Typing Rules of the Pure Calculus.

[11] See e.g. [3, Exercise 6.1.10].

[12] See e.g. [24, Theorem 4.1 (and Fig. 6)] or [31, Theorem 1 (and Definition 20 from the full version)].

A.1 Well-Filteredness

A give a proof of Lemma 4 in order to illustrate Proposition 3 in a simple case.

Lemma 4. *The rule* (WF) *is sound.*

Proof. We shall apply Proposition 3 to the Scott domain $[\![\sigma]\!]$. Let $f \in [\![\sigma \to \tau]\!]$ such that $[\![\bigwedge_{i\in I} \psi_i]\!] \subseteq f^{-1}([\![\varphi]\!])$. Note that $f^{-1}([\![\varphi]\!])$ is Scott-open since f is Scott-continuous while $[\![\varphi]\!]$ is Scott-open by Lemma 3.

Let $\mathcal{F}$ be the set of all $[\![\bigwedge_{j\in J} \psi_j]\!]$, where J ranges over all finite subsets of I. We check the assumptions of Proposition 3.

- First, $\mathcal{F}$ is filtering since it is non-empty (as $\emptyset$ is a finite subset of I) and since given $[\![\bigwedge_{j\in J} \psi_j]\!]$ and $[\![\bigwedge_{k\in K} \psi_k]\!]$ in $\mathcal{F}$, we have $[\![\bigwedge_{\ell\in J\cup K} \psi_\ell]\!] \in \mathcal{F}$ with $[\![\bigwedge_{\ell\in J\cup K} \psi_\ell]\!] \subseteq [\![\bigwedge_{j\in J} \psi_j]\!], [\![\bigwedge_{k\in K} \psi_k]\!]$.
- Second, it follows from Lemmas 2 and 3 that $\mathcal{F}$ consists of compacts saturated subsets of $[\![\sigma]\!]$.
- Third, we have

$$\begin{aligned}[\![\textstyle\bigwedge_{i\in I} \psi_i]\!] &= \textstyle\bigcap_{i\in I}[\![\psi_i]\!] \\ &= \textstyle\bigcap_{J\subseteq_{\text{fin}} I} \bigcap_{j\in J}[\![\psi_j]\!] \\ &= \textstyle\bigcap_{J\subseteq_{\text{fin}} I}[\![\bigwedge_{j\in J} \psi_j]\!] \\ &= \textstyle\bigcap \mathcal{F}\end{aligned}$$

Now we are done since by Proposition 3 there is some $[\![\bigwedge_{j\in J} \psi_j]\!] \in \mathcal{F}$ such that $[\![\bigwedge_{j\in J} \psi_j]\!] \subseteq f^{-1}([\![\varphi]\!])$. □

A.2 Main Results

We prove Lemma 5 and our Main Theorem 3.

Lemma 5. *Given $\varphi, \psi \in \mathcal{N}(\tau)$, if $[\![\psi]\!] \subseteq [\![\varphi]\!]$, then $\psi \vdash_\tau \varphi$ is derivable in the extension of Fig. 3 (Sect. 2.2) with Eq.* (2).

Proof. The general strategy is to reduce to the finite case (Proposition 2), by using Proposition 3, but without using the rule (WF).

Let $\varphi, \psi \in \mathcal{N}(\tau)$ such that $[\![\psi]\!] \subseteq [\![\varphi]\!]$. Since $\varphi \in \mathcal{N}(\tau)$, we have $\varphi = \bigwedge_{k\in K} \varphi_k$ with $\varphi_k \in \mathcal{L}_{\mathcal{O}}(\tau)$. Hence, for each $k \in K$ we have $[\![\psi]\!] \subseteq [\![\varphi_k]\!]$. Thanks to the right-rule for $\bigwedge$ in Fig. 3, we can therefore reduce to the case of $\varphi \in \mathcal{L}_{\mathcal{O}}(\tau)$.

We now assume $\varphi \in \mathcal{L}_{\mathcal{O}}(\tau)$, with $\varphi = \bigvee_{k\in K} \varphi_k$ and $\varphi_k \in \mathcal{L}_\wedge(\tau)$. Since $\psi \in \mathcal{N}(\tau)$, using Example 7 we can actually put ψ in $\bigvee\bigwedge$-form: we have $\psi \dashv\vdash \bigvee_{i\in I} \bigwedge_{j\in J_i} \psi_{i,j}$ with $\psi_{i,j} \in \mathcal{L}_\wedge(\tau)$. If $[\![\psi]\!] \subseteq [\![\varphi]\!]$, then for all $i \in I$ we have $[\![\psi_i]\!] \subseteq [\![\varphi]\!]$. Thanks to the left-rule for $\bigvee$ in Fig. 3, we can therefore reduce to the case where ψ is of the form $\bigwedge_{i\in I} \psi_i$ with $\psi_i \in \mathcal{L}_\wedge(\tau)$.

Assume $[\![\bigwedge_{i\in I} \psi_i]\!] \subseteq [\![\varphi]\!]$ with $\psi_i \in \mathcal{L}_\wedge(\tau)$, and with $\varphi \in \mathcal{L}_{\mathcal{O}}(\tau)$ as above. We use Proposition 3. Similarly as in the proof of Lemma 4, let $\mathcal{F}$ be the set of all $[\![\bigwedge_{j\in J} \psi_j]\!]$, where J ranges over all finite subsets of I. The assumptions of Proposition 3 are checked similarly as in the proof of Lemma 4. Again similarly as in the proof of Lemma 4, there is some finite $J \subseteq I$ such that $[\![\bigwedge_{j\in J} \psi_j]\!] \subseteq [\![\varphi]\!]$.

Since $\bigwedge_{i\in I}\psi_i \vdash \bigwedge_{j\in J}\psi_j$, we are done if we show that $\bigwedge_{j\in J}\psi_i \vdash \varphi$ is derivable. Note that $\bigwedge_{j\in J}\psi_j \in \mathcal{L}_\wedge(\tau)$ since J is finite.

Assume that $[\![\bigwedge_{j\in J}\psi_j]\!] = \emptyset$. By Proposition 2 we have $\bigwedge_{j\in J}\psi_j \vdash \mathsf{False}$, from which we get $\bigwedge_{j\in J}\psi_i \vdash \varphi$.

Otherwise, by Lemma 2 there is some finite $d \in [\![\tau]\!]$ such that $\uparrow d = [\![\bigwedge_{j\in J}\psi_j]\!]$. Hence $d \in [\![\varphi]\!]$, and there is some $k \in K$ such that $d \in [\![\varphi_k]\!]$. But this implies $[\![\bigwedge_{j\in J}\psi_j]\!] \subseteq [\![\varphi_k]\!]$, and $\bigwedge_{j\in J}\psi_j \vdash \varphi_k$ is derivable by Proposition 2. We then obtain $\bigwedge_{j\in J}\psi_i \vdash \varphi$ using the right-rule for $\bigvee$. □

We now turn to our main result (Theorem 3). Given a typing context $\mathcal{E} = x_1 : U_1, \dots, x_n : U_n$, we write $[\![\mathcal{E}]\!]$ for $[\![U_1]\!] \times \cdots \times [\![U_n]\!]$.

Theorem 3 (Main Result). *If $\mathcal{E} \vdash M : T$ is sound and normal then $\mathcal{E} \vdash M : T$ is derivable in the system of Sect. 2.3 extended with Eq.* (2).

Proof. Thanks to Proposition 4, we only have to consider the case of a normal judgment $\mathcal{E} \vdash M : T$ in which the type T is normal. The general idea of the proof is somehow similar to that of Lemma 5: we reduce to the finite case (Theorem 2), by using Proposition 3, but without using the rule (WF).

Since T is normal, it is of the form $\{\tau \mid \varphi\}$ with $\varphi \in \mathcal{N}(\tau)$. Similarly as in Lemma 5 (but using the right-rule for $\bigwedge$ in Fig. 5), we can reduce to the case of $\varphi \in \mathcal{L}_\mathcal{O}(\tau)$, with φ of the form $\bigvee_{k\in K}\varphi_k$, where $\varphi_k \in \mathcal{L}_\wedge(\tau)$.

Assume $\mathcal{E} = \mathcal{E}', x : U$. Since U is normal, it is of the form $\{\sigma \mid \psi\}$, with $\psi \in \mathcal{N}(\sigma)$. Again similarly as in Lemma 5, using Example 7 we can actually put ψ in $\bigvee\bigwedge$-form: we have $\psi \dashv\vdash \bigvee_{i\in I}\bigwedge_{j\in J_i}\psi_{i,j}$ with $\psi_{i,j} \in \mathcal{L}_\wedge(\sigma)$. For each $i \in I$, the judgment $\mathcal{E}', x : \{\sigma \mid \psi_i\} \vdash M : \{\tau \mid \varphi\}$ is sound (since so is $\mathcal{E} \vdash M : T$). Hence, using the left-rule for $\bigvee$ in Fig. 5, we can reduce to the case where ψ is a $\bigwedge$ of formulae in $\mathcal{L}_\wedge(\sigma)$.

Repeating the above for each declaration $(x : U) \in \mathcal{E}$, we can assume that $\mathcal{E}$ is of the form $x_1 : U_1, \dots, x_n : U_n$, where $U_i = \{\sigma_i \mid \psi_i\}$ with $\psi_i = \bigwedge_{j\in J_i}\psi_{i,j}$ and $\psi_{i,j} \in \mathcal{L}_\wedge(\sigma_i)$.

We shall now apply Proposition 3 to the Scott domain $[\![|\mathcal{E}|]\!]$. Note that $[\![M]\!]$ is a Scott-continuous function $[\![|\mathcal{E}|]\!] \to [\![\tau]\!]$, so that $S := [\![M]\!]^{-1}([\![\varphi]\!])$ is open in $[\![|\mathcal{E}|]\!]$ by Lemma 3. Let $\mathcal{F}$ consist of all the

$$[\![\textstyle\bigwedge_{\ell\in L_1}\psi_{1,\ell}]\!] \times \cdots \times [\![\textstyle\bigwedge_{\ell\in L_n}\psi_{n,\ell}]\!]$$

where $L_1, \dots, L_n$ range over all finite subsets of $J_1, \dots, J_n$, respectively. It is easy to see that $\mathcal{F}$ and S meet the assumptions of Proposition 3, namely that $\mathcal{F}$ is a filtering family of compact saturated subsets of $[\![|\mathcal{E}|]\!]$ such that $\bigcap\mathcal{F} \subseteq S$.

Hence Proposition 3 applies, and there are finite $L_1 \subseteq J_1, \dots, L_n \subseteq J_n$ s.t.

$$[\![\textstyle\bigwedge_{j\in L_1}\psi_{1,j}]\!] \times \cdots \times [\![\textstyle\bigwedge_{j\in L_n}\psi_{n,j}]\!] \subseteq S$$

Using subtyping, we can therefore reduce to the sound judgment

$$x_1 : \left\{\sigma_1 \;\middle|\; \textstyle\bigwedge_{j\in L_1}\psi_{1,j}\right\}, \dots, x_n : \left\{\sigma_n \;\middle|\; \textstyle\bigwedge_{j\in L_n}\psi_{n,j}\right\} \vdash M : \{\tau \mid \varphi\}$$

Assume that for some i we have $[\![\bigwedge_{j\in L_i} \psi_{i,j}]\!] = \emptyset$. Then Proposition 2 yields $\bigwedge_{j\in L_i} \psi_{i,j} \vdash \mathsf{False}$ and we can conclude using the left-rule for $\bigvee$ in Fig. 5.

Otherwise, by Lemma 2 for each i there is some finite $e_i \in [\![\sigma_i]\!]$ such that $\uparrow e_i = [\![\bigwedge_{j\in L_i} \psi_{i,j}]\!]$. Recall that $\varphi = \bigvee_{k\in K} \varphi_k$ with $\varphi_k \in \mathcal{L}_\wedge(\tau)$. We have

$$\uparrow(e_1,\dots,e_n) = [\![\textstyle\bigwedge_{j\in L_1} \psi_{1,j}]\!] \times \cdots \times [\![\textstyle\bigwedge_{j\in L_n} \psi_{n,j}]\!] \subseteq \textstyle\bigcup_{k\in K}[\![M]\!]^{-1}([\![\varphi_k]\!])$$

Hence, for some $k \in K$ the judgment

$$x_1 : \left\{\sigma_1 \;\middle|\; \textstyle\bigwedge_{j\in L_1} \psi_{1,j}\right\}, \dots, x_n : \left\{\sigma_n \;\middle|\; \textstyle\bigwedge_{j\in L_n} \psi_{n,j}\right\} \vdash M : \{\tau \mid \varphi_k\}$$

is sound. We can now conclude by Theorem 2 and subtyping. □

References

1. Abramsky, S.: Domain theory in logical form. Ann. Pure Appl. Log. **51**(1–2), 1–77 (1991). https://doi.org/10.1016/0168-0072(91)90065-T
2. Abramsky, S., Jung, A.: Domain theory. In: Abramsky, S., Gabbay, D., T.S.E., M. (eds.) Handbook of Logic in Computer Science, chap. 1. Clarendon Press, Oxford (1995)
3. Amadio, R.M., Curien, P.L.: Domains and Lambda-Calculi. Cambridge Tracts in Theoretical Computer Science. Cambridge University Press (1998)
4. Baier, C., Katoen, J.P.: Principles of Model Checking. The MIT Press (2008)
5. Berger, U., Matthes, R., Setzer, A.: Martin Hofmann's case for non-strictly positive data types. In: Dybjer, P., Espírito Santo, J., Pinto, L. (eds.) Proceedings of TYPES 2018, Leibniz International Proceedings in Informatics (LIPIcs), vol. 130, pp. 1:1–1:22. Schloss Dagstuhl - Leibniz-Zentrum fuer Informatik (2019). https://doi.org/10.4230/LIPIcs.TYPES.2018.1
6. Bonsangue, M.M., Kok, J.N.: Infinite intersection types. Inf. Comput. **186**(2), 285–318 (2003). https://doi.org/10.1016/S0890-5401(03)00143-3
7. Bradfield, J., Stirling, C.: Modal mu-calculi. In: Blackburn, P., Van Benthem, J., Wolter, F. (eds.) Handbook of Modal Logic. Studies in Logic and Practical Reasoning, vol. 3, pp. 721–756. Elsevier (2007). https://doi.org/10.1016/S1570-2464(07)80015-2
8. Bradfield, J.C., Walukiewicz, I.: The mu-calculus and model checking. In: Clarke, E.M., Henzinger, T.A., Veith, H., Bloem, R. (eds.) Handbook of Model Checking, pp. 871–919. Springer, Cham (2018)
9. Bunge, M., Funk, J.: Singular Coverings of Toposes. Lecture Notes in Mathematics, vol. 1890. Springer, Heidelberg (2006)
10. Dickmann, M., Schwartz, N., Tressl, M.: Spectral Spaces. New Mathematical Monographs. Cambridge University Press, Cambridge (2019). https://doi.org/10.1017/9781316543870
11. Gehrke, M., van Gool, S.: Topological Duality for Distributive Lattices: Theory and Applications. Cambridge Tracts in Theoretical Computer Science. Cambridge University Press, Cambridge (2024)

12. Goubault-Larrecq, J.: Non-Hausdorff Topology and Domain Theory: Selected Topics in Point-Set Topology. New Mathematical Monographs, Cambridge University Press, Cambridge (2013). https://doi.org/10.1017/CBO9781139524438
13. Grädel, E., Thomas, W., Wilke, T. (eds.): Automata, Logics, and Infinite Games: A Guide to Current Research. LNCS, vol. 2500. Springer, Cham (2002)
14. Hodkinson, I., Reynolds, M.: Temporal logic. In: Blackburn, P., Van Benthem, J., Wolter, F. (eds.) Handbook of Modal Logic, Studies in Logic and Practical Reasoning, vol. 3, pp. 655–720. Elsevier (2007). https://doi.org/10.1016/S1570-2464(07)80014-0
15. Hofmann, M., Chen, W.: Abstract interpretation from Büchi automata. In: Henzinger, T.A., Miller, D. (eds.) Joint Meeting of the Twenty-Third EACSL Annual Conference on Computer Science Logic (CSL) and the Twenty-Ninth Annual ACM/IEEE Symposium on Logic in Computer Science (LICS), CSL-LICS 2014, Vienna, Austria, 14–18 July 2014, pp. 51:1–51:10. ACM (2014). https://doi.org/10.1145/2603088.2603127
16. Hofmann, M., Ledent, J.: A cartesian-closed category for higher-order model checking. In: 32nd Annual ACM/IEEE Symposium on Logic in Computer Science, LICS 2017, Reykjavik, Iceland, 20–23 June 2017, pp. 1–12. IEEE Computer Society (2017). https://doi.org/10.1109/LICS.2017.8005120
17. Huth, M., Jung, A., Keimel, K.: Linear types and approximation. Math. Struct. Comput. Sci. **10**(6), 719–745 (2000)
18. Jaber, G., Riba, C.: Temporal refinements for guarded recursive types. In: Yoshida, N. (ed.) Proceedins of ESOP 2021. Lecture Notes in Computer Science, vol. 12648, pp. 548–578. Springer, Cham (2021). https://doi.org/10.1007/978-3-030-72019-3_20
19. Johnstone, P.: Stone Spaces. Cambridge Studies in Advanced Mathematics. Cambridge University Press (1982)
20. Kobayashi, N., Tabuchi, N., Unno, H.: Higher-order multi-parameter tree transducers and recursion schemes for program verification. In: POPL 2010: Proceedings of the 37th Annual ACM SIGPLAN-SIGACT Symposium on Principles of Programming Languages, pp. 495–508. Association for Computing Machinery, New York (2010). https://doi.org/10.1145/1707801.1706355
21. Koskinen, E., Terauchi, T.: Local temporal reasoning. In: Proceedings of the Joint Meeting of the Twenty-Third EACSL Annual Conference on Computer Science Logic (CSL) and the Twenty-Ninth Annual ACM/IEEE Symposium on Logic in Computer Science (LICS). CSL-LICS 2014. Association for Computing Machinery, New York (2014). https://doi.org/10.1145/2603088.2603138
22. Levy, P.B.: Call-By-Push-Value. Semantics Structures in Computation. Springer, Dordrecht (2003). https://doi.org/10.1007/978-94-007-0954-6
23. Levy, P.B.: Call-by-push-value. ACM SIGLOG News **9**(2), 7–29 (2022). https://doi.org/10.1145/3537668.3537670
24. Nanjo, Y., Unno, H., Koskinen, E., Terauchi, T.: A fixpoint logic and dependent effects for temporal property verification. In: Proceedings of the 33rd Annual ACM/IEEE Symposium on Logic in Computer Science, LICS 2018, pp. 759–768. Association for Computing Machinery, New York (2018). https://doi.org/10.1145/3209108.3209204
25. Nygaard, M., Winskel, G.: Full abstraction for HOPLA. In: Amadio, R., Lugiez, D. (eds.) Proceedings of CONCUR 2003. Lecture Notes in Computer Science, vol. 2761, pp. 378–392. Springer, Cham (2003). https://doi.org/10.1007/978-3-540-45187-7_25

26. Pierce, B.C.: Types and Programming Languages, 1st edn. The MIT Press (2002)
27. Plotkin, G.: LCF considered as a programming language. Theor. Comput. Sci. **5**, 223–256 (1977)
28. Riba, C., Kejikian, A.: Infinitary Refinement Types for Temporal Properties in Scott Domains (2025). Full version, available on arXiv https://arxiv.org/abs/2502.11917
29. Riba, C., Stern, S.: Liveness properties in geometric logic for domain-theoretic streams. In: Proceedings of JFLA 2024 (2024). https://inria.hal.science/hal-04407194, full version available on arXiv https://arxiv.org/abs/2310.12763
30. Santocanale, L., Venema, Y.: Completeness for flat modal fixpoint logics. Ann. Pure Appl. Logic **162**(1), 55–82 (2010)
31. Sekiyama, T., Unno, H.: Temporal verification with answer-effect modification: dependent temporal type-and-effect system with delimited continuations. Proc. ACM Program. Lang. **7**(POPL) (2023). Full version available on arXiv at https://arxiv.org/abs/2207.10386
32. Skalka, C., Smith, S., Van Horn, D.: Types and trace effects of higher order programs. J. Funct. Program. **18**(2), 179–249 (2008). https://doi.org/10.1017/S0956796807006466
33. Streicher, T.: Domain-theoretic foundations of functional programming. World Scientific (2006). https://doi.org/10.1142/6284. https://www.worldscientific.com/doi/abs/10.1142/6284
34. Unno, H., Satake, Y., Terauchi, T.: Relatively complete refinement type system for verification of higher-order non-deterministic programs. Proc. ACM Program. Lang. **2**(POPL), 12:1–12:29 (2018). https://doi.org/10.1145/3158100
35. Vickers, S.: Topology via Logic. Cambridge University Press, Cambridge (1989)
36. Völzer, H., Varacca, D., Kindler, E.: Defining fairness. In: Abadi, M., de Alfaro, L. (eds.) Proceedings of CONCUR 2005. Lecture Notes in Computer Science, vol. 3653, pp. 458–472. Springer, Cham (2005). https://doi.org/10.1007/11539452_35
37. Winskel, G.: Linearity and nonlinearity in distributed computation. In: Ehrhard, T., Girard, J.Y., Ruet, P. (eds.) Linear Logic in Computer Science. London Mathematical Society Lecture Note Series. Cambridge University Press (2004)

On Tame Semantics for Interpretability Logic

Vicent Navarro Arroyo(✉) and Joost J. Joosten

Universitat de Barcelona, Barcelona, Spain
{vicent.navarro,jjoosten}@ub.edu

Abstract. We study modal logics of interpretability. These logics are propositional modal logics with a binary modality $\rhd$ and a unary modality $\Box$ that model formalised versions of relativized interpretability and provability respectively. The standard relational semantics for interpretability logics goes by the name of Veltman semantics. Veltman models have a unary accessibility relation R to model the unary $\Box$ modality and a ternary accessibility relation S to model the binary modality $\rhd$.

Models can possess wild behaviour and in a sense cannot be tree-like. In this paper we study if we can tame the complexity of the needed models by resorting to a slightly tweaked notion of semantics. We prove soundness and completeness for this new semantics which follows from the right notion of bisimulation.

The motivation for this study is rooted in a long-standing open question to determine $\mathbf{IL}(\mathsf{All})$, the interpretability logic of all reasonable arithmetical theories. In this paper we strengthen a conjecture formulated in [5] and show that the new conjecture is consistent with the literature so far.

Keywords: Interpretabilty logic · Relational semantics · Modal logic

1 Introduction

We focus on a modal language with the $\Box$ and $\rhd$ modalities, where the first one is interpreted as "provable in theory T". When T can code syntax and is of minimal strength, it can express $\Box_T(x)$, meaning x is the Gödel number of a provable sentence in T. In this setup, T can prove facts about its own provability, like $T \vdash \Box_T(p \to q) \to (\Box_T\, p \to \Box_T\, q)$ for any T-sentences p and q. The set of modal sentences provable in this way is called T's provability logic.

The modal logic GL of provability is well-studied and is the provability logic of any theory with sufficient arithmetic and the totality of the exponentiation function [6,12].

Relative interpretations generalize provability, with $p \rhd_T q$ meaning "there is a translation from T's symbols to T-formulas such that anything provable in $T + q$ is provable in $T + p$". Interpretability logics, which have a unary modality $\Box$ and a binary modality $\rhd$, correspond to theories' interpretability relations, with $\Box_T$ and $\rhd_T$ as their interpretations.

D. Kozen and R. de Queiroz (Eds.): WoLLIC 2025, LNCS 15942, pp. 194–210, 2026.
https://doi.org/10.1007/978-3-031-99536-1_12

Interpretability logics are less stable than provability logics. For example, the logic for full induction is **IL**M [1,11], while finitely axiomatised theories have **IL**P [15], which differs from **IL**M. For theories like Primitive Recursive Arithmetic, the interpretability logic is still unknown [2].

This raises the question of determining **IL**(All), the collection of principles provable in any theory T of some minimal strength, whether T is finitely axiomatisable, containing full induction, or by otherwise. This question of determining **IL**(All) has been open for around thirty years, though steady progress has been made [4,8,14,16]. The current state of the art is presented in [5], where a new conjecture is proposed, formulated in semantic terms. This paper aims to be a first attempt to provide syntactical (partial) characterizations of the conjecture.

2 Prerequisites

2.1 Logics

This section provides the foundational background on interpretability logics.

Definition 1 (Syntax of interpretability logic). *We denote by* $\mathsf{Form}_{\mathbf{IL}}$ *the set of formulas of the modal language of interpretability logic. This is the smallest set that contains* $\bot$, $\top$, *a countably infinite set of propositional variables, and is closed under the Boolean connectives, the unary modal operator* $\Box$, *and the binary modal operator* $\rhd$. *As usual,* $\Diamond$ *abbreviates* $\neg\Box\neg$.

To reduce parentheses, we omit outer ones and fix the following binding order: $\neg$, $\Box$, and $\Diamond$ bind strongest; $\vee$ and $\wedge$ follow; then $\rhd$; and finally $\to$. For example, $p \rhd q \to p \wedge \Box r \rhd q \wedge \Box$ r abbreviates $[(p \rhd q) \to ((p \wedge \Box r) \rhd (q \wedge \Box r))]$.

Definition 2 (Arithmetical T-realization). *Given an arithmetic theory T, an* ***arithmetical T-realization*** *maps propositional variables p to arithmetical sentences p^*. This is extended to* $\mathsf{Form}_{\mathbf{IL}}$ *by defining it to commute with boolean connectives, setting* $(A \rhd B)^* = A^* \rhd_T B^*$, *and* $(\Box A)^* = \Box_T A^*$. *An interpretability principle of T is a formula provable in T under any such realization, and the interpretability logic of T, denoted* **IL**(T), *is the set of these principles.*

Definition 3 (IL(All)). *The interpretability logic of all numberized theories,* **IL**(All), *is the set of formulas φ such that* $\forall T \forall * \; T \vdash \varphi^*$. *Here T ranges over all theories T so that* $T \rhd \mathsf{S}^1_2$. *Here,* S^1_2 *is Buss's theory of bounded arithmetic [3].*

Definition 4 (IL logic). *The logic* **IL** *is the smallest set of formulas being closed under the rules of Necessitation and of Modus Ponens, that contains all tautological formulas and all instantiations of the following axiom schemata.*

1. L1: $\Box(A \to B) \to (\Box A \to \Box B)$
2. L2: $\Box A \to \Box\Box A$
3. L3: $\Box(\Box A \to A) \to \Box A$
4. J1: $\Box(A \to B) \to A \rhd B$
5. J2: $(A \rhd B) \wedge (B \rhd C) \to A \rhd C$
6. J3: $(A \rhd C) \wedge (B \rhd C) \to A \vee B \rhd C$
7. J4: $A \rhd B \to (\Diamond A \to \Diamond B)$.
8. J5: $\Diamond A \rhd A$.

Definition 5 (Extensions of IL). *Let us consider the following principles.*

1. $\mathsf{W} := A \rhd B \to A \rhd B \wedge \Box\neg A$,
2. $\mathsf{M} := A \rhd B \to A \wedge \Box C \rhd B \wedge \Box C$,
3. $\mathsf{M}_0 := A \rhd B \to \Diamond A \wedge \Box C \rhd B \wedge \Box C$,
4. $\mathsf{P} := A \rhd B \to \Box(A \rhd B)$.

Let X *be a set of axiom schemata. We denote by* **IL**X *the smallest set of formulas closed under Modus Ponens and Necessitation, containing all tautologies, all instances of the axiom schemata of* **IL**, *and those of* X.

2.2 Relational Semantics

The semantics of interpretability logic is a Kripke-like semantics. As the signature of our language is countable, we shall only consider countable models.

Definition 6 (Proto-frame). *A* ***proto-frame*** *is a triple* $\mathcal{F} = \langle W, R, S\rangle$. *Here* W *is a nonempty countable set of worlds,* R *a binary relation on* W, *and* S *is a set of binary relations on* W *indexed by elements of* W *so that* R *is conversely-well founded (Noetherian) and* $yS_xz \to xRy \,\&\, xRz$.

Definition 7 (IL-frames). *An* ***IL-frame*** *or Veltman frame* $\mathcal{F}$ *is a proto-frame satisfying that, for every* $x, y, z \in W$, $xRy \,\&\, yRz \to xRz$, $xRy \to yS_xy$, $xRy \,\&\, yRz \to yS_xz$ *and* $uS_xv \,\&\, vS_xw \to uS_xw$.

Remark 1. *From now on, for any binary relations* Q *and* T, $xQyTz$ *stands for* $xQy \,\&\, yTz$. *We often write* $\langle W, R, \{S_x\}_{x\in W}\rangle$ *instead of* $\langle W, R, S\rangle$.

Definition 8 (IL-model). *An* ***IL-model*** *is a quadruple* $\mathcal{M} = \langle W, R, S, V\rangle$. *Here* $\langle W, R, S\rangle$ *is an* **IL**-*frame and* $V : \mathsf{Prop} \to \mathcal{P}(W)$. *We write* $w \Vdash p$ *for* $\langle w, p\rangle \in V$, *where* $\Vdash$ *is the forcing relation and, by extension:*

1. $w \Vdash \neg A$ *iff* $w \nVdash A$.
2. $w \Vdash A \to B$ *iff* $w \nVdash A$ *or* $w \Vdash B$.
3. $w \Vdash' \Box A$ *iff* $\forall v\, (wRv \to v \Vdash, A)$.
4. $w \Vdash A \rhd B$ *iff* $\forall u\, (wRu \,\&\, u \Vdash A \to \exists v\, (uS_wv \,\&\, v \Vdash B))$.

Remark 2. W *is the universe of the model and its elements are called worlds. We denote by* $x{\upharpoonright}$ *the set* $\{y \in W : xRy\}$, *and by* $R{\upharpoonright}x$ *the set* $\{\langle y, z\rangle \in R : y, z \in x{\upharpoonright}\}$.

Additionally, for the sake of brevity, we will write $xRy \Vdash A$ *and* $xS_yz \Vdash A$ *instead of* $xRy \,\&\, y \Vdash A$ *and* $xS_yz \,\&\, z \Vdash A$, *respectively.*

Definition 9 (Truth). *An* **IL**-*model* $\mathcal{M} = \langle W, R, S, V\rangle$ *validates a formula* φ, *written* $\mathcal{M} \models \varphi$, *if* $w \Vdash \varphi$ *for all* $w \in W$. *An* **IL**-*frame* $\mathcal{F} = \langle W, R, S\rangle$ *validates* φ, *denoted* $\mathcal{F} \models \varphi$, *if* $\langle \mathcal{F}, V\rangle \models \varphi$ *for every valuation* V, *where* $\langle \mathcal{F}, V\rangle$ *abbreviates the model* $\langle W, R, S, V\rangle$. *An* **IL**-*frame or* **IL**-*model validates a scheme* X *if it validates all its instances. An instance of* X *is understood as a substitution* σ *yielding* X^σ, *though we omit formal details, as the meaning is clear. Accordingly, we define* $\mathcal{F} \models \mathsf{X}$ *iff* $\forall\sigma(\mathcal{F} \models \mathsf{X}^\sigma)$; $\mathcal{M} \models \mathsf{X}$ *iff* $\forall\sigma(\mathcal{M} \models \mathsf{X}^\sigma)$. *An* **IL**-*frame (or* **IL**-*model) that validates* X *is called an* **IL**X-*frame (or* **IL**X-*model), respectively.*

Some schemes are characterised by formulas of first or higher predicate logic.

Definition 10 (Frame condition). *If* X *is a scheme of* **IL**, *a formula* $\mathcal{C}$ *in first or higher order predicate logic is a* ***frame condition*** *of* **IL**X *whenever* $\mathcal{F} \models \mathcal{C}$ *iff* $\mathcal{F} \models$ X.

Definition 11 (Horn logic). *A formula* ϕ *is an* ***atom*** *in the language* $\{R, S\}$ *if it is of the form* aRb *or* $cS_e d$. *A first order formula* φ *is a* ***Horn clause*** *if it is the universal closure of* $(\phi_1 \wedge \ldots \wedge \phi_n) \to \psi$, *where* ϕ_i *and* ψ *are atoms. An axiomatic extension* **IL**X *of* **IL** *is a* ***Horn logic*** *if the principle* X *has a frame condition expressible as a set of Horn clauses in the language* $\{R, S\}$.

Remark 3. **IL**M, **IL**P *and* **IL**M$_0$ *are Horn logics. However,* **IL**W *is not a Horn logic because its frame condition is a second order formula (see [10]).*

See Lemma 4 in Appendix A for the frame conditions of **IL**M, **IL**P and **IL**M$_0$.

3 On Intersections of ILP and ILM

The latest conjecture for **IL**(All) [5] is formulated as a convoluted form of intersection. In this section we will formulate it and show that all currently known principles in **IL**(All) indeed fall under the new conjecture.

3.1 On Theorem Intersection

IL(All) is contained both in **IL**M and in **IL**P. It is not hard to check that the principle $A \rhd \Diamond B \to \Box(A \rhd \Diamond B)$ is in the intersection of **IL**P and **IL**M. Nevertheless, in [17] it is shown to not pertain to **IL**(All). As a consequence, **IL**(All) $\neq$ **IL**M $\cap$ **IL**P. The new conjecture for **IL**(All) is formulated in terms of closure conditions on frames and the purpose of the next subsection is to take a closer look at them.

3.2 Frame Closure

For a proto-frame $\langle W, R, \{S_x\}_{x\in W}\rangle$, its closure under some condition is the smallest proto-frame $\langle W, R', \{S'_x\}_{x\in W}\rangle$ such that $R \subseteq R'$ and $S_x \subseteq S'_x$, for each x, satisfying such condition. Before explicitly defining the closures, we have to introduce the impurities.

Definition 12 (IL-impurities). *An* **IL**-*impurity on a proto-frame* $\mathcal{F}_n$ *is a tuple* I *having one of the following forms.*

1. $I_1 = \langle 1, a, b, c\rangle$ *with* $\mathcal{F} \models aRbRc \wedge \neg(aRc)$.
2. $I_2 = \langle 2, a, b\rangle$ *with* $\mathcal{F} \models aRb \wedge \neg(bS_a b)$.
3. $I_3 = \langle 3, a, b, c, d\rangle$ *with* $\mathcal{F} \models bS_a cS_a d \wedge \neg(bS_a d)$.
4. $I_4 = \langle 4, a, b, c\rangle$ *with* $\mathcal{F} \models aRbRc \wedge \neg(bS_a c)$.

Definition 13 (M-, P- and M$_0$-impurities). *An* **IL**M- , **IL**P- *or* **IL**M$_0$*-impurity on a proto-frame* $\mathcal{F}_n$ *is a tuple* I *having the following form, respectively.*

1. $I_{\mathsf{M}} = \langle 5, a, b, c, d\rangle$ *with* $\mathcal{F} \models aRbS_a cRd \wedge \neg bRd$.
2. $I_{\mathsf{P}} = \langle 6, a, b, c, d\rangle$ *with* $\mathcal{F} \models aRbRcS_a d \wedge \neg cS_b d$.
3. $I_{\mathsf{M}_0} = \langle 7, a, b, c, d, e\rangle$ *with* $\mathcal{F} \models aRbRcS_a dRe \wedge \neg bRe$.

We can extend each proto-frame to an **IL**-frame.

Lemma 1. *Let* $\mathcal{F} = \langle W, R, S\rangle$ *be a proto-frame. Then, there exists an adequate* **IL***-frame* $\mathcal{F}' = \langle W, R', S'\rangle$ *such that* $R \subseteq R'$ *and* $S \subseteq S'$.

Proof. Assume $\mathcal{F} = \langle W, R, S\rangle$ and let $<_{\mathbf{IL}}$ be the well-ordering on

$$C_{\mathbf{IL}} := (\{1\} \times W^3) \cup (\{2\} \times W^2) \cup (\{3\} \times W^4) \cup (\{4\} \times W^3)$$

induced by the occurrence order in some fixed enumeration of $C_{\mathbf{IL}}$. Define a chain starting with $\mathcal{F}_0 := \mathcal{F}$. Given some element $\mathcal{F}_n$ of the chain we define $\mathcal{F}_{n+1}$ as follows. Let I be the $<_{\mathbf{IL}}$-minimal impurity on $\mathcal{F}_n$. If I does not exists we set $\mathcal{F}_{n+1} := \mathcal{F}_n$. If there exists such I, $\mathcal{F}_{n+1}$ is set by the next cases.

(a) $\mathcal{F}_{n+1} := \langle W_n, R_n \cup \{\langle a, c\rangle\}, S_n\rangle$,
(b) $\mathcal{F}_{n+1} := \langle W_n, R_n, S_n \cup \{\langle a, b, b\rangle\}\rangle$,
(d) $\mathcal{F}_{n+1} := \langle W_n, R_n \cup \{\langle a, c\rangle\}, S_n \cup \{\langle a, b, c\rangle\}\rangle$,
(c) $\mathcal{F}_{n+1} := \langle W_n, R_n, S_n \cup \{\langle a, b, d\rangle\}\rangle$,

It is easy to prove by induction that each $\mathcal{F}_n$ is a proto-frame. We would need to check properties of proto-frames for cases (a)–(d), but we only check that $R_{n+1} := R_n \cup \{\langle a, c\rangle\}$ is Noetherian. See Lemma 5 for more details.

Now, we prove that $\mathcal{F}' := \cup_{i<\omega}\mathcal{F}_i$ is the adequate **IL**-frame that we wanted. We need to check the next properties but all of them have easy proofs bearing in mind that, for every $i < \omega$, $R_i \subseteq R_{i+1}$. The properties are: W is the domain of $\mathcal{F}'$, $R_0 \subseteq \cup_{i<\omega} R_i$, $S_0 \subseteq \cup_{i<\omega} S_i$, R is Noetherian on $\mathcal{F}'$ and $\mathcal{F}'$ satisfies all the requirements of an **IL**-frame.

We define the **IL**M-, **IL**P- and **IL**M$_0$-closures on a subclass of proto-frames.

Definition 14 (Pre-frame). *A proto-frame is a* ***pre-frame*** *if* $R^{\mathrm{tr}}; S^{\mathrm{tr}}$ *is Noetherian*[1].

Pre-frames avoid pathological cases. For an example of a pathological case check Example 2 in Appendix B.

Lemma 2 (ILM-, ILP-, ILM$_0$-closures). *Let* $\mathcal{F} = \langle W, R, S\rangle$ *be a pre-frame. Then, there exist an adequate* **IL**M*-frame* $\mathcal{F}_{\mathsf{M}}$*, an adequate* **IL**P*-frame* $\mathcal{F}_{\mathsf{P}}$ *and an adequate* **IL**M$_0$*-frame* $\mathcal{F}_{\mathsf{M}_0}$ *with* $R \subseteq R_{\mathsf{X}}$ *and* $S \subseteq S_{\mathsf{X}}$*, for* $\mathsf{X} \in \{\mathsf{M}, \mathsf{P}, \mathsf{M}_0\}$.

---

[1] R^{tr} is the transitive closure of R and ; denotes the composition operator on relations.

Proof. We focus on the **IL**M-closure. The proof is almost identical to that of Lemma 1. For pre-frames regarding the **IL**M-closure, impurities are either **IL**-impurities or M-impurities and to deal with M-impurities we define

(e) $\mathcal{F}_{n+1} := \langle W_n, R_n \cup \{\langle b, d\rangle\}, S_n\rangle$.

We should check all properties for proto-frames but we only check that, for case (e), R_{n+1} is Noetherian. See Lemma 6 for more details.

Finally, we have to check that $\mathcal{F}' := \cup_{i<\omega}\mathcal{F}_i$ is the adequate pre-frame that we wanted. All properties are proven as in Lemma 1, except for the Noetherianess of R. For more details check [7].

To construct frames from sets of relations we define the frame operator.

Definition 15. (Frame operator). *If $L = \{\phi_i\}_i$ is a set of atoms, we define the* **IL*-frame induced by*** *L, $\overline{\mathcal{F}(\bigwedge_i \phi_i)}^{\mathbf{IL}}$, as the universal closure of the smallest proto-frame that satisfies all literals. For brevity, we will write $\mathcal{F}(\bigwedge_i \phi_i)$.*

For an illustration, see Example 1 in Appendix B.

Albeit well-defined, the **IL**M-, **IL**P- and **IL**M$_0$-closures may not be **IL**-frames (see Example 3 in Appendix B). Therefore, asking what are the sufficient conditions for an **IL**M, **IL**P or **IL**M$_0$ closure to be an **IL**-frame is natural. In fact, all three share the same sufficient condition.

Lemma 3. *Given an* **IL**W *frame, its* **IL**M*,* **IL**P *and* **IL**M$_0$ *closures exist and define an* **IL**M*,* **IL**P *and* **IL**M$_0$ *frame respectively.*

Proof. For labeled proto-frames, the proofs are given in Lemma 6.1.5 and Lemma 7.1.13 of [7]. The only problem that may arise is that during closures one can generate infinite chains (of R or $S_x; R$). But infinite chains are blocked if you start out with an **IL**W frame. More details in Appendix A.

3.3 On the New Conjecture

We begin by recalling Conjecture 5.1 from [5], then introduce a new set $\mathsf{M} \cap_{\mathcal{F}} \mathsf{P}$ of Horn clauses that yields a strengthening of the conjecture. Finally, we show that the Slim and Broad series frame conditions from [5] are included in this set.

Let $\mathfrak{F}$ be a class of **IL**-frames. By **IL**$[\mathfrak{F}]$ we denote the interpretability logic corresponding to this class. That is, **IL**$[\mathfrak{F}] := \{A\colon \text{for all } \mathcal{F} \in \mathfrak{F}, \mathcal{F} \models A\}$. Let $F(x, y, z)$ denote any first or higher order formula in the language with a binary relation R and indexed binary relations S_u where the only free variables are x, y, z. We now define the following class of conditions.

$$\mathcal{C}_{\mathbf{IL}\mathsf{P}\cap_{\mathcal{S}}\mathbf{IL}\mathsf{M}} :=$$
$$\{F(x,y,z) \to xS_yz\colon \mathbf{IL}\mathsf{P} \models F(x,y,z) \to xS_yz \wedge \mathbf{IL}\mathsf{M} \models F(x,y,z) \to xS_yz\}.$$

We write **IL**P $\models F(x, y, z) \to yS_xz$ to mean that any **IL**-frame $\mathcal{F}$ satisfying **IL**P also satisfies $F(x, y, z) \to yS_xz$. Similarly for **IL**M $\models F(x, y, z) \to yS_xz$. The condition $F(x,y,z) \to xS_yz$ denotes its universal closure. The class $\mathcal{C}_{\mathbf{ILP}\cap_S\mathbf{ILM}}$ thus captures the S_x relations imposed by both **IL**M and **IL**P frame conditions. Also, we define $\mathfrak{All} := \{\mathcal{F} \models \mathbf{IL}\mathsf{W} \colon \forall C \in \mathcal{C}_{\mathbf{ILP}\cap_S\mathbf{ILM}}, \mathcal{F} \models C\}$.

The following conjecture was then formulated in [5].

Conjecture 1. **IL**(All)=**IL**[$\mathfrak{All}$].

We now define a fragment **IL**[$\mathfrak{all}$] of **IL**[$\mathfrak{All}$] that encompasses all known principles with first-order frame conditions in **IL**(All). To this end, we begin with some preliminary definitions.

Definition 16 (M ∩ P-closure). *Given a pre-frame* $\mathcal{F} = \langle W, R, S\rangle$*, its* M ∩ P-***closure*** *is* $\overline{\mathcal{F}}^{\mathsf{M}\cap\mathsf{P}} := \overline{\mathcal{F}}^{\mathsf{M}} \cap \overline{\mathcal{F}}^{\mathsf{P}} = \langle W, \overline{R}^{\mathsf{M}} \cap \overline{R}^{\mathsf{P}}, \overline{S}^{\mathsf{M}} \cap \overline{S}^{\mathsf{P}}\rangle$.

Definition 17 ($\mathsf{M} \cap_{\mathcal{F}} \mathsf{P}$-clause set). *We define the* $\mathsf{M} \cap_{\mathcal{F}} \mathsf{P}$*-clause set as* $\bigwedge_i \phi_i \to \varphi :\in \mathsf{M}\cap_{\mathcal{F}}\mathsf{P}$ *iff* $\overline{\mathcal{F}(\bigwedge_i \phi_i)}^{\mathsf{M}\cap\mathsf{P}} \models \varphi$ *whenever* $\{\phi_i\}_i \cup \{\varphi\}$ *is a set of atoms so that* $\mathcal{F}(\bigwedge_i \phi_i)$ *defines a proto-frame.*

Indeed, we can prove that $\mathsf{M} \cap_{\mathcal{F}} \mathsf{P}$ defines a fragment of **IL**[$\mathfrak{All}$]. Let us define the lower-case class of **IL**-frames $\mathfrak{all} := \{\mathcal{F} \models \mathbf{IL}\mathsf{W} \colon \forall C \in \mathsf{M} \cap_{\mathcal{F}} \mathsf{P}, \mathcal{F} \models C\}$.

Theorem 1 **IL**[$\mathfrak{all}$] $\subseteq$ **IL**[$\mathfrak{All}$].

Proof. **IL**[$\mathfrak{All}$] focuses on frame requirements of the form $F(x,y,z) \to xS_yz$, whereas elements of $\mathsf{M} \cap_{\mathcal{F}} \mathsf{P}$ allow implications like $\bigwedge_i \phi_i \to xRy$, which is equivalent to $\bigwedge_i \phi_i \to yS_xy$. Therefore, restricting to S relations poses no real issue. Moreover, any conjunction of atoms can of course be seen as a special sort of first or higher-order formula $F(x,y,z)$, which proves the inclusion.

In the following subsection, we show that the smaller set **IL**[$\mathfrak{all}$] entails all known first-order frame condition principles in **IL**(All). It remains unknown whether **IL**[$\mathfrak{all}$] $\subsetneq$ **IL**[$\mathfrak{All}$].

3.4 Two Series Are in $\mathsf{M} \cap_{\mathcal{F}} \mathsf{P}$

Definition 18 (Broad series). *For the* n*-element of the Broad series, its frame condition is* $\forall x_{n+1}x_0y_0y_{n+1}\,(\mathcal{B}_n(x_{n+1},x_0,y_0,y_{n+1}) \to \forall u\,(y_{n+1}Ru \to y_0S_{x_0}u))$. $\mathcal{B}_n$ *is set recursively as starting with* $\mathcal{B}_0(x_1,x_0,y_0,y_1) := x_1Rx_0Ry_0S_{x_1}y_1$*, then* $\mathcal{B}_{n+1}(x_{n+2},x_0,y_0,y_{n+2}) := \exists x_{n+1}, y_{n+1}\Big(x_{n+2}Rx_{n+1} \wedge \mathcal{B}_n(x_{n+1},x_0,y_0,y_{n+1}) \wedge y_{n+1}S_{x_{n+2}}y_{n+2}\Big)$. *We should denote by* B_n *the antecedent of the frame condition of the nth element of the Broad series.*

Definition 19 (Slim series). *The frame condition associated to the* n*-element of the Slim series is* $\forall w,x,y,z\,(wRxRyS_wz \to \mathcal{G}_n(x,y,z))$*, where the relation* $\mathcal{G}_n$ *is defined recursively as starting with* $\mathcal{G}_0(x,y,z) := \forall u\,(zRu \to yS_xu)$*, then* $\mathcal{G}_{n+1}(x,y,z) := \forall u\,(zRu \to yS_xu \wedge \forall v\,(uS_xv \to \mathcal{G}_n(z,u,v))$. *We should denote by* S_n *the antecedent of the frame condition of the nth element of the Slim series.*

Take a look at Figs. 2 and 3 in Appendix C for an illustration of the first elements of Broad and Slim series, respectively. Thereafter, we will proceed to prove that the frame conditions of the Broad and Slim series are elements of $\mathsf{M} \cap_{\mathcal{F}} \mathsf{P}$.

Theorem 2. *The Slim series is in* $\mathsf{M} \cap_{\mathcal{F}} \mathsf{P}$*-clause set.*

Proof. Using Lemma 7 in Appendix A we have $y_n S_{x_n} y_{n+1} \in \overline{\mathcal{F}(S_n)}^{\mathsf{M}}$ and $x_n R y_n \in \overline{\mathcal{F}(S_n)}^{\mathsf{M}}$. By the same lemma and the transitivity of S_{x_n}, we have that $y_n S_{x_n} y_{n+1} \in \overline{\mathcal{F}(S_n)}^{\mathsf{P}}$. Thus, for any $n \geq 0$, $y_n S_{x_n} y_{n+1} \in \overline{\mathcal{F}(S_n)}^{\mathsf{M} \cap \mathsf{P}}$.

Theorem 3. *The Broad series is in the* $\mathsf{M} \cap_{\mathcal{F}} \mathsf{P}$*-clause set.*

Proof. By Lemma 8 in Appendix A, we have that $x_0 R y_0 R z \in \overline{\mathcal{F}(B_n)}^{\mathsf{M}}$. Therefore, $y_0 S_{x_0} z \in \overline{\mathcal{F}(B_n)}^{\mathsf{M}}$. By the same lemma, we have that $y_n S_{x_0} y_{n+1} \in \overline{\mathcal{F}(B_n)}^{\mathsf{P}}$, then $y_{n+1} S_{x_0} z \in \overline{\mathcal{F}(B_n)}^{\mathsf{P}}$. By transitivity of S_{x_0}, $y_0 S_{x_0} z \in \overline{\mathcal{F}(B_n)}^{\mathsf{P}}$. Thus, $y_0 S_{x_0} z \in \overline{\mathcal{F}(B_n)}^{\mathsf{M} \cap \mathsf{P}}$.

4 A False Conjecture

The class $\mathbf{IL}[\mathfrak{all}]$ is defined semantically via $\mathsf{M} \cap_{\mathcal{F}} \mathsf{P}$. Knowing both the Broad and Slim series are in $\mathbf{IL}[\mathfrak{all}]$, it seems there is no simple syntactic representation.

4.1 Pencil Frames

A first attempt to get a grip on $\mathsf{M} \cap_{\mathcal{F}} \mathsf{P}$ might be to focus on those Horn clauses that imply an R-pair. For example, motivated by the fact that the frame condition of $\mathsf{M_0}$ is induced by M and by P, one may conjecture the following.

Conjecture 2. Consider an **IL**-frame $\mathcal{F} = \langle W, R, S \rangle$. Then, for any $x, y \in W$, we have that $x\overline{R}^{\mathsf{M}} y \wedge x\overline{R}^{\mathsf{P}} y \wedge \neg(xRy) \rightarrow x\overline{R}^{\mathsf{M_0}} y$.

However, the Slim hierarchy disproves the conjecture, as $\mathsf{R_1}$ implies an R-relation not implied by $\mathsf{M_0}$—e.g., $x_1 R y_2$ in $\mathcal{F}(S_1)$. One might similarly conjecture using $\mathsf{R_n}$ in place of $\mathsf{M_0}$, but this too is refuted by the following frame.

Theorem 4. *There exists an* **IL**-*frame, the Pencil frame,* $\mathcal{P}_1 = \langle W, \widetilde{R}, \widetilde{S} \rangle$, *with* $a, b \in W$ *such that* $a\overline{\widetilde{R}}^{\mathsf{M}} b \wedge a\overline{\widetilde{R}}^{\mathsf{P}} b \wedge \neg(a\widetilde{R}b) \wedge \neg(a\overline{\widetilde{R}}^{\mathsf{M_0}} b)$.

Proof. Take the **IL**-frame induced by $\{xRy_1Ry_2, xRz_1Rz_2, y_1S_xz_1, y_2S_xz_2\}$. See Fig. 4 in Appendix C for the depiction of the **IL**-frame and its closures. Note that $y_1\overline{\widetilde{R}}^{\mathsf{M}} y_2$, $y_1\overline{\widetilde{R}}^{\mathsf{P}} y_2$, and $\neg(y_1\widetilde{R}y_2)$. Also, $\neg(y_1\overline{\widetilde{R}}^{\mathsf{M_0}} y_2)$ since $\overline{\widetilde{R}}^{\mathsf{M_0}} = \widetilde{R}$.

As a matter of fact, we can generalize the Pencil frame to a family of **IL**-frames.

Definition 20 (Pencil-like frames). *We define the set* $\mathfrak{P}$ *as the set of all Pencil-like frames, that is, for any* $n \in \mathbb{N}$, $\mathcal{P}_n \in \mathfrak{P}$ *if*

$$\mathcal{P}_n \models xRy_1 \wedge \bigwedge_{1 \leq i \leq n} y_iRy_{i+1} \wedge xRz_1 \wedge \bigwedge_{1 \leq i \leq n} z_iRz_{i+1} \wedge \bigwedge_{1 \leq i \leq n} y_iS_xz_i.$$

4.2 On Confluence

A drawback with respect to modal definability of Pencil models is unnecessary confluence, where two paths from x to z_2 via different S_x transitions are possible. Confluence is known to complicate modal completeness proofs and it suggests the dotted arrow (Fig. 4d in Appendix C) cannot be a frame condition for any modal formula. While some confluence is inherent in interpretability logics (e.g., $xRyS_xz$ implies xRz), unraveling techniques show that every **IL**-model is bisimilar to a tree-like model for R relations.

Definition 21 (Tree-like IL-model). *An* **IL**-*model* $\mathcal{M} = \langle W, R, S, V\rangle$ *is* ***tree-like*** *if there exists a unique root regarding* R *(TL1) and, for every world except for the root, there is a immediate unique predecessor regarding* R_0*, where* xR_0y *iff* xRy *and* $\neg\exists z\colon xRzRy$ *(TL2).*

Definition 22 (Bisimulation between IL-models). *Two* **IL**-*models* $\mathcal{M} = \langle W, R, S, V\rangle$ *and* $\mathcal{M}' = \langle W', R', S', V'\rangle$ *are* ***bisimilar***, $\mathcal{M} \underline{\leftrightarrow} \mathcal{M}'$, *if there exists a non-empty relation* $Z \subseteq W \times W'$ *satisfying three conditions.*

1. ***In:*** *If* wZw', *then* $w \in V(p)$ *iff* $w' \in V'(p)$, $\forall p \in \mathsf{Prop}$.
2. ***Back:*** *If* wZw' *and there exists* $u \in W$ *such that* wRu, *then there exists* $u' \in W'$ *such that* $w'R'u'$ *and* uZu'. *Furthermore, if* $u'S'_{w'}v'$, *for some* $v' \in W'$, *then there exist* $v \in W$ *such that* uS_wv *and* vZv'.
3. ***Forth:*** *If* wZw' *and there exists* $u' \in W'$ *such that* $w'R'u'$, *then there exists* $u \in W$ *such that* wRu *and* uZu'. *Furthermore, if* uS_wv, *for some* $v \in W$, *then there exist* $v' \in W'$ *such that* $u'S'_{w'}v'$ *and* vZv'.

Use $\mathcal{M}, x \underline{\leftrightarrow} \mathcal{M}', x'$ *to indicate that there is a bisimulation connecting* x *and* x'. *If the models are clear, simply use* $x \underline{\leftrightarrow} x'$ *to denote that* x *and* x' *are bisimilar.*

In fact, bisimilar **IL**-models prove the same modal formulas.

Definition 23 (Invariant for bisimulation). *A modal formula* φ *is* ***invariant under bisimulation*** *if whenever* $x \underline{\leftrightarrow} x'$, *then* $x \Vdash \varphi$ *iff* $x' \Vdash \varphi$.

Theorem 5. *Modal formulas are invariant under bisimulation for* **IL**-*models.*

Proof. By induction on the structure of the formula. See Lemma 2.2 of [18].

For some types of **IL**-models we can find bisimilar models that are tree-like.

Definition 24 (Restrictions of IL-models). *If* $\mathcal{M} = \langle W, R, S, V\rangle$ *is an* **IL**-*model, then its* ***restriction*** *to* $w \in W$ *is a model* $\mathcal{M}{\upharpoonright}w = \langle W_{|w}, R_{|w}, S_{|w}, V_{|w}\rangle$ *where* $W_{|w} = w{\upharpoonright} \cup \{w\}$, $R_{|w} = \{uRv\colon u, v \in W_{|w}\}$, $S_{|w} = \{S_u\}_{u \in W_{|w}}$ *and* $V_{|w}\colon \mathsf{Prop} \to \mathcal{P}(W_{|w})$.

Theorem 6. *For each* **IL**-*model* $\mathcal{M} = \langle W, R, S, V\rangle$ *and world* $w_0 \in W$, $\mathcal{M}{\upharpoonright}w_0$ *is bisimilar to a tree-like* **IL**-*model* $\mathcal{M}' = \langle W', R', S', V'\rangle$ *that is* R-*wise, in other words, according to the relation* R.

Proof. Define $W' = \{(w_0 w_1 \dots w_n) \colon w_i \in W_{|w_0}, w_{i-1} R w_i, 0 \leq i \leq n\}$, i.e., the set of all R-paths in $\mathcal{M}\restriction w_0$. Set $R' := R_1^{\mathsf{tr}}$ where $\alpha R_1 \beta$ iff if $\alpha = (w_0 \dots w_n)$ and $w_n R_{|w_0} w_{n+1}$, then $\beta = (w_0 \dots w_{n+1})$. If $\mathsf{lt}(\alpha)$ is the last element of $\alpha \in W'$, set S'_α where $\beta S'_\alpha \gamma$ iff $\alpha R' \beta, \alpha R' \gamma$ and $\mathsf{lt}(\beta)(S_{|w_0})_{\mathsf{lt}(\alpha)} \mathsf{lt}(\gamma)$. It is easily seen that $\mathcal{F}' = \langle W', R', S' \rangle$ is an **IL**-frame. See Lemma 9 in Appendix A for more details.

Obviously, (w_0) is the root of $\mathcal{M}'$. The proof of condition (TL2) is in Lemma 10 in Appendix A. Furthermore, if $\alpha \in W'$, set $V'(\alpha) = V(\mathsf{lt}(\alpha))$.

We define the bisimulation between $\mathcal{M}\restriction w_0$ and $\mathcal{M}'$ by setting $Z \subseteq W_{|w_0} \times W'$ as $w Z \alpha$ iff $w = \mathsf{lt}(\alpha)$. We prove that Z defines a bisimulation between **IL**-models, but we only check the **Back** condition since **In** is trivial and **Forth** is analogous to **Back**. Assume $w Z w'$ with $w' = (w_0 \dots w)$. If $w R_{|w_0} v$, then, by Lemma 11, there is some $v' \in W'$ with $\mathsf{lt}(v') = v$ such that $w' R' v'$ and $v Z v'$. If $v' S'_{w'} u'$ where $\mathsf{lt}(u') = u$, then $v S_w u$ and $u Z u'$.

5 Minimal Veltman Semantics

In the previous section, we showed that every model is bisimilar to a tree-like model with respect to R. Here, we focus on frames and propose an alternative semantics that avoids certain confluences.

5.1 Reducing S Relations

We propose an alternative semantics for interpretability logics, focusing on removing many S relations for easier control, with the missing relations compensated by the truth definition of $\rhd$.

Definition 25 (Minimal Veltman frame). *Consider a non-empty countable set of worlds W, $R \subseteq W \times W$ and, for each $x \in W$, $S_x \subseteq R\restriction x \times R\restriction x$ with R transitive and Noetherian; for every $x \in W$, S_x is irreflexive and antitransitive; for every $x, y, z \in W$, $y S_x z \to \neg y R z$. Then, $\mathcal{F} = \langle W, R, \{S_x\}_{x \in W} \rangle$ is a **Minimal Veltman frame** or* MV*-frame and $\mathcal{C}^{\mathsf{MVF}}$ is the **class of*** MV***-frames**.*

Definition 26 (Minimal Veltman model). *A **Minimal Veltman model** (*MV*-model) is a tuple $\langle W, R, \{S_x\}_{x \in W}, V \rangle$, where $\langle W, R, \{S_x\}_{x \in W} \rangle$ is an* MV*-frame, and V : $\mathsf{Prop} \to \mathcal{P}(W)$ is a valuation. The forcing relation $\Vdash_{\mathsf{MV}}$ follows the standard definition for **IL**-models, except for the $\rhd$-modality:*[2]

$$\mathcal{M}, x \Vdash_{\mathsf{MV}} A \rhd B \iff \forall y (x R y \Vdash_{\mathsf{MV}} A \to \exists z\, y (R \cup S_x)^* z \Vdash_{\mathsf{MV}} B).$$

*Finally, we will denote the **class of*** MV***-models** as $\mathcal{C}^{\mathsf{MVM}}$.*

Validity for formulas and schemes in MV-models and MV-frames follows Definition 9, using $\Vdash_{\mathsf{MV}}$ and $\vDash_{\mathsf{MV}}$ for forcing and consequence, respectively.

In addition, **IL** is sound under Minimal Veltman semantics (MVS).

Theorem 7 (Soundness). **IL** $\vdash \varphi \Rightarrow \forall \mathcal{F} \in \mathcal{C}^{\mathsf{MVF}} \mathcal{F} \vDash_{\mathsf{MV}} \varphi$.

Proof. By induction on the length of the **IL**-proof of φ.

[2] Given a binary relation Z, we denote Z^* as the composition of 0 or more copies of Z. We set Z^+ as the composition of 1 or more copies of Z. In fact, $Z^+ = Z; Z^*$.

5.2 Frame Conditions

Theorem 8. *The frame conditions of* **IL**M, **IL**P *and* **IL**M$_0$ *in* MVS *are, respectively,* $xRyS_xzRu \to yRu$, $xRyRzS_xu \to zS_yu$ *and* $xRyRzS_x^*uRv \to yRv$.

Proof. We focus on the right-to-left implication of the frame condition of **IL**M. Let $\mathcal{F} = \langle W, R, S\rangle$ be a MV-frame and consider any $x \in W$ with a valuation V. Next, suppose $x \Vdash_{\mathsf{MV}} A \rhd B$ and $xRy \Vdash_{\mathsf{MV}} A \wedge \Box C$. Then, there is $z \in W$ such that $y(R \cup S_x)^*z \Vdash_{\mathsf{MV}} B$. For any $u \in W$ with zRu, we have yRu by induction on the number of S_x in $(R \cup S_x)^*$. Thus, $u \Vdash_{\mathsf{MV}} C$ and $z \Vdash_{\mathsf{MV}} \Box C$.

6 Completeness of MVS

6.1 Bisimulations Revisited

In this section we will prove that there is a bisimulation between **IL**-models and MV-models. We will use the completeness of Veltman semantics to prove the completeness of MV semantics and, as before, we wish to work with frames and not just models.

Definition 27 (Bisimulation between a ***MV*****-model and an IL-model).** *An* **IL**-*model* $\mathcal{M} = \langle W, R, S, V\rangle$ *and an* MV-*model* $\mathcal{M}' = \langle W', R', S', V'\rangle$ *are* ***bisimilar***, $\mathcal{M} \underline{\leftrightarrow} \mathcal{M}'$, *if there exists a nonempty relation* $Z \subseteq W \times W'$ *satisfying the following conditions.*

1. ***In:*** *If* wZw', *then* $w \in V(p)$ *iff* $w' \in V'(p)$, $\forall p \in \mathsf{Prop}$.
2. ***Back:*** *If* wZw' *and there exists* $u \in W$ *such that* wRu, *then there exists* $u' \in W'$ *such that* $w'R'u'$ *and* uZu'. *Furthermore, if* $u'(R' \cup S'_{w'})^*v'$, *for some* $v' \in W$, *then there exists* $v \in W$ *such that* uS_wv *and* vZv'.
3. ***Forth:*** *If* wZw' *and there exists* $u' \in W'$ *such that* $w'R'u'$, *then there exists* $u \in W$ *such that* wRu *and* uZu'. *Furthermore, if* uS_wv, *for some* $v \in W$, *then there exists* $v' \in W'$ *such that* $u'(R' \cup S'_{w'})^*v'$ *and* vZv'.

We keep the notation for bisimulation of Definition 22.

Analogously to the bisimulation between **IL**-models we have that modal formulas are invariant under bisimulation between **IL**-models and MV-models.

Theorem 9. *Modal formulas are invariant under bisimulation between* **IL**- *and* MV-*models.*

Proof. By induction on the structure of the formula.

As a matter of fact, all **IL**-models are bisimilar to a MV-model.

Theorem 10. *Each* **IL**-*model is bisimilar to a* MV-*model.*

Proof. Take Z the identity relation on the set of worlds. Define $R' = R$, $V' = V$ and uS'_xv iff $uS_xv \wedge u \neq v \wedge \neg uRv \wedge \forall w\big((uS_xwS_xv \wedge u \neq w) \to w = v\big)$.

6.2 Completeness

Finally, we would like to show that MV-semantics is complete.

Theorem 11 (Completeness). $\forall \mathcal{F} \in \mathcal{C}^{\mathsf{MVM}} \mathcal{F} \models_{\mathsf{MV}} \varphi \Rightarrow \mathbf{IL} \vdash \varphi$.

Proof. By contraposition, assume $\mathbf{IL} \nvdash \varphi$ for some formula φ. By completeness, there is an **IL**-model $\mathcal{M}$ such that $\mathcal{M}, w \nVdash \varphi$ for some world w. By Theorem 10, $\mathcal{M} \leftrightarrows \mathcal{M}'$, for some MV-model $\mathcal{M}'$, and $w \leftrightarrows w'$ for some world w' in $\mathcal{M}'$. By Theorem 9 in Appendix A, $w \Vdash \varphi$ iff $w' \Vdash_{\mathsf{MV}} \varphi$. Hence, $w' \nVdash_{\mathsf{MV}} \varphi$.

6.3 Confluence Revisited

As previously noted, avoiding confluence in frames is desirable. While not all instances can be eliminated, certain cases can, motivating the following nontrivial requirement on frames. We present the Unique Path Condition or UPath.

$$(uR^*aS_xbR^*v \wedge uR^*cS_xdR^*v) \rightarrow \langle a, b\rangle = \langle c, d\rangle. \qquad \text{(UPath)}$$

Definition 28. *A rooted* MV*-model is* ***tree-some*** *if it satisfies* (UPath).

Definition 29 (MV-bisimulation). *Two* MV*-models* $\mathcal{M} = \langle W, R, S, V\rangle$ *and* $\mathcal{M}' = \langle W', R', S', V'\rangle$ *are* MV*-**bisimilar*** *(*$\mathcal{M} \leftrightarrows_{\mathsf{MV}} \mathcal{M}'$*) if there is a nonempty relation* $Z \subseteq W \times W'$ *that satisfies the following conditions.*

1. ***In:*** *If* wZw'*, then* $w \in V(p)$ *iff* $w' \in V'(p)$*,* $\forall p \in \mathsf{Prop}$.
2. ***Back:*** *If* wZw' *and there exists* $u \in W$ *such that* wRu*, then there exists* $u' \in W'$ *such that* $w'R'u'$ *and* uZu'*. Furthermore, if* $u'(R' \cup S'_{w'})^*v'$*, for some* $v' \in W$*, then there exists* $v \in W$ *such that* $u(R' \cup S_w)^*v$ *and* vZv'.
3. ***Forth:*** *If* wZw' *and there exists* $u' \in W'$ *such that* $w'R'u'$*, then there exists* $u \in W$ *such that* wRu *and* uZu'*. Futhermore, if* $u(R' \cup S_w)^*v$*, for some* $v \in W$*, then there exists* $v' \in W'$ *such that* $u'(R' \cup S'_{w'})^*v'$ *and* vZv'.

We use notation for MV*-bisimulation similar to that of* **IL***-bisimulation.*

Of course, modal formulas are invariant under MV-bisimulation.

Theorem 12. *Modal formulas are invariant under* MV*-bisimulation.*

Proof. By induction on the structure of the formula.

Theorem 13. *For each* MV*-model* $\mathcal{M} = \langle W, R, S, V\rangle$ *and each world* $w_0 \in W$ *we have that* $\mathcal{M}{\restriction}w_0$ *is bisimilar to a tree-some* MV*-model* $\mathcal{M}' = \langle W', R', S', V'\rangle$.

Proof. W' is the set of labelled paths on $W_{|w_0}$. A path $\alpha = (w_0 w'_1 \dots w'_n)$ is labelled if, for each w'_i, either $w'_i := w_i$ iff $w_{i-1} R_{|w_0} w_i$, or $w'_i := \overline{w_i}^{w_j}$ iff $w_{i-1}(S_{|w_0})_{w_j} w_i$. Next, set $R' := R_2^{\mathrm{tr}}$ where $\alpha R_2 \beta$ iff either, if $\alpha = (w_0 w'_1 \dots w'_n)$ and $w_n R_{|w_0} w_{n+1}$ then $\beta = (w_0 w'_1 \dots w'_n w_{n+1})$, or if $\beta = (w_0 w'_1 \dots w'_n)$ then $w'_n = \overline{w_n}^{\mathsf{lt}(\alpha)}$. Here $\mathsf{lt}(\alpha)$ denotes the last element of α without the label. Next, for each $\alpha \in W'$, define $\beta S'_\alpha \gamma$ iff $\alpha R' \beta$ and $\mathsf{lt}(\beta)(S_{|w_0})_{\mathsf{lt}(\alpha)} \mathsf{lt}(\gamma)$.

By construction, $\mathcal{F}' = \langle W', R', S' \rangle$ is a MV-frame satisfying (UPath). Furthermore, for every $\alpha \in W'$, set $V'(\alpha) := V_{|w_0}(\mathsf{lt}(\alpha))$. Finally, define $Z \subseteq W_{|w_0} \times W'$ as $wZ\alpha$ iff $w = \mathsf{lt}(\alpha)$. The relation Z defines a bisimulation between $\mathcal{M}{\restriction}w_0$ and $\mathcal{M}'$.

This last theorem guarantees that we can avoid the Pencil model. However, the Slim and Broad series do work with tree-some frames.

6.4 Conclusion and Future Work

In this paper, we addressed several key topics. We began by examining the intersection of **IL**M and **IL**P, strengthening a conjecture from [5] through the definition of $\mathbf{IL}[\mathfrak{all}]$, a fragment of $\mathbf{IL}[\mathfrak{All}]$. We then demonstrated that $\mathbf{IL}[\mathfrak{all}]$ entails all known first-order frame conditions of $\mathbf{IL}(\mathsf{All})$, although it likely lacks a simple syntactic characterization. Motivated by the challenge of syntactically representing $\mathbf{IL}[\mathfrak{all}]$, we turned to the problem of unnecessary confluence, addressing it via unraveling techniques over tree-like structures. Finally, we introduced a new semantics—Minimal Veltman semantics—that mitigates certain confluences and proved its soundness and completeness using bisimulation.

In a forthcoming paper, we will explore the preservation of the M and P frame conditions under bisimulation. In particular, we will investigate whether every **IL**M- or **IL**P-model admits a bisimilar MV-model satisfying the corresponding M- or P-frame condition. We will also consider whether restricted **IL**M- or **IL**P-models can be unraveled into bisimilar tree-some MV-models that satisfy these frame conditions.

Acknowledgments. We thank Lucas Van Oudheusden Navarro for his valuable insights and questions throughout the development of this work. The paper has been funded through Spanish Ministry of Science and Innovation PID2023-149556NB-I00, Generalitat de Catalunya 2021 SGR 00348, 2022 DI 051 and ICREA Acadèmia. The referees suggested many improvements to an earlier version of this paper.

Disclosure of Interests. The authors have no competing interests to declare that are relevant to the content of this article.

Appendices

A Proofs

Lemma 4. *The frame conditions of* **IL**M, **IL**P *and* **IL**M_0 *are, respectively,* $xRyS_x zRu \to yRu$, $xRyRzS_x u \to zS_y u$ *and* $xRyRzS_x uRv \to yRv$.

Proof. See Sect. 14 of [9], Sect. 5 of [13] and Sect. 15 of [9], respectively.

Lemma 5. *Given the chain defined in Lemma 1, $R_{n+1} := R_n \cup \{\langle a, c\rangle\}$ is Noetherian.*

Proof. Suppose for a contradiction that there is an infinite sequence such that $\mathcal{F}_{n+1} \models x_0 R x_1 R \ldots$ Replace any occurrence of aRc by $aRbRc$ and leave the rest unchanged. This contradicts the fact that R is Noetherian on $\mathcal{F}_n$.

Lemma 6. *Given the chain defined in Lemma 2, $R_n := R_n \cup \{\langle b, d\rangle\}$ is Noetherian.*

Proof. Suppose for a contradiction that there exists an infinite sequence such that $\mathcal{F}_{n+1} \models x_1 R x_2 R \ldots$ Replace any occurence of bRd by $aRbS_a cRd$ and leave the rest unchanged. If there are infinitely many S_a-transitions in the new sequence we get a contradiction from the fact that $R^{\mathsf{tr}}; S^{\mathsf{tr}}$ is Noetherian on $\mathcal{F}_n$. Otherwise, we contradict with the Noetherianess of R on $\mathcal{F}_n$.

Lemma 7. *1. $\forall n \geq 0, \forall 0 \leq k \leq n$, $y_k R y_{k+1} \in \overline{\mathcal{F}(S_n)}^{\mathsf{M}}$.*
2. $\forall n \geq 0, \forall 0 \leq k \leq n$, $x_k R x_{k+1} \in \overline{\mathcal{F}(S_n)}^{\mathsf{P}}$.

Proof. By induction on $n \geq 0$.

Lemma 8. *1. $\forall n \geq 0 \forall k \leq n$ $y_{n-k} R z \in \overline{\mathcal{F}(B_n)}^{\mathsf{M}}$.*
2. $\forall n \geq 0 \forall k \leq n$ $y_k S_{x_0} y_{k+1} \in \overline{\mathcal{F}(B^*_n)}^{\mathsf{P}}$[3]*.*

Proof. By induction on $k \leq n$.

Lemma 9. *$\mathcal{F}' = \langle W', R', S'\rangle$ is an* **IL***-frame.*

Proof. We will only prove that R' is Noetherian. The rest of properties are trivial. In order to prove that R' is Noetherian it will suffice to check that R_1 is Noetherian since $R' = R_1^{\mathsf{tr}}$. For a contradiction, assume there is an infinite sequence such that $\mathcal{F}' \models \alpha^0 R_1 \alpha^1 R_1 \ldots$ If $\alpha^0 = (w_0 \ldots w_n)$, then, for every m, $\alpha^m = (w_0 \ldots w_{n+m})$ and $\mathcal{F} \models w_n R w_{n+m}$. This defines an infinite sequence $y_1, y_2, \ldots$ with $\mathcal{F} \models w_n R w_{n+1} R w_{n+2} \ldots$ Hence, we get a contradiction with the fact that R is Noetherian on $W_{|w_0}$.

Lemma 10. *The model $\mathcal{M}'$, as defined in Theorem 6, verifies condition* (TL2).

Proof. Consider $\beta \in W'$ different from (w_0) and assume $\alpha_0 R'_0 \beta$ and $\alpha_1 R'_0 \beta$. Thereby, $\alpha_0 R' \beta$ and $\neg\exists \gamma_0 \colon \alpha_0 R' \gamma_0 R' \beta$; and $\alpha_1 R' \beta$ and $\neg\exists \gamma_1 \colon \alpha_1 R' \gamma_1 R' \beta$. Then, $\alpha_0 R_1 \beta$ and $\alpha_1 R_1 \beta$. Consequently, $\beta = (w_0 w_1 \ldots w_{n+1}) = (w_0 w'_1 \ldots w'_{m+1})$ where $\alpha_0 = (w_0 w_1 \ldots w_n)$ and $\alpha_1 = (w_0 w'_1 \ldots w'_m)$, but that is only possible if $n = m$ and $w_i = w'_i$, for every $1 \leq i \leq n+1$. Thus, $\alpha_0 = \alpha_1$.

Lemma 11. *If $w R_{|w_0} v$ and $w' = (w_0 \ldots w)$, then there is some $v' \in W'$ with $w' R' v'$ and $\mathsf{It}(v') = v$.*

Proof. If v is an immediate successor of w, set $v' = (w_0 \ldots wv)$. If not, set $v' = (w_0 \ldots w u_0 \ldots u_m v)$, where $w u_0 \ldots u_m v$ is a sequence of immediate successors.

[3] $\mathcal{F}(B^*_n)$ is the subframe of $\mathcal{F}(B_n)$ without the world z. Note that $\mathcal{F}(B^*_n)$ is a subframe of $\mathcal{F}(B^*_{n+1})$ and $\overline{\mathcal{F}(B^*_n)}^{\mathsf{P}}$ is a subframe of $\overline{\mathcal{F}(B^*_{n+1})}^{\mathsf{P}}$.

B Examples

Example 1. Consider the set of atoms $L = \{xRy, yRz\}$, then the **IL**-frame induced by it is $\mathcal{F} = \langle W, R, S\rangle$ where $W = \{x, y, z\}$, $R = \{xRy, yRz, xRz\}$, $S_x = \{yS_xy, zS_xz, yS_xz\}$, $S_y = \{zS_yz\}$ and $S_z = \varnothing$.

Check Fig. 1 in Appendix C for an illustration of $\mathcal{F}$.

Example 2. Consider the proto-frame $\mathcal{F} = \langle W, R, S\rangle$ such that $W = \{\omega\} \cup \mathbb{N}$, $R := (\{w\} \times \mathbb{N}) \cup \{nR(n+1) \colon n \text{ is even}\}$; for every $n \in \mathbb{N}$, $S_n = \varnothing$ and $S_w := \{nS_w(n+1) \colon n \text{ is odd}\}$. It is easy to check that $R^{\text{tr}}; S^{\text{tr}}$ is not Noetherian and that its **IL**M-, **IL**P- and **IL**M$_0$-closures are now well-defined.

Example 3. For the **IL**M-, **IL**P- and **IL**M$_0$- closures, consider the **IL**- frames induced by $L_1 = \{xRy, yS_xz, zRu, uRy\}$, $L_2 = \{xRy, yRz, zS_xu, uRy\}$ and $L_3 = \{xRy, yRz, zS_xu, uRv, vRy\}$, respectively. Observe that none of them satisfy the **IL**W-frame condition.

C Figures

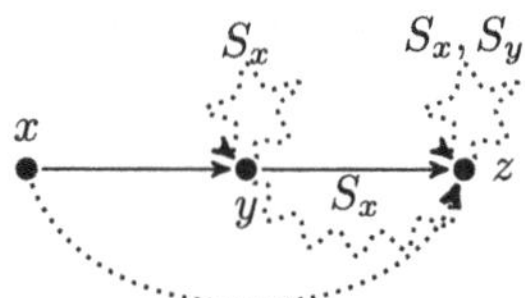

Fig. 1. **IL**-frame induced by L. The dotted arrows are the added R- and S-pairs.

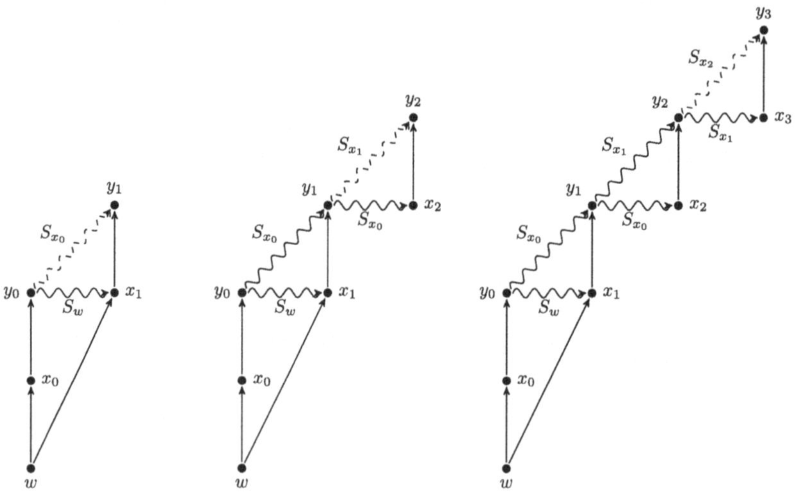

Fig. 2. From left to right we have depicted $\mathcal{F}(S_0)$ to $\mathcal{F}(S_2)$. Since $\mathcal{F}(S_{n+1})$ implies $\mathcal{F}(S_n)$ we have only depicted the content of $\mathcal{F}(S_{n+1})$ which is new w.r.t. $\mathcal{F}(S_n)$. As such we should read the pictures as: "if all un-dashed relations are as in the picture, then also the dashed relation should be present".

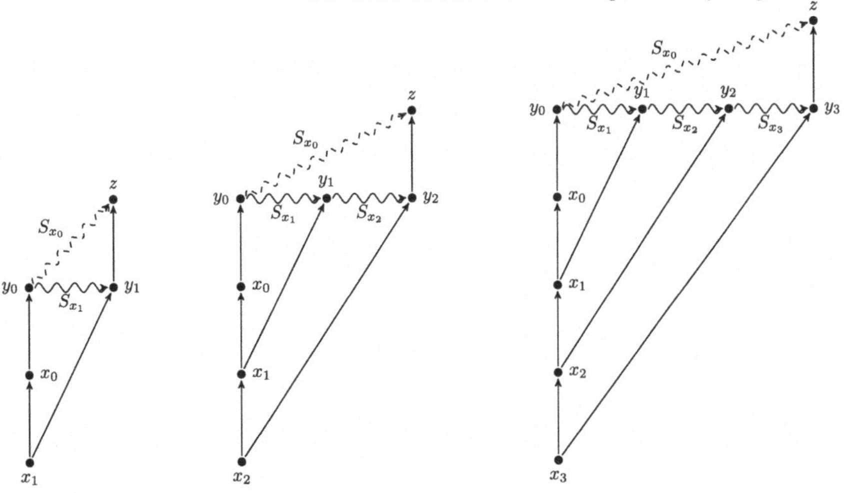

Fig. 3. From left to right we have depicted $\mathcal{F}(B_0)$ to $\mathcal{F}(B_2)$. We should read the pictures as: "if all un-dashed relations are as in the picture, then also the dashed relation should be present".

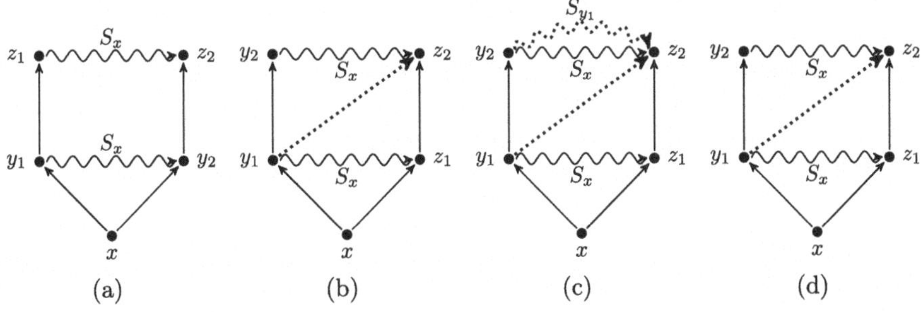

Fig. 4. (a) $\mathcal{P}_1$ (b) M-closure of $\mathcal{P}_1$ (c) P-closure of $\mathcal{P}_1$ (d) Intersection of the M and P closures of $\mathcal{P}_1$ with respect to R-relations. Dotted arrows represent the added pairs.

References

1. Berarducci, A.: The interpretability logic of peano arithmetic. J. Symb. Log. **55**(3), 1059–1089 (1990). https://doi.org/10.2307/2274474
2. Bilkova, M., Jongh, D., Joosten, J.J.: Interpretability in PRA. Ann. Pure Appl. Logic **161**(2), 128–138 (2009). https://doi.org/10.1016/j.apal.2009.05.012
3. Buss, S.: Bounded arithmetic. Bibliopolis, Napoli (1986). https://doi.org/10.2307/2274725
4. Goris, E., Joosten, J.J.: A new principle in the interpretability logic of all reasonable arithmetical theories. Logic J. IGPL **19**(1), 14–17 (2011). https://doi.org/10.1093/jigpal/jzp082
5. Goris, E., Joosten, J.J.: Two new series of principles in the interpretability logic of all reasonable arithmetical theories. J. Symb. Log. **85**(1), 1–25 (2020). https://doi.org/10.1017/jsl.2019.90

6. de Jongh, D., Jumelet, M., Montagna, F.: On the proof of Solovay's theorem. Stud. Logica. **50**, 51–69 (1991). https://doi.org/10.1007/BF00370387
7. Joosten, J.J.: Interpretability formalized. Ph.D. thesis, Utrecht University (2004). https://dspace.library.uu.nl/handle/1874/1275
8. Joosten, J.J., Visser, A.: The interpretability logic of all reasonable arithmetical theories. The new conjecture. Erkenntnis **53**(1-2), 3–26 (2000). https://doi.org/10.1023/A:1005657917054
9. Mas, J.: Interpretability logics and generalized Veltman semantics in Agda. Master's thesis, University of Barcelona (2021). https://hdl.handle.net/2445/173054
10. Mikec, L., Perkov, T., Vuković, M.: Decidability of interpretability logics $\mathbf{IL}\mathsf{M}_0$ and $\mathbf{IL}\mathsf{W}^*$. Logic J. IGPL **25**(5), 758–772 (2017). https://doi.org/10.1093/jigpal/jzx027
11. Shavrukov, V.Y.: The logic of relative interpretability over Peano arithmetic. Preprint, Steklov Mathematical Institute, Moscow (1988). (in Russian)
12. Solovay, R.M.: Provability interpretations of modal logic. Israel J. Math. **28**, 33–71 (1976). https://doi.org/10.1007/BF02757006
13. Veltman, F., De Jongh, D.: Provability logics for relative interpretability. In: Proceedings of the Summer School and Conference on Mathematical Logic (1990). https://doi.org/10.1007/978-1-4613-0609-2_3
14. Visser, A.: Preliminary notes on interpretability logic. Technical report. LGPS 29, Department of Philosophy, Utrecht University (1988). https://dspace.library.uu.nl/handle/1874/26292
15. Visser, A.: Interpretability logic. In: Petkov, P. (ed.) Mathematical Logic, Proceedings of the Heyting 1988 Summer School in Varna, Bulgaria, pp. 175–209. Plenum Press, Boston, New York (1990). https://doi.org/10.1007/978-1-4613-0609-2_13
16. Visser, A.: The formalization of interpretability. Stud. Logica. **50**(1), 81–106 (1991). https://doi.org/10.1007/BF00370389
17. Visser, A.: An overview of interpretability logic. In: Kracht, M., Rijke, M., Wansing, H. (eds.) Advances in Modal Logic 1996, pp. 307–359. CSLI Publications, Stanford, CA (1997)
18. Vrgoč, D., Vuković, M.: Bisimulations and bisimulation quotients of generalized veltman models. Logic J. IGPL **18**(6), 870–880 (2010). https://doi.org/10.1093/jigpal/jzp067

Constructive Modal Logics: Bi-nested Calculi and Bi-relational Countermodels

Han Gao(✉) and Nicola Olivetti

LIS, Aix-Marseille University, CNRS, Marseille, France
{gao.han,nicola.olivetti}@lis-lab.fr

Abstract. The logics **CK** and **WK** are two fundamental systems of constructive modal logics, which aim to provide an interpretation of modalities with an intuitionistic base. Semantics of these logics can be specified in terms of bi-relational models. We define bi-nested sequent calculi for these two systems. Our calculi are cut-free and only consist of invertible rules. Moreover, they support terminating proof-search under a suitable strategy. The main feature of the calculi is that they allow to directly construct countermodels in the bi-relational semantics from any failed proof.

Keywords: Nested sequent · Proof-search · Completeness

1 Introduction

Constructive modal logics belong to the family of intuitionistic modal logic, they are motivated by applications in computer science, including the Curry-Howard correspondence, knowledge representation, contextual reasoning [15], and more recently, game semantics [1]. The two fundamental systems are **CK** [4] and the older **WK**, where the latter is the propositional fragment of *constructive concurrent dynamic logic* [18]. The semantics of these systems can be defined in terms of bi-relational Kripke models, which include both a pre-order $\leq$ for accommodating intuitionistic propositional connectives and an accessibility relation R for modalities, without any frame condition connecting $\leq$ and R. For this reason **CK** and **WK** are considered 'more basic' or 'minimal' than well-known Fischer Servi/Simpson **IK** [5,15] which impose some confluence properties connecting the two relations.

From a proof-theoretic viewpoint, both **CK** and **WK** enjoy simple cut-free Gentzen calculi (see [6] for a proof-theoretical justification of **WK**). The proof-theory of them as well as some of their modal extensions has been further investigated in two directions. In the first one, the aim is to develop strongly terminating (cut-free) Gentzen calculi in the style of Dyckhoff' G4: a calculus of this kind for the $\Box$-fragment of **CK** was proposed in [12]. In [8] strongly terminating cut-free calculi for both **CK** and **WK** in the full language are proposed in the same vein. Moreover in that work strongly terminating *refutation* calculi are also defined for both logics; these calculi provide a countermodel construction for an unprovable

D. Kozen and R. de Queiroz (Eds.): WoLLIC 2025, LNCS 15942, pp. 211–227, 2026.
https://doi.org/10.1007/978-3-031-99536-1_13

sequent in an alternative *neighborhood* semantics. In the second direction, the interest is in developing (cut-free) structured and modular calculi, as proposed in [15] where a structured calculus for a multi-modal version of **CK** is proposed and in [17] where nested sequent calculi for **CK** and its extensions are proposed.

In our opinion proofs and countermodels hold an equal importance. Proofs serve as witnesses of validity or theoremhood, while (finite) countermodels serve as witnesses of non-validity. In particular we want to investigate cut-free calculi for **CK** and **WK** that provide not only a decision procedure, but also *direct countermodel extraction* in the original bi-relational semantics; that is from *any single* failed derivation of a sequent, it is possible to construct a finite countermodel of it. In this respect, none of the calculi proposed in the literature, with the partial exception of that in [8], fulfill this desideratum: [15,17] focus on syntactic cut-elimination without considering termination and semantic completeness. The refutation calculus in [8] allows for the extraction of a finite *neighborhood* model of an unprovable sequent; even if in principle, this model can be transformed into a bi-relational one (see [7]), the transformation is not straightforward and entails an exponential blow-up of the model.

This paper aims to define calculi for **CK** and **WK** which satisfy the above desiderata: they provide (i) a decision procedure for these logics and (ii) a direct countermodel construction in the original bi-relational semantics from *one single* failed proof. To this purpose, we adopt the proof-theoretic framework of bi-nested calculi, recently employed to cope with other variants of intuitionistic modal logics [2,3]. These calculi make use of two nesting structures corresponding to the two relations in bi-relational models: one for the pre-order and the other for modal accessibility. In this way, bi-nested calculi partially encode the bi-relational semantics into the syntax, without using labels and explicit relations on them as in e.g. [13]. This use of nesting is not new: it was first employed by Fitting [10]; a calculus with the same nesting was proposed to handle an extension of **CK** with (DP) [9]; more generally, calculi comprising various kinds of structures, in the style of display logic, were proposed to treat variants of (bi)-intuitionistic tense logics [11].

Aiming to define bi-nested calculi for **CK** and **WK**, an additional difficulty arises: the global forcing condition for $\Diamond$ involves a $\forall\exists$ combination for $\leq$ and R successors. It is not obvious how to capture this condition within bi-nested calculi. Our solution is to extend the language by a local $\Diamond$ which allows to decompose the $\forall\exists$-condition into two steps and formulate the rules smoothly for the global $\Diamond$. In this way then we obtain multiple-conclusion calculi with invertible rules. The calculi can be employed to obtain a terminating proof-search procedure under a suitable strategy. Thanks to the invertibility of the rules, the calculi support direct countermodel extraction in the sense mentioned above: from any non-axiomatic sequent occurring as a leaf of *any* failed proof, a finite *bi-relational* countermodel can be built. All in all we believe that bi-nested sequent calculus serves as a very flexible and powerful framework for obtaining *both* proofs and countermodel construction for multiple modal logics with an intuitionistic base.

2 Constructive Modal Logics CK and WK

In this section, we recap the bi-relational semantics and Hilbert-style axiom systems for the logic **CK** and **WK**.

Definition 1 (The language $\mathcal{L}$). *The set $\mathcal{L}$ of all formulas (denoted A, B, etc.) is generated by the following grammar:*

$$A ::= p \mid \bot \mid \top \mid (A \wedge A) \mid (A \vee A) \mid (A \supset A) \mid \Box A \mid \Diamond A$$

where p ranges over a countable set of propositional atoms At. *Besides, $\neg A$ is defined as $A \supset \bot$ and we omit most parentheses for readability. The size of a formula A is denoted as $|A|$.*

Definition 2 (Bi-relational Kripke model). *A bi-relational Kripke model is a quadruple $\mathcal{M} = (W, \leq, R, V)$ where W is a nonempty set of worlds, $\leq$ is a pre-order on W, R is a binary relation on W and $V : W \longrightarrow \wp(\mathsf{At})$ is a valuation on W satisfying monotonicity, which says $\forall x, y \in W, x \leq y$ implies $V(x) \subseteq V(y)$.*

Definition 3 (Forcing conditions). *Let $\mathcal{M} = (W, \leq, R, V)$ be a bi-relational Kripke model. The forcing conditions of a formula at a world $w \in W$ of $\mathcal{M}$ are defined as follows:*

$$\begin{array}{lll}
\mathcal{M}, w \Vdash p & \textit{iff} & p \in V(w); \qquad \mathcal{M}, w \Vdash \top; \\
\mathcal{M}, w \Vdash B \wedge C & \textit{iff} & \mathcal{M}, w \Vdash B \text{ and } \mathcal{M}, w \Vdash C; \\
\mathcal{M}, w \Vdash B \vee C & \textit{iff} & \mathcal{M}, w \Vdash B \text{ or } \mathcal{M}, w \Vdash C; \\
\mathcal{M}, w \Vdash B \supset C & \textit{iff} & \forall w' \in W \text{ with } w \leq w', \text{ if } \mathcal{M}, w' \Vdash B, \text{ then } \mathcal{M}, w' \Vdash C; \\
\mathcal{M}, w \Vdash \Box B & \textit{iff} & \forall w', v' \in W \text{ with } w \leq w' \text{ and } Rw'v', v \Vdash B; \\
\mathcal{M}, w \Vdash \Diamond B & \textit{iff} & \forall w' \in W \text{ if } w \leq w', \text{ then there is } v' \in W \text{ s.t. } Rw'v' \text{ and} \\
 & & \mathcal{M}, v' \Vdash B.
\end{array}$$

In addition, for constructive modal logics, inconsistent (also called fallible) worlds in the following sense are allowed: $W_\bot \subseteq W$ is a set of inconsistent worlds in $\mathcal{M}$ and closed under $\leq$ and R. For fallible worlds, we define

$$\begin{array}{lll}
\mathcal{M}, w \Vdash \bot & \textit{iff} & w \in W_\bot; \\
\mathcal{M}, w \Vdash p & & \text{for any } p \in \mathsf{At} \text{ if } w \in W_\bot.
\end{array}$$

We shall abbreviate $\mathcal{M}, w \Vdash A$ as $w \Vdash A$ if the model is clear from the context. A formula A in $\mathcal{L}$ is valid, denoted $\Vdash A$, if for any bi-relational model $\mathcal{M}$ and any world w in it, it holds that $\mathcal{M}, w \Vdash A$.

Note in **WK**, sets of fallible worlds are always empty. From the truth conditions and the closure property of $W_\bot$, as a result, we have formulas of the form $\bot \supset A$ always valid.

A Hilbert-style calculus $\mathcal{H}_{\mathbf{WK}}$ for **WK** consists of all the axioms and rules in Fig. 1 while a calculus $\mathcal{H}_{\mathbf{CK}}$ for **CK** contains all the axioms and rules except (k5). The systems were proven sound and complete with respect to the bi-relational semantics [14,18].

Theorem 1. *A formula is provable in $\mathcal{H}_{\mathbf{WK}}$ (resp. $\mathcal{H}_{\mathbf{CK}}$) iff it is valid.*

$$\begin{array}{ll} \text{k1} & \Box(A \supset B) \supset (\Box A \supset \Box B) \\ \text{k2} & \Box(A \supset B) \supset (\Diamond A \supset \Diamond B) \\ \text{k5} & \neg\Diamond\bot \end{array} \qquad \frac{A \supset B \qquad A}{B}\ \mathsf{mp} \qquad \frac{A}{\Box A}\ \mathsf{nec}$$

Fig. 1. Axioms and rules of constructive modal logics

3 Terminating Bi-nested Calculi

In this section, we provide bi-nested calculi for **CK** and **WK** which support terminating proof-search.

3.1 Bi-nested Calculi for Constructive Modal Logics

First we extend the modal language $\mathcal{L}$ by introducing auxiliary $\widehat{\Diamond}$-prefixed formulas. These formulas may occur in a bi-nested sequent and are used to capture the global semantics of $\Diamond$.

Let the extended language $\mathcal{L}^+ := \mathcal{L} \cup \{\widehat{\Diamond}\varphi \mid \varphi \in \mathcal{L}\}$ and we define bi-nested sequents as follows.

Definition 4 (Bi-nested sequent). *A bi-nested sequent S is defined as*

- *the empty sequent $\Rightarrow$ is a bi-nested sequent;*
- *$\Gamma \Rightarrow A_1, \ldots, A_k, \langle T_1 \rangle, \ldots, \langle T_n \rangle, [S_1], \ldots, [S_m]$ is a bi-nested sequent if Γ is a multiset of $\mathcal{L}$-formulas, $A_1, \ldots, A_k$ are $\mathcal{L}^+$-formulas, $S_1, \ldots, S_m, T_1, \ldots, T_n$ are bi-nested sequents where $k, m, n \in \mathbb{N}$.*

A bi-nested sequent has a two-sided form and allows two kinds of nested structures on the right, which are $\langle \cdot \rangle$, called an *implication block*, and $[\cdot]$, called a *modal block*. Intuitively speaking, implication blocks correspond to the upper worlds while modal blocks represent the accessible successors in a bi-relational model. In addition, we can see from the definition these auxiliary $\widehat{\Diamond}A$ formulas can only occur on the succedent of a bi-nested sequent. We will use S, T in this paper to denote bi-nested sequents and simply call them 'sequents' if it does not rise to any ambiguity. For a sequent $S = \Gamma \Rightarrow \Delta$, the formula part of Δ is denoted as $\mathsf{Fm}(\Delta)$, which is a multiset of $\mathcal{L}^+$-formulas.

Next we define some relations between sequents as well as the notion of context for specifying deep inference.

Definition 5. *Let $\Gamma_1 \Rightarrow \Delta_1, \Gamma_2 \Rightarrow \Delta_2$ be two sequents. We denote $\Gamma_1 \Rightarrow \Delta_1 \in_0^{\langle \cdot \rangle} \Gamma_2 \Rightarrow \Delta_2$ if $\langle \Gamma_1 \Rightarrow \Delta_1 \rangle \in \Delta_2$ and let $\in^{\langle \cdot \rangle}$ be the transitive closure of $\in_0^{\langle \cdot \rangle}$. Relations $\in_0^{[\cdot]}$ and $\in^{[\cdot]}$ for modal blocks are defined similarly. Besides, let $\in_0^+ = \in_0^{\langle \cdot \rangle} \cup \in_0^{[\cdot]}$ and finally let $\in^+$ be the reflexive-transitive closure of $\in_0^+$.*

A context $G\{\ \}$ is a part of an incomplete sequent G, serving as a placeholder to be filled with some other sequent.

$$\frac{}{G\{\Gamma, \bot \Rightarrow \Delta\}}(\bot_L) \quad \frac{}{G\{\Gamma \Rightarrow \top, \Delta\}}(\top_R) \quad \frac{}{G\{\Gamma, p \Rightarrow \Delta, p\}}(\text{id})$$

$$\frac{G\{A, B, \Gamma \Rightarrow \Delta\}}{G\{A \wedge B, \Gamma \Rightarrow \Delta\}}(\wedge_L) \quad \frac{G\{\Gamma \Rightarrow \Delta, A\} \quad G\{\Gamma \Rightarrow \Delta, B\}}{G\{\Gamma \Rightarrow \Delta, A \wedge B\}}(\wedge_R)$$

$$\frac{G\{\Gamma, A \Rightarrow \Delta\} \quad G\{\Gamma, B \Rightarrow \Delta\}}{G\{\Gamma, A \vee B \Rightarrow \Delta\}}(\vee_L) \quad \frac{G\{\Gamma \Rightarrow \Delta, A, B\}}{G\{\Gamma \Rightarrow \Delta, A \vee B\}}(\vee_R)$$

$$\frac{G\{\Gamma, A \supset B \Rightarrow A, \Delta\} \quad G\{\Gamma, B \Rightarrow \Delta\}}{G\{\Gamma, A \supset B \Rightarrow \Delta\}}(\supset_L) \quad \frac{G\{\Gamma \Rightarrow \Delta, \langle A \Rightarrow B\rangle\}}{G\{\Gamma \Rightarrow \Delta, A \supset B\}}(\supset_R)$$

$$\frac{G\{\Gamma, \Box A \Rightarrow \Delta, [\Sigma, A \Rightarrow \Pi]\}}{G\{\Gamma, \Box A \Rightarrow \Delta, [\Sigma \Rightarrow \Pi]\}}(\Box_L) \quad \frac{G\{\Gamma \Rightarrow \Delta, \langle \Rightarrow [\Rightarrow A]\rangle\}}{G\{\Gamma \Rightarrow \Delta, \Box A\}}(\Box_R)$$

$$\frac{G\{\Gamma, \Diamond A \Rightarrow \Delta, [A \Rightarrow]\}}{G\{\Gamma, \Diamond A \Rightarrow \Delta\}}(\Diamond_L) \quad \frac{G\{\Gamma \Rightarrow \Delta, \langle \Rightarrow \widehat{\Diamond} A\rangle\}}{G\{\Gamma \Rightarrow \Delta, \Diamond A\}}(\Diamond_R) \quad \frac{G\{\Gamma \Rightarrow \Delta, \widehat{\Diamond} A, [\Sigma \Rightarrow \Pi, A]\}}{G\{\Gamma \Rightarrow \Delta, \widehat{\Diamond} A, [\Sigma \Rightarrow \Pi]\}}(\widehat{\Diamond})$$

$$\frac{G\{\Gamma, \Gamma' \Rightarrow \Delta, \langle \Gamma', \Sigma \Rightarrow \Pi\rangle\}}{G\{\Gamma, \Gamma' \Rightarrow \Delta, \langle \Sigma \Rightarrow \Pi\rangle\}}(\text{trans})$$

Fig. 2. Bi-nested rules for constructive modal logics **WK** and **CK**

Definition 6 (Context). *A context $G\{\ \}$ is inductively defined as follows: the empty context $\{\ \}$ is a context; if $\Gamma \Rightarrow \Delta$ is a sequent and $G'\{\ \}$ is a context, then both $\Gamma \Rightarrow \Delta, \langle G'\{\ \}\rangle$ and $\Gamma \Rightarrow \Delta, [G'\{\ \}]$ are contexts.*

Moreover, we call $G\{\ \}$ an *implication context* if $S \in^{\langle\cdot\rangle} G\{S\}$ holds for an arbitrary sequent S; and *modal context* correspondingly.

Example 1. $G_1\{\ \} = p \Rightarrow q, \langle r \Rightarrow q \wedge s, [\{\ \}]\rangle$ is a modal context while $G_2\{\ \} = p \Rightarrow q, [r \Rightarrow q \wedge s, \langle\{\ \}\rangle]$ is an implication context. Let $S = s \Rightarrow$, then $G_1\{S\} = p \Rightarrow q, \langle r \Rightarrow q \wedge s, [s \Rightarrow]\rangle$ and $G_2\{S\} = p \Rightarrow q, [r \Rightarrow q \wedge s, \langle s \Rightarrow\rangle]$.

Definition 7 (Bi-nested sequent calculi for CK and WK). *Bi-nested rules for constructive modal logics are given in Fig. 2. A bi-nested sequent calculus for* **WK** *denoted* $\mathbf{C}_0$ *contains all of these rules. For* **CK***, the rules are the same while an additional requirement is added: $(\bot_L)$ is applied in a restricted way such that if $G\{\ \}$ is a modal context then $\mathsf{Fm}(\Delta) \neq \emptyset$. We denote the calculus for* **CK** *by* $\mathbf{C}_0^*$.

According to Definition 7, the only difference between $\mathbf{C}_0^*$ and $\mathbf{C}_0$ is the restriction imposed on $(\bot_L)$. Due to this reason, in the rest of the paper, mostly we will deal with both calculi simultaneously in order to avoid duplicative explanations and proofs. We use $\mathbf{C}$ to represent any of the two calculi.

We offer some remarks for the rules in $\mathbf{C}$. First, as usual, (id) is defined for propositional atoms, which can be easily generalized to arbitrary formulas. The logical rules, except $(\supset_R)$, are just the standard rules of an intuitionistic calculus in a nested form. From a bottom-up view, the rule $(\supset_R)$ introduces an implication block, which corresponds to a $\leq$-upper world in a bi-relational model. The (trans) rule, also called (Lift) in [10], transfers formulas from the lower worlds to upper ones along the pre-order. The modal rules decompose modal formulas by either creating new modal blocks or propagating subformulas into existing ones which correspond to R-accessible worlds. Moreover, we have an auxiliary $(\widehat{\Diamond})$ rule which also propagate subformulas into modal blocks. Note that if we consider a derivation $\mathcal{D}$ of a sequent S where S does not contain $\widehat{\Diamond}$-formulas, then any possible $\widehat{\Diamond}$-formulas occurring in $\mathcal{D}$ can only be introduced by backward applications of $(\Diamond_R)$.

A *derivation* in **C** is a directed tree $\mathcal{T}$, where the root is a sequent and children of each node are obtained by backward applications of some rule in **C**. A derivation is called a *proof* if all of its leaves are axioms. We say a sequent S is *provable* in **C** if there is a proof rooted by it; a formula A is provable if the corresponding sequent $\Rightarrow A$ is provable.

Proposition 1. *The following facts hold in* **C***:*

1. *all the rules are invertible.*
2. *the following weakening and contraction rules are admissible:*

$$\frac{G\{\Gamma \Rightarrow \Delta\}}{G\{\Gamma \Rightarrow \Delta, \mathcal{O}\}}\,(w_R) \quad \frac{G\{\Gamma \Rightarrow \Delta\}}{G\{A, \Gamma \Rightarrow \Delta\}}\,(w_L) \quad \frac{\Gamma \Rightarrow \Delta}{G\{\Gamma \Rightarrow \Delta\}}\,(w_C) \quad \frac{G\{\Gamma \Rightarrow \Delta, \mathcal{O}, \mathcal{O}\}}{G\{\Gamma \Rightarrow \Delta, \mathcal{O}\}}\,(c_R) \quad \frac{G\{\Gamma, A, A \Rightarrow \Delta\}}{G\{\Gamma, A \Rightarrow \Delta\}}\,(c_L)$$

   where in (w_R) *and* (c_R), $\mathcal{O}$ *can be either a formula or a block.*
3. *A sequent* $\Gamma \Rightarrow \Delta, \Diamond A$ *is provable iff* $\Gamma \Rightarrow \Delta, \Diamond A, \langle \Rightarrow \widehat{\Diamond} A\rangle$ *is provable.*

Proof. By induction on the height of a derivation.

Meanwhile, we can verify that any axiom in $\mathcal{H}_{\mathbf{WK}}$ or $\mathcal{H}_{\mathbf{CK}}$ is provable in the corresponding bi-nested calculus. As an example, we show the following

Example 2. Axiom (k2) is provable in **C**.

To show this, it suffices to show the sequent $\Box(A \supset B), \Diamond A \Rightarrow \Diamond B$ is provable. Let $\Gamma = \Box(A \supset B), \Diamond A$ and we have

$$\dfrac{\dfrac{\dfrac{\dfrac{}{\Gamma \Rightarrow \Diamond B, [A, A \supset B \Rightarrow A]}\,(\mathrm{id}) \qquad \dfrac{\mathcal{D}}{\Gamma \Rightarrow \Diamond B, [A, B \Rightarrow]}}{\Gamma \Rightarrow \Diamond B, [A, A \supset B \Rightarrow]}\,(\supset_L)}{\Gamma \Rightarrow \Diamond B, [A \Rightarrow]}\,(\Box_L)}{\Gamma \Rightarrow \Diamond B}\,(\Diamond_L)$$

where the sub-derivation $\mathcal{D}$ rooted by $\Gamma \Rightarrow \Diamond B, [A, B \Rightarrow]$ is

$$\dfrac{\dfrac{\dfrac{\dfrac{\dfrac{\dfrac{\dfrac{}{\Gamma \Rightarrow \Diamond B, [A, B \Rightarrow], \langle \Gamma \Rightarrow \widehat{\Diamond} B, [A, A \supset B \Rightarrow A]\rangle}\,(\mathrm{id}) \qquad \dfrac{}{\Gamma \Rightarrow \Diamond B, [A, B \Rightarrow], \langle \Gamma \Rightarrow \widehat{\Diamond} B, [A, B \Rightarrow B]\rangle}\,(\mathrm{id})}{\Gamma \Rightarrow \Diamond B, [A, B \Rightarrow], \langle \Gamma \Rightarrow \widehat{\Diamond} B, [A, A \supset B \Rightarrow B]\rangle}\,(\supset_L)}{\Gamma \Rightarrow \Diamond B, [A, B \Rightarrow], \langle \Gamma \Rightarrow \widehat{\Diamond} B, [A, A \supset B \Rightarrow]\rangle}\,(\widehat{\Diamond})}{\Gamma \Rightarrow \Diamond B, [A, B \Rightarrow], \langle \Gamma \Rightarrow \widehat{\Diamond} B, [A \Rightarrow]\rangle}\,(\Box_L)}{\Gamma \Rightarrow \Diamond B, [A, B \Rightarrow], \langle \Gamma \Rightarrow \widehat{\Diamond} B\rangle}\,(\Diamond_L)}{\Gamma \Rightarrow \Diamond B, [A, B \Rightarrow], \langle \Rightarrow \widehat{\Diamond} B\rangle}\,(\mathrm{trans})}{\Gamma \Rightarrow \Diamond B, [A, B \Rightarrow]}\,(\Diamond_R)$$

Lastly we establish the soundness of **C**. In order to show this, we first define the interpretation of a sequent, which is done by extending the forcing relation $\Vdash$ in Definition 3 to $\mathcal{L}^+$ as well as sequents and blocks therein.

Definition 8 (Interpretation). *Let $\mathcal{M} = (W, \leq, R, V)$ be a bi-relational model with a set of fallible worlds $W_\perp \subseteq W$ and $w \in W$. The satisfiability relation $\Vdash$ is extended to sequents as follows:*

$\mathcal{M}, w \Vdash \emptyset$	*iff* $w \in W_\perp$
$\mathcal{M}, w \Vdash \widehat{\Diamond} A$	*if there is* $v \in W$ *such that* Rwv *and* $v \Vdash A$;
$\mathcal{M}, w \Vdash [T]$	*if for every* v *with* $Rwv, \mathcal{M}, v \Vdash T$;
$\mathcal{M}, w \Vdash \langle T \rangle$	*if for every* w' *with* $w \leq w', \mathcal{M}, w' \Vdash T$
$\mathcal{M}, w \Vdash \Gamma \Rightarrow \Delta$	*if either* $\mathcal{M}, w \not\Vdash A$ *for some* $A \in \Gamma$ *or* $\mathcal{M}, w \Vdash \mathcal{O}$ *for some* $\mathcal{O} \in \Delta$, *where* $\mathcal{O}$ *is a formula or a block.*

S is called valid in $\mathcal{M}$ *iff $\mathcal{M}, w \Vdash S$ holds for each $w \in W$; furthermore, S is called* valid *iff it is valid in every model.*

Theorem 2 (Soundness). *If a formula A is provable in* **C**, *then it is valid.*

3.2 Termination

In this subsection, we provide a decision procedure for the two bi-nested calculi. Compared with the simple Gentzen calculi of **CK** and **WK**, which have strictly terminating variants, obtaining a terminating proof-search procedure for a bi-nested sequent calculus is more challenging. To define the procedure, we will introduce variants of the two bi-nested calculi and then prove that proof-search in the variants terminates under a suitable strategy.

At first we define **CC**, a variant of **C** where sequents are set-based instead of multiset-based and all the rules are in cumulative (or kleen'ed) forms. As usual, this reformulation is used to obtain a terminating calculus by preventing redundant backward applications of the rules and ensuring bounded size of sequents that can occur in a derivation. Rules in **CC** are defined as follows: - $(\perp_L)$, $(\top_R)$, (id), $(\Box_L)$, $(\Diamond_L)$, $(\widehat{\Diamond})$ and (trans) are in their original forms;
- $(\supset_R)$ is replaced by the following two rules:

$$A \in \Gamma \, \frac{G\{\Gamma \Rightarrow \Delta, A \supset B, B\}}{G\{\Gamma \Rightarrow \Delta, A \supset B\}} \, (\supset_{R_1}) \quad A \notin \Gamma \, \frac{G\{\Gamma \Rightarrow \Delta, A \supset B, \langle A \Rightarrow B \rangle\}}{G\{\Gamma \Rightarrow \Delta, A \supset B\}} \, (\supset_{R_2})$$

- other rules are modified by keeping the principal formula in the premise(s), e.g.

$$\frac{G\{A, B, A \wedge B, \Gamma \Rightarrow \Delta\}}{G\{A \wedge B, \Gamma \Rightarrow \Delta\}} \, (\wedge_L) \quad \frac{G\{\Gamma, A \supset B \Rightarrow A, \Delta\} \qquad G\{\Gamma, A \supset B, B \Rightarrow \Delta\}}{G\{\Gamma, A \supset B \Rightarrow \Delta\}} \, (\supset_L)$$

$$\frac{G\{\Gamma \Rightarrow \Delta, \Box A, \langle \Rightarrow [\Rightarrow A] \rangle\}}{G\{\Gamma \Rightarrow \Delta, \Box A\}} \, (\Box_R) \quad \frac{G\{\Gamma \Rightarrow \Delta, \Diamond A, \langle \Rightarrow \widehat{\Diamond} A \rangle\}}{G\{\Gamma \Rightarrow \Delta, \Diamond A\}} \, (\Diamond_R)$$

The notions of derivations and proofs in **CC** are defined similarly as in **C**. Due to the admissibility of weakening and contraction in **C**, we have a sequent is provable in **C** if and only if it is provable in **CC**.

To avoid redundant rule applications, we introduce saturation conditions associated with each rule application. These conditions will also be useful in the countermodel construction demonstrated in the next section.

Definition 9. *Let $\Gamma \Rightarrow \Delta$ be a sequent. Saturation condition associated with an application of a rule (r) in* **CC** *is defined in Fig. 3. Saturation conditions associated with other rules are defined as usual.*

$(\supset_L)$	If $A \supset B \in \Gamma$, then $A \in \Delta$ or $B \in \Gamma$.
$(\supset_R)$	If $A \supset B \in \Delta$, then either $A \in \Gamma$ and $B \in \Delta$, or there is $\langle \Sigma \Rightarrow \Pi \rangle \in \Delta$ with $A \in \Sigma$ and $B \in \Pi$.
$(\Box_R)$	If $\Box A \in \Delta$, then either there is $[\Lambda \Rightarrow \Theta] \in \Delta$ with $A \in \Theta$, or there is $\langle \Sigma \Rightarrow [\Lambda \Rightarrow \Theta], \Pi \rangle \in \Delta$ with $A \in \Theta$. there is $[\Lambda \Rightarrow \Theta] \in \Delta$ with $A \in \Theta$.
$(\Box_L)$	If $\Box A \in \Gamma$ and $[\Sigma \Rightarrow \Pi] \in \Delta$, then $A \in \Sigma$.
$(\Diamond_L)$	If $\Diamond A \in \Gamma$, then there is $[\Sigma \Rightarrow \Pi] \in \Delta$ with $A \in \Sigma$.
$(\Diamond_R)$	If $\Diamond A \in \Delta$, then either $\widehat{\Diamond} A \in \Delta$, or there is $\langle \Sigma \Rightarrow \Pi \rangle \in \Delta$ with $\widehat{\Diamond} A \in \Pi$.
$(\widehat{\Diamond})$	If $\widehat{\Diamond} A \in \Delta$, then for each $[\Sigma \Rightarrow \Pi] \in \Delta$, it holds $A \in \Pi$.
(trans)	If $\langle \Sigma \Rightarrow \Pi \rangle \in \Delta$, then $\Gamma \subseteq \Sigma$.

Fig. 3. Saturation conditions

We say a sequent is saturated with a rule (r) for some formula A, if it satisfies the saturation condition associated with (r) for A. A backward application of (r) to a sequent S is *redundant* if S already satisfies the corresponding saturation condition associated with (r).

To prevent redundant rule applications, we require two basic constraints for backward proof-search: (i) no rule is applied to an axiom; (ii) no rule is applied redundantly. However, these basic restrictions are not sufficient for ensuring termination. The following example demonstrates that non-redundant applications of rules can still result in loops in certain cases.

Example 3. Consider the sequent $\neg\Diamond p, \neg\Diamond q \Rightarrow \bot$, let $\Gamma = \neg\Diamond p, \neg\Diamond q$ and one branch in a derivation proceeds as follows

$$
\dfrac{\dfrac{\dfrac{\dfrac{\dfrac{\dfrac{\dfrac{\dfrac{\dfrac{\vdots}{\Gamma \Rightarrow \bot, \Diamond p, \Diamond q, \langle \Gamma \Rightarrow \widehat{\Diamond} q, \Diamond p, \Diamond q, \langle \Gamma \Rightarrow \widehat{\Diamond} p, \Diamond p, \Diamond q, \langle \Gamma \Rightarrow \widehat{\Diamond} q \rangle\rangle\rangle}}{\Gamma \Rightarrow \bot, \Diamond p, \Diamond q, \langle \Gamma \Rightarrow \widehat{\Diamond} q, \Diamond p, \Diamond q, \langle \Gamma \Rightarrow \widehat{\Diamond} p, \Diamond p, \Diamond q, \langle \Rightarrow \widehat{\Diamond} q \rangle\rangle\rangle}\,(\text{trans})}{\Gamma \Rightarrow \bot, \Diamond p, \Diamond q, \langle \Gamma \Rightarrow \widehat{\Diamond} q, \Diamond p, \Diamond q, \langle \Gamma \Rightarrow \widehat{\Diamond} p, \Diamond p, \Diamond q \rangle\rangle}\,(\Diamond_R)}{\Gamma \Rightarrow \bot, \Diamond p, \Diamond q, \langle \Gamma \Rightarrow \widehat{\Diamond} q, \Diamond p, \Diamond q, \langle \Gamma \Rightarrow \widehat{\Diamond} p \rangle\rangle}\,(\supset_L) \times 2}{\Gamma \Rightarrow \bot, \Diamond p, \Diamond q, \langle \Gamma \Rightarrow \widehat{\Diamond} q, \Diamond p, \Diamond q, \langle \Rightarrow \widehat{\Diamond} p \rangle\rangle}\,(\text{trans})}{\Gamma \Rightarrow \bot, \Diamond p, \Diamond q, \langle \Gamma \Rightarrow \widehat{\Diamond} q, \Diamond p, \Diamond q \rangle}\,(\Diamond_R)}{\Gamma \Rightarrow \bot, \Diamond p, \Diamond q, \langle \Gamma \Rightarrow \widehat{\Diamond} q \rangle}\,(\supset_L) \times 2}{\Gamma \Rightarrow \bot, \Diamond p, \Diamond q, \langle \Rightarrow \widehat{\Diamond} q \rangle}\,(\text{trans})}{\dfrac{\Gamma \Rightarrow \bot, \Diamond p, \Diamond q}{\Gamma \Rightarrow \bot}\,(\supset_L) \times 2}\,(\Diamond_R)
$$

The derivation comes to a loop as the innermost implication block of the top sequent, $\Gamma \Rightarrow \widehat{\Diamond} q$, is exactly the one already occurred on the sequent of line 4 from bottom. This is due to the situation that we have two $\Diamond$-formulas on the right and they can iteratively create new implication blocks and this process will not stop. Similarly loops may also occur due to iterated expansions of $\Box$-formulas on the succedent.

In order to deal with the loops and specify a proof-search strategy, we make use of a 'blocking' mechanism. This mechanism is used to 'block' certain rule applications to sequents which are 'equivalent' to another sequent that represent a lower world of it. Consequently, these blocked sequents will not be expanded.

Before that, we first divide all the cumulative rules of **CC** into three groups and define different levels of saturation: (R1): all propositional rules except $(\supset_R)$ together with $(\Diamond_L), (\Box_L)$ and $(\widehat{\Diamond})$; (R2): (trans); (R3): $(\supset_R), (\Box_R)$ and $(\Diamond_R)$.

Let $S = \Gamma \Rightarrow \Delta$, we denote by $\bar{\Delta}$ the sequent obtained by removing all the (nested) occurrences of $\langle\cdot\rangle$-blocks in Δ.[1]

Definition 10 (Saturation). *Let $S = \Gamma \Rightarrow \Delta$ be a sequent and not an axiom. S is called:*

- R1-saturated *if $\Gamma \Rightarrow \bar{\Delta}$ satisfies all the saturation conditions of R1 rules;*
- R2-saturated *if S is R1-saturated and S satisfies saturation conditions of R2 rules for $S_1 \in_0^{\langle\cdot\rangle} S$;*
- R3-saturated *if S is R2-saturated and S satisfies saturation conditions of R3 rules for formulas $A \supset B, \Box A, \Diamond A \in \Delta$.*

Finally, we define the notion of blocked sequents with the intention that these sequents will not be expanded further during the proof-search.

Definition 11 (Quasi-equivalence). *Let S_1, S_2 be two sequents where $S_1 = \Gamma_1 \Rightarrow \Delta_1, S_2 = \Gamma_2 \Rightarrow \Delta_2$. We say S_1 is quasi-equivalent to S_2, denoted as $S_1 \simeq S_2$, if $\Gamma_1 = \Gamma_2$ and $\mathsf{Fm}(\Delta_1) = \mathsf{Fm}(\Delta_2)$.*

Definition 12 (Blocked sequent). *Given a sequent S and $S_1, S_2 \in^+ S$, where $S_1 = \Gamma_1 \Rightarrow \Delta_1$ and $S_2 = \Gamma_2 \Rightarrow \Delta_2$. We say S_2 is blocked by S_1 in S, if S_1 is R2-saturated, $S_2 \in^{\langle\cdot\rangle} S_1$ and $S_1 \simeq S_2$. We say that a sequent $T \in^+ S$ is* blocked *in S if there exists $T' \in^+ S$ such that T is blocked by T' in S.*

Note that if S is a finite sequent, then for any $T \in^+ S$, checking whether it is blocked by some $T' \in^+ S$ can be effectively decided. We will simply say that T is blocked when $T \in^+ S$ is clear.

Back to Example 3, for the top sequent, continue with $(\supset_L) \times 2$, we have

$$\Gamma \Rightarrow \bot, \Diamond p, \Diamond q, \langle \Gamma \Rightarrow \widehat{\Diamond} q, \Diamond p, \Diamond q, \langle \Gamma \Rightarrow \widehat{\Diamond} p, \Diamond p, \Diamond q, \langle \Gamma \Rightarrow \widehat{\Diamond} q, \Diamond p, \Diamond q \rangle\rangle\rangle$$

The proof-search terminates as the innermost $\Gamma \Rightarrow \widehat{\Diamond} q, \Diamond p, \Diamond q$ is blocked.

[1] For example, let $\Delta = B, \langle \Sigma \Rightarrow \Pi \rangle, [\Lambda \Rightarrow [D \Rightarrow E, \langle P \Rightarrow Q \rangle]]$, then $\bar{\Delta} = B, [\Lambda \Rightarrow [D \Rightarrow E]]$.

Definition 13 (Global saturation). *Let S be a sequent and not an axiom. S is called* global-Ri-saturated *if for each $T \in^+ S$, T is Ri-saturated or blocked, where $i \in \{1, 2\}$; S is called* global-saturated *if for each $T \in^+ S$, T is R3-saturated or blocked.*

In order to specify the proof-search procedure, we make use of the following four macro-steps that extend a given derivation $\mathcal{D}$ by expanding a leaf S. Each procedure applies rules *non-redundantly* to some $T = \Gamma \Rightarrow \Delta \in^+ S$.

- **EXP1**$(\mathcal{D}, S, T) = \mathcal{D}'$ where $\mathcal{D}'$ is the extension of $\mathcal{D}$ obtained by applying R1-rules to every formula in $\Gamma \Rightarrow \bar{\Delta}$.
- **EXP2**$(\mathcal{D}, S, T) = \mathcal{D}'$ where $\mathcal{D}'$ is the extension of $\mathcal{D}$ obtained by applying R2-rules to blocks $\langle T_i \rangle \in \Delta$.
- **EXP3**$(\mathcal{D}, S, T) = \mathcal{D}'$ where $\mathcal{D}'$ is the extension of $\mathcal{D}$ obtained by applying R3-rules to formulas $A \supset B, \Box A, \Diamond A \in \Delta$.

It is easy to see that both **EXP2**$(\mathcal{D}, S, T)$ and **EXP3**$(\mathcal{D}, S, T)$ terminate as in either macro-steps only finitely formulas are processed. The proof for **EXP1**$(\mathcal{D}, S, T)$ is given in the appendix.

Proposition 2. *Let $\mathcal{D}$ be a finite derivation, S a finite leaf of $\mathcal{D}$ and $T \in^+ S$. For $i \in \{1, 2, 3\}$, each **EXPi**$(\mathcal{D}, S, T)$ terminates by producing a finite expansion of $\mathcal{D}$ where all sequents are finite.*

We now present the proof-search procedure PROC(A), see Algorithm 1. Given an input formula A it returns either a proof of A or a finite derivation with at least one global-saturated leaf. As we can see, due to the definition of blocked sequents, in the key step when checking loops and identifying two sequents, we do not go deeply into the nested structures but just compare formulas on the antecedent and succedent. This practice makes the procedure a substantial simplification compared to the algorithm in [2].

Invariance of saturations and the blocking situation are ensured during the repeated loop of the procedure.

Lemma 1. *Let S be a leaf of a derivation $\mathcal{D}$ of a formula A and $T \in^+ S$,*

1. *for every rule (r), if T satisfies the saturation condition of (r) on some formulas and/or blocks* before *the execution of the body of the repeat loop (line 3–14), then T satisfies the same condition on the involved formulas and blocks* after *the execution.*
2. *if T is blocked in S* before *the execution of the body of the repeat loop, then it remains blocked* after *it.*

Theorem 3 (Termination). *Let A be a formula. Proof-search for the sequent $\Rightarrow A$ terminates with a finite derivation in which all the leaves are axiomatic or there is one global-saturated leaf.*

4 Completeness

Adopting the decision procedure from the previous section, we show how to construct directly a countermodel of the formula at the root of a failed proof in **CC**. This further entails the completeness of the calculus.

Suppose S is a global-saturated leaf of a derivation of formula A in **CC**, we define the model associated with S as follows:

Algorithm 1: PROC(A)

Input: $\mathcal{D}_0 = \ \Rightarrow A$
initialization $\mathcal{D} = \mathcal{D}_0$;
repeat
    if *all the leaves of* $\mathcal{D}$ *are axiomatic* **then**
        return "PROVABLE" and $\mathcal{D}$
    else if *there is one non-axiomatic leaves of* $\mathcal{D}$ *that is global-saturated* **then**
        return "UNPROVABLE" and $\mathcal{D}$
    else
        select one non-axiomatic leaf S of $\mathcal{D}$ that is not global-saturated
        repeat
            if S *is global-R2-saturated* **then**
                for all $T \in^+ S$ such that T is a $\in^{\langle\cdot\rangle}$-minimal and not R3-saturated, check whether T is blocked in S, if not, let $\mathcal{D} = \mathbf{EXP3}(\mathcal{D}, S, T)$
            else if S *is global-R1-saturated* **then**
                for all $T \in^+ S$ that is not R2-saturated, let $\mathcal{D} = \mathbf{EXP2}(\mathcal{D}, S, T)$
            else
                for all $T \in^+ S$ that is not R1-saturated let $\mathcal{D} = \mathbf{EXP1}(\mathcal{D}, S, T)$
        until *FALSE*;
until *FALSE*;

Definition 14. *Let* $\mathcal{M}_S = (W_S, \leq_S, R_S, V_S)$ *where*

- $W_S = \{x_{\Phi \Rightarrow \Psi} \mid \Phi \Rightarrow \Psi \in^+ S\}$.
- *for pre-order, let* $x_{S_1} \leq^0_S x_{S_2}$ *iff one of the following holds: (i)* S_1 *is* S_2*; (ii)* $S_2 \in^{\langle\cdot\rangle}_0 S_1$*; (iii)* S_1 *is blocked by* S_2*. Take the transitive closure of* $\leq^0_S$ *as* $\leq_S$.
- *for accessibility relation, let* $R_S x_{S_1} x_{S_2}$ *iff* $S_2 \in^{[\cdot]}_0 S_1$.
- *for the set of fallible worlds, let* $W^0_\bot = \{x_{\Phi \Rightarrow \Psi} \in W_S \mid \bot \in \Phi\}$. *and take* $W_\bot$ *to be the minimal supset of* $W^0_\bot$ *closed under* $\leq$ *and* R.
- $V_S(x_{\Phi \Rightarrow \Psi}) = \{\bot\} \cup \mathsf{At}$ *if* $x_{\Phi \Rightarrow \Psi}$ *is fallible; otherwise,* $V_S(x_{\Phi \Rightarrow \Psi}) = \{p \mid p \in \Phi\}$

Proposition 3. *For a model* $\mathcal{M}_S$ *defined as above, we have*

1. *if* $x_{\Phi \Rightarrow \Psi} \in W^0_\bot$ *then* $\Phi \Rightarrow \Psi \in^{[\cdot]} S$ *and* $\mathsf{Fm}(\Psi) = \emptyset$*;*
2. *if* $x_{\Phi_1 \Rightarrow \Psi_1} \leq_S x_{\Phi_2 \Rightarrow \Psi_2}$*, then* $\Phi_1 \subseteq \Phi_2$*;*
3. $\mathcal{M}_S$ *satisfies the hereditary property.*

Lemma 2 (Truth lemma). *Let S be a global-saturated sequent contained in a derivation of a formula and $\mathcal{M}_S = (W_S, \leq_S, R_S, V_S)$ defined as above. For each $x_{\Phi\Rightarrow\Psi} \in W_S$, we have (a). if $A \in \Phi$, then $\mathcal{M}_S, x_{\Phi\Rightarrow\Psi} \Vdash A$; and (b). if $A \in \Psi$, then $M_S, x_{\Phi\Rightarrow\Psi} \nVdash A$.*

Proofs of the truth lemma differ for **CK** and **WK** due to the existence of fallible worlds. We provide the proof for **CK** in the appendix, which can be easily transformed into a proof for **WK** by ignoring the discussion on fallible worlds, making the proof even simpler. Following the truth lemma, we obtain

Theorem 4 (Completeness). *If a formula is valid, then it is provable in* **CC**.

We end this section with some examples.

Example 4. Consider formula $\Diamond(p \vee q) \supset \Diamond p \vee \Diamond q$ which is neither valid in **CK** nor **WK**. We initialize with the sequent $\Diamond(p \vee q) \Rightarrow \Diamond p \vee \Diamond q$, by backward proof-search, we obtain one saturated leaf as below

$$\begin{aligned} \Diamond(p \vee q) \Rightarrow \quad & \Diamond p \vee \Diamond q, \Diamond p, \Diamond q, [p \vee q, p \Rightarrow], \\ & \langle \Diamond(p \vee q) \Rightarrow \widehat{\Diamond} p, [p \vee q, q \Rightarrow p] \rangle, \\ & \langle \Diamond(p \vee q) \Rightarrow \widehat{\Diamond} q, [p \vee q, p \Rightarrow q] \rangle \end{aligned}$$

Denote this sequent by S, and further let $S_1 = p \vee q, p \Rightarrow$; $S_2 = \Diamond(p \vee q) \Rightarrow \widehat{\Diamond} p, [p \vee q, q \Rightarrow p]$; $S_3 = p \vee q, q \Rightarrow p$; $S_4 = \Diamond(p \vee q) \Rightarrow \widehat{\Diamond} q, [p \vee q, p \Rightarrow q]$; $S_5 = p \vee q, p \Rightarrow q$. Then we get a model $\mathcal{M}_S = (W, \leq, R, V)$ where $W = \{x_S, x_{S_1}, x_{S_2}, x_{S_3}, x_{S_4}, x_{S_5}\}$ and $W_\bot = \emptyset$; each world is reflexive and further $x_S \leq x_{S_2}$, $x_S \leq x_{S_4}$; $Rx_S x_{S_1}, Rx_{S_2} x_{S_3}$ and $Rx_{S_4} x_{S_5}$; $V(x_{S_1}) = V(x_{S_5}) = \{p\}$, $V(x_{S_3}) = \{q\}$ and $V(x_S) = V(x_{S_2}) = V(x_{S_4}) = \emptyset$. It is easy to verify $x_S \nVdash \Diamond(p \vee q) \supset \Diamond p \vee \Diamond q$.

Example 5. We consider the $\Diamond$-free formula $\neg\neg\Box\bot \supset \Box\bot$ which is suggested by Simpson in [16]. This formula is not valid in **CK**, but valid in stronger systems like **IK** and **FIK**. Initialize with $\neg\neg\Box\bot \Rightarrow \Box\bot$, by backward proof-search, we obtain a saturated sequent $S = \neg\neg\Box\bot \Rightarrow \langle \neg\neg\Box\bot \Rightarrow [\Rightarrow \bot], \langle \neg\neg\Box\bot, \Box\bot \Rightarrow \bot, \neg\Box\bot \rangle, \neg\Box\bot \rangle, \Box\bot$. Let $S_1 = \neg\neg\Box\bot \Rightarrow [\Rightarrow \bot], \langle \neg\neg\Box\bot, \Box\bot \Rightarrow \bot, \neg\Box\bot \rangle, \neg\Box\bot$; $S_2 = \neg\neg\Box\bot, \Box\bot \Rightarrow \bot, \neg\Box\bot$; $S_3 = \Rightarrow \bot$. Then we get a model $\mathcal{M}_S = (W, \leq, R, V)$ where $W = \{x_S, x_{S_1}, x_{S_2}, x_{S_3}\}$, $W_\bot = \emptyset$, each world is reflexive and $x_S \leq x_{S_1} \leq x_{S_2}$, $Rx_{S_1} x_{S_3}$, and $V(x) = \emptyset$ for every $x \in W_S$. Since $x_{S_3} \nVdash \bot$, it follows $x_{S_1} \nVdash \Box\bot$. Meanwhile $x_{S_2} \Vdash \Box\bot$, so $x_{S_i} \nVdash \neg\Box\bot$ holds for $i \in \{1, 2\}$, making $x_{S_1} \Vdash \neg\neg\Box\bot$. As a result, $x_S \nVdash \neg\neg\Box\bot \supset \Box\bot$.

5 Conclusion

We have defined complete bi-nested calculi for constructive modal logics **CK** and **WK**, which provide direct bi-relational countermodel extraction. Several topics merit further research. First of all, an obvious next step is to extend the calculi with axioms from the standard modal cube. This can be challenging in some cases, particularly since some logics (e.g., constructive S5) lack a semantic characterization in terms of bi-relational semantics. From the computational perspective, loop detection is performed by checking blocked sequents, we intend to investigate whether this checking can be replaced by a more efficient mechanism, in the light of the fact that these logics allow strongly terminating (but non-invertible) calculi. Moreover, we aim to investigate the size of countermodels built by our procedure, this would also be a first step to compare with countermodel constructions proposed in [8].

Appendix

This appendix includes selected proofs of some of our results.

Proof of Theorem 2. Given a rule (r) with empty context, i.e., of the form $\frac{S_1 \quad S_2}{S}$ or $\frac{S_1}{S}$, we say that (r) is *valid* iff for any model $\mathcal{M}$ and any world x in it, if $x \Vdash S_i$ holds for all $i \leq 2$, then $x \Vdash S$. We first need to show that every rule with empty context is valid. Most cases can be found in [2], in particular the auxiliary $(\widehat{\Diamond})$ is just the right rule for $\Diamond$ of the calculus in [2]. We only prove the case of $(\Diamond_R)$ here.

Assume for the sake of a contraction that $(\Diamond_R)$ with empty context is not valid, then there is a model $\mathcal{M}$ with w in it s.t. (a) $\mathcal{M}, w \Vdash \Gamma \Rightarrow \Delta, \langle \Rightarrow \widehat{\Diamond} A\rangle$ while (b) $\mathcal{M}, w \nVdash \Gamma \Rightarrow \Delta, \Diamond A$. From (b), we have (b1) $w \Vdash \bigwedge \Gamma$ and (b2) $w \nVdash \Diamond A$. Combining (b1) and (a), we see $w \Vdash \langle \Rightarrow A\rangle$, which means for any $w' \leq w$, it holds that (c) $w' \Vdash \widehat{\Diamond} A$. Meanwhile, by (b2), we see there is some w_0 s.t. for any $w_0' \geq w_0$, $w_0' \nVdash A$. Take w_0 to be w' in (c), there is some $w_1 \geq w_0$ s.t. $w_1 \Vdash A$, a contraction.

To complete the proof, we need to prove that each rule (r) in **C** preserves validity, i.e., for a model $\mathcal{M}$ and a world x in it, $x \Vdash G\{S_i\}$ implies $x \Vdash G\{S\}$. This can be shown by an easy induction on the structure of context. □

Proof of Proposition 2. We prove that $\mathbf{EXP1}(\mathcal{D}, S, T)$ terminates. First we give some preliminary definitions.

Modal degree for a formula F, denoted as $md(F)$, is defined as usual. Further, let Γ be a finite set of formulas, define $md(\Gamma) = md(\bigwedge \Gamma)$. For a sequent S of the following form

$$S = \Gamma \Rightarrow \Delta, [S_1], \ldots, [S_m], \langle T_1\rangle, \ldots, \langle T_n\rangle,$$

we set $md(S) =$

$$\max\{md(\Gamma), md(\Delta), md(S_1) + 1, \ldots, md(S_m) + 1, md(T_1), \ldots, md(T_n)\}.$$

A sequent S can be regarded as a tree $\mathcal{T}_S$ in the following sense: (i) the root of $\mathcal{T}_S$ is S; (ii) if $S_1 \in_0^{[\cdot]} S_2$, then S_1 is a child of S_2. We denote the height of $\mathcal{T}_S$ as $h(\mathcal{T}_S)$. It is easy to verify that $h(\mathcal{T}_S) \leq md(S)$. Moreover, we denote by $Sub(A)$ the set of subformulas of a formula A and let $Sub^+(A) = Sub(A) \cup \{\widehat{\Diamond} B \mid B \in Sub(A)\}$. Similar notions $Sub(S)$ and $Sub^+(S)$ for a sequent S are defined accordingly. Recall that $|Sub(S)| = \mathcal{O}(|S|)$ and further we have $|Sub^+(S)| = \mathcal{O}(|S|)$ as well.

We claim that for a derivation $\mathcal{D}_0$ rooted by T obtained by applying R1-rules to $\Gamma \Rightarrow \bar{\Delta}$, it holds (i) any T' occurring in $\mathcal{D}_0$ has size $\mathcal{O}(|T|^{|T|+1})$; and (ii). $\mathcal{D}_0$ is finitely-branching and with only branches of finite length. The proof is similar with that of [2, Proposition 45, 46]. With this claim, to show $\mathbf{EXP1}(\mathcal{D}, S, T)$ terminates, we only need to "appending" $\mathcal{D}_0$ by replacing every sequent T' in $\mathcal{D}_0$ by $G\{T'\}$ since $S = G\{T\}$ for some context $G\{\ \}$. □

Proof of Lemma 1. Proof for (1) is similar with [2, Lemma 47]. For (2), the procedure checks whether T is blocked in S at line 10, which implies that S is already global-R2-saturated, so is T. If T is blocked in S by some $T' \in^+ S$ in S, it follows $T \in^{\langle\cdot\rangle} T'$. Due to the $\in^{\langle\cdot\rangle}$-minimality, we have that T' is R3-saturated. Thus no rule can further modify the formula part of neither T nor T' during the execution of (the body of) the procedure. □

Lemma 3. *Given a formula A, let $\mathbf{Seq}(A)$ denote the set of sequents that may occur in any possible derivation with root $\Rightarrow A$ and $\mathbf{Seq}(A)/_{\simeq}$ be the quotient of $\mathbf{Seq}(A)$ with respect to quasi-equivalence $\simeq$ as defined in Definition 11. Then $\mathbf{Seq}(A)/_{\simeq}$ is finite.*

Proof. It suffices to show that the set $\Phi_A := \{\Gamma \Rightarrow \mathsf{Fm}(\Delta) \mid \Gamma \Rightarrow \Delta \in \mathbf{Seq}(A)\}$ is finite. Note that in the proof of Proposition 2, we already show for every sequent $\Gamma \Rightarrow \Delta \in \mathbf{Seq}_A$, the corresponding sequent $\Gamma \Rightarrow \bar{\Delta}$ has a bounded size. Since $Sub^+(\Gamma \Rightarrow \mathsf{Fm}(\Delta)) \subseteq Sub^+(\Gamma \Rightarrow \bar{\Delta}) \subseteq Sub^+(A)$, there are only finitely-many distinct $\Gamma \Rightarrow \mathsf{Fm}(\Delta)$, which makes Φ_A finite.

Proof of Theorem 3. We prove that PROC(A) terminates producing a finite derivation, where all leaves are axioms or there is one global-saturated leaf. According to the procedure, there must be one global-saturated leaf among the non-axiomatic ones, otherwise by steps from line 8, a non-axiomatic S would be taken and further expanded until it is global-saturated. Hence it suffices to prove that the procedure produces a finite derivation.

Let $\mathcal{D}$ be a derivation built by PROC(A). First we claim that all the branches of $\mathcal{D}$ are finite. Suppose for the sake of a contradiction that $\mathcal{D}$ contains an infinite branch $\mathcal{B} = S_0, \ldots, S_i, \ldots$. The branch is generated by applying repeatedly $\mathbf{EXP1}(\cdot), \mathbf{EXP2}(\cdot)$ and $\mathbf{EXP3}(\cdot)$ to each S_i. Since each of these sub-procedures terminates, the three of them must infinitely alternate on the branch. It is easy to see that if $T_i \in^+ S_i$ satisfies a saturation condition for a rule (r), it will still satisfy it in all S_j with $j > i$. This further implies that the branch must contain infinitely many phases of $\mathbf{EXP3}(\cdot)$ which generates new implication blocks at each time. By Lemma 1, if $T_i \in^+ S_i$ satisfies a saturation condition for a rule (r) or is blocked in some S_i it will remain so in all S_j with $j > i$. In other words, further steps in the branch cannot "undo" a fulfilled saturation condition or "unblock" a blocked sequent. Thus we can conclude that the branch must contain infinitely many phases of **EXP3**$(\cdot)$ each time applied to an unblocked sequent in some S_i. This entails that $\mathcal{B}$ contains infinitely many sequents that are not $\simeq$-equivalent, which contradicts with Lemma 3. Thus $\mathcal{D}$ contains branches with only finite length.

To conclude, observe that $\mathcal{D}$ is a finitely-branching tree, which means it has a finite number of branches at each fork (namely each node/sequent has at most two successors, as the rules in **CC** are at most binary), therefore $\mathcal{D}$ is finite. □

Proof of Proposition 3. To prove (1) we need to consider the cases of **WK** and **CK** separately. If $\mathbf{CC} = \mathbf{CC}_0$, $\mathcal{M}_S$ is a model for **WK**, then the set of fallible worlds is empty, making (1) holds trivially. Otherwise $\mathbf{CC} = \mathbf{CC}_0^*$, $\mathcal{M}_S$ is a model for **CK**. For (1), since $x_{\Phi\Rightarrow\Psi} \in W_\bot^0$, we have $\bot \in \Phi$. If $\Phi \Rightarrow \Psi \in^{\langle\cdot\rangle} S$ or $\mathsf{Fm}(\Psi) \neq \emptyset$, either satisfies the restriction on $(\bot_L)$ for $\mathbf{C}_0^*$, then it will make S an axiom instead of a saturated sequent. Thus it must be the case as claimed in (1).

For (2), we only verify the basic cases for the pre-order in the model construction. the case of (i) is trivial; (ii) is ensured by the saturation condition associated with (trans); (iii) is ensured by the definition of blocked sequent. The induction step on the transitive closure is direct. For (3), from (2) and the definition of valuation, we directly have the hereditary property holds for atoms, i.e., if $x_{\Phi_1\Rightarrow\Psi_1} \leq_S x_{\Phi_2\Rightarrow\Psi_2}$ and $x_{\Phi_1\Rightarrow\Psi_1} \Vdash p$, then $x_{\Phi_2\Rightarrow\Psi_2} \Vdash p$. Hereditary property for an arbitrary formula the follows via an induction on formula complexity. □

Proof of Lemma 2. Assume S is a global-saturated sequent in the calculus $\mathbf{CC}_0^*$.

If $x_{\Phi\Rightarrow\Psi} \in W_\bot$, then for (a) $x_{\Phi\Rightarrow\Psi}$ satisfies any arbitrary formula; for (b), $\mathsf{Fm}(\Psi) = \emptyset$. Hence the lemma holds directly. Otherwise, $x_{\Phi\Rightarrow\Psi}$ is not fallible, we establish the proof by induction on the complexity of A. In the following proof, we abbreviate $x_{\Phi\Rightarrow\Psi}, W_S, \leq_S, R_S, V_S$ as x, W, R, V and only verify the case when $A = \Diamond B$ or $A = \Box B$. Other cases are relatively trivial.

- Let $\Diamond B \in \Phi$. Note that $\Phi \Rightarrow \Psi$ satisfies the saturation condition associated with $(\Diamond_L)$ for $\Diamond B$ whether the sequent itself is blocked or not. To show $x \Vdash \Diamond B$, consider an arbitrary $y \geq x$ and it suffices to find some z s.t. Ryz and $z \Vdash B$. Assume $y = x_{\Sigma\Rightarrow\Pi}$, by Proposition 3, we have $\Phi \subseteq \Sigma$, hence $\Diamond B \in \Sigma$ as well. Then by the saturation condition associated with $(\Diamond_L)$, there is some $[\Lambda \Rightarrow \Theta] \in \Sigma$ s.t. $B \in \Lambda$. It follows from the model construction that $Ryx_{\Lambda\Rightarrow\Theta}$. By IH, we have $x_{\Lambda\Rightarrow\Theta} \Vdash B$. Take $z = x_{\Lambda\Rightarrow\Theta}$, we conclude $x \Vdash \Diamond B$.
- Let $\Diamond B \in \Psi$. Assume for the sake of a contradiction that $x \Vdash \Diamond B$, then for any $y \geq x$, there is some z s.t. Ryz and $z \Vdash B$. Since $(\Diamond_R)$ is an R3-rule, we need to consider if $\Phi \Rightarrow \Psi$ is blocked or not. If it is not blocked, then $\Phi \Rightarrow \Psi$ satisfies the saturation conditions associated with $(\Diamond_R)$ for $\Diamond B$, which means one of the two cases holds:
  1. $\widehat{\Diamond} B \in \Psi$. In this situation, since $x \leq x$, we just take $y = x$, then there is some $x_{\Lambda\Rightarrow\Theta}$ s.t. $Rxx_{\Lambda\Rightarrow\Theta}$ and $x_{\Lambda\Rightarrow\Theta} \Vdash B$. Recall $x_{\Phi\Rightarrow\Psi}$ is not fallible, if $x_{\Lambda\Rightarrow\Theta} \in W_\bot$, it must be the case $x_{\Lambda\Rightarrow\Theta} \in W_\bot^0$. Since $\Lambda \Rightarrow \Theta$ satisfies the saturation condition for $(\widehat{\Diamond})$, we have $B \in \Theta$ making $\mathsf{Fm}(\Theta)$ is non-empty,

it implies $x_{\Lambda \Rightarrow \Theta} \notin W^0_\bot$. Thus $x_{\Lambda \Rightarrow \Theta} \notin W_\bot$. Since $B \in \Theta$, by IH, we see $x_{\Lambda \Rightarrow \Theta} \nVdash B$, a contraction.
2. there is $\langle \Sigma \Rightarrow \Pi \rangle \in \Phi$ s.t. $\widehat{\Diamond} B \in \Pi$. By definition, $x \leq x_{\Sigma \Rightarrow \Pi}$. Take $y = x_{\Sigma \Rightarrow \Pi}$, then the proof proceeds as in (1).

Otherwise, $\Phi \Rightarrow \Psi$ is blocked by some unblocked $\Sigma \Rightarrow \Pi$, then $\Sigma \Rightarrow \Pi \simeq \Phi \Rightarrow \Psi$ which implies $\mathsf{Fm}(\Pi) = \mathsf{Fm}(\Psi)$. Thus $\Diamond B \in \Pi$ as well. Given that $\Sigma \Rightarrow \Pi$ is R3-saturated, it satisfies the saturation condition associated with $(\Diamond_R)$ for $\Diamond B$. Applying the argument above for the unblocked case to $\Sigma \Rightarrow \Pi$, then we have $x_{\Sigma \Rightarrow \Pi} \nVdash \Diamond B$. Since $\Phi \Rightarrow \Psi$ is blocked by $\Sigma \Rightarrow \Pi$, by model construction, we have $x \leq x_{\Sigma \Rightarrow \Pi}$. By the hereditary property, we conclude $x \nVdash \Diamond B$.

- Let $\Box B \in \Phi$. $\Phi \Rightarrow \Psi$ satisfies the saturation condition associated with $(\Box_L)$ for $\Box B$ regardless of whether the sequent itself is blocked or not. Assume for the sake of a contradiction that $x \nVdash \Box B$. Then there exists $x_{\Sigma \Rightarrow \Pi}, x_{\Lambda \Rightarrow \Theta}$ denoted as x_1, x_2 s.t. $x \leq x_1, Rx_1x_2$ and $x_2 \nVdash B$. By IH, we see that $B \notin \Lambda$. Since $x \leq x_{\Sigma \Rightarrow \Pi}$, by Proposition 3, $\Phi \subseteq \Sigma$, making $\Box B \in \Sigma$ as well. Then by the saturation condition associated with $(\Box_L)$, we have $B \in \Lambda$, a contraction.
- Let $\Box B \in \Psi$. Since $(\Box_R)$ is an R3-rule, it is necessary to distinguish whether $\Phi \Rightarrow \Psi$ is blocked or not. Assume that $\Phi \Rightarrow \Psi$ is not blocked, then it satisfies the one of the two saturation conditions associated with $(\Box_R)$ for $\Box B$:
  1. there is a block $[\Lambda \Rightarrow \Theta] \in \Psi$ with $B \in \Theta$. This means that $\mathsf{Fm}(\Theta)$ is non-empty, which further implies $x_{\Lambda \Rightarrow \Theta} \notin W_\bot$. By IH, we have $x_{\Lambda \Rightarrow \Theta} \nVdash B$. By model construction, we have $x \leq x$ and $Rxx_{\Lambda \Rightarrow \Theta}$, so $x \nVdash \Box B$.
  2. there is a block $\langle \Omega \Rightarrow [\Lambda \Rightarrow \Theta], \Xi \rangle \in \Psi$ with $B \in \Theta$. Denote the sequent $\Omega \Rightarrow [\Lambda \Rightarrow \Theta], \Xi$ by S_0. According to the model construction, we see that $x \leq x_{S_0}$ and $Rx_{S_0}x_{\Lambda \Rightarrow \Theta}$. Since $B \in \Theta$ thus $x_{\Lambda \Rightarrow \Theta} \notin W_\bot$. By IH we have $x_{\Lambda \Rightarrow \Theta} \nVdash B$ and then we conclude $x \nVdash \Box B$.

  Otherwise, $\Phi \Rightarrow \Psi$ is blocked by an unblocked sequent $\Sigma \Rightarrow \Pi \in^+ S$. By definition, $\Sigma \Rightarrow \Pi \simeq \Phi \Rightarrow \Psi$, which implies $\mathsf{Fm}(\Pi) = \mathsf{Fm}(\Psi)$, so $\Box B \in \Pi$ as well. Given that $\Sigma \Rightarrow \Pi$ is R3-saturated, it satisfies the saturation condition associated with $(\Box_R)$ for $\Box B$. Applying the argument above for the unblocked case to $\Sigma \Rightarrow \Pi$, then we have $x_{\Sigma \Rightarrow \Pi} \nVdash \Box B$. Since $\Phi \Rightarrow \Psi$ is blocked by $\Sigma \Rightarrow \Pi$, by model construction, we have $x \leq x_{\Sigma \Rightarrow \Pi}$. By the hereditary property, we conclude $x \nVdash \Box B$.

This completes our proof. □

References

1. Acclavio, M., Catta, D., Straßburger, L.: Game semantics for constructive modal logic. In: International Conference on Automated Reasoning with Analytic Tableaux and Related Methods, pp. 428–445. Springer, 2021
2. Balbiani, P., Gao, H., Gencer, C., Olivetti, N.: A natural intuitionistic modal logic: axiomatization and bi-nested calculus. In: Murano, A., Silva, A. (eds.), 32nd EACSL Annual Conference on Computer Science Logic (CSL 2024), volume 288 of Leibniz International Proceedings in Informatics (LIPIcs), pp. 13:1–13:21, Dagstuhl, Germany, 2024. Schloss Dagstuhl – Leibniz-Zentrum für Informatik. https://doi.org/10.4230/LIPIcs.CSL.2024.13

3. Balbiani, P., Gao, H., Gencer, C., Olivetti, N.: Local intuitionistic modal logics and their calculi. In: International Joint Conference on Automated Reasoning, pp. 78–96. Springer, 2024
4. Bellin, G., De Paiva, V., Ritter, E.: Extended curry-howard correspondence for a basic constructive modal logic. In: Proceedings of Methods for Modalities, vol. 2, 2001
5. Bierman, G.M., de Paiva, V.: On an intuitionistic modal logic. Stud. Log. **65**(3), 383–416 (2000). https://doi.org/10.1023/A:1005291931660
6. Dalmonte, T.: Wijesekera-style constructive modal logics. In: Fernández-Duque, D., Palmigiano, A., Pinchinat, S. (eds.), Advances in Modal Logic, AiML 2022, pp. 281–304. College Publications, 2022
7. Dalmonte, T., Grellois, C., Olivetti, N.: Intuitionistic non-normal modal logics: a general framework. J. Philos. Log. **49**(5), 833–882 (2020)
8. Dalmonte, T., Grellois, C., Olivetti, N.: Terminating calculi and countermodels for constructive modal logics. In: Das, A., Negri, S. (eds.), Automated Reasoning with Analytic Tableaux and Related Methods, pp. 391–408. Springer International Publishing, Cham, 2021
9. Das, A., Negri, S.: On intuitionistic diamonds (and lack thereof). In: Ramanayake, R., Urban, J. (eds.), Automated Reasoning with Analytic Tableaux and Related Methods - 32nd International Conference, TABLEAUX 2023, vol. 14278, LNCS, pp. 283–301. Springer, Cham (2023). https://doi.org/10.1007/978-3-031-43513-3_16
10. Fitting, M.: Nested sequents for intuitionistic logics. Notre Dame J. Form. Log. **55**(1), 41–61 (2014). https://doi.org/10.1215/00294527-2377869
11. Gore, R., Postniece, L., Tiu, A.: Cut-elimination and proof search for bi-intuitionistic tense logic. In: Beklemishev, L., Goranko, V., Shehtman, V., (eds.), Advances in Modal Logic, pp. 156–177. CSLI Publications, 2010
12. Iemhoff, R.: Terminating sequent calculi for two intuitionistic modal logics. J. Log. Comput. **28**(7), 1701–1712 (2018). https://doi.org/10.1093/logcom/exy026
13. Marin, S., Morales, M., Straßburger, L.: A fully labelled proof system for intuitionistic modal logics. J. Log. Comput. **31**(3), 998–1022 (2021). https://doi.org/10.1093/LOGCOM/EXAB020
14. Mendler, M., De Paiva, V.: Constructive ck for contexts. Context Representation and Reasoning (CRR-2005), p. 13, 2005
15. Mendler, M., De Paiva, V.: Cut-free gentzen calculus for multimodal ck. Inf. Comput. **209**(12), 1465–1490 (2011). Intuitionistic Modal Logic and Applications (IMLA 2008). https://doi.org/10.1016/j.ic.2011.10.003
16. Simpson, A.K.: The proof theory and semantics of intuitionistic modal logic, 1994
17. Straßburger, L., Das, A., Arisaka, R.: On nested sequents for constructive modal logics. Log. Methods Comput. Sci. **11** (2015)
18. Wijesekera, D.: Constructive modal logics I. Ann. Pure Appl. Log. **50**(3), 271–301 (1990). https://doi.org/10.1016/0168-0072(90)90059-B

Insensitive Games: Game Semantics for Modal Insensitivity

Can Başkent[1(✉)], David Gilbert[2], and Giorgio Venturi[3]

[1] Department of Computer Science, Middlesex University, London, UK
c.baskent@mdx.ac.uk

[2] Department of Philosophy, University of British Columbia, Vancouver, Canada
dave.gilbert@ubc.ca

[3] Dipartimento di Civiltá e Forme del Sapere, University of Pisa, Pisa, Italy
giorgio.venturi@unipi.it

Abstract. In this paper, we introduce a game theoretical semantics for a reflexive insensitive logic, and observe how classical semantic games needs to be altered to allocate reflexive insensitivity. Following, we extend semantic games to develop new games and new modalities. We prove the correctness theorems in each case.

Keywords: Game semantics · Reflexive Insensitivity · Semantic Insensitivity · Non-normal Modal Logics

1 Introduction

Insensitivity phenomenon in modal logic is the indifference of truth to the existence or non-existence of certain semantic properties. Reflexive-insensitivity is a well-known case where the logic is insensitive to the existence or non-existence of reflexive arrows in the relational model [12]. They were initially introduced to answer certain formal epistemic problems in modal logic such as contingency, essence and accident, and ignorance [11,13,15,17,18]. Recently, there has been a topological approach to the subject as well [5].

The idea of insensitivity is interesting from a game theoretical angle, too. Existence or non-existence of certain relational arrows describe the possibility or impossibility of certain moves in a game, which in turn impacts players' strategies. The game theoretical limitations that logics of insensitivities introduce to semantic games make such games of interest. Conversely, from a logical view point, semantic games offer an alternative semantics for such logical systems where the truth of a formula in a given model is established by playing a game. As such, semantic games introduce the element of strategising, thus rationality and choices, to logical discourse. An interesting research programme in this area is to develop semantic games for non-classical logics, where the non-classical elements in such logics generate rather interesting and *non-classical* games [1,2,6].

A proof theoretical analysis of the insensitivity phenomenon was discussed in [19]. The work focused on tableaux methods, reinforcing the analytical

D. Kozen and R. de Queiroz (Eds.): WoLLIC 2025, LNCS 15942, pp. 228–242, 2026.
https://doi.org/10.1007/978-3-031-99536-1_14

approaches to insensitivity. This is particularly important considering the BHK connection between proofs and truth, where to be true means to have a proof. Game semantics follows a similar pattern.

We start by introducing the formal system for reflexive-insensitivity. Let $\mathbf{P}$ be a set of countable propositional variables. We define the language of reflexive-insensitive modal logic $\mathcal{L}_\circ$ as follows in the Backus–Naur form

$$\varphi := p \mid \neg\varphi \mid \varphi \wedge \varphi \mid \varphi \vee \varphi \mid \circ\varphi \mid \bullet\varphi$$

where $p \in \mathbf{P}$.

The language of basic modal logic $\mathcal{L}_\Box$ is given as follows.

$$\varphi := p \mid \neg\varphi \mid \varphi \wedge \varphi \mid \varphi \vee \varphi \mid \Box\varphi \mid \Diamond\varphi$$

where, similarly, $p \in \mathbf{P}$.

We take the conditional arrow as an abbreviation: $\varphi \to \psi \equiv \neg\varphi \vee \psi$. Similarly, $\Diamond\varphi \equiv \neg\Box\neg\varphi$, dually. We prefer to keep both $\Diamond$ and $\Box$ modalities for game theoretical completeness of our treatment. The basic language of propositional logic, without the modal operators, will be denoted by $\mathcal{L}$.

A model $M = (W, R, V)$ is a triple where W is a non-empty set of worlds, R is a binary relation $R \subseteq W^2$ defined on W, and $V : W \mapsto 2^{\mathbf{P}}$ is a valuation function mapping worlds to sets of propositions that are satisfied there. In this model, the semantics for the Booleans are straight-forward. The semantics for the classical modalities and the $\circ$ and $\bullet$ operators are given as follows.

$$\begin{array}{lll}
M, w \models \Box\varphi & \text{iff} & \forall v.wRv \text{ implies } M, v \models \varphi \\
M, w \models \Diamond\varphi & \text{iff} & \exists v.wRv \text{ such that } M, v \models \varphi \\
M, w \models \circ\varphi & \text{iff} & M, w \not\models \varphi, \text{ or } \forall v.wRv \text{ implies } M, v \models \varphi \\
M, w \models \bullet\varphi & \text{iff} & M, w \models \varphi, \text{ and } \exists v.wRv \text{ such that } M, v \not\models \varphi
\end{array}$$

Using the language of basic modal logic, we then observe the following:

$$\circ\varphi \equiv \neg\varphi \vee \Box\varphi$$
$$\bullet\varphi \equiv \varphi \wedge \Diamond\neg\varphi$$

This paper is organised as follows. After briefly introducing the game semantics for classical modal logics, we develop a semantic game for reflexive-insensitive logics. After proving the correctness of semantic games, we then discuss how such games can be generalised to a broader class of logics of insensitivities.

2 Game Semantics for Classical Modal Logics, Briefly

Let $M = (S, R, V)$ be a model as before, and F be a frame based on M defined as $F = (S, R)$. Given a model, we construct modal semantic games.

Definition 1. *A semantic game is a tuple $\Gamma = (\pi, \rho, \sigma, F, w)$ where*

- *π is the set of players (with cardinality 2 in classical cases),*

- *ρ is the set of well-defined game rules,*
- *σ is the set of positions,*
- *F is the modal frame on which the game is played,*
- *w is the state in set S where the game starts.*

In classical modal logics, we have two players in π: the Verifier and the Falsifier. The Verifier's goal is to force the game to a win with true propositions whereas the Falsifier's goal is to force the game to a win with false propositions.

The positions σ depend on subformulas, players and states, and are determined by the game rules. The set σ is composed of tuples of the form (π_i, φ, w) where $\pi_i \in \pi$ is a player, $\varphi \in \mathcal{L}_\Box$ is a well-defined formula and $w \in S$ is a state. As such, the position will include the "turn function" which indicates which players are supposed to make a move at each position and at each state.

The rules ρ are defined inductively as transformations from a game position (π_i, φ, w) to a set of game positions $\{(\pi_j, \psi, v)\}_{j \in I}$ for $\pi_i, \pi_j \in \pi$, $I \subseteq \pi$ and $v \in S$. The players, formulas and the states in game positions are determined by the game rules and the relation R.

The set of accessible states from w is denoted by $R[w]$, and defined as usual: $R[w] := \{v : R(w, v)\}$.

Semantic games for classical modal logics are defined as follows.

Definition 2. *The tuple $\Gamma_\Box = (\varphi, \pi, \rho, \sigma, F, w)$ is a semantic game for classical modal logic with the language $\mathcal{L}_\Box$ for the formula $\varphi \in \mathcal{L}_\Box$, where $\pi = \{Verifier, Falsifier\}$, σ is the set of tuples (π_i, φ, w) for $\pi_i \in \pi$, $\varphi \in \mathcal{L}_\Box$ and $w \in S$, $F = (S, R)$ is the modal frame on which the game is played, and $w \in S$ is a state where the game starts.*

We define the set of positions σ inductively as follows, where $w \in S$:

- *(σ_p) If φ is atomic, then $(\pi_i, \varphi, w) \in \sigma$ for all $\pi_i \in \pi$,*
- *($\sigma_\neg$) If $\varphi = \neg\psi$, then $(\pi_i, \varphi, w) \in \sigma$ for all $\pi_i \in \pi$, and $(\pi_j, \psi, w) \in \sigma$ for some $\pi_j \in \pi$ depending on ψ's main connective;*
- *($\sigma_\wedge$) If $\varphi = \psi \wedge \chi$, then $(Falsifier, \varphi, w) \in \sigma$, and $(\pi_j, \psi, w), (\pi_k, \chi, w) \in \sigma$ for some $\pi_j, \pi_k \in \pi$ depending on ψ and χ's main connectives;*
- *($\sigma_\vee$) If $\varphi = \psi \vee \chi$, then $(Verifier, \varphi, w) \in \sigma$, and $(\pi_j, \psi, w), (\pi_k, \chi, w) \in \sigma$ for some $\pi_j, \pi_k \in \pi$ depending on ψ and χ's main connectives;*
- *($\sigma_\Box$) If $\varphi = \Box\psi$, then $(Verifier, \varphi, w) \in \sigma$, and $(\pi_j, \psi, v) \in \sigma$ for some $\pi_j \in \pi$ depending on ψ's main connective, and for all $v \in R[w]$;*
- *($\sigma_\Diamond$) If $\varphi = \Diamond\psi$, then $(Falsifier, \varphi) \in \sigma$, and $(\pi_j, \psi, v) \in \sigma$ for some $\pi_j \in \pi$ depending on ψ's main connective, and for all $v \in R[w]$.*

The set of rules ρ is defined as follows:

- *(ρ_p) If φ is atomic at w, the game terminates at w; and the Verifier wins if φ is true, the Falsifier wins if φ is false;*
- *($\rho_\neg$) If $\varphi = \neg\psi$ at w, the Falsifier and the Verifier switch roles, and the game continues with ψ at w;*

($\rho_\vee$) *If* $\varphi = \psi \vee \chi$ *at* w*, the Verifier chooses between* ψ *and* χ *at* w*;*
($\rho_\wedge$) *If* $\varphi = \psi \wedge \chi$ *at* w*, the Falsifier chooses between* ψ *and* χ *at* w*;*
($\rho_\Box$) *If* $\varphi = \Box\psi$*, the Falsifier chooses a state* $v \in R[w]$*, and the game continues with* ψ *at* v*;*
($\rho_\Diamond$) *If* $\varphi = \Diamond\psi$*, the Verifier chooses a state* $v \in R[w]$*, and the game continues with* ψ *at* v*.*

A brief explanation of this definition is in order. Let us consider the case for negation. For $\varphi = \neg\psi$, for any ψ, *all* players (which are the Verifier and the Falsifier, in the case of classical modal logic) make a move. By making that move, the position $(\pi_i, \neg\psi, w)$ is broken down into (π_j, ψ, w). If π_i was the Verifier, then π_j becomes the Falsifier, and *vice versa*. In some non-classical logical games, for example, for negation we can have $\pi_i = \pi_j$ –that is some players may *not* switch roles under negation [1]. Therefore, it is relatively straight-forward to extend Definition 2 to other logics.

Furthermore, the above definition is scaleable. It specifies the players, and more importantly the positions. In chess, for example, positions are given similarly. The position Be5 in coloumn 1, suggests that the player White moves Bishop to square e5, containing the same three components as in the tuples in σ: the player, the state and the proposition. The game rules, however, are given inductively where for each possible position, it specifies which moves are allowed and whose turn it is to make a move. As such, this definition can easily be extended to various other logics where alternative rules can be introduced.

The well-known correctness theorem of game semantics establishes the connection between modal semantic games and (classical) modal logic as follows.

Theorem 1. *Given a modal model* $M = (S, R, V)$ *and a modal semantic game* $\Gamma_\Box = (\varphi, \pi, \rho, \sigma, F, w)$*, we have*

$$M, w \models \varphi \text{ if and only if the Verifier has a winning strategy in } \Gamma_\Box \text{ at } w.$$

In classical modal logic, semantic games are two-player, zero-sum, competitive, determined and sequential with perfect information. It is, however, not a necessity to have all the aforementioned properties in a semantic game. Various non-classical logics force semantic games to be, for instance, a three-player, non-zero sum, cooperative, non-determined, non-sequential or concurrent [1–3,6]. Therefore, the relation between semantic games and logic are two directional: Given a logic, one can aim at developing a semantic game for that logic, or given a semantic game with various game theoretical properties, one can aim at engineering a logical system that matches with that game with the said properties. The current paper contributes to this research programme by examining logics of reflexive-insensitivity.

Let us now we examine what reflexive-insensitivity introduces to semantic games by focusing on the logic-to-games direction of the aforementioned relation.

3 Semantic Games for Reflexive-Insensitivity

The idea behind representing reflexive insensitivity game theoretically is to allow the players to have an *indifference* to the existence and the accessibility of some positions in the game board. Those positions will create certain strategic power for some players. Let us start with expanding Definition 2 to define semantic games for reflexive-insensitive logics.

Definition 3. *The tuple $\Gamma_\circ = (\varphi, \pi, \rho, \sigma, F, w)$ is a semantic game for reflexive-insensitive modal logic with the language $\mathcal{L}_\circ$ for the formula $\varphi \in \mathcal{L}_\circ$, where $\pi = \{Verifier, Falsifier\}$, σ is the set of tuples (π_i, φ, w) for $\pi_i \in \pi$, $\varphi \in \mathcal{L}_\Box$, and $w \in S$, $F = (S, R)$ is the modal frame where the game is played on, and $w \in S$ is a state where the game starts.*

We define the set of positions σ inductively as follows, where $w \in S$:

- *(σ_p) If φ is atomic, then $(\pi_i, \varphi, w) \in \sigma$ for all $\pi_i \in \pi$;*
- *($\sigma_\neg$) If $\varphi = \neg\psi$, then $(\pi_i, \varphi, w) \in \sigma$ for all $\pi_i \in \pi$, and $(\pi_j, \psi, w) \in \sigma$ for some $\pi_j \in \pi$ depending on ψ's main connective;*
- *($\sigma_\wedge$) If $\varphi = \psi \wedge \chi$, then $(Falsifier, \varphi, w) \in \sigma$, and $(\pi_j, \psi, w), (\pi_k, \chi, w) \in \sigma$ for some $\pi_j, \pi_k \in \pi$ depending on ψ and χ's main connectives;*
- *($\sigma_\vee$) If $\varphi = \psi \vee \chi$, then $(Verifier, \varphi, w) \in \sigma$, and $(\pi_j, \psi, w), (\pi_k, \chi, w) \in \sigma$ for some $\pi_j, \pi_k \in \pi$ depending on ψ and χ's main connectives;*
- *($\sigma_\circ$) If $\varphi = \circ\psi$, then $(Verifier, \varphi, w) \in \sigma$, and $(\pi_j, \neg\psi, w) \in \sigma$ and $(\pi_j, \psi, v) \in \sigma$ for some $\pi_j \in \pi$ depending on ψ's main connective, and for all $v \in R[w]$;*
- *($\sigma_\bullet$) If $\varphi = \bullet\psi$, then $(Falsifier, \varphi, w) \in \sigma$, and $(\pi_j, \psi, w) \in \sigma$ $(\pi_j, \psi, v) \in \sigma$ for some $\pi_j \in \pi$ depending on ψ's main connective, and for all $v \in R[w]$.*

The set of rules ρ is defined as follows:

- *(ρ_p) If φ is atomic at w, the game terminates at w; and the Verifier wins if φ is true, the Falsifier wins if φ is false;*
- *($\rho_\neg$) If $\varphi = \neg\psi$ at w, the Falsifier and the Verifier switch roles, and the game continues with ψ at w;*
- *($\rho_\vee$) If $\varphi = \psi \vee \chi$ at w, the Verifier chooses between ψ and χ at w;*
- *($\rho_\wedge$) If $\varphi = \psi \wedge \chi$ at w, the Falsifier chooses between ψ and χ at w;*
- *($\rho_\circ$) If $\varphi = \circ\psi$, the Verifier first chooses between remaining at the current state w and moving onto a state $v \in R[w]$. If he chooses to remain, then the game continues with $\neg\psi$ at w; if he chooses the latter, then the Falsifier makes another choice amongst the states in $R[w]$ where the game continues with ψ at a $v \in R[w]$;*
- *($\rho_\bullet$) If $\varphi = \bullet\psi$, the Falsifier first chooses between remaining at the current state w and moving onto a state $v \in R[w]$. If she chooses the former, the game continues with ψ at w; if she chooses the latter, the Verifier makes another choice amongst the states in $R[w]$ where the game continues with $\neg\psi$ at a $v \in R[w]$.*

The rules ($\rho_\circ$) and ($\rho_\bullet$) are more complicated than their modal counterparts ($\rho_\Box$) and ($\rho_\Diamond$), which were given in Definition 2. The main difference is that the modal operators $\circ$ and $\bullet$ force two sequential-moves with an alternating order of players. One player makes a choice and then "passes the ball" to the other player. Let us examine what they actually entail game theoretically by considering a simple example.

(a) The model M without the reflexive arrows.

(b) The model M' with the reflexive arrows.

Fig. 1. Models M and M', where the latter has reflexive arrows.

We start with a game for $\bullet p$ at a state w. In order to underline the reflexive-insensitivity of the logic, let us consider the following two models M and M', and evaluate $\bullet p$ at both w in M and w' in M', as given in Fig. 1.

Based on the above models M and M', we next construct game models, respectively at w and w', evaluating the formula $\bullet p$, given in Fig. 2. The player Falsifier is represented by F whereas the Verifier is by V where they get to make moves.

A closer inspection of the game tree given in Fig. 2b for M' shows how the reflexive arrows change the game tree. The moves l and r may seem to create a contradiction at first glance. However, the order of making a choice for the player F makes it impossible to make contradictory choices. Once the move l is made, r cannot be chosen at the same time. Therefore, the contradictory choices cannot be made – even if the players with opposing goals would rationally want to do so. Thus, the game becomes *insensitive* to the additional r moves, which can contradict *previous* moves of the opponent. This is the game theoretical characterisation of the insensitivity phenomenon within the context of semantic games. The strength of this approach is its *scalability* – it can be extended to other semantic modal insensitivities.

Another strength of the game semantic approach to insensitivity is that it resorts to "move priority order" to explain the phenomenon. Once a choice is made by a player, alternative moves are eliminated from the game tree. As a result of this, players can make two sequential moves without a contradiction. This is similar to Iterated Elimination of Strictly Dominated Strategies, which is already introduced into semantic games for the logics of non-sense [2]. However,

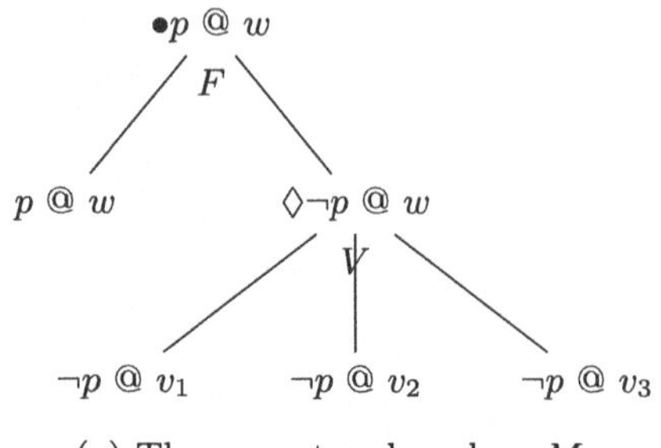

(a) The game tree based on M.

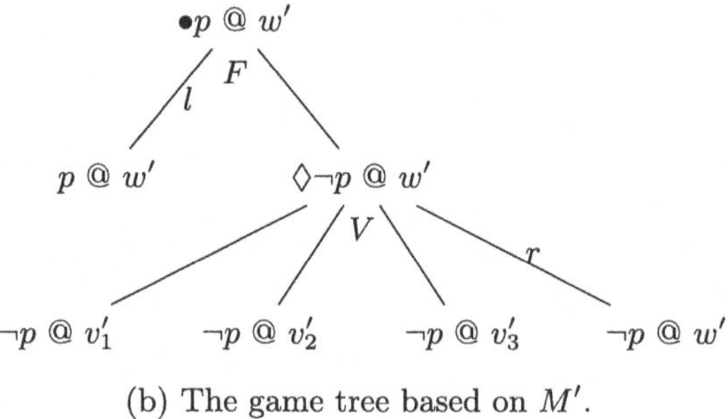

(b) The game tree based on M'.

Fig. 2. Game trees based on M and M', where the resolution of negated propositions $\neg p$ are omitted for easy read.

in the context of insensitive logics, it is not the strategies that are eliminated but redundant moves to which the game is insensitive. As such, semantic games for reflexive insensitivities extend the way sequentiality works in classical semantic games. Therefore, the non-classical element in such games is restricting the way that sequentiality of players' moves works.

A strategic power of insensitivity within the context of semantic games is worth noting. With the modalities $\circ$ and $\bullet$, players have the strategic power of *controlling the turns* in the game. They may choose to make a move themselves, or "pass the ball" to the opponent. This changes the strategic dynamic of the game that is familiar from the game semantics of standard modalities, given in rules $(\rho_\Box)$ and $(\rho_\Diamond)$ in Definition 2. Furthermore, this idea can be generalised for the sake of the games-to-logic direction. One can imagine a game where the players have certain power to control the turns, where a player's move may entail that first F then V, and then F again would make moves sequentially, following the said order. The logic that can match this strategic power may have some insensitivity to certain modal formulas. We discuss this idea in due time.[1]

[1] It is important to note that there is a sense of *completeness* in this bidirectional relation between logic and games from the insensitivity phenomena. The question of whether there exists a logic for every finite sequence of turns falls outside the scope of this paper.

Now, we test the ideas which we discussed earlier with a semantic game for the formula $\circ\varphi$ at w in M' with a slight abuse of the language for clarity. The game tree given in Fig. 3 illustrates the moves generated by reflexive arrows. The game remains strategically insensitive to the moves l and r.

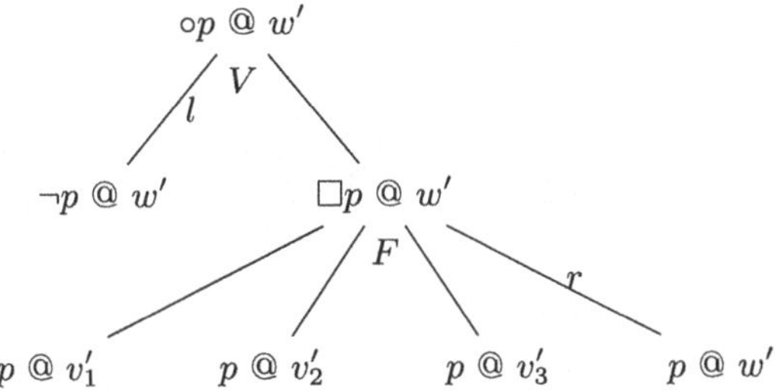

Fig. 3. Game tree for the semantic game for the formula $\circ\varphi$ at w' in model M'.

We now conclude this section with the following correctness theorem.

Theorem 2. *Given a reflexive-insensitive model* $M = (S, R, V)$ *and a reflexive-insensitive semantic game* $\Gamma_\circ = (\varphi, \pi, \rho, \sigma, F, w)$*, we have*

$M, w \models \varphi$ *if and only if the Verifier has a winning strategy for* φ *in* $\Gamma_\circ$ *at* w.

Similarly,

$M, w \not\models \varphi$ *if and only if the Falsifier has a winning strategy for* φ *in* $\Gamma_\circ$ *at* w.

4 Generalised Insensitive Games

An interesting dimension of game semantics for non-classical logics is that one can take advantage of game theoretical tools to develop new logics.

For instance, in the case of the logics of non-sense of Bochvar-Halldén, it is possible to extend the game semantics of such systems to engineer various extensions [2, 7–10, 14]. In the semantic games for Bochvar-Halldén logics, winning strategies of players form a partial order of *dominance*, reminiscent of the game theoretical method of *iterated elimination of strictly dominated strategies* (IESDS).

IESDS makes it possible to eliminate those strategies which are strictly dominated by other strategies. Carrying out this method step by step, one reaches a solution [16]. In logics of non-sense, this establishes truth and allows one to extend the standard 3-valued logic of non-sense of Bochvar-Halldén to a chain of n-valued logics of non-sense [2]. A similar method can also be a applied to diagrammatic reasoning in logic whilst establishing a connection between game semantics and diagrammatic reasoning in logic [3].

In the case of reflexive-insensitive logics, it is possible to develop an extension of $\Gamma_\circ$ games. The curious question is what the logics that correspond to these games would be. This is our goal in this section.

In $\Gamma_\circ$ games, moves in the form of "I play, and then you play" are allowed. This is a restriction in game semantics only because the shape of formulas determine the order of play. An immediate extension of $\Gamma_\circ$ would be to engineer games which would allow moves in the form of "I play, you play, and then I play again" for both players. This approach could also enable us to form a chain of games where it is possible to have games with moves "I play, you play, I play and then you play", and so on. Simply put, we already know the logic for semantic games with moves of the form "I play, and then you play", then what is the logic for semantic games which allow moves of the form "I play, you play, and then I play again"? That is what we answer in sequel.

We start with proposing the game rules with such moves. Let us denote such modalities with $\triangle$ and $\blacktriangle$. The game rules for the new modalities are given as follows.

($\rho_\triangle$) If $\varphi = \triangle\psi$, the Verifier first chooses between remaining at the current state w and moving onto a state $v \in R[w]$. If he chooses to remain, then the game continues with $\neg\psi$ at w; if he chooses the latter, then the Falsifier first chooses between remaining at state v in $R[w]$ and moving onto a state $u \in R[v]$. If the Falsifier chooses to remain at v, then the game continues with $\neg\psi$ at v. If the Falsifier chooses to move onto $t \in R[v]$, then the Verifier chooses a $t \in R[v]$ and the game continues with ψ at t.

($\rho_\blacktriangle$) If $\varphi = \blacktriangle\psi$, the Falsifier first chooses between remaining at the current state w and moving onto a state $v \in R[w]$. If he chooses to remain, then the game continues with ψ at w; if he chooses the latter, then the Verifier first chooses between remaining at state v in $R[w]$ and moving onto a state $u \in R[v]$. If the Verifier chooses to remain at v, then the game continues with psi at v. If the Verifier chooses to move onto $t \in R[v]$, then the Falsifier chooses a $t \in R[v]$ and the game continues with $\neg\psi$ at t.

The game trees for the formulas $\triangle p$ and $\blacktriangle p$ at state w are given as follows in Fig. 4, where $v \in R[w]$ and $u \in R[v]$.

It is possible to iterate the game rules to create a rule which is of the form "I play, you play, I play, then you play again". Let us briefly illustrate this case, too. For the four-turn moves, the corresponding modalities will be denoted by $\triangledown$ and $\blacktriangledown$. Consequently, let us call these moves ($\rho_\triangledown$) and ($\rho_\blacktriangledown$), and give them as follows.

($\rho_\triangledown$) If $\varphi = \triangledown\psi$, the Verifier first chooses between remaining at the current state w and moving onto a state $v \in R[w]$. If he chooses to remain, then the game continues with $\neg\psi$ at w; if he chooses the latter, then the Falsifier first chooses between remaining at state v in $R[w]$ and moving onto a state $t \in R[v]$. If the Falsifier chooses to remain at v, then the game continues with $\neg\psi$ at v. If the Falsifier chooses to move onto $t \in R[v]$, then the Verifier

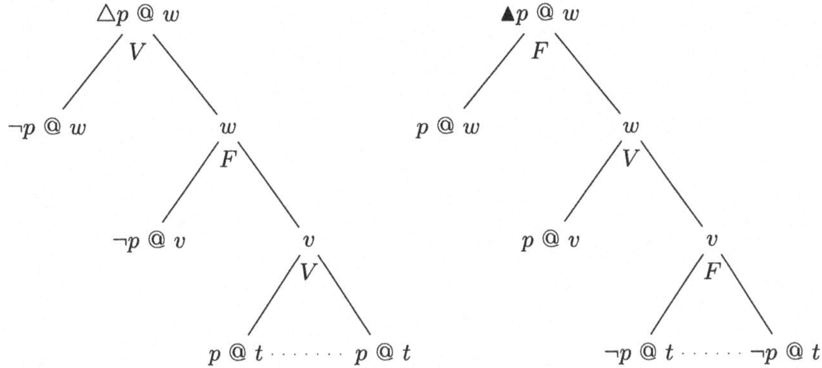

Fig. 4. The game trees for the formulas $\triangle p$ and $\blacktriangle p$ at state w, respectively, where $v \in R[w]$ and $t \in R[v]$.

at t first chooses between remaining at t and moving onto a state $u \in R[t]$. If the Verifier chooses to remain at t, then the game continues with $\neg\psi$ at t. If the Verifier chooses to move onto $u \in R[t]$, then the game continues with ψ at u.

($\rho_\blacktriangledown$) If $\varphi = \blacktriangledown\psi$, the Falsifier first chooses between remaining at the current state w and moving onto a state $v \in R[w]$. If he chooses to remain, then the game continues with ψ at w; if he chooses the latter, then the Verifier first chooses between remaining at state v in $R[w]$ and moving onto a state $t \in R[v]$. If the Verifier chooses to remain at v, then the game continues with *psi* at v. If the Verifier chooses to move onto $t \in R[v]$, then the Falsifier at t first chooses between remaining at t and moving onto a state $u \in R[t]$. If the Falsifier chooses to remain at t, then the game continues with ψ at t. If the Falsifier chooses to move onto $u \in R[t]$, then the game continues with $\neg\psi$ at u.

The game trees for the formulas $\triangledown p$ and $\blacktriangledown p$ at state w, respectively, where $v \in R[w]$, $u \in R[v]$, $t \in R[u]$, are given in Fig. 5.

Let us introduce the $\triangle, \blacktriangle$ and $\triangledown, \blacktriangledown$ operators to the basic language $\mathcal{L}$ which correspond to the game rules ($\rho_\triangle$), ($\rho_\blacktriangle$), ($\rho_\triangledown$) and ($\rho_\blacktriangledown$), and denote the language with these four modalities by $\mathcal{L}_\triangle$. Similarly, we denote the semantic games played in $\mathcal{L}_\triangle$ by $\Gamma_\triangle$, and define it in the usual way by extending Definition 2 by rules ($\rho_\triangle$), ($\rho_\blacktriangle$), ($\rho_\triangledown$) and ($\rho_\blacktriangledown$).

Now, what is the model theoretical semantics of $\triangle, \blacktriangle$ and $\triangledown, \blacktriangledown$ operators? We propose the following.

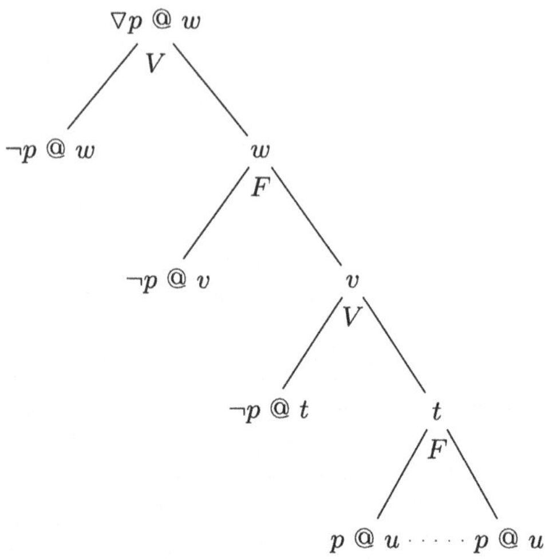

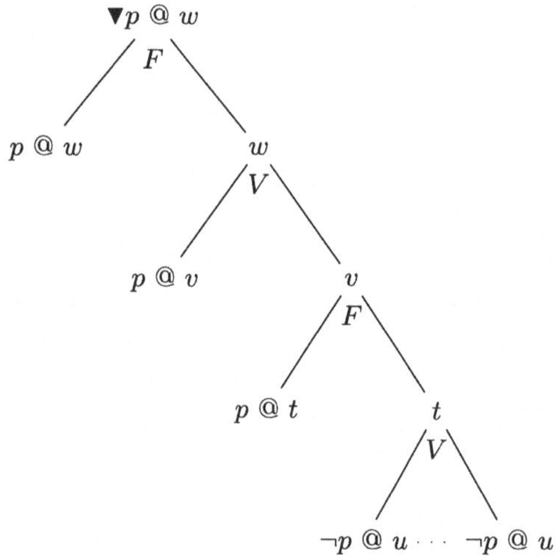

Fig. 5. The game trees for the formulas $\triangledown p$ and $\blacktriangledown p$ at state w, respectively, where $v \in R[w]$, $t \in R[v]$, $u \in R[t]$.

$$\begin{array}{lll} M, w \models \triangle\varphi & \text{iff} & M, w \not\models \varphi, \text{ or} \\ & & \forall v.wRv \text{ implies } (v \not\models \varphi \text{ and } (\exists t.vRt \text{ such that } t \models \varphi)) \\ M, w \models \blacktriangle\varphi & \text{iff} & M, w \models \varphi, \text{ and} \\ & & \exists v.wRv \text{ such that } (v \models \varphi \text{ implies } (\forall t.vRt \text{ implies } t \not\models \varphi)) \end{array}$$

$$\begin{array}{lll} M, w \models \triangledown\varphi & \text{iff} & M, w \not\models \varphi, \text{ or} \\ & & \forall v.wRv \text{ implies } (v \not\models \varphi \text{ and} \\ & & \quad (\exists t.vRt \text{ such that } (t \not\models \varphi \text{ or } (\forall u.tRu \text{ implies } u \models \varphi)))) \\ M, w \models \blacktriangledown\varphi & \text{iff} & M, w \models \varphi, \text{ and} \\ & & \exists v.wRv \text{ such that } (v \models \varphi \text{ implies} \\ & & \quad (\forall t.vRt \text{ implies } (t \models \varphi \text{ and } (\exists u.tRu \text{ and } u \not\models \varphi)))) \end{array}$$

We leave it to future work to examine the expressivity of the above modalities in $\mathcal{L}_\Box$ and $\mathcal{L}_\circ$ as well as the possibility to engineer various combinations of sequences of moves amongst the players.

What we demonstrated in this section is a methodology to generate logics based on various game theoretical *alterations* in semantic games. We took one simple step to form an alternating chain of orders, and it is very well possible to consider the cases that restrict the move orders to "I play, then I play again, then you play and then you play again" and so forth allowing various other combinations of strings of move orders. Such generalisations and their mathematical structures are left for future work.

We conclude this section with the following correctness theorem.

Theorem 3. *Given* $M = (S, R, V)$ *and a semantic game* $\Gamma_\triangle = (\varphi, \pi, \rho, \sigma, F, w)$, *we have*

$M, w \models \varphi$ *if and only if the Verifier has a winning strategy for* φ *in* $\Gamma_\triangle$ *at* w.

Similarly,

$M, w \not\models \varphi$ *if and only if the Falsifier has a winning strategy for* φ *in* $\Gamma_\triangle$ *at* w.

5 Conclusion

Various game theoretical conditions have a matching idea in logic. For example, the well-known solution method, "the iterated elimination of strictly dominated strategies", is captured by *strategy dominance* [2]. The current paper's contribution can be viewed within the remits of the same research programme.

In this paper, however, we used a much simpler idea from games: "pass the ball". Generalisation of this idea is straight-forward game theoretically with the help of some combinatorics. One can easily imagine a game of n-players, where some moves (that is modalities) enforce a player to pass the ball in a certain way between m-players. This would also help us to *engineer* a logical system with certain insensitivities. Similarly, various combinations of booleans and quantifiers, matching with a different order of players making moves in a certain order, can easily be motivated game theoretically. What is left is to explore the relationship between such sequences of moves and the insensitivity phenomenon. In this paper, particularly, this is how we captured reflexive-insensitivity game theoretically.

Finally, game semantics is helpful to present a diagrammatic reasoning for insensitive logics [3,4]. A visual representation of insensitivity is helpful to expand the strategic and game theoretical analysis to a broader class of insensitivities. What is next is to explore the relation between game trees for various semantic insensitivity and backward induction –a well-known method in game theory– from a diagrammatic view point.

We leave such ideas for future work.

A Appendix for Proofs

Proof (Theorem 2). The proof is by induction on the complexity of formulas. We skip the Boolean cases.

Let $M = (S, R, V)$ be a reflexive-insensitive model and $\Gamma_\circ$ be a reflexive-insensitive semantic game as defined earlier. We start with the case for $\varphi \equiv \circ\psi$.

Suppose $M, w \models \circ\psi$ for $w \in S$. Then, by the semantics of the $\circ$ modality, we have $M, w \not\models \psi$, or $\forall v.wRv$ implies $M, v \models \psi$.

Now, we have two cases to analyse. First, by the induction hypothesis for the Falsifier (applied to $M, w \not\models \psi$), we conclude that the Falsifier has a winning strategy at w for ψ. Second, by the induction hypothesis for the Verifier (applied to $M, v \models \psi$), we conclude that the Verifier has a winning strategy at v for all v with wRv. Furthermore, by the induction hypothesis for the Verifier for disjunction (applied to the main disjunction in the semantics of the $\circ$ modality), we conclude that the Verifier makes the first choice. Putting all together, we conclude that the Verifier first chooses either

(i) to stay at w and game continues with $\neg\psi$ at w, or

(ii) to move to a v in $R[w]$ so that the game continues with ψ at v in $R[w]$.

In the first case, since the Falsifier has a winning strategy for ψ at w, the Verifier has a winning strategy for $\neg\psi$ at w, by the case for the negation of this theorem. In the second case, as the Verifier is making the choice for $v \in R[w]$ and by the induction hypothesis for ψ at v, we conclude that the Verifier is still has a winning strategy at w. The very choice between these two cases is made by the Verifier, so either case, the Verifier has a winning strategy at w for the formula $\circ\psi$, by the game rule $\rho_\circ$ and the induction hypothesis. This concludes the truth-to-strategy direction of the proof.

For the converse direction, from strategy-to-truth, let us first suppose that the Verifier has a winning strategy in $\Gamma_\circ$ at w for the semantic game for the formula $\circ\psi$. By the game rule $(\rho_\circ)$ for $\circ\psi$ in $\Gamma_\circ$, the Verifier gets to make a move. He will choose either

(i) to remain at w so that the game continues with $\neg\psi$ at w, or

(ii) to move to $v \in R[w]$ so that the game continues with ψ at v.

In the first case, by the induction hypothesis of the very theorem, we conclude that $M, w \not\models \psi$. In the second case, using the same reasoning, we conclude that $M, v \models \psi$ for all $v \in R[w]$. Moreover, as the very first choice between the cases (i) and (ii) was carried out by the Verifier, by the induction hypothesis for the case for disjunction, we finally deduce that $M, w \not\models \psi$ or $M, v \models \psi$ for all $v \in R[w]$. Finally, by the semantics of the $\circ$ modality, we have $M, w \models \circ\psi$. This concludes the strategy-to-truth direction of the proof.

The argument for the Falsifier and the negation is almost identical.

The case for $\varphi \equiv \bullet\psi$ is similar, hence skipped.

This completes the proof.

Proof (Theorem 3). The proof is by induction on the complexity of formulas. We skip the Boolean cases. Therefore, we only prove the theorem for $\varphi = \triangle\psi$.

Let $M = (S, R, V)$ be a model and $\Gamma_\triangle$ be a semantic game as defined earlier. We start with the case for $\varphi \equiv \triangle\psi$.

Suppose $M, w \models \triangle\psi$ for $w \in S$. Then, by the semantics of the $\triangle$ modality, we have $M, w \not\models \psi$ or, $\forall v.wRv$ implies ($v \not\models \psi$ and ($\exists t.vRt$ such that $t \models \psi$)).

Now, we have two cases to analyse: cases (1) and (2). First, for the case (1), by the induction hypothesis for the Falsifier (applied to $M, w \not\models \psi$), we conclude that the Falsifier has a winning strategy for ψ at w. The second case is more complicated with two further sub-cases 2(a) and 2(b). First, for the case 2(a), by the induction hypothesis (applied to $v \not\models \psi$), Falsifier has a winning strategy at any state v in $R[w]$. Second, for the case 2(b), by the induction hypothesis (applied to $t \models \psi$) The Verifier has a winning strategy for some state t in $R[v]$. The very choice between the cases 2(a) and 2(b) is made by the Falsifier. And the choice between cases (1) and (2) is made by the Verifier, by the induction hypothesis for disjunction. Therefore, by the game rule $\rho_\triangle$ and the induction hypothesis, the Verifier has a winning strategy for $\triangle\psi$. This was truth-to-strategies direction.

For the converse, the strategies-to-truth direction, assume that the Verifier has a winning strategy in $\Gamma_\triangle$ at w for the semantic game for the formula $\triangle\psi$. Then, by the game rule $\rho_\triangle$, the Verifier makes the first choice. The Verifier chooses either

(Case 1): to remain at w so that the game continues with $\neg\psi$ at w, or

(Case 2): to move to $v \in R[w]$ where there the Falsifier chooses either

(Case 2a): to remain at v so that the game continues with $\neg\psi$ at v, or

(Case 2b): to move to $t \in R[v]$ where the Verifier chooses a $t \in R[v]$ and the game continues with ψ at t.

In Case 1, by the induction hypothesis of the very theorem, we conclude that $M, w \not\models \psi$. This is a choice made by the Verifier.

In Case 2, we have two sub-cases, (2a) and (2b), and the choice between Cases (2a) and (2b) is made by the Falsifier. If the Falsifier chooses (2a), then we conclude $M, v \not\models \psi$ for any $v \in R[w]$. If the Falsifier chooses (2b), then by the induction hypothesis, $M, t \models \psi$. The choice between the cases 1 and 2 is made by the Verifier whereas the choice between the cases (2a) and (2b) is made by the Falsifier. Putting all these together with the induction hypothesis, we conclude that $M, w \not\models \psi$ or, $\forall v.wRv$ implies ($v \not\models \psi$ and ($\exists t.vRt$ such that $t \models \psi$)). Finally, by the semantics of the $\triangle$ modality, we have $M, w \models \triangle\psi$. This concludes to strategies-to-truth direction.

The case for $\varphi = \nabla\psi$ is almost identical. Moreover, the cases for $\varphi = \blacktriangle\psi$ and $\varphi = \blacktriangledown\psi$ are similar.

This completes the proof.

References

1. Başkent, C.: Game theoretical semantics for some non-classical logics. J. Appl. Non-Classical Log. **26**(3), 208–39 (2016)
2. Başkent, C.: A game theoretical semantics for a logic of nonsense. In: Raskin, J.-F., Bresolin, D. (eds.) Proceedings of the 11th International Symposium on Games, Automata, Logics, and Formal Verification (GandALF 2020). Electronic Proceedings in Theoretical Computer Science, vol. 326, pp. 66–81 (2020)

3. Başkent, C.: Playing games with diagrams: truth diagrams and game semantics. In: Lemanski, J., et al. (eds.) 14th International Conference on the Theory and Application of Diagrams (DIAGRAMS 2024). LNAI, vol. 14981, pp. 300–315. Springer (2024)
4. Başkent, C.: Truth diagrams for some non-classical and modal logics. J. Appl. Non-Classical Log. **34**(4), 517–560 (2024)
5. Başkent, C., Gilbert, D., Venturi, G.: A logic of isolation. In: Studer, T., Metcalfe, G., de Queiroz, R. (eds.) Logic, Language, Information, and Computation (WoLLIC 2024). LNCS, vol. 14672, pp. 36–46 (2024)
6. Başkent, C., Carrasqueira, P.H.: A game theoretical semantics for a logic of formal inconsistency. Log. J. IGPL **28**(5), 936–952 (2020)
7. Bochvar, D.: On a three-valued logical calculus and its application to the analysis of contradictions. Matematicheskii Sbornik **4**(46), 287–308 (1937)
8. Bochvar, D.: On a three-valued logical calculus and its application to the analysis of the paradoxes of the classical extended functional calculus. Hist. Philos. Log. **2**(1–2), 87–112 (1981)
9. Ciuni, R., Ferguson, T.M., Szmuc, D.: Logics based on linear orders of contaminating values. J. Log. Comput. **29**(5), 631–663 (2019)
10. Ferguson, T.M.: Logics of nonsense and parry systems. J. Philos. Log. **44**(1), 65–80 (2015)
11. Gilbert, D., Kubyshkina, E., Petrolo, M., Venturi, G.: Logics of Ignorance and Being Wrong. Log. J. IGPL **30**(5), 870–885 (2021)
12. Gilbert, D., Venturi, G.: Reflexive insensitive modal logics. Rev. Symb. Log. **9**(1), 167–180 (2016)
13. Gilbert, D., Venturi, G.: Neighborhood semantics for logics of unknown truths and false beliefs. Australas. J. Log. **14**(1), 246–267 (2017)
14. Halldén, S.: The logic of nonsense. Uppsala Universitets Årsskrift (1949)
15. Marcos, J.: Logics of essence and accident. Bull. Sect. Log. **34**(1), 43–56 (2005)
16. Osborne, M.J., Rubinstein, A.: A Course in Game Theory. MIT Press (1994)
17. Steinsvold, C.: A note on logics of ignorance and borders. Notre Dame J. Formal Log. **49**(4), 385–392 (2008)
18. Steinsvold, C.: Being wrong: logics for false belief. Notre Dame J. Formal Log. **52**(3), 245–253 (2011)
19. Venturi, G., Yago, P.T.: Tableaux for essence and contingency. Log. J. IGPL **29**(5), 719–738 (2021)

Index Set Complexity for Congruence Lattices of Lattices

Bjørn Kjos-Hanssen[1(✉)] and Paul Kim Long V. Nguyen[2]

[1] University of Hawai'i at Mānoa, Honolulu, Hawai'i, USA
bjoernkh@hawaii.edu
[2] Agnes Scott College, Decatur, GA, USA
pnguyen@agnesscott.edu

Abstract. We analyze computable algebras (in the sense of universal algebra) in terms of index set complexity, specifically as regards their congruence lattices. We characterize simplicity of lattices as complete at the level Π^0_2, mirroring a result of Khoussainov and Morozov (2010) for groups. Finiteness of the congruence lattice is proved complete at the level Σ^0_3; and subdirect irreducibility at the level Σ^0_3.

Keywords: subdirect irreducibility · index set complexity · simple lattice · congruence lattice

1 Introduction

Computability researchers study computable rings, computable groups and computable algebras in general, in the sense of universal algebra. In this paper we study properties of the congruence lattice of computable universal algebras and their complexity. In particular we show computable lattices witness Π^0_2-completeness of being simple, as well witnessing the Σ^0_3-completeness of having finitely many congruences. We also examine the complexity of subdirect irreducibility, which we determine to be Σ^0_3-complete.

Complexity of properties of computable algebras have been studied previously and is an area of active research. In the finite case, for instance, it has been shown that for a finite algebra **A**, calculating **Con** (**A**) and determining whether **A** is simple are both complete for the class **NL** (nondeterministic logarithmic space) [2, Theorem 2.3,2.4]. Freese also showed algorithmic complexity results involving Malcev conditions in 2009 [5]. In the infinite case, Khoussainov and Morozov [8] showed simplicity to be Π^0_2-complete, witnessable by groups (see Definition 12). They also showed the property "to have finitely many congruences" to be Σ^0_3-complete, again witnessable by groups, as well as showing that the property "having a congruence lattice with the increasing chain property" is Π^1_1-complete along with the same result for the decreasing chain property.

The results in this article appeared in the doctoral dissertation of the second author, who thanks Ralph Freese and J.B. Nation for useful discussions. This work was partially supported by a grant from the Simons Foundation (#704836 to Bjørn Kjos-Hanssen).

D. Kozen and R. de Queiroz (Eds.): WoLLIC 2025, LNCS 15942, pp. 243–259, 2026.
https://doi.org/10.1007/978-3-031-99536-1_15

The study of the complexity of being subdirectly irreducible in particular has also been conducted by others, particularly in the finite case. In a 1997 paper, Freese showed one could decide if a finite computable lattice is subdirectly irreducible in time $O(n^2)$ where n is the cardinality of the lattice in question. In 2002, Bergman and Slutzki showed that for finite computable algebras subdirect irreducibility is **NL**-complete [2, Theorem 2.4] while also showing that directed graphs witness this complexity. We free ourselves of the finiteness restriction, and examine the complexity of these properties for possibly infinite algebras.

1.1 Definitions and Background

Definition 1 (algebra). *An* algebra $\mathbf{A}$ *is a tuple* (A, F) *in which* A *is a nonempty set and* $F = \{f_i\}_{i\in I}$ *is a sequence of functions where* $f_i : A^{n_i} \to A$ *and* $n_i \in \omega$ *for all* i *for some set* I *[1, Definition 1.1].*

Definition 2 (subalgebra). *If* $\mathbf{A} = (A, \{f_i : A^{n_i} \to A\}_{i\in I})$ *is an algebra, and* $B \subseteq A$ *where* $B \neq \emptyset$*, we call* $\mathbf{B} = (B, \{f_i \restriction B^{n_i}_{i\in I}\})$ *a* subalgebra *of* $\mathbf{A}$ *if* $f_i \restriction B^{n_i}$ *maps into* B*.*

Definition 3 (computable algebra). *A* computable algebra $\mathbf{A}$ *is a tuple*

$$(A, F = (f_0, f_1, \ldots)),$$

where

1. $A \subseteq \omega$ *is computable and* $A \neq \emptyset$*,*
2. F *is a uniformly computable sequence of functions, which are either the empty set or computable operations on* A*, and*
3. *there exists a computable function* $\sigma : \omega \to \omega \cup \{\uparrow\}$ *where for any* $k \in \omega$*, if* $\sigma(k) \in \omega$*,* f_k *is a computable operation from* $A^{\sigma(k)}$ *to* A*. If* $\sigma(k) =\uparrow$*, then* $f_k = \emptyset$*.*

We call A *and* F *the* domain *and* operations *of the computable algebra* $\mathbf{A}$ *respectively. We call* σ *the* rank function *for* $\mathbf{A}$ *and the value* $\sigma(k)$ *the* rank *of* f_k*. If* $\sigma(k) =\uparrow$*, we say operation* f_k *does not exist.*

Often, as a notational convention, we will assume implicitly that the domain of $\mathbf{A}$ is A, and the operations of $\mathbf{A}$ are $(f_0, f_1, \ldots)$.

Definition 4 (computable subalgebra). *Given a computable algebra* $\mathbf{A} = (A, F)$*, if* B *is a computable subset of* A*, we say* $\mathbf{B} = (B, F)$ *is a* computable subalgebra *of* $\mathbf{A}$*, if* $\mathbf{B}$ *is a computable algebra.*

While it would be tempting to require A to simply be an initial segment of ω, by only requiring A to be a computable subset of ω, we allow for the definition of computable subalgebra to be the intuitive one.

Definition 5 (uniformly computable algebras). *A sequence of computable algebras* $\{\mathbf{A}_i = (A_i, F_i = (f_{i,0}, f_{i,1}, \ldots))\}_{i<\omega}$ *is uniformly computable if*

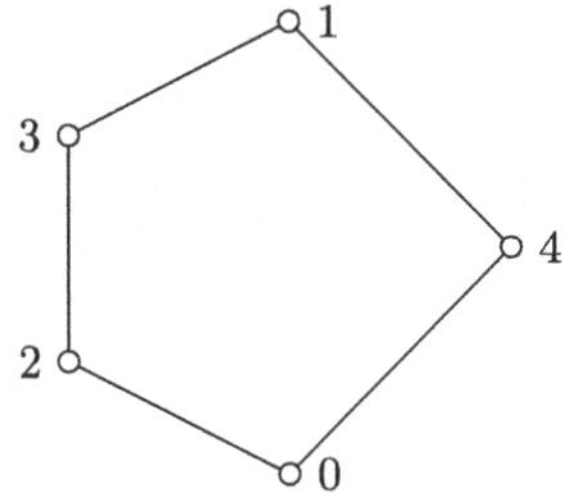

Fig. 1. The diagram of the lattice N_5

(1) their characteristic functions $\{A_i\}$ *and rank functions* $\{\sigma_i\}$ *are uniformly computable, and*
(2) there is a computable function $f(i,j,x)$ *with*

$$f(i,j,x) = f_{i,j}(x_1, x_2, \ldots, x_{\sigma_i(j)})$$

for all $x = \langle x_1, x_2, \ldots, x_{\sigma_i(j)} \rangle \in \omega$.

The *diagram* of a finite order (or finite lattice) is a graphical representation of that order. The elements are represented by circles. The circles representing the elements a and b are connected by an arc if one covers the other. In particular, if $b \prec a$, then the circle representing a is higher than the circle representing b [7, Section 2.1].

Example 1. Suppose we have a lattice $\mathbf{N_5} = (\{0,1,2,3,4\}, (\wedge, \vee))$, where $0 \prec 2 \prec 3 \prec 1$, $0 \prec 4 \prec 1$, and 4 is incomparable to 2 and 3. Then Fig. 1 is a diagram of N_5.

In practice however, in this paper we will often informally give "diagrams" for infinite lattices by using ellipses and the reader's imagination. We do so in the introduction of the following well-known family of lattices.

Definition 6. *For* $n \in \omega$ *or* $n = \omega$*, define* $\mathbf{M}_n = (M_n, (f_1 := \wedge, f_2 := \vee))$ *as follows. Let* $M_n = \{0, 1, \ldots, n+1\}$ *if* $n \in \omega$*, and* $M_n = \omega$ *when* $n = \omega$*. Let* $0 <_L 1$ *and for all* $m > 1 \in M_n$ *let* $x <_L m <_L y$ *if and only if* $x = 0$ *and* $y = 1$*. This results in the lattice represented in Fig. 2. This defines a family of lattices,* $\{\mathbf{M}_n\}_{n<\omega+1}$*.*

Definition 7 (substitution property). *Let* $\mathbf{A} = (A, (f_0, f_1, \ldots))$ *be a computable algebra and* θ *a binary relation on* A*. We use the shorthand* $a \ \theta \ b$ *if* $(a,b) \in \theta$*.*

We say θ *has the* substitution property *if for every* $n \in \omega$ *where* $\sigma(n) \neq \uparrow$*, we have that*

$$a_1 \ \theta \ b_1, a_2 \ \theta \ b_2, \ldots, a_{\sigma(n)} \ \theta \ b_{\sigma(n)}$$

implies

$$f_n(a_1, a_2, \ldots, a_{\sigma(n)}) \ \theta \ f_n(b_1, b_2, \ldots, b_{\sigma(n)}).$$

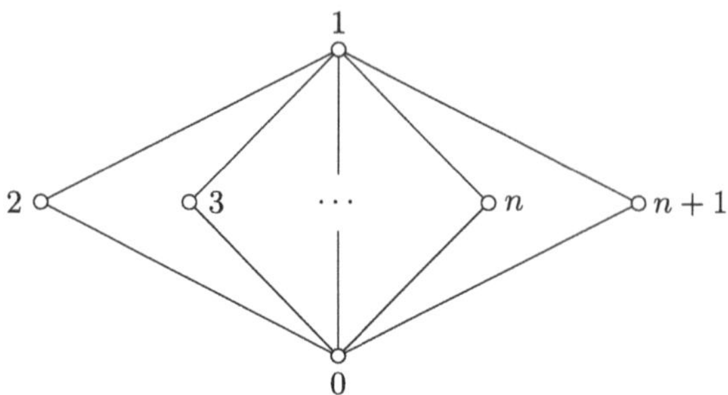

Fig. 2. The lattice $\mathbf{M}_n$

Intuitively, a relation has the substitution property if it "respects" the operations of an algebra. In the case where the relation is also reflexive, symmetric, and transitive we distinguish it from other relations.

Definition 8 (congruence). *If* $\mathbf{A}$ *is a computable algebra, and* θ *a binary relation on* A*, we say* θ *is a* congruence *if* θ *is an equivalence relation which has the substitution property. The set of all congruences of* $\mathbf{A}$ *we call* $\mathbf{Con}\,(\mathbf{A})$*. For* $a \in A$*, we define the* congruence class of "a" under θ *as the set* $\{b \in A : a\ \theta\ b\}$ *and denote this* $[\![a]\!]_\theta$*. Occasionally, when the context is clear we will suppress the subscript and write only* $[\![a]\!]$*.*

Congruences of algebras correspond to homomorphic images of that algebra, in the sense that every congruence induces a homomorphism, namely the map from the algebra to its congruence classes. Every algebra $\mathbf{A}$ has congruences $0_A = \{(x, x) : x \in A\}$ and $1_A = A \times A$. If these two congruences are the same, then $|A| = 1$ and we call $\mathbf{A}$ *trivial.* If $\mathbf{Con}\,(A) = \{0_A, 1_A\}$ and $\mathbf{A}$ is not trivial, then we call $\mathbf{A}$ *simple.*

It is known for instance that the lattice $\mathbf{M}_n$ is simple when $n \geq 3$. We will use this fact heavily.

Definition 9 (principal congruence). *Given a computable algebra* $\mathbf{A}$*, and elements* $a, b \in A$*, we say*

$$\mathrm{Cg}_{\mathbf{A}}\,(a, b) = \bigcap\{\theta \in \mathbf{Con}\,(\mathbf{A}) : (a, b) \in \theta\}.$$

It is known that $\mathrm{Cg}_{\mathbf{A}}\,(a, b)$ *is a congruence on* $\mathbf{A}$ *[1, Prop 1.23] and is thus the smallest congruence* θ *where* $a\ \theta\ b$*. As before, when the context is clear, we will suppress the subscript and just write* $\mathrm{Cg}\,(a, b)$*.*

Principal congruences are useful for proving general facts about $\mathbf{Con}\,(\mathbf{A})$, for instance the following lemma concerning principal congruences in lattices will be extremely useful, and oftentimes used implicitly.

Lemma 1. *If* $\mathbf{L}$ *is a lattice and* $a \leq b \in L$*, then for all* $x, y \in [a, b]_L$*,* $(x, y) \in \mathrm{Cg}\,(a, b)$*.*

Proof. Since $(a, b), (x, x) \in \mathrm{Cg}(a, b)$ we have by the Substitution Property that $(a, x) = (x \wedge a, x \wedge b) \in \mathrm{Cg}_{\mathbf{L}}(a, b)$. Similarly we have $(a, y) \in \mathrm{Cg}_{\mathbf{L}}(a, b)$. By transitivity $(x, y) \in \mathrm{Cg}_{\mathbf{L}}(a, b)$.

Using this lemma it is possible, for instance, to easily show that $\mathbf{M}_n$ is simple when $n \geq 3$ from the proof that $\mathbf{M}_3$ is simple [1, Lemma 2.9].

We will also use another useful theorem, a consequence of Dilworth [4, Lemma 2.1].

Theorem 1. *If* $\mathbf{L}$ *is a lattice, and* $a \leq_L b$ *then for* $\mathrm{Cg}_{\mathbf{L}}(a, b)$ *the following are equivalent:*

1. $[\![a]\!] = [a, b]_L$ *and for all* $x \notin [a, b]_L$, $[\![x]\!] = \{x\}$;
2. *for all* $x \in \mathbf{L}$, *if* $x \notin [a, b]_L$ *then* $(x <_L b \Rightarrow x <_L a)$ *and* $(a <_L x \Rightarrow b <_L x)$.

1.2 Completeness of Properties of Computable Algebras

We use the main definition from Khoussainov and Morozov [8, Main Definition].

Definition 10 (m-reducibility [11, 7.1]). *A set* A *is* many-one reducible *to* B *denoted* $(A \leq_m B)$ *if there exists a computable function* f *such that for all* a,

$$a \in A \Leftrightarrow f(a) \in B.$$

We abbreviate many-one reducible as m-reducible. If $A \leq_m B$ *and* $B \leq_m A$ *we say* $A \equiv_m B$.

Definition 11 ($\mathcal{J}$-complete property of an algebra). *Let* $\mathcal{J} \subseteq 2^\omega$ *(where* 2^ω *is the power set of* ω*) be closed downward under m-reducibility. We say that the property* $\mathcal{P}$ *of algebras in a class* $\mathcal{K}$ *is* $\mathcal{J}$-complete, *if the following is true:*

(1) For all uniformly computable sequences of algebras $\{\mathbf{A}_i\}_{i<\omega}$ *in* $\mathcal{K}$,

$$\{i : \mathbf{A}_i \text{ satisfies } \mathcal{P}\} \in \mathcal{J}.$$

(2) There exists a uniformly computable sequence of algebras $\{\mathbf{A}_i\}_{i<\omega}$ *in* $\mathcal{K}$ *for which for all* $J \in \mathcal{J}$,

$$J \leq_m \{i : \mathbf{A}_i \text{ satisfies } \mathcal{P}\}.$$

If the class $\mathcal{K}$ *is the class of all algebras, we suppress mention of it and simply say that the property* $\mathcal{P}$ *is* $\mathcal{J}$*-complete. If a property* $\mathcal{P}$ *satisfies property (1) we say* $\mathcal{P}$ *is a* $\mathcal{J}$-property *(in* $\mathcal{K}$*). If it satisfies property (2) we say* $\mathcal{P}$ *is* $\mathcal{J}$-hard *(in* $\mathcal{K}$*).*

We also introduce the notion of a class of algebras $\mathcal{S}$ *witnessing* $\mathcal{J}$-completeness for a class $\mathcal{K}$.

Definition 12 (witnessing $\mathcal{J}$-completeness). *If a property $\mathcal{P}$ is $\mathcal{J}$-complete in $\mathcal{K}$, and if there exists a uniformly computable sequence of algebras in a subclass $\mathcal{S}$ of a class $\mathcal{K}$ witnessing that $\mathcal{P}$ is $\mathcal{J}$-*hard *in $\mathcal{K}$, we say that $\mathcal{S}$ witnesses the $\mathcal{J}$-completeness of $\mathcal{P}$ in $\mathcal{K}$.*

Intuitively, this means that knowing the solution to determine if any $s \in \mathcal{S}$ has property $\mathcal{P}$ is sufficient to determine if any $k \in \mathcal{K}$ has property $\mathcal{P}$, and as such, $\mathcal{S}$ is somehow sufficiently complex in property $\mathcal{P}$ to understand the property in general.

Given a sequence of uniformly computable algebras $\{\mathbf{A}_i\}$ and some subset S of that sequence, the set $\{i : \mathbf{A}_i \in S\}$ is called the *index set* of S. In 2010, Khoussainov and Morozov [8] proved the following concerning properties of computable algebras:

(1) The simplicity is Π_2^0-complete,
(2) The property "to have finitely many congruences" is Σ_3^0-complete.

In proving statement (1) and (2), Khoussainov and Morozov proved that computable groups witness Π_2^0-completeness of being simple as well as witnessing Σ_3^0-completeness of having finitely many congruences. We prove that lattices are also sufficient, i.e. groups can be replaced by lattices, and thus also give alternate proofs for (1) and (2) as corollaries. In addition, we examine the complexity of subdirect irreduciblility which will be defined below.

In order to prove these results we will need a bit more theory.

Definition 13 (basic translation). *Given an algebra $\mathbf{A} = (A, \{f_i\}_{i<\omega})$, fix $i \in \omega$ and let $n = \sigma(i)$. Furthermore, let $j < n$, and $a_0, \ldots, a_{n-1} \in A$. Then*

$$u(x) = f_i(a_0, a_1, \ldots, a_{j-1}, x, a_{j+1}, \ldots, a_{n-1})$$

is a basic translation operation.

Definition 14 (translation). *Given an algebra $\mathbf{A} = (A, \{f_i\}_{i<\omega})$, the translations are a class of functions from A into A, defined as follows:*

(1) The identity function $u(x) = x$ and the basic translations are translations;
(2) If u and v are translations so is the composition.
(3) Nothing else is a translations operation.

The next result is one implicitly used and proved by Malcev, (see [6, Theorem 1.10.3] for a treatment of this).

Theorem 2 (Malcev's Lemma). *For an algebra $\mathbf{A}$, $(a, b) \in \mathrm{Cg}_{\mathbf{A}}(c, d)$ if and only if there exist $n < \omega$, a sequence $a = z_0, z_1, \ldots, z_n = b$ of elements of A and a sequence of translations $u_0, \ldots, u_{n-1}$ such that*

$$\{u_i(c), u_i(d)\} = \{z_i, z_{i+1}\}$$

for all $i < n$.

Corollary 1. *If* $\mathbf{B}$ *is a subalgebra of* $\mathbf{A}$*, and* $(a,b) \in \mathrm{Cg}_{\mathbf{B}}(c,d)$*, then* $(a,b) \in \mathrm{Cg}_{\mathbf{A}}(c,d)$*.*

Furthermore, this gives that if $\mathrm{Cg}_{\mathbf{B}}(c,d) = \mathrm{Cg}_{\mathbf{B}}(x,y)$*, then* $\mathrm{Cg}_{\mathbf{A}}(c,d) = \mathrm{Cg}_{\mathbf{A}}(x,y)$*.*

Proof. Since $(a,b) \in \mathrm{Cg}_{\mathbf{B}}(c,d)$, there exists a sequence of elements in B and translations that satisfy Malcev's Lemma. But these will still satisfy Malcev's Lemma in $\mathbf{A}$, which gives $(a,b) \in \mathrm{Cg}_{\mathbf{A}}(c,d)$.

Using our standard encoding for sequences of numbers, every basic transition $u(x) = f_i(a_0, a_1, \ldots, a_{j-1}, x, a_{j+1}, \ldots, a_{n-1})$ of an algebra $\mathbf{A}$ can be encoded computably as an element of ω, by encoding the sequence

$$(i, j, a_0, a_1, \ldots, a_{n-1}).$$

Furthermore, since any translation is just a sequence of compositions of basic translations and the identity function, we can encode any translation as a finite sequence of encoded basic transitions.

Lemma 2. *Given a computable algebra* $\mathbf{A}$ *and* $c,d \in A$*, the set* $\mathrm{Cg}_{\mathbf{A}}(c,d)$ *is* Σ^0_1*.*

We omit the easy proof. We will also need a technical lemma concerning simple lattices.

Lemma 3. *Suppose*

1. $M = [0_M, 1_M]_L, N = [0_N, 1_N]_L$ *are simple sublattices of a lattice* $\mathbf{L}$*,*
2. $\{1_M, 0_N\} \subseteq M \cap N$*,*
3. $1_M \neq 0_N$*, and*
4. $[0_M, 1_N]_L = M \cup N$*.*

Then $[0_M, 1_N]_L$ *is simple.*

Proof. Let $a \neq b \in M \cup N$. If $a,b \in M$, then since M simple, for all $x,y \in M$, we have $(x,y) \in \mathrm{Cg}_{\mathbf{L}}(a,b)$. But then $(1_M, 0_N) \in \mathrm{Cg}_{\mathbf{L}}(a,b)$, so since N is simple, we have for all $x,y \in N$, $(x,y) \in \mathrm{Cg}_{\mathbf{L}}(1_M, 0_N) \subseteq \mathrm{Cg}_{\mathbf{L}}(a,b)$. So $\mathrm{Cg}_{\mathbf{L}}(a,b) = 1_{[0_M,1_N]_L}\mathbf{L}$. The same argument works with $a,b \in N$. Thus we only need to consider the case where $a \in M \setminus N$ and $b \in N \setminus M$.

In that case $a \vee 1_M = 1_M$, and $b \vee 1_M \in N$, we would have two distinct elements of N related, so the above argument applies. Thus $[0_M, 1_N]_L$ is simple.

The assumptions of Lemma 3 are illustrated in Fig. 3.

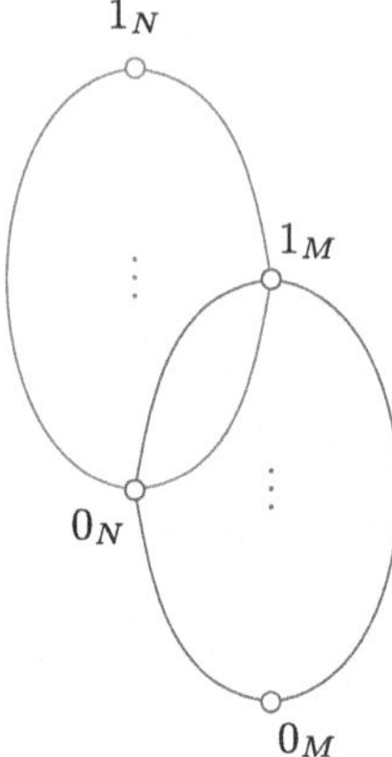

Fig. 3. An illustration of $[0_M, 1_N]_L$

2 Witnessing Complexity via Computable Lattices

In the next two chapters, in order to show the hardness of various properties, we will construct various sequences of computable lattices, $\{\mathbf{L}_b\}_{b<\omega}$. In doing so, for convenience, we will define each in terms of the partial order determined by $\wedge$ and $\vee$, being careful to ensure that calculating the meet and join of any two elements is computable. In particular, we construct each $\mathbf{L}_b$ in stages, by defining a series of sublattices $\mathbf{L}_{b,s} = (L_{b,s}, (\wedge_{b,s}, \vee_{b,s}))$, where

$$L_{b,s} \subseteq L_{b,s+1}, \wedge_{b,s} \subseteq \wedge_{b,s+1}, \text{ and } \vee_{b,s} \subseteq \vee_{b,s+1}$$

for all $s \in \omega$. Furthermore $\{L_{b,s}\}$ will be uniformly computable in s, and

$$\mathbf{L}_b = \left(\bigcup_{s<\omega} L_{b,s} = \omega, \left(\wedge_b = \bigcup_{s<\omega} \wedge_{b,s}, \vee_b = \bigcup_{s<\omega} \vee_{b,s} \right) \right).$$

The benefit in defining our lattices this way, is to ensure that they are 1) computable and 2) lattices. We define all the relations on $L_{b,s}$ in terms of a partial order, in such a way that the meets and joins will be computable. In fact, in $\mathbf{L}_b$, for any $x, y \in \omega$, since the meet and join operations are nested, the value of $x \vee y$ does not change once it is encountered. So we need only go to an s large enough that $x, y \in L_{b,s}$, and we can find $x \wedge y$ and $x \vee y$ there. This ensures our operations are computable. In order to ensure our algebras are indeed lattices we use a result found in Quackenbush [10]. The theorem, due to Lasker [10], is the following one:

Theorem 1. *Let $\mathcal{P}$ be a finite partial order with a planar diagram. If there is at most one element of $\mathcal{P}$ which has no cover and at most one element which covers no point then $\mathcal{P}$ is a lattice.*

This theorem allows us to ensure that our algebras $\mathbf{L}_{b,s}$ are lattices by making sure they have planar diagrams. Since this will give every pair of elements in ω a greatest lower bound and least upper bound, provided that $\mathbf{L}_b$ is a poset, we have that $\mathbf{L}_b$ is a lattice.

When defining these lattices, we will often want to add an element between two other elements in the intuitive way. We introduce a notion, we call "*just between*" to allow us to do that.

Definition 15 (just between). *Given a lattice* $\mathbf{L} = (L, (\wedge, \vee))$*, and* $a, b \in L$*. We say* c *is* just between a *and* b *if*

$$a \prec c \prec b \text{ and } (\forall d \in L)(c <_L d \Leftrightarrow d \geq_L b) \text{ and } (\forall d \in L)(c >_L d \Leftrightarrow d \leq_L a).$$

We will denote this

$$a \prec\!\!\prec c \prec\!\!\prec d \text{ in } L.$$

2.1 Simple Computable Lattices

Theorem 2. *Computable lattices witness the* Π_2^0*-completeness of being simple.*

Proof. We first show that, given a uniformly computable sequence of algebras $\{\mathbf{A}_i\}$,

$$\{i : \mathbf{A}_i \text{ is simple}\} \in \Pi_2^0.$$

This is shown by noting that in a simple algebra $\mathbf{A}_i$, if $a \neq b$, then $\mathrm{Cg}\,(a, b) = 1_{A_i}$. Thus $\{i : \mathbf{A}_i$ is simple$\}$ equals

$$\{i : (\forall a, b, c, d)(a, b, c, d \in A_i, c \neq d \rightarrow (a, b) \in \mathrm{Cg}\,(c, d))\} =$$
$$\{i : (\forall a, b, c, d)(\exists x)(\neg(a, b, c \neq d \in A_i) \text{ or } R(a, b, c, d, x) = 1)\},$$

which is Π_2^0, where R is as in the proof of Lemma 2.

Now suppose B is Π_2^0. Then it has been shown [11, Lemma before 14.XV] that there exists a uniformly computable sequence of boolean functions $\{P_b(t)\}_{b<\omega}$ such that

$$b \in B \Leftrightarrow (\overset{\infty}{\exists} t)(P_b(t) = 1),$$

where $(\overset{\infty}{\exists} t)$ means "there exist infinitely many t". We construct a sequence of lattices $\{\mathbf{L}_b\}_{b<\omega}$ with the property that $\mathbf{L}_b$ is simple if and only if $b \in B$. This will give $B \equiv_m \{b : \mathbf{L}_b$ is simple$\}$ via the identity function. We define each in stages, and will also define a helper function $T(s)$ which will, informally, be the "top" of the lattice as currently defined by stage s.

Stage 0: We start every $\mathbf{L}_b$ with the lattice operations in Fig. 4. We also let $T(0) = 3$, in keeping with our desire to have $T(0)$ point at the top after stage s. For technical reasons which will be clear later, we also let $T(-1) = 2$. We note that $L_{b,0} = \{0, 1, \ldots, 5\}$.

Stage s: We will define lattice operations for all elements less than (in the standard sense) and including $8 + 3s$. In particular, we just define our lattice

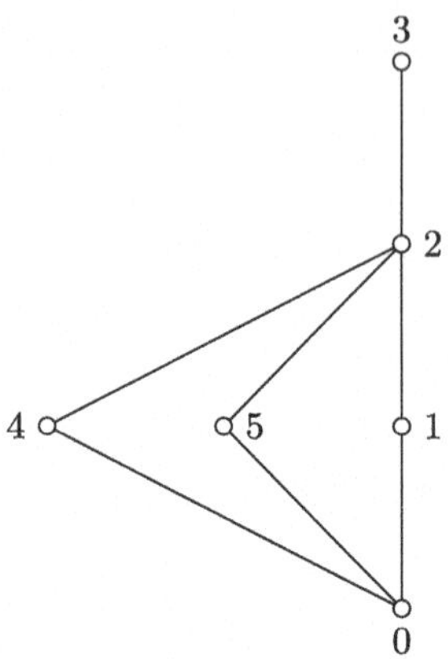

Fig. 4. The initial lattice

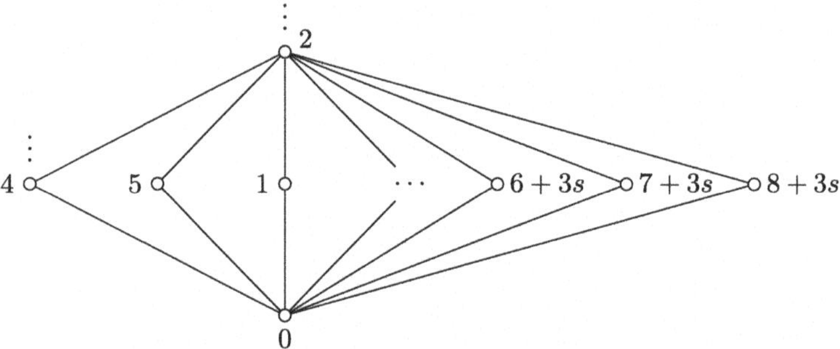

Fig. 5. Placement of nodes when $P_b(s) = 0$

operations for additional elements $6 + 3s, 7 + 3s$ and $8 + 3s$. Let $L_{b,s} = L_{b,s-1} \cup \{6 + 3s, 7 + 3s, 8 + 3s\}$.

If $P_b(s) = 0$, then for $6 \leq i \leq 8$ and $n \leq 8 + 3s$, let

$$0 \prec\!\!\prec (i + 3s) \prec\!\!\prec 2$$

in $L_{b,s}$ (see Fig. 5).

Since we have not put anything above $T(s)$, we let $T(s) = T(s-1)$.

Otherwise, if $P_b(s) = 1$, we place $6 + 3s$ at the top, covering $T(s-1)$, i.e. for $n \in L_{b,s}, n \leq_L 6 + 3s$. Furthermore let

$$T(s-1) + 1 \prec\!\!\prec 7 + 3s, 8 + 3s \prec\!\!\prec T(s-1).$$

Since we changed the top, we also let $T(t) = 6 + 3t$ (see Fig. 6).

We claim under this construction,

$$B = \{b : \mathbf{L}_b \text{ is simple}\}.$$

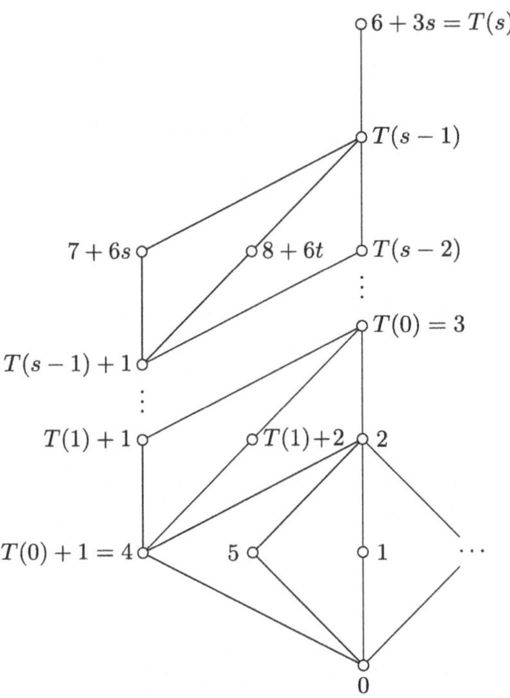

Fig. 6. Placement of nodes when $P_b(s) = 1$

Suppose $b \notin B$. Then there exists s_0 such that for all $s \geq s_0, P_b(s) = 0$. Thus, for all $s \geq s_0$, $T(s) = T(s_0)$. Also, ther e exists some maximal $s_1 < s_0$ where $T(s_0) \succ T(s_1)$. By Theorem 1 we have that $0_{L_b} \neq \text{Cg}\,(T(s_0), T(s_1)) \neq 1_{L_b}$. Thus $\mathbf{L}_b$ is not simple.

On the other hand, assume $b \in B$. Let s_k = the kth index s such that $T(s) > T(s-1)$. Since $b \in B$, this sequence is defined for all $k \in \omega$. Also let $s_0 = -1$. Then $T(s_k) \prec T(s_{k+1})$ for $k \in \omega$. See Fig. 7. Note $[0, T(s_0)]_L$ is isomorphic to $\mathbf{M}_n$ for some $n < \omega+1$, which is simple. Since for every $k > 0$, we have $[T(s_k)+1, T(s_k)]_L$ isomorphic to $\mathbf{M}_3$ by construction, also simple, then by Lemma 3, we have that for any k, $[0, T(s_k)]_L$ is a simple sublattice. We claim this shows $\mathbf{L}_b$ is simple, since for any $a \neq b$, $c \neq d$, there exists some s_k above all of them in the lattice theoretical sense, which gives $(c, d) \in \text{Cg}\,(a, b)$ inside of $[0, T(s_k)]_L$. But this gives a sequence required by Theorem 2 which will exist in the superlattice $\mathbf{L}_b$. Thus $a \neq b$ forces $(c, d) \in \text{Cg}\,(a, b)$, which gives that $\mathbf{L}_b$ is simple.

For space reasons, the proof that the computable lattices witness the Σ^0_3-completeness of having finitely many congruences is in the Appendix.

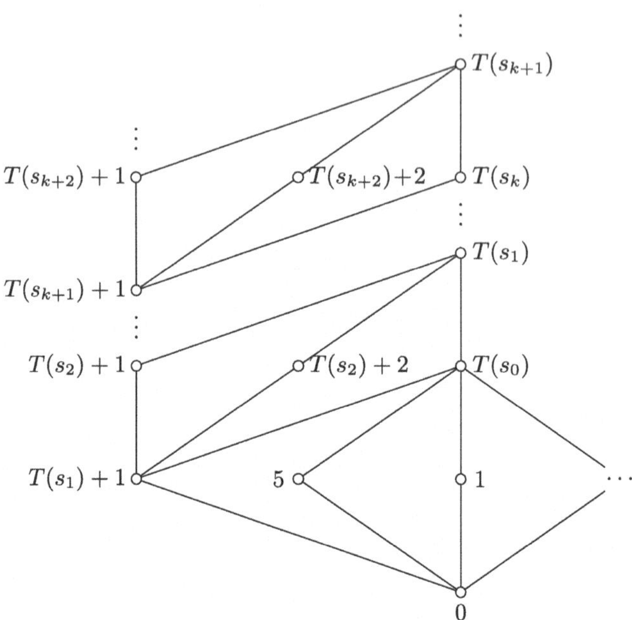

Fig. 7. $\mathbf{L}_b$ when $b \in B$

3 Subdirect Irreducibility of Computable Algebras

Definition 16 (subdirectly irreducible). *A computable algebra* $\mathbf{A}$ *is* subdirectly irreducible *if there exist two elements* $a \neq b \in A$*, such that for any* $0_{\mathbf{A}} \neq \theta \in \mathbf{Con}\,(\mathbf{A})$*, we have* $(a, b) \in \theta$*. The congruence* $\mathrm{Cg}\,(a, b)$ *is called the* monolith *of* $\mathbf{A}$*.*

This definition is equivalent to the one more commonly seen, that a universal algebra $\mathbf{A}$ is subdirectly irreducible when $|A| > 1$ and whenever $\mathbf{A}$ is isomorphic to a subalgebra of a direct product of algebras, then $\mathbf{A}$ is isomorphic to a subalgebra of one of the factors. In 1944, Birkhoff proved the subdirect representation theorem [3, Theorem 2] of universal algebra which states that every algebra is subdirectly representable by its subdirectly irreducible quotients.

We show that subdirect irreducibility is Σ^0_3-complete in [9]; we omit the proof here for space reasons.

A Finitely Many Congruences

Theorem 3. *The computable lattices witness the* Σ^0_3*-completeness of having finitely many congruences.*

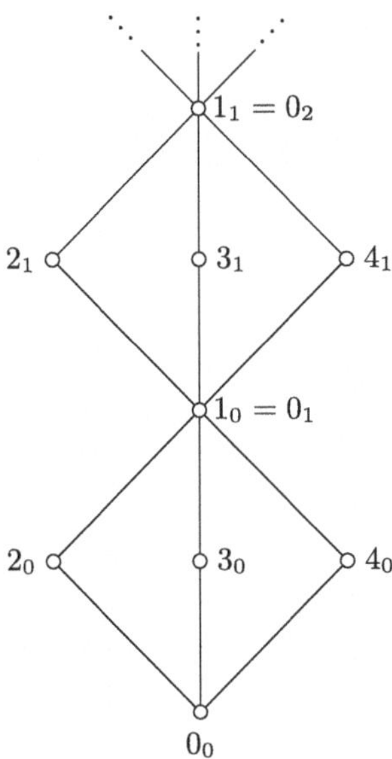

Fig. 8. The initial lattice $\mathbf{L}_{b,-1}$.

Proof. We first show property (1) of Definition 11. Suppose an algebra $\mathbf{A}$ has infinitely many congruences. Note that for any $\theta \in \mathbf{Con}(\mathbf{A})$, $\theta = \bigcup_{(a,b)\in\theta} \mathrm{Cg}(a,b)$. Thus if there were only finitely many principal congruences, say n, then there would be at most 2^n many congruences. Thus we must have infinitely many principal congruences. On the other hand, if an algebra has finitely many congruences, then surely it has finitely many principal ones. Thus an algebra has finitely many congruences if and only if it has finitely many principal ones. Thus an algebra $\mathbf{A}$ has finitely many congruences if and only if

$$(\exists x = \langle a_0, b_0, a_1, b_1, \ldots, a_k, b_k\rangle)(\forall a, b)(\exists i \leq k)\left(\mathrm{Cg}(a,b) = \mathrm{Cg}(a_i, b_i)\right),$$

so "having finitely many congruences" is a Σ_3^0 property.

Now we show property (2) of Definition 11. Since B is Σ_3^0, there is a uniformly computable sequence of relations $\{P_b(i,j)\}_{b<\omega}$ where

$$b \in B \Leftrightarrow (\exists i)(\overset{\infty}{\exists} j)(P_b(i,j) = 1)$$

[11, Theorem 14.XVII and 14.XV]. We construct a sequence of lattices where

$$B = \{b : \mathbf{L}_b \text{ has finitely many congruences}\},$$

which will show property (2) under the identity function. As before, we shall build $\mathbf{L}_b$ in stages. At stage -1, let $L_{b,-1} = \{2n : n \in \omega\}$ for each b. For the purposes of notation, let $i_k = 2(i + 4k)$ for $i < 5$. Note then that $1_k = 0_{k+1}$ for all k. For uniformity we will write $1_{-1} = 0_0$. We let $0_k \prec\!\!\prec 2_k, 3_k, 4_k \prec\!\!\prec 1_k$

Table 1. The values of s and its relation to $\bar{\imath}(s)$ and $\bar{\jmath}(s)$

$\bar{\jmath}(s)$ \ $\bar{\imath}(s)$	0	1	2	3	4	$\cdots$
0	0					
1	1	2				
2	3	4	5			
3	6	7	8	9		
4	10	11	12	13	14	
$\vdots$			$\vdots$			

in $0, 2, 4, \ldots, 4_k$ for all $k \in \omega$. Note that since $1_k = 0_{k+1} <_L 1_{k+1}$ for all k, we have $1_m <_L 1_n$ if and only if $m < n$. This process yields the lattice $\mathbf{L}_{b,-1} = (2\omega, (\wedge_0, \vee_0))$ shown in Fig. 8.

For notation, let $\omega_{-1} = \omega \cup \{-1\}$. We define a family of helper functions $c_s(n)$ on ω_{-1}. Let $c_{-1}(n) = n$ for all $n \in \omega_{-1}$. Given $s \in \omega$, let $\bar{\imath}(s)$ and $\bar{\jmath}(s)$ be the numbers where $\bar{\imath}(s) \le \bar{\jmath}(s)$ and $s = \frac{\bar{\jmath}(s)(\bar{\jmath}(s)+1)}{2} + \bar{\imath}(s)$. This is the inverse of the enumeration of the lower triangle of an $\omega \times \omega$ matrix shown in Table 1. Note that $\bar{\jmath}$ is increasing in s.

For $s \in \omega$ let

$$c_s(n) = \begin{cases} c_{s-1}(n) & \text{if } P_b(\bar{\imath}(s), \bar{\jmath}(s)) = 0 \text{ or } n < \bar{\imath}(s), \\ c_{s-1}(n+1) & \text{otherwise.} \end{cases}$$

We show some important properties of this family of functions.

Lemma 4. *$c_{s-1}(n)$ is strictly increasing in n for all $s \in \omega$.*

Proof. We proceed by induction on s. If $s = 0$, then $c_{s-1}(n) = c_{-1} = n$ which is strictly increasing.

Suppose c_{s-1} is strictly increasing. If $P_b(\bar{\imath}(s), \bar{\jmath}(s)) = 0$, then $c_s = c_{s-1}$ so c_s is strictly increasing. On the other hand, if $P_b(\bar{\imath}(s), \bar{\jmath}(s)) = 1$, then $c_s(n) = c_{s-1}(n)$ for all $n < \bar{\imath}(s)$, so c_s is strictly increasing on $-1, 0, 1, \ldots, \bar{\imath}(s) - 1$. For $n \ge \bar{\imath}(s)$, $c_s(n) = c_{s-1}(n+1)$, so c_s is strictly increasing on $\bar{\imath}(s), \bar{\imath}(s)+1, \bar{\imath}(s)+2, \ldots$. Furthermore,

$$c_s(\bar{\imath}(s) - 1) = c_{s-1}(\bar{\imath}(s) - 1) < c_{s-1}(\bar{\imath}(s) + 1) = c_s(\bar{\imath}(s)).$$

Thus c_s is strictly increasing on all of ω_{-1}.

Corollary 2. *Fix $n \in \omega_{-1}$. $c_{s-1}(n)$ is increasing in s for $s \in \omega$.*

Proof. This follows immediately from Lemma 4 and the fact that either $c_s(n) = c_{s-1}(n)$ or $c_s(n) = c_{s-1}(n+1) > c_{s-1}(n)$. Thus $c_s(n) \ge c_{s-1}(n)$.

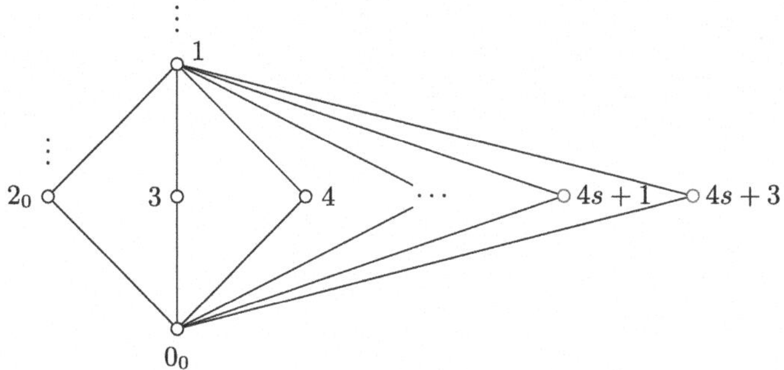

Fig. 9. Placement of nodes when $P_b(\bar{i}(s), \bar{j}(s)) = 0$.

Lemma 5. *Let $s_0 < s_1$, and fix $n \in \omega_{-1}$. Then $c_{s_0}(n) < c_{s_1}(n)$ if and only if there exists some s where $s_0 < s \le s_1$, $P_b(\bar{i}(s), \bar{j}(s)) = 1$ and $\bar{i}(s) \le n$.*

Proof. ($\Leftarrow$) Suppose there exists some s where $s_0 < s \le s_1$, $P_b(\bar{i}(s), \bar{j}(s)) = 1$, and $\bar{i}(s) \le n$. Then

$$\begin{aligned} c_{s_0}(n) &\le c_{s-1}(n) s_0 < s \text{ and Corollary 2} \\ &< c_{s-1}(n+1) \text{Lemma 4} \\ &= c_s(n) \neg\left(P_b(\bar{i}(s), \bar{j}(s)) = 0 \text{ or } n < \bar{i}(s)\right), \text{ definition of } c_s \\ &\le c_{s_1}(n). s \le s_1 \text{ and Corollary 2} \end{aligned}$$

($\Rightarrow$). Suppose for all s where $s_0 < s \le s_1$, we have$P_b(\bar{i}(s), \bar{j}(s)) = 0$ or $\bar{i}(s) > n$. Then for all m where $0 < m \le s_1 - s_0$, we have $s_0 < s_0 + m \le s_1$. So $P_b(\bar{i}(s_0 + m), \bar{j}(s_0 + m)) = 0$ or $\bar{i}(s_0 + m) > n$. Thus by definition of c_s, $c_{s_0+m}(n) = c_{s_0+m-1}(n)$ for all m where $0 < m \le s_1 - s_0$, and hence $c_{s_0+m}(n) = c_{s_0}(n)$ for all valid $0 < m \le s_1 - s_0$. Thus $c_{s_0}(n) = c_{s_1}(n)$.

Lemma 6. *If $b \notin B$, for any $n \in \omega_{-1}$, there exists an $s_n \in \omega$ where for all $s \ge s_n$, we have $c_s(n) = c_{s_n}(n)$. That is, $c_s(n)$ is eventually constant in s.*

Proof. Fix $n \in \omega_{-1}$. If $b \notin B$, then since

$$b \in B \Leftrightarrow (\exists i)(\overset{\infty}{\exists} j)(P_b(i,j) = 1),$$

for all i, there exists a j_i where for all $j \ge j_i$, we have $P_b(i,j) = 0$. Let $J = \max(j_0, j_1, \ldots, j_n, (n+1))$. Let $s_n = \frac{J(J+1)}{2}$. Note that this is just choosing s_n so that $\bar{j}(s_n) = J$ and $\bar{i}(s_n) = 0$. Then for any $s \ge s_n$, since $\bar{j}$ is increasing, we have $\bar{j}(s) \ge J$. Thus whenever $\bar{i}(s) \le n$, we have $P_b(\bar{i}(s), \bar{j}(s)) = 0$. Thus for all $s \ge s_n$ we have $P_b(\bar{i}(s), \bar{j}(s)) = 0$ or $n < \bar{i}(s)$, which gives $c_s(n) = c_{s-1}(n)$ for all $s > s_n$. Thus $c_s(n) = c_{s_n}(n)$ for all $s > s_n$.

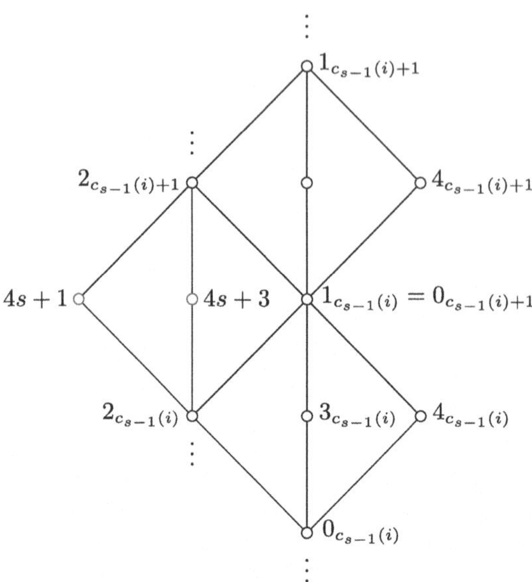

Fig. 10. Placement of nodes when $P_b(\bar{i}(s), \bar{j}(s)) = 1$, and $i = \bar{i}(s)$.

Finally, our last lemma regarding c_s.

Lemma 7. *If $b \in B$, then there exists n where $c_s(m)$ is eventually constant in s for all $m \leq n$, but $c_s(n+1)$ is unbounded in s.*[1]

Keeping these facts in mind, we now define our lattices.

At stage s, let $L_{b,s} = L_{b,s-1} \cup \{4s+1, 4s+3\}$. If $P_b(\bar{i}(s), \bar{j}(s)) = 0$, let

$$0_0 \lessdot 4s+1, 4s+3 \lessdot \qquad 1_0 \text{ in } L_{b,s}.\text{(see Figure 9)}$$

If $P_b(\bar{i}(s), \bar{j}(s)) = 1$, we let $2_{c_{s-1}(\bar{i}(s))} \lessdot 4s+1, 4s+3 \lessdot 2_{c_{s-1}(\bar{i}(s))+1}$ in $L_{b,s}$ (see Fig. 10). We claim $\mathbf{L}_b$ has finitely many congruences if and only if $b \in B$. For this we prove a couple lemmas.

Lemma 8. *At any stage s, $1_{c_s(n-1)}$ and $1_{c_s(n)}$ satisfy the conditions of Theorem 1 for all $n \in \omega$ in $\mathbf{L}_{b,s}$. Also, for any $x \in \mathbf{L}_{b,s}$, we have $x \in [1_{c_s(k-1)}, 1_{c_s(k)}]_{L_{b,s}}$ for some $m \in \omega$.*

Lemma 9. *For all $s \in \omega$, $[I_{c_{s-1}(n-1)}, 1_{c_{s-1}}(n)]_L$ is a simple sublattice of $\mathbf{L}_{b,s-1}$.*

Suppose $b \in B$. By Lemma 7 there exists an i_0 where $c_s(i_0 - 1)$ is eventually constant but $c_s(i_0)$ is unbounded. Let s_0 be a stage where if $s > s_0$, $c_s(i_0 - 1) = c_{s_0}(i_0 - 1)$. We claim that $\mathbf{X} = \{x : x \geq_L 1_{c_{s_0}(i_0-1)}\}$ is a simple sublattice.

Let $a \neq b, c, d \geq_L 1_{c_{s_0}(i_0-1)}$. Since $c_s(i_0)$ is unbounded in s, there exists some $s > s_0$ where $a, b, c, d \leq_L 1_{c_s(i)}$. But by Lemma 9, $[1_{c_{s_0}}(i_0 - 1), 1_{c_s}(i_0)]_L$

[1] We omit the proofs of Lemmas 7, 8 and 9 due to space limitations.

is simple, so $c, d \in \mathrm{Cg}(a, b)$. This gives $\mathbf{X}$ simple. If $i_0 = 1$, $\mathbf{X} = \mathbf{L}_b$ so we would be finished. So suppose $i_0 > 1$. Then $I_{s,0}$ is simple for all $s > s_0$, by Lemma 8. But $[1_{s,0}, 1_{s,i_0-1}]_L$ is finite and unchanging for all $s > s_0$. Thus can only be finitely many principal congruences with elements in $[1_{s,0}, 1_{s,i_0-1}]_L$. Fix an element $x_0 \in X$ where $x_0 \succ 1_{c_{s_0}(i_0-1)}$. Then for any $x \neq 1_{c_{s_0}(i_0-1)}$ where $x \in X$ and any $y \notin X$, $y <_L 1_{c_{s_0}(i_0-1)}$, so $(x, 1_{c_{s_0}(i_0-1)}) \in \mathrm{Cg}(x, y)$ by Lemma 1. But $\mathbf{X}$ is simple so this gives $(x, x_0) \in \mathrm{Cg}(x, y)$. But the same argument gives $(x, x_0) \in \mathrm{Cg}(x_0, y)$. Thus there are only finitely many principal congruences with an element in X and one outside. A similar argument can be given for $I_{s,0}$. Thus there are only finitely many principal congruences.

If $b \notin B$, then suppose for the purposes of contradiction that there were only N many congruences. By Lemma 6, $c_s(n)$ is eventually constant. Take s_0 large enough that for all $s \geq s_0$, you have $c_s(n)$ is constant for all $n \leq N + 2$. By Lemma 8 and Theorem 1, $\mathrm{Cg}\left(1_{c_{s_0}(m)}, 1_{c_{s_0}(m+1)}\right) \neq \mathrm{Cg}\left(1_{c_{s_0}(n)}, 1_{c_{s_0}(n+1)}\right)$ if $m \neq n$ and $m, n \leq N + 2$. Thus there are at least $N + 1$ principal congruences, a contradiction. Therefore there are infinitely many congruences.

References

1. Bergman, C.: Universal algebra, volume 301 of Pure and Applied Mathematics (Boca Raton). CRC Press, Boca Raton, FL, 2012. Fundamentals and selected topics
2. Bergman, C., Slutzki, G.: Computational complexity of some problems involving congruences on algebras. Theor. Comput. Sci. **270**(1–2), 591–608 (2002)
3. Birkhoff, G.: Subdirect unions in universal algebra. Bull. Am. Math. Soc. **50**, 764–768 (1944)
4. Dilworth, R.P.: The structure of relatively complemented lattices. Ann. Math. **2**(51), 348–359 (1950)
5. Freese, R., Valeriote, M.A.: On the complexity of some Maltsev conditions. Int. J. Algebra Comput. **19**(1), 41–77 (2009)
6. Grätzer, G.: Universal Algebra, second edition. Springer, New York (2008). With appendices by Grätzer, Bjarni Jónsson, Walter Taylor, Robert W. Quackenbush, Günter H. Wenzel, and Grätzer and W. A. Lampe
7. Grätzer, G.: Lattice theory: foundation. Birkhäuser/Springer Basel AG, Basel (2011)
8. Khoussainov, B., Morozov, A.: On index sets of some properties of computable algebras. In: Ferreira, F., Löwe, B., Mayordomo, E., Mendes Gomes, L. (eds.) CiE 2010. LNCS, vol. 6158, pp. 219–228. Springer, Heidelberg (2010). https://doi.org/10.1007/978-3-642-13962-8_25
9. Nguyen, P.K.L.V.: Complexity of index sets of computable lattices. ProQuest LLC, Ann Arbor, MI, 2014. Thesis (Ph.D.)–University of Hawai'i at Manoa
10. Robert, W.: Quackenbush. Planar lattices. In: Proceedings of the University of Houston Lattice Theory Conference (Houston, Tex., 1973), pp. 512–518 (1973). Dept. Math., Univ. Houston, Houston, Tex., 1973
11. Rogers, H.: Theory of Recursive Functions and Effective Computability, 2nd edn. MIT Press, Cambridge, MA (1987)

The Satisfiability Problem in a Separation Logic of Relations

Nicolas Peltier(✉)

Univ. Grenoble Alpes, CNRS, LIG, 38000 Grenoble, France
nicolas.peltier@imag.fr

Abstract. The separation logic of relations (SLR) is a generalization of separation logic (SL) which is useful to describe complex structures like graphs and relational databases. SLR extends SL by interpreting heaps as (multi)sets of relational atoms instead of partial functions. This paper addresses the satisfiability problem for SLR formulas with additional shape constraints (called *patterns*) expressing conditions such as uniqueness of atoms or functionality of relations. We show that the satisfiability problem is 2-EXPTIME-complete when (dis)equalities over existential variables are excluded from the considered patterns, and undecidable otherwise.

1 Introduction

Separation Logic (SL) [6,9] is widely employed in program verification to reason about code that manipulates dynamically allocated memory. SL formulas describe *heaps*, i.e., partial finite functions that map certain memory locations to tuples of other locations. SL formulas are built using atomic expressions like $x \mapsto (y_1, \ldots, y_k)$, which assert that the location associated with x is the sole allocated one (i.e., the heap domain is a singleton ℓ, where ℓ is the value of x) and that this location points to the tuple $(y_1, \ldots, y_k)$. To denote disjoint unions of heaps, SL introduces the separating conjunction $*$. Recently, an extension of SL has been introduced [1,2,7] to reason on more complex structures, based on arbitrary relations. This extended logic, known as Separation Logic of Relations (SLR), generalizes SL by allowing arbitrary (potentially non-functional) relations, where heaps are interpreted as sets of atomic expressions of the form $p(\ell_1, \ldots, \ell_n)$, where p is a relation and $\ell_1, \ldots, \ell_n$ are locations. SLR offers a flexible framework for describing diverse data structures, such as graphs, hypergraphs, relational databases, and software or hardware architectures. SL is a specific instance of SLR, restricted to a single functional relation $\mapsto$. Like SL, SLR can be extended with inductively defined predicates and fixpoint semantics, enabling the description of unbounded structures. In this paper, we focus on testing the satisfiability of SLR formulas over multisets of atoms, under additional constraints (also called *patterns*) on the shape of the structure. These constraints may, for example, assert that certain atoms and/or locations appear at most n times in a structure (for some fixed $n \in \mathbb{N}$), or that a relation satisfies some

This work has been partially funded by the French National Research Agency project ANR-21-CE48-0011.

D. Kozen and R. de Queiroz (Eds.): WoLLIC 2025, LNCS 15942, pp. 260–277, 2026.
https://doi.org/10.1007/978-3-031-99536-1_16

properties such as functionality. This problem generalizes the satisfiability problem for SL or for SLR over sets (as studied in [2,3]). In [3], it is proved that satisfiability is EXPTIME-complete for SL formulas, and in [2] it is shown that satisfiability belongs to 2-EXPTIME for a specific fragment of SLR that encodes reconfigurable architectures. Our work broadens these approaches by addressing more general classes of structures and arbitrary shape constraints. The shape constraints corresponding to SL [3] are related to the functional nature of the heap and assert that the same location cannot be allocated twice, whereas the *configuration logic* of [2] allows for structures defined as sets of relational atoms of some specific form. The structures we consider are arbitrary multisets of atoms $p(\ell_1, \ldots, \ell_n)$, and the constraints we handle allow us to exclude structures that contain substructures of specific shapes, which strictly generalizes previous approaches (see Sect. 3 for more details). We demonstrate that the problem is 2-EXPTIME-complete when the shape constraints exclude disequalities over existential variables, and undecidable otherwise. Due to space constraints, some proofs are deferred to the appendix.

2 Definitions

We define the syntax and semantics of the logic SLR. We first briefly review some basic notations and definitions. For any function f, *dom*(f) denotes the domain of f, and for any finite set S, *card*(S) denotes the number of elements in S. A multiset S is a function mapping elements to natural numbers, where $S(x)$ denotes the number of instances of x in S (called the *multiplicity* of x in S). The sum of two multisets S_1, S_2 is defined as usual: $(S_1 + S_2)(x) = S_1(x) + S_2(x)$.

We consider 3 disjoints sets of symbols: a countably infinite set of *variables* $\mathcal{V}$ and two sets of *predicate symbols*, $\mathcal{P}_{\mathtt{H}}$ and $\mathcal{P}_{\mathtt{I}}$, called *heap predicates* and *inductive predicates*, respectively. Each symbol $P \in \mathcal{P}_{\mathtt{H}} \cup \mathcal{P}_{\mathtt{I}}$ is associated with a unique arity $ar(P) \geq 0$. The predicates in $\mathcal{P}_{\mathtt{H}}$ are used to define the relational structures on which the formulas are interpreted, whereas those in $\mathcal{P}_{\mathtt{I}}$ denote inductively-defined structures of unbounded size. The set of *SLR-formulas* (or simply formulas) is inductively defined as follows:

$$\mathtt{emp} \mid (x \approx y) \mid (x \not\approx y) \mid P(x_1, \ldots, x_n) \mid \phi_1 \vee \phi_2 \mid \phi_1 * \phi_2 \mid \exists x \psi$$

where $x, y, x_1, \ldots, x_n$ are variables, $P \in \mathcal{P}_{\mathtt{H}} \cup \mathcal{P}_{\mathtt{I}}$, $n = ar(P)$, and ϕ_1, ϕ_2, ψ are SLR-formulas. As in SL, emp is a special atom denoting empty structures and $*$ is a special conjunction (called *separating conjunction*) denoting a union of structures. Negation and standard conjunction are not used (as in the usual fragment of SL called *symbolic heaps*). A formula of the form emp or $P(x_1, \ldots, x_n)$ with $P \in \mathcal{P}_{\mathtt{H}} \cup \mathcal{P}_{\mathtt{I}}$ (resp. $x \approx y$ or $x \not\approx y$) is called a *spatial atom* (resp. an *equational atom*). An *atom* is a spatial atom or an equational atom. For all $S \subseteq \mathcal{P}_{\mathtt{H}} \cup \mathcal{P}_{\mathtt{I}}$, an S-*atom* is an atom of the form $P(x_1, \ldots, x_n)$ with $P \in S$. For any formula ϕ, we denote by $fv(\phi)$ the set of variables freely occurring in ϕ. Formulas are taken up to all the usual properties of the logical symbols: associativity and commutativity of $*$, commutativity of $\approx$ and $\not\approx$, neutrality of emp for $*$, contraction of equational atoms for $*$ (i.e., $\phi * \phi = \phi$ if ϕ is an equational atom), α-renaming, commutativity of $\exists$ (i.e. $\exists x \exists y \phi$ and $\exists x \exists y \phi$ are taken as identical) and up to transformation into prenex form. Any empty $*$-conjunction, e.g., $\phi_1 * \cdots * \phi_n$

with $n = 0$, is taken as $\mathtt{emp}$. For any finite sequence of variables $\boldsymbol{x} = (x_1, \ldots, x_n)$, $\exists \boldsymbol{x}\, \phi$ denotes the formula $\exists x_1 \ldots \exists x_n\, \phi$. A *substitution* is a total function from variables to variables. The *domain* of a substitution σ, denoted by $dom(\sigma)$, is the set of variables x such that $\sigma(x) \neq x$. A substitution of domain $\{x_1, \ldots, x_n\}$ with $\sigma(x_i) = y_i$ is denoted by $\{x_i \mapsto y_i \mid i = 1, \ldots, n\}$. Formulas are interpreted over structures defined as follows:

Definition 2.1. *Let $\mathcal{L}$ be a countably infinite fixed set of* locations. *A* heap atom *is an expression of the form $p(\ell_1, \ldots, \ell_n)$, where $p \in \mathcal{P}_{\mathrm{H}}$, $n = ar(p)$ and $\ell_1, \ldots, \ell_n \in \mathcal{L}$. A* structure *is a pair $(\mathfrak{s}, \mathfrak{h})$, where:*

- *$\mathfrak{s}$ is a store, i.e., a partial function from $\mathcal{V}$ to $\mathcal{L}$, with a finite domain.*
- *$\mathfrak{h}$ is an* R-heap *(or simply a* heap*), i.e., a finite multiset of heap atoms.*

We denote by $\mathcal{L}(\mathfrak{h})$ the set of locations ℓ that occur in some heap atom in $\mathfrak{h}$, i.e., $\mathcal{L}(\mathfrak{h}) = \{\ell_i \mid p(\ell_1, \ldots, \ell_n) \in \mathfrak{h}, 1 \leq i \leq n\}$.

Any store $\mathfrak{s}$ can be extended into a function mapping $\mathcal{P}_{\mathrm{H}}$-atoms with variables in $dom(\mathfrak{s})$ to heap atoms: $\mathfrak{s}(p(x_1, \ldots, x_n)) = p(\mathfrak{s}(x_1), \ldots, \mathfrak{s}(x_n))$.

Remark 2.2. Unlike [2,7], we define heaps as multisets rather than sets. This approach has the advantage of making the composition of heaps form a total function, while also broadening the applicability of the results to encompass multigraphs. Importantly, this generalization entails no loss of expressiveness, as we can enforce the condition that each atom appears at most once using a pattern within the language (see Sect. 3).

The semantics of predicates in $\mathcal{P}_{\mathrm{I}}$ is defined by inductive rules:

Definition 2.3. *A* set of inductive definitions *(SID) is a set of* rules *that are expressions of the form $P(x_1, \ldots, x_n) \Leftarrow \phi$, where $P \in \mathcal{P}_{\mathrm{I}}$, $ar(P) = n$, $x_1, \ldots, x_n$ are pairwise distinct variables and ϕ is a formula with $fv(\phi) \subseteq \{x_1, \ldots, x_n\}$.*

We write $P(y_1, \ldots, y_n) \Leftarrow_{\mathcal{R}} \psi$ if $P(y_1, \ldots, y_n)$ can be transformed into ψ using one of the rules in $\mathcal{R}$, i.e., if $\mathcal{R}$ contains a rule $P(x_1, \ldots, x_n) \Leftarrow \phi$ with $\psi = \phi\{x_i \mapsto y_i \mid i = 1, \ldots, n\}$.

Definition 2.4. *The* satisfiability relation $\models_{\mathcal{R}}$ *is the least relation such that $(\mathfrak{s}, \mathfrak{h}) \models_{\mathcal{R}} \phi$ if $dom(\mathfrak{s}) \supseteq fv(\phi)$ and one of the following conditions holds:*

- *$\phi = \mathtt{emp}$ and $\mathfrak{h} = \emptyset$.*
- *$\phi = (t \approx s)$ (resp. $(t \not\approx s)$), $\mathfrak{h} = \emptyset$ and $\mathfrak{s}(t) = \mathfrak{s}(s)$ (resp. $\mathfrak{s}(t) \neq \mathfrak{s}(s)$). Note that both formulas are satisfied only on empty heaps.*
- *ϕ is an $\mathcal{P}_{\mathrm{H}}$-atom $p(x_1, \ldots, x_n)$ and $\mathfrak{h} = \{p(\mathfrak{s}(x_1), \ldots, \mathfrak{s}(x_n))\}$. The formula asserts that $p(\mathfrak{s}(x_1), \ldots, \mathfrak{s}(x_n))$ is the* only *element in $\mathfrak{h}$, with multiplicity* 1.
- *ϕ is a $\mathcal{P}_{\mathrm{I}}$-atom and there exists a formula ψ such that $\phi \Leftarrow_{\mathcal{R}} \psi$ and $(\mathfrak{s}, \mathfrak{h}) \models_{\mathcal{R}} \psi$.*
- *$\phi = \phi_1 * \phi_2$ and there exist heaps $\mathfrak{h}_1, \mathfrak{h}_2$ such that $\mathfrak{h} = \mathfrak{h}_1 + \mathfrak{h}_2$ and $(\mathfrak{s}, \mathfrak{h}_i) \models_{\mathcal{R}} \phi_i$ for all $i = 1, 2$. Note that, in contrast to SL, $\mathfrak{h}_1, \mathfrak{h}_2$ are not necessarily disjoint. The operator $+$ denotes the sum of the two multisets.*
- *$\phi = \exists x \psi$ and there exists a location ℓ such that $(\mathfrak{s}', \mathfrak{h}) \models_{\mathcal{R}} \psi$, where $\mathfrak{s}'$ denotes a store of domain $dom(\mathfrak{s}) \cup \{x\}$ such that $\mathfrak{s}'(x) = \ell$ and $\mathfrak{s}'(y) = \mathfrak{s}(y)$ if $y \in dom(\mathfrak{s}) \setminus \{x\}$.*

A structure $(\mathfrak{s}, \mathfrak{h})$ *such that* $(\mathfrak{s}, \mathfrak{h}) \models_{\mathcal{R}} \phi$ *is an* $\mathcal{R}$-model *of* ϕ. *A formula is* satisfiable *if it has at least one* $\mathcal{R}$*-model.*

Remark 2.5. Note that equational atoms are true only in structures with an empty heap. This convention has the advantage of simplifying the syntax: equational constraints may be expressed without having to use the standard conjunction.

It is clear that the semantics of formulas does not depend on the name of the locations but only on the relations between these locations. Consequently, the locations occurring in a structure can be renamed arbitrarily without affecting the truth values of the formulas in the structure. This may be formalized by the proposition below. For any heap $\mathfrak{h}$ and mapping $\lambda : \mathcal{L} \to \mathcal{L}$, we denote by $\lambda(\mathfrak{h})$ the heap defined by the relations: $\lambda(\emptyset) = \emptyset$, $\lambda(p(\ell_1, \ldots, \ell_n)) = p(\lambda(\ell_1), \ldots, \lambda(\ell_n))$ and $\lambda(\mathfrak{h}_1 + \mathfrak{h}_2) = \lambda(\mathfrak{h}_1) + \lambda(\mathfrak{h}_2)$.

Proposition 2.6. *Let* λ *be any injective mapping from* $\mathcal{L}$ *to* $\mathcal{L}$. *Let* $(\mathfrak{s}, \mathfrak{h})$ *be a structure and let* ϕ *be a formula. Then:* $(\mathfrak{s}, \mathfrak{h}) \models_{\mathcal{R}} \phi \iff (\lambda \circ \mathfrak{s}, \lambda(\mathfrak{h})) \models_{\mathcal{R}} \phi$.

Proof. By an immediate induction on the satisfiability relation.

3 The $\mathcal{S}$-Satisfiability Problem

Definition 3.1. *A* pattern ϕ *is a formula containing no predicate symbol in* $\mathcal{P}_{\mathtt{I}}$ *and no disjunction. It is* non-equational *if, moreover, it contains no occurrence of* $\approx$ *or* $\not\approx$, *and* $\exists$-restricted *if for all atoms* $x \approx y$ *or* $x \not\approx y$ *occurring in* ϕ, *neither* x *nor* y *occurs as an existentially quantified variable in* ϕ. *The* width *of* ϕ *is defined as the number of occurrences of spatial atoms in* ϕ: $\mathtt{width}(p(x_1, \ldots, x_n)) = 1$, $\mathtt{width}(x \approx y) = \mathtt{width}(x \not\approx y) = 0$, $\mathtt{width}(\phi_1 * \phi_2) = \mathtt{width}(\phi_1) + \mathtt{width}(\phi_2)$ *and* $\mathtt{width}(\exists x\, \phi) = \mathtt{width}(\phi)$.

Up to transformation into prenex form, a pattern of width k may be written in the form: $\exists \boldsymbol{x}\, (*_{i=1}^{m} (y_i \approx y_i') * *_{i=1}^{n} (z_i \not\approx z_i') * *_{i=1}^{k} p_i(\boldsymbol{u}_i))$, where $m, n, k \geq 0$, $\boldsymbol{x}$ is a possibly empty sequence of variables, $y_i, y_i', z_i, z_i' \in \mathcal{V}$, $p_i \in \mathcal{P}_{\mathtt{H}}$ and $\boldsymbol{u}_i$ is a sequence of variables.

Definition 3.2. *A structure* $(\mathfrak{s}, \mathfrak{h})$ *is* compatible with *a set of patterns* $\mathcal{S}$ *if there is no* $\mathfrak{h}' \subseteq \mathfrak{h}$ *and no* $\phi \in \mathcal{S}$ *such that* $(\mathfrak{s}, \mathfrak{h}') \models_{\mathcal{R}} \phi$.

The problem we are considering in this paper (termed the *$\mathcal{S}$-satisfiability problem*) is to determine, given a formula ϕ, a set of rules $\mathcal{R}$ and a set of patterns $\mathcal{S}$, whether there exists an $\mathcal{R}$-model of ϕ that is compatible with $\mathcal{S}$. Note that the formulas in $\mathcal{S}$ are interpreted negatively, i.e., assert conditions that *cannot* be satisfied by any substructure. In particular, the standard satisfiability problem in Separation Logic may be encoded as follows: the set $\mathcal{P}_{\mathtt{H}}$ contains a unique symbol $\mathtt{H}$ denoting the heap, with arity $k+1$, where k denotes a number of record fields. An atom $\mathtt{H}(x_0, \ldots, x_k)$ asserts that location x_0 is allocated and refers to the tuple of locations $(x_1, \ldots, x_k)$. The set $\mathcal{S}$ contains a unique formula which guarantees that the same location cannot be allocated twice: $\exists x, y_1, \ldots, y_k, z_1, \ldots, z_k\, (\mathtt{H}(x, y_1, \ldots, y_k) * \mathtt{H}(x, z_1, \ldots, z_k))$. The *configuration logic* of [2] is encoded by considering a set $\mathcal{P}_{\mathtt{H}}$ containing a monadic predicate $x \mapsto [x]$ (asserting that x denotes a component in the architecture), a family of n-ary predicates $x_1, \ldots, x_n \mapsto \langle x_1.p_1, \ldots, x_n.p_n \rangle$ (denoting interactions, for every $n \in \mathbb{N}$ and ports $p_1, \ldots, p_n$) and predicates $x \mapsto x@q$ (asserting that component x is in state q). The set $\mathcal{S}$ contains the formulas $\exists x\,([x] * [x])$ and $\exists x_1, \ldots, x_n\,(\langle x_1.p_1, \ldots, x_n.p_n\rangle) * \langle x_1.p_1, \ldots, x_n.p_n\rangle)$, which assert that each component or interaction occurs only once, as well as the formulas $\exists x\,(x@q * x@q')$ for all distinct states q, q' (asserting that each component is in only one state). Numerous variations are possible. For instance we may consider structures encoding multigraphs, then $\mathcal{S}$ will contain a formula of the form $\exists x\,(\mathtt{node}(x) * \mathtt{node}(x))$ (as nodes occur at most once in a graph) but no formula $\exists x, y\,(\mathtt{edge}(x, y) * \mathtt{edge}(x, y))$ (as multiple edges are permitted). We may also consider sets $\mathcal{S}$ containing formulas with equality. For instance assume that $\mathcal{P}_{\mathrm{H}}$ contains two predicates `next` and `prev` denoting pointers in a doubly linked list, then the formula $\exists x, y, z\,(\mathtt{next}(x, y) * \mathtt{prev}(y, z) * x \not\approx z)$ asserts that these pointers are well-defined, in the sense that the previous element of the next element of x is necessarily x. However, the latter formula is not $\exists$-restricted, and as we shall demonstrate, the satisfiability problem is undecidable in this case.

4 Decision Procedure

In the present section, we devise an algorithm to solve the $\mathcal{S}$-satisfiability problem, assuming that all the patterns in $\mathcal{S}$ are $\exists$-restricted (but the input formula may be arbitrary). We show that this algorithm operates in doubly exponential time. The algorithm follows a standard technique (see, e.g., [3, 8]), which consists in constructing an abstraction of the set of models of the input formula. This abstraction is finite (which ensures termination) and contains enough information to determine if the abstracted model is compatible with $\mathcal{S}$. The information stored in the abstraction includes the set of free variables V, an equivalence relation $\sim$, denoting the equality relation over these variables, and a finite set Σ of non-equational patterns satisfied over subparts of the heap.

To formalize this notion of abstraction, we need to introduce some notations. Let $<$ be any total order on variables (fixed throughout this paper). For every equivalence relation $\sim$ on some set of variables V (which will always be clear from the context), we denote by $x\downarrow_\sim$ the smallest (w.r.t. $<$) variable $y \in V$ such that $x \sim y$. For every formula ϕ such that $fv(\phi) \subseteq V$, we denote by $\phi\downarrow_\sim$ the formula $\phi\sigma$, where $\sigma = \{x \mapsto x\downarrow_\sim \mid x \in V\}$. The formula ϕ is *$\sim$-normalized* if $\phi\downarrow_\sim = \phi$.

Definition 4.1. *A* abstraction *is a tuple $(V, \sim, \Sigma)$ where V is a finite set of variables, $\sim$ is an equivalence relation on V, and Σ is a finite set of non-equational $\sim$-normalized patterns.*

Definition 4.4 yields a simple criterion to check that the structures that are captured by a given abstraction satisfy a given $\exists$-restricted pattern. To this purpose, we first introduce a notion of subsumption, which captures a very simple restricted form of entailment:

Definition 4.2. *A formula ϕ* subsumes *a formula ψ if ϕ and ψ are respectively of the form: $\exists y_1, \ldots, y_m\,(\phi'\sigma)$. and $\exists x_1, \ldots, x_n\,\exists y_1, \ldots, y_m\,\phi'$, where σ is any substitution of domain $\{x_1, \ldots, x_n\}$.*

As explained before, formulas are taken modulo α-renaming and commutativity of $\exists$: for instance the formula $\exists x\, p(x, y)$ subsumes the formula $\exists u\, \exists v\, p(u, v)$ because these formulas may be written $\exists x\, p(x, v)\sigma$ and $\exists v\, \exists x\, p(x, v)$ (respectively), with $\sigma = \{v \mapsto y\}$. The following proposition is immediate to prove:

Proposition 4.3. *If ϕ subsumes ψ and $(\mathfrak{s}, \mathfrak{h}) \models_{\mathcal{R}} \phi$ then $(\mathfrak{s}, \mathfrak{h}) \models_{\mathcal{R}} \psi$.*

Definition 4.4. *Let ϕ be an $\exists$-restricted pattern. We write $(V, \sim, \Sigma) \triangleright \phi$ if ϕ is of the form $\exists z\, (*_{i=1}^{n} (x_i \approx x_i') * *_{i=1}^{m} (y_i \not\approx y_i') * \phi')$ and:*

- *For all $i \in \{1, \ldots, n\}$, $x_i, x_i' \in V$ and $x_i \sim x_i'$.*
- *For all $i \in \{1, \ldots, m\}$, $y_i, y_i' \in V$ and $y_i \not\sim y_i'$.*
- *The set Σ contains a formula subsuming $\exists z\, \phi'$.*

Note that, because ϕ is $\exists$-restricted, the variables x_i, x_i', y_i, y_i' cannot occur in z.

We define an algorithm to construct, given a formula ϕ, a set of abstractions which capture all the models of ϕ (in a sense that will be specified later). This set is constructed by structural induction on ϕ, using a fixpoint computation to handle inductive predicates (see Definition 4.5). In what follows, we often denote an equivalence relation $\sim$ by giving a set of equations $x \sim y$, with the implicit meaning that $\sim$ is the smallest reflexive, symmetric and transitive relation on V such that $(x \sim y) \in S \implies x \sim y$ (where V is fixed by the context). For instance $\emptyset$ denotes the relation $\sim$ such that $x \sim y \iff (x = y \wedge x \in V)$. To simplify notations, we assume that the equality $fv(\phi_1) = fv(\phi_2)$ holds for all disjunctions $\phi_1 \vee \phi_2$ (this property can easily be enforced by replacing each formula ϕ_i by $\phi_i * *_{x \in fv(\phi_{3-i}) \setminus fv(\phi_i)} (x \approx x)$). Similarly, we also assume that the equality $fv(\phi) = fv(p(\boldsymbol{x}))$ holds for all rules $p(x) \Leftarrow \phi$ (again, this property can be enforced by adding dummy equations $x \approx x$ into ϕ).

Definition 4.5. *For every formula ϕ, we denote by $\mathcal{A}_k(\phi)$ the set of abstractions defined inductively as follows.*

- *If $\phi = \mathtt{emp}$ then $\mathcal{A}_k(\phi) = \{(\emptyset, \emptyset, \{\mathtt{emp}\})\}$.*
- *If $\phi = x \approx y$ then $\mathcal{A}_k(\phi) = \{(\{x, y\}, \{x \sim y\}, \{\mathtt{emp}\})\}$.*
- *If $\phi = x \not\approx y$ then $\mathcal{A}_k(\phi) = \{(\{x, y\}, \emptyset, \{\mathtt{emp}\})\}$.*
- *If $\phi = p(x_1, \ldots, x_n)$ with $p \in \mathcal{P}_{\mathtt{H}}$ then $\mathcal{A}_k(\phi)$ is the set of abstractions of the form $(\{x_1, \ldots, x_n\}, \sim, \{\mathtt{emp}, \phi\downarrow_\sim\})$, where $\sim$ is an equivalence relation on $\{x_1, \ldots, x_n\}$.*
- *If $\phi = P(x_1, \ldots, x_n)$ with $P \in \mathcal{P}_{\mathtt{I}}$ then $\mathcal{A}_k(\phi) = \bigcup_{\phi \Leftarrow_{\mathcal{R}} \psi} \mathcal{A}_k(\psi)$.*
- *If $\phi = \phi_1 \vee \phi_2$ then $\mathcal{A}_k(\phi) = \mathcal{A}_k(\phi_1) \cup \mathcal{A}_k(\phi_2)$.*
- *If $\phi = \phi_1 * \phi_2$, $(V_i, \sim_i, \Sigma_i) \in \mathcal{A}_k(\phi_i)$ (for all $i \in \{1, 2\}$) and $\sim$ is any equivalence relation on $V_1 \cup V_2$ that agrees with $\sim_i$ on V_i, then $\mathcal{A}_k(\phi)$ contains the abstraction:*

$$\left(V_1 \cup V_2, \quad \sim, \quad \{ (\phi_1 * \phi_2)\downarrow_\sim \mid \phi_i \in \Sigma_i, \mathtt{width}(\phi_1) + \mathtt{width}(\phi_2) \leq k \} \right)$$

- *If $\phi = \exists x\, \psi$ and $(V', \sim', \Sigma') \in \mathcal{A}_k(\psi)$ then $\mathcal{A}_k(\phi)$ contains the abstraction $(V, \sim, \Sigma)$ where $V = V' \setminus \{x\}$, $\sim$ is the restriction of $\sim'$ to V and $\Sigma = \{\exists x\, \xi \mid \xi \in \Sigma'\}$. We assume, by α-renaming, that $y < x$ for all $y \in fv(\phi)$.*

Lemmata 4.6 and 4.7 relate the set of abstractions $\mathcal{A}_k(\phi)$ to the models of ϕ. More precisely, Lemma 4.6 states that every abstraction $A \in \mathcal{A}_k(\phi)$ can be associated with a model of ϕ which satisfies all the properties stated in A (as defined in Definition 4.4). For all $V \subseteq \mathcal{V}$ and for all $k \in \mathbb{N}$, we denote by $\mathtt{Pt}(V, k)$ the set of non-equational patterns ϕ such that $fv(\phi) \subseteq V$ and $\mathtt{width}(\phi) \leq k$.

Lemma 4.6. *For every formula ϕ and for every abstraction $A = (V, \sim, \Sigma)$ in $\mathcal{A}_k(\phi)$ there exists a structure $(\mathfrak{s}, \mathfrak{h})$ satisfying the following properties:*

1. $(\mathfrak{s}, \mathfrak{h}) \models_{\mathcal{R}} \phi$.
2. *For all $x, y \in V$, $x \sim y \iff \mathfrak{s}(x) = \mathfrak{s}(y)$.*
3. *If $\psi \in \mathtt{Pt}(V, k)$, $(\mathfrak{s}, \mathfrak{h}') \models_{\mathcal{R}} \psi$ and $\mathfrak{h}' \subseteq \mathfrak{h}$ then Σ contains a formula subsuming $\psi \downarrow_{\sim}$.*

Conversely, Lemma 4.7 states a form of completeness: for every model $(\mathfrak{s}, \mathfrak{h})$ of ϕ, $\mathcal{A}_k(\phi)$ contains some abstraction containing the properties fulfilled by $(\mathfrak{s}, \mathfrak{h})$.

Lemma 4.7. *Let ϕ be a formula with $V = fv(\phi)$ and $(\mathfrak{s}, \mathfrak{h})$ be an $\mathcal{R}$-model of ϕ, with $dom(\mathfrak{s}) = V$. The set $\mathcal{A}_k(\phi)$ contains an abstraction $A = (V, \sim, \Sigma)$ such that:*

1. *For all $x, y \in V$, $x \sim y \iff \mathfrak{s}(x) = \mathfrak{s}(y)$.*
2. *For all $\psi \in \Sigma$, there exists $\mathfrak{h}' \subseteq \mathfrak{h}$ such that $(\mathfrak{s}, \mathfrak{h}') \models_{\mathcal{R}} \psi$.*

Theorem 4.8 gives the decision procedure for testing $\mathcal{S}$-satisfiability and Corollary 4.9 states the main results of this section.

Theorem 4.8. *Let ϕ be a formula, with $V = fv(\phi)$, and let $\mathcal{S}$ be a set of $\exists$-restricted patterns such that $\mathtt{width}(\psi) \leq k$, for all $\psi \in \mathcal{S}$. The two following statements are equivalent.*

- *The formula ϕ admits an $\mathcal{R}$-model $(\mathfrak{s}, \mathfrak{h})$ that is compatible with $\mathcal{S}$.*
- *The set $\mathcal{A}_k(\phi)$ contains an abstraction A of domain V such that $A \not\triangleright \psi$, for all $\psi \in \mathcal{S}$.*

Corollary 4.9. *The $\mathcal{S}$-satisfiability problem is in* 2-EXPTIME *for sets of restricted patterns $\mathcal{S}$. If the size of the formulas in $\mathcal{S}$ is bounded by a constant, then the problem is* EXPTIME*-complete.*

5 Lower Bound

In this section, we show that $\mathcal{S}$-satisfiability is 2-EXPTIME-hard (for $\exists$-restricted patterns). The proof is based on a reduction from the membership problem for alternating Turing machines.

Definition 5.1. *An* Alternating Turing Machine *(ATM) is a tuple $M = (Q, \Gamma, \delta, q_0, g)$ where:*

- *Q is a finite set of* states.
- *Γ is a finite alphabet, containing a special symbol* B, *called the* blank *symbol.*

- $\delta \subseteq Q\times\Gamma\times Q\times\Gamma\times\{\leftarrow,\rightarrow\}$ *is the* transition relation. *The transition* $(q,a,q',b,\mu) \in \delta$ *specifies that, in state* q*, upon reading symbol* a*, the machine may move to state* q'*, write* b *to the tape and move the head by one to the left (if* $\mu =\leftarrow$*) or to the right (if* $\mu = \rightarrow$*).*
- $q_0 \in Q$ *is the* initial state.
- $g : Q \rightarrow \{\vee, \wedge\}$ *partitions the set of states into* existential *(*$g(q) = \vee$*) and* universal *(*$g(q) = \wedge$*) states.*

A *configuration* of an ATM $M = (Q,\Gamma,\delta,q_0,g)$ is a tuple (q,w,i) where $q \in Q$ is the current state, $w : \mathbb{N} \rightarrow \Gamma$ is a *tape*, encoding a finite word on Γ, denoted by a function giving the symbol $w(j)$ stored in every cell $j \in \mathbb{N}$, where the set $\{j \in \mathbb{N} \mid w(j) \neq \text{B}\}$ is finite, and $i \in \mathbb{N}$ is the current position of the head on the tape. For any tape w and integer i, we denote by $w[i \leftarrow a]$ the tape w' which satisfies $w'(i) = a$ and $w'(j) = w(j)$ for all $j \neq i$. Let $i^{\leftarrow} \stackrel{\text{def}}{=} i - 1$ if $i > 0$ (where $0^{\leftarrow}$ is undefined) and $i^{\rightarrow} \stackrel{\text{def}}{=} i + 1$. We assume that, since 0 denotes the leftmost position on the tape, no transition moves the head left of 0. The *step relation* of M is a relation between configurations, defined as follows: $(q,w,i)\rightarrow (q',w',j)$ iff there exists a transition $(q,a,q',b,\mu) \in \delta$ such that $w(i) = a$, $w' = w[i \leftarrow b]$ and $j = i^{\mu}$ (assuming i^{μ} is defined, i.e., either $i > 0$ or $\mu =\rightarrow$). The set of *accepting configurations* is defined inductively as follows. A configuration (q,w,i) is accepting if one of the following conditions holds: (i) $g(q) = \vee$ and there exists a configuration (q',w',j) such that $(q,w,i) \rightarrow (q',w',j)$ and (q',w',j) is accepting. (ii)$g(q) = \wedge$ and all configurations (q',w',j) such that $(q,w,i)\rightarrow (q',w',j)$ are accepting. In particular, if $g(q) = \wedge$ (resp. $g(q) = \vee$) and δ contains no transition of the form (q,a,q',b,μ) then (q,w,i) is always (resp. never) accepting. A standard (non deterministic) Turing machine is an ATM where there are no transitions from universal states, which are thus accepting states. An ATM *accepts* a word $a_0.\ldots.a_n \in (\Gamma\setminus\{\text{B}\})^*$ if the configuration $(q_0, w_0, 0)$ is accepting, with $w_0(i) = a_i$ if $0 \le i \le n$ and $w_0(i) = \text{B}$ otherwise. The *membership problem* (M,w) asks the following: given an ATM $M = (Q,\Gamma,\delta,q_0,g)$ and a word w does M accept w ?

For any tape w, we denote by $|w|$ the length of w: $|w| = card(\{j \in \mathbb{N} \mid w(j) \neq \text{B}\})$. The ATM M is *exponential-space bounded* if there exists a constant c such that for every configuration (q,w,i) with $(q_0,w_0,0) \rightarrow^* (q,w,i)$, $|w| \le c.2^{p(|w_0|)}$, for some constant c and polynomial function p. The complexity class **AEXPSPACE** is the class of membership problems where M is exponential-space bounded. It is known that AEXPSPACE = co-AEXPSPACE = 2-EXPTIME [4], where co-AEXPSPACE is the complement class of AEXPSPACE[1].

In the following, we shall consider the membership problem (M,ϵ), where ϵ denotes the empty word. This is without loss of generality; indeed, let (M,w) be any instance of the membership problem, and let c and p be the constant and polynomial function witnessing the fact that M is exponential-space bounded. Let M_w be an ATM that produces w starting from input ϵ. Clearly, M_w uses at most $|w|$ working space, thus the machine $M_w; M$, which runs M_w on the empty word and then continues with M, runs in space $c \cdot 2^{p(|w|)}$ and accepts ϵ if and only if M accepts w. If N denotes any natural number with

[1] Every ATM can be complemented in linear time, by simply interchanging the existential with the universal states, thus all alternating classes are closed under complement.

$N \geq \log_2(c) + p(w)$, then $M_w; M$ runs in space 2^N and moreover, (M, w) and (M_w, ϵ) have the same answer. Therefore, we assume from now on that $M = (Q, \Gamma, \delta, q_0, g)$ is an ATM started in the configuration $(q_0, w_0, 0)$ with $w_0(j) = \text{B}$ for all $j \in \mathbb{N}$ and that M runs in space at most 2^N on the empty input word, where N is bounded by a polynomial in the length of w. We define a formula ϕ and a set of patterns $\mathcal{S}$ (of polynomial size w.r.t. M and N) such that ϕ is $\mathcal{S}$-satisfiable iff the configuration $(q_0, w_0, 0)$ is accepting. This reduction ensures that any problem in AEXPSPACE is polynomially reducible to the $\mathcal{S}$-satisfiability problem, thus that the latter problem is 2-EXPTIME-hard.

All symbols $x \in \Gamma \cup \{0, 1, \leftarrow, \rightarrow\}$ are associated with pairwise distinct variables in $\mathcal{V}$, also denoted by x to simplify notations and improve readability. These variables occur freely in the formula ϕ and in the set of patterns $\mathcal{S}$ and must be passed as parameters to every predicate in $\mathcal{P}_\text{I}$. For readability, we take this as implicit in the rules given below, i.e., any atom $P(\boldsymbol{x})$ with $P \in \mathcal{P}_\text{I}$ should be read $P(\boldsymbol{x}, \boldsymbol{y})$ where $\boldsymbol{y}$ is the sequence of variables in $\Gamma \cup \{0, 1, \leftarrow, \rightarrow\}$ (with any fixed order).

We first define a predicate P which generates heaps denoting tapes of exponential size. The tape is encoded using a symbol $t \in \mathcal{P}_\text{H}$. Each cell in the tape is associated with a number encoded in binary and the atom $t(x, y_1, \ldots, y_N, z)$ is used to assert that the cell numbered $y_1, \ldots, y_N$ in the tape x contains the symbol z. We also use a predicate $h \in \mathcal{P}_\text{H}$ to denote the position of the head in the tape: $h(x, y_1, \ldots, y_N)$ states that the head of tape x points to the cell number $(y_1, \ldots, y_N)$. The predicate P positions the head arbitrarily and call a predicate P' which generates the content of each cell in the tape, starting from the one numbered $0, \ldots, 0$.

$$P(x) \Leftarrow \exists y_1, \ldots, y_N\, (h(x, y_1, \ldots, y_N) * P'(x, 0, \ldots, 0) * \mathop{\huge *}_{i=1}^{N} d(y_i))$$

$$d(x) \Leftarrow x \approx 0 \qquad\qquad d(x) \Leftarrow x \approx 1$$

The atom $P'(x, y_1, \ldots, y_N)$ chooses the content $z \in \Gamma$ of the cell numbered $y_1, \ldots, y_N$ and allocates the corresponding atom $t(x, y_1, \ldots, y_N, z)$. If $y_1, \ldots, y_N$ is not $(1, \ldots, 1)$ then it recursively calls P' on the next cell. To this purpose, one needs to increase $y_1, \ldots, y_N$ by 1. This can be done by adding different rules for each $i \in \{1, \ldots, N\}$, where i denotes the index of the rightmost digit in $y_1, \ldots, y_N$ that is equal to 0. In each of these rules, we add conditions stating that y_i is 0 and that $y_{i+1}, \ldots, y_N = 1$, so that the next cell is necessarily numbered $(y_1, \ldots, y_{i-1}, 1, 0 \ldots, 0)$. Note that, in all cases, one rule is required for each $z \in \Gamma$.

$$P'(x, y_1, \ldots, y_N) \Leftarrow (t(x, y_1, \ldots, y_N, z) * P'(x, y_1, \ldots, y_{i-1}, 1, 0 \ldots, 0) * y_i \approx 0 * \mathop{\huge *}_{j=i+1}^{N} (y_j \approx 1)) \quad \text{for all } z \in \Gamma \text{ and } i \in \{1, \ldots, N\}$$

$$P'(x, y_1, \ldots, y_N) \Leftarrow t(x, y_1, \ldots, y_N, z) * \mathop{\huge *}_{j=1}^{n} (y_j \approx 1) \quad \text{for all } z \in \Gamma$$

We introduce a predicate $a \in \mathcal{P}_\text{H}$ which will encode the actions applied on the tapes: $a(x, y, u, v, w)$ states that the tape y is obtained from a tape x by replacing the symbol u occurring at the head position by v, then by applying the move w on the head. We then introduce a predicate $q \in \mathcal{P}_\text{I}$ for every state $q \in Q$, generating potential derivations from state q. More precisely, the atom $q(x)$ allocates the action applied on a tape x at state q and the new tape y, then calls the predicate $q'(y)$ corresponding to the target state. If

$g(q) = \vee$ then one transition is chosen undeterministically in every rule, yielding one action and one tape, whereas if $g(q) = \wedge$ then all transitions corresponding to the state q and some (arbitrarily chosen) symbol a must be applied, yielding several actions and tapes in the same rule. Note that, at this point, we do not check that the content of the tape x is coherent with the selected transition (such conditions will be asserted later, by formulas in $\mathcal{S}$).

$$q(x) \Leftarrow \exists y\,(a(x,y,a,b,\mu) * P(y) * q'(y))$$
$$\text{for all } q,a,q',b,\mu \text{ such that } g(q) = \vee \text{ and } (q,a,q',b,\mu) \in \delta$$

$$q(x) \Leftarrow \exists y_1,\dots,y_N \mathop{\ast}_{i=1}^{n} (a(x,y_i,a,b_i,\mu_i) * P(y_i) * q_i(y_i))$$
$$\text{for all } q \text{ such that } g(q) = \wedge,\ \text{for all } a \in \Gamma$$
$$\text{where } \{(q,a,q_i,b_i,\mu_i) \mid i \in \{1,\dots,n\}\} \text{ is the set of transitions of the form } (q,a,q',b,\mu)$$

We then define a set of patterns $\mathcal{S}$ which assert various constraints ensuring that the derivation encoded by the construction above is valid, i.e., that the applied transitions are in coherence with the tape content. The first formula states that the initial tape x_0 is empty. To this purpose it suffices to check that it contains no cell of the form $t(x_0,y_1,\dots,y_N,z)$ with $z \notin \text{B}$, which is asserted by adding the following pattern in $\mathcal{S}$ (remind that $\mathcal{S}$-satisfiability is defined by excluding all structures containing a subheap satisfying one of the patterns in $\mathcal{S}$):

$$\exists y_1,\dots,y_N\ t(x_0,y_1,\dots,y_N,z) \quad \text{for all } z \neq \text{B}$$

Similarly, to encode the fact that the head initially points to $(0,\dots,0)$, we introduce patterns ruling out all atoms $h(x_0,y_1,\dots,y_N)$ where $y_i = 1$ for some $i \in \{1,\dots,N\}$:

$$\exists y_1,\dots,y_{N-1}\ h(x_0,y_1,\dots,y_{i-1},1,y_i,y_{N-1}) \quad \text{for all } i \in \{1,\dots,N\}$$

We then encode the relation between tapes and actions. We first check that, if the structure contains an atom $a(x,x',u,v,w)$ (meaning that tape x' is obtained from x by replacing a by b and applying move w), then necessarily the cell corresponding to the head position in x must contain a in x and b in x'. As the head position in encoded by an atom $h(x,y_1,\dots,y_N)$, this yields the following pattern:

$$\exists x,x',y_1,\dots,y_N\ (a(x,x',u,v,w) * h(x,y_1,\dots,y_N)$$
$$* t(x,y_1,\dots,y_N,z) * t(x',y_1,\dots,y_N,z'))$$
$$\text{for all } u,v \in \Gamma,\ \text{for all } w \in \{\leftarrow,\rightarrow\} \text{ and for all } z,z' \in \Gamma \text{ with } z \neq u \text{ or } z' \neq v$$

By excluding structures containing heaps satisfying the above pattern, we ensure that the head of x points to a cell containing u in x and v in x'. To state that all the cells other than the one numbered $y_1,\dots,y_N$ are unaffected by the above action, we introduce the following formulas:

$$\exists x,x',y_1,\dots,y_{N-1},y'_1,\dots,y'_{N-1}\ (a(x,x',u,v,w) * h(x,y_1,\dots,y_i,y,y_{i+1},\dots,y_{N-1})$$
$$* t(x,y_1,\dots,y_i,y',y_{i+1},\dots,y_{N-1},z) * t(x,y_1,\dots,y_i,y',y_{i+1},\dots,y_{N-1},z'))$$
$$\text{for all } i \in \{0,\dots,N-1\},\ \text{for all } y,y' \in \{0,1\} \text{ and for all } z,z' \in \Gamma \text{ with } y \neq y' \text{ and } z \neq z'$$

Here the head points to the cell numbered $(y_1, \ldots, y_i, y, y_{i+1}, \ldots, y_{N-1})$ (where y is some particular distinguished digit, that is fixed in each rule). The pattern rules out structures in which a cell numbered $y_1, \ldots, y_i, y', y_{i+1}, \ldots, y_{N-1}$ (where y' is some digit distinct from y) has distinct content in x and x'. This is stated by allocating atoms of the form $t(x, y_1, \ldots, y_i, y', y_{i+1}, \ldots, y_{N-1}, z)$ and $t(x, y_1, \ldots, y_i, y', y_{i+1}, \ldots, y_{N-1}, z')$ (with $z, z' \in \Gamma$ and $z \neq z'$). One such formula is added for all $i \in \{0, \ldots, N-1\}$ and for all distinct digits y, y' and symbols z, z', and ruling out all these patterns ensures that the content of any cell other than that of head of x is the same in x and x'.

The next two formulas encode the effect of a move to the right. They state that if the current head position is numbered $(y_1, \ldots, y_i, 0, 1 \ldots, 1)$ then the position after the move should be $(y_1, \ldots, y_i, 1, 0 \ldots, 0)$. As the constraints are expressed negatively, this is stated by discarding positions that differ from the latter sequence of digits. To state that the positions are not identical, we ensure that they differ by at least one digit (the last one that is distinct in both sequence). To this purpose, we assume that j denotes the index of the rightmost faulty digit. The first formula covers the case where this digit occurs inside the suffix $1, 0, \ldots, 0$. The case $j = i + 1$ covers the case where the first digit in the sequence is 0 instead of 1, while the case $j > i + 1$ occurs when one of the 0 is 1 instead of 0.

$$\begin{aligned}\exists x, x', y_1, \ldots, y_{j-1}\ (a(x, x', u, v, \rightarrow) * h(x, y_1, \ldots, y_i, 0, 1, \ldots, 1) \\ * h(x', y_1, \ldots, y_i, y_{i+1}, \ldots, y_{j-1}, u, 0, \ldots, 0)) \\ \text{for all } u, v \in \Gamma \text{ and } i, j \in \{1, \ldots, N\} \text{ where } j > i \\ \text{and either } j = i + 1 \text{ and } u = 0 \text{ or } j > i + 1 \text{ and } u = 1\end{aligned}$$

The formula below covers the case where the suffix is correct, but the faulty digit occurs inside the prefix $y_1, \ldots, y_i$.

$$\begin{aligned}\exists x, x', y_1, \ldots, y_i, y'_1, \ldots, y'_{j-1}\ (a(x, x', u, v, \rightarrow) * h(x, y_1, \ldots, y_{j-1}, y, y_{j+1}, \ldots, y_i, 0, 1, \ldots, 1) \\ * h(x', y'_1, \ldots, y'_{j-1}, y', y_{j+1}, \ldots, y_i, 1, 0, \ldots, 0) \\ \text{for all } u, v \in \Gamma, y, y' \in \{0, 1\} \text{ and } i, j \in \{1, \ldots, N-1\}, \text{ where } j \leq i \text{ and } y \neq y'\end{aligned}$$

Similar patterns can be added to encode the effect of the moves to the left (they are omitted for conciseness). The next formula ensures that all the tapes are pairwise distinct:

$$\exists x\, (h(x, 0, \ldots, 0) * h(x, 0, \ldots, 0))$$

It is easy to check that the formula $P(x_0) * q_0(x_0)$ admits a model compatible with the above patterns iff the configuration $(q_0, w_0, 0)$ is accepting. This yields the following:

Theorem 5.2. *The $\mathcal{S}$-satisfiability problem is 2-EXPTIME-hard for $\exists$-restricted sets of patterns $\mathcal{S}$.*

6 Undecidability Result

We now show that the $\mathcal{S}$-satisfiability problem is undecidable if the patterns under consideration are not $\exists$-restricted, i.e., if disequations[2] containing existential variables are allowed inside formulas in $\mathcal{S}$. The proof goes by a reduction from the halting problem on ATM (TM are sufficient but the reduction is given for ATM for the sake of uniformity). The encoding we use is similar to that of Sect. 5, except that cell numbers are represented as locations (linked by a predicate `next`) rather than sequences of digits. Because disequalities on existential variables are now allowed, we can assert that two cell numbers (denoted by locations) x and y are distinct using the formula $x \not\approx y$. This eliminates the need to explicitly instantiate x and y with distinct sequences of digits, as was done in Sect. 5 and greatly simplifies the encoding.

We consider any ATM $M = (Q, \Gamma, \delta, q_0, g)$ and encode accepting derivations starting from an empty tape. The rules of the predicate P are adapted as follows. Instead of generating a tape of exponential size, they generate a tape of arbitrary size, in which the cell numbers are encoded as locations, chained using `next`. The variables y_0 and y_f denote the first and last cell numbers, respectively, and $t(x, y, z)$ asserts that the cell numbered y in tape x contains the symbol z.

$$
\begin{array}{lll}
P(x, y_0, y_f) & \Leftarrow \exists y\ (h(x, y) * P'(x, y_0, y_f)) & \\
P'(x, y, y_f) & \Leftarrow \exists y'\ (t(x, y, z) * P'(x, y', y_f) * \mathtt{next}(y, y') * y \not\approx y_f) & \text{for all } z \in \Gamma \\
P(x, y, y_f) & \Leftarrow (t(x, y, z) * y \approx y_f) & \text{for all } z \in \Gamma
\end{array}
$$

The predicates corresponding to states are defined as in Sect. 5. The definition of the set of patterns $\mathcal{S}$ is adapted as follows. In contrast to Sect. 5, we also need to ensure that there is no move to the right of the last cell and that the predicate `next` is functional (note that the same atom $\mathtt{next}(x, y)$ may occur several times in the structure).

$$\exists y\, t(x_0, y, z) \quad \text{for all } z \neq \text{B} \qquad\qquad \exists y\ (h(x_0, y) * y \neq y_0)$$

$$\exists x, x', y\ (a(x, x', u, v, w) * h(x, y) * t(x, y, z) * t(x', y, z'))$$
$$\text{for all } u, v \in \Gamma,\ w \in \{\leftarrow, \rightarrow\} \text{ and } z, z' \in \Gamma \text{ with } z \neq u \text{ or } z' \neq v$$

$$\exists x, x', y, y'\ (a(x, x', u, v, w) * h(x, y) * y \not\approx y' * t(x, y', z) * t(x', y', z'))$$
$$\text{for all } u, v \in \Gamma,\ w \in \{\leftarrow, \rightarrow\} \text{ and } z, z' \in \Gamma \text{ such that } z \neq z'$$

$$\exists x, x', y, y', y''\ (a(x, x', u, v, \rightarrow) * h(x, y) * \mathtt{next}(y, y') * h(x', y'') * y'' \not\approx y') \quad \forall u, v \in \Gamma$$
$$\exists x\ (h(x, y_0) * h(x, y_0))$$

$$\exists x, x'\ (a(x, x', u, v, \rightarrow) * h(x, y_f)) \quad \texttt{\% no move to the right of the last cell}$$
$$\exists y, y_1, y_2\ (\mathtt{next}(y, y_1) * \mathtt{next}(y, y_2) * y_1 \not\approx y_2) \qquad \texttt{next is functional}$$

The formula $P(x_0) * q_0(x_0)$ admits a model compatible with the above patterns iff the configuration $(q_0, \epsilon, 0)$ is accepting. As M is arbitrary, we get:

Theorem 6.1. *The $\mathcal{S}$-satisfiability problem is undecidable for non $\exists$-restricted sets of patterns $\mathcal{S}$.*

[2] Note that the equations containing existential variables are not problematic as they can always be eliminated using the equivalence: $\exists x\, (x \approx y * \phi) \equiv \phi\{x \mapsto y\}$.

7 Conclusion

We developed a doubly exponential algorithm to check the satisfiability of formulas in the separation logic of relations, under additional constraints defined by sets of patterns of a specific form that are excluded from the structures. We proved that this algorithm is optimal and that the problem becomes undecidable when a more general class of patterns is considered. These results significantly advance existing satisfiability testing algorithms for certain variants of separation logic and provide a clearer boundary for the types of properties that can be imposed on structures without losing the decidability of the satisfiability problem. Importantly, unlike [5] (which focuses on a decidable fragment of the entailment problem in SLR), our approach imposes no restrictions on the inductive rules defining the semantics of the predicate symbols; the only limitations apply to the patterns. We plan to extend this algorithm to target more expressive languages. Specifically, we aim to broaden the logic to represent structures that include data interpreted over fixed theories, such as arithmetic.

A Proof of Lemma 4.6

The proof proceeds by induction on the set $\mathcal{A}_k(\phi)$.

- Assume that $\phi = \mathtt{emp}$ and $A = (\emptyset, \emptyset, \{\mathtt{emp}\})$, i.e., $V = \emptyset = fv(\phi)$, $\sim$ is empty and $\Sigma = \{\mathtt{emp}\}$. Let $\mathfrak{s}$ be an arbitrary store, and let $\mathfrak{h} = \emptyset$. By definition, $(\mathfrak{s}, \mathfrak{h}) \models_{\mathcal{R}} \phi$, hence Assertion 1 holds. Assertion 2 trivially holds because $V = \emptyset$. Moreover, the only formula $\psi \in \mathtt{Pt}(V, k)$ such that $(\mathfrak{s}, \mathfrak{h}') \models_{\mathcal{R}} \psi$ for some $\mathfrak{h}' \subseteq \mathfrak{h}$ is $\mathtt{emp}$ (as the only atoms in formulas in $\mathtt{Pt}(V, k)$ are $\mathcal{P}_{\mathtt{H}}$-atoms or $\mathtt{emp}$, and no $\mathcal{P}_{\mathtt{H}}$-atom can be satisfied on an empty heap), thus Assertion 3 holds (as $\mathtt{emp}$ subsumes itself).
- Assume that $\phi = (x \approx y)$ and $A = (\{x, y\}, \{x \sim y\}, \{\mathtt{emp}\})$, i.e., $V = \{x, y\} = fv(\phi)$, $u \sim v$ holds for all $u, v \in V$ (remember that $\sim$ is closed under reflexivity, symmetry and transitivity) and $\Sigma = \{\mathtt{emp}\}$. Let $\mathfrak{s}$ be an arbitrary store such that $\mathfrak{s}(x) = \mathfrak{s}(y)$ and let $\mathfrak{h} = \emptyset$. It is clear that Assertions 1 and 2 hold. As in the previous case, the only formula $\psi \in \mathtt{Pt}(V, k)$ such that $(\mathfrak{s}, \mathfrak{h}') \models_{\mathcal{R}} \psi$ for some $\mathfrak{h}' \subseteq \mathfrak{h}$ is $\mathtt{emp}$, thus Assertion 3 holds.
- Assume that $\phi = (x \not\approx y)$ and $A = (\{x, y\}, \emptyset, \{\mathtt{emp}\})$, i.e., $V = \{x, y\} = fv(\phi)$, $u \sim v$ holds iff $u = v$ and $\Sigma = \{\mathtt{emp}\}$. Let $\mathfrak{s}$ be an arbitrary store such that $\mathfrak{s}(x) \neq \mathfrak{s}(y)$ and let $\mathfrak{h} = \emptyset$. As in the previous cases, it is straightforward to check that Assertions 1, 2, and 3 hold.
- Assume that $\phi = p(x_1, \ldots, x_n)$ with $p \in \mathcal{P}_{\mathtt{H}}$ and that the abstraction $\mathcal{A}_k(\phi)$ is of the form $(\{x_1, \ldots, x_n\}, \sim, \{\mathtt{emp}, \phi\downarrow_{\sim}\})$, where $\sim$ is an equivalence relation on $\{x_1, \ldots, x_n\}$. Then $V = \{x_1, \ldots, x_n\} = fv(\phi)$ and $\Sigma = \{\mathtt{emp}, \phi\downarrow_{\sim}\}$. Let $\mathfrak{s}$ be any store such that $\mathfrak{s}(x_i) = \mathfrak{s}(x_j)$ iff $x_i \sim x_j$ (such a store always exists as $\mathcal{L}$ is infinite). Assertion 2 holds by definition of $\mathfrak{s}$. Let $\mathfrak{h}$ be the heap $\{p(\mathfrak{s}(x_1), \ldots, \mathfrak{s}(x_n))\}$. By definition of $\mathfrak{h}$, $(\mathfrak{s}, \mathfrak{h}) \models_{\mathcal{R}} \phi$, i.e., Assertion 1 holds. Now, consider any formula $\psi \in \mathtt{Pt}(V, k)$ such that $(\mathfrak{s}, \mathfrak{h}') \models_{\mathcal{R}} \psi$, for some $\mathfrak{h}' \subseteq \mathfrak{h}$. We show that ψ is subsumed by a formula in Σ. The result is immediate if $\mathfrak{h}' = \emptyset$, as necessarily $\psi = \mathtt{emp}$ in this case, and $\mathtt{emp}$ occurs in Σ. Otherwise, we must have $\mathfrak{h}' = \mathfrak{h}$. Since $\psi \in \mathtt{Pt}(V, k)$, ψ is of the form $\exists \mathbf{y} *_{i=1}^{m} p_i(z_i^1, \ldots, z_i^{n_i})$ with $p_i \in \mathcal{P}_{\mathtt{H}}$. As $\mathfrak{h}$ is of cardinality 1 and $(\mathfrak{s}, \mathfrak{h}) \models_{\mathcal{R}} \psi$, we must

have $m = 1$ (as every atom $p_i(z_i)$ is satisfied only on heaps of cardinality 1). Thus, there exists a store $\mathfrak{s}'$, coinciding with $\mathfrak{s}$ on all variables not occurring in $\boldsymbol{y}$ such that $(\mathfrak{s}', \mathfrak{h}) \models_{\mathcal{R}} p_1(z_1^1, \dots, z_1^{n_1})$. By definition of $\mathfrak{h}$, this entails that $p_1 = p$, $n_1 = n$ and that $\mathfrak{s}'(z_1^i) = \mathfrak{s}(x_i)$ for all $i \in \{1, \dots, n\}$. Consequently, $z_1^i \downarrow_\sim = x_i \downarrow_\sim$ for all i such that $z_1^i \in \{x_1, \dots, x_n\}$. Let σ be a substitution mapping every variable z_1^i occurring in $\boldsymbol{y}$ to $x_i \downarrow_\sim$. We get $p(z_1^1, \dots, z_1^n) \downarrow_\sim \sigma = \phi \downarrow_\sim$, so that $\psi \downarrow_\sim$ is subsumed by the formula $\phi \downarrow_\sim$ that occurs in Σ. Hence Assertion 3 holds.

- Assume that $\phi = P(x_1, \dots, x_n)$ and $A \in \mathcal{A}_k(\xi)$ for some ξ such that $\phi \Leftarrow_{\mathcal{R}} \xi$. By the induction hypothesis, there exists a model $(\mathfrak{s}, \mathfrak{h})$ of ξ such that Assertions 2 and 3 hold. As every model of ξ is also a model of ϕ, Assertion 1 is also satisfied.
- Assume that $\phi = \phi_1 \vee \phi_2$ and $A \in \mathcal{A}_k(\phi_i)$ for some $i \in \{1, 2\}$. By the induction hypothesis, there exists a model $(\mathfrak{s}, \mathfrak{h})$ of ϕ_i such that Assertions 2 and 3 hold. As every model of ϕ_i is also a model of ϕ, we get the result.
- Assume that $\phi = \phi_1 * \phi_2$ and that $\mathcal{A}_k(\phi_i)$ contains abstractions $(V_i, \sim_i, \Sigma_i) \in \mathcal{A}_k(\phi_i)$ (for all $i \in \{1, 2\}$), where $V = V_1 \cup V_2$, $\sim$ agrees with $\sim_i$ on V_i, and Σ is the tuple $\{(\phi_1 * \phi_2)\downarrow_\sim \mid \phi_i \in \Sigma_i, \mathtt{width}(\phi_1) + \mathtt{width}(\phi_2) \le k\}$. By the induction hypothesis, there exist structures $(\mathfrak{s}_i, \mathfrak{h}_i)$ such that $(\mathfrak{s}_i, \mathfrak{h}_i) \models_{\mathcal{R}} \phi_i$; $x \sim_i y \iff \mathfrak{s}_i(x) = \mathfrak{s}_i(y)$ (for all $x, y \in V_i$); and if $\psi \in \mathtt{Pt}(V_i, k)$ and $(\mathfrak{s}_i, \mathfrak{h}') \models_{\mathcal{R}} \psi$ for some $\mathfrak{h}' \subseteq \mathfrak{h}_i$ then Σ_i contains a formula subsuming $\psi \downarrow_{\sim_i}$. Let $\mathfrak{s}$ be any store such that the equivalence $x \sim y \iff \mathfrak{s}(x) = \mathfrak{s}(y)$ holds for all $x, y \in V$. By definition, Assertion 2 is satisfied. Let $\mathcal{L}_1, \mathcal{L}_2$ be disjoint infinite subsets of $\mathcal{L}$, which are also disjoint from $\mathfrak{s}(V)$. As $\sim$ agrees with $\sim_i$ on all variables in V_i, we get $\mathfrak{s}(x) = \mathfrak{s}(y) \iff \mathfrak{s}_i(x) = \mathfrak{s}_i(y)$ for all $x, y \in V_i$. Thus one can construct an injective mapping λ_i from $\mathfrak{s}_i(V_i) \cup \mathcal{L}(\mathfrak{h}_i)$ to $\mathfrak{s}(V_i) \cup \mathcal{L}_i$ such that $\lambda_i(\mathfrak{s}_i(x)) = \mathfrak{s}(x)$, for all $x \in V_i$, and $\lambda_i(\ell) \in \mathcal{L}_i$ if $\ell \notin \mathfrak{s}(V_i)$. By Proposition 2.6 we have $(\lambda_i \circ \mathfrak{s}_i, \gamma(\mathfrak{h}_i)) \models_{\mathcal{R}} \phi_i$, thus (as $\mathfrak{s}$ coincides with $\lambda_i \circ \mathfrak{s}_i$ on every variable occurring in $V_i = fv(\phi_i)$), we get $(\mathfrak{s}, \lambda_i(\mathfrak{h}_i)) \models_{\mathcal{R}} \phi_i$. Let $\mathfrak{h} = \lambda_1(\mathfrak{h}_1) + \lambda_2(\mathfrak{h}_2)$. By definition, we have $(\mathfrak{s}, \mathfrak{h}) \models_{\mathcal{R}} \phi_1 * \phi_2 = \phi$, hence Assertion 1 holds. It only remains to show that Assertion 3 is satisfied. Consider a formula $\psi \in \mathtt{Pt}(V, k)$ such that $(\mathfrak{s}, \mathfrak{h}') \models_{\mathcal{R}} \psi$ for some $\mathfrak{h}' \subseteq \mathfrak{h}$. We must show that Σ contains a formula subsuming $\psi \downarrow_\sim$. By definition of $\mathfrak{h}$, $\mathfrak{h}'$ must be of the form $\mathfrak{h}'_1 + \mathfrak{h}'_2$ where $\mathfrak{h}'_i \subseteq \lambda_i(\mathfrak{h}_i)$. Moreover, the formula ψ is of the form $\exists \boldsymbol{y} *_{i=1}^{n} p_i(z_i)$ with $p_i \in \mathcal{P}_{\mathrm{H}}$. We assume by α-renaming that $\boldsymbol{y}$ contains no variable in V. As $(\mathfrak{s}, \mathfrak{h}') \models_{\mathcal{R}} \psi$, there exists a store $\mathfrak{s}'$, coinciding with $\mathfrak{s}$ on all variables not occurring in $\boldsymbol{y}$, such that $(\mathfrak{s}', \mathfrak{h}') \models_{\mathcal{R}} \xi$. Let σ be any substitution mapping every variable y in $\boldsymbol{y}$ to an arbitrary chosen variable $y' \in V$ such that $\mathfrak{s}(y') = \mathfrak{s}'(y)$, if such a variable exists, otherwise $y\sigma = y$. By definition, $(\mathfrak{s}', \mathfrak{h}') \models_{\mathcal{R}} \xi\sigma$, and for all variables y occurring in $\boldsymbol{y}$ and $\xi\sigma$, we must have $\mathfrak{s}'(y) \notin \mathfrak{s}(V)$. As each atom $p_i(z_i)$ is satisfied only on heaps of size 1, one can partition the set $\{1, \dots, n\}$ into sets I_1, I_2 such that $i \in I_j$ iff the part of the heap that corresponds to $p_i(z_i)$ is in I_j. Let $\xi_j = *_{i \in I_j} p_i(\boldsymbol{x}_i)$, we get $(\mathfrak{s}', \mathfrak{h}'_j) \models_{\mathcal{R}} \xi_j\sigma$ and $\xi = \xi_1 * \xi_2$ (up to AC of $*$). Let $\boldsymbol{y}_j$ be the sequence of the variables in $\boldsymbol{y}$ that occur in $\xi_j\sigma$, we get $(\mathfrak{s}, \mathfrak{h}'_j) \models_{\mathcal{R}} \exists \boldsymbol{y}_j \xi_j\sigma$. Since $\psi \in \mathtt{Pt}(V, k)$, necessarily $\mathtt{width}(\psi) \le k$, i.e., $n \le k$, so that $\mathtt{width}(\exists \boldsymbol{y}_j \xi_j) = card(I_j) \le k$. As $(\mathfrak{s}', \mathfrak{h}'_j) \models_{\mathcal{R}} \xi_j\sigma$, for every variable $x \in fv(\xi_j)$, we have $\mathfrak{s}'(x) \in \mathcal{L}(\mathfrak{h}'_j) \subseteq \mathcal{L}(\lambda_j(\mathfrak{h}_j))$. Thus if moreover $x \in V \setminus V_j$, then by definition of λ_j (since $\mathcal{L}(\lambda_j(\mathfrak{h}_j)) \subseteq \mathfrak{s}(V_j) \cup \mathcal{L}_j$ and $\mathcal{L}_j \cup \mathfrak{s}(V) = \emptyset$) there must exist some variable $x' \in V_j$ such that $\mathfrak{s}(x) = \mathfrak{s}(x')$. Let θ_j be a substitution mapping every such variable $x \in (V \cap fv(\xi_j)) \setminus V_j$ to a variable $x' \in V_j$ with the same value in $\mathfrak{s}$.

We get $(\mathfrak{s}, \mathfrak{h}'_j) \models_{\mathcal{R}} \exists \boldsymbol{y}_j \xi_j \sigma \theta_j$, thus (as $fv(\exists \boldsymbol{y}_j \xi_j \theta_j) \subseteq V_j$) $(\lambda \circ \mathfrak{s}_j, \mathfrak{h}'_j) \models_{\mathcal{R}} \exists \boldsymbol{y}_j \xi_j \sigma \theta_j$. Using Proposition 2.6, we deduce that $(\mathfrak{s}_j, \mathfrak{h}_j) \models_{\mathcal{R}} \exists \boldsymbol{y}_j \xi_j \sigma \theta_j$, so that (by the induction hypothesis) Σ_j contains a formula ψ'_j subsuming $\exists \boldsymbol{y}_j \xi_j \sigma \theta_j \downarrow_{\sim_j}$. By definition of the subsumption relation, the formula ψ'_j is of the form $\exists \boldsymbol{y}'_j \xi_j \sigma \theta_j \eta_j \downarrow_{\sim_j}$, where η_j is a substitution and $\boldsymbol{y}'_j$ is the subsequence of the variables in $\boldsymbol{y}_j$ that do not occur in the domain of η_j. Then Σ necessarily contains the formula $(\psi'_1 * \psi'_1) \downarrow_{\sim}$. Up to prenex form, and using the fact that $\sim_1$ and $\sim_2$ are included in $\sim$, the formula $(\psi'_1 * \psi'_2) \downarrow_{\sim}$ may be written on the form: $\exists \boldsymbol{y}'_1 \exists \boldsymbol{y}'_2 (\xi_1 \sigma \theta_1 \eta_1 * \xi_2 \sigma \theta_2 \eta_2) \downarrow_{\sim}$. By definition $x\theta_i \downarrow_{\sim} = x \downarrow_{\sim}$ (as $x \sim x\theta_i$) thus $(\psi'_1 * \psi'_2) \downarrow_{\sim}$ is of the form: $\exists \boldsymbol{y}'_1 \exists \boldsymbol{y}'_2 (\xi_1 * \xi_2) \sigma \eta \downarrow_{\sim}$, where $x\eta = x\eta_1 \eta_2 \downarrow_{\sim}$, i.e., of the form $\exists \boldsymbol{y}'_1 \exists \boldsymbol{y}'_2 (\xi_1 * \xi_2) \downarrow_{\sim} \sigma'$, with $x\sigma' = x\sigma\eta \downarrow_{\sim}$. Therefore, $(\psi'_1 * \psi'_2) \downarrow_{\sim}$ subsumes the formula $\psi \downarrow_{\sim}$.

- Assume that $\phi = \exists x \phi'$ and that there exists $(V', \sim', \Sigma') \in \mathcal{A}_k(\phi')$ such that $V = V' \setminus \{x\}$, $\sim$ is the restriction of $\sim'$ to V and $\Sigma = \{\exists x \xi \mid \xi \in \Sigma'\}$. By the induction hypothesis there exists a structure $(\mathfrak{s}, \mathfrak{h})$ such that $(\mathfrak{s}, \mathfrak{h}) \models_{\mathcal{R}} \phi'$, $x \sim' y \iff \mathfrak{s}(x) = \mathfrak{s}(y)$ (for all $x, y \in V'$) and for all formulas $\psi \in \mathtt{Pt}(V', k)$ and heaps $\mathfrak{h}' \subseteq \mathfrak{h}$, if $(\mathfrak{s}, \mathfrak{h}') \models_{\mathcal{R}} \psi$ then Σ' contains a formula subsuming $\psi \downarrow_{\sim'}$. This entails that Assertions 1 and 2 hold (as ϕ is a logical consequence of ϕ' and $V \subseteq V'$). Consider a formula $\psi \in \mathtt{Pt}(V, k)$ and a heap $\mathfrak{h}' \subseteq \mathfrak{h}$ such that $(\mathfrak{s}, \mathfrak{h}') \models_{\mathcal{R}} \psi$. As $V \subseteq V'$, we deduce that $\psi \in \mathtt{Pt}(V', k)$, so that Σ' contains a formula ξ subsuming $\psi \downarrow_{\sim'}$. By definition, ψ must be of the form $\exists \boldsymbol{y} \exists \boldsymbol{z} \psi'$ and there exists a substitution σ of domain $\boldsymbol{y}$ such that $\xi = \exists \boldsymbol{z} (\psi' \downarrow_{\sim'} \sigma)$. We may assume by α-renaming that $\boldsymbol{y}$ and $\boldsymbol{z}$ contain no variable in V' (hence x does not occur in $\boldsymbol{y}$ or $\boldsymbol{z}$). Then Σ contains the formula $\exists x \xi$. Since (by the assumption in Definition 4.5), $y < x$ holds for all $y \in fv(\phi)$, we have $u \downarrow_{\sim} = u \downarrow_{\sim'}$ for all variables $u \neq x$. Since x cannot occur in $fv(\psi')$ (as $\psi \in \mathtt{Pt}(V, k)$, thus $fv(\psi) \subseteq V$, and x does not occur in $\boldsymbol{y}$ or $\boldsymbol{z}$), we get $\xi = \exists \boldsymbol{z} (\psi' \downarrow_{\sim} \sigma)$. If $x \notin fv(\xi)$ then $\exists x \xi = \xi$ subsumes $\psi \downarrow_{\sim}$ and the proof is completed. Otherwise, $\boldsymbol{y}$ contains a variable y such that $y\sigma = x$, then $\boldsymbol{y}$ is of the form $(\boldsymbol{y}', y)$. Up to α-renaming, $\exists x \xi$ is of the form $\exists y \xi\{x \mapsto y\}$ and we get $\exists y \xi\{x \mapsto y\} = \exists y \exists \boldsymbol{z} (\psi' \downarrow_{\sim} \sigma')$, where σ' is the restriction of σ' to the variables distinct from y, with $\psi \downarrow_{\sim} = \exists \boldsymbol{y}' \exists y \exists \boldsymbol{z} \psi' \downarrow_{\sim}$, so that $\exists x \xi$ subsumes $\psi \downarrow_{\sim}$.

B Proof of Lemma 4.7

The proof is by induction on the satisfiability relation.

- If $\phi = \mathtt{emp}$, then by Definition 4.5, $\mathcal{A}_k(\phi)$ contains an abstraction $(\emptyset, \emptyset, \{\mathtt{emp}\})$. By definition, $V = \emptyset$ and $\mathfrak{h} = \emptyset$, so that the two assertions of the lemma trivially hold.
- If $\phi = (x \approx y)$, then, by Definition 4.5, $\mathcal{A}_k(\phi)$ contains an abstraction $(\{x, y\}, \{x \sim y\}, \{\mathtt{emp}\})$. By definition, $V = \{x, y\}$, $\mathfrak{s}(x) = \mathfrak{s}(y)$ and $\mathfrak{h} = \emptyset$, so that we get $u \sim v \iff \mathfrak{s}(u) = \mathfrak{s}(v)$ (for all $u, v \in V$) and $(\mathfrak{s}, \mathfrak{h}) \models_{\mathcal{R}} \mathtt{emp}$.
- If $\phi = (x \not\approx y)$, then, by Definition 4.5, $\mathcal{A}_k(\phi)$ contains an abstraction $(\{x, y\}, \emptyset, \{\mathtt{emp}\})$. By definition, $V = \{x, y\}$, $\mathfrak{s}(x) \neq \mathfrak{s}(y)$ and $\mathfrak{h} = \emptyset$, so that $u \sim v \iff \mathfrak{s}(u) = \mathfrak{s}(v)$ (for all $u, v \in V$) and $(\mathfrak{s}, \mathfrak{h}) \models_{\mathcal{R}} \mathtt{emp}$.
- If $\phi = p(x_1, \dots, x_n)$ with $p \in \mathcal{P}_{\mathtt{H}}$ then $V = \{x_1, \dots, x_n\}$ and, by Definition 4.5, $\mathcal{A}_k(\phi)$ contains an abstraction $(\{x_1, \dots, x_n\}, \sim, \{\mathtt{emp}, \phi \downarrow_{\sim}\})$, where $\sim$ is the equivalence relations of V such that $u \sim v \iff \mathfrak{s}(u) = \mathfrak{s}(v)$ (for all $u, v \in V$). By Definition 2.4,

$\mathfrak{h} = \{p(\mathfrak{s}(x_1), \ldots, \mathfrak{s}(x_n))\}$, so that $(\mathfrak{s}, \mathfrak{h}) \models_{\mathcal{R}} \phi$, and therefore $(\mathfrak{s}, \mathfrak{h}) \models_{\mathcal{R}} \phi\downarrow_{\sim}$. Moreover, we also have $(\mathfrak{s}, \emptyset) \models_{\mathcal{R}} \mathtt{emp}$, with $\emptyset \subseteq \mathfrak{h}$.

- If ϕ is a $\mathcal{P}_{\mathrm{I}}$-atom, then by definition $(\mathfrak{s}, \mathfrak{h}) \models_{\mathcal{R}} \psi$ for some formula ψ such that $\phi \Leftarrow_{\mathcal{R}} \psi$. Note that (as the right-hand side of inductive rules contains all the variables in the left-hand side) necessarily $fv(\psi) = fv(\phi) = V$. By the induction hypothesis, $\mathcal{A}_k(\psi)$ contains an abstraction $A = (V, \sim, \Sigma)$ such that $x \sim y \iff \mathfrak{s}(x) = \mathfrak{s}(y)$ (for all $x, y \in V$) and for all $\psi \in \Sigma$, there exists $\mathfrak{h}' \subseteq \mathfrak{h}$ such that $(\mathfrak{s}, \mathfrak{h}') \models_{\mathcal{R}} \psi$. By Definition 4.5, $A \in \mathcal{A}_k(\phi)$.
- If $\phi = \phi_1 \vee \phi_2$, then by definition $(\mathfrak{s}, \mathfrak{h}) \models_{\mathcal{R}} \phi_i$ for some $i \in \{1, 2\}$. By the above assumption on disjunctions, $fv(\phi_i) = V$. By the induction hypothesis, $\mathcal{A}_k(\phi_i)$ contains an abstraction $A = (V, \sim, \Sigma)$ such that $x \sim y \iff \mathfrak{s}(x) = \mathfrak{s}(y)$ (for all $x, y \in V$) and for all $\psi \in \Sigma$, there exists $\mathfrak{h}' \subseteq \mathfrak{h}$ such that $(\mathfrak{s}, \mathfrak{h}') \models_{\mathcal{R}} \psi$. By Definition 4.5, $A \in \mathcal{A}_k(\phi)$.
- If $\phi = \phi_1 * \phi_2$, then by definition, there exist heaps $\mathfrak{h}_1, \mathfrak{h}_2$ such that $(\mathfrak{s}, \mathfrak{h}_i) \models_{\mathcal{R}} \phi_i$ for all $i \in \{1, 2\}$, and $\mathfrak{h} = \mathfrak{h}_1 + \mathfrak{h}_2$. Let $V_i = fv(\phi_i)$. By the induction hypothesis, $\mathcal{A}_k(\phi_i)$ contains an abstraction $A_i = (V_i, \sim_i, \Sigma_i)$ such that $x \sim_i y \iff \mathfrak{s}(x) = \mathfrak{s}(y)$ (for all $x, y \in V_i$) and for all $\psi \in \Sigma_i$, there exists $\mathfrak{h}' \subseteq \mathfrak{h}_i$ such that $(\mathfrak{s}, \mathfrak{h}') \models_{\mathcal{R}} \psi$. Let $\sim$ be the equivalence relation such that $x \sim y \iff \mathfrak{s}(x) = \mathfrak{s}(y)$ (for all $x, y \in V$). By definition, $\sim$ coincides with $\sim_i$ on V_i. Moreover, $V = V_1 \cup V_2$. By Definition 4.5, $\mathcal{A}_k(\phi)$ contains the abstraction $(V, \sim, \Sigma)$ with $\Sigma = \{(\phi_1 * \phi_2)\downarrow_{\sim} \mid \phi_i \in \Sigma_i, \mathtt{width}(\phi_1) + \mathtt{width}(\phi_2) \leq k\}$. Let $\psi \in \Sigma$. By definition, $\psi = (\psi_1 * \psi_2)\downarrow_{\sim}$ with $\psi_i \in \Sigma_i$, so that there exists $\mathfrak{h}'_i$ with $\mathfrak{h}'_i \subseteq \mathfrak{h}_i$ and $(\mathfrak{s}, \mathfrak{h}'_i) \models_{\mathcal{R}} \psi_i$ (for all $i \in \{1, 2\}$). This entails that $(\mathfrak{s}, \mathfrak{h}'_1 + \mathfrak{h}'_2) \models_{\mathcal{R}} (\psi_1 * \psi_2)\downarrow_{\sim} = \psi$ with $\mathfrak{h}'_1 + \mathfrak{h}'_2 \subseteq \mathfrak{h}_1 + \mathfrak{h}_2 = \mathfrak{h}$.
- If $\phi = \exists x\, \psi$ then by definition there exists a store $\mathfrak{s}'$ coinciding with $\mathfrak{s}$ on any variable other than x such that $(\mathfrak{s}', \mathfrak{h}) \models_{\mathcal{R}} \psi$. By the induction hypothesis, we deduce that $\mathcal{A}_k(\psi)$ contains an abstraction $(V', \sim', \Sigma')$ such that $V' = fv(\psi)$, $u \sim v \iff \mathfrak{s}'(u) = \mathfrak{s}'(v)$ (for all $u, v \in V'$) and $\forall \psi \in \Sigma'\ \exists \mathfrak{h}' \subseteq \mathfrak{h}$ s.t. $(\mathfrak{s}', \mathfrak{h}') \models_{\mathcal{R}} \psi$. By Definition 4.5, $\mathcal{A}_k(\phi)$ contains an abstraction $(V' \setminus \{x\}, \sim, \Sigma)$, where $\sim$ is the restriction of $\sim'$ to $V' \setminus \{x\}$ and $\Sigma = \{\exists x\, \xi \mid \xi \in \Sigma'\}$. We have $V' \setminus \{x\} = fv(\psi) \setminus \{x\} = fv(\phi) = V$. Moreover, if $x \in V$ then $\mathfrak{s}(u) = \mathfrak{s}'(u)$, so that the equivalence $u \sim v \iff \mathfrak{s}(u) = \mathfrak{s}(v)$ holds for all $u, v \in V$. Finally, if $\psi \in \Sigma$, then $\psi = \exists x\, \xi$ with $\xi \in \Sigma'$, so that there exists $\mathfrak{h}' \subseteq \mathfrak{h}$ with $(\mathfrak{s}', \mathfrak{h}') \models_{\mathcal{R}} \xi$. This entails that $(\mathfrak{s}, \mathfrak{h}') \models_{\mathcal{R}} \exists x\, \xi = \psi$.

C Proof of Theorem 4.8

We establish the two implications.

$\Rightarrow$ Let $(\mathfrak{s}, \mathfrak{h})$ be a model of ϕ that is compatible with $\mathcal{S}$, i.e., $(\mathfrak{s}, \mathfrak{h}') \not\models_{\mathcal{R}} \psi$ for all $\psi \in \mathcal{S}$ and for all $\mathfrak{h}' \subseteq \mathfrak{h}$. By Lemma 4.7, $\mathcal{A}_k(\phi)$ contains an abstraction $A = (V, \sim, \Sigma)$ such that $x \sim y \iff \mathfrak{s}(x) = \mathfrak{s}(y)$ (for all $x, y \in V$) and $\forall \psi \in \Sigma, \exists \mathfrak{h}' \subseteq \mathfrak{h},\ (\mathfrak{s}, \mathfrak{h}') \models_{\mathcal{R}} \psi$. Assume that there exists $\psi \in \mathcal{S}$ such that $A \triangleright \psi$. By definition, this entails that ψ is of the form $\exists z\, (*_{i=1}^{n} (x_i \approx x'_i) * *_{i=1}^{m} (y_i \not\approx y'_i) * \xi)$ where $x_i, x'_i, y_i, y'_i \in V$, $x_i \sim x'_i$ (for all $i \in \{1, \ldots, n\}$), $y_i \not\sim y'_i$ (for all $i \in \{1, \ldots, m\}$), and Σ contains a formula ξ' subsuming $\exists z\, \xi$. Using the above equivalence, we deduce that $\mathfrak{s}(x_i) = \mathfrak{s}(x'_i)$ (for all $i \in \{1, \ldots, n\}$), and $\mathfrak{s}(y_i) \neq \mathfrak{s}(y'_i)$ (for all $i \in \{1, \ldots, m\}$), so that $(\mathfrak{s}, \emptyset) \models_{\mathcal{R}} *_{i=1}^{n} (x_i \approx x'_i) * *_{i=1}^{m} (y_i \not\approx y'_i)$. Moreover, as $\xi' \in \Sigma$, there exists $\mathfrak{h}' \subseteq \mathfrak{h}$ such that $(\mathfrak{s}, \mathfrak{h}') \models_{\mathcal{R}} \xi'$.

By Proposition 4.3, we deduce that $(\mathfrak{s}, \mathfrak{h}') \models_{\mathcal{R}} \exists z\, \xi$. Consequently, we get: $(\mathfrak{s}, \mathfrak{h}') \models_{\mathcal{R}} \exists z\, (*_{i=1}^{n}(x_i \approx x_i') * *_{i=1}^{m}(y_i \not\approx y_i') * \xi)$, i.e. $(\mathfrak{s}, \mathfrak{h}') \models_{\mathcal{R}} \psi$, thus leading to a contradiction of the assumption that $(\mathfrak{s}, \mathfrak{h})$ is compatible with $\mathcal{S}$.

$\Leftarrow$ Assume that $\mathcal{A}_k(\phi)$ contains an abstraction $A = (V, \sim, \Sigma)$ of domain V such that $A \not\triangleright \psi$, for all $\psi \in \mathcal{S}$. By Lemma 4.6, we deduce that there exists a structure $(\mathfrak{s}, \mathfrak{h})$ such that $(\mathfrak{s}, \mathfrak{h}) \models_{\mathcal{R}} \phi$, $x \sim y \iff \mathfrak{s}(x) = \mathfrak{s}(y)$ (for all $x, y \in V$) and for all $\psi \in \mathtt{Pt}(V, k)$, if $(\mathfrak{s}, \mathfrak{h}') \models_{\mathcal{R}} \psi$ for some $\mathfrak{h}' \subseteq \mathfrak{h}$ then ψ is subsumed by some formula in Σ. Assume that $(\mathfrak{s}, \mathfrak{h})$ is not compatible with $\mathcal{S}$, i.e., that there exist $\psi \in \mathcal{S}$ and $\mathfrak{h}' \subseteq \mathfrak{h}$ such that $(\mathfrak{s}, \mathfrak{h}') \models_{\mathcal{R}} \psi$. By definition, ψ must be of the form $\exists z\, (*_{i=1}^{n}(x_i \approx x_i') * *_{i=1}^{m}(y_i \not\approx y_i') * \xi)$ with $n \geq 0$, $m \geq 0$ and ξ contains no equational atom. As $\mathcal{S}$ is $\exists$-restricted, x_i, x_i', y_i, y_i' occur in V. Therefore we get by the above equivalence: $x_i \sim x_i'$ (for all $i \in \{1, \dots, n\}$) and $y_i \not\sim y_i'$ (for all $i \in \{1, \dots, m\}$). Moreover, $(\mathfrak{s}, \mathfrak{h}') \models_{\mathcal{R}} \exists z\, \xi$. By the hypothesis of the lemma, $\mathtt{width}(\psi) \leq k$, so that $\mathtt{width}(\xi) \leq k$ and thus $\exists z\, \xi \in \mathtt{Pt}(V, k)$. By the implication above, we deduce that there exists a formula $\xi' \in \Sigma$ that subsumes $\exists z\, \xi$, so that $A \triangleright \psi$, which contradicts our hypothesis.

D Proof of Corollary 4.9

By Theorem 4.8, to test whether a formula ϕ is $\mathcal{S}$-satisfiable, it is sufficient to compute the set $\mathcal{A}_k(\phi)$ (for $k = \mathtt{width}(\mathcal{S})$) and verify whether it contains an abstraction A such that $A \not\triangleright \psi$ for all $\psi \in \mathcal{S}$. To achieve this, one needs to compute all the sets $\mathcal{A}_k(\phi'\sigma)$, where ϕ' is a formula occurring in ϕ or $\mathcal{R}$, and σ is a substitution. Up to a renaming of variables, the number of such formulas is simply exponential w.r.t. the size of ϕ and $\mathcal{R}$. It is clear that the size of the formulas in $\mathtt{Pt}(V, k)$ is polynomial w.r.t. the size of ϕ and $\mathcal{S}$. Consequently, the number of formulas in $\mathtt{Pt}(V, k)$ is exponential, and the number of subsets of $\mathtt{Pt}(V, k)$ is doubly exponential. Since the number of equivalence relations $\sim$ over a set V is simply exponential w.r.t. *card*(V), we deduce that the number of abstractions to consider is doubly exponential w.r.t. the size of ϕ, $\mathcal{S}$, and $\mathcal{R}$. Meanwhile, the size of these abstractions is simply exponential. Therefore, the algorithm runs in doubly exponential time.

If the size of the formulas in $\mathcal{S}$ is bounded, then k is also bounded, and the size of the formulas in $\mathtt{Pt}(V, k)$ is bounded as well. Consequently, the number of abstractions becomes simply exponential, and the algorithm runs in exponential time. Hence, the problem is EXPTIME-complete, as EXPTIME-hardness follows from the EXPTIME-hardness of the satisfiability problem in standard SL [3].

References

1. Ahrens, E., Bozga, M., Iosif, R., Katoen, J.: Reasoning about distributed reconfigurable systems. Proc. ACM Program. Lang. **6**(OOPSLA2), 145–174 (2022)
2. Bozga, M., Bueri, L., Iosif, R.: Decision problems in a logic for reasoning about reconfigurable distributed systems. In: Blanchette, J., Kovács, L., Pattinson, D. (eds.) IJCAR 2022. LNCS, vol. 13385, pp. 691–711. Springer, Cham (2022). https://doi.org/10.1007/978-3-031-10769-6_40

3. Brotherston, J., Fuhs, C., Pérez, J.A.N., Gorogiannis, N.: A decision procedure for satisfiability in separation logic with inductive predicates. In: Henzinger, T.A., Miller, D., (eds.), Joint Meeting of the Twenty-Third EACSL Annual Conference on Computer Science Logic (CSL) and the Twenty-Ninth Annual ACM/IEEE Symposium on Logic in Computer Science (LICS), CSL-LICS '14, Vienna, Austria, July 14 - 18, 2014, pp. 25:1–25:10. ACM (2014)
4. Chandra, A.K., Kozen, D., Stockmeyer, L.J.: Alternation. J. ACM **28**(1), 114–133 (1981)
5. Echenim, M., Peltier, N.: A direct procedure to test entailment in a separation logic of relations. Research report (under review) (2024). https://lig-membres.imag.fr/peltier/RSL.pdf
6. Ishtiaq, S.S., O'Hearn, P.W.: Bi as an assertion language for mutable data structures. ACM SIGPLAN Not. **36**, 14–26 (2001)
7. Kuncak, V., Rinard, M.: Generalized records and spatial conjunction in role logic. In: Giacobazzi, R. (ed.) SAS 2004. LNCS, vol. 3148, pp. 361–376. Springer, Heidelberg (2004). https://doi.org/10.1007/978-3-540-27864-1_26
8. Peltier, N.: An EXPTIME-complete entailment problem in separation logic. In: Metcalfe, G., Studer, T., de Queiroz, R. (eds.) WoLLIC 2024. LNCS, vol. 14672, pp. 157–174. Springer, Cham (2024)
9. Reynolds, J.: Separation logic: a logic for shared mutable data structures. In: Proceedings of LICS 2002 (2002)

Graded Relation Updates in Modal Logic

Raul Fervari[1,2(✉)], Daniel Figueiredo[3], and Manuel A. Martins[3]

[1] FAMAF, Universidad Nacional de Córdoba, Córdoba, Argentina
[2] Consejo Nacional de Investigaciones Científicas y Técnicas, Buenos Aires, Argentina
rfervari@unc.edu.ar
[3] CIDMA and Department of Mathematics, Universidade de Aveiro, Aveiro, Portugal

Abstract. This paper introduces a fuzzy approach to modal logics with graded relation updates. Specifically, we develop relation-changing modal logics where modalities modify the membership degree of a pair of elements in the accessibility relation. Our framework encompasses variants of local swap, sabotage, and bridge modalities. We motivate our approach via examples, and provide bisimulation notions for each logic, together with their corresponding characterization theorems. We also prove that model-checking for these logics is PSpace-complete, exactly as in the non-fuzzy cases.

Keywords: Modal Logic · Fuzzy Models · Relation Updates · Bisimulation · Model-checking

1 Introduction

Graphs are one of the most fundamental structures in computer science and mathematics, since they enable us to represent any kind of relationship between entities. Examples of their application are databases, software systems, multi-agent scenarios, just to name a few. In turn, it is natural to have a formalism for describing and reasoning about graphs, aiming to define, analyze, and manipulate these relationships. This enables, for instance, to perform more rigorous and efficient computations.

A well-known paradigm to reason about graphs is Modal Logic [10,11], a family of logical formalisms specially tailored to acting on this kind of structures. In general, modal logics provide a good balance between expressive power (typically, in the spectrum between Classical Propositional Logic (CPL) and First-Order Logic (FOL)) and computational behaviour. For instance, the satisfiability problem for the Basic Modal Logic, one of the simplest modal logics, is PSpace-complete, whereas its model-checking problem is in PTime. Moreover, this approach includes an important perspective on the subject, since it allows to represent how a given graph evolves or changes due to the application of certain

The original version of the chapter has been revised. The Chapter 17 reference has been corrected. A correction to this chapter can be found at https://doi.org/10.1007/978-3-031-99536-1_23

D. Kozen and R. de Queiroz (Eds.): WoLLIC 2025, LNCS 15942, pp. 278–292, 2026.
https://doi.org/10.1007/978-3-031-99536-1_17

actions. For instance, modeling dynamic aspects of graphs are useful in graph games [9], information flow [17] and software verification [28], to name a few. It turns out that modal logic is still a good candidate in order to model a great diversity of updates, with applications in all these fields of interest.

Different modal logics were born to represent updates in different components of a graph (the set of states, the accessibility relation and/or the labeling on states, see e.g. [19,27] for discussions on the different types of updates). Among these logics, those updating the accessibility relation have received particular attention, with so-called Relation-Changing Logics [3,4,18]. One of the reasons of the importance of this particular family is their applications, for instance to give a logical framework of *sabotage games* (see e.g. [5,8]). Another reason, from a more theoretically perspective, is that in the aforementioned works, relation-changing logics were investigated in a structured way, allowing a deep understanding of the intrinsic properties of this kind of updates, and of dynamic logics in general. In fact, this systematic study enabled, for instance, a general mechanization of dynamic logics to verify their properties (see [19]), and to determine the limits for obtaining well-behaved fragments (see, e.g., [1]).

Relation-changing modal logics in a classical setting are the first step towards a more general theory. To the best of our knowledge, there is no investigation about graded variants of relation-changing logics. This paper aims to fill this gap, by investigating relation updates in a fuzzy setting, in which instead of considering *crisp* relations (i.e., for any pair of elements they are connected or not), there is a function establishing the *membership degree* of every pair of elements with respect to a relation. In doing so, following the terminology of e.g. [4], we consider three kind of updates on edges: swapping, deleting (denoted as 'sabotage') and adding (denoted as 'bridge'). In a graded setting, this corresponds to swapping, deleting or adding some value on the membership function. All these updates are considered in a local flavour, i.e., the changes are performed over edges that are adjacent to the evaluation point. We revisit properties of the logics in a graded setting. Precisely, we investigate bisimulation notions and corresponding characterization theorems, and show that the model-checking problem for these logics is PSpace-complete, exactly the same complexity as the crisp cases.

Related Work. The modal logic paradigm is not the only way to capture updates in a graph-shaped model. In a slightly different approach, we need to mention switch graphs, initially proposed in [22] in the context of reactive systems. In short, switch graphs are state transition structures that update their accessibility relation based on the edges crossed, and whose structural changes are codified in the model itself by incorporating high-order edges (i.e., edges connecting two other edges instead of states). Due to their versatility, these structures have been used for modelling several case-studies. Several variants such as paraconsistent [16] and fuzzy (see e.g. [14,15]) switch graphs were also introduced. These variants of reactive graphs were proposed to approach different case-studies, from computer science [21] to biological [20,29] and pharmaeconomic [25] frameworks.

While reactive graphs are used as a modelling tool, the modal logics used to study such case-studies do not present any operators to trigger the so-called reactivity. Instead, all reconfiguration are encoded using the mentioned "higher-level" edges and regular modal logic can be used to explore the unfolded model. In this work we look into a different approach, where the proposed syntax already embeds the relation-changing operator. Nevertheless, it still has the potential to, for example, assess the safety of systems where concurrent processes occur, such as in some biological frameworks. Indeed, many cellular biochemical dynamics are triggered by components competing to bind the same cell receptors. This is the case, for example, with antibodies produced by the immune system to prevent viruses from binding to healthy cells [33], or carbon monoxide intoxication that competes with oxygen [24]. Also, the same mechanisms are present in some diseases such as cancer, where caspases, which induces cellular death, play a central role [12]. Indeed, due to the large number of components in a cell and the stochastic nature of the processes, biological contexts require a qualitative approach rather than an exact quantitative one. The existence of a edge – which may represent cellular death as a consequence of enough caspases binding to a cell – depends not only of the amount of that component in the cellular environment, but also on the chance of meeting cell receptors. While this is virtually guaranteed to occur at high caspase concentrations, intermediate levels may lead to uncertain scenarios. Thus, we believe that sabotage, swap and bridge operators can be naturally applied to the study of these systems, where the main relation changes to be expected are due to resource consumption and biological components synthesis.

Outline of the Paper. In Sect. 2, we review the fundamental concepts of fuzzy logic, including the syntax and semantics of the basic fuzzy modal logic. In Sect. 3 we propose fuzzy versions of sabotage, swap, and bridge modalities. Then, in Sect. 4, we define appropriate notions of bisimulation and prove a modal invariance theorem under these notions. In Sect. 5 we prove that the model-checking problem for the logics we introduce is PSpace-complete. We conclude the paper with final remarks and some directions for future research in Sect. 6.

2 Preliminaries

In this section, we introduce some basic definitions that will be used along the paper. In particular, we define the notion of t-norm, that is crucial to introduce a semantics with fuzzy values. These notions are inspired by *fuzzy algebras* [23].

A *t-norm* is a binary operation $* : [0,1] \times [0,1] \to [0,1]$ satisfying the following conditions: (i) $*$ is *commutative* and *associative*; (ii) $*$ is *non-decreasing* in both arguments; and (iii) $1 * x = x$ and $0 * x = 0$ for all $x \in [0,1]$. A *continuous t-norm* is a t-norm that is a continuous mapping of $[0,1] \times [0,1]$ into $[0,1]$ (in the usual sense). Some important examples of continuous t-norms are presented in Fig. 1.

One important notion when we intend to use fuzzy semantics to interpret propositional sentences is the choice of the most appropriate notion of implication (see [7]). In CPL, the implication $A \to B$ is true if and only if the truth-value of A is less than or equal to the truth-value of B. On $[0,1]$, $A \to B$

should be interpreted as an operation $x \Rightarrow y$ (called residuum in fuzzy settings) which should be *non-increasing* in x and *non-decreasing* in y (with x, y interpreting A, B, respectively). This leads to the definition of the residuum $\Rightarrow$ as: $x * z \leq y$ iff $z \leq (x \Rightarrow y)$.

Then it follows that $x \Rightarrow y$ is the maximal z satisfying $x*z \leq y$. The following lemma guarantees the existence of such a maximal element (see [23] for details).

t-norm	Definition	Implication $a \Rightarrow b$	Negation $\sim a$
Łukasiewicz	$\max(0, a+b-1)$	$\min(1, 1-a+b)$	$1-a$
Gödel	$\min(a, b)$	1 if $a \leq b$, else b	1 if $a = 0$, else 0
Product	$a \cdot b$	1 if $a \leq b$, else b/a	1 if $a = 0$, else 0

Fig. 1. Łukasiewicz, Gödel, and Product *t*-norms, along with their implications and negations.

Lemma 1 ([23]). *Let $*$ be a continuous t-norm. Then there is a unique operation $x \Rightarrow y$ satisfying, for all $x, y, z \in [0,1]$, the condition: $x * z \leq y$ iff $z \leq (x \Rightarrow y)$, namely: $x \Rightarrow y = \max\{z \mid x * z \leq y\}$.*

The operation $x \Rightarrow y$ from Lemma 1 is called the *residuum* of the *t*-norm. In what follows, context will disambiguate the *t*-norm we are using whenever we take some particular residuum $\Rightarrow$. The respective residuum/implication for each presented *t*-norm is displayed also in Fig. 1.

The residuum $\Rightarrow$ defines in a natural way a negation $\sim x := (x \Rightarrow 0)$. In general this negation is not involutive. Again, these can be visualized in Fig. 1.

Most fuzzy modal logics have semantics based on *t*-norms and a residuum (for recent investigations on fuzzy modal logics, see e.g. [30–32]). Therefore, in what follows, we consider a generic continuous *t*-norm T and its residuum $\Rightarrow$. We begin by defining the basic modal language.

Definition 1. *Let* Prop *be a set of atomic propositions, the set of modal formulas* Form *is given by the following BNF:*

$$\varphi, \psi ::= p \mid \bot \mid \varphi \wedge \psi \mid \varphi \rightarrow \psi \mid \Diamond\varphi,$$

where $p \in$ Prop. *Other connectives can be introduced by definition (see [23]):*

$$\begin{aligned} \varphi \underline{\wedge} \psi &:= \varphi \wedge (\varphi \rightarrow \psi), && \textit{weak conjunction} \\ \varphi \vee \psi &:= ((\varphi \rightarrow \psi) \rightarrow \psi) \underline{\wedge} ((\psi \rightarrow \varphi) \rightarrow \varphi), && \textit{disjunction} \\ \neg\varphi &:= \varphi \rightarrow \bot. && \textit{negation} \end{aligned}$$

Kripke semantics is generalized in the fuzzy context in a natural way. More precisely, we introduce the notion of "fuzzy Kripke model", a generalization of standard Kripke models where instead of relations between elements we have "degrees of membership" between them.

Definition 2 (Fuzzy Models). *A* fuzzy frame *is a tuple* $\mathfrak{F} = (W, R)$ *where* W *is a set of states and* $R : W^2 \to [0,1]$ *is a membership function indicating the membership degree of each edge.*

A fuzzy Kripke model *is a triple* $\mathfrak{M} = (W, R, V)$ *where* (W, R) *is a fuzzy frame and* $V : \mathsf{Prop} \to 2^W$ *is the valuation function. Let* $w \in W$*, the pair* $(\mathfrak{M}, w)$ *is called a (fuzzy)* pointed model*, with parentheses usually dropped.*

The weight given by $R(w, w')$ in a fuzzy context describes the membership degree of the transition (w, w'). Notice that the valuation function we consider is *crisp* (i.e., is either 0 or 1), but a fuzzy version can also be defined (see, e.g. [13]). The choice of crisp vs. fuzzy valuation varies among the different approaches of fuzzy logics. Also notice that classical Kripke models are fuzzy Kripke models where R is also crisp ($R(w, v) = 0$, if $(w, v) \notin R$).

Definition 3. *Let* $\mathfrak{M} = (W, R, V)$ *be a fuzzy Kripke model,* $w \in W$*, and let* T *be a continous t-norm. The semantics of a formula* φ *is given recursively by a function* $[\![\cdot]\!]^w_{\mathfrak{M}} : \mathsf{Form} \to [0,1]$ *as:*

$$
\begin{array}{lcl}
[\![p]\!]^w_{\mathfrak{M}} & = & \begin{cases} 1 & \text{if } w \in V(p) \\ 0 & \text{otherwise} \end{cases} \\
[\![\bot]\!]^w_{\mathfrak{M}} & = & 0 \\
[\![\varphi \wedge \psi]\!]^w_{\mathfrak{M}} & = & T([\![\varphi]\!]^w_{\mathfrak{M}}, [\![\psi]\!]^w_{\mathfrak{M}}) \\
[\![\varphi \to \psi]\!]^w_{\mathfrak{M}} & = & [\![\varphi]\!]^w_{\mathfrak{M}} \Rightarrow [\![\psi]\!]^w_{\mathfrak{M}} \\
[\![\Diamond\varphi]\!]^w_{\mathfrak{M}} & = & \sup_{w' \in W} \big(T(R(w, w'), [\![\varphi]\!]^{w'}_{\mathfrak{M}})\big).
\end{array}
$$

Note that the negation is not necessarily involutive. So the $\Box$ modal operator has to be considered as a primitive. Rigorously, in this paper we are considering a $\Diamond$-fragment of the full modal fuzzy logic, but this is enough for our purposes.

3 Fuzzy Relation Updates and Associated Modal Logics

We proceed to introduce the different notions of fuzzy relation-changing operators. Herein, we provide local versions of swap, sabotage and bridge (following the terminology in e.g. [4,18]), although global versions could be also defined.

3.1 (Local) Fuzzy Swap Operator

We start by generalizing the swap operator introduced and studied in [3,4,18]. The operator $\langle \mathsf{sw} \rangle_x$, with $x \in [0,1]$, is interpreted as a fuzzy version of the swap modality. The value x can be seen as the minimum degree of existence that allows us to cross an edge. After its evaluation, this operator reduces the degree of existence of the crossed edge by the value x and adds it to the edge with the opposite orientation. We now present formally the language that we will use for the fuzzy swap logic that we will call here $\mathsf{ML}(\langle \mathsf{sw} \rangle_x)$.

Definition 4. *Let* Prop *be a set of atomic propositions, the set of formulas* Form_{sw} *is given by the following BNF:*

$$\varphi, \psi ::= p \mid \bot \mid \varphi \wedge \psi \mid \varphi \rightarrow \psi \mid \Diamond\varphi \mid \langle \mathsf{sw} \rangle_x \varphi,$$

where $p \in$ Prop *and* $x \in [0, 1]$.

As an example of how we will interpret $\langle \mathsf{sw} \rangle_x$, let us consider the models in Fig. 2. Suppose that the initial model $\mathfrak{M}$ is the one on the left, with evaluation point w, and that we want to evaluate a formula $\langle \mathsf{sw} \rangle_{0.6}\varphi$ there. This formula indicates that first we need to find a successor of w with membership degree of *at least* 0.6. With this condition we mimic the guard *"there exists a successor..."* which is present in $\Diamond$-like modalities, for instance in the local swap operator from [3]. In the example, the successor w' that verifies $R(w, w') \geq 0.6$ is v, since $R(w, v) = 0.7$, $R(w, w) = 0$ and $R(w, u) = 0.5$ (in this paper, the absence of an arrow between x and y will indicate that $R(x, y) = 0$). Secondly, if such a successor exists, we need to evaluate the formula φ at such a successor, but on the model where the membership function between the two involved states changed. In our example, the membership R between w and v needs to be *swapped.* We need to be precise about what 'swapping' means, as one can think that the values of $R(w, v)$ and $R(v, w)$ are changed by the other. Our proposal follows exactly the formal definition in [18], and it is adapted to handle membership values: we simply transfer the value 0.6 from $R(w, v)$ to $R(v, w)$. This is reflected in the model in the center in Fig. 2, which we call $\mathfrak{M}^{0.6}_{*(w,v)}$.

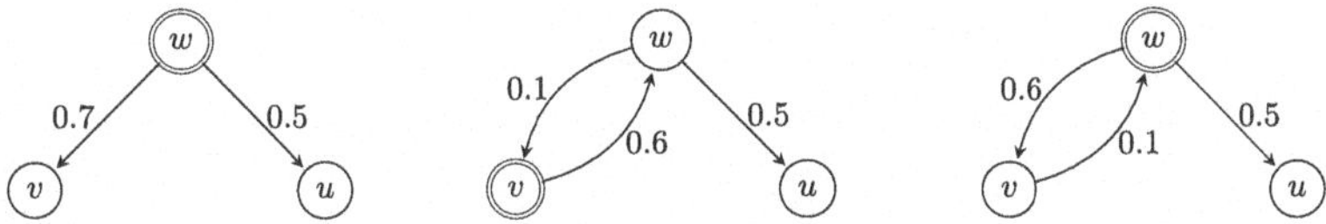

Fig. 2. Example of fuzzy swap.

Definition 5. *Let* $\mathfrak{M} = (W, R, V)$ *be a fuzzy Kripke model,* $w \in W$*, and let* T *be a t-norm. The semantics of a formula* φ *is given by a function* $[\![\cdot]\!]^w_{\mathfrak{M}} : \mathsf{Form}_{sw} \rightarrow [0, 1]$*, extending the one in Definition 3 as:*

$$[\![\langle \mathsf{sw} \rangle_x \varphi]\!]^w_{\mathfrak{M}} \quad = \sup_{\{w' : R(w,w') \geq x\}} \left(T(R(w, w'), [\![\varphi]\!]^{w'}_{\mathfrak{M}^x_{*(w',w)}})\right),$$

where, for fixed values of w' *and* x, $\mathfrak{M}^x_{*(w',w)} = (W, R^x_{*(w',w)}, V)$ *with* $R^x_{*(w',w)}$ *defined in the following way:*

$$R^x_{*(w',w)}(v, u) = \begin{cases} \min(R(v, u) + x, 1) & \textit{if } (v, u) = (w', w) \textit{ and } w \neq w' \\ R(v, u) - x & \textit{if } (v, u) = (w, w') \textit{ and } w \neq w' \\ R(v, u) & \textit{otherwise.} \end{cases}$$

Notice that while the first case of the definition above, we need to take the 'min' between the updated value and 1, the second case is simply defined as $R(v,u) - x$, without making sure this value remains above 0. The reason is that such a condition is checked in the semantics of $\langle \mathsf{sw} \rangle_x$ (as we take those w' such that $R(w,w') \geq x$). Moreover, the semantics of $\langle \mathsf{sw} \rangle_x$ takes into account the value of $R(w,w)$ before the update to calculate the final evaluation value, similarly to what is done in [13] for Gödel Modal Logic. Finally, such as it is the case in classic swap logic, a loop is kept unchanged whenever is crossed.

The next result states that $\langle \mathsf{sw} \rangle_0$ corresponds to the usual diamond in fuzzy modal logic.

Proposition 1. *For any φ, and $\mathfrak{M}, w$, we have that $[\![\Diamond\varphi]\!]^w_{\mathfrak{M}} = [\![\langle \mathsf{sw} \rangle_0\varphi]\!]^w_{\mathfrak{M}}$.*

Moreover, it is also easy to see that $\langle \mathsf{sw} \rangle_1$ corresponds to the classical local swap operator, considering $R(x,y) = 0$ equivalent to say in a classical setting that $(x,y) \notin R$.

Below we evaluate $\langle \mathsf{sw} \rangle_{0.6}\langle \mathsf{sw} \rangle_{0.5}p$ in the model on the left of Fig. 2 (the updated model $(\mathfrak{M}^{0.6}_{*(w,v)})^{0.5}_{*(v,w)}$ is the one on the right). The symbol p is considered to be true everywhere in the model.

$$[\![\langle \mathsf{sw} \rangle_{0.6}\langle \mathsf{sw} \rangle_{0.5}p]\!]^w_{\mathfrak{M}} = T\big(0.7, [\![\langle \mathsf{sw} \rangle_{0.5}p]\!]^v_{\mathfrak{M}^{0.6}_{*(w,v)}}\big) = T(0.7, 0.6)$$

. In case we are considering the product semantics we get 0.42. If we deal with Łukasiewicz we have 0.3, while for Gödel semantics we obtain 0.6.

3.2 (Local) Fuzzy Sabotage Operator

Here we generalize the sabotage operator introduced and studied in e.g. [3–5, 18]. We start by introducing the syntax of the logic that we call herein $\mathsf{ML}(\langle \mathsf{sb} \rangle_x)$.

Definition 6. *Let* Prop *be a set of atomic propositions, the set of formulas* Form_{sb} *is given by the following BNF:*

$$\varphi, \psi ::= p \mid \bot \mid \varphi \wedge \psi \mid \varphi \rightarrow \psi \mid \Diamond\varphi \mid \langle \mathsf{sb} \rangle_x\varphi,$$

where $p \in$ Prop and $x \in [0,1]$.

Similarly to the fuzzy swap case, we add the operator $\langle \mathsf{sb} \rangle_x$ with $x \in [0,1]$ and, again, the value x can be seen as the minimum degree of existence that allows us to cross an edge. This operator also reduces the degree of existence of the crossed edge by the value x but does not add it to any other edge. Therefore, the operator $\langle \mathsf{sb} \rangle_x$ can be seen as a resource "consumption" in a model.

Let $\mathfrak{M}$ be the model on the left in Fig. 3. Let us evaluate $\langle \mathsf{sb} \rangle_{0.8}\varphi$ at w, with local sabotage semantics. It is clear that the only successor w' verifying $R(w,w') \geq 0.8$ is t. Thus after the evaluation of $\langle \mathsf{sb} \rangle_{0.8}$, $R(w,t)$ is updated to 0, as we reduced the existence of $R(w,t)$ by 0.8 (exacly its value). As in classical local sabotage, φ is evaluated at t in the udpated model, called here $\mathfrak{M}^{0.8}_{-(w,t)}$.

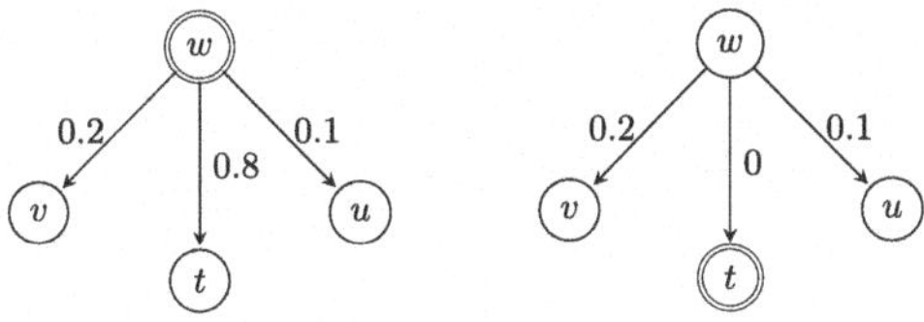

Fig. 3. Example of fuzzy sabotage.

Definition 7. *The function* $[\![\cdot]\!]^w_{\mathfrak{M}} : \mathsf{Form}_{sb} \to [0,1]$ *extends that of Definition 3 as:*

$$[\![\langle \mathsf{sb}\rangle_x \varphi]\!]^w_{\mathfrak{M}} = \sup_{\{w':R(w,w')\geq x\}} \left(T(R(w,w'), [\![\varphi]\!]^{w'}_{\mathfrak{M}^x_{-(w,w')}})\right),$$

where, for fixed values of w' *and* x, $\mathfrak{M}^x_{-(w,w')} = (W, R^x_{-(w,w')}, V)$ *where* $R^x_{-(w,w')}$ *is defined in the following way:*

$$R^x_{-(w,w')}(v,v') = \begin{cases} R(v,v') - x & \text{if } (v,v') = (w,w') \\ R(v,v') & \text{otherwise.} \end{cases}$$

Again, we note that $\langle \mathsf{sb}\rangle_1$ corresponds to the usual local sabotage operator while $\langle \mathsf{sb}\rangle_0$ corresponds to the usual diamond in fuzzy modal logic as stated in next proposition.

Proposition 2. *For any* φ, *and* $\mathfrak{M}, w$, *we have that* $[\![\Diamond\varphi]\!]^w_{\mathfrak{M}} = [\![\langle \mathsf{sb}\rangle_0 \varphi]\!]^w_{\mathfrak{M}}$.

3.3 (Local) Fuzzy Bridge Operator

The bridge operator introduced and studied in e.g. [3,4,18] can also be generalized to this context. We add the operator $\langle \mathsf{br}\rangle_x$ with $x \in [0,1]$ where the value x can be added to the degree of an edge. The resulting logic is called $\mathsf{ML}(\langle \mathsf{br}\rangle_x)$.

Definition 8. *Let* Prop *be a set of atomic propositions, the set of formulas* Form_{br} *is given by the following BNF:*

$$\varphi, \psi ::= p \mid \bot \mid \varphi \wedge \psi \mid \varphi \to \psi \mid \Diamond\varphi \mid \langle \mathsf{br}\rangle_x \varphi,$$

where $p \in \mathsf{Prop}$ *and* $x \in [0,1]$.

Similarly to the previous cases, we add the operator $\langle \mathsf{br}\rangle_x$ with $x \in [0,1]$. Here the value x can be seen as the degree we assign to an edge with degree less than x to allow us to cross the edge.

Let $\mathfrak{M}$ be the model on the left in Fig. 4. Let us evaluate $\langle \mathsf{br}\rangle_{0.6}\varphi$ at w, with local bridge semantics. There are two successors w' verifying $R(w,w') \leq 0.6$, which are t, v. Thus after the evaluation of $\langle \mathsf{br}\rangle_{0.6}$, either $R(w,t)$ is updated to 0.6 and the rest remains unchanged, or $R(w,v)$ is updated to 0.6 and the rest remains unchanged. As in classical local bridge, φ is evaluated at t and v in the corresponding updated models, called here $\mathfrak{M}^{0.6}_{+(w,t)}$, $\mathfrak{M}^{0.6}_{+(w,v)}$, respectively. The evaluation at w of $\langle \mathsf{br}\rangle_{0.6}\varphi$ would be the supremum of the two values.

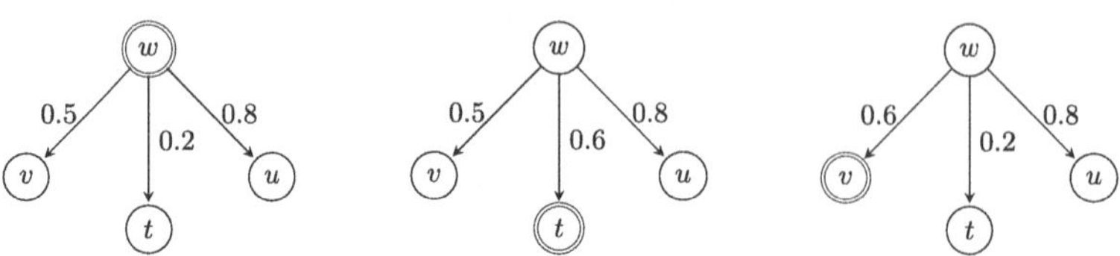

Fig. 4. Example of fuzzy bridge.

Definition 9. *The function* $[\![\cdot]\!]^w_{\mathfrak{M}} : \mathsf{Form}_{br} \to [0,1]$ *extends that of Definition 3 as:*

$$[\![\langle \mathsf{br} \rangle_x \varphi]\!]^w_{\mathfrak{M}} \quad = \quad \sup_{\{w' : R(w,w') < x\}} \big(T(x, [\![\varphi]\!]^{w'}_{\mathfrak{M}^x_{+(w,w')}})\big),$$

where, for fixed values of w' *and* x, $\mathfrak{M}^x_{+(w,w')} = (W, R^x_{+(w,w')}, V)$ *where* $R^x_{(w,w')}$ *is defined in the following way:*

$$R^x_{+(w,w')}(v,v') = \begin{cases} x & \text{if } (v,v') = (w,w') \text{ and } R(w,w') < x \\ R(v,v') & \text{otherwise.} \end{cases}$$

We note that $\langle \mathsf{br} \rangle_1$ corresponds to the usual operator of bridge logic.

4 Bisimulations and Invariance

In this section we discuss a crucial notion to investigate the expressivity of a logic: the concept of bisimulation. With this definition at hand, we are able to characterize in a way how much differences the logic is able to detect between models. This is in general stated by an *invariance* property that establishes that bisimilar models satisfy the same formulas (over the corresponding language). Thus, finding the right definition of bisimulation for each respective logic is of great importance. Below we introduce bisimulations and corresponding invariance theorems for the logics introduced in the previous section.

Definition 10 (Swap/sabotage-bisimulations). *Let* $\mathfrak{M} = (W, R, V)$ *and* $\mathfrak{M}' = (W', R', V')$ *be two fuzzy Kripke models and* x *in*$[0,1]$. *A relation* $Z \subseteq (W \times [0,1]^{W^2}) \times (W' \times [0,1]^{W'^2})$ *is called an* x-swap *(respectively* x-sabotage*)* bisimulation *if and only if,* $(w, E)Z(w', E')$ *implies:*

- **atom:** $w \in V(p)$ *iff* $w' \in V'(p)$, *for all* $p \in \mathsf{Prop}$;
- **swap-zig (resp. sab-zig):** *for any* $v \in W$ *such that* $E(w,v) \geq x$, *exists* $v' \in W'$ *s.t.* $E'(w',v') \geq E(w,v)$ *and* $(v, E^x_{*(w,v)})Z(v', E'^x_{*(w',v')})$ *(resp.* $(v, E^x_{-(w,v)})Z(v', E'^x_{-(w',v')})$*);*
- **swap-zag (resp. sab-zag):** *for any* $v' \in W'$ *such that* $E'(w',v') \geq x$, *exists* $v \in W$ *s.t.* $E(w,v) \geq E'(w',v')$ *and* $(v, E^x_{*(w,v)})Z(v', E'^x_{*(w',v')})$ *(resp.* $(v, E^x_{-(w,v)})Z(v', E'^x_{-(w',v')})$*).*

We say that $\mathfrak{M}, w$ *and* $\mathfrak{M}', w'$ *are* x*-swap (resp.* x*-sabotage) bisimilar and denoted by* $\mathfrak{M}, w \leftrightarroweq^{\leftarrow}_{x} \mathfrak{M}, w'$ *(resp.* $\mathfrak{M}, w \leftrightarroweq^{-}_{x} \mathfrak{M}', w'$*) iff there is an* x*-swap (resp.* x*-sabotage) bisimulation* Z *such that* $(w, R)E(w', R')$*. They are swap (resp. sabotage) bisimilar and we denote it by* $\mathfrak{M}, w \leftrightarroweq^{\leftarrow} \mathfrak{M}', w'$ *(resp.* $\mathfrak{M}, w \leftrightarroweq^{-} \mathfrak{M}', w'$*), if they are* x*-swap (resp.* x*-sabotage) bisimilar for all* $x \in [0, 1]$*.*

We state below the intended result.

Theorem 1. (Invariance under swap/sabotage bisimulation.). *Let* $\mathfrak{M} = (W, R, V)$ *and* $\mathfrak{M}' = (W', R', V')$ *be two fuzzy Kripke models,* $w \in W, w' \in W'$*.*

- *If* $\mathfrak{M}, w \leftrightarroweq^{\leftarrow} \mathfrak{M}', w'$*, then,* $[\![\varphi]\!]^{w}_{\mathfrak{M}} = [\![\varphi]\!]^{w'}_{\mathfrak{M}'}$ *for all formula* $\varphi \in \mathsf{Form}_{sw}$*.*
- *If* $\mathfrak{M}, w \leftrightarroweq^{-} \mathfrak{M}', w'$*, then,* $[\![\varphi]\!]^{w}_{\mathfrak{M}} = [\![\varphi]\!]^{w'}_{\mathfrak{M}'}$ *for all formula* $\varphi \in \mathsf{Form}_{sb}$*.*

Proof. Let $\mathfrak{M}, w$ and $\mathfrak{M}', w'$ be swap bisimilar or sabotage bisimilar. For each corresponding set of formulas, we prove that $[\![\varphi]\!]^{w}_{\mathfrak{M}} = [\![\varphi]\!]^{w'}_{\mathfrak{M}'}$ by induction over the structure of formulas.

During the proof, $\langle\ominus\rangle_x$ is used whenever the argument can be applied to both $\langle\mathsf{sw}\rangle_x$ and $\langle\mathsf{sb}\rangle_x$. Consequently, $\ominus$-zig and $\ominus$-zag refer to either swap-zig and swap-zag or sab-zig and sab-zag. As a consequence, $E^{x}_{\ominus(w,v)}$ refers to either $E^{x}_{*(w,v)}$ or $E^{x}_{-(w,v)}$; and $\mathfrak{M}^{x}_{\ominus(w',v')}$ refers to either $\mathfrak{M}^{x}_{*(w',v')}$ or $\mathfrak{M}^{x}_{-(w',v')}$, according to the context.

- For $p \in \mathsf{Prop}$, $[\![p]\!]^{w}_{\mathfrak{M}} = [\![p]\!]^{w'}_{\mathfrak{M}'}$ by definition of bisimulation (atom).
- The case of $\perp$ is trivial.
- $[\![\varphi \wedge \psi]\!]^{w}_{\mathfrak{M}} = T([\![\varphi]\!]^{w}_{\mathfrak{M}}, [\![\psi]\!]^{w}_{\mathfrak{M}})$. Using the inductive hypothesis, we conclude that $T([\![\varphi]\!]^{w}_{\mathfrak{M}}, [\![\psi]\!]^{w}_{\mathfrak{M}}) = T([\![\varphi]\!]^{w'}_{\mathfrak{M}'}, [\![\psi]\!]^{w'}_{\mathfrak{M}'})$, which is equal to $[\![\varphi \wedge \psi]\!]^{w'}_{\mathfrak{M}'}$.
- $[\![\varphi \to \psi]\!]^{w}_{\mathfrak{M}} = [\![\varphi]\!]^{w}_{\mathfrak{M}} \Rightarrow [\![\psi]\!]^{w}_{\mathfrak{M}}$. Using the inductive hypothesis, we conclude that $[\![\varphi]\!]^{w}_{\mathfrak{M}} \Rightarrow [\![\psi]\!]^{w}_{\mathfrak{M}} = [\![\varphi]\!]^{w'}_{\mathfrak{M}'} \Rightarrow [\![\psi]\!]^{w'}_{\mathfrak{M}'}$, which is equal to $[\![\varphi \to \psi]\!]^{w'}_{\mathfrak{M}'}$.
- For each $x \in [0, 1]$, $[\![\langle\ominus\rangle_x\varphi]\!]^{w}_{\mathfrak{M}} = \sup_{\{w':R(w,w')\geq x\}} T(R(w, v), [\![\varphi]\!]^{v}_{\mathfrak{M}^{x}_{\ominus(w,v)}})$. By definition, $\ominus$-zig implies that, for each $v \in W$, s.t. $E(w, v) \geq x$, exists $v' \in W'$ s.t. $E'(w', v') \geq E(w, v)$ and $(v, E^{x}_{\ominus(w,v)})Z(v', E'^{x}_{\ominus(w',v')})$.
  Using the inductive hypothesis, we have $[\![\varphi]\!]^{v}_{\mathfrak{M}^{x}_{\ominus(w,v)}} = [\![\varphi]\!]^{v'}_{\mathfrak{M}'^{x}_{\ominus(w',v')}}$. This implies that $T(E(w, v), [\![\varphi]\!]^{v}_{\mathfrak{M}^{x}_{\ominus(w,v)}}) \leq T(E(w', v'), [\![\varphi]\!]^{v'}_{\mathfrak{M}^{x}_{\ominus(w',v')}})$, due to the monotonicity of t-norms.
  As a result, we conclude that $\sup_{\{w':R(w,w')\geq x\}} T(R(w, w'), [\![\varphi]\!]^{v}_{\mathfrak{M}^{x}_{\ominus(w,v)}})$
  $$\leq \sup_{\{w':R(w,w')\geq x\}} T(R'(w', v'), [\![\varphi]\!]^{v'}_{\mathfrak{M}^{x}_{\ominus(w',v')}}) = [\![\langle\ominus\rangle_x\varphi]\!]^{w'}_{\mathfrak{M}'}.$$
  Using an analogous argument (with $\ominus$-zag instead of $\ominus$-zig), we conclude that $[\![\langle\ominus\rangle_x\varphi]\!]^{w'}_{\mathfrak{M}'} \leq [\![\langle\ominus\rangle_x\varphi]\!]^{w}_{\mathfrak{M}}$. With both inequalities the equality follows. □

We move to $\mathsf{ML}(\langle\mathsf{br}\rangle_x)$, which slightly differs from the previous cases.

Definition 11 (Bridge-bisimulation). *Let* $\mathfrak{M} = (W, R, V)$, $\mathfrak{M}' = (W', R', V')$ *be two fuzzy Kripke models,* $w \in W$, $w' \in W'$ *and* x *in*$[0,1]$. *A relation* $Z \subseteq (W \times [0,1]^{W^2}) \times (W' \times [0,1]^{W'^2})$ *is an* x-bridge bisimulation *if and only if,* $(w, E)Z(w', E')$ *implies:*

atom: $w \in V(p)$ *iff* $w' \in V'(p)$, *for all* $p \in \mathsf{Prop}$;
bridge-zig: *for any* $v \in W$ *such that* $E(w,v) < x$, *exists* $v' \in W'$ *s.t.* $x > E'(w',v')$ *and* $(v, E^x_{+(w,v)})Z(v', E'^x_{+(w',v')})$;
bridge-zag: *for any* $v' \in W'$ *such that* $E'(w',v') < x$, *exists* $v \in W$ *s.t.* $x > E(w,v)$ *and* $(v, E^x_{+(w,v)})Z(v', E'^x_{+(w',v')})$.

We say that $\mathfrak{M}, w$ *and* $\mathfrak{M}', w'$ *are* x*-bridge bisimilar (denoted* $\mathfrak{M}, w \leftrightarrows^+_x \mathfrak{M}', w'$*) iff there is an* x*-bridge bisimulation* Z *such that* $(w, R)E(w', R')$. *They are bridge bisimilar (denoted* $\mathfrak{M}, w \leftrightarrows^+ \mathfrak{M}', w'$*), if they are* x*-bridge bisimilar for all* $x \in [0,1]$.

Theorem 2 (Invariance under bridge-bisimulation). *Let* $\mathfrak{M} = (W, R, V)$ *and* $\mathfrak{M}' = (W', R', V')$ *be two fuzzy Kripke models. If* $\mathfrak{M}, w \leftrightarrows^+ \mathfrak{M}', w'$, *then* $[\![\varphi]\!]^w_{\mathfrak{M}} = [\![\varphi]\!]^{w'}_{\mathfrak{M}'}$, *for every formula* $\varphi \in \mathsf{Form}_{br}$.

Proof. Let $\mathfrak{M}, w$ and $\mathfrak{M}', w'$ be bridge bisimilar. We prove that $[\![\varphi]\!]^w_{\mathfrak{M}} = [\![\varphi]\!]^{w'}_{\mathfrak{M}'}$ by induction over the structure of formulas. Propositional cases are omitted here.

- For each $x \in [0,1]$, $[\![\langle \mathsf{br} \rangle_x \varphi]\!]^w_{\mathfrak{M}} = \sup_{\{w' : R(w,w') < x\}} T(x, [\![\varphi]\!]^v_{\mathfrak{M}^x_{+(w,v)}})$. By bridge-zig we have that, for each $v \in W$ s.t. $E(w,v) < x$, exists $v' \in W'$ s.t. $E'(w',v') < x$ and $(v, E^x_{+(w,v)})Z(v', E'^x_{+(w',v')})$.
  Using the inductive hypothesis, we have $[\![\varphi]\!]^v_{\mathfrak{M}^x_{+(w,v)}} = [\![\varphi]\!]^{v'}_{\mathfrak{M}'^x_{+(w',v')}}$. This implies that $T(x, [\![\varphi]\!]^v_{\mathfrak{M}^x_{+(w,v)}}) = T(x, [\![\varphi]\!]^{v'}_{\mathfrak{M}^x_{+(w',v')}})$.
  As result, we conclude that
  $$\sup_{\{w' : R(w,w') < x\}} T(x, [\![\varphi]\!]^v_{\mathfrak{M}^x_{+(w,v)}}) \leq \sup_{\{w' : R(w,w') < x\}} T(x, [\![\varphi]\!]^{v'}_{\mathfrak{M}^x_{+(w',v')}}) = [\![\langle \mathsf{br} \rangle_x \varphi]\!]^{w'}_{\mathfrak{M}'}.$$
  Using an analogous argument (with bridge-zag instead of bridge-zig), we get $[\![\langle \mathsf{br} \rangle_x \varphi]\!]^{w'}_{\mathfrak{M}'} \leq [\![\langle \mathsf{br} \rangle_x \varphi]\!]^w_{\mathfrak{M}}$. With both inequalities the equality follows. □

5 Model-Checking

In this section we tackle the problem of characterizing the computational complexity of the model-checking problem for relation-changing logics over fuzzy structures. In order to do so, we will combine ideas and results for model-checking standard relation-changing logics [4,18], and from model-checking in a fuzzy setting [6,26]. Precisely, we will prove that the complexity in the fuzzy relation-changing framework is PSpace-complete, exactly as in the standard case.

We start by defining the **model-checking** problem under consideration.

Input: A finite fuzzy Kripke model $\mathfrak{M}$, a state w of $\mathfrak{M}$, and a formula φ.
Output: $[\![\varphi]\!]^w_{\mathfrak{M}}$.

The following result establishes an upper-bound for the complexity of the model-checking problem. It is worth noticing that in what follows, we consider that the s-norm, t-norm, implication $\Rightarrow$, sup and arithmetic operations can be all be computed in $\mathsf{O}(1)$ time (i.e., in constant time).

Lemma 2. *The model-checking problem for* $\mathsf{ML}(\langle \mathsf{sw} \rangle_x)$, $\mathsf{ML}(\langle \mathsf{sb} \rangle_x)$ *and* $\mathsf{ML}(\langle \mathsf{br} \rangle_x)$ *is in* PSpace.

Proof. The result follows by a standard labelling algorithm (see, e.g. [10] for details), that for each state of the model, it computes the membership value corresponding to each subformula of the input formula at such a state. For each state w of the input model $\mathfrak{M} = (W, R, V)$, and each ψ a subformula of φ, compute $[\![\psi]\!]^w_{\mathfrak{M}}$ by following the semantics of each operator.

For the propositional connectives, the algorithm does not use extra memory except for its recursive calls. For the modal operators ($\langle \mathsf{br} \rangle_x$, $\langle \mathsf{sb} \rangle_x$, and $\langle \mathsf{sw} \rangle_x$), we need to keep a counter for all the states of the model, as their evaluation at a given state require to recursively call the algorithm over the successors of the state, and to inspect the value of the membership function between them. Counters use logarithmic space. Also, recursive calls for $\langle \mathsf{br} \rangle_x$, $\langle \mathsf{sb} \rangle_x$, and $\langle \mathsf{sw} \rangle_x$ need to consider updated models, but only a polynomial number of them. Each updated model uses a polynomial amount of space, but this memory is reclaimed after the recursive call. The number of recursive call is linear w.r.t. the size of the formula. Thus, the algorithm uses polynomial space. □

Then, we obtain the intended result.

Theorem 3. *The model-checking problem for the logics* $\mathsf{ML}(\langle \mathsf{sw} \rangle_x)$, $\mathsf{ML}(\langle \mathsf{sb} \rangle_x)$ *and* $\mathsf{ML}(\langle \mathsf{br} \rangle_x)$ *is* PSpace*-complete.*

Proof. Harndess follows since model-checking the crisp cases is already PSpace-complete [4,18]. Completeness follows from Lemma 2. □

6 Conclusion and Future Work

This paper introduces the initial steps in studying relation changes over fuzzy graphs, focusing on sabotage, swap, and bridge operators. In doing so, we propose a fuzzy modal logic to reason about the dynamics of such modal changes. We define bisimulations for these logics, show the modal invariance under bisimulation, and prove that their model-checking problems are PSpace-complete.

Our research paves the way to several new questions. From a theoretical standpoint, it would be valuable to explore other types of relation changes (in particular global versions of those discussed here), as well as situations where propositional valuations are also fuzzy. Another avenue for investigation involves identifying the appropriate conditions that ensure the reciprocal of the invariance theorem. Moreover, it would be interesting to formalize and verify our results using proof assistants, generalizing the mechanization of non-fuzzy cases from [19], and to define appropriate proof systems extending those in [2]. Finally, it could be interesting to find fragments of fuzzy relation-changing modal logics with good computational properties.

On the applied side, we believe that this approach could be highly beneficial for identifying key components in biological models, which usually comprise a wide number of elements. Also, it can be useful for addressing issues related to resource availability in transportation and assignment problems, and un multi-agent systems in general.

Furthermore, we are interested in examining model changes within probabilistic relation models. The condition that the sum of all transitions from a state must equal 1 leads to a different interpretation of traditional model change operators. Finally, we aim to extend this work to an arbitrary residuated lattice A, rather than limiting ourselves to the special case over $[0, 1]$.

Acknowledgments. Raul Fervari was supported by Agencia I+D+i grant PICT 2021-00400, the EU H2020 research and innovation program under the Marie Skłodowska-Curie grant agreements 101008233 (MISSION), the IRP SINFIN, and SeCyT-UNC grant 33620230100178CB. Daniel Figueiredo and Manuel Martins were supported by Portuguese funds through the CIDMA, under the FCT project UIDB/04106/2025.

References

1. Areces, C., van Ditmarsch, H., Fervari, R., Maubert, B., Schwarzentruber, F.: Copy and remove as dynamic operators. J. Appl. Non Class. Logics **31**(3–4), 181–220 (2021)
2. Areces, C., Fervari, R., Hoffmann, G.: Tableaux for relation-changing modal logics. In: Fontaine, P., Ringeissen, C., Schmidt, R.A. (eds.) FroCoS 2013. LNCS (LNAI), vol. 8152, pp. 263–278. Springer, Heidelberg (2013). https://doi.org/10.1007/978-3-642-40885-4_19
3. Areces, C., Fervari, R., Hoffmann, G.: Swap logic. Logic J. IGPL **22**(2), 309–332 (2014). https://doi.org/10.1093/JIGPAL/JZT030
4. Areces, C., Fervari, R., Hoffmann, G.: Relation-changing modal operators. Logic J. IGPL **23**(4), 601–627 (2015). https://doi.org/10.1093/jigpal/jzv020
5. Aucher, G., van Benthem, J., Grossi, D.: Modal logics of sabotage revisited. J. Log. Comput. **28**(2), 269–303 (2018)
6. Baaz, M., Fermüller, C.G., Salzer, G.: Automated deduction for many-valued logics. In: Robinson, J.A., Voronkov, A. (eds.) Handbook of Automated Reasoning (in 2 volumes), pp. 1355–1402. Elsevier and MIT Press (2001)
7. Baczyński, M., Jayaram, B.: Fuzzy Implications, Studies in Fuzziness Soft Computing, vol. 231. Springer, Berlin (2008). https://doi.org/10.1007/978-3-540-69082-5
8. Benthem, J.: An essay on sabotage and obstruction. In: Hutter, D., Stephan, W. (eds.) Mechanizing Mathematical Reasoning. LNCS (LNAI), vol. 2605, pp. 268–276. Springer, Heidelberg (2005). https://doi.org/10.1007/978-3-540-32254-2_16

9. van Benthem, J., Liu, F.: Graph games and logic design. In: Liu, F., Ono, H., Yu, J. (eds.) Knowledge, Proof and Dynamics, pp. 125–146. Springer, Singapore (2020)
10. Blackburn, P., van Benthem, J.: Modal logic: a semantic perspective. In: Handbook of Modal Logic, pp. 1–84. Elsevier (2006). https://doi.org/10.1016/s1570-2464(07)80004-8
11. Blackburn, P., de Rijke, M., Venema, Y.: Modal Logic. Cambridge University Press, Cambridge (2002). https://doi.org/10.1017/CBO9781107050884
12. Boice, A., Bouchier-Hayes, L.: Targeting apoptotic caspases in cancer. Biochimica et Biophysica Acta (BBA)-Mol. Cell Res. **1867**(6), 118688 (2020)
13. Caicedo, X., Rodríguez, R.O.: Standard gödel modal logics. Stud. Logica. **94**(2), 189–214 (2010)
14. Campos, S., Santiago, R., Martins, M.A., Figueiredo, D.: Aggregation-based operations for reversal fuzzy switch graphs. Fuzzy Sets Syst. **466**, 108273 (2023). https://doi.org/10.1016/J.FSS.2022.03.015
15. Campos, S., Santiago, R., Martins, M.A., Figueiredo, D.: Introduction to reversal fuzzy switch graph. Sci. Comput. Program. **216**, 102776 (2022). https://doi.org/10.1016/J.SCICO.2022.102776
16. Costa, D., Figueiredo, D., Martins, M.A.: Relation-changing models meet paraconsistency. J. Logical Algebraic Methods Program. **133**, 100870 (2023). https://doi.org/10.1016/J.JLAMP.2023.100870
17. van Ditmarsch, H., van der Hoek, W., Kooi, B.: Dynamic Epistemic Logic. Springer, Cham (2007). https://doi.org/10.1007/978-1-4020-5839-4
18. Fervari, R.: Relation-Changing Modal Logics. Ph.D. thesis, Universidad Nacional de Córdoba (2014)
19. Fervari, R., Trucco, F., Ziliani, B.: Verification of dynamic bisimulation theorems in Coq. J. Logical Algebraic Methods Program. **120**, 100642 (2021). https://doi.org/10.1016/J.JLAMP.2021.100642
20. Figueiredo, D., Barbosa, L.S.: Reactive models for biological regulatory networks. In: Chaves, M., Martins, M.A. (eds.) MLCSB 2018. LNCS, vol. 11415, pp. 74–88. Springer, Cham (2019). https://doi.org/10.1007/978-3-030-19432-1_5
21. Figueiredo, D., Martins, M.A., Barbosa, L.S.: A note on reactive transitions and Reo connectors. In: It's All About Coordination: Essays to Celebrate the Lifelong Scientific Achievements of Farhad Arbab, pp. 57–67. Springer (2018). https://doi.org/10.1007/978-3-319-90089-6_4
22. Gabbay, D., Marcelino, S.: Global view on reactivity: switch graphs and their logics. Ann. Math. Artif. Intell. **66**(1), 131–162 (2012)
23. Hájek, P.: Metamathematics of fuzzy logic, Trends Log. Stud. Log. Libr., vol. 4. Dordrecht: Kluwer Academic Publishers (1998)
24. Jasani, S.: Chapter 147 - smoke inhalation. In: Silverstein, D.C., Hopper, K. (eds.) Small Animal Critical Care Medicine (Second Edition), pp. 785–788. W.B. Saunders, St. Louis, second edition edn. (2015). https://doi.org/10.1016/B978-1-4557-0306-7.00147-1, https://www.sciencedirect.com/science/article/pii/B9781455703067001471
25. Mendes, D., Figueiredo, D., Alves, C., Penedones, A., Costa, B., Batel-Marques, F.: Impact of the Covid-19 pandemic on cancer screenings in Portugal. Cancer Epidemiol. **88**, 102496 (2024)
26. Pan, H., Li, Y., Cao, Y., Ma, Z.: Model checking fuzzy computation tree logic. Fuzzy Sets Syst. **262**, 60–77 (2015)
27. Plaza, J.: Logics of public communications. Synthese **158**(2), 165 (2007)

28. Reynolds, J.C.: Separation logic: a logic for shared mutable data structures. In: 17th IEEE Symposium on Logic in Computer Science (LICS 2002), pp. 55–74. IEEE Computer Society (2002). https://doi.org/10.1109/LICS.2002.1029817
29. Santiago, R., Martins, M.A., Figueiredo, D.: Introducing fuzzy reactive graphs: a simple application on biology. Soft. Comput. **25**(9), 6759–6774 (2021). https://doi.org/10.1007/s00500-020-05353-1
30. Vidal, A.: On modal expansions of t-norm based logics with rational constants. Ph.D. thesis, Universitat de Barcelona (2015)
31. Vidal, A., Esteva, F., Godo, L.: On modal extensions of product fuzzy logic. J. Log. Comput. **27**(1), 299–336 (2017)
32. Vidal, A., Esteva, F., Godo, L.: Axiomatizing logics of fuzzy preferences using graded modalities. Fuzzy Sets Syst. **401**, 163–188 (2020)
33. Wilson, I.A., Stanfield, R.L.: 50 years of structural immunology. J. Biol. Chem. **296** (2021)

Proof Search in Classical Propositional Logic with Partial Proof Terms

José Espírito Santo(✉) and Ana Catarina Sousa

Centre of Mathematics, University of Minho, Braga, Portugal
jes@math.uminho.pt

Abstract. Partial (i.e. unfinished) proofs can be represented by partial proof terms. These are proof terms expressing gaps in incomplete derivations with the help offormal sequents, that is, sequents occurring as proper components of the syntax of proof terms. Our previous paper applied this methodology to intuitionistic propositional logic, to show that focusing in sequent calculus corresponds to intercalation in bidirectional natural deduction. The main goal of this paper is to extend these results to classical logic, using the same methodology. We consider the focused sequent calculus LKT and a bidirectional natural deduction system with alternative conclusions, NKT. In the latter system the admissible typing rule for structural substitution is in fact an elimination rule for an implications which is an alternative conclusion.

Keywords: Proof search · Partial proof term · Partial derivation · Proof state · Focusing · Intercalation · Classical propositional logic

1 Introduction

In a previous paper [19], we proposed *partial proof terms* as a new tool in the study of proof search. Partial proof terms are proof terms where sequents may occur as proper components of the term in order to represent "holes", that is, unfinished portions of a proof. Such *partial proofs*, exhibiting unspecified components (unspecified except for the sought sequent), are the mundane objects handled by the search process, more than finished proofs. In [19], the case study was intuitionistic implicational logic, both in the sequent and natural deduction formats. More precisely, we studied two proof search procedures, focusing [1,13] in the focused sequent calculus LJT [12] and intercalation [20,21] in a bidirectional [5] natural deduction system NJT, and showed them to be isomorphic.

In this paper, we investigate whether the correspondence between focusing in LJT and intercalation in NJT can be lifted for classical logic, using the same tools of our previous paper. For classical logic the precise definition of the proof systems and associated search procedures is less off-the-shelf. Sequent calculus LKT has its origin in linear logic [4] but has not been developed as a sequent calculus with proof terms; and the intercalation calculus of [20] is not a natural deduction system in the tradition of Parigot's classical natural deduction and

D. Kozen and R. de Queiroz (Eds.): WoLLIC 2025, LNCS 15942, pp. 293–308, 2026.
https://doi.org/10.1007/978-3-031-99536-1_18

the corresponding $\lambda\mu$-calculus [18] – a tradition we will adopt in this paper. The precise definition of systems LKT and NKT and associated search procedures is already a contribution. Then we confirm that the methodology of partial proof terms can give an adequate representation of the two search procedures. Finally, using such representation, we are able to prove that the correspondence of procedures previously observed in the intuitionistic case indeed lifts to the classical case.

This is a contribution to *idealized proof search* [19], a theoretical middle ground between proof theory and computer science. In such middle ground, one takes proof search as an object of study, but not necessarily with the perspective of automation, implementation or performance. The usual proof systems $\mathcal{S}$ are taken as a reference, a criterion for the well-formedness of complete proofs, but new artifacts are developed: an extension $\mathcal{S}_\partial$ of $\mathcal{S}$ to "type" partial proof terms, or equivalently, to determine which *partial sequents* do represent proof states found in the search process of a given sequent; and a rewriting system, acting on partial proof terms, to express search rules, typically one per inference rule of $\mathcal{S}$, showing how the inference rule contributes to the dynamics of the search.

Such two-layered organization is also reflected in the organization of the present paper. Proof systems LKT and NKT are presented and developed in Sects. 2 and 4, while the associated artifacts are studied in Sect. 3 and 5. The comparison between focusing and intercalation is found in Sect. 6. Section 7 discusses related and future work. Technical details are given in Appendix A.

2 Sequent Calculus LKT

In this paper, formulas A, B are either atoms p or absurdity $\perp$ or implications $A \supset B$. In this section, we consider the focused, cut-free sequent calculus LKT for classical propositional logic. It is a variant of the T-fragment of $\overline{\lambda}\mu\tilde{\mu}$ [3]; it is also the classical version of LJT [12,19].

The sequent calculus LKT handles three kinds of sequents, $\Gamma \vdash A|\Delta$ and $\Gamma; A \vdash \Delta$ and $\Gamma \mid\!\!- \Delta$, ranged over by σ, τ, and ζ, respectively. In the second form, the sequent shows a distinguished formula A in the left-hand side (LHS), which we call the **focus** of the sequent. In the first form, the sequent also shows a distinguished formula, now in the right-hand side (RHS), which is not a focus, but just a **selected** or **active conclusion**.

Here, and elsewhere, Γ ranges over sets of pairs (x, A), written $(x : A)$ and understood as assumptions. We additionally assume a set of **co-variables**, ranged over by a, b; and Δ ranges over sets of pairs (a, A), written $(a : A)$ and understood as **alternative conclusions**. In Γ (resp. Δ), each variable x (resp. co-variable) occurs in at most one assumption (resp. alternative conclusion).

The inference rules of LKT are given in Fig. 1. They are the axiom AX, the right and left introduction rules ($R\supset$, $L\supset$) for implication, the left introduction rule for absurdity ($L\perp$) and three structural rules: i) the **activation rule** ACT, which selects a formula in the RHS; ii) the left contraction rule $LCTR$, which

$$\frac{\Gamma, x:A \vdash B|\Delta}{\Gamma \vdash A \supset B|\Delta}\ R\supset \qquad \frac{\Gamma \models a:A,\Delta}{\Gamma \vdash A|\Delta}\ ACT$$

$$\frac{\Gamma, x:A; A \vdash \Delta}{\Gamma, x:A \models \Delta}\ LCTR \qquad \frac{\Gamma, x:A \vdash B|a:A \supset B,\Delta}{\Gamma \models a:A \supset B,\Delta}\ RCTR$$

$$\frac{}{\Gamma; p \vdash a:p,\Delta}\ AX \qquad \frac{}{\Gamma; \bot \vdash \Delta}\ L\bot \qquad \frac{\Gamma \vdash A|\Delta \quad \Gamma; B \vdash \Delta}{\Gamma; A \supset B \vdash \Delta}\ L\supset$$

Fig. 1. *LKT*. Sequents handled: $\Gamma \vdash A|\Delta$ and $\Gamma; A \vdash \Delta$ and $\Gamma \models \Delta$.

takes a formula out of the focus and contracts it with another occurrence of the same formula already present in Γ; iii) the **right contraction** rule $RCTR$, which does an implicit right introduction of $A \supset B$ and contracts this formula with another occurrence of the same formula already present in Δ.

LKT can be understood as an extension of LJT with "multiple conclusions". To see this, think of sequents $\Gamma \vdash A$ and $\Gamma; A \vdash p$ of LJT as, respectively, the sequents $\Gamma \vdash A|\cdot$ and $\Gamma; A \vdash \star : p$ of LKT, where $\cdot$ is the empty Δ. The constructor $\star$ can be thought of as the unique, implicit, intuitionistic co-variable. The inference rules of LKT, when acting on these restricted sequents, define deduction as in LJT: erase Δ in rule $R\supset$ and the left premiss of rule $L\supset$; the axiom concludes $\Gamma; p \vdash \star : p$; rule $RCTR$ does not apply, as its premiss is beyond the considered restrictions; Δ has the form $\star : p$ in rule $L\bot$, as well as in the right premiss and conclusion of rule $L\supset$; finally, rules $LCTR$ and ACT and the third form of sequents is hidden inside the deduction: from $\Gamma, x : A; A \vdash \star : p$ get $\Gamma, x : A \models \star : p$ by $LCTR$; then obtain $\Gamma, x : A \vdash p|\cdot$, by ACT. This simulates the effect of left contraction rule of LJT.

Proof terms t, u, commands c and proof lists l of LKT are defined by:

$$t, u ::= \lambda x^A.t \mid \mu a^A.c \qquad c ::= \langle x \mid l\rangle \mid \langle \lambda x^A.t \mid a\rangle \qquad l ::= a \mid \mathsf{abort} \mid u::l$$

LKT with proof terms handles three kinds of sequents $\Gamma \vdash t : A|\Delta$ and $\Gamma; l : A \vdash \Delta$ and $\Gamma \overset{c}{\models} \Delta$, called **total sequents**, with the rules in Fig. 2. Each proof constructor witnesses the use of a certain inference. Therefore, if $\Gamma \vdash t : A|\Delta$ is derivable, t encodes the derivation of $\Gamma \vdash A|\Delta$. Admissible inference rules are witnessed by admissible proof-term operations.

Theorem 1 (Admissible cut rules of ***LKT*****).** *Consider the equations in Fig. 3. The cut rules (1) to (7) in Fig. 4 are admissible in LKT.*

Proof. For a more precise statement of the theorem, see Appendix A. For all t, c and l, the sizes $|t|$, $|c|$ and $|l|$ are defined by simultaneous structural recursion on t, c and l as follows: $|\lambda x^A.t| = 1 + |t|$, $|\mu a^A.c| = 1 + |c|$, $|\langle x \mid l\rangle| = 2 + |l|$, $|\langle \lambda x^A.t \mid a\rangle| = 3 + |t|$, $|a| = 1$, $|\mathsf{abort}| = 1$ and $|u::l| = 1 + |u| + |l|$. The proof of items (1) to (7) is made by simultaneous induction on the lexicographically ordered pairs: $(|A|, 1, |t|)$, $(|A|, 1, |c|)$, $(|A|, 1, |l|)$, $(|A|, 0, |u|)$, $(|A|, 0, |c|)$, $(|A|, 0, |l'|)$ and $(|A|, 0, |u|)$. □

$$\frac{\Gamma, x : A \vdash t : B|\Delta}{\Gamma \vdash \lambda x^A.t : A \supset B|\Delta}\ R\supset \qquad \frac{\Gamma \overset{c}{\vdash} a : A, \Delta}{\Gamma \vdash \mu a^A.c : A|\Delta}\ ACT$$

$$\frac{\Gamma, x : A; l : A \vdash \Delta}{\Gamma, x : A \overset{\langle x \,|\, l\rangle}{\vdash} \Delta}\ LCTR \qquad \frac{\Gamma, x : A \vdash t : B|a : A \supset B, \Delta}{\Gamma \overset{\langle \lambda x^A.t \,|\, a\rangle}{\vdash} a : A \supset B, \Delta}\ RCTR$$

$$\frac{}{\Gamma; a : p \vdash a : p, \Delta}\ AX \qquad \frac{}{\Gamma; \mathsf{abort} : \bot \vdash \Delta}\ L\bot \qquad \frac{\Gamma \vdash u : A|\Delta \quad \Gamma; l : B \vdash \Delta}{\Gamma; u :: l : A \supset B \vdash \Delta}\ L\supset$$

Fig. 2. *LKT* with proof terms. Sequents: $\Gamma \vdash t : A|\Delta$ and $\Gamma; l : A \vdash \Delta$ and $\Gamma \overset{c}{\vdash} \Delta$

$$\begin{aligned}
[u/x](\lambda y^A.t) &= \lambda y^A.[u/x]t \\
[u/x](\mu a^A.c) &= \mu a^A.[u/x]c \\[1ex]
[u/x]\langle x \,|\, l\rangle &= u@[u/x]l \\
[u/x]\langle y \,|\, l\rangle &= \langle y \,|\, [u/x]l\rangle \;\; (y \neq x) \\
[u/x]\langle \lambda y^A.t \,|\, a\rangle &= \langle \lambda y^A.[u/x]t \,|\, a\rangle \\[1ex]
[u/x]a &= a \\
[u/x]\mathsf{abort} &= \mathsf{abort} \\
[u/x](t :: l) &= ([u/x]t) :: ([u/x]l) \\[1ex]
(\lambda y^A.t)@a &= \langle \lambda y^A.t \,|\, a\rangle \\
(\lambda y^A.t)@(u :: l) &= ([u/y]t)@l \\
(\mu a^A.c)@l &= ([l/a]c)
\end{aligned}$$

$$\begin{aligned}
[l/a]\langle x \,|\, l'\rangle &= \langle x \,|\, [l/a]l'\rangle \\
[u :: l/a]\langle \lambda x^A.t \,|\, a\rangle &= ([u/x]([u :: l/a]t))@l \\
[l/a]\langle \lambda x^A.t \,|\, b\rangle &= \langle \lambda x^A.[l/a]t \,|\, b\rangle \;\; (b \neq a) \\[1ex]
[l/a]a &= l \\
[l/a]b &= b \;\; (b \neq a) \\
[l/a]\mathsf{abort} &= \mathsf{abort} \\
[l/a](u :: l') &= ([l/a]u) :: ([l/a]l') \\[1ex]
[l/a](\lambda x^A.t) &= \lambda x^A.[l/a]t \\
[l/a](\mu b^B.c) &= \mu b^B.[l/a]c
\end{aligned}$$

Fig. 3. Equations for *LKT*

3 Proof Search in *LKT*

Proof search in *LKT* proceeds by bottom-up application of inference rules and obeys the **focusing** discipline: first we invert $R\supset$ to decompose implications in the RHS. This phase is explicitly finished by one application of *ACT*. Next there is an alternative: either we focus on a formula in the LHS, through rule *LCTR*, and, as long as the focus formula is an implication, we keep the focus on the succedent of the implication, as we apply $L\supset$ – this is very much as what happens in *LJT*; or we pick an implication in the RHS, decide this formula results from an introduction with contraction, and return to the inversion phase – this is the new option offered by rule *RCTR*.

We intend to represent this process as a rewriting system acting on **partial proof terms**, which are proof terms expressing gaps in incomplete derivations with the help of **formal sequents**, that is, sequents occurring as proper components of the syntax of proof terms. The system *LKT* with proof terms is grown to LKT_∂ with partial proof terms.

$$\frac{\Gamma \vdash u : A|\Delta \quad \Gamma, x : A \vdash t : B|\Delta}{\Gamma \vdash [u/x]t : B|\Delta}\ (1) \qquad \frac{\Gamma \vdash u : A|\Delta \quad \Gamma, x : A \overset{c}{\vdash} \Delta}{\Gamma \overset{[u/x]c}{\vdash} \Delta}\ (2)$$

$$\frac{\Gamma \vdash u : A|\Delta \quad \Gamma, x : A; l : B \vdash \Delta}{\Gamma; [u/x]l : B \vdash \Delta}\ (3) \qquad \frac{\Gamma \vdash u : A|\Delta \quad \Gamma; l : A \vdash \Delta}{\Gamma \overset{u@l}{\vdash} \Delta}\ (4)$$

$$\frac{\Gamma \overset{c}{\vdash} \Delta, a : A \quad \Gamma; l : A \vdash \Delta}{\Gamma \overset{[l/a]c}{\vdash} \Delta}\ (5) \qquad \frac{\Gamma; l' : B \vdash \Delta, a : A \quad \Gamma; l : A \vdash \Delta}{\Gamma; [l/a]l' : B \vdash \Delta}\ (6)$$

$$\frac{\Gamma \vdash u : B|\Delta, a : A \quad \Gamma; l : A \vdash \Delta}{\Gamma \vdash [l/a]u : B|\Delta}\ (7)$$

Fig. 4. Admissible cut rules of LKT

The proof terms for LKT_∂ are generated as follows:

$$\begin{array}{rl} \text{(Partial proof terms)} & t, u ::= \lambda x^A.t \mid \mu a^A.c \mid \underline{\sigma} \\ \text{(Partial proof lists)} & l ::= a \mid \mathsf{abort} \mid u{::}l \mid \underline{\tau} \\ \text{(Partial commands)} & c ::= \langle x \mid l \rangle \mid \langle \lambda x^A.t \mid a \rangle \mid \underline{\zeta} \end{array}$$

where $\underline{\sigma}$ ranges over *formal term sequents*, $\underline{\Gamma \vdash A|\Delta}$, which are term sequents as partial proof terms; $\underline{\tau}$ ranges over *formal list sequents*, $\underline{\Gamma; A \vdash \Delta}$, which are list sequents as partial proof lists; and $\underline{\zeta}$ ranges over *formal command sequents*, $\underline{\Gamma \vdash \Delta}$, which are command sequents as partial commands.

The typing system of LKT_∂ handles **partial sequents** $\Xi \Vdash t : \sigma$ and $\Xi \Vdash l : \tau$ and $\Xi \Vdash c : \zeta$ with the rules given in Fig. 5, generating **partial derivations**. Lists of formal sequents are ranged over by Ξ, and written $[\underline{\sigma}, \underline{\tau}, \underline{\tau'}]$ for instance. For such lists, we use ϵ to denote the empty list and $\Xi_1 @ \Xi_2$ to denote concatenation.

A partial sequent $\Xi \Vdash t : \sigma$ derivable in LKT_∂ represents a **proof state** found in the process of proof search in LKT: Ξ contains a list of **proof obligations** and σ is the **goal sequent**. The formal sequents in Ξ are those occurring in t. The derivations of LKT_∂ are partial because they contain occurrences of special rules named ∂, which is where proof obligations are created. Proof obligations can be fulfilled by reducing t according to reduction rules given in Fig. 6. If all the proof obligations in Ξ are fulfilled (i.e. reduced away), the partial proof term t is converted into a proof term of the sequent σ. Similar considerations apply to $\Xi \Vdash l : \tau$ and and $\Xi \Vdash c : \xi$.

The reduction rules in Fig. 6 formalize the verbal explanation of the search procedure in the first paragraph of this section. There is a reduction rule for each inference rule of LKT. A **redex** is a formal sequent.

The reduction rules determine three different binary relations: one on partial proof terms, one on partial proof lists, and one on partial commands. We use $\to$ to denote the compatible closure of these binary relations and $\twoheadrightarrow$ to denote

$$\dfrac{}{[\underline{\sigma}] \Vdash \underline{\sigma} : \sigma}\,\partial \qquad \dfrac{}{[\underline{\tau}] \Vdash \underline{\tau} : \tau}\,\partial \qquad \dfrac{}{[\underline{\zeta}] \Vdash \underline{\zeta} : \zeta}\,\partial$$

$$\dfrac{}{\epsilon \Vdash a : (\Gamma; p \vdash a : p, \Delta)}\,AX \qquad \dfrac{}{\epsilon \Vdash \mathsf{abort} : (\Gamma; \bot \vdash \Delta)}\,E\bot \qquad \dfrac{\Xi \Vdash c : (\Gamma \mid\!\!- a : A, \Delta)}{\Xi \Vdash \mu a^A.c : (\Gamma \vdash A|\Delta)}\,ACT$$

$$\dfrac{\Xi \Vdash t : (\Gamma, x : A \vdash B|a : A \supset B, \Delta)}{\Xi \Vdash \langle \lambda x^A.t \,|\, a\rangle : (\Gamma \mid\!\!- a : A \supset B, \Delta)}\,RCTR \qquad \dfrac{\Xi \Vdash l : (\Gamma, x : A; A \vdash \Delta)}{\Xi \Vdash \langle x \,|\, l\rangle : (\Gamma, x : A \mid\!\!- \Delta)}\,LCTR$$

$$\dfrac{\Xi \Vdash t : (\Gamma, x : A \vdash B|\Delta)}{\Xi \Vdash \lambda x^A.t : (\Gamma \vdash A \supset B|\Delta)}\,RI \qquad \dfrac{\Xi_1 \Vdash u : (\Gamma \vdash A|\Delta) \quad \Xi_2 \Vdash l : (\Gamma; B \vdash \Delta)}{\Xi_1 @ \Xi_2 \Vdash u :: l : (\Gamma; A \supset B \vdash \Delta)}\,LI$$

Fig. 5. LKT_∂: LKT with partial proof terms

$$\begin{array}{rr}
(SIR) & \underline{\Gamma \mid\!\!- a : A \supset B, \Delta} \to \langle \lambda x^A.(\underline{\Gamma, x : A \vdash B|a : A \supset B, \Delta}) \,|\, a\rangle \\
(KIR) & \underline{\Gamma \vdash A \supset B|\Delta} \to \lambda x^A.(\underline{\Gamma, x : A \vdash B|\Delta}) \\
(FIR) & \underline{\Gamma \vdash A|\Delta} \to \mu a^A.(\underline{\Gamma \mid\!\!- a : A, \Delta}) \\
(SFL) & \underline{\Gamma, x : A \mid\!\!- \Delta} \to \langle x \,|\, (\underline{\Gamma, x : A; A \vdash \Delta})\rangle \\
(KFL) & \underline{\Gamma; A \supset B \vdash \Delta} \to (\underline{\Gamma \vdash A|\Delta}) :: (\underline{\Gamma; B \vdash \Delta}) \\
(FFL_{atm}) & \underline{\Gamma; p \vdash a : p, \Delta} \to a \\
(FFL_{ab}) & \underline{\Gamma; \bot \vdash \Delta} \to \mathsf{abort}
\end{array}$$

Fig. 6. Reduction rules for proof search in LKT. The names of the rules stand for: start inversion right, keep inversion right, finish inversion right, start focus left, keep focus left, finish focus left (atomic and absurdity).

the reflexive and transitive closure of $\to$. The reduction rules also determine a relation $\Xi \to \Xi'$: if the redex of a rule is in Ξ, in Ξ' the redex is replaced by the formal sequents of the *contractum.*

There are three technical results, detailed in Appendix A: (1) **Conservativity**: derivability is partial derivability from the empty list of proof obligations; (2) **Record of search**: if a sequent $\Xi \Vdash t : \sigma$ is derivable in LKT_∂, then the partial proof term t records a run of proof search that starts from σ, in the sense that $\underline{\sigma} \twoheadrightarrow t$; (3) **Subject reduction**: If $\Xi \Vdash t : \sigma$ and $t \to t'$, then $\Xi' \Vdash t' : \sigma$ for some Ξ' such that $\Xi \to \Xi'$. From these, we arrive at the main result of this section, which can be roughly described like this: if $\sigma = (\Gamma \vdash A|\Delta)$, then proof search finds a proof t for σ iff $\underline{\sigma} \twoheadrightarrow t$.

Theorem 2 (Proof search as normalization) . *(1) LKT derives $\Gamma \vdash t : A|\Delta$ iff $\underline{\sigma} \twoheadrightarrow t$, where $\underline{\sigma} = \underline{\Gamma \vdash A|\Delta}$. (2) LKT derives $\Gamma; l : A \vdash \Delta$ iff $\underline{\tau} \twoheadrightarrow l$, where $\underline{\tau} = \underline{\Gamma; A \vdash \Delta}$. (3) LKT derives $\Gamma \mid\!\!\stackrel{c}{-} \Delta$ iff $\underline{\zeta} \twoheadrightarrow c$, where $\underline{\zeta} = \underline{\Gamma \mid\!\!- \Delta}$.*

Proof. The "only if" statements follow from conservativity and record of search. As to the "if" statement, let us prove the first. Suppose $\underline{\sigma} \twoheadrightarrow t$, where $\underline{\sigma} = \underline{\Gamma \vdash A|\Delta}$. Notice $[\underline{\sigma}] \Vdash \underline{\sigma} : \sigma$. By subject reduction, $\Xi \Vdash t : \sigma$, for some Ξ. But t is total, so $\Xi = \epsilon$. By conservativity, LKT derives $\Gamma \vdash t : A|\Delta$. □

$$\frac{\Gamma, x : A \vdash B|\Delta}{\Gamma \vdash A \supset B|\Delta}\ I\supset \qquad \frac{\Gamma \mid\!\!\!- a : A, \Delta}{\Gamma \vdash A|\Delta}\ ACT$$

$$\frac{\Gamma \rhd \bot |\Delta}{\Gamma \mid\!\!\!- \Delta}\ E\bot \qquad \frac{\Gamma \rhd p|a : p, \Delta}{\Gamma \mid\!\!\!- a : p, \Delta}\ PSS \qquad \frac{\Gamma, x : A \vdash B|a : A \supset B, \Delta}{\Gamma \mid\!\!\!- a : A \supset B, \Delta}\ CTR$$

$$\frac{}{\Gamma, x : A \rhd A|\Delta}\ A \qquad \frac{\Gamma \rhd A \supset B|\Delta \quad \Gamma \vdash A|\Delta}{\Gamma \rhd B|\Delta}\ E\supset$$

Fig. 7. *NKT*. Sequents handled: $\Gamma \vdash A|\Delta$ and $\Gamma \rhd A|\Delta$ and $\Gamma \mid\!\!\!- \Delta$

4 Natural Deduction System *NKT*

NKT is a system of natural deduction which handles three kinds of sequents, $\Gamma \vdash A|\Delta$ and $\Gamma \rhd A|\Delta$ and $\Gamma \mid\!\!\!- \Delta$, ranged over by σ, ρ and ζ, respectively. Following [18], sequents have **alternative conclusions**, collected in Δ. In the first kind, A is active. In the third kind, all conclusions are passive. In the second kind, A is the **focus** of the sequent. See Fig. 7 for the inference rules.

In a derivation, the formulas in the focus constitute the elimination part of a branch, starting with an assumption, containing a sequence of formulas figuring as main premiss of inferences $E\supset$, down to an atom p or to $\bot$. The coercion to a sequent $\Gamma \vdash A|\Delta$ requires two steps: first, the atom p is made **passive** by rule PSS, or $\bot$ is eliminated by rule $E\bot$; second, one of the alternative conclusions in Δ is made **active** by rule ACT. The introduction part of the branch thus started can be grown downwards by applications of $I\supset$, or through a kind of *detour* made possible by rule CTR, where $A \supset B$ is implicitly introduced and immediately made passive and contracted with $a : A \supset B$ present in the set of alternative conclusions; in order to return to the introduction mode, ACT must be used, but there is no guarantee that $a : A \supset B$ will be activated later on.

NKT can also be understood as an extension of *NJT* [19] with "multiple conclusions". To see this, think of sequents $\Gamma \vdash A$ and $\Gamma \rhd A$ of *NJT* as, respectively, the sequents $\Gamma \vdash A|\cdot$ and $\Gamma \rhd A|\cdot$ of *NKT*, where $\cdot$ is the empty Δ. The inference rules of *NKT*, when acting on these restricted sequents, define deduction as in *NJT*: erase Δ in rules $I\supset$ and $E\supset$; the axiom concludes $\Gamma, x : A \rhd A|\cdot$; rule CTR does not apply, as its premiss is beyond the considered restrictions; and rules PSS and ACT and the third form of sequents are hidden inside the following derivation: From $\Gamma \rhd p|\cdot$ we get $\Gamma \rhd p|a : p$ though weakening; then we get $\Gamma \mid\!\!\!- a : p$ through PSS; finally we get $\Gamma \vdash p|\cdot$ through ACT. This simulates the inclusion of derivability of $\Gamma \rhd p$ in derivability of $\Gamma \vdash p$ enjoyed by *LJT*.

Proof terms M, statements S and neutral terms H of *NKT* are defined by:

$$M, N ::= \lambda x^A.M \mid \mu a^A.S \qquad S ::= \mathsf{abort}(H) \mid a(H) \mid a(\lambda x^A.M) \qquad H ::= x \mid HN$$

$$\frac{\Gamma, x : A \vdash M : B|\Delta}{\Gamma \vdash \lambda x^A.M : A \supset B|\Delta}\ I\supset \qquad \frac{\Gamma \overset{S}{\models} a : A, \Delta}{\Gamma \vdash \mu a^A.S : A|\Delta}\ ACT$$

$$\frac{\Gamma \rhd H : \perp |\Delta}{\Gamma \overset{\mathsf{abort}(H)}{\models} \Delta}\ E\perp \qquad \frac{\Gamma \rhd H : p|a : p, \Delta}{\Gamma \overset{a(H)}{\models} a : p, \Delta}\ PSS \qquad \frac{\Gamma, x : A \vdash M : B|a : A \supset B, \Delta}{\Gamma \overset{a(\lambda x^A.M)}{\models} a : A \supset B, \Delta}\ CTR$$

$$\frac{}{\Gamma, x : A \rhd x : A|\Delta}\ A \qquad \frac{\Gamma \rhd H : A \supset B|\Delta \quad \Gamma \vdash N : A|\Delta}{\Gamma \rhd HN : B|\Delta}\ E\supset$$

Fig. 8. NKT with proof terms. Sequents: $\Gamma \vdash M : A|\Delta$ and $\Gamma \rhd H : A|\Delta$ and $\Gamma \overset{S}{\models} \Delta$

NKT with proof terms handles sequents $\Gamma \vdash M : A|\Delta$ and $\Gamma \rhd H : A|\Delta$ and $\Gamma \overset{S}{\models} \Delta$ with the rules in Fig. 8. Notice the invariant: if $\Gamma \overset{S}{\models} \Delta, b :\perp$ is derivable, then b is not free in S and $\Gamma \overset{S}{\models} \Delta$ is derivable. Similarly for M and H.

Proposition 1. (Generalization of *PSS*). *Let* $\mathsf{pass}(a, A, H)$ *be the statement defined by recursion on* A *as follows:* $\mathsf{pass}(a, p, H) = a(H)$*;* $\mathsf{pass}(a, \perp, H) = \mathsf{abort}(H)$*;* $\mathsf{pass}(a, A \supset B, H) = a(\lambda x^A.\mu b^B.\mathsf{pass}(b, B, H(\mu a^A.\mathsf{pass}(a, A, x))))$*. Then the following rules are admissible in* NKT*:*

$$\frac{\Gamma \rhd H : A|a : A, \Delta}{\Gamma \overset{\mathsf{pass}(a,A,H)}{\models} a : A, \Delta}\ PASS \qquad \frac{\Gamma \rhd H : A|a : A, \Delta}{\Gamma \vdash \mu a^A.\mathsf{pass}(a, A, H) : A|\Delta}$$

Proof. The first is proved by induction A. The second follows from the first. □

Proposition 2 (Double negation elim.) . NKT *derives* $(A \supset\perp) \supset\perp\vdash A|$.

For the benefit of the next theorem, and as done in [19] in the context of system NJT, we introduce **extended neutral terms**: an extended neutral term is either a neutral term, or a term considered as a neutral term, called a **head term** and denoted $hd(M)$. Extended neutral terms are ranged over by $\mathbb{H}$. Next we introduce the auxiliary form of sequent $\Gamma \blacktriangleright \mathbb{H} : A$, which is an abbreviation defined by the following two rules

$$\frac{\Gamma \rhd H : A|\Delta}{\Gamma \blacktriangleright H : A|\Delta} \qquad \frac{\Gamma \vdash M : A|\Delta}{\Gamma \blacktriangleright hd(M) : A|\Delta} \tag{1}$$

Given $\mathbb{H}$, we define statements $a(\!|\mathbb{H}|\!)$ and $\mathsf{abort}(\!|\mathbb{H}|\!)$ satisfying the typing rules:

$$\frac{\Gamma \blacktriangleright hd(M) : A|a : A, \Delta}{\Gamma \overset{a(\!|hd(M)|\!)}{\models} a : A, \Delta} \qquad \frac{\Gamma \blacktriangleright \mathbb{H} : p|a : p, \Delta}{\Gamma \overset{a(\!|\mathbb{H}|\!)}{\models} a : p, \Delta} \qquad \frac{\Gamma \blacktriangleright \mathbb{H} :\perp |\Delta}{\Gamma \overset{\mathsf{abort}(\!|\mathbb{H}|\!)}{\models} \Delta}$$

$$[N/x](\lambda y^C.M) = \lambda y^C.[N/x]M$$
$$[N/x](\mu a^B.S) = \mu a^B.[N/x]S$$

$$[N/x](\mathsf{abort}(H)) = \mathsf{abort}(\!|[N/x]H|\!)$$
$$[N/x](a(H)) = a(\!|[N/x]H|\!)$$
$$[N/x](a(\lambda y^C.M)) = a(\lambda y^C.[N/x]M)$$

$$[N/x]x = hd(N)$$
$$[N/x]y = y \ (y \neq x)$$
$$[N/x](HM) = ([N/x]H)@([N/x]M)$$

$$H@N = HN$$
$$(hd(M))@N = hd(M@N)$$

$$[@N/a](c(H)) = c([@N/a]H), \ (c \neq a)$$
$$[@N/a](a(\lambda x^A.M)) = a(\!|hd([N/x]([@N/a]M))|\!)$$
$$[@N/a](c(\lambda x^A.M)) = c(\lambda x^A.[@N/a]M), \ (c \neq a)$$
$$[@N/a]\mathsf{abort}(H) = \mathsf{abort}([@N/a]H)$$

$$[@N/a]x = x$$
$$[@N/a](HM) = ([@N/a]H)([@N/a]M)$$

$$[@N/a](\lambda y^C.M) = \lambda y^C.[@N/a]M$$
$$[@N/a](\mu c^C.S) = \mu c^C.[@N/a]S$$

$$(\lambda y^A.M)@N = [N/y]M$$
$$(\mu a^{A \supset B}.S)@N = \mu a^B.[@N/a]S$$

Fig. 9. Equations for NKT

$$\frac{\Gamma \vdash N : A|\Delta \quad \Gamma, x : A \vdash M : B|\Delta}{\Gamma \vdash [N/x]M : B|\Delta} \ (1) \qquad \frac{\Gamma \vdash N : A|\Delta \quad \Gamma, x : A \stackrel{S}{\vdash} \Delta}{\Gamma \stackrel{[N/x]S}{\vdash} \Delta} \ (2)$$

$$\frac{\Gamma \vdash N : A|\Delta \quad \Gamma, x : A \rhd H : B|\Delta}{\Gamma \blacktriangleright [N/x]H : B|\Delta} \ (3) \qquad \frac{\Gamma \blacktriangleright \mathbb{H} : A \supset B|\Delta \quad \Gamma \vdash N : A|\Delta}{\Gamma \blacktriangleright \mathbb{H}@N : B|\Delta} \ (4)$$

$$\frac{\Gamma \vdash M : A \supset B|\Delta \quad \Gamma \vdash N : A|\Delta}{\Gamma \vdash M@N : B|\Delta} \ (5) \qquad \frac{\Gamma \stackrel{S}{\vdash} a : A \supset B, \Delta \quad \Gamma \vdash N : A|\Delta}{\Gamma \stackrel{[@N/a]S}{\vdash} a : B, \Delta} \ (6)$$

$$\frac{\Gamma \rhd H : C|a : A \supset B, \Delta \quad \Gamma \vdash N : A|\Delta}{\Gamma \rhd [@N/a]H : C|a : B, \Delta} \ (7) \qquad \frac{\Gamma \vdash M : C|a : A \supset B, \Delta \quad \Gamma \vdash N : A|\Delta}{\Gamma \vdash [@N/a]M : C|a : B, \Delta} \ (8)$$

Fig. 10. Admissible rules of NKT

The definition is as follows: $a(\!|H|\!) = a(H)$; $a(\!|hd(\mu b^A.S)|\!) = [a/b]S$; $a(\!|hd(\lambda x^C.M)|\!) = a(\lambda x^C.M)$; $\mathsf{abort}(\!|H|\!) = \mathsf{abort}(H)$; $\mathsf{abort}(\!|hd(\mu b^{\perp}.S)|\!) = S$.

Theorem 3 (Admissible rules of NKT**).** *Consider the equations in Fig. 9. The rules (1) to (8) in Fig. 10 are admissible in* NKT.

Proof. For a more precise statement of the theorem, see Appendix A. For all M, S and H, the sizes $|M|$, $|S|$ and $|H|$ are defined by simultaneous structural recursion on M, S and H as follows: $|\lambda x^A.M| = 1 + |M|$, $|\mu a^A.S| = 1 + |S|$, $|\mathsf{abort}(H)| = 1 + |H|$, $|a(H)| = |H|$, $a(\lambda x^A.M) = 1 + |\lambda x^A.M|$, $|x| = 1$ and $|HN| = |H| + |N|$. We also put $|hd(M)| = 1 + |M|$ The proof of items (1) to (8) is made by simultaneous induction on the lexicographically ordered pairs: $(|A|, |M|)$, $(|A|, |S|)$, $(|A|, |H|)$, $(f(\mathbb{H}, A, B), |\mathbb{H}|)$, $(|A|+|B|, |M|)$, $(|A|+|B|, |S|)$, $(|A|+|B|, |H|)$ and $(|A|+|B|, |M|)$, where $f(H, A, B) = 0$ and $f(hd(M), A, B) = |A| + |B|$. □

The constructor $a(M)$ of the $\lambda\mu$-calculus is split in NKT into $a(M)$ and $a(H)$, with M even restricted to a λ-abstraction. This has an impact on the operation $[@N/a]_{-}$. It is a "structural substitution" [2,18], but it only looks for occurrences of a of the form $a(\lambda x^A.M)$. For this reason, the typing rules (6), (7) and (8) of Fig. 10 are in fact **elimination rules for alternative implications**.

5 Proof Search in *NKT*

Proof search in NKT extends the process in NJT. First, as in focusing, implications in the RHS are decomposed by inversion of rule $I\supset$. This phase is explicitly stopped by an application of rule ACT, producing a certain sequent $\Gamma \models \Delta$. Next there is an alternative: either we change direction and decompose implications by top-down application of rule $E\supset$, starting from an assumption chosen in Γ by rule A, until we compute $\perp$ or an atom p (the latter we hope to see in Δ) – this is very much like in NJT; or we pick an implication in Δ, decide this formula results from an introduction with contraction, and return to the inversion phase – this is the new option offered by rule CTR.

To formalize this process, we extend NKT to NKT_∂, in a similar way as we extended before LKT to LKT_∂ – but here we will be more succinct. Partial proof terms, head terms and statements are generated as follows:

$$M, N ::= \lambda x^A.M \mid \mu a^A.S \mid \underline{\sigma} \qquad\qquad H ::= x \mid HN$$
$$S ::= \mathsf{abort}(H) \mid a(H) \mid a(\lambda x^A.M) \mid \underline{\zeta} \mid \mathsf{ab}(H, \underline{\rho})$$

where $\underline{\sigma}$ ranges over *formal proof term sequents*; $\underline{\rho}$ ranges over *formal neutral term sequents*, which are neutral term sequents as partial neutral terms; and $\underline{\zeta}$ ranges over *formal statement sequents*, which are statement sequents as partial statements.

The typing system of NKT_∂ handles **partial sequents** $\Xi \Vdash M : \sigma$ and $\Xi \Vdash H : \rho$ and $\Xi \Vdash S : \zeta$ with the rules given in Fig. 11. The second ∂-rule says that $\mathsf{ab}(H, \underline{\rho})$ is the gap between the sequent $\rho = (\Gamma \rhd A|\Delta)$, obtained according to H, and the sequent $\Gamma \models \Delta$.

The search process described in the first paragraph of this section is formalized with the rules of Fig. 12. Notice how $a(H)$ is generated when finishing the focus down phase, while $a(\lambda x^A.M)$ signals the start of the right inversion phase. Notice also that a redex is not necessarily a formal sequent.

As for LKT_∂, we prove for NKT_∂ conservativity, record of search, and subject reduction (details in Appendix A), and then:

Theorem 4 (Proof search as normalization) . *(1) NKT derives $\Gamma \vdash M : A|\Delta$ iff $\underline{\Gamma \vdash A|\Delta} \twoheadrightarrow M$. (2) NKT derives $\Gamma \overset{S}{\models} \Delta$ iff $\underline{\Gamma \models \Delta} \twoheadrightarrow S$. (3) NKT derives $\Gamma \rhd H : A|\Delta$ iff $\underline{\Gamma \models \Delta} \twoheadrightarrow \mathsf{ab}(H, (\underline{\Gamma \rhd A|\Delta}))$.*

6 Focusing Versus Bidirectionality

First we present the bijection between LKT_∂-terms and NKT_∂-terms. The translations $\Theta : LKT_\partial \to NKT_\partial$ and $\Psi : NKT_\partial \to LKT_\partial$ are defined in Fig. 13.

$$\frac{}{[\underline{\sigma}] \Vdash \underline{\sigma} : \sigma}\ \partial \qquad \frac{\Xi \Vdash H : \rho \quad \rho = (\Gamma \rhd A|\Delta)}{\Xi @ [\underline{\rho}] \Vdash \mathsf{ab}(H, \underline{\rho}) : (\Gamma \mathrel{|\!\!-} \Delta)}\ \partial \qquad \frac{}{[\underline{\zeta}] \Vdash \underline{\zeta} : \zeta}\ \partial$$

$$\frac{}{\epsilon \Vdash x : (\Gamma, x : A \rhd A|\Delta)}\ A \qquad \frac{\Xi \Vdash H : (\Gamma \rhd \bot |\Delta)}{\Xi \Vdash \mathsf{abort}(H) : (\Gamma \mathrel{|\!\!-} \Delta)}\ E\bot \qquad \frac{\Xi \Vdash S : (\Gamma \mathrel{|\!\!-} a : A, \Delta)}{\Xi \Vdash \mu a^A.S : (\Gamma \vdash A|\Delta)}\ ACT$$

$$\frac{\Xi \Vdash M : (\Gamma, x : A \vdash B|a : A \supset B, \Delta)}{\Xi \Vdash a(\lambda x^A.M) : (\Gamma \mathrel{|\!\!-} a : A \supset B, \Delta)}\ CTR \qquad \frac{\Xi \Vdash H : (\Gamma \rhd p|a : p, \Delta)}{\Xi \Vdash a(H) : (\Gamma \mathrel{|\!\!-} a : p, \Delta)}\ PSS$$

$$\frac{\Xi \Vdash M : (\Gamma, x : A \vdash B|\Delta)}{\Xi \Vdash \lambda x^A.M : (\Gamma \vdash A \supset B|\Delta)}\ I\supset \qquad \frac{\Xi_1 \Vdash H : (\Gamma \rhd A \supset B|\Delta) \quad \Xi_2 \Vdash N : (\Gamma \vdash A|\Delta)}{\Xi_1 @ \Xi_2 \Vdash HN : (\Gamma \rhd B|\Delta)}\ E\supset$$

Fig. 11. NKT_∂: NKT with partial proof terms

$$\begin{array}{rr}
(SIR) & \underline{\Gamma \mathrel{|\!\!-} a : A \supset B, \Delta} \to a(\lambda x^A.(\underline{\Gamma, x : A \vdash B|a : A \supset B, \Delta})) \\
(KIR) & \underline{\Gamma \vdash A \supset B|\Delta} \to \lambda x^A.(\underline{\Gamma, x : A \vdash B|\Delta}) \\
(FIR) & \underline{\Gamma \vdash A|\Delta} \to \mu a^A.(\underline{\Gamma \mathrel{|\!\!-} a : A, \Delta}) \\
(SFD) & \underline{\Gamma, x : A \mathrel{|\!\!-} \Delta} \to \mathsf{ab}(x, (\underline{\Gamma, x : A \rhd A|\Delta})) \\
(KFD) & \mathsf{ab}(H, (\underline{\Gamma \rhd A \supset B|\Delta})) \to \mathsf{ab}(H(\underline{\Gamma \vdash A|\Delta}), (\underline{\Gamma \rhd B|\Delta})) \\
(FFD_{atm}) & \mathsf{ab}(H, (\underline{\Gamma \rhd p|a : p, \Delta})) \to a(H) \\
(FFD_{abs}) & \mathsf{ab}(H, (\underline{\Gamma \rhd \bot |\Delta})) \to \mathsf{abort}(H)
\end{array}$$

Fig. 12. Reduction rules for proof search in NKT. The names of the rules stand for: start inversion right, keep inversion right, finish inversion right, start focus down, keep focus down, finish focus down (atomic and absurdity).

Let us name as $L\text{–}Terms$, $Lists$ and $Commands$ the three sets of expressions defined simultaneously by the grammar of LKT_∂, and analogously use the names $N\text{–}Terms$, $Neutrals$ and $Statements$ for NKT_∂. The map $\Theta : L\text{–}Terms \to N\text{–}Terms$ is defined together with $\Theta : Neutrals \times Lists \to Statements$ and $\Theta : Commands \to Statements$ by simultaneous recursion on $t \in L\text{–}Terms$, $l \in Lists$ and $c \in Commands$. The map $\Psi : N\text{–}Terms \to L\text{–}Terms$ is defined together with $\Psi : Neutrals \times Lists \to Commands$ and $\Psi : Statements \to Commands$ by simultaneous recursion on $M \in N\text{–}Terms$, $H \in Neutrals$ and $S \in Statements$.

Theorem 5 ($LKT_\partial \cong NKT_\partial$). *(1) $\Theta\Psi M = M$ and $\Psi\Theta t = t$. (2) $t \to t'$ in LKT_∂ iff $\Theta t \to \Theta t'$ in NKT_∂. (3) $M \to M'$ in NKT_∂ iff $\Psi M \to \Psi M'$ in LKT_∂.*

The previous theorem says that reduction of $t \in LKT_\partial$ is isomorphic to reduction of $M = \Theta t \in NKT_\partial$. If we consider the particular case of $t = M = \underline{\sigma}$, and given that, according to Theorems 2 and 4, reduction in LKT_∂ (resp. NKT_∂) implements proof search in LKT (resp. NKT), we may conclude:

Corollary 1. *Proof search in LKT is isomorphic to proof search in NKT.*

$$\begin{aligned} \Theta(\lambda x^A.t) &= \lambda x^A.\Theta t \\ \Theta(\mu a^A.c) &= \mu a^A.\Theta c \\ \Theta(\underline{\sigma}) &= \underline{\sigma} \\ \\ \Theta(H,a) &= a(H) \\ \Theta(H,\mathsf{abort}) &= \mathsf{abort}(H) \\ \Theta(H,u::l) &= \Theta(H\Theta u,l) \\ \Theta(H,(\underline{\Gamma;A\vdash\Delta})) &= \mathsf{ab}(H,(\underline{\Gamma\rhd A|\Delta})) \\ \\ \Theta(\langle x\,|\,l\rangle) &= \Theta(x,l) \\ \Theta(\langle\lambda x^A.t\,|\,a\rangle) &= a(\lambda x^A.\Theta t) \\ \Theta(\underline{\zeta}) &= \underline{\zeta} \end{aligned}$$

$$\begin{aligned} \Psi(\lambda x^A.M) &= \lambda x^A.\Psi M \\ \Psi(\mu a^A.A) &= \mu a^A.\Psi S \\ \Psi(\underline{\sigma}) &= \underline{\sigma} \\ \\ \Psi(x,l) &= \langle x\,|\,l\rangle \\ \Psi(HN,l) &= \Psi(H,\Psi N::l) \\ \\ \Psi(\mathsf{abort}(H)) &= \Psi(H,\mathsf{abort}) \\ \Psi(a(H)) &= \Psi(H,a) \\ \Psi(a(\lambda x^A.M)) &= \langle\lambda x^A.\Psi M\,|\,a\rangle \\ \Psi(\mathsf{ab}(H,(\underline{\Gamma\rhd A|\Delta}))) &= \Psi(H,(\underline{\Gamma;A\vdash\Delta})) \\ \Psi(\underline{\zeta}) &= \underline{\zeta} \end{aligned}$$

Fig. 13. Translations $\Theta : LKT_\partial \to NKT_\partial$ and $\Psi : NKT_\partial \to LKT_\partial$

7 Final Remarks

We have to briefly recall here certain comparisons detailed in our previous paper [19]. The area of theorem proving has inspired the theoretical development of type theories with meta-variables and explicit substitutions [14–16]. Compared with partial proof terms, these are more powerful, and more complex, tools working at a different level of abstraction. For the results aimed in the present paper, we do not need all that power. Also, the first author and two co-authors developed in a series of papers [8–10] "coinductive proof search", employing proof terms with meta-variables X^σ typed with a sequent σ. The focus in that series has been on decision problems and the representation of the entire search space determined by a sequent. We refer to [19] for detailed comparisons with open derivations [11] and rewriting logic [17].

Sieg and co-authors studied proof search directly in natural deduction, through the intercalation calculus [20,21]. Here we distinguish between intercalation as a proof search strategy in natural deduction from the specific intercalation calculi developed in the cited papers. NKT follows the intercalation strategy, but differs greatly from the intercalation calculus.

In fact, NKT is a striking version of the $\lambda\mu$-calculus, with the typing rules for "structural substitution" [2,18] flagrantly being elimination rules for implication. In [7] one finds another variant of $\lambda\mu$ and its T-fragment, in perfect correspondence, regarding cut-elimination vs normalization, with the $\overline{\lambda}\mu\tilde{\mu}$-calculus and its T-fragment of [3], respectively. But the systems of [7], being aligned with those of [3], have a different syntactic organization. In addition, [7] is not a study of proof search.

An interesting project is to experiment with partial proof terms in the study of the combination of proof search with cut-elimination/normalization.

Acknowledgements. The authors were partially financed by Portuguese Funds through FCT (Fundação para a Ciência e Tecnologia) within Projects UID/00013: Centro de Matemática da Universidade do Minho (CMAT/UM).

A Technical Supplements

A.1 Supplements for Section 2

Theorem 1 (Admissible cut rules of LKT). Consider the equations in Fig. 3. In LKT one has:

(1) For all A, t: if $\Gamma \vdash u : A|\Delta$ and $\Gamma, x : A \vdash t : B|\Delta$, then the equations define the proof term $[u/x]t$ and $\Gamma \vdash [u/x]t : B|\Delta$.
(2) For all A, c: if $\Gamma \vdash u : A|\Delta$ and $\Gamma, x : A \stackrel{c}{\vdash} \Delta$, then the equations define the command $[u/x]c$ and $\Gamma \stackrel{[u/x]c}{\vdash} \Delta$.
(3) For all A, l: if $\Gamma \vdash u : A|\Delta$ and $\Gamma, x : A; l : B \vdash \Delta$, then the equations define the proof list $[u/x]l$ and $\Gamma; [u/x]l : B \vdash \Delta$.
(4) For all A, u: if $\Gamma \vdash u : A|\Delta$ and $\Gamma; l : A \vdash \Delta$, then the equations define the command $u@l$ and $\Gamma \stackrel{u@l}{\vdash} \Delta$.
(5) For all A, c: if $\Gamma \stackrel{c}{\vdash} \Delta, a : A$ and $\Gamma; l : A \vdash \Delta$, then the equations define the command $[l/a]c$ and $\Gamma \stackrel{[l/a]c}{\vdash} \Delta$.
(6) For all A, l': if $\Gamma; l' : B \vdash \Delta, a : A$ and $\Gamma; l : A \vdash \Delta$, then the equations define the proof list $[l/a]l'$ and $\Gamma; [l/a]l' : B \vdash \Delta$.
(7) For all A, u: if $\Gamma \vdash u : B|\Delta, a : A$ and $\Gamma; l : A \vdash \Delta$, then the equations define the proof term $[l/a]u$ and $\Gamma \vdash [l/a]u : B|\Delta$.

In particular, the cut rules (1) to (7) in Fig. 4 are admissible in LKT.

A.2 Supplements for Section 3

Proposition 3 (Conservativity) . *(1) LKT derives $\Gamma \vdash t : A|\Delta$ iff LKT_∂ derives $\epsilon \Vdash t : (\Gamma \vdash A|\Delta)$. (2) LKT derives $\Gamma; l : A \vdash \Delta$ iff LKT_∂ derives $\epsilon \Vdash l : (\Gamma; A \vdash \Delta)$. (3) LKT derives $\Gamma \stackrel{c}{\vdash} \Delta$ iff LKT_∂ derives $\epsilon \Vdash c : (\Gamma \vdash\!\!\!- \Delta)$.*

Proof. The "only if" statements are proved by simultaneous induction on the derivations of $\Gamma \vdash t : A|\Delta$, $\Gamma; l : A \vdash \Delta$ and $\Gamma \stackrel{c}{\vdash} \Delta$. The proof of the "if" statements is by simultaneous induction on the derivations of $\Xi \Vdash t : (\Gamma \vdash A|\Delta)$, $\Xi \Vdash l : (\Gamma; A \vdash \Delta)$ and $\Xi \Vdash c : (\Gamma \vdash\!\!\!- \Delta)$. □

Proposition 4 (Record of search). . *(1) If $\Xi \Vdash t : \sigma$ then $\underline{\sigma} \twoheadrightarrow t$. (2) If $\Xi \Vdash l : \tau$ then $\underline{\tau} \twoheadrightarrow l$. (3) If $\Xi \Vdash c : \zeta$ then $\underline{\zeta} \twoheadrightarrow c$.*

Proof. By simultaneous induction on the derivations of $\Xi \Vdash t : \sigma$, $\Xi \Vdash l : \tau$ and $\Xi \Vdash c : \zeta$. We illustrate one case: suppose $c = \langle x \,|\, l \rangle$ and the derivation of $\Xi \Vdash c : \zeta$ ends with $LCTR$. Then $\underline{\zeta} = \underline{\Gamma, x : A \vdash\!\!\!- \Delta} \to \langle x \,|\, \underline{(\Gamma, x : A; A \vdash \Delta)} \rangle \twoheadrightarrow \langle x \,|\, l \rangle$, where the first step is by SFL and the rest of reduction is by IH. Notice that c dictates and records the search from $\underline{\zeta}$.

Proposition 5. (Subject reduction for LKT_∂).

1. *If $\Xi \Vdash t : \sigma$ and $t \to t'$, then there is Ξ' such that $\Xi \to \Xi'$ and $\Xi' \Vdash t' : \sigma$.*
2. *If $\Xi \Vdash l : \tau$ and $l \to l'$, then there is Ξ' such that $\Xi \to \Xi'$ and $\Xi' \Vdash l' : \tau$.*
3. *If $\Xi \Vdash c : \zeta$ and $c \to c'$, then there is Ξ' such that $\Xi \to \Xi'$ and $\Xi' \Vdash c' : \zeta$.*

Proof. By simultaneous induction on $t \to t'$, $l \to l'$ and $c \to c'$. □

A.3 Supplements for Section 4

Proposition 2 (Double negation elim.). NKT derives $(A \supset \perp) \supset \perp \vdash A|$.

$$\dfrac{}{y : (A \supset \perp) \supset \perp, x : A \rhd x : A | b : \perp, a : A}\ A$$

$$\dfrac{y : (A \supset \perp) \supset \perp, x : A \rhd x : A | b : \perp, a : A}{y : (A \supset \perp) \supset \perp, x : A \mid\!\!\xrightarrow{\mathsf{pass}(a,A,x)} b : \perp, a : A}\ PASS$$

$$\dfrac{y : (A \supset \perp) \supset \perp, x : A \mid\!\!\xrightarrow{\mathsf{pass}(a,A,x)} b : \perp, a : A}{y : (A \supset \perp) \supset \perp, x : A \vdash \mu b^{\perp}.\mathsf{pass}(a, A, x) : \perp\ | a : A}\ ACT$$

$$\dfrac{y : (A \supset \perp) \supset \perp, x : A \vdash \mu b^{\perp}.\mathsf{pass}(a, A, x) : \perp\ | a : A}{y : (A \supset \perp) \supset \perp \vdash \lambda x^{A}.\mu b^{\perp}.\mathsf{pass}(a, A, x) : A \supset \perp\ | a : A}\ I_{\supset}$$

$$\dfrac{(*) \qquad y : (A \supset \perp) \supset \perp \vdash \lambda x^{A}.\mu b^{\perp}.\mathsf{pass}(a, A, x) : A \supset \perp\ | a : A}{y : (A \supset \perp) \supset \perp \rhd y(\lambda x^{A}.\mu b^{\perp}.\mathsf{pass}(a, A, x)) : \perp\ | a : A}\ E_{\supset}$$

$$\dfrac{y : (A \supset \perp) \supset \perp \rhd y(\lambda x^{A}.\mu b^{\perp}.\mathsf{pass}(a, A, x)) : \perp\ | a : A}{y : (A \supset \perp) \supset \perp \mid\!\!\xrightarrow{\mathsf{abort}(y(\lambda x^{A}.\mu b^{\perp}.\mathsf{pass}(a,A,x)))} a : A}\ E\perp$$

$$\dfrac{y : (A \supset \perp) \supset \perp \mid\!\!\xrightarrow{\mathsf{abort}(y(\lambda x^{A}.\mu b^{\perp}.\mathsf{pass}(a,A,x)))} a : A}{y : (A \supset \perp) \supset \perp \vdash \mu a^{A}.(\mathsf{abort}(y(\lambda x^{A}.\mu b^{\perp}.\mathsf{pass}(a, A, x)))) : A|}\ ACT$$

where $(*)$ is the proof: $\dfrac{}{y : (A \supset \perp) \supset \perp \rhd y : (A \supset \perp) \supset \perp\ | a : A}\ A$. □

Theorem 3 (Admissible rules of NKT). Consider the equations in Fig. 9. In NKT one has:

(1) For all A, M: if $\Gamma \vdash N : A|\Delta$ and $\Gamma, x : A \vdash M : B|\Delta$, then the equations define the proof term $[N/x]M$ and $\Gamma \vdash [N/x]M : B|\Delta$.
(2) For all A, S: if $\Gamma \vdash N : A|\Delta$ and $\Gamma, x : A \mid\!\!\xrightarrow{S} \Delta$, then the equations define the statement $[N/x]S$ and $\Gamma \mid\!\!\xrightarrow{[N/x]S} \Delta$.
(3) For all A, H: if $\Gamma \vdash N : A|\Delta$ and $\Gamma, x : A \rhd H : B|\Delta$, then the equations define the extended neutral term $[N/x]H$ and $\Gamma \blacktriangleright [N/x]H : B|\Delta$.
(4) For all $A, B, \mathbb{H}$: if $\Gamma \blacktriangleright \mathbb{H} : A \supset B|\Delta$ and $\Gamma \vdash N : A|\Delta$, then the equations define the extended neutral term $\mathbb{H}@N$ and $\Gamma \blacktriangleright \mathbb{H}@N : B|\Delta$.
(5) For all A, B, M: if $\Gamma \vdash M : A \supset B|\Delta$ and $\Gamma \vdash N : A|\Delta$, then the equations define the proof term $M@N$ and $\Gamma \vdash M@N : B|\Delta$.
(6) For all A, B, S: if $\Gamma \mid\!\!\xrightarrow{S} a : A \supset B, \Delta$ and $\Gamma \vdash N : A|\Delta$, then the equations define the statement $[@N/a]S$ and $\Gamma \mid\!\!\xrightarrow{[@N/a]S} a : B, \Delta$.
(7) For all A, B, H: if $\Gamma \rhd H : C|a : A \supset B, \Delta$ and $\Gamma \vdash N : A|\Delta$, then the equations define the neutral term $[@N/a]H$ and $\Gamma \rhd [@N/a]H : C|a : B, \Delta$.
(8) For all A, B, M: if $\Gamma \vdash M : C|a : A \supset B, \Delta$ and $\Gamma \vdash N : A|\Delta$, then the equations define the proof term $[@N/a]M$ and $\Gamma \vdash [@N/a]M : C|a : B, \Delta$.

In particular, the rules (1) to (8) in Fig. 10 are admissible in NKT.

A.4 Supplements for Section 5

Proposition 6 (Conservativity). . *(1) NKT derives $\Gamma \vdash M : A|\Delta$ iff NKT_{∂} derives $\epsilon \Vdash M : (\Gamma \vdash A|\Delta)$. (2) NKT derives $\Gamma \rhd H : A|\Delta$ iff NKT_{∂} derives $\epsilon \Vdash H : (\Gamma \rhd A|\Delta)$. (3) NKT derives $\Gamma \mid\!\!\xrightarrow{S} \Delta$ iff NKT_{∂} derives $\epsilon \Vdash S : (\Gamma \mid\!\!\xrightarrow{} \Delta)$.*

Proof. The "only if" statements are proved by simultaneous induction on the derivations of $\Gamma \vdash M : A|\Delta$, $\Gamma \rhd H : A|\Delta$ and $\Gamma \overset{S}{\vdash} \Delta$. The proof of the "if" statements is by simultaneous induction on the derivations of $\Xi \Vdash M : (\Gamma \vdash A|\Delta)$, $\Xi \Vdash H : (\Gamma \rhd A|\Delta)$ and $\Xi \Vdash S : (\Gamma \vdash \Delta)$. □

Proposition 7 (Record of search). . *(1) If $\Xi \Vdash M : \sigma$ then $\underline{\sigma} \twoheadrightarrow M$. (2) If $\Xi \Vdash S : \zeta$ then $\underline{\zeta} \twoheadrightarrow S$. (3) If $\Xi \Vdash H : (\Gamma \rhd A|\Delta)$ then $\underline{\Gamma \vdash \Delta} \twoheadrightarrow$* $\mathsf{ab}(H, \underline{(\Gamma \rhd A|\Delta)})$.

Proof. By simultaneous induction on the derivations of $\Xi \Vdash M : \sigma$, $\Xi \Vdash S : \zeta$ and $\Xi \Vdash H : (\Gamma \rhd A|\Delta)$. □

Proposition 8. (Subject reduction for NKT_∂).

1. *If $\Xi \Vdash M : \sigma$ and $M \to M'$, then there is Ξ' such that $\Xi \to \Xi'$ and $\Xi' \Vdash M' : \sigma$.*
2. *If $\Xi \Vdash S : \zeta$ and $S \to S'$, then there is Ξ' such that $\Xi \to \Xi'$ and $\Xi' \Vdash S' : \zeta$.*
3. *If $\Xi \Vdash H : \rho$ and $H \to H'$, then there is Ξ' such that $\Xi \to \Xi'$ and $\Xi' \Vdash H' : \rho$.*

Proof. By simultaneous induction on $M \to M'$, $H \to H'$ and $S \to S'$. □

A.5 Supplements for Section 6

Theorem 5 ($LKT_\partial \cong NKT_\partial$)**.**

1. $\Theta\Psi M = M$ and $\Psi\Theta t = t$.
2. $t \to t'$ in LKT_∂ iff $\Theta t \to \Theta t'$ in NKT_∂.
3. $M \to M'$ in NKT_∂ iff $\Psi M \to \Psi M'$ in LKT_∂.

Proof. The proof of item 1 is also an extension of the proof found in [6]. One proves $\Theta\Psi M = M$, $\Theta\Psi(H, l) = \Theta(H, l)$ and $\Theta\Psi S = S$ by simultaneous induction on M, H and S; and one proves $\Psi\Theta t = t$, $\Psi\Theta(H, l) = \Psi(H, l)$ and $\Psi\Theta c = c$ by simultaneous induction on t, l and c. Using item 1, one obtains the "if" statements of items 2 and 3 from the "only if" statements. It remains to prove the latter.

The "only if" statement of item 2 is proved together with: (1) if $l \to l'$ in LKT_∂ then $\Theta(H, l) \to \Theta(H, l')$ in NKT_∂, for all H; and (2) if $c \to c'$ in LKT_∂ then $\Theta c \to \Theta c'$ in NKT_∂. The proof is by simultaneous induction on $t \to t'$, $l \to l'$ and $c \to c'$. □

References

1. Andreoli, J.: Logic programming with focusing proofs in linear logic. J. Log. Comput. **2**(3), 297–347 (1992)
2. Ariola, Z.M., Herbelin, H.: Control reduction theories: the benefit of structural substitution. J. Funct. Program. **18**(3), 373–419 (2008)

3. Curien, P., Herbelin, H.: The duality of computation. In: Odersky, M., Wadler, P. (eds.) Proceedings of the Fifth ACM SIGPLAN International Conference on Functional Programming (ICFP 2000), Montreal, Canada, September 18-21, 2000, pp. 233–243. ACM (2000)
4. Danos, V., Joinet, J.B., Schellinx, H.: LKQ and LKT: sequent calculi for second order logic based upon dual decompositions of classical implication. In: Girard, J.Y. (ed.) Advances in Linear Logic, pp. 211–224. Cambridge University Press (1995)
5. Dunfield, J., Krishnaswami, N.: Bidirectional typing. ACM Comput. Surv. **54**(5), 98:1–98:38 (2022)
6. Dyckhoff, R., Pinto, L.: Cut-elimination and a permutation-free sequent calculus for intuitionistic logic. Stud. Logica. **60**(1), 107–118 (1998)
7. Espírito Santo, J.: Towards a canonical classical natural deduction system. Ann. Pure Appl. Log. **164**(6), 618–650 (2013)
8. Espírito Santo, J., Matthes, R., Pinto, L.: Decidability of several concepts of finiteness for simple types. Fundam. Inform. **170**(1–3), 111–138 (2019)
9. Espírito Santo, J., Matthes, R., Pinto, L.: Inhabitation in simply typed lambda-calculus through a lambda-calculus for proof search. Math. Struct. Comput. Sci. **29**(8), 1092–1124 (2019)
10. Espírito Santo, J., Matthes, R., Pinto, L.: A coinductive approach to proof search through typed lambda-calculi. Ann. Pure Appl. Logic **172**(10), 103026 (2021)
11. Geuvers, H., Jojgov, G.I.: Open proofs and open terms: a basis for interactive logic. In: Bradfield, J. (ed.) CSL 2002. LNCS, vol. 2471, pp. 537–552. Springer, Heidelberg (2002). https://doi.org/10.1007/3-540-45793-3_36
12. Herbelin, H.: A λ-calculus structure isomorphic to Gentzen-style sequent calculus structure. In: Pacholski, L., Tiuryn, J. (eds.) CSL 1994. LNCS, vol. 933, pp. 61–75. Springer, Heidelberg (1995). https://doi.org/10.1007/BFb0022247
13. Liang, C., Miller, D.: Focusing and polarization in linear, intuitionistic, and classical logic. Theor. Comput. Sci. **410**, 4747–4768 (2009)
14. Muñoz, C.A.: Dependent types and explicit substitutions: a meta-theoretical development. Math. Struct. Comput. Sci. **11**(1), 91–129 (2001)
15. Muñoz, C.A.: Proof-term synthesis on dependent-type systems via explicit substitutions. Theor. Comput. Sci. **266**(1–2), 407–440 (2001)
16. Nanevski, A., Pfenning, F., Pientka, B.: Contextual modal type theory. ACM Trans. Comput. Log. **9**(3), 23:1–23:49 (2008)
17. Olarte, C., Pimentel, E., Rocha, C.: A rewriting logic approach to specification, proof-search, and meta-proofs in sequent systems. J. Log. Algebraic Methods Program. **130**, 100827 (2023)
18. Parigot, M.: Lambda-mu-calculus: an algorithmic interpretation of classical natural deduction. In: Voronkov, A. (ed.) LPAR 1992. LNCS, vol. 624, pp. 190–201. Springer, Heidelberg (1992). https://doi.org/10.1007/BFb0013061
19. Espírito Santo, J., Sousa, A.C.: Partial proof terms in the study of idealized proof search. In: Kohlhase, A., Kovács, L. (eds.) Intelligent Computer Mathematics - 17th International Conference, CICM 2024, Montréal. LNCS, vol. 14960, pp. 279–297. Springer, Cham (2024). https://doi.org/10.1007/978-3-031-66997-2_16
20. Sieg, W., Byrnes, J.: Normal natural deduction proofs (in classical logic). Stud. Logica. **60**(1), 67–106 (1998)
21. Sieg, W., Cittadini, S.: Normal natural deduction proofs (in non-classical logics). In: Hutter, D., Stephan, W. (eds.) Mechanizing Mathematical Reasoning. LNCS (LNAI), vol. 2605, pp. 169–191. Springer, Heidelberg (2005). https://doi.org/10.1007/978-3-540-32254-2_11

A Significance-Based Account of *Ceteris paribus* Counterfactuals

Avgerinos Delkos[1] and Marianna Girlando[2(✉)]

[1] University of Birmingham, Birmingham, UK
[2] University of Amsterdam, Amsterdam, Netherlands
m.girlando@uva.nl

Abstract. When evaluating a counterfactual statement, it is often convenient to specify conditions that ought to be kept unchanged. Formally, this can be done by associating to each counterfactual a *ceteris paribus* set of formulas, specifying the facts that "ought to be kept unchanged". *Ceteris paribus* counterfactuals originate in the debate between D. Lewis and Fine in the 1970s, and have been captured in formal accounts. However, these accounts are merely based on 'counting' formulas, and can yield counterintuitive results. In this paper, we develop a novel approach to evaluate *ceteris paribus* counterfactuals at (weakly) centered sphere models, by taking into account the 'significance' of formulas that ought to be kept unchanged. Hypothetical states that keep the most significant formulas unchanged will be prioritized in the evaluation of a counterfactual. We show that the resulting notion of validity coincides with theoremhood in Lewis' conditional logics VC or VW.

Keywords: *Ceteris paribus* · Sphere semantics · Conditional logics

1 Introduction

Counterfactuals are sentences allowing to reason about hypothetical states of affairs. For instance: "If Nixon had pressed the button, there would have been a nuclear holocaust". We will use this counterfactual, due to Fine [3] and known as *Nixon counterexample* (*nc*), as our running example. Several classes of possible-world models have been introduced to interpret counterfactuals, among which *sphere models* and *preferential models* [1,9], both encoding notions of similarity between states. To evaluate a counterfactual $A > B$ at a world x, one checks whether B holds in states that satisfy A and which are most similar to x.

Ceteris paribus counterfactuals, with *ceteris paribus* (*cp* for short) meaning "all other things being equal", specify additional conditions to be taken into account when evaluating counterfactuals. *Cp*-counterfactuals were introduced by D. Lewis in [10] as an answer to Fine's critique of sphere models in [3]. Fine observed that, in relation to (*nc*) above, a world where a small miracle prevents the launch of the missile is more similar to the actual world than a world where a nuclear holocaust occurs. Hence, the counterfactual (*nc*) is counterintuitively

D. Kozen and R. de Queiroz (Eds.): WoLLIC 2025, LNCS 15942, pp. 309–325, 2026.
https://doi.org/10.1007/978-3-031-99536-1_19

evaluated as false: at the state closest to the actual world and at which Nixon pushes the button there is no nuclear holocaust (but a small miracle occurs). To obtain the correct evaluation, Lewis proposed to transform (nc) into a *cp*-counterfactual: "If Nixon had pressed the button, *and no miracle occurred*, there would have been a nuclear holocaust". While the similarity ordering among states is left intentionally vague in Lewis' account, the idea of specifying an appropriate context for the evaluation of counterfactuals has received widespread attention in the literature. Most notably, theories of *cp*-counterfactuals based on selection-function semantics were developed in [11,16], while in [14,15] a *cp*-preferential operator is introduced, an approach later formalised in [12][1].

Our contribution stems from the works of P. Girard and M.A. Triplett, who define in [4,5] an analysis of *cp*-counterfactuals within centered preferential models. They introduce a *cp*-counterfactual $[A, \Gamma]B$, to be understood as Lewis' counterfactual operator $A > B$ where the truth values of formulas in Γ ought to be kept unchanged when evaluating the counterfactual. The formula $[A, \Gamma]B$ can be evaluated at a world x by 'updating' the preorder relation of preferential models in three different ways. In their first proposal, which we call *strict evaluation*, only worlds which agree with x on all formulas in Γ are considered for the evaluation. This operation amounts to check satisfiability of $(A \wedge \bigwedge \Gamma) > B$ at x. However, several worlds might fail to satisfy $A \wedge \bigwedge \Gamma$, thus trivializing the result. This can be remedied by relaxing the strict evaluation into two 'prioritisations' [4,5]: *naïve counting* and *maximal supersets*, which ultimately rely on 'counting' the number of formulas in Γ satisfied by the worlds. However, it is easy to find examples of *cp*-counterfactuals whose evaluations under the aforementioned relaxed prioritisations yield counterintuitive results (Remark 4.6).

In this paper, we introduce the *disagreement update*, which takes into account a notion of 'significance' of formulas in Γ to re-arrange worlds in a system of spheres. Intuitively, worlds which 'agree the most' with the actual world over the most significant formulas in Γ will be moved 'closest' to the actual world, and will thus make a difference for the evaluation. Formally, we shall first associate to each formula a *weight*, measuring its implausiblity w.r.t. the actual state. This notion, generalised to sets of formulas, allows us to identify the significant formulas for the evaluation of a *cp*-counterfactual. The system of spheres is updated by taking the weight of specific sets of formulas into account. The counterfactual is then evaluated in the updated model. This fine-grained update, which does not solely rely on counting formulas, permits us to overcome the problems encountered when evaluating a *cp*-counterfactual with the prioritarisations from [4,5].

Our update gives rise to logics VW^{d} and VC^{d}, *cp*-versions of Lewis' logics VW and VC, and characterized by weakly centered and centered sphere models[2]. We show that validity in VW^{d} and VC^{d} coincides with validity in VW and VC.

---

[1] *Premise semantics* is another approach that also allows to formalise *cp*-reasoning, by establishing causal links between sentences. Refer, e.g., to [6–8].

[2] Our account is based on sphere models, as these allow for an intuitive definition of weights. However, our definitions can easily be adapted to preferential structures.

The paper is structured as follows. After introducing the semantics in Sect. 2, in Sect. 3 we define weight and significance. Section 4 presents the disagreement update and compares it with the prioritisations from [4,5]. Then, Sect. 5 proves soundness and completeness of our logics, while Sect. 6 concludes with some directions for future work.

2 Preliminaries

Given a countable list of propositional atoms $\mathsf{Atm} = \{p_0, p_1, p_2, \dots\}$, the formulas of the language $\mathcal{L}^{>}_{cp}$ are generated as follows: $A ::= p \mid \bot \mid A \to A \mid A >^{\Gamma} A$. We set $\neg A := A \to \bot$, and we can standardly define the other propositional connectives. For simplicity, we often write $\bar{p}$ instead of $\neg p$. A *literal* is a propositional atom p or its negation $\bar{p}$. We set $\bar{\bar{p}} = p$. The operator $>^{\Gamma}$ is the *cp*-counterfactual conditional, with Γ, the *cp*-set, being a finite set of literals of $\mathcal{L}^{>}_{cp}$[3]. We take Γ to be *paired*, that is: for any atom p, it holds that $p \in \Gamma$ iff $\bar{p} \in \Gamma$. A formula $A >^{\Gamma} B$ reads "If A had been the case, and all things in Γ were unchanged, then B would have been the case". When Γ is empty, $A >^{\Gamma} B$ corresponds to Lewis' counterfactual conditional, and we write it as $A > B$. We denote by $\mathcal{L}^{>}$ the language of Lewis' logics, obtained by setting $\Gamma = \varnothing$ in $\mathcal{L}^{>}_{cp}$.

By requiring *cp*-sets to be paired, we guarantee that both a literal and its negation are taken into account for the evaluation, following the intuition that, if p should be 'kept unchanged', the same should hold for $\bar{p}$. Moreover, since the worlds are classical, we have that a world always satisfies some literal in a given *cp*-set. We now introduce sphere models, from [9].

Definition 2.1. A *sphere model* $\mathcal{M} = \langle W, S, v \rangle$ is composed of a non-empty set of worlds W, a valuation function $v : \mathsf{Atm} \longrightarrow \mathcal{P}(W)$, and a sphere function $S : W \longrightarrow \mathcal{P}(\mathcal{P}(W))$ which associates to each world $x \in W$ a *system of spheres* $S(x)$. We denote by $\alpha, \beta, \dots$ the elements of $S(x)$, called *spheres*. S satisfies the properties of *non-emptiness*: For any $x \in W$, and for any $\alpha \in S(x)$, $\alpha \neq \varnothing$; and *nesting*: For any $x \in W$, $\alpha, \beta \in S(x)$, either $\alpha \subseteq \beta$ or $\beta \subseteq \alpha$. Then, a *weakly centered sphere model* is a sphere model satisfying *weak centering*: for any $x \in W$, for any $\alpha \in S(x)$, $x \in \alpha$. A *centered sphere model* is a sphere model satisfying *centering*, that is, for any $x \in W$, $\{x\} \in S(x)$[4].

Definition 2.2. The satisfaction relation of literals at a world x of $\mathcal{M}$ is defined as $\mathcal{M}, x \Vdash p$ *iff* $x \in v(p)$ and $\mathcal{M}, x \Vdash \bar{p}$ *iff* $x \notin v(p)$.

In this paper, we restrict our analysis to *finite* sphere models. We shall define the satisfaction of general formulas in (weakly) centered sphere models in Sect. 4, after introducing the elements needed to evaluate *cp*-counterfactuals.

---

[3] We could have easily allowed $\bot$-formulas, $\to$-formulas and $>^{\Delta}$-formulas with $\Delta = \varnothing$ in *cp*-sets. We chose not to do it, to simplify the definitions in Sects. 3 and 4.

[4] Due to nesting, at any centered sphere model it holds that for any $\alpha \in S(x)$, $\{x\} \subseteq \alpha$.

3 From Weight to Significance

To evaluate *cp*-counterfactuals, we shall refine the prioritisations from [4,5] by differentiating literals w.r.t. their significance. We consider literals for convenience; the notions we will introduce can be easily extended to compound formulas. To illustrate what we mean by 'significance', let h be a formula stating that a tossed coin lands on the heads side, and p be a formula expressing some law of physics. While satisfying or failing to satisfy h represents a small change in the state of the world, a world where p does not hold would be very different from a world where p is true. Consequently, when considering things that 'ought to remain unchanged' p is a much more relevant, or significant, formula than h.

We shall formalize this intuition by first associating to each literal a *weight*, measuring how (im)plausible the literal is in a system of spheres. We will then generalise this notion to sets of literals, and illustrate the role of significance in evaluating *cp*-counterfactuals. We use G, H as meta-variables for literals.

For this section, let us fix a (weakly) centered model $\mathcal{M} = \langle W, S, v\rangle$, some $x \in W$ and a system of spheres $S(x)$. Thanks to nesting and (weak) centering, $S(x)$ can be ordered w.r.t set inclusion: $S(x) = \{\alpha_0, \ldots, \alpha_n\}$ with $\alpha_i \subseteq \alpha_{i+1}$, for each $i < n$ and $x \in \alpha_0$. For S set, let $|S|$ denote the number of elements of S.

The weight of a literal G relative to $\mathcal{M}$ and x is defined by taking into account the number of worlds satisfying G and the position of such worlds in $S(x)$. The weight is meant to indicate how implausible a literal is w.r.t. the actual world: namely, a literal G satisfied by several worlds in a sphere is considered 'highly plausible', and will have a low weight, while a literal H satisfied by fewer worlds in the same sphere is considered 'less plausible' than G and will have higher weight. Moreover, the definition takes into account the position of the worlds within the spheres, with literals satisfied by worlds in inner spheres being 'more plausible' than those satisfied by worlds in outer spheres. Thus, the weight of a literal is defined by counting the worlds in each sphere satisfying it, starting from the innermost sphere. Formally:

Definition 3.1. For any literal $G \in \mathcal{L}_{cp}^{>}$, the *weight of* G *relative to* $\mathcal{M}$ *and* x, denoted by $\mathbf{w}_x(G)$, is the list of natural numbers $(w_0^G, .., w_n^G)$, where $w_0^G = |\{u \in \alpha_0 \mid u \Vdash A\}|$ and for $1 \leq i \leq n$:

- If $\alpha_i = \alpha_{i-1}$, then $w_i^G = w_{i-1}^G$;
- If $\alpha_i \supset \alpha_{i-1}$, then $w_i^G = |\{u \in \alpha_i \backslash \alpha_{i-1} \mid u \Vdash G\}|$.

We next introduce a relation $\trianglelefteq_x$ to compare literals according to their weights. Literals smaller w.r.t. $\trianglelefteq_x$ have lower weight, and are thus the 'more plausible' ones. The definition matches Lewis's intuition, according to which worlds in innermore spheres are 'smaller' w.r.t. the similarity preorder than worlds in outermore spheres.

Definition 3.2. Let $\mathbf{w}_x(G) = (w_0^G, .., w_n^G)$ and $\mathbf{w}_x(H) = (w_0^H, .., w_n^H)$, for some G, H literals and $n \geq 0$. We compare $\mathbf{w}_x(G)$ and $\mathbf{w}_x(H)$ inverse lexicographically, that is: for the first $l \leq n$ such that $w_l^G \neq w_l^H$, set $\mathbf{w}_x(H) \prec_{xel} \mathbf{w}_x(G)$ iff

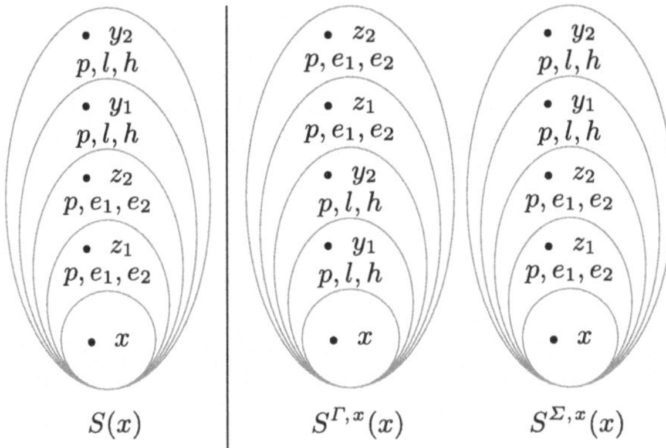

Fig. 1. Left: The atoms are interpreted as follows: p means Nixon presses the button, e_1 means Technical error 1 occurs, e_2 means Technical error 2 occurs, l means The launch is successful and h means There is a nuclear holocaust. The system of spheres $S(x)$ within $\mathcal{M} = \langle W, S, v\rangle$, for $W = \{x, z_1, z_2, y_1, y_2\}$, $S(z_i) = \{\{z_i\}\}$ and $S(y_i) = \{\{y_i\}\}$ for $i \in \{1, 2\}$, and $S(x) = \{\{x\}, \{x, z_1\}, \{x, z_1, z_2\}, \{x, z_1, z_2, y_1\}, \{x, z_1, z_2, y_1, y_2\}\}$. Moreover, $v(p) = \{z_1, z_2, y_1, y_2\}$; $v(e_1) = v(e_2) = \{z_1, z_2\}$; and $v(l) = v(h) = \{y_1, y_2\}$. **Right:** Updated systems of spheres $S^{\Gamma,x}(x)$ and $S^{\Sigma,x}(x)$. Refer to Definition 4.2 and Example 4.5.

$w_l^G < w_l^H$. We say that H *has less or equal weight than* G, in symbols $H \trianglelefteq_x$, iff $\mathbf{w}_x(H) \preceq_{xel} \mathbf{w}_x(G)$. We write $H =_x G$ iff $H \trianglelefteq_x G$ and $G \trianglelefteq_x H$.

In finite models, the weight of a literal will be one of $2^{|W|}$ possible distinct values (lists). Literals falsified by all worlds in $\bigcup S(x)$ have the highest weight (and are the most implausible ones), while literals satisfied by all worlds have the lowest weight (and are the most plausible). It is easy to see that the relation $\trianglelefteq_x$ induces a well ordering among literals. Moreover, in centered models, $\mathbf{w}_x(G) \neq \mathbf{w}_x(\bar{G})$, for any literal G. The following shows that the weights of a literal and its negation behave 'dually'. The proof is in Appendix A.1.

Proposition 3.3. *For G, H literals, if $H \trianglelefteq_x G$ then $\bar{G} \trianglelefteq_x \bar{H}$.*

Example 3.4. Consider the centered model $\mathcal{M}$ to the left of Fig. 1, representing a variation of Nixon's counterexample. Propositions e_1 and e_2 represent two minor technical errors, which prevent the missile from launching. Since these are small changes w.r.t. the actual world when compared to a nuclear holocaust, worlds satisfying e_1 and e_2 are closer to x than worlds satisfying h in $S(x)$.

The two errors, even when considered together, represent a less significant change than the miracle from Fine's example (nc). Considering *two* very small changes is a problem for approaches that evaluate *cp*-counterfactuals by 'counting' the number of formulas which worlds (fail to) satisfy. As we will argue in Example 4.5 and Remark 4.6, our approach can handle such cases.

The weights of literals are calculated as follows: $\mathbf{w}_x(p) = (0,1,1,1,1)$; $\mathbf{w}_x(\bar{p}) = (1,0,0,0,0)$; $\mathbf{w}_x(e_1) = \mathbf{w}_x(e_2) = (0,1,1,0,0)$; $\mathbf{w}_x(l) = \mathbf{w}_x(h) = (0,0,0,1,1)$; $\mathbf{w}_x(\bar{l}) = (1,1,1,0,0) = \mathbf{w}_x(\bar{h})$. Comparing the weights according to Definition 3.2 yields: $\bar{h} =_x \bar{l} \blacktriangleleft_x \bar{e}_1 =_x \bar{e}_2 \blacktriangleleft_x \bar{p} \blacktriangleleft_x p \blacktriangleleft_x e_1 =_x e_2 \blacktriangleleft_x h =_x l$.

Next, we define weights of sets of literals. This amounts to calculating the weights of all the literals in the set, and ordering them from higher to lower (left to right). The resulting lists are compared lexicographically. Formally:

Definition 3.5. For a set of literals $\Gamma = \{G_1, .., G_m\}$, the *weight of Γ relative to $\mathcal{M}$ and x*, written $\mathbf{w}_x(\Gamma)$, is the list of weights of literals $(w_1, .., w_m)$ where, for $i < m$ and $j, k \leq m$, we set $w_i = \mathbf{w}_x(G_j)$ and $w_{i+1} = \mathbf{w}_x(G_k)$ if and only if $G_k \trianglelefteq_x G_j$. We set $\mathbf{w}_x(\varnothing) = (0)$.

Definition 3.6. For Γ, Δ sets of literals, let $\mathbf{w}_x(\Gamma) = \{c_1, .., c_m\}$ and $\mathbf{w}_x(\Delta) = \{d_1, .., d_k\}$, for some $m, k \geq 0$. We compare $\mathbf{w}_x(\Gamma)$ and $\mathbf{w}_x(\Delta)$ lexicographically, that is: for the first $l \leq \min\{m, k\}$ such that $c_l \neq d_l$, set $\mathbf{w}_x(\Gamma) \prec_{lex} \mathbf{w}_x(\Delta)$ if and only if $c_l \trianglelefteq_x d_l$. If, for all $l \leq min\{m, k\}$ it holds that $d_l = c_l$, we set $\mathbf{w}_x(\Gamma) \preceq_{lex} \mathbf{w}_x(\Delta)$ if and only if $m \leq k$. We say that Γ *has less or equal weight than Δ relative to $\mathcal{M}, x$*, in symbols $\Gamma \trianglelefteq_x \Delta$, iff $\mathbf{w}_x(\Gamma) \preceq_{lex} \mathbf{w}_x(\Delta)$. We write $\Gamma =_x \Delta$ whenever $\Gamma \trianglelefteq_x \Delta$ and $\Delta \trianglelefteq_x \Gamma$.

The next result, whose proof is in Appendix A.1, shows that the subset relation is monotone over weights.

Proposition 3.7. *For Γ, Δ sets of literals with $\Gamma \subseteq \Delta$, it holds that $\Gamma \trianglelefteq_x \Delta$.*

When evaluating *cp*-counterfactuals, we will calculate the weights of specific sets of literals - namely, the literals in a *cp*-set that are different between the actual world and other possible worlds. Proposition 3.3 naturally induces a spectrum of weights of literals, from low (low implausibility) to high (high implausibility). If a literal G is placed at the low end of the spectrum, its negation $\bar{G}$ is dually placed at the high end. Those pairs (literals and their negations) which find themselves closer to the ends of this spectrum are precisely the ones which will be crucial for the evaluation. To evaluate a *cp*-counterfactual, we will 're-arrange' the worlds in a system of spheres, according to the (im)plausibility of the literals in the *cp*-set that the worlds (fail to) satisfy. Thus, the 'significant' pairs of literals for the evaluation will be those that have very low and very high implausibility, as worlds satisfying or failing to satisfy them will 'move' very close to or very far from the actual world in the updated system of spheres.

Formally, we say that a literal G is *at least as significant* as a literal H iff $\{G, \bar{G}\} \trianglelefteq_x \{H, \bar{H}\}$. In Example 3.4, it holds that $\{e_1, \bar{e_1}\} \trianglelefteq_x \{h, \bar{h}\}$, as $\max\{\mathbf{w}_x(e_1), \mathbf{w}_x(\bar{e}_1)\} = e_1 \blacktriangleleft_x h = \max\{\mathbf{w}_x(h), \mathbf{w}_x(\bar{h})\}$. Similarly, $\{e_2, \bar{e}_2\} \trianglelefteq_x \{h, \bar{h}\}$, whence h is more significant than e_1 and e_2. Also, since $\mathbf{w}_x(l) = \mathbf{w}_x(h)$, we conclude that l is more significant than e_1 and e_2.

4 Evaluating *cp*-counterfactuals

In this section we discuss how to evaluate a *cp*-counterfactual $A >^{\Gamma} B$ at a world x of a (weakly) centered sphere model $\mathcal{M}$. We shall first 're-arrange', or 'update', the system of spheres $S(x)$ by calculating, for each world y, the weight of the *disagreement set* between x and y, that is, the set of literals in Γ which are satisfied at x but not at y. Intuitively, the worlds whose disagreement sets have low weights are the 'most plausible', as they differ less from the actual world x. We define the updated system of spheres $S^{\Gamma,x}(x)$ by accordingly placing such worlds in the innermost spheres. The Lewis counterfactual $A > B$ is then evaluated at the system of spheres $S^{\Gamma,x}(x)$. We start by defining disagreement sets and the corresponding disagreement update at (weakly) centered sphere models.

Definition 4.1. For $\mathcal{M} = \langle W, S, v\rangle$, $x, y \in W$ and Γ *cp*-set of literals, the *disagreement set of y w.r.t. Γ and x* is $\mathsf{D}(x,y)^{\Gamma} = \{G \in \Gamma \mid x \Vdash G \textit{ iff } y \nVdash G\}$.

Definition 4.2. Given a (weakly) centered model $\mathcal{M} = \langle W, S, v\rangle$, $x \in W$ and a *cp*-set Γ, the *disagreement update of $\mathcal{M}$ at x and Γ*, denoted $\mathcal{M}^{\Gamma,x} = \langle W^{\Gamma,x}, S^{\Gamma,x}, v^{\Gamma,x}\rangle$, is defined by setting $W^{\Gamma,x} = W$ and $v^{\Gamma,x} = v$. To define $S^{\Gamma,x}$, we first define the spheres of $S^{\Gamma,x}(x)$. For $n \in \{\mathbf{w}_x(\mathsf{D}(x,y)^{\Gamma}) \mid y \in \bigcup S(x)\}$, let $\sigma_n = \{y \in \bigcup S(x) \mid \mathbf{w}_x(\mathsf{D}(x,y)^{\Gamma}) \preceq_{lex} n\}$. Then, for each n and for each $|\bigcup S(x)| > i \geq 0$, we inductively define 'subspheres' σ_{n_i} of σ_n:

$$\sigma_{n_0} = \sigma_{n-1} \cup \{y \in (\sigma_n \backslash \sigma_{n-1}) \mid \text{for all } z \in (\sigma_n \backslash \sigma_{n-1}), \alpha \in S(x), \text{ if } z \in \alpha \text{ then } y \in \alpha\}$$
$$\sigma_{n_{i+1}} = \sigma_{n_i} \cup \{y \in (\sigma_n \backslash \sigma_{n_i}) \mid \text{for all } z \in (\sigma_n \backslash \sigma_{n_i}), \alpha \in S(x), \text{ if } z \in \alpha \text{ then } y \in \alpha\}$$

Finally, set $S^{\Gamma,x}(x) = \{\sigma_{n_i}\}_{n,i}$ and for all $y \neq x$, $S^{\Gamma,x}(y) = S(y)$.

From the definition it follows that, for every i, $\sigma_{n-1} \subseteq \sigma_{n_i} \subseteq \sigma_n$. Moreover, since $\mathcal{M}$ is finite, $\sigma_{n_j} = \sigma_n$, for some $j \leq |\bigcup S(x)|$. Intuitively, for any n weight of some disagreement sets of worlds in $S(x)$, the sphere σ_n contains exactly all worlds whose disagreement set w.r.t Γ and x has weight at most n (according to $\trianglelefteq_x$ or, equivalently, to $\preceq_{lex}$). The subspheres σ_{n_i} are then needed to 'distinguish' between worlds y_1, y_2 whose disagreement sets have the same wights, but which are placed within different spheres in $S(x)$. In this case, we want y_1 and y_2 to be placed in distinct spheres in $S^{\Gamma,x}(x)$, whence the introduction of the subspheres. Next, we show that the models obtained through the updates are sphere models (the proof is in the Appendix A.2).

Lemma 4.3. *Given $\mathcal{M}$, x and Γ, $\mathcal{M}^{\Gamma,x}$ satisfies non-emptiness and nesting. Moreover, if $\mathcal{M}$ is (weakly) centered then $\mathcal{M}^{\Gamma,x}$ is (weakly) centered.*

We now define satisfaction of formulas. We use the following shorthands: $\alpha \Vdash^{\exists} A$ *iff* there is $y \in \alpha$ s.t. $y \Vdash A$, and $\alpha \Vdash^{\forall} A$ *iff* for all $y \in \alpha, y \Vdash A$.

Definition 4.4. The satisfaction relation of formulas $A \in \mathcal{L}_{cp}^{>}$ at a world x of a model $\mathcal{M}$ is defined by adding to the clauses in Definition 2.2 the following:

- $\mathcal{M}, x \not\Vdash \bot$;
- $\mathcal{M}, x \Vdash A \to B$ *iff* $\mathcal{M}, x \not\Vdash A$ or $\mathcal{M}, x \Vdash B$;
- $\mathcal{M}, x \Vdash A > B$ *iff* there is $\alpha \in S(x)$ such that $\alpha \Vdash^{\exists} A$, then there is $\beta \in S(x)$ such that $\beta \Vdash^{\exists} A$ and $\beta \Vdash^{\forall} A \to B$;
- $\mathcal{M}, x \Vdash A >^{\Gamma} B$ *iff* $\mathcal{M}^{\Gamma,x}, x \Vdash A > B$.

We say that A is *valid in weakly centered* (resp. *centered*) *models under the disagreement update*, in symbols $\models^{\mathsf{VW^d}} A$ (resp. $\models^{\mathsf{VC^d}} A$), iff $\mathcal{M}, x \Vdash A$ holds for all worlds x and all weakly centered (resp. centered) models $\mathcal{M}$.

The clause for $>$ above corresponds to the truth condition for Lewis counterfactual. Thus, when restricted to formulas in $\mathcal{L}^{>}$, validity in (weakly) centered sphere models under the disagreement update coincides with validity in (weakly) centered sphere models. Formally, for $A \in \mathcal{L}^{>}$, we say that A is *valid in weakly centered* (resp. *centered*) *sphere models*, denoted by $\models^{\mathsf{VW}} A$ (resp. $\models^{\mathsf{VC}} A$) *iff* $\mathcal{M}, x \Vdash A$ holds for all worlds x and all weakly centered (resp. centered) models $\mathcal{M}$. These sets of validities identify Lewis' logics VW and VC respectively.

The sets of formulas valid under the disagreement update at (weakly) centered sphere models in turn give rise to two logics, which we denote by $\mathsf{VW^d}$ and $\mathsf{VC^d}$. We have just observed that, for $A \in \mathcal{L}^{>}$, $\models^{\mathsf{VW}} A$ *iff* $\models^{\mathsf{VW^d}} A$ and $\models^{\mathsf{VC}} A$ *iff* $\models^{\mathsf{VC^d}} A$. In the next section, we shall prove that similar statements hold for formulas of $\mathcal{L}^{>}_{cp}$, thus establishing soundness and completeness of $\mathsf{VW^d}$ and $\mathsf{VC^d}$ w.r.t. Lewis' logics VW and VC respectively. We conclude this section by illustrating with an example the satisfiability under the disagreement update, and comparing our updates with the prioritarisations from the literature.

Example 4.5. Recall the model $\mathcal{M}$ from Example 3.4. Since worlds satisfying e_1 and e_2 are closer to x than worlds satisfying h, the counterfactual from Nixon's counterxample $p > h$ is evaluated as false at $S(x)$, that is: $\mathcal{M}, x \not\Vdash p > h$. Let us now consider the *cp*-sets $\Gamma = \{e_1, e_2, \bar{e}_1, \bar{e}_2\}$, $\Sigma = \Gamma \cup \{l, \bar{l}\}$ and the *cp*-counterfactuals $p >^{\Gamma} h$ and $p >^{\Sigma} h$. They respectively express "If Nixon had pressed the button, and no technical errors occurred, there would have been a nuclear holocaust" and "If Nixon had pressed the button, no technical errors occurred, but the launch was not successful, there would have been a nuclear holocaust." Intuitively, the first sentence should be evaluated as true, and the second as false. We evaluate the *cp*-counterfactuals in our framework.

Continuing from Example 3.4, we need to consider the disagreement sets of each world w.r.t. x, and compare their weights (Definition 3.6), considering Γ and Σ respectively. The disagreements sets are: $\mathsf{D}(x,x)^{\Gamma} = \mathsf{D}(x,y_1)^{\Gamma} = \mathsf{D}(x,y_2)^{\Gamma} = \varnothing$; $\mathsf{D}(x,z_1)^{\Gamma} = \mathsf{D}(x,z_2)^{\Gamma} = \Gamma$ and $\mathsf{D}(x,y_1)^{\Sigma} = \mathsf{D}(x,y_2)^{\Sigma} = \{l, \bar{l}\}$; and $\mathsf{D}(x,z_1)^{\Sigma} = \mathsf{D}(x,z_2)^{\Sigma} = \Gamma$. Comparison of their weights yields: $\varnothing =_x \mathsf{D}(x,x)^{\Gamma} =_x \mathsf{D}(x,y_1)^{\Gamma} =_x \mathsf{D}(x,y_2)^{\Gamma} \lhd_x \mathsf{D}(x,z_1)^{\Gamma} =_x \mathsf{D}(x,z_2)^{\Gamma} =_x \Gamma$ and $\Gamma =_x \mathsf{D}(x,z_1)^{\Sigma} =_x \mathsf{D}(x,z_2)^{\Sigma} \lhd_x \mathsf{D}(x,y_1)^{\Sigma} =_x \mathsf{D}(x,y_2)^{\Sigma} =_x \{l, \bar{l}\}$. The two updated systems of spheres $S^{\Gamma,x}(x)$ and $S^{\Sigma,x}(x)$ are displayed on the right of Fig. 1. It holds that $\mathcal{M}^{\Gamma,x}, x \Vdash p > h$, and $\mathcal{M}^{\Sigma,x}, x \not\Vdash p > h$. The disagreement update yields the intuitively correct result on both formulas (also refer to Fig. 2).

Observe that for $p >^{\Sigma} h$ the updated system of spheres $S^{\Sigma,x}(x)$ 'ranks' the worlds according to the significance of the literals in Σ they satisfy. Thus, worlds y_1, y_2 are placed in the outermost spheres, as they 'disagree' with x on l, the most significant literals in Σ.

cp-counterfactual	strict evaluation	naïve counting	maximal superset	disagreement update
$p >^{\Gamma} h$	✓	✓	✓	✓
$p >^{\Sigma} h$	✓	✓	×	×
$p >^{\Gamma} \bar{h}$	×	×	×	×
$p >^{\Sigma} \bar{h}$	✓	×	×	✓

Fig. 2. Results of evaluating *cp*-counterfactuals at world x of the model from Example 3.4. Symbol ✓ means that the formula is satisfiable at x, and × that it is not. Strict evaluation, naïve counting and maximal superset are from [4,5] (strict evaluation is called *ceteris paribus* there), while disagreement update is our proposed evaluation.

Remark 4.6 (Comparison with [4,5]*).* We now consider the prioritisations *naïve counting* and *maximal supersets* defined by Girard and Triplett in [4,5]. These prioritarizations operate on preferential centered models, and detail how to 're-arrange' the preorder relation to evaluate formulas. Both notions rely on *agreement sets*, defined in [4] as $A^{\mathcal{M}}_{\Gamma}(x, y) = \{G \in \Gamma \mid x \Vdash G \text{ iff } y \Vdash G\}$. Naïve counting simply counts the number of formulas two worlds z, x agree on. Thus, a world y is 'closer' to x than z if $|A^{\mathcal{M}}_{\Gamma}(x, y)| \geq |A^{\mathcal{M}}_{\Gamma}(x, z)|$. Under maximal supersets, a world y is 'closer' to x than z if $A^{\mathcal{M}}_{\Gamma}(x, z) \subseteq A^{\mathcal{M}}_{\Gamma}(x, y)$. Our disagreement sets (Definition 4.1) are dual to the agreement sets, and the definitions in [4,5] can be easily adapted to sphere models. Unlike naïve counting and maximal supersets, our disagreement update differentiates formulas in *cp*-sets by taking into account their significance or, equivalently, by considering their weights. Instead, the prioritarisations of Girard and Triplett are based on 'counting' the number of formulas in specific sets. This can lead to counterintuitive evaluations of quite simple formulas. In Fig. 2 we report the results of evaluating *cp*-formulas in the centered model $\mathcal{M}$ from Example 3.4. While the maximal supersets evaluation gives the intuitively correct evaluation of the formulas considered in Example 4.5, none of the evaluations from [4] yields the intuitively correct result over formulas $p >^{\Gamma} \bar{h}$ and $p >^{\Sigma} \bar{h}$, which our disagreement update evaluates correctly as satisfiable and not satisfiable at $\mathcal{M}, x$.

Moreover, the *cp*-counterfactual under the strict evaluation of [4] is not *dynamic* (in the sense of Dynamic Epistemic Logic, refer, e.g., to [13]). The strict evaluation performs a 'one-step' update of the model. If the formula contains other *cp*-modalities, these are *not* taken into account. Girard and Triplett do not discuss whether naïve counting and maximal supersets allow for iterated updates. Our disagreement update allows to evaluate formulas $A >^{\Gamma} B$ where A and B are allowed to contain (possibly nested) *cp*-modalities.

5 Soundness and Completeness

We now turn to proving soundness and completeness of VW^{d} and VC^{d} with respect to the Lewis' logics VW and VC respectively. For this section, set $\mathsf{L} \in \{\mathsf{W}, \mathsf{C}\}$. We shall write VL (resp. VL^{d}) to denote VW or VC (resp. VW^{d} and VC^{d}).

Let us first illustrate our proof strategy. For convenience, we shall consider a language $\mathcal{L}_{cp}^{\preccurlyeq}$ having as primitive a different *cp*-operator: $\preccurlyeq^{\Gamma}$, the *ceteris paribus* version of the *comparative plausibility* operator $\preccurlyeq$, introduced by Lewis in [9]. We denote by $\mathcal{L}^{\preccurlyeq}$ the language featuring only the $\preccurlyeq$ operator (without *cp*-sets). The comparative plausibility and the conditional operator are interdefinable, and it is easy to show that the same holds for their *cp*-versions. Then, we shall prove that for any $A \in \mathcal{L}_{cp}^{\preccurlyeq}$, it holds that $\models^{\mathsf{VL}} \hat{A}$ iff $\models^{\mathsf{VL}^{\mathsf{d}}} A$, where $\hat{A} \in \mathcal{L}^{\preccurlyeq}$ is a formula equisatisfiable with A but having empty *cp*-sets.

Constructing formula $\hat{A}$ is far from trivial, but it allows us to relate the *cp*-counterfactual evaluated in the disagreement update with Lewis' counterfactuals. The construction is based on ideas from [5], adapted to the disagreement update. Soundness and completeness of VL^{d} w.r.t. VL then follow immediately. We choose the (*cp*-)comparative plausibility as our primitive operators because their truth conditions are simpler than the ones for the (*cp*-)counterfactual, and thus simplify the construction.

We start by defining the languages $\mathcal{L}_{cp}^{\preccurlyeq}$ and $\mathcal{L}^{\preccurlyeq}$. The formulas of $\mathcal{L}_{cp}^{\preccurlyeq}$ are generated from a countable set of propositional atoms Atm, by means of the grammar $A{::=}p \mid \bot \mid A \rightarrow A \mid A \preccurlyeq^{\Gamma} A$, where $p \in \mathsf{Atm}$ and Γ *cp*-set of literals of $\mathcal{L}_{cp}^{\preccurlyeq}$ (so Γ is finite and paired). As before, we write $A \preccurlyeq B$ for $A \preccurlyeq^{\varnothing} B$. We denote by $\mathcal{L}^{\preccurlyeq}$ the language generated by the above grammar with the restriction that $\Gamma = \varnothing$. The operator $A \preccurlyeq B$ is read as "A is at least as plausible as B", and $A \preccurlyeq^{\Gamma} B$ is its *cp*-version: "All things in Γ being equal, A is at least as plausible as B". Moreover, following Lewis, we define $\Diamond A{:=}\neg(\bot \preccurlyeq A)$.

Given a (weakly) centered model $\mathcal{M}$, a world x and a *cp*-set Γ, the disagreement update of $\mathcal{M}$ is defined as in Definition 4.1. Then, satisfiability of a formula $A \preccurlyeq^{\Gamma} B$ at a world of a (weakly) centered model is defined as follows:

- $\mathcal{M}, x \Vdash A \preccurlyeq B$ *iff* for all $\alpha \in S(x)$, if $\alpha \Vdash^{\exists} B$, then $\alpha \Vdash^{\exists} A$;
- $\mathcal{M}, x \Vdash A \preccurlyeq^{\Gamma} B$ *iff* $\mathcal{M}^{\Gamma,x}, x \Vdash A \preccurlyeq B$.

Again, the clause for $\preccurlyeq$ corresponds to Lewis' satisfiability condition for the comparative plausibility at nested sphere models [9]. Lewis showed that the comparative plausibility and the counterfactual are interdefinable, and this result easily extends to our framework. We omit the proof, which is routine from [9].

Lemma 5.1. *For $\mathcal{M}$ (weakly) centered sphere model and x world, it holds that:*

1. *For $A, B \in \mathcal{L}_{cp}^{>}$, $\mathcal{M}, x \Vdash A >^{\Gamma} B$ iff $\mathcal{M}, x \Vdash (\bot \preccurlyeq^{\Gamma} A) \vee \neg((A \wedge \neg B) \preccurlyeq^{\Gamma} (A \wedge B))$*
2. *For $A, B \in \mathcal{L}_{cp}^{\preccurlyeq}$, $\mathcal{M}, x \Vdash A \preccurlyeq^{\Gamma} B$ iff $\mathcal{M}, x \Vdash ((A \vee B) >^{\Gamma} \bot) \vee ((A \vee B) >^{\Gamma} \neg A)$*

In light of Lemma 5.1, with an abuse of notation we say that, for $A \in \mathcal{L}_{cp}^{>}$, A is *valid in weakly centered* (resp. *centered*) *models models under the disagreement update*, in symbols $\models^{\mathsf{VW}^{\mathsf{d}}} A$ (resp. $\models^{\mathsf{VC}^{\mathsf{d}}} A$), iff $\mathcal{M}, x \Vdash A$ holds for all worlds x and all weakly centered (resp. centered) models $\mathcal{M}$. Similarly, for $A \in \mathcal{L}^{\preccurlyeq}$, we write $\models^{\mathsf{VW}} A$ and $\models^{\mathsf{VC}} A$ to denote validity in Lewis' logics VW and VC respectively. The following immediately holds, since satisfaction of $A \in \mathcal{L}^{\preccurlyeq}$ within VL and VL^{d} remains unchanged, as no updates are performed in VL^{d}.

Fact 5.2. For $A \in \mathcal{L}^{\preccurlyeq}$, it holds that $\models^{\mathsf{VL}} A$ iff $\models^{\mathsf{VL}^{\mathsf{d}}} A$.

Next, we investigate the relation of *cp*-comparative plausibility formulas with their correspondents in Lewis' language $\mathcal{L}^{\preccurlyeq}$, aiming at translating $\mathcal{L}^{\preccurlyeq}_{cp}$ formulas into equisatisfiable $\mathcal{L}^{\preccurlyeq}$ formulas. The construction depends on the model chosen to evaluate $\mathcal{L}^{\preccurlyeq}_{cp}$-formulas. Lemma 5.4 shows how to 'eliminate' the $\preccurlyeq^{\Gamma}$ operator from a formula $A \preccurlyeq^{\Gamma} B$ of $\mathcal{L}^{\preccurlyeq}_{cp}$; then, by recursively iterating the construction, Proposition 5.5 effectively translates every $\mathcal{L}^{\preccurlyeq}_{cp}$-formula into a $\mathcal{L}^{\preccurlyeq}$-formula.

Definition 5.3. For any model $\mathcal{M}$, world x and Γ *cp*-set of formulas, the *forcing set of* Γ, x is defined as $[\![x]\!]_{\Gamma} = \{G \in \Gamma \mid x \Vdash G\}$ and its complement as $[\![x]\!]^{c}_{\Gamma} = \{G \in \Gamma \mid x \nVdash G\}$. Moreover, let the *set of paired subsets of* Γ be $\mathsf{Pr}(\Gamma) = \{\lambda \subseteq \Gamma \mid \lambda \text{ is paired}\}$.

For $A \in \mathcal{L}^{\preccurlyeq}_{cp}$, let $cp^{\preccurlyeq}(A)$ denote the number of *cp*-connectives with non-empty *cp*-sets occurring in A. If $A \in \mathcal{L}^{\preccurlyeq}_{cp}$ and $cp^{\preccurlyeq}(A) = 0$, then $A \in \mathcal{L}^{\preccurlyeq}$. The proof of the following Lemma can be found in Appendix A.3.

Lemma 5.4. *Take* $F = A \preccurlyeq^{\Gamma} B \in \mathcal{L}^{\preccurlyeq}_{cp}$, *with* $\Gamma \neq \varnothing$. *For* $\mathcal{M}$ *(weakly) centered model and world* x, $\mathcal{M}, x \Vdash F$ *iff* $\mathcal{M}, x \Vdash \hat{F}$, *where* $\hat{F}$ *is the formula:*

$$\hat{F} = \bigwedge_{\lambda \in \mathsf{Pr}(\Gamma)} \Bigg[^{1} \Bigg(^{2} \bigwedge_{\mathsf{Pr}(\Gamma) \ni \lambda' \lhd_x \lambda} \neg \Diamond \big(A \wedge \bigwedge [\![x]\!]_{\Gamma \setminus \lambda'}\big) \Bigg)^{2} \rightarrow \\ \rightarrow \Bigg(^{3} \Big(\bigvee_{\mathsf{Pr}(\Gamma) \ni \lambda'' \unlhd_x \lambda} \big(A \wedge \bigwedge [\![x]\!]_{\Gamma \setminus \lambda''}\big)\Big) \preccurlyeq \big(B \wedge \bigwedge [\![x]\!]_{\Gamma \setminus \lambda}\big) \Bigg)^{3} \Bigg]^{1}. \tag{1}$$

Intuitively, if $cp^{\preccurlyeq}(A) = cp^{\preccurlyeq}(B) = 0$, we set $\hat{F} \in \mathcal{L}^{\preccurlyeq}$; else, $\hat{F} \in \mathcal{L}^{\preccurlyeq}_{cp}$. Due to Definition 4.4, the statement is well defined. Formula $\hat{F}$ 'describes' the updated sphere model using formulas in $\mathcal{L}^{\preccurlyeq}$. The paired sets $\lambda \in \mathsf{Pr}(\Gamma)$ represent the disagreement sets between worlds in $\bigcup S(x)$ and the actual world x. Thus, each λ can be thought of as representing a degree of disagreement w.r.t. the actual world. We can say that, e.g., $\mathsf{D}(x,u)^{\Gamma} \unlhd_x \lambda$, for some $u \in \bigcup S(x)$. Informally, whenever this happens we will say that "u disagrees from x less or equal to λ". For some $z \in \bigcup S$ and $\lambda' \in \mathsf{Pr}(\Gamma)$, $z \Vdash \bigwedge [\![x]\!]_{\Gamma \setminus \lambda'}$ means that z satisfies all the formulas in $\Gamma \setminus \lambda'$ which are also satisfied in x. Consequently, the set of formulas z and x disagree upon is a subset of λ', from which we obtain $\mathsf{D}(x,z)^{\Gamma} \unlhd_x \lambda'$. Considering worlds that satisfy (conjunction of) formulas within $\Gamma \setminus \lambda'$ which x satisfies then corresponds to selecting a world which disagrees from x less or equal to λ'. Then, $\hat{F}$ is a conjunction of formulas, one for each $\lambda \in \mathsf{Pr}(\Gamma)$. Let us fix an arbitrary such λ, corresponding to the disagreement set $\mathsf{D}(x,u)^{\Gamma}$ of some world $u \in \bigcup S(x)$. The formula within parentheses 2 in (5.4) above states that for any choice of $\lambda' \in \mathsf{Pr}(\Gamma)$ such that $\lambda' \lhd_x \lambda$, there is no world that disagrees less or equal to λ' with x and that satisfies A. The formula in parenthesis 3 says that if there is a world $v \in \alpha \in S(x)$ that disagrees less or equal to λ with x and that satisfies B, then there exists a world $y \in \alpha$ which disagrees less or equal to λ with x and that satisfies A. This is exactly the truth condition for $\preccurlyeq$-formulas. Then, for each choice of λ, either there is a world u' which satisfies A and such that $\mathsf{D}(x,u')^{\Gamma} \unlhd_x \mathsf{D}(x,u)^{\Gamma}$, thus making the formula in parenthesis 2 false or, if no such u' exists, then the formula in 3 needs to be satisfied.

Next, we generalize Lemma 5.4 to arbitrary formulas of $\mathcal{L}_{cp}^{\preccurlyeq}$ and conclude with soundness and completeness results. Both proofs are in Appendix A.3.

Proposition 5.5. *For $A \in \mathcal{L}_{cp}^{\preccurlyeq}$, $\mathcal{M}$ (weakly) centered sphere model and x world, there is $\hat{A} \in \mathcal{L}^{\preccurlyeq}$ such that $\mathcal{M}, x \Vdash A$ iff $\mathcal{M}, x \Vdash \hat{A}$.*

Theorem 5.6. *For $A \in \mathcal{L}_{cp}^{>}$, there is $\hat{A} \in \mathcal{L}^{\preccurlyeq}$ such that $\models^{\mathsf{VL}^{\mathsf{d}}} A$ iff $\models^{\mathsf{VL}} \hat{A}$.*

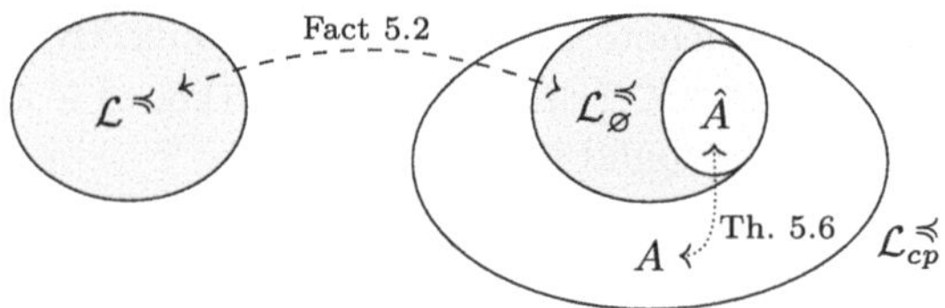

Fig. 3. Relationship between sets of valid formulas. $\mathcal{L}^{\preccurlyeq}$ (resp. $\mathcal{L}_{cp}^{\preccurlyeq}$) is the set of formulas of $\mathcal{L}^{\preccurlyeq}$ (resp. $\mathcal{L}_{cp}^{\preccurlyeq}$) valid at (weakly) centered sphere models. $\mathcal{L}_{\varnothing}^{\preccurlyeq}$ is the subset of valid $\mathcal{L}_{cp}^{\preccurlyeq}$-formulas having empty *cp*-sets, coinciding with the set of $\mathcal{L}^{\preccurlyeq}$-valid formulas (Fact 5.2). Formulas $A \in \mathcal{L}_{cp}^{\preccurlyeq} \setminus \mathcal{L}_{\varnothing}^{\preccurlyeq}$ are s.t. $cp^{\preccurlyeq}(A) > 0$. By Theorem 5.6 valid $\mathcal{L}_{cp}^{\preccurlyeq}$-formulas with non-empty *cp*-sets are mapped into a fragment of valid $\mathcal{L}_{\varnothing}^{\preccurlyeq}$-formulas.

By definition, the formula $\hat{A}$ is either a formula of $\mathcal{L}^{\preccurlyeq}$ (in case all its *cp*-sets are empty) or a formula expressible in the language of $\mathcal{L}^{\preccurlyeq}$. Thus, by Fact 5.2 and Theorem 5.6, the set of valid formulas of VL^{d} coincides with the set of valid formulas of VL (refer to Fig. 3). Since Lewis defined axiom systems for logics VL in [9], Theorem 5.6 also provides us with an axiomatization for logics VL^{d}.

6 Conclusions and Future Work

In this paper we introduced an innovative way of evaluating *cp*-counterfactuals, by updating the worlds of a sphere model according to the significance of literals, which we measured by calculating the weights of specific sets of literals associated to each world in a system of spheres. The disagreement update, performed on (weakly) centered sphere models, gives rise to logics VW^{d}, VC^{d}, which we showed to be complete with respect to Lewis' logics VW and VC.

We plan to extend our analysis of *cp*-counterfactuals in various directions. We wish to deepen the study of the comparative plausibility operator $\preccurlyeq^{\Gamma}$ (following [2], in non-nested models), and compare it to the preferential *cp*-operator introduced in [12]. Furthermore, we wish to explore additional constraints on *cp*-sets, such as, e.g., allowing *cp*-counterfactuals to occur within *cp*-sets, or requiring *cp*-sets to be consistent or closed under subformulas. Finally, we plan to include *impossible worlds* in our account, following ideas from [16]. Thanks to our approach, we could distinguish between different kinds of impossible worlds, allowing for a nuanced evaluation of counterfactuals within impossible states.

A Appendix

A.1 Proofs from Section 3

Proof (of Proposition 3.3). Let $\mathbf{w}_x(G) = (w_0^G, \ldots, w_n^G)$, $\mathbf{w}_x(H) = (w_0^H, .., w_n^H)$, $\mathbf{w}_x(\bar{G}) = (w_0^{\bar{G}}, .., w_n^{\bar{G}})$ and $\mathbf{w}_x(\bar{H}) = (w_0^{\bar{H}}, .., w_n^{\bar{H}})$. From Definition 3.1 it follows that, since worlds are classical, for any $l \leq n$ it holds that $w_l^{\bar{G}} < w_l^{\bar{H}}$ if and only if $w_l^H < w_l^G$. Now suppose $H \blacktriangleleft_x G$. Then, for the first $k \leq n$ such that $w_k^G \neq w_k^H$, it holds that $w_k^G < w_k^H$. Thus, $w_k^{\bar{H}} < w_k^{\bar{G}}$, and $\bar{G} \blacktriangleleft_x \bar{H}$. If $H =_x G$, then for all $k \leq n$, $w_k^G = w_k^H$, and thus $w_k^{\bar{G}} = w_k^{\bar{H}}$, hence $\bar{G} =_x \bar{H}$. □

Proof (of Proposition 3.7). We only cover the case when $\Gamma \subset \Delta$. So, we have that $\Delta \backslash \Gamma \neq \varnothing$. Then, for some $0 \leq n < l$, we have that $\mathbf{w}_x(\Gamma) = (\mathbf{w}_x(c_1), .., \mathbf{w}_x(c_n))$ and $\mathbf{w}_x(\Delta) = (\mathbf{w}_x(d_1), .., \mathbf{w}_x(d_{n+l}))$. If there is some $G \in \Delta \backslash \Gamma$ such that for some $H \in \Gamma$ it holds that $H \blacktriangleleft_x G$, then by definition $\Gamma \lhd_x \Delta$. Otherwise, if for all literals $G \in \Delta \backslash \Gamma$ and all literals $H \in \Gamma$ it holds $G \trianglelefteq_x H$, then we conclude that $\Gamma \lhd_x \Delta$ because $n < n + l$. □

A.2 Proofs from Section 4

Proof (of Lemma 4.3). Non-emptiness and nesting of $S^{\Gamma,x}(x)$ immediately follow from Definition 4.2. Moreover, $\mathbf{w}_x(\mathsf{D}(x,x)^{\Gamma}) = \min\{\mathbf{w}_x(\mathsf{D}(x,y)^{\Gamma}) \mid y \in \bigcup S(x)\}$. Thus, if $\mathcal{M}$ is weakly centered, then for all $\alpha \in S^{\Gamma,x}(x)$ we have $x \in \alpha$, hence $\mathcal{M}^{\Gamma,x}$ is weakly centered. If $\mathcal{M}$ is centered, then by definition $\{x\} \in S^{\Gamma,x}(x)$. So we conclude that $\mathcal{M}^{\Gamma,x}$ is centered.

A.3 Proofs from Section 5

The following notion of *agreement set* is the dual of the disagreement set, which we took as primitive to define our updates (Definition 4.1). The following Lemma makes their duality explicit. For technical convenience, both the Definition and the Lemma will be used in the proof of Lemma 5.4.

Definition A.1. For $\mathcal{M} = \langle W, S, V \rangle$ (weakly) centered sphere model, worlds $x, y \in W$ and a *cp*-set of literals Γ, the *agreement set of* y *w.r.t.* Γ, x is the set $\mathsf{A}(x,y)^\Gamma = \{G \in \Gamma \mid x \Vdash G \textit{ iff } y \Vdash G\}$.

Lemma A.2. *For a (weakly) centered model* $\mathcal{M}$*, worlds* $x, y, z \in \bigcup S(x)$ *and* cp*-set* Γ*, it holds that:*

1. $\Gamma = \mathsf{A}(x,y)^\Gamma \cup \mathsf{D}(x,y)^\Gamma$;
2. $\mathsf{D}(x,y)^\Gamma \trianglelefteq_x \mathsf{D}(x,z)^\Gamma$ *iff* $\mathsf{A}(x,z)^\Gamma \trianglelefteq_x \mathsf{A}(x,y)^\Gamma$.

Proof. Item 1 is an immediate consequence of the definition of agreement and disagreement sets, considering that Γ is paired. We also note that by definition, $\mathsf{A}(x,y)^\Gamma \cap \mathsf{D}(x,y)^\Gamma = \varnothing$. To prove one direction of Item 2, assume that $\mathbf{w}_x(\mathsf{A}(x,z)^\Gamma) \preceq_{lex} \mathbf{w}_x(\mathsf{A}(x,y)^\Gamma)$. We shall first prove that:

$$\mathbf{w}_x(\mathsf{A}(x,z)^\Gamma \setminus \mathsf{A}(x,y)^\Gamma) \preceq_{lex} \mathbf{w}_x(\mathsf{A}(x,y)^\Gamma \setminus \mathsf{A}(x,z)^\Gamma) \tag{2}$$

If $\mathsf{A}(x,y)^\Gamma \cap \mathsf{A}(x,z)^\Gamma = \varnothing$ we immediately obtain that (2) holds. Otherwise, there are literals $G_1, \ldots, G_n \in \mathsf{A}(x,z)^\Gamma \cap \mathsf{A}(x,y)^\Gamma$. Removing $\mathbf{w}_x(G_1), \ldots, \mathbf{w}_x(G_n)$ from both lists $\mathbf{w}_x(\mathsf{A}(x,z)^\Gamma)$ and $\mathbf{w}_x(\mathsf{A}(x,y)^\Gamma)$ does not alter the order w.r.t. $\preceq_{lex}$, as we remove the same elements from both lists. Thus, $\mathbf{w}_x(\mathsf{A}(x,z)^\Gamma) \setminus (\mathbf{w}_x(G_1), \ldots, \mathbf{w}_x(G_n)) \preceq_{lex} \mathbf{w}_x(\mathsf{A}(x,y)^\Gamma) \setminus (\mathbf{w}_x(G_1), \ldots, \mathbf{w}_x(G_n))$, whence we conclude that (2) holds.

From Item 1 it easily follows that $(\mathsf{A}(x,y)^\Gamma \setminus \mathsf{A}(x,z)^\Gamma) = (\mathsf{D}(x,z)^\Gamma \setminus \mathsf{D}(x,y)^\Gamma)$ and $(\mathsf{A}(x,z)^\Gamma \setminus \mathsf{A}(x,y)^\Gamma) = (\mathsf{D}(x,y)^\Gamma \setminus \mathsf{D}(x,z)^\Gamma)$. From these and (2) we obtain:

$$\mathbf{w}_x(\mathsf{D}(x,y)^\Gamma \setminus \mathsf{D}(x,z)^\Gamma) \preceq_{lex} \mathbf{w}_x(\mathsf{D}(x,z)^\Gamma \setminus \mathsf{D}(x,y)^\Gamma) \tag{3}$$

To conclude the proof, we need to show that the following holds:

$$\mathbf{w}_x(\mathsf{D}(x,y)^\Gamma) \preceq_{lex} \mathbf{w}_x(\mathsf{D}(x,z)^\Gamma) \tag{4}$$

If $\mathsf{D}(x,y)^\Gamma \cap \mathsf{D}(x,z)^\Gamma = \varnothing$, then (4) immediately follows from (3). Otherwise, there are literals $H_1, \ldots, H_k \in \mathsf{D}(x,z)^\Gamma \cap \mathsf{D}(x,y)^\Gamma$. Adding $\mathbf{w}_x(H_1), \ldots, \mathbf{w}_x(H_k)$ in both lists $\mathbf{w}_x(\mathsf{D}(x,z)^\Gamma)$ and $\mathbf{w}_x(\mathsf{D}(x,y)^\Gamma)$ does not alter the order w.r.t. $\preceq_{lex}$, as we add the same number of elements to each list, with the same value. Thus, from (4) we obtain that $(\mathbf{w}_x(\mathsf{D}(x,y)^\Gamma \setminus \mathsf{D}(x,z)^\Gamma)) \cup (\mathbf{w}_x(H_1), \ldots, \mathbf{w}_x(H_k)) \preceq_{lex} (\mathbf{w}_x(\mathsf{D}(x,z)^\Gamma \setminus \mathsf{D}(x,y)^\Gamma)) \cup (\mathbf{w}_x(H_1), \ldots, \mathbf{w}_x(H_k))$, from which (4) immediately follows.

The converse direction of Clause 2 is proved similarly. □

Proposition A.3. *For any (weakly) centered sphere* $\mathcal{M}$*, and* $x, v \in \bigcup S(x)$*,* Γ cp*-set and* $\lambda \in \mathsf{Pr}(\Gamma)$*, it holds that:*

1. $\mathsf{A}(x,v)^\Gamma = (\llbracket x \rrbracket_\Gamma \cap \llbracket v \rrbracket_\Gamma) \cup (\llbracket x \rrbracket_\Gamma^c \cap \llbracket v \rrbracket_\Gamma^c)$;
2. $\mathsf{D}(x,v)^\Gamma = (\llbracket x \rrbracket_\Gamma \cap \llbracket v \rrbracket_\Gamma^c) \cup (\llbracket x \rrbracket_\Gamma^c \cap \llbracket v \rrbracket_\Gamma)$;
3. $\mathcal{M}, v \Vdash \bigwedge \llbracket x \rrbracket_{\Gamma \setminus \lambda}$ *if and only if* $\mathsf{D}(x,v)^\Gamma \subseteq \lambda$;
4. $\mathcal{M}, v \Vdash \bigwedge \llbracket x \rrbracket_\lambda$ *if and only if* $\lambda \subseteq \mathsf{A}(x,v)^\Gamma$;
5. *if* $\mathsf{D}(x,v)^\Gamma \subseteq \lambda$ *then* $\mathbf{w}_x(\mathsf{D}(x,v)^\Gamma) \preceq_{lex} \mathbf{w}_x(\lambda)$.

Proof (sketch). Item 1 states that the agreement set of x and v in Γ corresponds to the set of literals in Γ which x and v both satisfy, plus the set of literals in Γ that both x and v do not satisfy. Similarly, Item 2 defines the disagreement set of x and v in Γ as the literals in Γ that x satisfies but v does not, plus the set of literals in Γ that v satisfies, but x does not. Both statements follow from Definition 3.5 and the definition of $[\![x]\!]^c_\Gamma$. To prove Item 3, observe that $v \Vdash \bigwedge[\![x]\!]_{\Gamma\setminus\lambda}$ if and only if for any literal $G \in \Gamma\setminus\lambda$, if $x \Vdash G$ then $v \Vdash G$ (and also if $x \nVdash G$ then $v \nVdash G$). Since x and v assign the same value to literals in $\Gamma\setminus\lambda$ then, by Definition 4.1, $\Gamma\setminus\lambda = \mathsf{A}(x,v)^{\Gamma\setminus\lambda}$. Since agreement and disagreement sets are complementary (Lemma A.2), we obtain $\mathsf{D}(x,v)^{\Gamma\setminus\lambda} = \varnothing$, which is equivalent to $\mathsf{D}(x,v)^\Gamma \subseteq \lambda$. The proof of Item 4 is similar to that of Item (3) and Item 5 is a special case of Proposition 3.7. □

Proof (of Lemma 5.4). For one direction, assume $\mathcal{M}, x \Vdash A \preccurlyeq^\Gamma B$. Then, by definition, $\mathcal{M}^{\Gamma,x}, x \Vdash A \preccurlyeq B$ which means that for all $\hat{\alpha} \in S^{\Gamma,x}(x)$, if $\hat{\alpha} \Vdash^\exists B$, then $\hat{\alpha} \Vdash^\exists A$. Let $\lambda \in \mathsf{Pr}(\Gamma)$ such that:

$$\mathcal{M}, x \models \bigwedge_{\mathsf{Pr}(\Gamma)\ni\lambda'\lhd_x\lambda} \neg\Diamond(A \wedge \bigwedge[\![x]\!]_{\Gamma\setminus\lambda'}) \tag{5}$$

We need to show that x satisfies the formula within parentheses 3. Consider any world $v \in \bigcup S(x)$ such that $\mathcal{M}, v \Vdash B \wedge \bigwedge[\![x]\!]_{\Gamma\setminus\lambda}$ (observe that, if no such world exists, then the formula in parentheses 3 is vacuously satisfied, and we are done). Then, $\mathcal{M}, v \Vdash B$ and $\mathcal{M}, v \Vdash \bigwedge[\![x]\!]_{\Gamma\setminus\lambda}$. By 3 of Proposition A.3 we conclude that $\mathsf{D}(x,v)^\Gamma \subseteq \lambda$. Therefore, by Item 5 of Proposition A.3, and by definition, we have that $\mathsf{D}(x,v)^\Gamma \unlhd_x \lambda$. Since $\mathcal{M}, v \Vdash B$ and $v \in \bigcup S(x)$, then for some sphere $\hat{\alpha} \in S^{\Gamma,x}(x)$ we have that $v \in \hat{\alpha} \in S^{\Gamma,x}(x)$, and thus $\hat{\alpha} \Vdash^\exists B$. Choose the smallest such sphere $\hat{\alpha}$. This sphere will contain only worlds z such that $\mathsf{D}(x,z)^\Gamma \unlhd_x \mathsf{D}(x,v)^\Gamma$. By assumption, $\hat{\alpha} \Vdash^\exists A$, that is, there is a $y \in \hat{\alpha}$ such that $y \models A$, and $\mathsf{D}(x,y)^\Gamma \unlhd_x \mathsf{D}(x,v)^\Gamma$. However, it cannot be that $\mathsf{D}(x,y)^\Gamma \lhd_x \mathsf{D}(x,v)^\Gamma$, because by taking $\lambda' = \mathbf{w}_x(\mathsf{D}(x,y)^\Gamma)$ we would obtain that $x \models \Diamond(A \wedge (\bigwedge[\![x]\!]_{\Gamma\setminus\lambda'}))$, contradicting (5). Thus, we have that $\mathsf{D}(x,y)^\Gamma =_x \mathsf{D}(x,v)^\Gamma$. Since $v \models B \wedge \bigwedge[\![x]\!]_{\Gamma\setminus\lambda}$ and $v \in \bigcup S(x)$, we also have that for some $\alpha \in S(x)$, $v \in \alpha$ and $\alpha \Vdash^\exists B \wedge \bigwedge[\![x]\!]_{\Gamma\setminus\lambda}$. To conclude the proof, it remains to show that the following holds:

$$\alpha \Vdash^\exists \bigvee_{\mathsf{Pr}(\Gamma)\ni\lambda''\unlhd_x\lambda} (A \wedge \bigwedge[\![x]\!]_{\Gamma\setminus\lambda''}). \tag{6}$$

Take $\lambda'' = \mathsf{D}(x,y)^\Gamma$. Hence $y \models \bigwedge[\![x]\!]_{\Gamma\setminus\lambda''}$, by 3 of Proposition A.3. Thus $y \Vdash A \wedge \bigwedge[\![x]\!]_{\Gamma\setminus\lambda''}$, from which we obtain that:

$$y \Vdash \bigvee_{\mathsf{Pr}(\Gamma)\ni\lambda''\unlhd_x\lambda} (A \wedge \bigwedge[\![x]\!]_{\Gamma\setminus\lambda''}).$$

Since $y \in \bigcup S^{\Gamma,x}(x) = \bigcup S(x)$, there is a $\beta \in S(x)$ such that $y \in \beta$. However, since $\mathsf{D}(x,y)^\Gamma =_x \mathsf{D}(x,v)^\Gamma$ and since $y, v \in \hat{\alpha}$, we have either $\beta \subseteq \alpha$ or $\beta = \alpha$. In both cases we conclude that $y \in \alpha$, whence (6) holds.

To prove the converse direction of the Lemma, assume that:

$$\mathcal{M}, x \Vdash \bigwedge_{\lambda \in \mathsf{Pr}(\Gamma)} \Big[^1 \Big(^2 \bigwedge_{\mathsf{Pr}(\Gamma) \ni \lambda' \lhd_x \lambda} \neg \Diamond (A \wedge \bigwedge [\![x]\!]_{\Gamma \setminus \lambda'}) \Big)^2 \rightarrow$$
$$\rightarrow \Big(^3 \big(\bigvee_{\mathsf{Pr}(\Gamma) \ni \lambda'' \unlhd_x \lambda} (A \wedge \bigwedge [\![x]\!]_{\Gamma \setminus \lambda''})\big) \preccurlyeq (B \wedge \bigwedge [\![x]\!]_{\Gamma \setminus \lambda}) \Big)^3 \Big]^1. \quad (7)$$

Let us take an arbitrary $\hat{\alpha} \in S^{\Gamma, x}(x)$ such that $\hat{\alpha} \Vdash^{\exists} B$, i.e., let us suppose that there is a $v \in \hat{\alpha}$ such that $v \Vdash B$. We shall prove that $\hat{\alpha} \Vdash^{\exists} A$, i.e., we shall find an $y \in \hat{\alpha}$ such that $y \Vdash A$. Take $\lambda = \mathsf{D}(x, v)^{\Gamma}$. We distinguish two cases. First, suppose that the following holds:

$$\mathcal{M}, x \nVdash \bigwedge_{\mathsf{Pr}(\Gamma) \ni \lambda' \lhd_x \lambda} \neg \Diamond (A \wedge \bigwedge [\![x]\!]_{\Gamma \setminus \lambda'}).$$

This means that, for some $\lambda' \lhd_x \lambda$, there is a $y \in \bigcup S(x)$ such that $y \Vdash A \wedge \bigwedge [\![x]\!]_{\Gamma \setminus \lambda'}$. Then, by 3 of Proposition A.3 we have $\mathsf{D}(x, y)^{\Gamma} \subseteq \lambda'$. We conclude that $\mathsf{D}(x, y)^{\Gamma} \lhd_x \mathsf{D}(x, v)^{\Gamma}$. Thus, by Definition 4.2, $y \in \hat{\alpha}$, from which we obtain $\hat{\alpha} \Vdash^{\exists} A$, thus concluding the proof.

Next, suppose that the following holds:

$$\mathcal{M}, x \Vdash \bigwedge_{\mathsf{Pr}(\Gamma) \ni \lambda' \lhd_x \lambda} \neg \Diamond (A \wedge \bigwedge [\![x]\!]_{\Gamma \setminus \lambda'}).$$

Then, by (7), we obtain that:

$$\mathcal{M}, x \Vdash \big(\bigvee_{\mathsf{Pr}(\Gamma) \ni \lambda'' \unlhd_x \lambda} (A \wedge \bigwedge [\![x]\!]_{\Gamma \setminus \lambda''})\big) \preccurlyeq (B \wedge \bigwedge [\![x]\!]_{\Gamma \setminus \lambda}).$$

Since $\lambda = \mathsf{D}(x, v)^{\Gamma}$, by 3 of Proposition A.3 we have that $v \Vdash \bigwedge [\![x]\!]_{\Gamma \setminus \lambda}$. Moreover, by assumption, $v \Vdash B$, and therefore there is an $\alpha \in \bigcup S(x)$ such that $v \in \alpha$ and $\alpha \Vdash^{\exists} B \wedge (\bigwedge [\![x]\!]_{\Gamma \setminus \lambda})$. Then, always by assumption, we have that:

$$\alpha \Vdash^{\exists} \big(\bigvee_{\mathsf{Pr}(\Gamma) \ni \lambda'' \unlhd_x \lambda} A \wedge \bigwedge [\![x]\!]_{\Gamma \setminus \lambda''}\big).$$

Thus, for some $y \in \alpha$, it holds $y \Vdash A \wedge \bigwedge [\![x]\!]_{\Gamma \setminus \lambda''}$. Using Proposition A.3, we conclude that $\mathsf{D}(x, y)^{\Gamma} \subseteq \lambda''$ and $\mathsf{D}(x, y)^{\Gamma} \unlhd_x \mathsf{D}(x, v)^{\Gamma}$. By construction (Definition 4.2) we have that $y \in \hat{\alpha}$, and the proof is completed.

Proof (sketch, of 5.5). If $cp^{\preccurlyeq}(A) = 0$, set $\hat{A} = A \in \mathcal{L}^{\preccurlyeq}$, and the result immediately follows. Otherwise, if $cp^{\preccurlyeq}(A) = n > 0$, we 'decompose' formula A, evaluating its satisfiability at $\mathcal{M}, x$ (and possibly other worlds in the model). Whenever we encounter a subformula $B \preccurlyeq^{\Gamma} C$ with $\Gamma \neq \varnothing$, we apply Lemma 5.4. After n iterations of Lemma 5.4, we obtain a formula $\hat{A} \in \mathcal{L}^{\preccurlyeq}$ equisatisfiable with A. □

Proof (of Theorem 5.6). To prove one direction, take an arbitrary $A \in \mathcal{L}_{cp}^{\preccurlyeq}$ such that $\models^{\mathsf{VL}^d} A$. Then, for arbitrary $\mathcal{M}$, x, it holds that $\mathcal{M}, x \Vdash A$ and, by Lemma 5.1, there is a formula $B \in \mathcal{L}_{cp}^{\preccurlyeq}$ such that $\mathcal{M}, x \Vdash B$. By Proposition 5.5, $\mathcal{M}, x \Vdash \hat{B}$, for $\hat{B} \in \mathcal{L}^{\preccurlyeq}$. Then, since the above holds for arbitrary models, conclude that $\models^{\mathsf{VL}} \hat{B}$ and, again by Lemma 5.1, we have that there is $\hat{A} \in \mathcal{L}_{cp}^{>}$ such that $\models^{\mathsf{VL}} \hat{A}$. The converse direction is proved similarly. □

References

1. Burgess, J.: Quick completeness proofs for some logics of conditionals. Notre Dame J. Formal Log. **22** (1981). https://doi.org/10.1305/ndjfl/1093883341
2. Dalmonte, T., Girlando, M.: Comparative plausibility in neighbourhood models: axiom systems and sequent calculi. In: Fernández-Duque, D., Palmigiano, A., Pinchinat, S. (eds.) Advances in Modal Logic, AiML 2022, pp. 305–327. College Publications (2022). http://www.aiml.net/volumes/volume14/20-Dalmonte-Girlando.pdf
3. Fine, K.: Critical notice of Lewis, counterfactuals. Mind **84**(335), 451–458 (1975). https://www.jstor.org/stable/2253565
4. Girard, P., Triplett, M.A.: Ceteris paribus logic in counterfactual reasoning. In: Ramanujam, R. (ed.) Proceedings Fifteenth Conference on Theoretical Aspects of Rationality and Knowledge, TARK 2015, Carnegie Mellon University, Pittsburgh, USA, 4–6 June 2015. EPTCS, vol. 215, pp. 176–193 (2015). http://www.tark.org/proceedings/tark_jun4_15/TARK2015.13.pdf
5. Girard, P., Triplett, M.A.: Prioritised ceteris paribus logic for counterfactual reasoning. Synthese **195**(4), 1681–1703 (2017). https://doi.org/10.1007/s11229-016-1296-5
6. Goodman, N.: The problem of counterfactual conditionals. J. Philos. **44**(5), 113–128 (1947). https://www.jstor.org/stable/2019988
7. Kaufmann, S.: Causal premise semantics. Cogn. Sci. **37**(6), 1136–1170 (2013). https://doi.org/10.1111/cogs.12063
8. Kratzer, A.: Partition and revision: the semantics of counterfactuals. J. Philos. Log. **10**, 201–216 (1981). https://doi.org/10.1007/BF00248849
9. Lewis, D.: Counterfactuals. Blackwell, Oxford (1973)
10. Lewis, D.: Counterfactual dependence and time's arrow. Noûs **13**(4), 455–476 (1979). https://www.jstor.org/stable/2215339
11. Priest, G.: An Introduction to Non-classical Logic: From If to Is. Cambridge Introductions to Philosophy, 2nd edn. Cambridge University Press, Cambridge (2008). https://doi.org/10.1017/CBO9780511801174
12. Van Benthem, J., Girard, P., Roy, O.: Everything else being equal: a modal logic for ceteris paribus preferences. J. Philos. Log. **38**(1), 83–125 (2009). https://doi.org/10.1007/s10992-008-9085-3
13. Van Ditmarsch, H., van Der Hoek, W., Kooi, B.: Dynamic Epistemic Logic, vol. 337. Springer, Dordrecht (2007). https://doi.org/10.1007/978-1-4020-5839-4
14. Von Wright, G.H.: The Logic of Preference, vol. 40. Edinburgh University Press (1963)
15. Von Wright, G.H.: The logic of preference reconsidered. Theory Decis. **3**(2) (1972). https://doi.org/10.1007/BF00141053
16. Weiss, Y.: Semantics for counterpossibles. Australas. J. Log. **14**(4), 383–407 (2017). https://doi.org/10.26686/ajl.v14i4.4050 https://doi.org/10.26686/ajl.v14i4.4050

Tabular Intermediate Logics Comparison

Paweł Rzążewski[1,2] and Michał Stronkowski[1(✉)]

[1] Warsaw University of Technology, Warsaw, Poland
{pawel.rzazewski,michal.stronkowski}@pw.edu.pl
[2] University of Warsaw, Warsaw, Poland

Abstract. Tabular intermediate logics are intermediate logics characterized by finite posets treated as Kripke frames. For a poset $\mathbb{P}$, let $L(\mathbb{P})$ denote the corresponding tabular intermediate logic. We investigate the complexity of the following decision problem LogContain: given two finite posets $\mathbb{P}$ and $\mathbb{Q}$, decide whether $L(\mathbb{P}) \subseteq L(\mathbb{Q})$.

By Jankov's and de Jongh's theorem, the problem LogContain is related to the problem SPMorph: given two finite posets $\mathbb{P}$ and $\mathbb{Q}$, decide whether there exists a surjective p-morphism from $\mathbb{P}$ onto $\mathbb{Q}$. Both problems belong to the complexity class NP.

We present two contributions. First, we describe a construction which, starting with a graph $\mathbb{G}$, gives a poset $\mathsf{Pos}(\mathbb{G})$ such that there is a surjective locally surjective homomorphism (the graph-theoretic analog of a p-morphism) from $\mathbb{G}$ onto $\mathbb{H}$ if and only if there is a surjective p-morphism from $\mathsf{Pos}(\mathbb{G})$ onto $\mathsf{Pos}(\mathbb{H})$. This allows us to translate some hardness results from graph theory and obtain that several restricted versions of the problems LogContain and SPMorph are NP-complete. Among other results, we present a 18-element poset $\mathbb{Q}$ such that the problem to decide, for a given poset $\mathbb{P}$, whether $L(\mathbb{P}) \subseteq L(\mathbb{Q})$ is NP-complete.

Second, we describe a polynomial-time algorithm that decides LogContain and SPMorph for posets $\mathbb{T}$ and $\mathbb{Q}$, when $\mathbb{T}$ is a tree.

Keywords: Tabular intermediate logic · Logics comparison · p-morphism

1 Introduction

A (propositional) *intermediate logic* is a logic, i.e., a set of formulas closed under substitutions and *Modus Ponens*, lying between intuitionistic and classical logics. (See e.g. [4,17] for the necessary information on logic, [20] on the theory of computation, [7] on graph theory and [11] on posets. The essential concepts for this article are presented in Sect. 2.) Every poset $\mathbb{P}$ determines an intermediate logic $L(\mathbb{P})$. It consists of formulas that are true in $\mathbb{P}$ when $\mathbb{P}$ is interpreted as a Kripke frame. If $\mathbb{P}$ is finite, we say that $L(\mathbb{P})$ is *tabular*. We are interested in comparing such logics with respect to inclusion. In particular, we investigate the computational complexity of the following decision problem

D. Kozen and R. de Queiroz (Eds.): WoLLIC 2025, LNCS 15942, pp. 326–339, 2026.
https://doi.org/10.1007/978-3-031-99536-1_20

Problem: LogContain
Instance: A pair $\mathbb{P}$, $\mathbb{Q}$ of finite posets **Question:** Does it hold that $L(\mathbb{P}) \subseteq L(\mathbb{Q})$?

In [16] it was indicated that LogContain is NP-complete even under the restriction that the input posets have depth at most three. This is the starting point of our investigations: we are interested in understanding what makes instances of LogContain hard.

The problem LogContain is intrinsically related to p-morphisms, as we proceed to explain. Let $\mathbb{P}$ and $\mathbb{Q}$ be posets. A *p-morphism* (known also as a bounded morphism or a reduction) between $\mathbb{P}$ and $\mathbb{Q}$ is a mapping $h\colon X^{\mathbb{P}} \to X^{\mathbb{Q}}$ satisfying

(HP) for all $x, y \in X^{\mathbb{P}}$, if $x \leq^{\mathbb{P}} y$ then $h(x) \leq^{\mathbb{Q}} h(y)$ (*the homomorphism property*);

(BP) for all $x \in X^{\mathbb{P}}$ and $y \in X^{\mathbb{Q}}$, if $h(x) \leq^{\mathbb{Q}} y$ then there exists $z \in X^{\mathbb{P}}$ such that $x \leq^{\mathbb{P}} z$ and $h(z) = y$ (*the backward property*).

Let us recall crucial Jankov's and de Jongh's theorem [12–14]. Here $\uparrow^{\mathbb{P}} x$, for an element x of a poset $\mathbb{P}$, denotes the upset in $\mathbb{P}$ generated by x.

Theorem 1. *For every finite rooted poset $\mathbb{P}$ there exists a formula $\chi_{\mathbb{P}}$ such that, for each poset $\mathbb{Q}$, we have $\chi_{\mathbb{P}} \notin L(\mathbb{Q})$ if and only if $\mathbb{P}$ is a p-morphic image of $\uparrow^{\mathbb{Q}} x$ for some $x \in X^{\mathbb{Q}}$.*

Theorem 1 allows us, while studying LogContain, to focus only on p-morphisms, as the following direct corollary shows.

Corollary 2. *Let $\mathbb{P}$ and $\mathbb{Q}$ be finite posets. Then $L(\mathbb{P}) \subseteq L(\mathbb{Q})$ if and only if every poset $\uparrow^{\mathbb{Q}} y$, where y is minimal in $\mathbb{Q}$, is a p-morphic image of $\uparrow^{\mathbb{P}} x$ for some $x \in X^{\mathbb{P}}$. In particular, if both $\mathbb{P}$ and $\mathbb{Q}$ are rooted and have the same depth, then $L(\mathbb{P}) \subseteq L(\mathbb{Q})$ if and only if there is a surjective p-morphism from $\mathbb{P}$ onto $\mathbb{Q}$.*

The above considerations lead us to the following decision problem:

Problem: SPMorph
Instance: A pair $\mathbb{P}$, $\mathbb{Q}$ of finite posets **Question:** Does there exist a surjective p-morphism $h\colon \mathbb{P} \to \mathbb{Q}$?

It is evident that SPMorph belongs to the complexity class NP. By Corollary 2, the same holds for LogContain.

Graph-theoretic analogs of p-morphisms were studied in social sciences as early as the 1980s and 1990s, see e.g. [8,18,21]. They appeared under various names, like *locally surjective homomorphisms*, *role assignments* or *role colorings*. Computational aspects of locally surjective (and related locally bijective) graph homomorphisms were studied in e.g. [2,3,5,10,15,18]. (See e.g. [1] for historical information on p-morphisms.)

Our main contribution in this paper is the constructions that, for a graph $\mathbb{G}$, produces a poset $\mathrm{Pos}(\mathbb{G})$ and a rooted poset $\mathrm{Pos}_{\perp}(\mathbb{G})$, each of size linear in the size of $\mathbb{G}$, such that the following conditions are equivalent (see Theorem 6 and Corollary 15):

- There exists a surjective locally surjective homomorphism from $\mathbb{G}$ onto $\mathbb{H}$;
- There exists a surjective p-morphism from $\mathrm{Pos}(\mathbb{G})$ onto $\mathrm{Pos}(\mathbb{H})$;
- There exists a surjective p-morphism from $\mathrm{Pos}_\perp(\mathbb{G})$ onto $\mathrm{Pos}_\perp(\mathbb{H})$.

This allows us to transfer some hardness results from graphs to posets. We summarize them below. In what follows, by $\mathbb{P}\mathrm{ath}_2$ we denote the three-vertex path and by $\mathbb{K}_4$ we denote the complete graph on four vertices. The Hasse diagram of $\mathrm{Pos}_\perp(\mathbb{P}\mathrm{ath}_2)$ is depicted in Fig. 1 (some edges are plotted as dashed to improve visibility).

Theorem 3. *The problem* LogContain *is NP-complete even for inputs* $\mathbb{P}, \mathbb{Q}$, *where*

1. $\mathbb{P}$ *is of depth 5 and* $\mathbb{Q} = \mathrm{Pos}_\perp(\mathbb{P}\mathrm{ath}_2)$ (*in particular,* $\mathbb{Q}$ *has 18 elements*);
2. $\mathbb{P}$ *is of dimension at most 7, and its every element except for the root has at most 4 immediate successors and at most 12 successors in all, and* $\mathbb{Q} = \mathrm{Pos}_\perp(\mathbb{K}_4)$ (*in particular,* $\mathbb{Q}$ *has 29 elements*);
3. $\mathbb{P}$ *has pathwidth at most 20 and* $\mathbb{Q}$ *has pathwidth at most 17.*

Theorem 4. *The problem* SPMorph *is NP-complete even for inputs* $\mathbb{P}, \mathbb{Q}$, *where*

1. $\mathbb{P}$ *is of depth 4 and* $\mathbb{Q} = \mathrm{Pos}(\mathbb{P}\mathrm{ath}_2)$ (*in particular* $\mathbb{Q}$, *has 17 elements*);
2. $\mathbb{P}$ *is of dimension at most 7, and its every element has at most 4 immediate successors and at most 12 successors in all; and* $\mathbb{Q} = \mathrm{Pos}(\mathbb{K}_4)$ (*in particular,* $\mathbb{Q}$ *has 28 elements*);
3. $\mathbb{P}$ *has pathwidth at most 19 and* $\mathbb{Q}$ *has pathwidth at most 16.*

We finish the paper with one positive result. Namely, we present a polynomial-time algorithm that decides LogContain and SPMorph for posets $\mathbb{T}$ and $\mathbb{Q}$, when $\mathbb{T}$ is a tree.

2 Preliminaries

Here we provide basic definitions primarily in order to fix notation. A *poset* $\mathbb{P}$ is a structure consisting of the *carrier* set $X^{\mathbb{P}}$ and the order relation $\leq^{\mathbb{P}}$. Its *covering relation* is given by

$$\prec^{\mathbb{P}} = \{(x, y) : x, y \in X^{\mathbb{P}},\ x <^{\mathbb{P}} y,\ \text{there is no } z \in X^{\mathbb{P}} \text{ such that } x <^{\mathbb{P}} z <^{\mathbb{P}} y\}.$$

For an element x of a poset $\mathbb{P}$ the sets $\uparrow^{\mathbb{P}} x = \{y \in X^{\mathbb{P}} : x \leq^{\mathbb{P}} y\}$ and $\downarrow^{\mathbb{P}} x = \{y \in X^{\mathbb{P}} : y \leq^{\mathbb{P}} x\}$ are called (*principal*) *upset* and *downset* respectively. Clearly, both these sets are carriers of subposets of $\mathbb{P}$ with the order inherited from $\mathbb{P}$. We do not distinguish notationally these posets from their carriers. A poset $\mathbb{P}$ is *rooted* if there exists $r \in X^{\mathbb{P}}$ such that $\mathbb{P} = \uparrow^{\mathbb{P}} r$. The element r is then called the *root* of $\mathbb{P}$.

We say that an element x of a poset $\mathbb{P}$ is *of depth* n if $\uparrow x$ contains a chain of cardinality n but not a larger one. The *depth* of a poset is the maximum depth of its elements. We will use the following basic observation that follows from (BP).

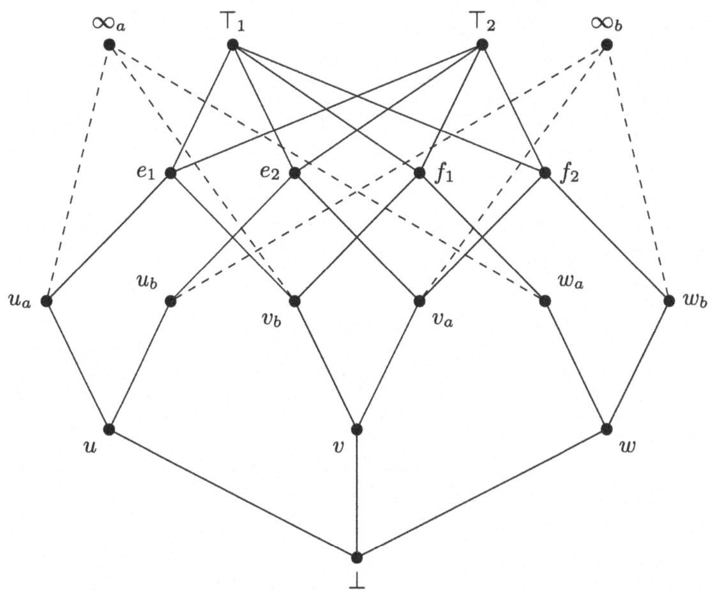

Fig. 1. The rooted poset $\mathrm{Pos}_\perp(\mathbb{P}\mathrm{ath}_2)$ for the three-vertex path $\mathbb{P}\mathrm{ath}_2$.

Observation 5. *Let $h\colon \mathbb{P} \to \mathbb{Q}$ be a p-morphism. Then, for $x \in X^{\mathbb{P}}$, the depth of $h(x)$ is not greater than the depth of x. Also the number of elements in $\uparrow^{\mathbb{Q}} h(x)$ is not greater than the number of elements in $\uparrow^{\mathbb{P}} x$. In particular, h maps maximal elements of $\mathbb{P}$ into maximal elements of $\mathbb{Q}$.*

Let us give a sketch of the proof of Corollary 2.

Proof of Corollary 2. Suppose that $L(\mathbb{P}) \subseteq L(\mathbb{Q})$ and let y be a minimal element of $\mathbb{Q}$. Let us consider a formula $\chi_{\uparrow^{\mathbb{Q}} y}$. Since the identity mapping on $\uparrow^{\mathbb{Q}} y$ is a p-morphism, by Theorem 1, $\chi_{\uparrow^{\mathbb{Q}} y} \notin L(\mathbb{Q})$. Hence, $\chi_{\uparrow^{\mathbb{Q}} y} \notin L(\mathbb{P})$ and, by Theorem 1, there exists $x \in X^{\mathbb{P}}$ such that $\uparrow^{\mathbb{Q}} y$ is a p-morphic image of $\uparrow^{\mathbb{P}} x$.

For the inverse implication, note that for any formula φ, we have $\varphi \in L(\mathbb{P})$ iff $\varphi \in L(\uparrow^{\mathbb{P}} x)$ for all $x \in X^{\mathbb{P}}$, and that p-morphisms preserve the satisfaction of formulas, see [4, Sec. 2.3]. The last statement follows from Observation 5. □

A *graph* $\mathbb{G}$ is a structure consisting of the set $V^{\mathbb{G}}$ of its *vertices* and a set $E^{\mathbb{G}}$ of its *edges*. An edge is a two-element subset of $V^{\mathbb{G}}$. The edge $\{u, v\}$ is denoted simply by uv. For graphs $\mathbb{G}$ and H a mapping $g\colon V^{\mathbb{G}} \to V^{\mathbb{H}}$ is called a *locally surjective homomorphism* if it satisfies

(HP) for all $u, v \in V^{\mathbb{G}}$, if $uv \in E^{\mathbb{G}}$ then $g(u)g(v) \in E^{\mathbb{H}}$ (*the homomorphism property*);

(BP) for all $u \in V^{\mathbb{G}}$ and $w \in V^{\mathbb{H}}$, if $g(u)w \in E^{\mathbb{H}}$ then there exists $v \in V^{\mathbb{G}}$ such that $uv \in E^{\mathbb{G}}$ and $g(v) = w$ (*the backward property*).

3 From Graphs to Posets

Our aim in this section is to provide a construction of the poset $\mathrm{Pos}(\mathbb{G})$ for a given graph $\mathbb{G}$, such that there exists a surjective locally surjective homomorphism from $\mathbb{G}$ onto $\mathbb{H}$ if and only if there is a surjective p-morphism from $\mathrm{Pos}(\mathbb{G})$ onto $\mathrm{Pos}(\mathbb{H})$. The construction of $\mathrm{Pos}(\mathbb{G})$ is inspired by the incidence poset of a graph [19]. For the application in logic, we will also consider a modification of $\mathrm{Pos}(\mathbb{G})$. Let $\mathrm{Pos}_{\bot}(\mathbb{G})$ be obtained from $\mathrm{Pos}(\mathbb{G})$ by adding a root $\bot$ to it. The poset $\mathrm{Pos}_{\bot}(\mathbb{P}\mathrm{ath}_2)$ for the three-element path graph $\mathbb{P}\mathrm{ath}_2$, with vertices u, v, w and edges $e = uv$, $f = vw$, is depicted in Fig. 1.

Let $\mathbb{G} = (V^{\mathbb{G}}, E^{\mathbb{G}})$ be a graph. The carrier of $\mathrm{Pos}(\mathbb{G})$ is given by

$$X^{\mathrm{Pos}(\mathbb{G})} = V^{\mathbb{G}} \cup V_a^{\mathbb{G}} \cup V_b^{\mathbb{G}} \cup E_1^{\mathbb{G}} \cup E_2^{\mathbb{G}} \cup \{\top_1, \top_2, \infty_a, \infty_b\},$$

where $V_a^{\mathbb{G}}$, $V_b^{\mathbb{G}}$ are copies of the vertex set $V^{\mathbb{G}}$ and $E_1^{\mathbb{G}}$, $E_2^{\mathbb{G}}$ are copies of the edge set $E^{\mathbb{G}}$. The copies of $v \in V^{\mathbb{G}}$ in $V_a^{\mathbb{G}}$ and in $V_b^{\mathbb{G}}$ are denoted by v_a and v_b respectively. Similarly, e_1 and e_2 are copies of $e \in E^{\mathbb{G}}$ in $E_1^{\mathbb{G}}$, $E_2^{\mathbb{G}}$ respectively. The purpose of the auxiliary elements $\top_1, \top_2, \infty_a, \infty_b$ is to *improve rigidity*, in a sense of eliminating unwanted p-morphisms between posets $\mathrm{Pos}(\mathbb{G})$ and $\mathrm{Pos}(\mathbb{H})$. Let

$$\begin{aligned}
\lhd = \{&(v, v_a), (v, v_b) : v \in V^{\mathbb{G}}\} \\
\cup\, \{&(v_a, \infty_a), (v_b, \infty_b) : v \in V^{\mathbb{G}}\} \\
\cup\, \{&(e_1, \top_1), (e_1, \top_2), (e_2, \top_1), (e_2, \top_2) : e \in E^{\mathbb{G}}\} \\
\cup\, \{&(v_a, \top_1), (v_b, \top_1), (v_a, \top_2), (v_b, \top_2) : v \in V^{\mathbb{G}} \text{ is isolated in } \mathbb{G}\}
\end{aligned}$$

The covering relation of $\mathrm{Pos}(\mathbb{G})$ is the expansion of $\lhd$ obtained by adding, for every $e = uv \in E^{\mathbb{G}}$, the covers $(u_a, e_i), (v_b, e_i)$ and $(u_b, e_j), (v_a, e_j)$ in such a way that $\{i, j\} = \{1, 2\}$.

Theorem 6. *Let $\mathbb{G}$, $\mathbb{H}$ be graphs such that $\mathbb{H}$ has at least one vertex, and let $\mathbb{P} = \mathrm{Pos}(\mathbb{G})$, $\mathbb{Q} = \mathrm{Pos}(\mathbb{H})$. Then there exists a surjective locally surjective homomorphism from $\mathbb{G}$ onto $\mathbb{H}$ if and only if there is a surjective p-morphism from $\mathbb{P}$ onto $\mathbb{Q}$.*

The proof of Theorem 6 is organized as follows. We start with consideration of a surjective p-morphism $h\colon \mathbb{P} \to \mathbb{Q}$. We show that h maps $V^{\mathbb{G}}$ onto $V^{\mathbb{H}}$ and the restriction of h to $V^{\mathbb{G}}$ is a surjective locally surjective homomorphism from $\mathbb{G}$ onto $\mathbb{H}$. Then we show that every surjective locally surjective homomorphism $g\colon \mathbb{G} \to \mathbb{H}$ extends to a surjective p-morphism from $\mathbb{P}$ onto $\mathbb{Q}$. We split the reasoning into a series of lemmas.

Lemma 7. *We have $h(\{\top_1, \top_2\}) \subseteq \{\top_1, \top_2\}$.*

Proof. We consider only $\top_1$. By Observation 5, $h(\top_1) \in \{\top_1, \top_2, \infty_a, \infty_b\}$. Suppose, for the sake of contradiction and without loss of generality, that $h(\top_1) = \infty_a$. Then, by (HP), $h({\downarrow}^{\mathbb{P}}\top_1) \subseteq {\downarrow}^{\mathbb{Q}}\infty_a$. Since we assumed that $\mathbb{H}$

has at least one vertex, say u, the four-element set $\{\top_1, \top_2, \infty_b, u_b\}$ is contained in $X^{\mathbb{Q}} \setminus {\downarrow}^{\mathbb{Q}}\infty_a$. And since $X^{\mathbb{P}} \setminus {\downarrow}^{\mathbb{P}}\top_1 = \{\top_2, \infty_a, \infty_b\}$ has three elements, we reach a contradiction with the surjectivity of h. □

Lemma 8. *We have* $h(\{\infty_a, \infty_b\}) = \{\infty_a, \infty_b\}$.

Proof. By Lemma 7 and (HP),

$$h(X^{\mathbb{P}} \setminus \{\infty_a, \infty_b\}) = h({\downarrow}^{\mathbb{P}}\top_1 \cup {\downarrow}^{\mathbb{P}}\top_2) \subseteq {\downarrow}^{\mathbb{Q}}\top_1 \cup {\downarrow}^{\mathbb{Q}}\top_2 = X^{\mathbb{H}} \setminus \{, \infty_a, \infty_b\}.$$

Thus the statement follows by the surjectivity of h. □

Lemma 9. *We have* $h(\{\top_1, \top_2\}) = \{\top_1, \top_2\}$.

Proof. By the surjectivity of h, there are $x_1, x_2 \in X^{\mathbb{P}}$ such that $h(x_1) = \top_1$ and $h(x_2) = \top_2$. By Lemma 8, $x_1, x_2 \notin \{\infty_a, \infty_b\}$. Thus $x_1 \leq^{\mathbb{P}} \top_i$ and $x_2 \leq^{\mathbb{P}} \top_j$ for some $i, j \in \{1, 2\}$. But then, by (HP), we infer that $h(\top_i) = \top_1$ and $h(\top_j) = \top_2$. This forces that $i \neq j$. Thus the lemma follows. □

Lemma 10. *We have* $h(E_1^{\mathbb{G}} \cup E_2^{\mathbb{G}}) \subseteq E_1^{\mathbb{H}} \cup E_2^{\mathbb{H}}$.

Proof. Let $e_1 \in E_1^{\mathbb{G}}$. By Observation 5, $h(e_1) \notin V^{\mathbb{H}} \cup V_b^{\mathbb{H}} \cup V_a^{\mathbb{H}}$. Indeed, for every $y \in V^{\mathbb{H}} \cup V_b^{\mathbb{H}} \cup V_a^{\mathbb{H}}$, the upset ${\uparrow}^{\mathbb{Q}}y$, has at least four elements y, $\top_1, \top_2$ and ∞_a or ∞_b, while ${\uparrow}^{\mathbb{P}}e_1$ has only three elements $e_1, \top_1, \top_2$. Suppose now that $h(e_1)$ is maximal in $\mathbb{Q}$. Then, by (HP), we would have $h(\top_1) = h(\top_2) = h(e_1)$. This contradicts Lemma 9. The argument for $e_2 \in E_2^{\mathbb{G}}$ is the same. □

Lemma 11. *If* $h(\infty_a) = \infty_a$ *then* $h(V_a^{\mathbb{G}}) \subseteq V_a^{\mathbb{H}}$ *and* $h(V_b^{\mathbb{G}}) \subseteq V_b^{\mathbb{H}}$. *If* $h(\infty_a) = \infty_b$ *then* $h(V_a^{\mathbb{G}}) \subseteq V_b^{\mathbb{H}}$ *and* $h(V_b^{\mathbb{G}}) \subseteq V_a^{\mathbb{H}}$.

Proof. Suppose that $h(\infty_a) = \infty_a$. Observe that $V_a^{\mathbb{G}} \subseteq {\downarrow}^{\mathbb{P}}\top_1 \cap {\downarrow}^{\mathbb{P}}\infty_a$. Thus, by (HP) and Lemma 7 and the assumption, for some $i \in \{1, 2\}$,

$$h(V_a^{\mathbb{G}}) \subseteq {\downarrow}^{\mathbb{P}}h(\top_1) \cap {\downarrow}^{\mathbb{P}}h(\infty_a) \subseteq {\downarrow}^{\mathbb{Q}}\top_i \cap {\downarrow}^{\mathbb{Q}}\infty_a = V^{\mathbb{H}} \cup V_a^{\mathbb{H}}$$

Suppose, for the sake of contradiction, that $h(v_a) \in V^{\mathbb{H}}$ for some $v \in V^{\mathbb{G}}$. Then, by (BP), there would exist $x \in {\uparrow}^{\mathbb{P}}v_a \setminus \{v_a\} \subseteq E_1^{\mathbb{G}} \cup E_2^{\mathbb{G}} \cup \{\infty_a, \top_1, \top_2\}$ such that $h(x) = \infty_b$. But, by Lemmas 7 and 10, and the assumption that $h(\infty_a) = \infty_a$, it is not the case. Thus $h(V_a^{\mathbb{G}}) \subseteq V_a^{\mathbb{H}}$. We infer analogically that $h(V_b^{\mathbb{G}}) \subseteq V_b^{\mathbb{H}}$.

The argument in the case when $h(\infty_a) = \infty_b$ is the same. □

Lemma 12. *We have* $h(V^{\mathbb{G}}) \subseteq V^{\mathbb{H}}$. *Moreover, for* $v \in V^{\mathbb{G}}$*: if* $f(\infty_a) = \infty_a$ *then* $h(v_a) = h(v)_a$ *and* $h(v_b) = h(v)_b$, *and if* $f(\infty_a) = \infty_b$ *then* $h(v_a) = h(v)_b$ *and* $h(v_b) = h(v)_a$.

Proof. By Lemma 8, $h(\infty_a) \in \{\infty_a, \infty_b\}$. We consider only the situation when $h(\infty_a) = \infty_a$. Let $v \in V^{\mathbb{G}}$. Then $v \leq^{\mathbb{P}} v_a, v_b$. Thus, by Lemma 11 and (HP), $h(v) \leq^{\mathbb{Q}} h(v_a) \in V_a^{\mathbb{H}}$ and $h(v) \leq^{\mathbb{Q}} h(v_b) \in V_b^{\mathbb{H}}$. By the definition of $\mathbb{Q}$, there exists at most one element w, which is in $V^{\mathbb{H}}$, such that $w \leq^{\mathbb{Q}} h(v_a), h(v_b)$. It follows that w exists and, in fact, $h(v) = w$. Moreover, by the definition of $\mathbb{Q}$, we have $h(v_a) = h(v)_a$ and $h(v_b) = h(v)_b$. □

Lemma 12 yields that the mapping $g\colon V^{\mathbb{G}} \to V^{\mathbb{H}}$, given by $g(v) = h(v)$ is well-defined.

Lemma 13. *The mapping g is a surjective locally surjective homomorphism from $\mathbb{G}$ onto $\mathbb{H}$.*

Proof. By Lemma 8, $h(\infty_a) \in \{\infty_a, \infty_b\}$. We consider only the case when $h(\infty_a) = \infty_a$.

By Lemmas 7, 8, 10, 11, and 12, the surjectivity of h yields that $h(V^{\mathbb{G}}) = V^{\mathbb{H}}$. Thus g is surjective.

Let us observe that, for an edge $e = uv \in E^{\mathbb{G}}$, we have $\{h(e_1), h(e_2\} = \{(g(u)g(v))_1, (g(u)g(v))_2\}$. In particular, $g(u)g(v)$ is an edge in $\mathbb{H}$. For this aim, let us suppose that $u_a, v_b <^{\mathbb{P}} e_1$ and $u_b, v_a <^{\mathbb{P}} e_2$. By Lemma 10 and (HP), we have $h(u_a), h(v_b) \leq^{\mathbb{Q}} h(e_1) \in E_1^{\mathbb{H}} \cup E_2^{\mathbb{H}}$ and $h(u_b), h(v_a) \leq^{\mathbb{Q}} h(e_2) \in E_1^{\mathbb{H}} \cup E_2^{\mathbb{H}}$. By Lemma 11 and the assumption that $h(\infty_a) = \infty_a$, we have $h(u)_a, h(v)_b \leq^{\mathbb{Q}} h(e_1)$ and $h(u)_b, h(v)_a \leq^{\mathbb{Q}} h(e_2)$. Since $V_a^{\mathbb{H}} \cap V_b^{\mathbb{H}} = \emptyset$, we have $h(u)_a \neq h(v)_b$ and $h(u)_b \neq h(v)_a$. Note that elements w_a and t_b, from the sets $V_a^{\mathbb{H}}$ and $V_b^{\mathbb{H}}$ respectively, have a common bound $f_i \in E_1^{\mathbb{H}} \cup E_2^{\mathbb{H}}$ if and only if $f = wt$. Thus the claim follows.

It follows directly from the above observation that g is a homomorphism. In order to see that g also satisfies (BP) for graphs, suppose, for some $u \in V^{\mathbb{G}}$ and $w \in V^{\mathbb{H}}$, that $f = h(u)w$ is an edge in $E^{\mathbb{H}}$. Then, by Lemma 12, $h(u_a) = h(u)_a \leq^{\mathbb{Q}} f_j$ for some $j \in \{1, 2\}$. By (BP), there exists $x \in {\uparrow^{\mathbb{P}}} u_a$ such that $h(x) = f_i$. Notice that, by Lemmas 7, 8, 11 and 12, $x = e_i$ for an edge e in $\mathbb{G}$ and an index $i \in \{1, 2\}$. We infer that $e = uv$, for some $v \in V^{\mathbb{G}}$, and, by the observation, $f_j = h(e_i) = (h(u)h(v))_j$. Thus $h(v) = w$. This shows that g is locally surjective. □

With Lemma 13, we finish the first part of the proof of Theorem 6. Now, we consider a surjective locally surjective homomorphism $g\colon \mathbb{G} \to \mathbb{H}$ and show that it may be extended to a surjective p-morphism $h\colon \mathbb{P} \to \mathbb{Q}$. We define h as follows

$$h(x) = \begin{cases} x & \text{if } x \in \{\top_1, \top_2, \infty_a, \infty_b\}, \\ g(u) & \text{if } x = u \in V^{\mathbb{G}}, \\ g(u)_a & \text{if } x = u_a \text{ for } u \in V^{\mathbb{G}}, \\ g(u)_b & \text{if } x = u_b \text{ for } u \in V^{\mathbb{G}}, \\ (g(u)g(v))_j & \text{if } x = (uv)_i \in E^{\mathbb{G}},\ u_a, v_b <^{\mathbb{P}} (uv)_i \\ & \text{and } g(u)_a, g(v)_b <^{\mathbb{Q}} (g(u)g(v))_j \end{cases}$$

Lemma 14. *The mapping h is a surjective p-morphism.*

Proof. In what follows, we consider points that might seem not straightforward.

Checking that h is surjective: We verify that f_j, for $f \in E^{\mathbb{H}}$ and $j \in \{1, 2\}$, is in the range of h. Let $f = wt$. Then either $w_a, t_b <^{\mathbb{Q}} f_j$ or $w_b, t_a <^{\mathbb{Q}} f_j$. Without loss of generality, we assume that $w_a, t_b <^{\mathbb{Q}} f_j$. By the surjectivity of g, there exists $u \in V^{\mathbb{G}}$ such that $g(u) = w$. By (BP) for graphs, there exists $v \in V^{\mathbb{G}}$ such that $g(w) = t$ and $e = uv \in E^{\mathbb{G}}$. We have $u_a, v_b <^{\mathbb{P}} e_i$ for some $i \in \{1,2\}$. Then $h(e_i) = f_j$ by the definition of h.

Checking that h is a homomorphism: We verify that $h(x) \leq^{\mathbb{Q}} h(y)$ when $x = u_a$ and $y = e_i$, where $e = uv \in E^{\mathbb{G}}$ and $u_a, v_b <^{\mathbb{P}} e_i$. Then $h(u_a) = g(u)_a$ and $h(e_i) = (g(u)g(v))_j$, where $g(u)_a, g(v)_b <^{\mathbb{Q}} (g(u)g(v))_j$. Hence, $h(u_a) <^{\mathbb{Q}} h(e_i)$.

Checking that h satisfies (BP): Suppose that $h(x) \leq^{\mathbb{Q}} y$. We consider the case when $x = u_a \in V_a^{\mathbb{G}}$ and $y = (g(u)w)_j \in E_j^{\mathbb{H}}$. Then also $h(u_a) = g(u)_a$ and $w_b <^{\mathbb{Q}} (g(u)w)_j$. We have $g(u)w \in E^{\mathbb{H}}$ and, by (BP) for graphs, there exists $v \in V^{\mathbb{G}}$ such that $g(v) = w$ and $uv \in E^{\mathbb{G}}$. Hence $u_a, v_b <^{\mathbb{P}} (uv)_i$, for some $i \in \{1,2\}$, and $h((uv)_i) = (g(u)w)_j$. □

This finishes the proof of Theorem 6. We have the following consequence for rooted posets.

Corollary 15. *Let $\mathbb{G}$, $\mathbb{H}$ be graphs such that $\mathbb{H}$ has at least one vertex. Then there exists a surjective locally surjective homomorphism from $\mathbb{G}$ onto $\mathbb{H}$ if and only if there is a surjective p-morphism from* $\mathrm{Pos}_\perp(\mathbb{G})$ *onto* $\mathrm{Pos}_\perp(\mathbb{H})$.

The proof is straightforward and is omitted.

4 Hardness Results

The constructions in Sect. 3 allow us to translate certain hardness results from the world of graphs to the world of posets. Let LSHom denotes the problem where we are given two graphs $\mathbb{G}$ and $\mathbb{H}$, and we need to decide if there exists a locally surjective homomorphism g from $\mathbb{G}$ to $\mathbb{H}$. In the recalled results, $\mathbb{H}$ will be connected. Thus, if g exists, it is surjective.

Note that the posets constructed in Sect. 3 have depth (i.e., the number of elements in a longest chain) bounded by 4 in case of $\mathrm{Pos}(\mathbb{G})$ and by 5 in case of $\mathrm{Pos}_\perp(\mathbb{G})$.

Fiala and Paulusma [10, Theorem 1] proved that LSHom remains NP-hard even if $\mathbb{H}$ is any fixed connected graph on at least 3 vertices, such as a three-vertex path $\mathbb{P}\mathrm{ath}_2$. Note that $\mathrm{Pos}(\mathbb{P}\mathrm{ath}_2)$ has 17 elements and $\mathrm{Pos}_\perp(\mathbb{P}\mathrm{ath}_2)$ has 18 elements. Thus, we immediately obtain the following result.

Corollary 16. *The problem* LogContain *(resp.,* SPMorph*) is NP-complete for inputs $\mathbb{P}$, $\mathbb{Q}$ of depth 5 (resp., 4) and $\mathbb{Q} = \mathrm{Pos}_\perp(\mathbb{P}\mathrm{ath}_2)$ (resp. $\mathbb{Q} = \mathrm{Pos}(\mathbb{P}\mathrm{ath}_2)$). In particular, $\mathbb{Q}$ is of constant size.*

The structure of $\mathbb{P}$ can be restricted even further. Kratochvíl showed in [15, Corollary 4.2] that LSHom is NP-complete for inputs $\mathbb{G}$, $\mathbb{K}_4$, where $\mathbb{K}_4$ is the complete graph on four vertices, and $\mathbb{G}$ is three-regular (i.e., every vertex is of degree 3). This result was improved by Bílka et al. in [2, Theorem 2] by showing that we may restrict to a planar three-regular graph $\mathbb{G}$.

It is straightforward to verify that the construction in Sect. 3 preserves the boundedness of degrees (with the exception for the element $\perp$ of $\mathrm{Pos}_\perp(\mathbb{G})$.

Lemma 17. *Let $\mathbb{G}$ be a graph. If every vertex of $\mathbb{G}$ has degree at most k, where $k \geq 2$, then every element of* $\mathrm{Pos}(\mathbb{G})$ *has at most $k+1$ immediate successors, and at most $2k+6$ successors in total.*

Next, let us exploit the planarity of $\mathbb{G}$. For information on the dimension of a poset, see e.g. [11, Chap. 7].

Lemma 18. *Let $\mathbb{G}$ be a finite planar graph, then the dimension of* $\mathrm{Pos}(\mathbb{G})$ *and of* $\mathrm{Pos}_\perp(\mathbb{G})$ *is at most 7.*

Proof. We observe that the subposet of $\mathrm{Pos}(\mathbb{G})$ induced by $V^{\mathbb{G}} \cup E_1^{\mathbb{G}}$ or, symmetrically, by $V^{\mathbb{G}} \cup E_2^{\mathbb{G}}$ is isomorphic to the *incidence poset* of $\mathbb{G}$. As shown by Schnyder [19], the incidence poset of a planar graph has dimension at most 3. Let $\leq_1, \leq_2, \leq_3$ be linear extensions of $\leq \, = \, \leq^{\mathrm{Pos}(\mathbb{G})} \cap (V^{\mathbb{G}} \cup E_1^{\mathbb{G}})^2$ whose intersection is $\leq$.

We expand $\leq_1$ and $\leq_2$ as follows. Each element v is replaced by three elements (in order): $v \prec v_b \prec v_a$, and each element e_1 by two elements $e_2 \prec e_1$. Next, we add the elements $\top_1 \prec \top_2 \prec \infty_a \prec \infty_b$ as the four largest elements in the order. Next, we expand $\leq_3$ similarly. Each element v is replaced by three elements (in order): $v \prec v_a \prec v_b$ and each element e_1 by two elements $e_1 \prec e_2$. Next, we add the elements $\infty_b \prec \infty_a \prec \top_2 \prec \top_1$ as the four largest elements in that order. Let $\leq_1', \leq_2'$ and $\leq_3'$ be the obtained linear extensions of $\leq^{\mathrm{Pos}(\mathbb{G})}$.

Note that their intersection is *almost* $\leq^{\mathrm{Pos}(\mathbb{G})}$, with the exception that the element ∞_a is larger than all elements in $E_1^{\mathbb{G}} \cup E_2^{\mathbb{G}} \cup V_b^{\mathbb{G}}$, and ∞_b, is larger than all elements in $E_1^{\mathbb{G}} \cup E_2^{\mathbb{G}} \cup V_a^{\mathbb{G}}$, and $u_b, v_a \leq e_i$ when $u_a, v_b \leq e_i$ (while they should be incomparable). We remedy this by adding four new linear extensions $\leq_4$, $\leq_5$, $\leq_6$ and $\leq_7$. In $\leq_4$ we have (elements in $V^{\mathbb{G}}$) $<_4$ (elements in $V_a^{\mathbb{G}}$) $<_4$ ∞_a $<_4$ (elements in $V_b^{\mathbb{G}}$) $<_4$ ∞_b $<_4$ (elements in $E_1^{\mathbb{G}} \cup E_2^{\mathbb{G}}$) $<_4$ $\top_1, \top_2$. The order $\leq_5$ is similar to $\leq_4$ but with swapped places for a and b. In $\leq_6$ we have (elements in $V^{\mathbb{G}}$) $<_6$ (elements in $\{u_a, v_b \in V_a^{\mathbb{G}} \cup V_b^{\mathbb{G}} : u_a, v_b <^{\mathrm{Pos}(\mathbb{G})} (uv)_1\}$) $<_6$ (elements in $E_1^{\mathbb{G}}$) $<_6$ (elements in $\{u_a, v_b \in V_a^{\mathbb{G}} \cup V_b^{\mathbb{G}} : u_a, v_b <^{\mathrm{Pos}(\mathbb{G})} (uv)_2\}$) $<_6$ (elements in $E_2^{\mathbb{G}}$) $<_6$ $\infty_a, \infty_b \top_1, \top_2$. The order $\leq_7$ is similar to $\leq_7$ but with swapped places for 1 and 2. One can readily verify that the intersection of $\leq_1', \leq_2', \leq_3', \leq_4, \leq_5, \leq_6, \leq_7$ is exactly $\leq^{\mathrm{Pos}(\mathbb{G})}$, and thus the dimension of $\mathrm{Pos}(\mathbb{G})$ is at most 7.

Note that inserting $\perp$ to the orders $\leq_1', \leq_2', \leq_3', \leq_4, \leq_5, \leq_6, \leq_7$ as the minimum element yields 7 linear extensions whose intersection is $\leq^{\mathrm{Pos}_\perp(\mathbb{G})}$, so the dimension of $\mathrm{Pos}_\perp(\mathbb{G})$ is also at most 7. □

Combining these lemmas with the hardness result of Bílka et al. in [2, Theorem 2], we obtain the following.

Corollary 19. *The problem* LogContain *(resp.,* SPMorph*) is NP-complete for inputs $\mathbb{P}, \mathbb{Q}$ of dimension at most 7, and its every element (except for the root in case of* LogContain*) has at most 4 immediate successors and at most 12 successors in all, and $\mathbb{Q} = \mathrm{Pos}_\perp(\mathbb{K}_4)$ (resp. $\mathbb{Q} = \mathrm{Pos}(\mathbb{K}_4)$).*

Now let us turn our attention to the case that $\mathbb{H}$ is not considered fixed. Chaplick et al. [5, Theorem 1] showed that LSHom remains NP-hard for inputs $\mathbb{G}, \mathbb{H}$, where $\mathbb{G}$ is of pathwidth at most 4 and $\mathbb{H}$ is of pathwidth at most 3. We observe that the construction in Sect. 3 preserves pathwidth, up to a constant factor. Here, by the pathwidth of a poset we mean the pathwidth of its cover graph, i.e., we do not include edges that *follow* by transitivity. Formally, $\mathbb{G}$ is the *cover graph* of a poset $\mathbb{P}$ if $V^{\mathbb{G}} = X^{\mathbb{P}}$ and $xy \in E^{\mathbb{G}}$ if $x \prec^{\mathbb{P}} y$ or $y \prec^{\mathbb{P}} x$. (For information on pathwidth, see [7, Chap. 12].)

Lemma 20. *If* $\mathbb{G}$ *has pathwidth* $k \geq 1$*, then* $\mathrm{Pos}(\mathbb{G})$ *has pathwidth at most* $3k+7$ *and* $\mathrm{Pos}_{\perp}(\mathbb{G})$ *has pathwidth at most* $3k+8$.

Proof. Consider a path decomposition $\mathcal{P}$ of $\mathbb{G}$ with width at most k, i.e., each of its bag has at most $k+1$ elements. We modify it into a path decomposition of $\mathrm{Pos}(\mathbb{G})$. First, consider an edge $e = uv$ of $\mathbb{G}$ and choose one bag X^e of $\mathcal{P}$ that contains both u and v; it exists as $\mathcal{P}$ is a path decomposition. We create two new bags $X_1^e = X_1^e \cup \{e_1\}$ and $X_2^e = X_2^e \cup \{e_2\}$, and insert them to $\mathcal{P}$ immediately after X_e. We repeat this for every edge $e \in E^{\mathbb{G}}$, always picking for X_e a bag of the original decomposition $\mathcal{P}$.

We denote the obtained sequence of bags by $\mathcal{P}'$. Next, for each bag X of $\mathcal{P}'$, we replace it by $X \cup \{v_a, v_b \colon v \in X\}$. Finally, we add the elements $\top_1, \top_2, \infty_a, \infty_b$ to every bag. It is straightforward to verify that the obtained sequence is a path decomposition of $\mathrm{Pos}(\mathbb{G})$ and each of its bag has at most

$$3(k+1)+1+4 = 3k+8$$

elements. Thus, $\mathrm{Pos}(\mathbb{G})$ has pathwidth at most $3k+7$.

To obtain a path decomposition of $\mathrm{Pos}_{\perp}(\mathbb{G})$, we need to insert $\perp$ into every bag, increasing its size by 1. □

This, combined with the aforementioned hardness result, yields the following.

Corollary 21. *The problem* LogContain *(resp.,* SPMorph*) is NP-complete for inputs* $\mathbb{P}, \mathbb{Q}$ *when* $\mathbb{P}$ *has pathwidth at most 20 (resp., 19) and* $\mathbb{Q}$ *has pathwidth at most 17 (resp., 16).*

5 Algorithm for Trees

In [9, Corollary 8] Fiala and Paulusma provided a polynomial-time algorithm that checks, for given finite graphs $\mathbb{G}$ and $\mathbb{H}$, where $\mathbb{G}$ is a tree, if there exists a locally surjective homomorphism from $\mathbb{G}$ to $\mathbb{H}$. This section contains a poset analog of this result.

A finite poset $\mathbb{T}$ is a tree if it has a root and its every principal downset $\downarrow^{\mathbb{T}} t$ forms a chain.

Theorem 22. *There is a polynomial-time algorithm answering* SPMorph *and* LogContain *for given finite posets* $\mathbb{T}$ *and* $\mathbb{Q}$*, where* $\mathbb{T}$ *is a tree.*

We split the proof of Theorem 22 into a series of lemmas. Here the posets $\mathbb{T}$ and $\mathbb{Q}$ are fixed. We also assume that $\mathbb{Q}$ has a root. We do so, as otherwise there is no surjective p-morphism from $\mathbb{T}$ onto $\mathbb{Q}$ anyway.

For $t \in X^{\mathbb{T}}$ let

$$Q_t = \{q \in X^{\mathbb{Q}} : \text{there exists a surjective } p\text{-morphism from } {\uparrow}^{\mathbb{T}} t \text{ onto } {\uparrow}^{\mathbb{Q}} q\}.$$

Clearly, there exists a surjective p-morphism from $\mathbb{T}$ onto $\mathbb{Q}$ iff the root of $\mathbb{Q}$ is in Q_r, where r is the root of $\mathbb{T}$. The algorithm we are going to present computes sets Q_t for $t \in X^{\mathbb{T}}$ recursively. Clearly, for a leaf t in $\mathbb{T}$ (i.e., for a maximal element of $\mathbb{T}$) the set Q_t consists of maximal elements in $\mathbb{Q}$. Once we have computed Q_s for every immediate successor s of t, we can compute Q_t. When we find the root of $\mathbb{Q}$ in one of Q_t, we can answer the question in SPMorph affirmatively. Indeed, by the next lemma, then the root of $\mathbb{Q}$ also belongs to Q_r, where r is a root of $\mathbb{T}$.

Lemma 23. *Let s, t be elements in $\mathbb{T}$ and p, q be elements in $\mathbb{Q}$. Suppose that $s \leq^{\mathbb{T}} t$, $p \leq^{\mathbb{Q}} q$ and $p \in Q_t$. Then $q \in Q_s$.*

Proof. Let us suppose that there exists a surjective p-morphism $h\colon {\uparrow}^{\mathbb{T}} t \to {\uparrow}^{\mathbb{Q}} p$. By (BP), there exists $t' \geq t$ such that $h(t') = q$. Let u be any maximal element of ${\uparrow}^{\mathbb{Q}} q$. We define a mapping $k\colon {\uparrow}^{\mathbb{T}} s \to {\uparrow}^{\mathbb{Q}} q$ by

$$k(x) = \begin{cases} h(x) & \text{if } x \geq^{\mathbb{T}} t', \\ q & \text{if } x \leq^{\mathbb{T}} t', \\ u & \text{otherwise.} \end{cases}$$

By (BP), k is surjective. Let us check that k is a homomorphism. It is clear that (HP) holds for every $x < y$, where $x \in {\uparrow}^{\mathbb{T}} t' \cup {\downarrow}^{\mathbb{T}} t'$. Otherwise, $k(x) = u$. Then, since $\mathbb{T}$ is a tree, $y \notin {\uparrow}^{\mathbb{T}} t' \cup {\downarrow}^{\mathbb{T}} t'$. Hence, $k(y) = u$ and (HP) holds also in this case. The satisfaction of (BP) by k follows from the satisfaction of (BP) by h. □

In what follows, it will be convenient to have a notation for the set of immediate successors of p in the poset $\mathbb{P}$. Let us denote this set by $\mathrm{isucc}^{\mathbb{P}}(p)$.

Suppose that t is an element of $\mathbb{T}$, and we have already computed all sets Q_s, where $s \in \mathrm{isucc}^{\mathbb{T}}(t)$. By Lemma 23, $\bigcup\{Q_s : s \in \mathrm{isucc}^{\mathbb{T}}(t)\} \subseteq Q_t$. Besides this, it appears that we only need to check if $q \in Q_t$ for those q that have all successors in $\bigcup\{Q_s : s \in \mathrm{isucc}^{\mathbb{T}}(t)\}$.

Lemma 24. *Let t be an element of $\mathbb{T}$ and q be en element of $\mathbb{Q}$. If $q \in Q_t$ then $\mathrm{isucc}^{\mathbb{Q}}(q) \subseteq \bigcup\{Q_s : s \in \mathrm{isucc}^{\mathbb{T}}(t)\}$.*

Proof. Let $h\colon {\uparrow}^{\mathbb{T}} t \to {\uparrow}^{\mathbb{Q}} q$ be a surjective p-morphism. Let $p \in \mathrm{isucc}^{\mathbb{Q}}(q)$. By (BP), there exists $t' \in {\uparrow}^{\mathbb{T}} t \setminus \{t\}$ such that $h(t') = p$. Hence, $p \in Q_{t'}$. Let s be the immediate successor of t such that $s \leq^{\mathbb{T}} t'$. By Lemma 23, $p \in Q_s$. □

Thus, having computed Q_s for every immediate successor s of t, it only remains to decide which elements in $X^{\mathbb{Q}} \setminus \bigcup\{Q_s : s \in \operatorname{isucc}^{\mathbb{T}}(t)\}$ and with all immediate successors in $\bigcup\{Q_s : s \in \operatorname{isucc}^{\mathbb{T}}(t)\}$, belong to Q_t. We do it with the help of Hopcroft-Karp algorithm for finding a maximum matching in a bipartite graph, see e.g. [6, p. 763].

For $t \in X^{\mathbb{T}}$ and $q \in X^{\mathbb{Q}}$, let $\mathbb{G}_{t,q}$ be the bipartite graph with the parts $\operatorname{isucc}^{\mathbb{T}}(t)$ and $\operatorname{isucc}^{\mathbb{Q}}(q)$. A pair sp is an edge in $\mathbb{G}_{t,q}$ if $p \in Q_s$.

Lemma 25. *Let t be an element of $\mathbb{T}$ and q be an element of $\mathbb{Q}$. Assume that $q \notin \bigcup\{Q_s : s \in \operatorname{isucc}^{\mathbb{T}}(t)\}$. Then $q \in Q_t$ if and only if there exists a matching in $\mathbb{G}_{t,q}$ with n edges, where $n = |\operatorname{isucc}^{\mathbb{Q}}(q)|$.*

Proof. Suppose that there exists a matching M in $\mathbb{G}_{t,q}$ consisting of n edges $\{s_1p_1, \ldots, s_np_n\}$. Let $h_j \colon {\uparrow}^{\mathbb{T}} s_j \to {\uparrow}^{\mathbb{Q}} s_j$ be surjective p-morphisms witnessing this. Let u be any maximal vertex in ${\uparrow}^{\mathbb{Q}} q$. Then the mapping $h \colon {\uparrow}^{\mathbb{T}} t \to {\uparrow}^{\mathbb{Q}} q$, given by

$$h(x) = \begin{cases} h_j(x) & \text{if } x \in {\uparrow}^{\mathbb{T}} s_j, \\ q & \text{if } x = t, \\ u & \text{otherwise,} \end{cases}$$

is a surjective p-morphism.

Let us now assume that there exists a surjective p-morphism $h \colon {\uparrow}^{\mathbb{T}} t \to {\uparrow}^{\mathbb{Q}} q$. For an immediate successor p of q there exists a successor t_p of t such that $h(t_p) = p$. Let s_p be the unique immediate successor of t such that $t \prec^{\mathbb{T}} s_p \leq^{\mathbb{T}} t_p$. Then, by (HP), $h(s_p) \in \{q, p\}$. But, by the assumption that $q \notin \bigcup\{Q_s : s \in \operatorname{isucc}^{\mathbb{T}}(t)\}$, we have $h(s_p) \neq q$. This shows that $p \in Q_{s_p}$. Also, since $h(s_p) = p$, we have $s_p \neq s_{p'}$ if $p \neq p'$. Consequently, $\{s_pp : p \in \operatorname{isucc}^{\mathbb{Q}}(q)\}$ is a matching in $\mathbb{G}_{t,q}$ with n edges. □

Lemmas 23, 24, 25 and the presented discussion shows that the following Algorithm 1 correctly answers the question in SPMorph. By Corollary 2 and Lemma 23, it also correctly answers the questions in LogContain. Notice that Algorithm 1 visits each element t in $\mathbb{T}$ at most once and, for fixed t, each vertex in $\mathbb{Q}$ at most once. The Hopcroft-Karp algorithm, for $\mathbb{G}_{t,q}$, runs in time $O((|\operatorname{isucc}^{\mathbb{T}}(t)| + |\operatorname{isucc}^{\mathbb{T}}(t)|)^{2.5})$. Hence, Algorithm 1 runs in polynomial time.

Finally, incorporating constructions from Lemmas 23 and 25 into Algorithm 1 allows us to find a p-morphism from $\mathbb{T}$ onto $\mathbb{Q}$, if one exists, in polynomial time.

Acknowledgement. The first author was supported by the European Research Council (ERC) under the European Union's Horizon 2020 research and innovation programme, grant agreement no 948057 (BOBR).

Disclosure of Interests. The authors have no competing interests.

Algorithm 1: Solving SPMorph & LogContain for a tree $\mathbb{T}$ and a poset $\mathbb{Q}$

```
Input: A finite tree 𝕋 and a poset ℚ
if ℚ is not rooted then Return No
S ← the set of leaves in T
for t ∈ S do
  └ Q_t ← the set of maximal elements in ℚ
for t maximal in 𝕋 \ S do
  | Q_t ← ⋃{Q_s : s ∈ isucc^𝕋(t)}
  | for q in ℚ such that isucc^ℚ(q) ⊆ ⋃{Q_s : s ∈ isucc^𝕋(t)} ∌ q do
  |   | if G_{t,q} has a |isucc^ℚ(q)|-matching /* Hopcroft-Karp algorithm */
  |   | then
  |   └   └ if q is the root of ℚ then return Yes else Q_t ← Q_t ∪ {q}
  └ S ← S ∪ {t}
return No
```

References

1. Baeten, J.C.M., Sangiorgi, D.: Concurrency theory: a historical perspective on coinduction and process calculi. In: Computational logic, pp. 399–442. Amsterdam: Elsevier/North Holland (2014)
2. Bílka, O.r., Jirásek, J., Klavík, P., Tancer, M., Volec, J.: On the complexity of planar covering of small graphs. In: Graph-theoretic concepts in computer science, Lecture Notes in Comput. Sci., vol. 6986, pp. 83–94. Springer, Heidelberg (2011). https://doi.org/10.1007/978-3-642-25870-1_9
3. Bulteau, L., Dabrowski, K.K., Köhler, N., Ordyniak, S., Paulusma, D.: An algorithmic framework for locally constrained homomorphisms. SIAM J. Discret. Math. **38**(2), 1315–1350 (2024). https://doi.org/10.1137/22M1513290
4. Chagrov, A., Zakharyaschev, M.: Modal logic, Oxford Logic Guides, vol. 35. The Clarendon Press, Oxford University Press, New York (1997). Oxford Science Publications
5. Chaplick, S., Fiala, J., van 't Hof, P., Paulusma, D., Tesař, M.: Locally constrained homomorphisms on graphs of bounded treewidth and bounded degree. Theoretical Comput. Sci. **590**, 86–95 (2015). https://doi.org/10.1016/j.tcs.2015.01.028, fundamentals of Computation Theory
6. Cormen, T.H., Leiserson, C.E., Rivest, R.L., Stein, C.: Introduction to algorithms. Cambridge, MA: MIT Press, 3rd ed. edn. (2009)
7. Diestel, R.: Graph theory, graduate texts in mathematics, vol. 173. Springer, Heidelberg, fourth edn. (2010). https://doi.org/10.1007/978-3-642-14279-6
8. Everett, M.G., Borgatti, S.: Role colouring a graph. Math. Social Sci. **21**(2), 183–188 (1991). https://doi.org/10.1016/0165-4896(91)90080-B
9. Fiala, J., Paulusma, D.: Comparing universal covers in polynomial time. Theory Comput. Syst. **46**(4), 620–635 (2010). https://doi.org/10.1007/s00224-009-9200-z
10. Fiala, J.r., Paulusma, D.: A complete complexity classification of the role assignment problem. Theoret. Comput. Sci. **349**(1), 67–81 (2005). https://doi.org/10.1016/j.tcs.2005.09.029
11. Harzheim, E.: Ordered sets, Advances in Mathematics (Springer), vol. 7. Springer, New York (2005)

12. Jankov, V.A.: On the relation between deducibility in intuitionistic propositional calculus and finite implicative structures. Dokl. Akad. Nauk SSSR **151**, 1293–1294 (1963)
13. de Jongh, D., Yang, F.: Jankov's theorems for intermediate logics in the setting of universal models. In: Logic, language, and computation. In: 8th International Tbilisi Symposium on Logic, Language, and Computation, TbiLLC 2009, Bakuriani, Georgia, September 21–25, 2009. Revised selected papers, pp. 53–76. Berlin: Springer (2011). https://doi.org/10.1007/978-3-642-22303-7_5
14. de Jongh, D.H.J.: Investigations on the intuitionistic propositional calculus. ProQuest LLC, Ann Arbor, MI thesis (Ph.D.)–The University of Wisconsin - Madison (1968)
15. Kratochvíl, J.: Regular codes in regular graphs are difficult. Discrete Math. **133**(1–3), 191–205 (1994). https://doi.org/10.1016/0012-365X(94)90026-4
16. Mata, A., Stronkowski, M.: Comparison of tabular intermediate logics. Abstract at TACL conference, Coimbra (2022)
17. Mints, G.: A short introduction to intuitionistic logic. The University Series in Mathematics, Kluwer Academic/Plenum Publishers, New York (2000)
18. Pekeč, A., Roberts, F.S.: The role assignment model nearly fits most social networks. Math. Soc. Sci. **41**(3), 275–293 (2001). https://doi.org/10.1016/S0165-4896(00)00064-0
19. Schnyder, W.: Planar graphs and poset dimension. Order **5**(4), 323–343 (1989). https://doi.org/10.1007/BF00353652
20. Sipser, M.: Introduction to the theory of computation. Thompson, Boston, MA (2006)
21. White, D.R., Reitz, K.P.: Graph and semigroup homomorphisms on networks of relations. Soc. Netw. **5**(2), 193–234 (1983). https://doi.org/10.1016/0378-8733(83)90025-4

Insignificant Choice Polynomial Time
A Logic Capturing PTIME

Klaus-Dieter Schewe(✉)

Institut Nationale Polytechnique de Toulouse/IRIT CNRS, Toulouse, France
kd.schewe@gmail.com

Abstract. In this article choiceless polynomial time (CPT) is extended using non-deterministic Abstract State Machines (ASMs), which are restricted by three conditions: (1) choice is restricted to choice among atoms; (2) update sets in a state must be isomorphic; (3) for any two isomorphic update sets on states S and S', respectively, the sets of update sets of the corresponding successor states are isomorphic. The restrictions can be incorporated into the semantics of ASM rules such that update sets are only yielded, if the conditions are satisfied. Furthermore, the conditions can be checked in polynomial time on a simulating Turing machine. Finally, the conditions imply global insignificance, i.e. the final result is independent from the choices. These properties suffice to show that the ASMs restricted this way define a logic capturing PTIME, which we call insignificant choice polynomial time (ICPT).

Keywords: abstract state machine · non-determinism · insignificant choice · polynomial time · PTIME logic · descriptive complexity · Gurevich's conjecture

This article is dedicated to my former student, colleague, collaborator and friend Qing Wang (1972–2025). She will live on in our memories and our sincere appreciation for her personality and her inspiring research contributions.

1 Introduction

In 1982 Chandra and Harel raised the question whether there is a computation model over structures that captures PTIME rather than Turing machines that operate over strings [8]. As there is typically a huge gap between the abstraction level of an algorithm and the one of Turing machines, Gurevich formulated a new thesis based on the observation that "if an abstraction level is fixed (disregarding low-level details and a possible higher-level picture) and the states of an algorithm reflect all the relevant information, then a particular small instruction

K.-D. Schewe—A full version of this paper is available in [21].

Part of this work is supported by the ANR project EBRP:EventB-Rodin-Plus under grant no. ANR-19-CE25-0010.

D. Kozen and R. de Queiroz (Eds.): WoLLIC 2025, LNCS 15942, pp. 340–356, 2026.
https://doi.org/10.1007/978-3-031-99536-1_21

set suffices to model any algorithm, never mind how abstract, by a generalised machine very closely and faithfully". This led to the definition of Abstract State Machines (ASMs), formerly known as evolving algebras [16].

Nonetheless, in 1988 Gurevich formulated the conjecture that there is no logic[1] capturing PTIME [15]. If true an immediate implication would be that PTIME differs from NP. Among the most important results in descriptive complexity theory (see Immerman's monograph [19]) are Fagin's theorem stating that the complexity class NP is captured by the existential fragment of second-order logic [10], and the theorem by Immerman and Vardi stating that over ordered structures the complexity class PTIME is captured by first-order logic plus inflationary fixed-point [18,24]. Thus, if there is a logic capturing PTIME, it must be included[2] in $\exists$SO and extend IFP[FO]. As an extension by increase of order can be ruled out, the argumentation concentrates on the addition of generalised quantifiers, but there is very little evidence that all of PTIME can be captured by adding a simple set of quantifiers to IFP[FO] (see e.g. the rather detailed discussion in Libkin's monograph [20, 204f.]).

Another strong argument supporting Gurevich's conjecture comes from the work of Blass, Gurevich and Shelah on choiceless polynomial time (CPT), which exploits a polynomial time-bounded version of deterministic ASMs supporting unbounded parallelism, but no choice [4]. CPT extends IFP[FO], subsumes other models of computation on structures such as relational machines [2] and reflective relational machines [1], but still captures only a fragment of PTIME. As shown in [4, Thm. 42, 43] some PTIME problems such as Parity or Bipartite Matching cannot be expressed in CPT, and for extensions of CPT by adding quantifiers such as counting the perspective of capturing PTIME remains as elusive as for IFP[FO], as all arguments given by Libkin in [20, 204f.] also apply to CPT.

If true, another consequence of Gurevich's conjecture would be that complexity theory could not be based as a whole on more abstract models of computations on structures such as ASMs. In particular, it would not be possible to avoid dealing with string encodings using Turing Machines. However, this consequence appears to be less evident in view of the ASM success stories. Gurevich's important sequential ASM thesis provides a purely logical definition of the notion of sequential algorithm and shows that these are captured by sequential ASMs [17], which provides solid mathematical support for the "new thesis" formulated by Gurevich in 1985. Generalisations of the theory have been developed for unbounded parallel algorithms [11], recursive algorithms [6], concurrent algorithms [5], and for reflective algorithms [22]. In addition, the usefulness of ASMs for high-level development of complex systems is stressed by Börger and Stärk in [7]. Furthermore, logics that enable reasoning about ASMs have been developed for deterministic ASMs by Stärk and Nanchen [23] based on ideas from Glavan and Rosenzweig that had already been exploited for CPT [14],

[1] Gurevich's definition of "logic" is to be understood in a very general way comprising computation models over structures, so it actually provides a formalisation of the problem formulated by Chandra and Harel.

[2] using a careful definition of "inclusion".

and extended to non-deterministic ASMs by Ferrarotti, Schewe, Tec and Wang [12], the latter work leading to a fragment of second-order logic with Henkin semantics.

Therefore, we dared to doubt that Gurevich's conjecture is true, in particular, as the choiceless fragment of PTIME is captured by a version of deterministic ASMs. Same as others [3,13] we saw that non-deterministic ASMs could be used, for which the choices have no effect on the final result, but global insignificance cannot be decided [9]. We found a different *local insignificance condition* to solve this problem, which can be expressed syntactically, and together with a restriction of choices to atoms can be checked in polynomial time. This, however, is not yet restrictive enough, as global insignificance is not implied. This can be easily repaired by another condition taming the branching in ASMs, so we call this additional condition *branching condition.* This brings up the challenge to show that this condition can also be checked in PTIME.

For this, the behavioural theories of ASMs [11,17] come to help. It turns out that bounded exploration witnesses can be successively exploited to reduce the states that are required in the branching condition to representatives of W-similarity classes, where W is a bounded exploration witness generalised to non-deterministic ASMs. In this article we summarise our findings with the main result that PTIME insignificant choice ASMs (icASMs) define a logic capturing PTIME, where the icASMs are defined by choices restricted to atoms and being locally insignificant, and ASM rules satisfying the branching condition.

Due to space restrictions we assume familiarity with ASMs and define a version of non-deterministic ASMs analogous to the one in [4], i.e. we assume a fixed finite input structure, and consider only hereditarily finite sets as objects. This is then used to define PTIME-bounded ASMs. Details are contained in the extended version of this paper [21]. Section 2 is dedicated to the introduction of insignificant choice. We start with motivating examples, and then formally restrict our computation model to PTIME-bounded insignificant choice ASMs satisfying the local insignificance conditions. This leads to the definition of the complexity class ICPT. In order to show that this logic captures PTIME we first show how to effectively translate PTIME-bounded insignificant choice ASMs to Turing machines. These run in polynomial time, if the local insignificance and branching conditions can be checked in polynomial time for all states. In Sect. 3 we show this is indeed possible. The most important lemma in the proof is a reduction lemma, which shows that the branching condition only depends on certain W-similarity classes, where W is a bounded exploration witness. Section 4 summarises the main result of this article, the capture of PTIME. All proofs except the one for the decisive reduction lemma are either given in an appendix or in [21].

2 Insignificant Choice

We assume familiarity with the basic concepts of ASMs. In general, ASMs including their foundations, semantics and usage in applications are the subject of the detailed monograph by Börger and Stärk [7]. We adopt specific ASMs as in [4], i.e. we consider base sets that are defined as sets of hereditarily finite sets. Detailed definitions are given in [21] and for reasons of space restrictions are omitted here. The main extensions to the ASMs in [4] are the use of choice- and call-rules:

choice. If v is a variable, t is a term with $v \notin \mathit{fr}(t)$, and $r(v)$ is a rule, then also **choose** $v \in \{x \mid x \in \mathit{Atoms} \wedge x \in t\}$ **do** $r(v)$ **enddo** is a rule.
call. If $t_0, t_1, \dots, t_n$ are terms and N is an ASM with a rule that does not use choice nor call, then also $t_0 \leftarrow N(t_1, \dots, t_n)$ is a rule.

Note that choice rules only permit to choose among atoms, which is a severe syntactic restriction compared to the common ASM choice rules [7]. Call rules as used in [6] allow us to treat some subcomputations by called ASMs as a single step of the calling ASM. The terms $t_1, \dots, t_n$ define the input for the called machine, which after termination returns a value that is then assigned to a location defined by the term t_0. We further assume that if a function symbol f is shared by a called ASM N and the calling ASM M, then locations with this function symbol are only read by N, i.e. f never appears in an update set defined by N.

2.1 Polynomial-Time-Bounded ASMs

Not all atoms and sets are active in the sense that they appear as value or argument of a location with defined value. We therefore define active objects as follows.

Definition 2.1. Let S be a state with base set B. An object $a \in B$ is called *critical* iff a is an atom or $a \in \{0, 1\}$ or a is the value of a location ℓ of S or there is a location $\ell = (f, \bar{a})$ with $\mathrm{val}_S(\ell) \neq \emptyset$ and a appears in $\bar{a}$. An object $a \in B$ is called *active* in S iff there exists a critical object a' with $a \in \mathit{TC}(a')$.

In addition, if $R = S_0, S_1, \dots$ is a run of an ASM, then we call an object $a \in B$ *active* in R iff a is active in at least one state S_i of R.

In order to define a polynomial time bound on an ASM we have to count steps of a run. If we only take the length of a run, each step would be a macrostep that involves many elementary updates, e.g. the use of unbounded parallelism does not impose any restriction on the number of updates in an update set employed in a transition from one state to a successor state, nor does the size of the critical objects. So we have to take the size of update sets and the size of critical objects into account as well. As critical objects are hereditarily finite sets, their sizes can be estimated by the cardinality of their transitive closures. We therefore adopt the notion of PTIME bound from CPT [4].

Definition 2.2. A *PTIME (bounded) ASM* is a triple $\tilde{M} = (M, p(n), q(n))$ comprising an ASM M and two integer polynomials $p(n)$ and $q(n)$, in which every called ASM is also PTIME bounded. A *run* of $\tilde{M}$ is an initial segment of a run of M of length at most $p(n)$ and a total number of at most $q(n)$ active objects, where n is the size of the input in the initial state of the run.

We say that a PTIME ASM $\tilde{M}$ *accepts* the input structure I iff there is a run of $\tilde{M}$ with initial state generated by I and ending in a state, in which *Halt* holds and the value of *Output* is 1. Analogously, a PTIME ASM $\tilde{M}$ *rejects* the input structure I iff there is a run of $\tilde{M}$ with initial state generated by I and ending in a state, in which *Halt* holds and the value of *Output* is 0.

2.2 Insignificant Choice Polynomial Time

We now formalise the observation above concerning insignificant choice. We first define *globally insignificant* ASMs, for which the final outcome does not depend on the choices. Global insignificance is a property, which in essence has already been investigated in [3,13], but in general is undecidable. Therefore, we also introduce *locally insignificant* ASMs (icASMs) that are characterised by two restrictions to ASMs. We will show that icASMs are globally insignificant, and they can be used to define the logic of insignificant choice polynomial time (ICPT).

In the following we use standard ASM notation and write $S + \Delta$ for the uniquely defined state S' that results from applying the update set Δ to the state S. If Δ is consistent, we have

$$\mathrm{val}_{S'}(\ell) = \begin{cases} v & \text{if } (\ell, v) \in \Delta \\ \mathrm{val}_S(\ell) & \text{else} \end{cases} ,$$

which is extended to $S + \Delta = S$ for inconsistent update sets Δ [[7], Def. 2.4.6].

Definition 2.3. An ASM M is *globally insignificant* iff for every run $S_0, \dots, S_k$ of length k such that *Halt* holds in S_k, every $i \in \{0, \dots, k-1\}$ and every update set $\Delta \in \boldsymbol{\Delta}(S_i)$ there exists a run $S_0, \dots, S_i, S'_{i+1}, \dots, S'_m$ such that $S'_{i+1} = S_i + \Delta$, *Halt* holds in S'_m, and *Output* $=$ **true** (or **false**, respectively) holds in S_k iff *Output* $=$ **true** (or **false**, respectively) holds in S'_m.

A *globally insignificant PTIME ASM* is a PTIME ASM $\tilde{M} = (M, p(n), q(n))$ with a globally insignificant ASM M.

Note that for a globally insignificant PTIME ASM $\tilde{M}$ whenever an input structure I is accepted by $\tilde{M}$ (or rejected, respectively) then every run on input structure I is accepting (or rejecting, respectively). Further note that the global insignificance restriction is a semantic one expressed by means of runs.

Definition 2.4. An ASM M is *locally insignificant* (for short: M is an icASM) iff the following two conditions are satisfied:

local insignificance condition. For every state S any two update sets $\Delta, \Delta' \in \boldsymbol{\Delta}(S)$ are isomorphic, and we can write $\boldsymbol{\Delta}(S) = \{\sigma\Delta \mid \sigma \in G\}$ with a set G of isomorphisms fixing the base set of S and $\Delta \in \boldsymbol{\Delta}(S)$. The isomorphisms in G are defined as products of transpositions given by the choice subrules of the rule r of M.

branching condition. For any states S, S' and any two isomorphic update sets $\Delta \in \boldsymbol{\Delta}(S)$ and $\Delta' = \sigma(\Delta) \in \boldsymbol{\Delta}(S')$ we have $\sigma(\boldsymbol{\Delta}(S + \Delta)) = \boldsymbol{\Delta}(S' + \Delta')$, i.e. the isomorphism σ defines an isomorphism between the sets of update sets on the corresponding successor states of S and S', respectively.

A *PTIME (bounded) icASM* is a PTIME ASM $\tilde{M} = (M, p(n), q(n))$ with an icASM M.

Note that called submachines are considered as single steps, so subcomputations can be hidden by such calls, but the contribution to complexity is taken into account. The conditions of Definition 2.4 must hold for the calling machine, but of course any object returned by a called ASM will somehow enter the update sets.

Proposition 2.1. *Every icASM is globally insignificant.*

The easy induction proof is given in Appendix A. Defining a PTIME icASM to solve a particular decision problem can be rather tricky, but we will later see that PTIME icASMs arise quite naturally for PTIME decision problems, and most importantly they permit a straightforward simulation by deterministic PTIME Turing machines.

Our aim is to show that with PTIME icASMs we can define a logic capturing PTIME in the sense of Gurevich [15]. We will use the definitions of PTIME logic and logic capturing PTIME in exactly the same way as in [4].

Definition 2.5. The complexity class *insignificant choice polynomial time* (ICPT) is the collection of pairs (K_1, K_2), where K_1 and K_2 are disjoint classes of finite structures of the same signature, such that there exists a PTIME icASM that accepts all structures in K_1 and rejects all structures in K_2.

2.3 Effective Translation

The effective translation of PTIME icASMs to Turing machines follows from the following lemma. The straighforward proof is given in [21].

Proposition 2.2. *For every icASM M with input signature Υ_0 there exists a deterministic Turing machine T_M simulating M. The machine T_M takes ordered versions of structures I over Υ_0 as input and accepts iff M accepts I. The translation from M to T_M is effective and compositional in the rule of M.*

We see immediately, that the construction in the proof of Proposition 2.2 results in a PTIME Turing machine, if M is a PTIME icASM and the checks of the local insignificance and branching conditions can be executed in polynomial time. The straighforward proof of Proposition 2.3 can be found in [21].

Proposition 2.3. *Assume that checks of the branching condition of an arbitrary ASM rule r and the local insignificance condition of choice subrules of r can be executed on a Turing machine in polynomial time. Then for a PTIME icASM $\tilde{M} = (M, p(n), q(n))$ the simulating Turing machine T_M in Proposition 2.2 runs in polynomial time.*

With these two lemmata we can concentrate on the remaining properties of PTIME logics. We have to show that icASMs have a recursive syntax and that the checks of the local insignificance and branching conditions can be executed on a Turing machine in polynomial time. The latter problem will be addressed in the next subsection. For the recursive syntax we simply keep choice rules and global rules of ASMs as defined above (this obviously preserves the recursive syntax we have for arbitrary ASMs), but we modify their semantics.

For a choice rule r' of the form **choose** $v \in \{\ \mathrm{x} \mid Atoms \wedge x \in t\}$ **do** $r(v)$ **enddo** we define that the set of yielded update sets is $\emptyset$, if the local insignificance condition is violated, i.e. we get $\boldsymbol{\Delta}^{ic}_{r',\zeta}(S) =$

$$\begin{cases} \bigcup\limits_{\substack{a \in Atoms \\ a \in val_{S,\zeta}(t)}} \boldsymbol{\Delta}_{r(a),\zeta(v\mapsto a)}(S) & \text{if for all } b, c \in Atoms \text{ with } b, c \in val_{S,\zeta}(t) \text{ and} \\ & \text{all } \Delta \in \boldsymbol{\Delta}_{r(b),\zeta(v\mapsto b)}(S), \Delta' \in \boldsymbol{\Delta}_{r(c),\zeta(v\mapsto c)}(S) \\ & \text{there exists an isomorphism } \sigma \text{ with } \sigma(\Delta) = \Delta' \\ \emptyset & \text{else} \end{cases}$$

Analogously, if r' is the complete closed rule of an icASM (not one of its component rules), we modify its semantics (i.e. the semantics of update sets that determine the successor states) as well defining that the set of yielded update sets is $\emptyset$, if the branching condition is violated, i.e. we get

$$\boldsymbol{\Delta}^{ic}_{r'}(S) = \begin{cases} \boldsymbol{\Delta}_{r'}(S) & \text{if for all states } S' \text{ and all update sets } \Delta \in \boldsymbol{\Delta}_{r'}(S), \\ & \Delta' \in \boldsymbol{\Delta}_{r'}(S') \text{ such that } \sigma(\Delta) = \Delta' \text{ holds for some} \\ & \text{isomorphism } \sigma \text{ we have } \sigma(\boldsymbol{\Delta}_{r'}(S + \Delta)) = \boldsymbol{\Delta}_{r'}(S' + \Delta') \\ \emptyset & \text{else} \end{cases}$$

Note that with this modified semantics for every state S we either have $\boldsymbol{\Delta}^{ic}_{r}(S) = \boldsymbol{\Delta}_{r}(S)$ or $\boldsymbol{\Delta}^{ic}_{r}(S) = \emptyset$. Then the proof of Lemma 2.1 will continue to hold for these modified machines, in particular, all machines are locally and globally insignificant. The only difference to the "normal" ASM semantics is that runs are truncated, if the local insignificance or branching conditions are violated, i.e. such machines will not accept (nor reject) any structure.

3 Polynomial Time Verification

In order to simulate a PTIME icASM by a PTIME Turing machine we still need to prove that the local insignificance and branching conditions can be checked on a Turing machine in polynomial time. The proof of the following proposition is given in Appendix A.

Proposition 3.1. *Let $\tilde{M} = (M, p(n), q(n))$ be an PTIME ASM with rule r. Then for every state S of M it can be checked in polynomial time, if for any two update sets $\Delta, \Delta' \in \boldsymbol{\Delta}_r(S)$ there exists an isomorphism σ with $\sigma(\Delta) = \Delta'$, where σ is defined by a product of those transpositions determined by the choice rules in r.*

3.1 The Branching Condition

Checking the branching condition for a PTIME ASM $\tilde{M} = (M, p(n), q(n))$ with rule r will be much more difficult, as for a given state S and an update set $\Delta \in \boldsymbol{\Delta}(S)$ we have to consider all states S', for which there exists an isomorphic update set $\Delta' = \sigma(\Delta) \in \boldsymbol{\Delta}(S')$. At first sight it seems impossible that a condition that involves all states S' could be verified in polynomial time. We will therefore investigate how to reduce the number of pairs (S', Δ') that need to be checked to finitely many, independent from the input structure.

We say that a pair (S', Δ') with a state S' and an update set $\Delta' \in \boldsymbol{\Delta}_r(S')$ with $\Delta' = \sigma(\Delta)$ for some isomorphism σ *satisfies BC with respect to* (S, Δ) iff $\sigma(\boldsymbol{\Delta}_r(S + \Delta)) = \boldsymbol{\Delta}_r(S' + \Delta')$ holds. Lemmata 3.1 and 3.2 cover the easy cases. Proofs can be found in [21].

Lemma 3.1. *For every update set $\Delta' \in \boldsymbol{\Delta}_r(S)$ it can be checked in polynomial time on a Turing machine, if (S, Δ') satisfies BC.*

Lemma 3.2. *If (S_1, Δ_1) satisfies BC and S_2 is isomorphic to S_1, i.e. $\tau(S_1) = S_2$ holds for some isomorphism τ and hence $\Delta_2 = \tau(\Delta_1) \in \boldsymbol{\Delta}_r(S_2)$, then also (S_2, Δ_2) satisfies BC.*

3.2 Bounded Exploration Witnesses

In order to further reduce the pairs (S', Δ'), for which BC satisfaction needs to be checked, we introduce *bounded exploration witnesses*, which we generalise from those used in the parallel ASM thesis [11] to arbitrary non-deterministic ASMs.

We use the notation $\langle t \mid \varphi \rangle_V$ for multiset comprehension terms, where t is a term defined over the signature of an ASM, φ is a Boolean term, and V is the set of free variables in the multiset comprehension term. In particular, we must have $fr(t) \subseteq fr(\varphi) \cup V$. Then the evaluation of terms defined in the previous section generalises to multiset comprehension terms in the usual way, i.e.

$$val_{S,\zeta}(\langle t \mid \varphi \rangle_V) = \langle val_{S,\zeta'}(t) \mid val_{S,\zeta'}(\varphi), \zeta'(v) = \zeta(v) \text{ for all } v \in V \rangle \ ,$$

where S is a state and ζ is a variable assignment. For closed multiset comprehension terms the evaluation does not depend on the variable assignment ζ, so we can simply write $val_S(\langle t \mid \varphi \rangle_V)$.

As we deal with choice rules, we consider more general multiset comprehension terms $\langle t \mid \varphi \rangle_V$, in which the term t is itself a multiset comprehension term. Such terms will be called *witness terms*. Clearly, the evaluation of a closed witness term in a state S results in a multiset of multisets of objects. We say that states S and S' *coincide* on a set W of closed witness terms iff $val_S(\alpha) = val_{S'}(\alpha)$ holds for all $\alpha \in W$.

Definition 3.1. A *bounded exploration witness* for an ASM M with rule r is a finite set W of closed witness terms such that for any two states S_1, S_2 of M that coincide on W we have $\boldsymbol{\Delta}_r(S_1) = \boldsymbol{\Delta}_r(S_2)$.

For an ASM rule r with free variables $fr(r) = V$ we can define a (standard) set W_r of witness terms with free variables in V. If r is closed, then also all witness terms in W_r are closed. For a rule r the set W_r of witness terms is defined as follows:

(1) If r is a **skip** rule, then we simply have $W_r = \{\langle\langle\rangle_\emptyset\rangle_\emptyset\}$.
(2) If r is an assignment rule $f(t_1, \dots, t_n) := t_0$ with $V = \bigcup_{0\le i\le n} fr(t_i)$, then we have $W_r = \{\langle\langle(t_0, \dots, t_n) \mid \mathbf{true}\rangle_V\rangle_V\}$.
(3) If r is a branching rule **if** φ **then** r_1 **else** r_2 **endif** with $V_0 = fr(\varphi)$, $V_1 = fr(r_1)$ and $V_2 = fr(r_2)$, thus $fr(r) = V_0 \cup V_1 \cup V_2$, we have

$$\begin{aligned} W_r = \{\langle\langle\varphi \mid \mathbf{true}\rangle_{V_0} \mid \mathbf{true}\rangle_{V_0}\}\cup \\ \{\langle\langle t \mid \psi \wedge \varphi\rangle_{V_0\cup V_1'} \mid \chi\rangle_{V_0\cup V_1} \mid \langle\langle t \mid \psi\rangle_{V_1'} \mid \chi\rangle_{V_1} \in W_{r_1}\}\cup \\ \{\langle\langle t \mid \psi \wedge \neg\varphi\rangle_{V_0\cup V_2'} \mid \chi\rangle_{V_0\cup V_2} \mid \langle\langle t \mid \psi\rangle_{V_2'} \mid \chi\rangle_{V_2} \in W_{r_2}\}\ . \end{aligned}$$

(4) If r is a parallel rule **forall** $v \in t$ **do** $r(v)$ **enddo** with $V_0 = fr(t)$ and $V = fr(r(v))$, we have $fr(r) = (V \cup V_0) - \{v\}$ and

$$\begin{aligned} W_r = \{\langle\langle t' \mid \psi \wedge v \in t\rangle_{(V'\cup V_0)-\{v\}} \mid \chi\rangle_{(V\cup V_0)-\{v\}} \mid \langle\langle t' \mid \psi\rangle_{V'} \mid \chi\rangle_V \in W_{r(v)}\}\cup \\ \{\langle\langle t' \mid \psi \wedge v \notin t\rangle_{(V'\cup V_0)-\{v\}} \mid \chi\rangle_{(V\cup V_0)-\{v\}} \mid \langle\langle t' \mid \psi\rangle_{V'} \mid \chi\rangle_V \in W_{r(v)}\}\ . \end{aligned}$$

(5) If r is a choice rule **choose** $v \in \{x \mid x \in Atoms \wedge x \in t\}$ **do** $r(v)$ **enddo** with $V_0 = fr(t)$ and $V = fr(r(v))$, then $fr(r) = (V \cup V_0) - \{v\}$ and

$$\begin{aligned} W_r = \\ \{\langle\langle t' \mid \psi\rangle_{(V'\cup V_0)-\{v\}} \mid \chi \wedge v \in Atoms \wedge v \in t\rangle_{(V\cup V_0)-\{v\}} \mid \langle\langle t' \mid \psi\rangle_{V'} \mid \chi\rangle_V \in W_{r(v)}\}\cup \\ \{\langle\langle t' \mid \psi\rangle_{(V'\cup V_0)-\{v\}} \mid \chi \wedge (v \notin Atoms \vee v \notin t)\rangle_{(V\cup V_0)-\{v\}} \mid \langle\langle t' \mid \psi\rangle_{V'} \mid \chi\rangle_V \in W_{r(v)}\}\ . \end{aligned}$$

(6) If r is a call rule $t_0 \leftarrow N(t_1, \dots, t_n)$ with $V = \bigcup_{i=0}^{n}$ and $t_0 = f(t_1', \dots, t_m')$, then we have

$$W_r = \{\langle\langle(t_1', \dots, t_m', t_1, \dots, t_n) \mid \mathbf{true}\rangle_V\rangle_V\}\ .$$

In [21] the following proposition is shown. The structural induction proof is omitted here.

Proposition 3.2. *If r is the rule of an ASM M, then the standard set W_r of witness terms constructed above is a bounded exploration witness for M.*

3.3 A Reduction Lemma

We will now show that BC satisfaction only depends on W-similarity classes for a fixed bounded exploration witness W.

Definition 3.2. Let M be an ASM with rule r and bounded exploration witness W. For a state S of M we obtain an equivalence class $\sim_S$ on W by $\alpha \sim_S \alpha'$ iff $val_S(\alpha) = val_S(\alpha')$. Then two states S and S' are called *W-similar* iff $\sim_S = \sim_{S'}$ holds.

Lemma 3.3. *Let M be an ASM with rule r and bounded exploration witness W. For a state S of M and an update set $\Delta \in \boldsymbol{\Delta}_r(S)$ assume that (S_1, Δ_1) satisfies BC with respect to (S, Δ). Let S_2 be another state of M, and assume that the update set $\Delta_2 \in \boldsymbol{\Delta}_r(S_2)$ is isomorphic to Δ. If $S_1 + \Delta_1$ and $S_2 + \Delta_2$ are W-similar, then also (S_2, Δ_2) satisfies BC with respect to (S, Δ).*

Proof. Without loss of generality we can assume that the sets of atoms A_1 and A_2 in the base sets of S_1 and S_2, respectively, are disjoint. Otherwise we could replace S_2 by an isomorphic copy S_2' with a base set that is isomorphic to the one of S_1. If η is an isomorphism with $\eta(S_2) = S_2'$, we get $\Delta' = \eta(\Delta_2) \in \boldsymbol{\Delta}_r(S_2')$, and clearly Δ_2' is isomorphic to Δ. Furthermore, as $S_1 + \Delta_1$ and $S_2 + \Delta_2$ are W-similar, also $S_1 + \Delta_1$ and $S_2' + \Delta_2'$ are W-similar. Thus, if we show the lemma for S_1 and S_2', we get that (S_2', Δ_2') satisfies BC. Then we can apply Lemma 3.2, which shows that also (S_2, Δ_2) satisfies BC as claimed.

Now let σ, τ be isomorphisms with $\sigma(\Delta) = \Delta_1$ and $\tau(\Delta) = \Delta_2$. As we assume that (S_1, Δ_1) satisfies BC, we know that $\sigma(\boldsymbol{\Delta}_r(S + \Delta)) = \boldsymbol{\Delta}_r(S_1 + \Delta_1)$ holds.

Consider the state $S_3 = \sigma\tau^{-1}(S_2)$ and the update set $\Delta_3 = \sigma\tau^{-1}(\Delta_2) = \Delta_1 \in \boldsymbol{\Delta}_r(S_3)$. Hence also $\sigma\tau^{-1}(S_2 + \Delta_2) = S_3 + \Delta_1$ holds. Then for every witness term $\alpha \in W$ such that $val_{S_3+\Delta_1}(\alpha)$ contributes to an update set we get

$$val_{S_3+\Delta_1}(\alpha) = val_{\sigma\tau^{-1}(S_2+\Delta_2)}(\alpha) = \sigma\tau^{-1}(val_{S_2+\Delta_2}(\alpha)) \stackrel{(*)}{=} val_{S_1+\Delta_1}(\alpha) \; .$$

That is, $S_3 + \Delta_1$ and $S_1 + \Delta_1$ coincide on the subset of W containing all witness terms needed to determine $\boldsymbol{\Delta}_r(S_3 + \Delta_1)$. Using the defining property of bounded exploration witnesses plus the strengthening remark above we conclude that $\boldsymbol{\Delta}_r(S_1 + \Delta_1) = \boldsymbol{\Delta}_r(S_3 + \Delta_1)$, hence $\sigma(\boldsymbol{\Delta}_r(S + \Delta)) = \sigma\tau^{-1}(\boldsymbol{\Delta}_r(S_2 + \Delta_2))$ and further $\tau(\boldsymbol{\Delta}_r(S + \Delta)) = \boldsymbol{\Delta}_r(S_2 + \Delta_2)$ as claimed.

It remains to show the validity of the equality $(*)$ above. For this let

$$\alpha = \langle\langle t(x_1, \dots, x_n, y_1, \dots, y_m) \mid \varphi(x_1, \dots, x_n, y_1, \dots, y_m)\rangle_{\{y_1, \dots, y_m\}} \mid \psi(y_1, \dots, y_m)\rangle_{\emptyset}$$

and let $val_{S_2+\Delta_2}(\alpha) = \langle M_1, \dots, M_r\rangle$ with $(c_0, \dots, c_k) \in M_i$. Then there exist atoms $a_1, \dots, a_m$ and objects $b_1, \dots, b_n$ such that $\psi(a_1, \dots, a_m)$, $\varphi(b_1, \dots, b_n, a_1, \dots, a_m)$ and $(c_0, \dots, c_k) = t(b_1, \dots, b_n, a_1, \dots, a_m)$ hold in $S_2 + \Delta_2$.

If $(c_0, \dots, c_k)$ is an update tuple in $\Delta' \in \boldsymbol{\Delta}_r(S_2 + \Delta_2)$, i.e. for some dynamic function symbol $f \in \Upsilon$ we have $((f, (c_1, \dots, c_k)), c_0) \in \Delta'$, then also $t(b_1', \dots, b_n', a_1, \dots, a_m) = (c_0', \dots, c_k')$ defines an update $((f, (c_1', \dots, c_k')), c_0') \in \Delta'$, provided that in $S_2 + \Delta_2$ $\varphi(b_1', \dots, b_n', a_1, \dots, a_m)$ holds. This follows from the construction of witness terms for parallel rules.

Likewise, for atoms $a_1', \dots, a_m'$ with $a_i' = \sigma_i(a_i)$ such that $\psi(a_1', \dots, a_m')$ holds in $S_2 + \Delta_2$ we get $\sigma_1 \dots \sigma_m(\Delta') \in \boldsymbol{\Delta}_r(S_2 + \Delta_2)$. Thus, the value $val_{S_2+\Delta_2}(\alpha)$ of the witness term α is completely determined by $\boldsymbol{\Delta}_r(S_2 + \Delta_2)$.

As $S_2 + \Delta_2$ and $S_1 + \Delta_1$ are W-similar, the same holds for $val_{S_1+\Delta_1}(\alpha)$, hence $\sigma\tau^{-1}(val_{S_2+\Delta_2}(\alpha)) = \pi(val_{S_1+\Delta_1}(\alpha))$ holds with some isomorphism π. Due to Lemma 3.2 we get $\pi = id$, which shows (∗) and completes the proof of the lemma. □

Lemma 3.3 implies that in order to check the branching condition for a given state S and an update set $\Delta \in \boldsymbol{\Delta}_r(S)$ it suffices to consider those pairs (S', Δ'), where $S' + \Delta'$ are representatives of W-similarity classes. The number of W-similarity classes only depends on W (and thus on the rule r of the ASM M), but not on the input structure. Furthermore, there must exist an isomorphism σ with $\sigma(\Delta) = \Delta'$, so it may be the case that not all W-similarity classes need to be considered.

3.4 PTIME Verification of the Branching Condition

The W-similarity classes correspond to partitions λ of W, say $W = \bigcup_{i=1}^{\ell} \{\alpha_1^i, \dots, \alpha_{\lambda_i}^i\}$. For these we obtain a formula

$$\varphi_\lambda \equiv \bigwedge_{1 \le i \le \ell} \left(\bigwedge_{1 \le j < k \le \ell} \alpha_j^i = \alpha_k^i \wedge \bigwedge_{\substack{2 \le i' \le \ell \\ i < i'}} \alpha_1^i \neq \alpha_1^{i'} \right) \tag{1}$$

such that $val_S(\varphi_\lambda) = 1$ holds iff the state S belongs to the W-similarity class defined by λ. As W contains nested conditions from the branching subrules of the ASM rule r of the ASM M, many of these formulae φ_λ are equivalent to **false**, i.e. the partition λ does not define a W-similarity class.

As the values of the witness terms in W in a state S determine the update sets in $\boldsymbol{\Delta}_r(S)$, we obtain a transition relation $\to$ on partitions of W that define W-similarity classes. Due to the normalisation of the ASM rule r we have $\lambda_1 = \lambda_2$, whenever $\lambda_1 \to \lambda'$ and $\lambda_2 \to \lambda'$ hold. This transition relation will be used in the construction of states S' and update sets $\Delta' \in \boldsymbol{\Delta}_r(S')$ such that Δ' is isomorphic to a given update set $\Delta \in \boldsymbol{\Delta}_r(S)$ and $S' + \Delta'$ is a representative of a W-similarity class.

With the following lemma we complete the proof that the branching condition in a state S can be verified on a Turing maching in polynomial time. The proof is given in Appendix A.

Proposition 3.3. *Let S be a state of a PTIME ASM M with rule r, and let $\Delta \in \boldsymbol{\Delta}_r(S)$. Then it can be checked in polynomial time on a simulating Turing machine, whether for every state S' and every $\Delta' \in \boldsymbol{\Delta}_r(S')$ that is isomorphic to Δ the pair (S', Δ') satisfies BC with respect to (S, Δ).*

4 The Capture of PTIME

We now present our main result, the capture of PTIME by ICPT. The proof comprises two parts, an easier one showing PTIME ⊆ ICPT, which in essence requires to simulate a PTIME Turing machine by an icASM, and a more difficult one showing ICPT $\subseteq$ PTIME, which integrates all other results about ICPT from the previous subsections. A sketch of the proof is given in Appendix A, while the full proof is contained in [21].

Theorem 4.1. *ICPT is a logic capturing PTIME on arbitrary finite structures.*

Theorem 4.1 shows indeed that ICPT defines a logic capturing PTIME:

(1) The sentences of the logic are PTIME icASMs. For their syntax we simply adopt ASM rules, so $Sen(\Upsilon)$ is a recursive set. However, we use a modified semantics for choice rules and for the closed rules associated with an ASM, which permits empty sets of update sets, if the defining conditions of icASMs are violated.
(2) The modified semantics for choice rules yields an empty set of update sets in a state, if the local insignificance condition is violated. Likewise, the rule of an ASM yields an empty set of update sets in all states, in which the branching condition is violated. By adopting this modified semantics we enforce that the ASMs are icASMs.
(3) For the SAT relation a sentence φ is satisfied by a structure I iff φ as an icASM accepts the input structure I. Clearly, this also gives a recursive relation.
(4) In Theorem 4.1 we proved that each PTIME icASM $\tilde{M} = (M, p(n), q(n))$ can be effectively translated into a deterministic PTIME Turing machine T_M, which accepts exactly the standard encodings of ordered versions of input structures I for M iff M accepts I.

5 Conclusion

In this article we proved that ICPT, a logic defined by restricted non-deterministic ASMs, captures PTIME thereby refuting Gurevich's conjecture from 1988 and providing an answer to Chandra's and Harel's question from 1982. To summarise, ICPT is based on three conditions: (1) choice is restricted to choice among atoms, (2) choices must satisfy that update sets in a state must be isomorphic, and (3) for any two isomorphic update sets on states S and S', respectively, the sets of update sets of the corresponding successor states are isomorphic.

A Selected Proofs

Proof (of Proposition 2.1). Let $S_0, S_1, S_2, \dots$ and $S_0', S_1', S_2', \dots$ be runs of M with $S_0 = S_0'$. We show for every $i \geq 0$ that $\boldsymbol{\Delta}(S_i)$ and $\boldsymbol{\Delta}(S_i')$ are isomorphic. As all update sets in $\boldsymbol{\Delta}(S_i)$ are pairwise isomorphic by the local insignificance condition, and likewise all update sets in $\boldsymbol{\Delta}(S_i')$ are pairwise isomorphic, then all update sets in $\Delta_i \in \boldsymbol{\Delta}(S_i)$ are isomorphic to all $\Delta_i' \in \boldsymbol{\Delta}(S_i')$.

Hence, for $((\mathit{Halt}, ()), b) \in \Delta_i$ with a truth value b we also get $((\mathit{Halt}, ()), b) \in \Delta_i'$, i.e. terminating runs have the same length. Analogously, for $((\mathit{Output}, ()), b) \in \Delta_i$ with a truth value b we also get $((\mathit{Output}, ()), b) \in \Delta_i'$, i.e. the last update to *Output* is the same in both runs, which implies the claimed global insignificance.

As for the claimed condition itself we use induction over i. For $i = 0$ there is nothing to show. Let $S_{i+1} = S_i + \Delta$. If we assume $\sigma(\boldsymbol{\Delta}(S_i)) = \boldsymbol{\Delta}(S_i')$, we obtain an isomorphism σ' with $\sigma'(\Delta) = \Delta' \in \boldsymbol{\Delta}(S_i')$ for $S_{i+1}' = S_i' + \Delta'$. By the branching condition we obtain $\sigma'(\boldsymbol{\Delta}(S_{i+1})) = \boldsymbol{\Delta}(S_{i+1}')$ as claimed. □

Proof (of Proposition 3.1). Consider a Turing machine T_M simulating M as constructed in Proposition 2.2. In order to check the local insignificance condition this machine can produce (encodings of) all update sets in $\boldsymbol{\Delta}_r(S)$ and write them onto some tape. Any object in one of these update sets must be active, and $q(n)$ is a polynomial bound on the number of active objects. Furthermore, r makes choices only among atoms, so for each choice there are at most n update sets. Consequently, for each choice subrule there are at most $n - 1$ transpositions mapping one chosen atom to another one. As the number of choice subrules in r is fixed, there is a polynomial bound on the number of possible isomorphisms σ between update sets.

Therefore, we can fix one update set $\Delta \in \boldsymbol{\Delta}_r(S)$, then apply all these possible isomorphisms σ to Δ and write the resulting update sets onto some tape. The application of σ is merely a syntactic replacement of atoms, so it can be done in linear time in the size of Δ.

Finally, the simulating Turing machine needs to check, if each of the computed update sets $\sigma(\Delta)$ appears in the list of update sets in $\boldsymbol{\Delta}_r(S)$ and vice versa. Such a comparison requires again polynomial time in the size of the update sets and the number of update sets, hence this can be done in polynomial time. Altogether the check that update sets $\Delta, \Delta' \in \boldsymbol{\Delta}_r(S)$ are pairwise isomorphic is done by T_M in polynomial time. □

Proof (of Proposition 3.3). Due to Lemma 3.3 it suffices to check that (S', Δ') satisfies BC only for those pairs, for which $S' + \Delta'$ are representatives of W-similarity classes. These classes only depend on the finite bounded exploration witness W and not on S nor Δ.

Given such a pair (S', Δ') with $\Delta' = \sigma(\Delta)$ for some isomorphism σ, the simulating Turing machine can determine all update sets $\bar{\Delta} \in \boldsymbol{\Delta}_r(S + \Delta)$ and write then onto some tape. The number of these update sets is polynomially bounded as well as the size of each $\bar{\Delta}$ and the critical values therein. Then the isomorphism σ can be applied to all these update sets $\bar{\Delta}$. This is merely a syntactic replacement of atoms, hence requires at most polynomial time.

In the same way the machine can compute in polynomial time all update sets $\bar{\Delta}' \in \boldsymbol{\Delta}_r(S' + \Delta')$ and write these onto another tape. Then it can be checked in polynomial time, if the two sets of update sets $\sigma(\boldsymbol{\Delta}_r(S + \Delta))$ and $\bar{\Delta}' \in \boldsymbol{\Delta}_r(S' + \Delta')$ coincide.

Therefore, it remains to show that all representatives of W-similarity classes that take the form $S' + \Delta'$ and isomorphisms σ with $\sigma(\Delta) = \Delta'$ can be computed in polynomial time. For this consider also the run $S_0, \dots, S_k$ that leads to the given state S, i.e. $S_k = S$. For $j = 0, \dots, k-1$ let $\Delta_j \in \boldsymbol{\Delta}_r(S_j)$ be an update set with $S_j + \Delta_j = S_{j+1}$. In addition let $\Delta_k = \Delta$.

We can assume that the simulating Turing machine has written all these update sets $\Delta_0, \dots, \Delta_k$ onto some dedicated tape. Due to the polynomial restriction of active objects and the polynomial bound on the length of a run, the memorisation of the update sets causes only a polynomial time overhead. In addition, with every update $(\ell, v) \in \Delta_j$ let the Turing machine keep the previous value of the location ℓ, i.e. it stores $val_{S_j}(\ell)$ together with the update. This memorisation of update sets allows the simulating Turing machine to process backwards through the run starting from the given state S.

Now let $\lambda_1, \dots, \lambda_m$ be all the partitions of W that determine W-similarity classes, and let $\rightarrow$ denote the transition relation on the set of these partitions, i.e. we have $\lambda_i \rightarrow \lambda_j$ iff there are states S_i and S_j in the W-similarity classs defined by λ_i and λ_j, respectively, for which $S_j = S_i + \Delta_i$ holds for some update set $\Delta_i \in \boldsymbol{\Delta}_r(S_i)$. Furthermore, let φ_{λ_i} be the condition defined in (1), i.e. a state S_i satisfies φ_{λ_i} iff S_i is in the W-similarity class defined by λ_i.

Assume that $S \models \varphi_{\lambda_p}$ and $S + \Delta \models \varphi_{\lambda_q}$ with $\lambda_p \rightarrow \lambda_q$. Then the pair (S, Δ) for the W-similarity class defined by λ_q. The simulating Turing machine can further determine the W-similarity class of $S' + \Delta'$ for each $\Delta' \in \boldsymbol{\Delta}_r(S)$, which defines further pairs (S', Δ') that need to be checked. In the worst case all $\Delta' \in \boldsymbol{\Delta}_r(S)$ need to be considered, in which case Lemma 3.1 shows that checking BC satisfaction can be done in polynomial time.

This leaves those W-similarity classes defined by λ_s with $\lambda_p \rightarrow \lambda_s$, for which there is no representative $S + \Delta'$. For these cases we need other states S' with $S' \models S_{\lambda_p}$. We can exclude $S' \models \varphi_{\lambda_{p'}}$ for $p' \neq p$, as for such states there cannot exist an update set $\Delta' \in \boldsymbol{\Delta}_r(S')$.

As we have $\lambda_p \rightarrow \lambda_s$, there must be some condition ψ not in φ_{λ_p} that can give rise to an update set in $\boldsymbol{\Delta}_r(S')$, but not in $\boldsymbol{\Delta}_r(S)$. Hence there must exist an ancestor state S_i of S with update sets $\Delta_i, \Delta_i' \in \boldsymbol{\Delta}_r(S_i)$ such that $S_i + \Delta_i' \models \psi$, but $S_i + \Delta_i \not\models \psi$. The simulating Turing machine can find such an ancestor by backward processing in polynomial time through the run.

Fix such an ancestor state. We can assume that the local insignificance and branching conditions have already been checked successfully for all ancestor states $S_0, \dots, S_{\ell-1}$ of S. Then we know that there exists an isomorphism σ with $\sigma(\Delta_i) = \Delta_i'$, which arises from checking the local insignificance condition for S_i. Then we obtain a run $S_0', \dots, S_\ell'$ with $S_j' = S_j$ for all $j \le i$ and $S_{j+1}' = S_j' + \Delta_j'$ for $j \ge i$ with update sets $\Delta_j' = \sigma(\Delta_j) \in \boldsymbol{\Delta}_r(S_j')$. In particular, for $S' = S_\ell'$ we have an update set $\Delta' = \sigma(\Delta) \in \boldsymbol{\Delta}_r(S')$, and $S' + \Delta' \models \varphi_{\lambda_s}$. This construction of (S', Δ') and σ takes in total polynomial time.

The simulating Turing machine proceeds in this way, until for all W-similarity classes defined by $\lambda_{p'}$ with $\lambda_p \rightarrow \lambda_{p'}$ a representative $S' + \Delta'$ together with an isomorphism between Δ and Δ' has been found. As the number of W-similarity classes only depends on W, the whole process requires polynomial time as claimed, which completes the proof of the lemma. $\square$

Proof (of Theorem 4.1). For ***PTIME*** $\subseteq$ ***ICPT*** consider a PTIME problem represented by a Boolean query ϕ and a signature for input structures I for ϕ. Then there exists a PTIME Turing machine T accepting standard encodings of ordered versions of I iff I satisfies ϕ. In particular, T is order-invariant. Furthermore, if T accepts the standard encoding of an ordered version of I, it also accepts the standard encoding of any ordered version of any structure J that is isomorphic to I.

We need to construct a PTIME icASM that simulates the given Turing machine T. As the input for T is the standard encoding of an ordered structure $(I, <)$, whereas for an icASM we only have the unordered structure I as input, we have to first create an ordered version $(I, <)$ and then build the standard encoding with respect to this order $<$. Therefore, we define a PTIME icASM that comprises three steps:

(1) First we show that with a PTIME icASM, i.e. a PTIME ASM that satisfies the local insignificance and branching conditions, we can construct an arbitrary order on the set of atoms of $State(I)$, so we obtain an ordered structure $(I, <)$.
(2) Then using an ASM rule CREATE_ENCODING we build the standard binary encoding of $(I, <)$ (see [20, p.88]), which can be done by a PTIME ASM without choice. In particular, the local insignificance condition is trivially satisfied. As in the first step an arbitrary order $<$ on the set of atoms was constructed, there exists an isomorphism between any of these orders. Consequently, such an isomorphism maps the different standard encodings onto each other, which implies that the simulating ASM satisfies the branching condition.
(3) In the third and most important step we use an ASM rule RUN_SIMULATION to simulate T (see [7, p.289]), which is defined by calling another PTIME ASM without choice. In particular, this deterministic ASM satisfies the local insignificance condition. As the called deterministic ASM is handled as a single step of the calling ASM, the fact that T is order-invariant and the class of accepted structures is closed under isomorphisms implies that also the branching condition is satisfied.

We omit the details of the combined PTIME icASM (see [21]). We obtain an ASM which only exploits choices among atoms. We show that the conditions of Definition 2.4 are satisfied, and hence the constructed ASM is a PTIME icASM.

Concerning the local insignificance condition in a state S we have $|\boldsymbol{\Delta}_r(S)| = 1$, whenever $val_S(mode) \in \{\text{init}, \text{build-tm}, \text{simulate-tm}\}$ holds, in which case there is nothing to show. In case $val_S(mode) = \text{create-order}$ holds, a choice is made, an atom $a \in A$ is selected and the corresponding update set Δ_a contains updates $((<, (a', a)), \textbf{true})$ for all $a' \in A^c$ as well as $((A, ()), A_{new})$ with $A_{new} = \text{val}_S(A) - \{a\}$, and $((A^c, ()), A^c_{new})$ with $A^c_{new} = \text{val}_S(A^c) \cup \{a\}$. In case $val_S(A) = \{a\}$ holds, there is an additional update $((mode, ()), \text{build-tm}) \in \Delta_a$. These update sets are parameterised by the selected atom a. For two different choices a_1, a_2 let σ be the isomorphism defined by the transposition of a_1 and a_2. Then $\sigma(\Delta_{a_1}) = \Delta_{a_2}$ holds.

Concerning the branching condition we have to distinguish several cases depending on the value of the location *mode*. We only show the case $val_S(mode) = \text{init}$ (for the other cases see [21]). Consider states S, S' and update sets $\Delta \in \boldsymbol{\Delta}_r(S)$, $\Delta' \in \boldsymbol{\Delta}_r(S')$, and assume that there is an isomorphism σ with $\sigma(\Delta) = \Delta'$.

If $val_S(mode) = \text{init}$ holds, we have $((mode, ()), \text{create-order}) \in \Delta$, so an isomorphism σ mapping Δ to Δ' only exists for $S' = S$ and $\Delta' = \Delta$. In this case every isomorphism σ preserves Δ, because *Atoms* and $\emptyset$ are invariant under isomorphisms. As above $\boldsymbol{\Delta}_r(S + \Delta) = \boldsymbol{\Delta}_r(S' + \Delta')$ contains update sets Δ_a for all atoms a, where Δ_a contains only updates $((A, ()), Atoms - \{a\})$ and $((A^c, ()), \{a\})$ plus eventually $((mode, ()), \text{build-tm})$ in case $Atoms = \{a\}$. Clearly, every isomorphism σ maps the set $\{\Delta_a \mid a \in Atoms\}$ of update sets onto itself.

For **ICPT** $\subseteq$ **PTIME** assume a PTIME icASM $\tilde{M} = (M, p(n), q(n))$. Analogously to the proof of [4, Thm.3] we create a simulating PTIME Turing machine, which takes strings encoding ordered versions of input structures I of $\tilde{M}$ as input.

As shown in Proposition 2.2 we can effectively construct a simulating Turing machine. Every step of M is simulated by first checking the branching condition, then applying the rule r of M. For every choice subrule the local insignificance condition is checked. Due to Proposition 3.1 these checks are performed in polynomial time. Due to Proposition 3.3 also the check of the branching condition is performed in polynomial time. Due to Proposition 2.3 the simulating Turing machine is deterministic, because global insignificance holds by Proposition 2.1 and thus choices can be replaced by selecting always the smallest atom in the order added to the input structure. Furthermore, the polynomial bounds of $\tilde{M}$ guarantee that the simulating Turing machine accepts in polynomial time. □

References

1. Abiteboul, S., Papadimitriou, C.H., Vianu, V.: The power of reflective relational machines. In: Proceedings of the Ninth Annual Symposium on Logic in Computer Science (LICS 1994), pp. 230–240. IEEE Computer Society (1994)
2. Abiteboul, S., Vianu, V.: Generic computation and its complexity. In: Koutsougeras, C., Vitter, J.S., (eds) Proceedings of the 23rd Annual ACM Symposium on Theory of Computing (STOC 1991), pp. 209–219. ACM (1991)
3. Arvind, V., Biswas, S.: Expressibility of first order logic with a nondeterministic inductive operator. In: Brandenburg, F.J., Vidal-Naquet, G., Wirsing, M. (eds.) STACS 1987. LNCS, vol. 247, pp. 323–335. Springer, Heidelberg (1987). https://doi.org/10.1007/BFb0039616
4. Blass, A., Gurevich, Y., Shelah, S.: Choiceless polynomial time. Ann. Pure Appl. Logic **100**, 141–187 (1999)
5. Börger, E., Schewe, K.-D.: Concurrent Abstract State Machines. Acta Informatica **53**(5), 469–492 (2016)
6. Börger, E., Schewe, K.-D.: A behavioural theory of recursive algorithms. Fund. Inform. **177**(1), 1–37 (2020)

7. Börger, E., Stärk, R.: Abstract State Machines. Springer-Verlag, Berlin Heidelberg New York (2003)
8. Chandra, A.K., Harel, D.: Structure and complexity of relational queries. J. Comput. Syst. Sci. **25**(1), 99–128 (1982)
9. Dawar, A., Richerby, D.: Fixed-point logics with nondeterministic choice. J. Log. Comput. **13**(4), 503–530 (2003)
10. Fagin, R.: Generalized first-order spectra and polynomial-time recognizable sets. In: Karp, R., ed. SIAM-AMS Proceedings, no. 7, pp. 43–73 (1974)
11. Ferrarotti, F., Schewe, K.-D., Tec, L., Wang, Q.: A new thesis concerning synchronised parallel computing - simplified parallel ASM thesis. Theor. Comp. Sci. **649**, 25–53 (2016)
12. Ferrarotti, F., Schewe, K.-D., Tec, L., Wang, Q.: A unifying logic for non-deterministic, parallel and concurrent abstract state machines. Ann. Math. Artif. Intell. **83**(3–4), 321–349 (2018)
13. Gire, F., Hoang, H.K.: An extension of fixpoint logic with a symmetry-based choice construct. Inf. Comput. **144**(1), 40–65 (1998)
14. Glavan, P., Rosenzweig, D.: Communicating evolving algebras. In: E. Börger et al., editors, Computer Science Logic, 6th Workshop (CSL '92), vol. 702 of Lecture Notes in Computer Science, pp. 182–215. Springer (1992)
15. Gurevich, Y.: Logic and the challenge of computer science. In: E. Börger, ed. Current Trends in Theoretical Computer Science, pp. 1–57. Computer Science Press (1988)
16. Gurevich, Y.: Evolving algebras 1993: Lipari Guide. In: E. Börger, ed. Specification and Validation Methods, pp. 9–36. Oxford University Press (1995)
17. Gurevich, Y.: Sequential abstract state machines capture sequential algorithms. ACM Trans. Comp. Logic **1**(1), 77–111 (2000)
18. Immerman, N.: Relational queries computable in polynomial time. Inf. Control **68**(1–3), 86–104 (1986)
19. Immerman, N.: Descriptive Complexity. Graduate texts in computer science. Springer (1999)
20. Libkin, L.: Elements of finite model theory. Texts in Theoretical Computer Science. An EATCS Series. Springer (2004)
21. Schewe, K.-D.: Insignificant choice polynomial time. CoRR, abs/2005.04598, version 8 (2025)
22. Schewe, K.-D., Ferrarotti, F.: Behavioural theory of reflective algorithms I: reflective sequential algorithms. Sci. Comput. Program. **223**, 102864 (2022)
23. Stärk, R., Nanchen, S.: A logic for abstract state machines. J. Univ. Comput. Sci. **7**(11) (2001)
24. Vardi, M.Y.: The complexity of relational query languages (extended abstract). In: Lewis, H.R., et al., eds. Proceedings of the 14th Annual ACM Symposium on Theory of Computing (STOC 1982), pp. 137–146. ACM (1982)

Counterexamples to Import-Export in Conditionals: A Logical Analysis

Eric Raidl[1] and Gilberto Gomes[2(✉)]

[1] Cluster of Excellence 'Machine Learning for Science', Eberhard Karls Universität, Tübingen, Germany
eric.raidl@uni-tuebingen.de

[2] UENF, Campos dos Goytacazes, Brazil
ggomes.ggomes@gmail.com

Abstract. It is usually considered that $A \rightarrowtail (B \rightarrowtail C)$ (i) implies and (ii) is implied by $(A \wedge B) \rightarrowtail C$. (i) is called Import (IM) and (ii) Export (EX). IM seems to be valid for natural language conditionals, but here we present counterexamples to EX, such as: *If he uses cocaine every weekend and hides it from his family, he is already addicted*, but not: *If he uses cocaine every weekend, then if he hides it from his family, he is already addicted.* Gibbard's collapse theorem depends on IM-EX and Simplification (Conjunction Elimination). Here we use the implicative conditional for a logical analysis of IM-EX. We show that possibilistic versions of IM and EX are respectively valid and invalid for the implicative conditional, in accordance with what is observed in natural language conditionals. We conclude that this supports the adequacy of the implicative conditional for analysing the implicative use of natural language conditionals. We also conclude that the implicative conditional is immune to Gibbard's collapse theorem, since it invalidates both IM-EX and Simplification.

Keywords: Implicative conditional · Import · Export · Gibbard's proof · Simplification · Conjunction Elimination

1 Introduction

The equivalence between *If A, then if B, then C* and *If A and B, then C* is called the principle of Import-Export (or Importation and Exportation, IM-EX), which is valid for the material conditional (i.e., when $\rightarrowtail$ is interpreted as $\supset$ in the following formula). [1]

$$(A \rightarrowtail (B \rightarrowtail C)) \equiv ((A \wedge B) \rightarrowtail C) \qquad \text{IM-EX}^1$$

Import-Export is usually considered to apply to the natural language use of conditional sentences (Edgington, 2020; McGee, 1989). However, we present several counterexamples to it here. As an equivalence, the principle is a conjunction of two principles, namely the entailment from the first to the second of the above-mentioned conditionals, and the entailment from the second to the first. The former is called importation

[1] $\rightarrowtail$ is used here for a generic conditional; $\equiv$ for the material biconditional (material equivalence); $\supset$ for the material conditional.

D. Kozen and R. de Queiroz (Eds.): WoLLIC 2025, LNCS 15942, pp. 357–368, 2026.
https://doi.org/10.1007/978-3-031-99536-1_22

(IM) because the antecedent of the embedded conditional is 'imported' to antecedent of the main conditional (as a conjunct), and the latter exportation (EX) because the second conjunct of the antecedent is 'exported' to an embedded conditional.[2]

$$(A \rightarrowtail (B \rightarrowtail C)) \supset ((A \wedge B) \rightarrowtail C) \qquad \text{IM}$$
$$((A \wedge B) \rightarrowtail C) \supset (A \rightarrowtail (B \rightarrowtail C)) \qquad \text{EX}$$

It seems that no example in natural language invalidates importation, but the counterexamples provided here invalidate exportation, and thus the conjunction of importation and exportation.

The rest of the paper is organized as follows. Section 2 presents the counterexamples and the pattern they follow. In Sect. 3, we discuss Gibbard's collapse theorem, which relies on the supposed validity of IM-EX and purports to prove that any conditional stronger than the material conditional collapses to the latter. Section 4 brings a brief presentation of the implicative conditional, the operator that will be used for our analysis of IM-EX. Section 5 discusses the possibilistic principles that are characteristic of the implicative conditional, because possibilitic versions of IM and EX will be necessary for our subsequent analysis.[3] Section 6 then presents our logical analysis of IM-EX for the implicative conditional. We show that possibilistic IM is valid and possibilistic EX invalid for the implicative conditional. Section 7 relates this analysis to the counterexamples of Sect. 2. Finally, Sect. 8 contains our conclusions, and the Appendix A all the proofs.

2 Counterexamples to Import-Export

(1) If you sell your car and buy a bike, you'll have money for the trip.
(2) If you sell your car, then if you buy a bike, you'll have money for the trip.
(3) If you study for one hour and watch TV for the rest of the evening, you'll pass the test tomorrow.
(4) If you study for one hour, then if you watch TV for the rest of the evening, you'll pass the test tomorrow.
(5) If you exceed the speed limit and put other people's lives at risk, you'll be fined.
(6) If you exceed the speed limit, then if you put other people's lives at risk, you'll be fined.
(7) If you sell your tickets for the concert and buy new ones for some other date, then you'll be able to come to my party.
(8) If you sell your tickets for the concert, then if you buy new ones for some other date, you'll be able to come to my party.

The pattern of these counterexamples is clear. There is a reason for adding a conjunct to the antecedent, but this conjunct does not participate in the implicative relation between the first conjunct and the consequent. There is no conditional 'connection'

[2] Whitehead and Russell (1927/1963, p. 110) trace the name *exportation* to Peano.

[3] Sections 4 and 5 are based on previous works by the authors.

between the second conjunct and the consequent.[4] It is only the truth of the first conjunct that functions as a sufficient condition for the truth of the consequent, without any help from the second conjunct. For this reason, when Exportation is applied to (1), (3), (5) and (7), which all make good sense, a bad result is obtained. (2), (4), (6) and (8) all seem to say that if the antecedent of the main conditional is true, then the embedded conditional is true, but the latter seems to imply a connection between its antecedent and its consequent which does not exist. They all seem to imply that the antecedent of the embedded conditional is also necessary to form a sufficient condition for the truth of the consequent, when in fact it is not. In view of these and other similar counterexamples, it can be concluded that Exportation is far from being a fact of natural language usage, and efforts to preserve Import-Export in conditional logic may be viewed as misguided, as far as a representation of conditionals used in natural reasoning is intended.

3 Gibbard's Collapse Theorem

Gibbard (1981, pp. 234–235) used Import-Export as a premise in his proof that any indicative conditional connective (if it is a propositional function at all) reduces to the material conditional. In addition to Import-Export, Gibbard's demonstration relies on Simplification (Conjunction Elimination), considered as a logical entailment that implies the truth of the corresponding indicative conditional . Due to the shortcomings of the material conditional for an analysis of natural language conditionals, however, he considers that the collapse of any stronger conditional to the material conditional supports his thesis that conditionals are not propositions. Kratzer (2012, pp. 87–88) similarly uses Gibbard's proof to discredit any conditional operator stronger than the material conditional and prepare the way for her theory that conditionals are the restriction of a modal claim implicit in the consequent.

Fitelson (2013) notes that Gibbard's proof is in fact an informal argument, rather than a strict proof. He proposes a formalization of Gibbard's collapse theorem, in which the first two axioms are Import-Export and Simplification. Egré, Rossi, and Sprenger (2023) investigate the Gibbardian collapse in three-valued logics. They argue that Gibbard's collapse result may be better described as stating that we cannot have two conditional connectives that satisfy both Import-Export and Simplification, where one is strictly stronger than the other, and where the weaker satisfies Modus Ponens. Since the results of Gibbard, Fitelson, and Egré, Rossi and Sprenger all rest on Import-Export and Simplification, a logic that does not contain either of these will not be prone to the Gibbardian collapse (or at least, the mentioned proofs will not go through).

4 The Implicative Conditional

The implicative conditional is a conditional operator that was proposed by Burks (1955) for causal conditionals, and by Gomes (2005, 2013, 2020) for a wider class of implicative conditionals. This conditional was also investigated by Priest (1999) and Gherardi

[4] In some examples, such as (2) and (4), the addition of *even* to the nested conditional, making it a concessive conditional, would make the sentence acceptable, but for others, such as (6) and (8), this would not work. Only the transformation of the embedded conditional into an unconditional, by replacing *if* with *whether or not*, could make them acceptable.

and Orlandelli (2021). The implicative conditional is a strengthening of Pizzi's consequential conditional (Gomes, Pizzi, & Raidl, 2025; Pizzi, 1991, an operator that was praised by McCall (2012, p. 443) for using ordinary modal logic as a basis for connexive semantics. The motivation, semantics and axiomatization of the logic of the implicative conditional were studied by Raidl and Gomes (2024). Soundness and completeness of a logic for the implicative conditional with respect to reflexive Kripke models were proved in Raidl and Gomes (2024), based on the method of definable conditionals introduced by Raidl (2021a). The axiomatic system IC of the implicative conditional is obtained as translationally equivalent to the normal modal logic KT. For our analysis of Import-Export, we use the logic of the implicative conditional IC.

According to the theory of the implicative conditional (symbolized as $\Rightarrow$), a natural language sentence used in reasoning as an implicative conditional is analysed as:

def IC $A \Rightarrow B := \neg \Diamond(A \wedge \neg B) \wedge \Diamond A \wedge \Diamond \neg B$

The first conjunct expresses the strict conditional by the impossibility of $A \wedge \neg B$, the second and third conjuncts add the possibilistic conditions $\Diamond A$ and $\Diamond \neg B$, and the whole formula implies $\Diamond \neg A$, $\Diamond B$, $\Diamond(A \wedge B)$, and $\Diamond(\neg A \wedge \neg B)$. The possibility of the conjunction $\neg A \wedge B$ is left undetermined by this definition. If $\neg A \wedge B$ is possible, we have an asymmetrical implicative conditional ($A \Rightarrow B$ and $\neg(B \Rightarrow A)$), and if it is impossible, we have an implicative biconditional ($A \Leftrightarrow B$).[5]

Equivalent ways of expressing the implicative conditional are:[6]

$$\Box(A \supset B) \wedge \Diamond A \wedge \Diamond \neg B$$
$$\Box(A \supset B) \wedge \neg\Box(A \supset \neg B) \wedge \neg\Box(\neg A \supset B)$$
$$A \prec B \wedge \Diamond A \wedge \Diamond \neg B$$
$$A \prec B \wedge \neg(A \prec \neg B) \wedge \neg(\neg A \prec B)$$

Some important principles of the implicative conditional are Aristotle's Thesis (AT), Weak Boethius' Thesis (wBT) and Aristotle's Second Thesis (AT2):[7]

$$\neg(A \Rightarrow \neg A) \qquad \text{AT}$$
$$(A \Rightarrow B) \supset \neg(A \Rightarrow \neg B) \qquad \text{wBT}$$
$$(A \Rightarrow B) \supset \neg(\neg A \Rightarrow B) \qquad \text{AT2}$$

Some other important properties are the invalidity of Symmetry (S) and of Conditional Excluded Middle (CEM, which is equivalent to the converse of wBT). That is, the following are invalid (Raidl & Gomes, 2024)

$$(A \Rightarrow B) \equiv (B \Rightarrow A) \qquad \text{S}$$
$$\neg(A \Rightarrow \neg B) \supset (A \Rightarrow B) \qquad \text{CEM}$$

[5] Two other conditionals bear some similarity to the implicative conditional. The so-called weak super-strict conditional drops the third conjunct of the definition of the implicative conditional (Gherardi, Orlandelli, & Raidl, 2024). The neutral conditional uses the variably strict conditional conjoined to $\Diamond A$ (Raidl, 2019; 2021b; 2023).

[6] $\prec$ symbolizes the strict conditional (following C. I. Lewis).

[7] See Raidl and Gomes (2024, Fact 4).

5 Possibilistic Principles in the Logic of the Implicative Conditional

Since the truth of the implicative conditional $A \Rightarrow B$ requires the contingency of A and of B, no implicative conditional can be valid (Raidl & Gomes, 2024, Fact 3). However, the satisfaction of these modal requirements may imply the truth of some implicative conditionals. In fact, the conjunction of the possibility of antecedent and the possibility of the negated consequent of any valid strict conditional will imply the corresponding implicative conditional (Raidl & Gomes, 2024, p. 21). For example, the fact that Simplification is valid for the strict conditional entails that there is a valid material implication from $\Diamond(A \wedge B) \wedge \Diamond \neg A$ to the implicative conditional version of Simplification:

$$\vdash (A \wedge B) \dashv\!\!3\, A$$
$$\vdash (\Diamond(A \wedge B) \wedge \Diamond \neg A) \supset ((A \wedge B) \Rightarrow A)$$

The latter principle is called Possibilistic Simplification (PSI).

When the principle in question is a conditional that has an implicative conditional in its consequent, it may just as well be necessary to conjoin some possibilistic premise(s) to the antecedent of the principle. For example, for Disjunctive Weakening,

$$(A \rightarrowtail B) \supset (A \rightarrowtail (B \vee C)) \qquad \text{DW}$$

it is necessary to add the conjunct $\Diamond \neg(B \vee C)$ to the antecedent, giving rise to Possibilistic Disjunctive Weakening (PDW):

$$((A \Rightarrow B) \wedge \Diamond \neg(B \vee C)) \supset (A \Rightarrow (B \vee C)) \qquad \text{PDW}$$

It is not necessary to add $\Diamond A$, by contrast, because this is already implied by the premise $A \Rightarrow B$.

For Rational Monotonicity,

$$((A \rightarrowtail C) \wedge \neg(A \rightarrowtail \neg B) \supset ((A \wedge B) \rightarrowtail C) \qquad \text{RM}$$

it is only necessary to supplement the antecedent with $\Diamond B$, yielding Possibilistic Rational Monotonicity, since $\Diamond A$ and $\Diamond \neg C$ are already implied by $A \Rightarrow C$ (Raidl & Gomes, 2024, p. 29, 42):

$$((A \Rightarrow C) \wedge \neg(A \Rightarrow \neg B) \wedge \Diamond B) \supset ((A \wedge B) \Rightarrow C) \qquad \text{PRM}$$

Sometimes, however, it is not necessary to include any possibilistic premise, because the contingency of the antecedent and the consequent of the implicative conditional in the conclusion of the principle is already completely implied by the premise of the principle. For example, this is the case of Transitivity,[8]

$$((A \Rightarrow B) \wedge (B \Rightarrow C)) \supset (A \Rightarrow C) \qquad \text{TR}$$

since $A \Rightarrow B$ implies $\Diamond A$, and $B \Rightarrow C$ implies $\Diamond \neg C$.

[8] It is also the case of Conjunction of Consequents (AND).

6 Logical Analysis of Import-Export for $\Rightarrow$

With regard to Import-Export, the original, unrestricted, implications (IM and EX) are both invalid for the implicative conditional. (Proofs for all results are found in Appendix A.)

Theorem 1. *Exportation is invalid for* $\Rightarrow$ *in reflexive Kripke models.*

Theorem 2. *Importation is invalid for* $\Rightarrow$ *in reflexive Kripke models.*

Invalidity of IM and EX is really due to the fact that $A \Rightarrow (B \Rightarrow C)$ imposes other modal constraints than $(A \wedge B) \Rightarrow C$. Indeed,
$(A \wedge B) \Rightarrow C$ imposes:

(i) $\Diamond(A \wedge B)$
(ii) $\Diamond \neg C$
(iii) $\Box((A \wedge B) \supset C)$

$A \Rightarrow (B \Rightarrow C)$ imposes:

(a) $\Diamond A$
(b) $\Diamond \neg(B \Rightarrow C)$
(c) $\Box(A \supset (B \Rightarrow C))$

Importation fails essentially because $\Diamond A$ (a) does not imply $\Diamond(A \wedge B)$ (i), even in the presence of the other assumptions (b)-(c). Exportation fails essentially because (iii) (whether or not in conjunction with (i), (ii)) does not imply (c), which requires $\Box(A \supset \Diamond B)$, $\Box(A \supset \Diamond \neg C)$ and $\Box(A \supset \Box(B \supset C))$.

We now examine the validity or invalidity of possibilistic versions of IM and EX. Raidl and Gomes (2024) and Gomes et al. (2025) note that the implicative conditional fails to validate certain principles but, as mentioned in the previous section, validates possibilistic versions of these principles. Namely, the Identity Conditional (ID), Simplification (SI), Strengthening of the Antecedent (SA), Factor Law (FL), Rational Monotonicity (RM), Superclassicality (SC), Disjunctive Weakening (DW) and Right Weakening (RW) are invalid, and are replaced by the possibilistic versions PID, PSI, PM,[9] PFL, PRM, PSC, PDW and PRW, where 'P' stands for *Possibilistic*.

The possibilistic version of a principle X of the form

$$F \supset (A \rightarrowtail C)$$

is to add to the premise formula (F) the possibility of the antecedent ($\Diamond A$) and the possibility of the negated consequent ($\Diamond \neg C$) of the implied implicative conditional. The new principle is then

$$(F \wedge \Diamond A \wedge \Diamond \neg C) \supset (A \Rightarrow C)$$

which we will call here PPX, where 'PP' stand for the two new possibility assumptions. For some principles, one of the possibility assumptions can be dropped, since the

[9] Possibilistic Monotonicity, the possibilistic version of SA.

premise formula (F) already implies it. When only the first possibility assumption ($\Diamond A$) is explicitly present, we will here call the possibilistic version P1X, and when only the second ($\Diamond \neg B$) is explicitly present, we will call the possibilistic version P2X.[10]

The possibilistic versions of EX and IM are as follows:

$$(((A \wedge B) \Rightarrow C) \wedge \Diamond A \wedge \Diamond \neg(B \Rightarrow C)) \supset (A \Rightarrow (B \Rightarrow C)) \qquad \text{PPEX}$$
$$(((A \wedge B) \Rightarrow C) \wedge \Diamond A) \supset (A \Rightarrow (B \Rightarrow C)) \qquad \text{P1EX}$$
$$(((A \wedge B) \Rightarrow C) \wedge \Diamond \neg(B \Rightarrow C)) \supset (A \Rightarrow (B \Rightarrow C)) \qquad \text{P2EX}$$
$$((A \Rightarrow (B \Rightarrow C)) \wedge \Diamond(A \wedge B) \wedge \Diamond \neg C) \supset ((A \wedge B) \Rightarrow C) \qquad \text{PPIM}$$
$$((A \Rightarrow (B \Rightarrow C)) \wedge \Diamond(A \wedge B)) \supset ((A \wedge B) \Rightarrow C) \qquad \text{P1IM}$$
$$((A \Rightarrow (B \Rightarrow C)) \wedge \Diamond \neg C) \supset ((A \wedge B) \Rightarrow C) \qquad \text{P2IM}$$

In general, X implies P1X, P2X, and each of these implies PPX. The converses need not be true. However, sometimes the converses hold, when one of the possibilistic assumptions is redundant. For example:

Fact 1. *In Kripke models:*

1. PPEX *is equivalent to* P2EX,
2. P1EX *is equivalent to* EX.

However, in reflexive Kripke models, PPIM does not imply P1IM, because the antecedent of P1IM is not sufficient to imply $\Diamond \neg C$. Similarly, PPIM does not imply P2IM, because the antecedent of P2IM is not sufficient to imply $\Diamond(A \wedge B)$. Hence, while there are really just two exportation principles – EX and P2EX – there are 4 distinct importation principles: IM, P1IM, P2IM and PPIM.

Theorem 3. *All Possibilistic Exportations (*PPEX, P1EX, P2EX*) are invalid for $\Rightarrow$ in reflexive Kripke models.*

Theorem 4. PPIM *is valid for $\Rightarrow$ in reflexive Kripke models.*

While all Exportation principles are invalid, the Possibilistic Importation principle PPIM is valid. By contrast, one can prove that the stronger P1IM and P2IM are invalid (in a similar manner as IM is).

7 The Correspondence Between the Logical Analysis and the Behaviour of Inferences in Natural Language Conditionals

Going back to a general principle X of the form $F \supset (A \rightarrowtail C)$, we can say that, when applied to the implicative conditional, it must be fully possibilistic, that is, the premise of the principle must include, either explicitly or by implication, both possibility assumptions $\Diamond A$ and $\Diamond \neg C$. Thus, there is in fact only one fully possibilistic version that contains no redundancy for each principle of this form. For Exportation, it is P2EX,

[10] According to this convention, PM would be called P1M, PRW would be called P2RW, and PSI would be called PPSI, for example.

for Importation, it is PPIM, and these may thus be more simply called PEX and PIM, respectively.

The validity of Possibilistic Importation (PIM) and the invalidity of Possibilistic Exportation (PEX) for the implicative conditional follow the validity of IM and invalidity of EX for the strict conditional.[11] In fact, the strict conditional is at the core of the implicative conditional, and the only difference between them is that the implicative conditional requires that both the antecedent and the consequent be contingent. These possibility assumptions do not alter, however, the essential validity of Importation and invalidity of Exportation for the strict conditional, only requiring the replacement of these principles by their possibilistic versions.

We have seen, in Sect. 2, that (2), (4), (6) and (8) are not intuitively adequate as inferences from (1), (3), (5) and (7), respectively, because they suggest a connection between the antecedent and the consequent of the embedded conditional, which does not exist. Let us check whether this intuitive failure of inference is well explained by the invalidity of PEX, which, as we prove, derives from the truth conditions provided by the logical definition of the implicative conditional.

Let us consider (1) and (2), repeated here for convenience:

(1) If you sell your car and buy a bike, you'll have money for the trip.
(2) If you sell your car, then if you buy a bike, you'll have money for the trip.

(1) makes good sense, but it seems unreasonable to assert (2), and even paradoxical, because it suggests that buying the bike would somehow contribute to having the money for the trip. Interpreting (1) as an implicative conditional means that it is possible for you to sell your car and buy a bike, it is possible for you not to have the money for the trip, but it is impossible, all other things being equal, for you to sell your car, buy a bike, and not have money for the trip.[12]

Now let us see why interpreting (2) and its embedded conditional as implicative makes (2) false, thus explaining its intuitive unacceptability. Consider the following reflexive model (where A = *you will sell your car*, B = *you will buy a bike*, C = *you will have money for the trip*):

$$w_{\neg A,\neg B,\neg C} \longrightarrow v_{A,B,C} \longrightarrow u_{\neg A,B,\neg C} \qquad (1)$$

This means that, in the possible world w, A, B and C are false; in the possible world v, they are true; and in the possible world u, A and C are false and B is true. Example (1) is true in w since $A \wedge B$ is true in v, $\neg C$ is true in w and $A \wedge B \wedge \neg C$ is false in any possible world.

Let us recall the formula of PEX:

$$(((A \wedge B) \Rightarrow C) \wedge \Diamond\neg(B \Rightarrow C)) \supset (A \Rightarrow (B \Rightarrow C)) \qquad \text{PEX}$$

[11] Proofs of the last two are left to the reader.

[12] It is assumed that in the situation considered, the money you will get for the car is certainly more than the sum of the price of a bike and the money needed for the trip.

Applying this formula to examples (1)(2), we could thus write:

Example (1) $\wedge \Diamond \neg(B \Rightarrow C) \supset$ Example (2)

We have seen that (1) is true in w. The possibilistic condition $\Diamond \neg(B \Rightarrow C)$ is also true in w. This is because $B \wedge \neg C$ is true in u; hence, it is possible in v; hence $B \Rightarrow C$ is false in v; hence, $\Diamond \neg(B \Rightarrow C)$ is true in w. However, PEX fails for (1), since (2) is false in w. In fact, for (2) to be true in w, $A \wedge \neg(B \Rightarrow C)$ would have to be impossible, but it is possible in w, since true in v.

In other words, in a possible situation in which I have sold my car, the implicative conditional *If you buy a bike, then you'll have money for the trip* would be false, because it would still have been possible for me not to have sold my car, to buy a bike, and not to have money for the trip. (Only the concessive conditional *Even if you buy a bike, you'll still have money for the trip* would be true.) Thus, the implicative conditional with an embedded implicative conditional *If you sell your car, then if you buy a bike, then you'll have money for the trip* is false.

A similar reasoning can be applied to the other counterexamples.

8 Conclusions

The validity of PIM and invalidity of PEX for the logical implicative conditional mirror the observation that in natural language, Importation seems always to be a possible inference, while there are clear counterexamples to Exportation. Obviously, we are not arguing that natural language sentences of the form *If A and B, then C* never imply *If A, then if B, then C*. They often do, but not always. As a theorem, Exportation is invalid, even in its possibilistic version, but many instances of it in natural language may hold.

The correspondence between the behaviour of these inferences in natural language and in the logic of the implicative conditional may be viewed as a confirmation of the adequacy of this logic for analysing the implicative use of conditional sentences in natural language.

Because Gibbard's proof depends on IM-EX and Simplification, which are both invalid for the implicative conditional, we also conclude that the latter is immune to Gibbardian collapse.

Acknowledgments. Comments by an anonymous reviewer were useful in improving the article. Eric Raidl's work was funded by the Deutsche Forschungsgemeinschaft (EXC number 2064/1, project no. 390727645).

Author contributions. GG wrote Sects. 1–5 and 7–8. ER wrote Sect. 6 and Appendix A. Both authors contributed to and revised the whole paper.

Disclosure of Interests. The authors have no competing interests to declare that are relevant to the content of this article.

A Proofs

Proof of Theorem 1*:* We show that there is a world in a model such that

1. $(A \wedge B) \Rightarrow C$ (all of $\Diamond(A \wedge B)$, $\Diamond \neg C$, $\Box((A \wedge B) \supset C)$), is true;
2. $A \Rightarrow (B \Rightarrow C)$ (one of $\Diamond A$, $\Box(A \supset (B \Rightarrow C))$, $\Diamond \neg(B \Rightarrow C)$, namely the last) is false.

Consider the reflexive and symmetrical model with two worlds w, v, such that A, B, C are true in w, and only A is true in v (B and C are false), symbolized by the graph

$$w_{ABC} \longleftrightarrow v_A \tag{2}$$

At w all (1) is true. Indeed, $A \wedge B$ is true in w, hence $\Diamond(A \wedge B)$ is true in w, due to reflexivity. $\neg C$ is true in v, hence $\Diamond \neg C$ is true in w, since wRv. And $(A \wedge B) \supset C$ is true in w, since C is true, and it is also true in v, since B is false so that $A \wedge B$ is false. Hence since w, v are all accessible worlds from w, $\Box((A \wedge B) \supset C)$ is true in w.

But at w one of (2) is false, namely the last: note that $\Diamond \neg(B \Rightarrow C)$ is equivalent to the disjunction $\Diamond \Box \neg B \vee \Diamond \Box C \vee \Diamond \Diamond(B \wedge \neg C)$. Thus it suffices to show that each of the three disjuncts are false at w. In w we have $\Box \Diamond B$, since a B-world (w) can be accessed from w as from v and hence from all accessible worlds from w. Hence $\Diamond \Box \neg B$ is false at w. In w we also have $\Box \Diamond \neg C$, since a $\neg C$-world (v) can be accessed from w as from v. Hence $\Diamond \Box C$ is false at w. In w, $\Diamond \Diamond(B \wedge \neg C)$ is also false, since there is simply no $B \wedge \neg C$ world available.

In what follows, we simply give the graph. □

Proof of Theorem 2*:* In the reflexive model

$$w_C \longrightarrow v_A \longrightarrow u_{BC} \tag{3}$$

at w:

1. $A \Rightarrow (B \Rightarrow C)$ (all of $\Diamond A$, $\Box(A \supset (B \Rightarrow C))$, $\Diamond \neg(B \Rightarrow C)$, namely $\Diamond \Box \neg B$) is true;
2. but $(A \wedge B) \Rightarrow C$ is false (namely $\Diamond(A \wedge B)$).

□

Proof of Fact 1*:* $(A \wedge B) \Rightarrow C$ already implies $\Diamond(A \wedge B)$ and hence implies $\Diamond A$, so that this possibility assumption is redundant in PPEX and in P1EX. Hence P2EX is equivalent to PPEX, and P1EX is equivalent to EX. □

Proof of Theorem 3*:* P1EX is equivalent to EX (Fact 1). But EX is invalid (Theorem 1). Hence P1EX is invalid.

Since PPEX and P2EX are equivalent (Fact 1), it suffices to prove invalidity of P2EX. In the reflexive model

$$w_{ABC} \longrightarrow v_A \longrightarrow u_B \tag{4}$$

at w:

1. $(A \wedge B) \Rightarrow C$ (all of $\Diamond(A \wedge B)$, $\Diamond \neg C$, $\Box((A \wedge B) \supset C))$ and $\Diamond \neg(B \Rightarrow C)$ are true (for the last, since $B \wedge \neg C$ is true in u);
2. but $A \Rightarrow (B \Rightarrow C)$ (i.e. one of the following $\Diamond A$, $\Diamond \neg(B \Rightarrow C)$, $\Box(A \supset (B \Rightarrow C)))$ is false, namely the last, since $A \wedge \Diamond(B \wedge \neg C)$ is true at v.

□

Proof of Theorem 4*:* We use standard reasoning in KT. Assume $A \Rightarrow (B \Rightarrow C)$, and in addition $\Diamond(A \wedge B)$ and $\Diamond \neg C$. Then, to show that $(A \wedge B) \Rightarrow C$, it suffices to prove $\Box((A \wedge B) \supset C)$. From $A \Rightarrow (B \Rightarrow C)$ we have $\Box(A \supset (B \Rightarrow C))$. We thus obtain $\Box(A \supset (\Box(B \supset C) \wedge \Diamond B \wedge \Diamond \neg C))$ by DEF. Hence also $\Box(A \supset \Box(B \supset C))$. But $\Box(\Box X \supset X)$. Therefore $\Box(\Box(B \supset C) \supset (B \supset C))$. Hence $\Box(A \supset (B \supset C))$. Therefore $\Box((A \wedge B) \supset C)$. Hence we have proved $(A \wedge B) \Rightarrow C$. □

References

Burks, A.W.: Dispositional statements. Philoso. Sci. **22**(3), 175–193 (1955). https://doi.org/10.1086/287422

Edgington, D.: Indicative conditionals. In: E. N. Zalta (Ed.), The Stanford Encyclopedia of Philosophy (Fall 2020 ed.). Metaphysics Research Lab, Stanford University (2020). https://plato.stanford.edu/archives/fall2020/entries/conditionals/

Egré, P., Rossi, L., Sprenger, J.: Gibbardian collapse and trivalent conditionals. In: Kaufmann, S., Over, D.E., Sharma, G. (eds.) Conditionals. Palgrave MacMillan (2023)

Fitelson, B.: Gibbards collapse theorem for the indicative conditional: an axiomatic approach. In: Bonacina, M.P., Stickel, M.E., (eds.), Automated Reasoning and Mathematics: Essays in Memory of William W. McCune, pp. 181–188. Berlin: Springer (2013)

Gherardi, G., Orlandelli, E.: Super-strict implications. Bull. Sect. Logic 50(1), 1–34 (2021). https://doi.org/10.18778/0138-0680.2021.02

Gherardi, G., Orlandelli, E., Raidl, E.: Proof systems for super-strict implication. Stud. Logica. **112**, 249–294 (2024). https://doi.org/10.1007/s11225-023-10048-3

Gibbard, A.: Two recent theories of conditionals. In: Harper, W.L., Stalnaker, R., Pearce, G., (Eds.), Ifs: Conditionals, belief, decision, chance and time, pp. 211– 247. Dordrecht: Springer Netherlands (1981). https://doi.org/10.1007/978-94-009-9117-0_10

Gomes, G.: Ordinary language conditionals (2005). https://www.academia.edu/93865496/Ordinary_Language_Conditionals_2005 (Manuscript)

Gomes, G.: Pensamento e linguagem nas afirmações condicionais. DELTA: Documentação de Estudos em Linguística Teórica e Aplicada, **29**(1), 121–134 (2013).https://doi.org/10.1590/s0102-44502013000100006

Gomes, G.: Concessive conditionals without 'even if' and nonconcessive conditionals with 'even if'. Acta Analytica 35(1), 1–21 (2020). https://doi.org/10.1007/s12136-019-00396-y

Gomes, G., Pizzi, C., Raidl, E.: Consequential implication and the implicative conditional. Log. Logical Philoso. (2025). https://doi.org/10.12775/LLP.2025.001

Kratzer, A.: Modals and conditionals. Oxford University Press (2012)

McCall, S.: A history of connexivity. In: D.M. Gabbay, F.J. Pelletier, J. Woods (Eds.), Logic: A history of its Central Concepts, vol. 11, pp. 415–449. Amsterdam: North-Holland (2012). https://doi.org/10.1016/b978-0-444-52937-4.50008-3

McGee, V.: Conditional probabilities and compounds of conditionals. Philos. Rev. **98**, 485–542 (1989)

Pizzi, C.: Decision procedures for logics of consequential implication. Notre Dame J. Formal Log. **32**(4), 618–636 (1991). https://doi.org/10.1305/ndjfl/1093635934

Priest, G.: Negation as cancellation, and connexive logic. Topoi **18**, 14–148 (1999). https://doi.org/10.1023/A:1006294205280

Raidl, E.: Completeness for counter-doxa conditionals – using ranking semantics. Rev. Symbol. Logic **12**(4), 861–891 (2019). https://doi.org/10.1017/S1755020318000199

Raidl, E.: Definable conditionals. Topoi, 40(1), 87–105 (2021a). https://doi.org/10.1007/s11245-020-09704-3

Raidl, E.: Strengthened conditionals. In: Liao, B., Wáng, Y.N., (eds.), Context, Conflict and Reasoning. Logic in Asia Series, pp. 139–155. Singapore: Springer (2021b). https://doi.org/10.1007/978-981-15-7134-3_11

Raidl, E.: Neutralization, Lewis' doctored conditional, or another note on "A connexive conditional". Logos Episteme **14**(1), 101–118 (2023). https://doi.org/10.5840/logos-episteme20231415

Raidl, E., Gomes, G.: The implicative conditional. J. Philos. Log. **53**, 1–47 (2024). https://doi.org/10.1007/s10992-023-09715-6

Whitehead, A.N., Russell, B.: Principia mathematica (2nd ed.). Cambridge University Press (1927/1963)

Correction to: Graded Relation Updates in Modal Logic

Raul Fervari, Daniel Figueiredo, and Manuel A. Martins

Correction to:
Chapter 17 in: D. Kozen and R. de Queiroz (Eds.): *Logic, Language, Information, and Computation*, LNCS 15942, https://doi.org/10.1007/978-3-031-99536-1_17

The book was published with a typo of chapter 17 in this book ID (665315_1_En). In Chapter 17, we have followed MS for reference 21, noticed that in the paper:

Fervari, R., Figueiredo, D., Martins, M.A. (2026). Graded Relation Updates in Modal Logic. In: Kozen, D., de Queiroz, R. (eds) Logic, Language, Information, and Computation. WoLLIC 2025. Lecture Notes in Computer Science, vol 15942. Springer, Cham. https://doi.org/10.1007/978-3-031-99536-1_17 (https://link.springer.com/chapter/10.1007/978-3-031-99536-1_17) there is a reference to the paper:

Figueiredo, D., Martins, M.A., Barbosa, L.S. (2018). A note on reactive transitions and Reo connectors. In: It's All About Coordination: Essays to Celebrate the Lifelong Scientific Achievements of Farhad Arbab, pp. 57–67. Springer. https://doi.org/10.1007/978-3-319-90089-6_4 (https://link.springer.com/chapter/10.1007/978-3-319-90089-6_4)

The updated version of this chapter can be found at https://doi.org/10.1007/978-3-031-99536-1_17

D. Kozen and R. de Queiroz (Eds.): WoLLIC 2025, LNCS 15942, p. C1, 2026.
https://doi.org/10.1007/978-3-031-99536-1_23

Author Index

D. Kozen and R. de Queiroz (Eds.): WoLLIC 2025, LNCS 15942, p. 369, 2026.
https://doi.org/10.1007/978-3-031-99536-1

The manufacturer's authorised representative in the EU is Springer Nature Customer Service Centre GmbH, Europaplatz 3, 69115 Heidelberg, Germany. If you have any concerns regarding our products, please contact ProductSafety@springernature.com

Printed and bound by CPI Group (UK) Ltd, Croydon, CR0 4YY

29/04/2026

02099511-0003